D1823313

STEWART PARKER

From one Northern
Irish writer to another : . . .
. . . was this our lives too?
all our love Rachel

Mum & Dad
Christmas 2012.

Stewart Parker

A Life

Marilynn Richtarik

OXFORD
UNIVERSITY PRESS

OXFORD

UNIVERSITY PRESS

Great Clarendon Street, Oxford, OX2 6DP,
United Kingdom

Oxford University Press is a department of the University of Oxford.
It furthers the University's objective of excellence in research, scholarship,
and education by publishing worldwide. Oxford is a registered trade mark of
Oxford University Press in the UK and in certain other countries

First Edition published in 2012

Impression: 1

British Library Cataloguing in Publication Data

Data available

Library of Congress Cataloging in Publication Data

Data available

ISBN 978–0–19–969503–4

Printed in Great Britain by
MPG Books Group, Bodmin and King's Lynn

This book is dedicated to the friends of
Stewart Parker, old and new

Preface

Belfast in the mid-1970s ranked among the least auspicious places imaginable for a playwright to attempt to launch a career. For years, both republican and loyalist paramilitaries had employed random attacks on civilians to underline their demands that Northern Ireland should break or maintain its ties with the United Kingdom. Not surprisingly, people stayed close to home at night, and all but one of the city's few theatres had closed. Nevertheless, when Stewart Parker completed *Spokesong* (1975), the play that would establish his international reputation, he felt 'desperate for it to be seen first by a Belfast audience'. He and a group of friends and collaborators launched a fund-raising campaign to try to mount an independent production, but they ended up, as he recalled bitterly ten years later, 'with just one positive response—an offer of £75 from British Rail. As an ironist, I felt very keenly the poetic aptness of this donor, whose services I would later engage to take a one-way journey out.' In the event, *Spokesong* did not receive an indigenous Belfast production until 1989, by which time it had been staged in Dublin, London, New York City, Belgium, Denmark, Finland, Canada, Sweden, the Netherlands, Norway, Australia, New Zealand, and in regional theatres all over the United States. Parker, meanwhile, had given up on Belfast as a base, moving first to Edinburgh and then to London, where he died of stomach cancer in 1988 at the age of 47. As James Joyce had discovered before him, though, he found that leaving home need not entail abandoning it intellectually or emotionally.[1]

The overarching theme of this book is the relationship between Stewart Parker and Belfast. In many ways, this is a familiar story of Irish artistic exile. Like Joyce, Samuel Beckett, and Sean O'Casey, Parker spent much of his life outside Ireland (including the most productive years of his play-writing career). The year before he died, though, he proclaimed himself happy to be called a 'Belfast playwright'; indeed, he said, 'it's the only kind of description that makes any sense to me'.[2] This identity constituted a matter of choice for him as well as of birth. The child of working-class Protestant parents, Parker attended Queen's University Belfast in the 1960s as one of the beneficiaries of the Education Act that put state-funded higher education within the reach of people from backgrounds like his. Fascinated by American poetry and popular culture, he dreamed of emigrating, and from 1964 until 1969 he lived and taught in the US. There he bore intent witness to the civil rights movement, Vietnam War protests, and political violence, going home to Northern Ireland in August 1969 (the same week the British Army arrived to attempt to quell sectarian disturbances) because he had come to feel that he would never be more than an observer in North America. To get below the surface of things, he had to grapple with his birthplace, which he loved and hated in equal measure.

Parker brought back with him a heightened political awareness and a sense of the role of 'cultural revolutionaries' in instigating social change. When he returned to Belfast in 1969, he returned spiritually as well as physically, determined to address himself to the city instead of continuing to try to escape or transcend it. Inspired by a former teacher, John Malone, he had already begun to take an interest in local history, especially those aspects of it that demonstrated that sectarian divisions need not be a timeless condition of Northern Irish life. By 1967, for example, Parker had started to research the United Irish movement of the 1790s for a play he planned to write on Henry Joy McCracken, one of the Belfast leaders of the 1798 rebellion (work that issued over fifteen years later in his 1984 masterpiece *Northern Star*).

The Troubles really made Parker into a 'Belfast playwright', though, by giving new urgency to his private project of imagining alternatives to Northern Ireland's stalemate. Throughout his career, however, he rejected pressure to take sides or to make the violence itself the subject of his plays. Instead, his interest lay in getting behind the symptoms of cultural division and finding new and unexpected angles from which to examine it. Sometimes Parker's independent attitude manifested itself in metaphorical approaches to Northern Ireland: *Kingdom Come* (1978), for example, recreates the social and political configuration of the North on a fictional Caribbean island. He also illuminated the forces activating the Northern crisis by displacing the action in time, as in *Northern Star*, to focus on the causes of the Troubles rather than merely their effects. Whatever his formal strategy, Parker's writing reflects his individualism, liberal humanism, and the socialist perspective that helped him evade sectarian pitfalls.

Many of Parker's best dramatic works, most written after he moved away from the city for good in 1978, can be described as Belfast history plays. From *Spokesong*, the protagonist of which is a bicycle salesman obsessed with his dead grandparents, to Parker's last play, *Pentecost* (1987), the city of Belfast looms larger than any nation—deliberately so, I think, since Protestants and Catholics there may not be able to agree on whether they are British or Irish, but they all know where they live. 'Citizens of Belfast...', McCracken declaims repeatedly in *Northern Star*, addressing not only his contemporaries in the play but generations to come in the theatre. It is in the implied audience for his plays that Parker is most quintessentially a 'Belfast playwright'. He conceived of drama as a ritual communal act, and his ideal imagined audience was usually a Belfast one. His entire career, by means of which he wedded himself to his native place through a creative engagement with its history, declared his faith in people's capacity to be educated into tolerance and appreciation of one another. As his friend and contemporary Seamus Heaney puts it, Parker gave people 'a renewed trust in the very possibility of trust itself'.[3]

Joyce and Parker shared more than ambivalent exile. As Joyce's work captures the multifarious life of Dublin, Parker's work, taken as a whole, comprises one of the most serious efforts by a Northern Irish writer to present Belfast in all its variety, with characters of different ages, classes, occupations, religious and political associations, and periods. From the shipyard workers of his first successful radio play, killed during the building of *Titanic*, to the misguided musicians of *Catchpenny Twist* (1977), the Protestant revolutionaries of *Northern Star*, and the bewildered refugees of *Pentecost*, set during the Ulster Workers' Council Strike of 1974,

Parker's aim of holding a mirror up to Belfast never faltered. Shortly before he died he wrote a synopsis for a screenplay about an upwardly mobile couple who own a wine bar and a sportswear boutique, signalling his intention to continue to explore new facets of life in Belfast.

In 1976, Parker discussed Joyce, his greatest influence, in terms that also describe what makes his own work compelling, citing his sense of humour, 'verbal felicity', and 'positive vision of life'. Perhaps most important to Parker, Joyce 'had a sense of the poetry of fact, of using actual information about things in a way that transcends documentary and gives you an insight into people's lives, relationships and history'. Both men put extensive research into their writing, but the work they produced combines meticulous attention to detail with radical formal experimentation. For his play *Nightshade* (1980), which features an undertaker, Parker studied the theory of embalming but also decided that his protagonist should be an amateur magician. One of the main characters in *Spokesong*, a play inspired by the historical fact that John Boyd Dunlop invented the pneumatic tyre in Belfast, is the Trick Cyclist, who punctuates the action with fancy riding and cabaret songs, in addition to taking several parts in the play. In *Northern Star*, Parker underlines the way in which decisions made in the 1790s continued to influence Irish politics in the 1970s and beyond by including in the play seven scenes corresponding to the seven ages of man and seven stages of the United Irish movement, each written in the style of a different Irish dramatist. 'I've always loved theatricality', Parker remarked in 1985. 'Playwrights write for themselves in that sense. You write the sort of plays you've always wanted to see.'[4]

Despite his tragically foreshortened life, Parker produced a rich and varied body of work. However, a number of factors have combined to obscure his achievement. The first has to do with the nature of drama itself. Most artists deal with commercial constraints to a certain extent, but playwrights are at the mercy of the whims and priorities of others to an extraordinary degree. In the other literary genres, a writer controls, more or less, the final form of his or her work. A dramatist does not have this privilege. A script, no matter how polished, is only the blueprint for a performance. Unless a play is produced, and produced well, it cannot achieve its apotheosis. Unfortunately, as Parker learned early in his career, 'It needs a combination of good luck and miraculous intervention to get a play presented properly.'[5]

First, a playwright (or his or her agent) has to interest a producer in the script. Someone appropriate must be found to direct it. Then, actors need to be recruited to play the characters. These, ideally, should be the right age and have the right 'look' for their roles, as well as having the talents and skills to perform them convincingly. There are also a host of other people who contribute to a play's success or lack of it: the set, lighting, and costume designers; composer; musicians; construction crew; stage manager; house manager; and so on. But even when the people with whom you wish to work also want to work with you, they may not be available to do so. The most committed producers may be unable to find a suitable venue in which to mount the play, or the dates offered by a desirable venue may be less than desirable. And even with all the goodwill and theatrical acumen in the world at its disposal, a production may fail for lack of money to pull it off in style. All in all, the ability to make a living solely as a dramatist, which Parker did for twelve years—as a writer for the stage as well as for radio, television, and the cinema—is a remarkable achievement in itself.

The central part that luck, both good and bad, inevitably plays in a dramatist's life can be illustrated by two examples from Parker's career. The initial production of a play is supremely important. Unless a play attracts plenty of positive attention on its first outing, it is unlikely to be picked up by other theatre managements, it will probably not be published, and it is apt to sink without a trace. In 1975, Parker catapulted into the consciousness of both British and Irish theatre enthusiasts when his first play, *Spokesong*, became the surprise hit of the Dublin Theatre Festival. Critics from both London and Dublin hailed the advent of a major new writing talent, and *Spokesong* opened in 1976 at a fringe venue in London, from which it transferred, the following year, to the West End. The play was subsequently produced in many countries. *Spokesong* is an innovative and enjoyable work, but without its triumph in Dublin events would probably not have unfolded as they did. And one reason a first play by an unknown playwright, produced in an inconvenient and ill-appointed theatre on a minuscule budget, received the accolades that it did was because most of the other offerings at that year's Festival were uninspired. As Parker informed his friend Alfred Gingold, 'almost everything else in the Festival was so virulently denounced that we emerged a clear success'.[6]

Two years later, with his second play, Parker had a wholly different experience of the Dublin Theatre Festival. *Catchpenny Twist* opened at the Peacock, the Abbey Theatre's studio space, in a slot immediately preceding the Festival, receiving mixed reviews from the Dublin critics (who had also been divided on the merits of *Spokesong*). The final three days of the play's run coincided with the start of the Festival, and these performances were sold out, with patrons paying for standing room. This time, though, the play closed before the London-based critics arrived in town. Two and a half years—during which Parker's career lost valuable momentum—elapsed before *Catchpenny Twist* was seen in London, when the Kings Head pub theatre (which had also produced *Spokesong*) presented it. Like *Spokesong*, *Catchpenny Twist* proved a hit at this venue, but a proposed transfer to the West End fell through because the Kings Head had no money to put into it and because one of the leading actors had more lucrative film and television offers. It has rarely been produced since. Now, many would assume that because *Catchpenny Twist* has not fared as well as *Spokesong* it must not be as good a play, but I would suggest that the relative quality of the two scripts is most assuredly only part of the story.

In general, Parker had better luck with the productions of his television plays than with his stage plays. Fortunately, his television work survives in a permanent form, since television drama is usually preserved by the companies that produce it. On the other hand, despite its thus being fixed in a way that theatre is not, television drama is an evanescent genre. Television plays may be repeated once or twice after their initial transmission, but then they tend to fade from view entirely, and they are even less likely than stage plays to be published. Moreover, because they are frozen in the conventions of the time in which they were made, they date quickly. The populist in Parker thrilled to the possibility of mass audiences presented by television, calling it in 1986 'not merely the real national theatre, but a multi-national one to boot'.[7] None the less, he knew that stage plays are more critical to a playwright's long-term literary reputation, and he took his stage writing most seriously, subsidizing it with television and film work. Although a stage play is realized only in the moment of performance, making it one of the most ephemeral arts of all, it is in being continually recreated on stage that a dramatist's words truly live.

Another reason for Parker's relative obscurity may be that his plays are difficult to do well. He understood that 'a play has to be written in a form which can withstand any number of brutalisations and distortions. It has to be robust enough to take companies in different places and at all levels of talent. It has to be as tough as an old boot at the same time as being sensitive as a flower.' Parker's passion for theatricality, however, constantly pushed him to test the limits of what could be done in a theatre. Stephen Rea, an actor who worked closely with both Parker and Brian Friel, compares them by saying that Friel's great skill as a dramatist is to write good, solid plays that cannot be ruined by indifferent productions. Parker's work, in contrast, is more daringly experimental—the only problem with that being that it is hard to know if a play really works without seeing it in an excellent production with a uniformly strong cast.[8] One clue regarding the different approaches of these two outstanding Irish dramatists may lie in the fact that Friel knew almost nothing about theatre when he decided to turn his hand to drama, and he always tried to write in such a way as to maintain the maximum degree of authorial control over the proceedings. Parker, in contrast, was involved with all aspects of making theatre from his early teen years (he even, for a time, considered becoming a professional actor), and he relished the risk-taking and collaborative possibilities that his style of writing entailed. He set other theatre practitioners almost insurmountable challenges, trusting that they would find ways to surmount them. Given the technical demands of his plays, it is particularly regrettable that Parker lacked a theatrical home and the opportunity to work over time with a stable company of actors.

The scattered nature of Parker's output has also contributed to an underestimation of what he accomplished in his lifetime. Parker wrote drama for four different media, in addition to poetry and prose. One of the pleasures of surveying the entire body of his work lies in seeing the inventive ways in which he dealt with the distinctive features of different genres and media, but very few people until now have been in a position to evaluate his work as a whole. The biography reveals him as a prolific and flexible writer.

Parker's Northern origins have further complicated the reception of his work. He considered himself to be Irish, even an Irish nationalist, but his Protestant and unionist background made it hard for him to identify with the prevailing ethos of the Republic of Ireland. There, he was regarded with some reserve by the arts community because he also, and equally, thought of himself as British and looked as naturally to London as to Dublin. As many of his stage plays premièred in Britain as in Dublin, but Parker's dual allegiance often meant that he seemed 'too British' in the Republic and 'too Irish' in Britain. His insistence on writing about

Belfast further alienated him from both the London and the Dublin cultural establishments.

Only towards the end of his life did Parker begin to receive significant Northern Irish productions of his stage plays, and the Lyric Players Theatre production of *Northern Star* in 1984 and the Field Day Theatre Company production of *Pentecost* in 1987 marked highlights of his career. Parker loved the way these productions were assessed in political as well as artistic terms and the fact that they attracted audiences who did not usually attend the theatre. By this time, though, he felt that he had come to the end of a major phase in his writing. He had said what he had to say about the Northern situation and was preparing to strike out into different territory. Had he lived, he would also have moved into directing, at least of his own work (he had already arranged to direct the television play he was writing when he died).

Parker's untimely death was the biggest reason for his overshadowing in the last years of the twentieth century. Here, again, a comparison with Brian Friel may be helpful. If Friel had died at 47, audiences would never have enjoyed *Faith Healer, Translations*, or *Dancing at Lughnasa*—or any of the other plays he wrote after 1976. Parker died at the height of his powers, and what he wrote about playwright Sam Thompson is equally true of himself: 'His death was a grievous loss to Irish drama, for there is no doubt that he had many plays still in him.'[9] However much we may regret the Parker plays we shall never get to see, though, he left more than enough good work behind to be judged a writer of the first order.

When I became interested in Stewart Parker, in 1989, much of his work remained unavailable. *Spokesong* had been published by the theatrical firm Samuel French, *Catchpenny Twist* by both French and The Gallery Press, *Nightshade* by Co-Op Books (affiliated with the Irish Writers' Co-operative), and Parker's late 'triptych'—consisting of *Northern Star, Heavenly Bodies*, and *Pentecost*—by Oberon Press. I read all these in Oxford's Bodleian Library, along with two pamphlets of Parker's poetry issued in conjunction with the Belfast Festival at Queen's University in the late 1960s (in a series that also included pamphlets by Seamus Heaney, Derek Mahon, and Michael Longley); Parker's lecture *Dramatis Personae*, privately printed in Belfast in 1986; and his radio play *The Iceberg*, published in the literary journal *The Honest Ulsterman* in 1975. Another radio play, *The Kamikaze Ground Staff Reunion Dinner*, had been included in a Methuen volume, *Best Radio Plays of 1980*. But what of Parker's television plays, with their intriguing titles (*I'm a Dreamer Montreal; Iris in the Traffic, Ruby in the Rain; Radio Pictures*)? What of his other stage and radio plays? And what of the man himself, who had died only the previous year? Despite the quality of his writing, there had been at that time little scholarly attention to him. Terence Brown, Andrew Parkin, Elmer Andrews, and Claudia Harris had written pioneering academic articles on Parker, but there was not much else.

Nowadays, my curiosity could be more easily satisfied. Recent years have witnessed a steady growth of interest in Parker. Mark Phelan and his colleagues in the new Drama Department of Queen's University organized the first international conference devoted to Stewart Parker in the autumn of 2008 to mark the twentieth anniversary of his death, and several volumes of Parker's writings have been published in the past decade. Methuen's *Plays: 1* and *Plays: 2*, introduced by Lynne Parker and Stephen Rea, made most of Parker's stage plays available to a new generation in 2000. *Paddy Dies*, a selection of Parker's poetry edited by Kate Newmann and Philip Hobsbaum, was issued by Summer Palace Press in 2004. In *Television Plays* (Litteraria Pragensia, 2008), Clare Wallace presents eleven of Parker's television scripts, along with a critical introduction. Gerald Dawe, Maria Johnston, and Clare Wallace offer a collection of his prose pieces in *Dramatis Personae & Other Writings* (Litteraria Pragensia, 2008), and Dawe and Johnston also collaborated on the preparation of *High Pop: The Irish Times Column 1970–1976*, a volume collecting Parker's popular music criticism (Lagan Press, 2008). Moreover, critical essays devoted to Irish drama increasingly feature Parker's work.

There have also been a number of notable revivals of Parker's plays of late. Three of them made an especially significant impact. Dublin's Rough Magic Theatre Company, under the direction of Lynne Parker, presented *Pentecost* during the 1995 Dublin Theatre Festival, winning the Irish Life Festival Choice Award for the best Irish production that year. The company revived the production for a tour of Ireland and a four-week run at the Donmar Warehouse in London the following year, and again in 2000 when it was included in the Island: Arts from Ireland festival at Washington, DC's John F. Kennedy Center for the Performing Arts. Then, in 1998 (the 200th anniversary of the 1798 rebellion), Belfast's Tinderbox Theatre Company, in collaboration with the Field Day Theatre Company and the Belfast Festival at Queen's, mounted a production of *Northern Star* in the First Presbyterian Church on Rosemary Street, a site associated with the United Irishmen. Stephen Rea directed this in a manner that took full advantage of the historically resonant space. And in 2004, Lynne Parker directed *Heavenly Bodies*, which had not been produced since the playwright revised it just months before his death, as part of a special summer season celebrating the 100th anniversary of the Abbey Theatre. *Heavenly Bodies*, about the nineteenth-century Irish dramatist Dion Boucicault, was presented in the Peacock at the same time that *The Shaughraun*, one of Boucicault's popular melodramas, was being performed upstairs on the main stage, prompting a reviewer for the *Irish Times* to comment that it had quickly become apparent to her that the former production was 'far more than an interesting footnote' to the Boucicault 'blockbuster', adding that 'the relationship may actually be the other way around'.[10] These superb and well-received productions of Parker's last three stage plays helped to bring the scripts to the attention of younger theatre professionals.

In 1991, however, the only way to learn the things I wanted to know was to write the book I wanted to read. That year I applied for a fellowship from the Institute of Irish Studies at Queen's, proposing to complete my doctoral thesis on Field Day and then begin work on a critical biography of Parker. I received in response an uncommonly delightful rejection letter from R. H. Buchanan, the Institute's director, explaining that there had been a surplus of good candidates already holding the doctorate, but adding that the Stewart Parker Trust might support my project. The Trust, I subsequently learned from its secretary, John Fairleigh, existed to help emerging Irish playwrights rather than fledgling academics, but Fairleigh sent a copy of my fellowship application to Lesley Bruce, Parker's partner and the executor of his estate. Shortly thereafter, I received a letter from her telling me that she possessed Parker's papers and inviting me to contact her if I ever got the opportunity to pursue my research into his life and work. This came in 1993, when I won a Killam Postdoctoral Fellowship at the University of British Columbia in Vancouver, having been encouraged to apply by John Wilson Foster, a professor in the English Department who hailed from Belfast. And so, that autumn, I embarked on an undertaking the dimensions and difficulty of which I could hardly have imagined.

During the two years I lived in Vancouver, I spent literally half my time in other places—in England, Ireland, Northern Ireland, Scotland, the US, other parts of Canada, even Spain—on the trail of Stewart Parker. I spent many weeks in London, going through the contents of Parker's study and talking with Lesley Bruce, whose patience, insight, and openness made the rest of my work possible. Her loss remained fresh when I began my research, and the process of recalling Parker incredibly painful for her, yet she sacrificed her peace of mind (and at least one play of her own) to the perpetuation of his memory, and for that I can never thank her enough. Parker's family, too, welcomed and assisted me, and I talked early on with Parker's father Herbie, as well as with his brother George, sister-in-law Margaret, sister Joan, brother-in-law Joe, nieces Lynne and Julie, and members of his extended family. I also visited friends and collaborators of Parker far and wide. In the book, information obtained by talking with people is cited in the notes using a name and date only. Additional details are provided in the References section under the heading 'Interviews and Conversations with the Author'. In the text, I treat these oral comments like printed works, referring to people's remarks in the present tense even in cases where I know my informant has since died.

Most people, though, however much they may remember, are unreliable about dates and details. I was thus fortunate in the quality of Parker's personal archive. In his late twenties, he had been commissioned by Sam Thompson's literary executor to prepare the popular Northern dramatist's papers for deposit in the Belfast Central Library. Parker found these, to put it mildly, in a state of daunting disarray. Up to that point, his own 'archive' had resembled Thompson's, consisting mainly of a cardboard box into which he threw business-related letters. Although Parker never got around to sorting through these (one of my own first jobs), the experience of imposing order on Thompson's jumbled souvenirs made him henceforth more self-conscious about his own literary remains. The organizational system he eventually devised entailed a box file for each play he wrote, in which he placed loose notes or photocopies made in the planning stages for it, successive drafts of the script, related correspondence (down to fan letters from people he had never met), programmes and/or publicity material from productions of it, and copies of reviews. Although Parker's collections of reviews were rarely comprehensive, the box files always offered an invaluable starting place. (Early in his play-writing career, he pasted reviews into a large scrapbook—a practice he abandoned after a few years. Playwrights are often asked to provide potential producers with press clippings, and this is hard to do when they are affixed in an album.)

Letters make priceless biographical sources because in them writers describe and explain (usually in more detail than would seem necessary in a private diary entry) the events and activities filling their days. Parker wrote a great many letters to a wide range of people. Unfortunately, few people save the letters they receive. Even fewer are both willing and able to produce them for a biographer. I am therefore profoundly grateful to those I met who fell into that last category, especially to Shaun Davey, John Gilbert, Alfred Gingold, Philip Hobsbaum, Ken and June Lambla, Nancy McKibbin, and Bea MacLeod, who shared with me collections of letters spanning a number of years. Parker himself did not, as a rule, preserve personal correspondence addressed to him. However, he did save letters pertaining to his work. He also frequently kept copies of important business letters he wrote. Sometimes these would be photocopies or duplicates. In other cases, he would retain the handwritten draft of a letter which he would then, presumably, type and send. I have cited these as 'draft' letters. While the versions received by the addressees may have differed slightly in wording, I have assumed that their content remained substantially the same.

Most useful of Parker's personal papers were the journals he kept from 1966 until his death. These vary in comprehensiveness. In the late 1960s, for example, Parker wrote only occasional entries; he did not keep a journal during most of 1972; his 1973 journal consists entirely of one-line entries, since the date book he possessed that year did not provide room for more, and 1974's entries are only marginally less sketchy; Parker's journal from the second half of 1982 through 1984 reverted to being sporadic, reflecting an upheaval in his personal life; and by 1987 he had stopped writing daily entries and kept only Filofax pages with brief notations. From 1975 to 1986, however, the period spanning the heart of Parker's professional play-writing career, his journals provide a concise record of his daily activities. With their aid, I constructed an outline chronology of Parker's life that served as an essential reference to me while writing, and dates mentioned in the biography are derived from the journals unless otherwise indicated.

In the text, I use the words 'journal' and 'diary' interchangeably to refer to this record. I prefer 'journal', though, as helping to dispel the impression readers might have of its containing intimately personal reflections. Parker wrote the occasional confessional entry (and I quote many of these), but his journal entries mostly comprise brief factual accounts of: (1) his work progress (pages written, pieces posted, rehearsals or meetings attended, letters received, conversations regarding these matters); (2) people met with, or other significant activities; (3) books read, television programmes watched, and plays, films, and concerts attended; (4) the state of his health (a natural preoccupation for a survivor of childhood cancer); and (5) meals eaten. His relatively rare private musings usually focus on his worries at the time. In short, the journals, taken alone, do not convey a sense of Parker that people who knew him in person would recognize. Friends agree that Parker enjoyed nothing better than chatting with all sorts of people, in whom he took a genuine interest. Highly attuned to the world around him, he experienced a quick trip to the shops as full of incident. He appeared carefree, had an infectious laugh and a keen sense of humour, hardly ever complained or got angry, and did not seem to take himself all that seriously. In the journals, he comes across as an intensely ambitious and dedicated writer whose work stood at the centre of his life. Both sets of impressions are 'true'—though each only partially.

In addition to his journals, Parker kept a series of notebooks throughout his writing career. These contain ideas for writing projects, notes and research towards them, drafts of poems and song lyrics, snatches of dialogue and one-liners, observations on life and art, potential titles and character names, and other memorable verbal formulations. Many of these show up in his completed work, but much time might elapse between an entry and its use by Parker. In 1987, he described his writing process to Deirdre Purcell:

> The glimmerings of the plays come together over a period of months, even years. It's a very gradual process. The plays have been around in my head for much longer than even I realise. . . . I spend a lot of time thinking, just thinking—probably not enough—but a lot. At some point, even at the beginning, I get a title. It can be a kind of magnet around which all these things cluster. And when enough things cluster, I can start out.[11]

Parker's writing notebooks support this description. Full of significance to anyone familiar with his body of work, they would probably read like gibberish to other people. Most surprising is their sketchiness. Clearly Parker carried his detailed plans for work in progress in his head, because I rarely found anything more than outline schemata and brief notes written down.

Parker often used a single notebook for several years. In the 1960s, he kept most of his work notes in his journal. Moving into the 1970s, when he adopted the date book format for his journal and disciplined himself to write daily entries, he began making work notes in a different place. He kept one notebook through to the end of 1973, one from 1974 to 1978, one in 1978 and 1979, one from 1980 to early 1988, and yet another until his death. (He used separate notebooks for his research and notes towards a film screenplay he wrote in 1984 and his 1986 play *Heavenly Bodies*.) Through cross-referencing with the journals, I dated some individual notes with precision, which allowed me to estimate many others. In the text, I cite all quoted entries as 'notebook', along with, where possible, an approximate date.

As a mature writer Parker generally did his most serious work late at night, starting after dinner and carrying on until 2, 3, or even 4 a.m. He wrote, in the first instance, in longhand on pads of foolscap paper, and he set himself a quota of three pages a night. The resulting manuscript drafts cannot be called 'rough'. Parker wrote deliberately, sometimes stopping to think for half an hour before committing another line to paper—in any case, the actual writing of a play had usually been preceded by months or years of thinking about it. While writing the initial draft of a script, he listened to music (usually early choral or instrumental music) quietly in the background. He also drank whiskey, sometimes quite a lot, at this stage, but there was nothing bacchanalian about his solitary imbibing. In this context, Parker used the whiskey, the music, and the lateness of the hour to help him turn off his critical faculty and access his dream consciousness, where he could concentrate on listening to the voices in his head. A highly rational person, Parker nevertheless believed implicitly that a playwright needed, above all, a certain kind of impressionability. He put this idea in his notebook early in 1981:

> Plays are all about people w/ obsessions of a concentrated kind. That's why (or because) the kind of writer who gravitates towards the theatre is the most intensely obsessive kind. Erudition he can do without, and lyric grace, and a whole vision of society. But he must be subject to possession. Both divine and diabolic.
>
> He is as a medium, speaking with other voices.

Despite his determination to tackle political issues in his work, Parker regarded character as central to drama, telling an interviewer that 'I want to go to the theatre to see interesting people doing exciting things', and he regarded fidelity to his characters as his foremost responsibility as a dramatist.[12]

Once he completed the manuscript draft of a play, Parker shaped and refined it in accordance with his own ends. This sober, daylight activity began when he typed the play, revising as he went. The typed version of a script was the first he would show anyone else: the 'first' draft. Ideally, he would finish this at least several months before a play went into production. Then, shortly before rehearsals began, Parker would revise the play again, addressing any concerns raised by the director or producer. He liked to be personally involved with productions of his plays, and he often did further rewriting during the rehearsal period. Rarely, however, did he make drastic changes from the manuscript to the 'final' version. His revisions consisted more usually of tweaking the dialogue, clarifying the themes, and streamlining the action.

While I have attempted to convey some sense of the genesis and development of each of Parker's works, this book is not a detailed study of the texts' evolution through successive drafts. Nor is it a survey of the criticism that now exists on his work or an exhaustive exploration of Parker's literary influences. Rather, I have sought to tell the life story of a charismatic and courageous person. This, necessarily, is framed by the story of the turbulent times through which he lived in Belfast. I agree with Anthony Curtis that 'A biography is essentially a work of history, a unique kind of genre filtering history through the life of an outstanding individual, integrating the public archive with the private archive.' Such integration is especially valuable when considering Northern Ireland in the second half of the twentieth century, since it challenges the generalizations and stereotypes that obstruct our view of the past. As John Wilson Foster declared in a 1985 lecture on the 'critical condition' of Ireland: 'It is a plurality of voices we precisely need in Ireland in order to interrupt the tiresome duologue of recent history. . . . One is tempted to exclaim: let ungovernable choirs of dissonant voices rain down on us in Ireland! Let the forests be invisible for the trees!'[13] The more I learned about Parker's life, the more interest it held for me. I would not have begun this project, however, had I not also been convinced that Stewart Parker should be regarded as an important writer. Thus, I also provide readings of his literary works, in the hope that these will serve as starting points for other critics and in the firm belief that his writing gains resonance when examined in the contexts of his life and times.

Despite Parker's assertion, in 1986, that 'each of the plays is an entry in the private book of reckoning for my own journey', when I began this research I did not think of him as an especially autobiographical writer.[14] Rather, I believed that most people's lack of knowledge about Northern Ireland would cause them to miss the subtleties of his work, and this context chiefly concerned me. The more deeply I delved into his life, however, the more I realized how much his personal circumstances also fed into his creative writing. From Chapter 8 on, the chapters of the biography each form themselves naturally around one or two stage plays of the period. Earlier chapters cover Parker's childhood and education, the amputation of his left leg when he was 19, the years he spent living in the US, his youthful writings, his decision to return to Belfast, and his experience of life in that city during the worst of the violence of the 1970s. Starting with Chapter 5, each chapter begins with a paragraph surveying its contents.

Marilynn Richtarik

Atlanta, Georgia
17 March 2012

Acknowledgements

In the preparation of this biography, I have accrued debts of gratitude that I can never hope to repay. My husband, Matt Bolch, and our sons, Walker and Declan Bolch, have had to share my attentions with Stewart Parker for as long as they have known me, and they have done so without (much) complaint; I give thanks for them every day. I am grateful to Lesley Bruce and to Parker's family for their support of my efforts, and to John Kelly, John Fairleigh, John Wilson Foster, Edna Longley, and Gerald Dawe for encouraging my interest in its early stages. Parker's agents past and present, Marc Berlin and Alexandra Cann, have also been helpful. A number of organizations funded various parts of the research and writing of this book, and I thank the American Council of Learned Societies, the American Philosophical Society, Georgia State University, Green College of the University of British Columbia, the Hambidge Center for Creative Arts and Sciences, Jesus College Oxford, the Killam Trust, the National Endowment for the Humanities, the National Humanities Center, the Research Triangle Foundation of North Carolina, the Rhodes Trust, and the University of British Columbia. I am also grateful to everyone who supported my grant applications, successful and unsuccessful: Tony Bradley, Elizabeth Butler Cullingford, John Fairleigh, Jay Farness, John Wilson Foster, Adrian Frazier, Beth Gylys, Seamus Heaney, John Kelly, Richard Kirkland, Robert Paul Lamb, Edna Longley, Lucy McDiarmid, Frank McGuinness, Derek Mahon, Paul Muldoon, Christopher Murray, Donna Potts, Richard Russell, George Watson, and Stephen Watt. Many friends (and sources who became friends) invited me to stay with them on my research trips, and their hospitality enlivened my days as well as enabling me to stretch my travel money further. With fond memories, I wish to thank especially Marcus Patton and Joanna Mules, George and Margaret Parker, Sam and Hortensia Fannin, John Gilbert and Rena McAllister, Mimi Kingsley and Helen Nesbitt, Joan and Kate Newmann, Tony and Patty Bradley, Steph Pickering, George and Jo Watson, Sam and Joan McCready, Ken and June Lambla, Chris Avery, Joanne Woolway, Jonathan Levin, Annie Dawes, Lucy and Colin Kidd, Anne Skeldon and Paul Dauncey, and Joan and Peter Pyne. My mother, shortly before her death, accompanied me on several of my early research expeditions, and my recollections of them are intimately connected with my memory of her loving presence and wisdom. The members of the Triangle Irish Studies Group, particularly Weldon Thornton, Michael Moses, and Richard Russell, offered good fellowship during the year I spent in North Carolina (1998/9) and influenced my reading of Parker's play *Pentecost*.

I have been fortunate while writing to have had a number of perceptive readers. Sam Fannin, Lesley Bruce, Lynne Parker, Modupe Labode, Matt Bolch, and my agent, Jonathan Williams, read every chapter and made invaluable suggestions. I am hugely indebted to Oxford University Press's anonymous readers both for their positive reports on the book and for practical counsel regarding cuts and edits. Two of my research assistants, Shannon Gilstrap and Dan Vollaro, also offered editorial advice on the first half of the book. A number of my sources have given me comments on individual chapters or sections of chapters, and, although I will not list them all here, I am thankful to each and every one. The members of the Biography Group at the National Humanities Center (1998/9) were a wonderful first audience for Chapters 1 and 2 and raised provocative theoretical issues: Janet Beizer, Jonathan Bush, Ed Friedman, Rochelle Gurstein, Tony La Vopa, R. W. B. Lewis, Elizabeth McHenry, Wilfrid Prest, Suzanne Raitt, Ashraf Rushdy, and Bertram and Anne Wyatt-Brown. Adrian Frazier included an extract from an earlier version of Chapter 2 in a special issue of *The Irish Review* that he edited and gave me helpful tips regarding biography as a genre. Michael Parker read and commented on the first two chapters. The various incarnations of the Works In Progress Group of Georgia State University's Department of English offered useful reactions to Chapters 4, 5, 6, and 8: Tanya Caldwell, Stephen Dobranski, Michael Galchinsky, Pitt Harding, Jim Hirsh, Chris Kocela, Mary Lamb, Scott Lightsey, Pearl McHaney, Randy Malamud, David Payne, Mary Ramsey, LeeAnne Richardson, Renée Schatteman, and Paul Schmidt. My colleagues Randy Malamud and Ian Almond also read sections of the book outside of the WIP Group. The past and present chairs of my department, Robert Sattelmeyer and Matthew Roudané, showed remarkable patience in waiting for this work to come to fruition, Patricia Bryan and Marta Hess helped me with the necessary accounting, Greg George and Richard Gordon provided technical support, and Margaret Mills Harper offered encouragement. My research assistants, Jan Rieman, Mary Carter, Shannon Gilstrap, Joe Anderson, and Dan Vollaro, did their jobs cheerfully and well, and Lisa Anderson helped me track down some sources on a voluntary basis.

Thanks are also due to the staffs of the various libraries and archives I have accessed, including the BBC Northern Ireland Community Archive; BBC Northern Ireland Document Archive; BBC Radio Archives; BBC Written Archives Centre; Belfast Central Library; Bodleian Library; British Library Newspapers; Cornell University Library; Field Day Theatre Company; Hamilton College Library; Linen Hall Library; National Humanities Center Library; National Library of Ireland; Pullen Library, Georgia State University; Queen's University Belfast Library (Special Collections); RTÉ Script Archives; University of British Columbia Library; University of Ulster at Coleraine Library; and Woodruff Library, Emory University (especially the Manuscript, Archives, and Rare Book Library).

I particularly wish to thank all the people who provided me with information, without whom this book could not have been written. I do not cite them all in the text, but each added to my picture of Stewart Parker and his contexts. These include (with my abject apologies to anyone I have inadvertently left off this list): Brenda Adams, Lucy Alcorn, Roy Alcorn, Michael Allen, Douglas Archibald, Jonathan Bardon, Brian Barfield, Michael Barnes, Paula Barnett, Ed Barrett, Fergus Bell, Marc Berlin, Tony Bicât, Scott Boltwood, John Boyd, Patty Bradley, Tony Bradley, Harry Bradshaw, Austin Briggs, Margaret Briggs, Rodney Brown, Terence Brown, Lesley Bruce, Charles Burrowes, Bridget Butter, Peter Butter, Ophelia Byrne, Brenda Callaghan, Sydney Callaghan, Alexandra Cann, Marvin Carlson, Geoffrey Carnall,

Douglas Carson, Mary Carson, Bill Carswell, Joan Parker Clements, Joe Clements, Nancy Cole, Stephen Cole, Gail Collins, Robert Cooper, Dan Crawford, Molly Crawford, Robert Crone, John Cronin, Dermot Crowley, Barbara Dalgarno, Shaun Davey, Liz Davidson, Gerald Dawe, Angélique Day, Seamus Deane, Pat Devlin, Keith Dewhurst, Liz Dickey, David Dickson, Jim Doan, Miche Doherty, Douglas Dowd, Noeleen Dowling, Cynthia Ellis, Stephen Enniss, David Evans, Sally Evans, John Fairleigh, Lorraine Brown Fannin, Sam Fannin, Peter Farago, Simon Farquhar, Christopher Fitz-Simon, Imelda Foley, Michael Foley, John Wilson Foster, Roy Foster, John Frost, Alan Gabbey, Brian Garrett, John Gilbert, Elgy Gillespie, Alfred Gingold, Bill Goldsmith, Maggie Goldsmith, Marvin Gowdy, Bill Granleese, Bob Granleese, Patrick Grant, Charles Grime, Eileen Halliday, Helen Hamilton, John Hamilton, David Hammond, William Harris, Ann Hasson, Denys Hawthorne, Charlotte Headrick, Seamus Heaney, Margaret Windham Heffernan, Neil Hertz, Ian Hill, Philip Hobsbaum, Maureen Horner, Marilyn Imrie, Lyn Innes, Carrie Jobes, Edwin Jobes, Jennifer Johnston, Jane Keenan, Terry Keenan, Douglas Kennedy, Susan Kenney, John Killen, Mimi Kingsley, Peter Kingsley, Richard Kirkland, Susan Knowles, Tony La Vopa, June Lambla, Ken Lambla, Gina Leishman, Laurence Lerner, Valerie Lilley, Dwight Lindley, Edna Longley, Michael Longley, Frank Lorenz, Grainne Loughran, Alison Lurie, Brian Lynch, Vivian Valvano Lynch, Rena McAllister, Róisin McAuley, Tony McAuley, Sean McCarthy, Jim McCloskey, James McConkey, Joan McCready, Sam McCready, Alf McCreary, Gerry McCrudden, Kevin McCrudden, Brian McGinn, Brian McIlroy, Ciaran McKeown, Brian McKibbin, Nancy McKibbin, Tom McLaughlin, Bernard MacLaverty, Bea MacLeod, Scott McMillin, Julie Parker McMullan, Niamh MacNamara, Aodán Mac Póilin, Joan Caldwell McQuoid, Julie MacRae, Angela McWhirter, George McWhirter, Derek Mahon, Ivan Marki, Jeanne Marki, Patrick Mason, Ronald Mason, Julia Mattingly, David Maxwell, Karen Maxwell, Catherine Miller, Joe Mills, Stanley Mills, Rex Mitchell, Vicki Moltke, Bill Morrison, John Morrow, Gerard Moses, Louis Muinzer, Paul Muldoon, Joanna Mules, Frank Murphy, May Neill, Colette Nelis, Helen Nesbitt, Joan Newmann, Carole Nimmons, Roy Nimmons, Sara O'Brien, Mary O'Connor, Patrick O'Connor, Mary O'Malley, Francie Nesbitt Oppel, Frank Ormsby, Jack Pakenham, G. H. Parker, George Parker, Kate Parker, Lynne Parker, Margaret Parker, Reeve Parker, Andrew Parkin, Marjorie Patterson, Marcus Patton, John Paul, Tom Paulin, Denis Payne, Mark Phelan, Seán Phillips, Steph Pickering, Sybil Allen Poole, Michael Quinn, Brian Rainey, Stephen Rea, Christina Reid, Jennie Renton, Eliza Robertson, Nicholas Round, Howard Schuman, Sally Schwartz, Brian Scott, Pat Scott, Tim Shields, Art Skidmore, Denis Smyth, Linda Southall, Randolph Splitter, Bert States, J. S. Stevenson, Mary Stewart, Nathaniel C. Strout, Ann Tannahill, Gerry Thompson, May Thompson, Warren Thompson, Frances Tomelty, Andrew Totten, Roberta Truesdale, Alan Tuttle, Elaine Urquhart, Brian Walker, George Watson, Tracy Weston, Winthrop Wetherbee, Joanne Woolway, Sylvia Wynne, and John Young.

I wish to thank the following for providing illustrations for the book and/or for allowing the reproduction of copyright material: Lesley Bruce, John Gilbert, Chris Hill, the Parker family, Lynne Parker, Amelia Stein, the 10th Belfast

Scout Group, and Andrew Totten. All reasonable effort has been made to contact the holders of copyright in images reproduced in this book. Any omissions will be rectified in future printings if notice is given to the publisher.

Finally, and by no means least, I am thankful to the people whose professional skills helped to make this book a reality, especially my agent Jonathan Williams, Commissioning Editor Jacqueline Baker, Assistant Commissioning Editor Ariane Petit, Production Editor Brendan Mac Evilly, copy-editor Joanna North, proof-reader Albert Stewart, typesetter J. Olivia Mary, Jenny Townsend, Shinn Uehara, and Matt Bolch.

M. R.

Contents

List of Plates

List of Abbreviations

DUP	Democratic Unionist Party
IRA	Irish Republican Army
NICRA	Northern Ireland Civil Rights Association
PD	People's Democracy
RUC	Royal Ulster Constabulary
SDLP	Social Democratic and Labour Party
UDA	Ulster Defence Association
UUP	Ulster Unionist Party
UUUC	United Ulster Unionist Council
UVF	Ulster Volunteer Force
UWC	Ulster Workers' Council

A Brief Chronology of Stewart Parker's Life and Major Works

20 October 1941   James Stewart Parker born in Belfast

1947–1952   attended Strand Primary School (not entered for the Eleven Plus exam owing to ill health)

1953–1955   attended Ashfield Boys' Secondary School

1955–1959   attended Sullivan Upper School in Holywood

1959–1963   completed the English Honours course at Queen's University Belfast with a 2.1 degree

17 May 1961   had his left leg amputated after being diagnosed with bone cancer

1963–1964   began work at Queen's on a Master's thesis on poetic drama (submitted in 1966); participated in Philip Hobsbaum's original Belfast Writers' Group

26 August 1964   married Kate Ireland and moved to the United States

1964–1967   employed as an instructor in English at Hamilton College in Clinton, New York

1966   *The Casualty's Meditation*, a pamphlet of poetry, published by the Belfast Festival in a series that also included pamphlets by Seamus Heaney, Michael Longley, and Derek Mahon

1967   *Speaking of Red Indians* (radio play) produced and transmitted by the BBC; a second Festival poetry pamphlet, *Maw*, published

1967–1969   employed as an instructor in English at Cornell University in Ithaca, New York; co-taught a bi-weekly writing class at Allenwood Prison Camp in Pennsylvania from February until July 1969

21 August 1969   arrived back in Belfast less than a week after British troops were sent to the city to try to quell sectarian violence

1970   published several personal articles in the *Irish Times* and then began writing a regular column on popular music, *High Pop*, that would run in that newspaper until 1976

1971   *Minnie and Maisie and Lily Freed* (radio play) and *Self Portrait* (radio talk) produced and transmitted by the BBC

1973   'Requiem' (dramatic poem) produced and transmitted by the BBC; from July until December, taught a weekly class at Long Kesh prison camp which included Gerry Adams as a student

1974   *The Iceberg* (radio play) produced by the BBC (transmitted in 1975)

1975   première of *Spokesong* (stage play) at the Dublin Theatre Festival

1976   production of *Spokesong* and première of *The Actress and the Bishop* (one-act stage play) at the Kings Head Theatre Club in Islington (London)

1977   received the Evening Standard's Most Promising Playwright Award for 1976; Kings Head production of *Spokesong* transferred to the Vaudeville Theatre in the West End; *I'm a Dreamer Montreal* (radio play) produced and transmitted by the BBC; première of *Catchpenny*

	Twist (stage play) on the Peacock stage of the Abbey Theatre, Dublin; *Catchpenny Twist* (television play) produced and transmitted by the BBC
1978	première of *Kingdom Come*, a musical written with composer Shaun Davey, at the Kings Head; *Spokesong* produced by the Long Wharf Theatre in New Haven, Connecticut; moved to Edinburgh; *I'm a Dreamer Montreal* (television play) produced by Thames Television (transmitted in 1979)
1979	*Spokesong* presented on Broadway at the Circle in the Square Theatre; *The Kamikaze Ground Staff Reunion Dinner* (radio play) produced and transmitted by the BBC; *I'm a Dreamer Montreal* (television version) won the Christopher Ewart-Biggs Memorial Award
1980	première of *Nightshade* on the Peacock stage of the Abbey Theatre; *The Kamikaze Ground Staff Reunion Dinner* (television play) produced by the BBC (transmitted in 1981)
1981	*The Kamikaze Ground Staff Reunion Dinner* (radio version) won a Giles Cooper Award; *Iris in the Traffic, Ruby in the Rain* (television film) produced and transmitted by the BBC
1982	*Joyce in June* (television play) produced and transmitted by the BBC; moved to London; separated from his wife, Kate
1983	moved in with Lesley Bruce and her daughter; première of *Pratt's Fall* at the Tron Theatre, Glasgow
1984	*The Traveller* (radio play) produced by the BBC (transmitted in 1985); *Blue Money* (television film) produced by Blue Money Productions and London Weekend Television and transmitted on the ITV network; première of *Northern Star* at the Lyric Players Theatre, Belfast
1985	*Radio Pictures* (television play) produced and transmitted by the BBC
1986	première of *Heavenly Bodies* at the Birmingham Repertory Theatre; *Dramatis Personae* (lecture) delivered and published in Belfast; *Lost Belongings* (six-part series of television films) produced by Euston Films in association with Channel Four and Primetime Television (transmitted in 1987 on Channel Four and the ITV network)
1987	première of *Pentecost* (stage play) in Derry by the Field Day Theatre Company; *Pentecost* received a Harvey's Award for Best New Play
2 November 1988	died of stomach cancer

1

A British Boyhood

At age 29, Stewart Parker recalled his life before birth:

> East Belfast was bombed in the Spring of 1941, and I wasn't born until October of
> that year. I don't know how I come to carry an image in my head of crowding into the
> air-raid shelter with all our neighbours. Maybe it's true that memories begin in the
> womb. More likely I dreamed the scene so intensely, it became true: and this kind of
> truth, the truth of memory and of literature, is more important than the trivial reality
> of what actually happened.[1]

Anyone growing up in Belfast in the 1940s and '50s would have imbibed the wartime experience from the city's collective memory. The Belfast Blitz of April and
May 1941 left hundreds dead and 15,000 homeless. During the Easter Raid of
15/16 April alone, over 700 people were killed and 1,500 injured. For weeks afterwards, those unable to flee Belfast left the city nightly to sleep in fields and ditches.
Others took refuge in air-raid shelters, singing to pass the time until the all-clear
sounded. Among them was Isobella (Belle) Parker, pregnant with her third child.
She started smoking out of sheer nervousness during these tense evenings, a habit
that eventually grew to sixty Gallaher's Blues a day. During Stewart's early childhood, the shelter, 'a symbol of the past', remained, along with the bomb crater that
served neighbourhood children for a pond.[2]

The advent of the Second World War had been greeted almost with relief in
Belfast, where the global Depression set in early and lingered late. Since 1920,
Northern Ireland had been the stepchild of the United Kingdom. Observers in
Britain recoiled from the vicious sectarian violence that engulfed it immediately
before and after partition. After these Troubles died down, the Unionist regime at
Stormont, left to its own devices domestically, restricted Catholic access to employment and social services and repressed the political aspirations of any it considered
enemies of the state, allowing the sectarian canker to fester. However, it lacked the
power to take actions that might have made Northern Ireland more competitive in
a world economy. Trade and monetary policy emanated from Westminster, and the
British government favoured 'mainland' Britain. Throughout the 1920s, Belfast
was the most disadvantaged industrial region in the UK, averaging one quarter of
all insured workers unemployed at any given time. Belfast's per capita income
before the war stood at about half of Britain's, and in 1938 it was estimated that
36 per cent of the city's population lived in 'absolute poverty'.[3]

British rearmament, beginning in 1935, helped alleviate these inequities. Belfast's
relative distance from Germany, surplus of skilled labour, and spare engineering

capacity made it a centre for war industries. Few dwelt on the possible negative consequences of being a vital part of the British war machine. People doubted that Belfast would be attacked, and, mindful of the nationalist minority, the British government hesitated to introduce conscription in Northern Ireland.[4]

After the fall of France and the Low Countries in 1940, however, Belfast acquired new strategic importance, placing it at greater risk. Pressured by German U-boats, British vessels detoured around Northern Ireland, which remained effectively defenceless.[5] The Easter Raid demonstrated the cost to civilians of inadequate preparation by both Westminster and Stormont. The force of the attack fell on residential districts north of the city centre (the German bombers likely mistook the Cavehill Waterworks for the harbour), but the real target had been Sydenham, an industrial area adjacent to the shipyards and Shorts aircraft factory, where Belle Parker lived with her husband, Herbie, and their two children, George and Joan, at 86 Larkfield Road.[6]

Belle and Herbie met in their mid-teens at the Willowfield Picture House and married shortly afterwards, in February 1932. The newly-weds rented a house on Palestine Street, behind Queen's University. George was born the next year; Joan followed four years later. The Larkfield Road house had been purchased by Herbie's parents, who intended to live there while his father commuted to his job in Larne, a harbour town north of Belfast. When this proved impracticable, Herbie's growing family took it over.[7]

Herbie's father, George Herbert Parker, worked as maintenance engineer at the Avoniel Distillery until it closed and then in a similar position at Northern Ireland Paper Mills, in Ballyclare and then in Larne. Though on call twenty-four hours a day, he received no pension when he retired. Belle's father, James Lynas, worked as a coppersmith at the Sirocco Works, which made tea-drying machinery for use in the far reaches of the Empire. He provided the purest splash of orange in Stewart Parker's family, signing Ulster's Solemn League and Covenant against Home Rule in 1912, joining the original Ulster Volunteer Force, fighting at the Somme in 1916, and marching every year in the July Twelfth parades. Nevertheless, when he learned once of plans to ambush a Catholic co-worker, he warned him, probably saving his life. A hearty man, who had played football for Ireland and for East Belfast's Glentoran (a career curtailed by wounds in his thighs and calves received during the First World War), he lived to be 93. Throughout his life, his damaged legs extruded bits of shrapnel.[8]

Herbie held various jobs, including selling Hoover cleaners door-to-door (a mortifying business for a man who was never 'forward'). Unemployed for a time during the Depression, he moved the family to Larne to stay with his parents and weekly cycled the twenty-two miles into Belfast to collect his dole money. Finally he found work as a tailor's cutter at Norman Duncan & Company, a firm that made women's housecoats and commercial clothing. He spent the rest of his working life there, retiring as a production manager. Belle, who trained as a bookbinder and worked briefly in a printer's office, stayed home after marrying.[9]

James Stewart Parker (always 'Stewart') was born on 20 October 1941, joining what he called later 'an average Unionist family, without being hard line'. His parents subscribed to the *Belfast Telegraph* and voted for the mainstream Unionist Party, eventually switching allegiance to the Northern Ireland Labour Party.[10] The neighbourhood being almost entirely Protestant, Stewart was exposed to the usual sectarian stereotypes, though not in any particularly virulent form. 'As a child,' he wrote, 'I went to a prod school in a prod neighbourhood and never remember being told to hate papists, nor did I ever fight one, in fact I probably never met one: but I grew up with an osmotic sense of their being different and a bit dangerous.'[11] As he put it in another context, 'Fenians lived out beyond the stockade somewhere and went to chapels instead of churches and walked out of the pictures before the Queen was played. They were too abstract to interest me much. The Free State was where my mother got me slabs of pink bubble gum and sticks of rock with Dundalk or Omeath down the middle of them.'[12]

The Parker family belonged to the Church of Ireland. Belle and Herbie, lax attenders themselves, sent their children to Sunday school at the church of St Brendan the Navigator. The patron of sailors and navigators, Brendan made an appropriate sponsor for a congregation in a shipyard district, but he is also renowned as a hero of Celtic legend. During Parker's childhood, he remarked, Brendan provided his one tenuous link to that other, Irish, Ireland, 'the invisible Celtic world of Ballymacarrett and Connsbrook and Connsbridge and the rest of Ireland beyond: an unsuspected skeleton under all the familiar surfaces'.[13]

'Saved' (briefly) by the Baptists at 13, Stewart began 'conducting revivalist meetings in friends' garages'—this proved a passing fancy. He taught Sunday school at St Brendan's as a teenager but gradually experienced a crisis of faith, as he explained years later:

> My conscience forbade me to speak in church any part of the Creed I couldn't accept any longer, and as the Sundays went by it became more and more pitted with gaps, phrases I would mouth but not speak. Finally there was nothing left but the first phrase, 'I believe in God', and when that went, I quit. Before this, however, there was the anguish of Confirmation followed by first Communion. When I touched the symbol of Christ's blood to my lips, I fully expected some cataclysmic retribution on my hypocritical body. Things like that are so important when you're sixteen.[14]

Parker's extended family lavished on music the passion that members of some Northern Irish clans spent on politics and religion. His maternal grandfather, James Lynas, loved music and encouraged his children to develop their abilities: Molly sang, and Belle played the violin, Carrie the piano, and Jim the mandolin. Even after George's birth, Belle and Carrie performed ballroom music at dances. Belle enjoyed music into her seventies, directing the family sing-songs at Christmas gatherings and performing her party piece, 'A Bird in a Gilded Cage'.[15]

On the Parker side, music tended to be associated with religious observance. Herbie's mother left the Church of Ireland, which she found lacking in enthusiasm, and joined the Baptist Church for its rousing hymns. In search of ever more musical and spiritual excitement, she switched to the Salvation Army Church after the move to Larne (and played the organ for them, although she could not read music). Herbie sang with the Grosvenor Hall male voice choir at the central Methodist mission, a group of about forty men who performed sacred music a cappella. He also belonged to a smaller ensemble called The Sundowners, whose repertoire consisted of Gene Autry-style 'singing cowboy' numbers about characters like 'Sioux City Sue' and 'Ragtime Cowboy Joe'. They had professional gigs at music halls in Belfast and sang on BBC radio broadcasts. The Sundowners broke up when they were offered engagements in England, since several of the men had families and did not wish to travel, but their regular rehearsals at the Parker home before that stood out in Stewart's mind long afterwards as one of the 'ingredients of romance' that fed his imagination in childhood.[16]

When Stewart was a teenager, his father (a skilled craftsman) yielded to his importuning and built him a guitar, which, as he put it, served as 'the vehicle of long hours of adolescent world-weariness up in my cold bedroom'. Like his Gran Parker, he taught himself to play by ear. With several friends he started a skiffle group called The Troubadours. Stewart led the band, singing and teaching the others how to play their instruments (tea chest bass, washboard and thimbles, acoustic guitar). They imitated their idols—Lonnie Donegan, Nancy Whiskey, and The Vipers—in songs such as Woody Guthrie's 'Grand Coulee Dam'. Later, rock 'n' roll took over, starting with Bill Haley's 'Rock Around the Clock' and followed by the Beatles ('Lennon and McCartney were my heroes', Parker recalled). He also recollected creating a sensation at his first school debate when he opposed a motion condemning the downward slide of 'culture' by opening his Dansette record-player and putting on Jerry Lee Lewis's 'Whole Lotta Shakin' Goin' On'.[17]

As befit a young man whose parents met in a cinema, other forms of popular culture likewise played important roles in Parker's youth. His family did not own a television while he was growing up, but radio provided information and diversion. Parker and his friend Bill Granleese loved *The Goon Show*, which Peter Sellers, Spike Milligan, and Harry Secombe created and starred in for the BBC from 1951 to 1960. Parker also saw plenty of movies, especially Westerns, at the Astoria on the Upper Newtownards Road and the Strand Picture House on the Holywood Road. Bill and Bob Granleese remember a camping trip with Stewart in the Mourne Mountains when they were teenagers, which climaxed in an excursion into Newcastle to see Elvis Presley's *Jailhouse Rock*.[18] Far and away Stewart's favourite film star, though, was Danny Kaye, whose performances sent him into convulsions of mirth.[19] Most of these entertainments were imported from Britain or the United States, with one notable exception: *The McCooeys*, a BBC Northern Ireland radio drama series that actor Joseph Tomelty wrote and performed in for seven years in the late 1940s and early 1950s. Centred on a Belfast family of 'unidentifiable religious background', this show stood out for its humorously realistic depiction of Northern Irish working-class life and use of local accents and expressions. Tremendously popular with people on both sides of the sectarian divide, it attracted a weekly audience of half a million. As an undergraduate at Queen's, Parker told a friend that he would have liked to have written for *The McCooeys*.[20]

The Belfast of Parker's earliest memories remained in some respects a Victorian city. Many of the public buildings and most of the houses dated from the nineteenth century, the period of the city's great expansion. Red brick dominated, and almost any street gave on to unobstructed vistas of the surrounding hills. In the more exclusive areas, the streets were lined with monkey puzzle trees, alternating here and there, incongruously, with lofty palms. Sydenham still bordered on green fields, and everything from bread and lemonade to coal was delivered to the door by men with horses and carts.[21] As an adult, Parker remembered with nostalgia the street hawkers of his childhood: 'Women would come out in their slippers with the hearth brush to sweep up the horse's droppings for garden manure. There was the rag and bone man, the herring man, the balloon man', and the coalbrick man, 'flying past covered in black dust, surrounded by the steam curling from the coalbrick he sat on, like a devil rising from the pit'. As late as the 1980s, Canadian Charles Foran identified the 'distinctive smell' of Belfast, intensified after the frequent rains, as coal smoke with an undertone of bog and peat: 'The smell of rural Ireland blended with the smell of industrial England.' Indoors, a musty fragrance prevailed because, although residents of the city burned sufficient coal to fill the air in lower-lying areas with soot and deposit a grey film on buildings and trees, there never seemed to be enough in those stringent post-war years to heat the people or the houses fully or to dispel the pervasive damp.[22]

Most streets were paved with cobblestones, so the air always rang with the clatter of traffic. (Around consecrated public buildings, like churches and the grand City Hall, the cobbles were covered with pine boards treated with tar to muffle the din.) Parker also recalled the constant 'distant clanging of the shipyard and the sudden roar from the test bench at Shorts', the 'baleful moans of foghorns from ships coming up [Belfast Lough]', and the rattle of trains passing by the bottom of the street. On weekdays people flocked to and from work on bicycles or in open trams, so full only the roof remained visible. On Sundays, though, work and play alike ceased, the swings in public playgrounds were tied up to keep children from violating the Sabbath, and in the quiet one could hear the traffic lights changing.[23]

By the end of the Second World War, however, Belfast stood on the verge of transformation. In the general election of July 1945, the Labour Party won a mandate for radical social change, and with legislation passed through the late 1940s the government created the British welfare state. At first those in charge at Stormont resisted following this lead, but Westminster overcame Unionist opposition to the legislative programme by offering to subsidize the cost of welfare laws in Northern Ireland.[24] Thus, various reforms in health, housing, and education were implemented at the behest of the British government which would have far-reaching effects in the North.

Of immeasurable importance to Parker was the creation in 1948 of the National Health Service—open to everyone, free, and effectively comprehensive. A more or less identical act passed through Stormont the same year, and, historian Jonathan Bardon writes, 'because of cruel neglect in the past, the impact of this new service was more profoundly felt in Belfast than in any city in Britain'. Stewart's parents called on the National Health on his behalf many times during his youth. At age 7, he got sunstroke on a family outing to Helen's Bay, and pleurisy set in as a complication. Stewart missed a year's schooling and had to refrain from strenuous activity for several additional years. He marvelled in later life about how such 'accidents' reinforced the personality traits that would make him a writer: 'All my inclinations, from the cradle, were towards passivity, stoicism and reflectiveness, and they were merely intensified by years of not being allowed to work up a sweat or lie in the sun, of constant x-rays and waiting-rooms pent up with blighted unhappy children.' At 11, Stewart had his appendix removed at Haypark Hospital—the first operation in his family. He observed that

> This event etched the world of hospitals on to my mind, and I suppose I have believed ever since that hospitals hold the secret of the human condition. In the clinics of earlier years I was constantly falling desperately in love with little girls whose legs were in callipers or whose faces were badged with a livid rash. Now surrounded by them in hospital I was wracked by the same overpowering emotion, the heart's response to the absolute isolation of suffering, first your own and then other people['s].[25]

Partly because of Stewart's 'smitten lungs', his family moved house shortly after he developed pleurisy, to 'the more rarefied air' of a new estate across the Holywood Road. Many people in Belfast were moving at this time, since a crash programme of house-building had begun right after the war. The distance between Larkfield Road and 12 Carolhill Park was small geographically but considerably greater in class terms. The family left a solidly working-class area for one that had been dominated by wealthy people, the owners and bosses of the industries employing most of their relations. These previous residents often resented new developments like Carolhill Park, so although the Parkers were heading up in the world in absolute terms, they might have been made to feel more self-conscious about their status. Parker himself dealt lightly with this class dislocation:

> Suddenly we were semi-detached and suburban, and a piece was no longer a piece but a packed lunch. But we were also adjacent to green fields, to a sports club and the estates of the landed gentry.
> These estates aroused in me, not an instinct for social equality, which was already strong, but a scientific curiosity.[26]

With Bill Granleese, whose family moved into the neighbourhood a few years after the Parkers, Stewart became an avid bird-watcher. For two or three years, the only period of Stewart's life when he arose cheerfully before dawn, the boys roamed the green spaces, identifying the many varieties of birds frequenting them. For some time, Stewart (extremely near-sighted though he did not realize it yet) merely pretended to see most of the things Bill pointed out to him; only after he got his first pair of glasses at the age of about 13 did he admit to bluffing before. Perhaps because of his poor eyesight, Stewart regarded listening to the dawn chorus for the first time as 'the supreme experience of our bird-watching mania'.[27]

Other encounters with the outdoors came through his involvement with the Boy Scouts. As a spindly 11-year-old he joined the 10th Belfast Scout Group, unusual then for not being affiliated with any particular church.[28] Stewart especially enjoyed the summer camping and youth hostelling excursions, usually to destinations in Britain such as Loch Lomond or the Northumberland fells. At the camp in Scotland, his first trip away from home, he remembered learning 'that I was incapable of homesickness.... I also discovered that you didn't have to be good at games to be well thought of... I was useless at any sport, but was never made to feel inadequate as a result—instead, each boy was encouraged to shine at whatever he *could* do. Which in my case was entertain.' Parker made his first day trip into the British capital from a Scout camp in Buckinghamshire in 1956, and he remarked in 1987 that 'living in London now over thirty years later, I am still sometimes reminded of the heady excitement of that first brief encounter with the city'. The adult Parker also recalled fondly the weekly Scout's Own sessions, 'discussion groups-cum-sing-songs', at which members took turns reading papers they had written and 'talked over moral values and general principles, in a humanist kind of way'. He remained in the group for four years, quitting only when he needed to start working 'flat out' at school in order to win a university scholarship.[29]

That a boy from Parker's background was even considering university owed much to another piece of British legislation. The 1944 Butler Act decreed that primary education would end at age 11, to be followed by free and compulsory secondary education provided by three types of schools—grammar, secondary, and technical—into which students would be channelled according to their performance in a competitive exam. This law would have revolutionary social effects throughout the UK as working-class children in large numbers gained access to a superior secondary education and a chance at university. In Northern Ireland the impact would be especially great since Catholics there had long been disproportionately disadvantaged. Both Catholics and Protestants were initially suspicious of the Education Act, however, fearing it would dilute the sectarian ethos of their schools. A bill extending the main provisions of the Butler Act to Northern Ireland did not pass until 1947, and it did nothing to mandate integration at the primary and secondary levels; real mixing between Protestants and Catholics would not take place until students arrived at Queen's. The substance of educational reform in Northern Ireland was to convert the old public elementary school system into a new primary and secondary system. Pupils completing primary school took a qualifying exam (the 'Eleven Plus') and, on the basis of it, the most 'able' 20 per cent were sent to grammar schools and the remaining 80 per cent to 'intermediate' secondary schools.[30]

Stewart attended Strand Primary School, which his brother George remembers as an ordinary Northern Irish school of the time, with strict discipline—pupils might be caned for serious infractions or have a 'duster' thrown at them for not paying attention—that 'didn't do us any harm'. Sam McCready, who attended Strand about five years before Stewart did, recalls some exacting teachers and a student body largely devoid of ambition other than (for the boys) obtaining a position at Shorts or the shipyards or (for the girls) leaving school for a job in a shop, followed, with luck, by marriage. Stewart's own recollections of Strand are considerably more lurid: 'This school was [permeated] with a heavy odour of depravity and madness, actually embodied in the fetid stench that hung in the air of the dining hall.... The teachers were likely to be faith healers or alcoholics; one elderly lady whose white powdered face I won't forget was a casebook sadist who sliced a ruler across your cold knuckles at every opportunity.' By the time he wrote this

passage (most of which was excised from the version of his autobiographical reflections aired by the BBC in 1971), Parker had been steeped in a 1960s' brand of
iconoclasm, but his political education had likely been preceded by an instinctive
abhorrence of regimentation. He resented most of all, in retrospect, the stifling of
his imagination. Clearly, too, things that did not make much of a negative impression on others who experienced them bothered him inordinately. He was, as he
described himself in a poem written around the time of his twenty-first birthday,
'A sickly sensitive child/All wrong for a shipyard district.'[31]

Adding insult to injury, Strand did not enter Stewart for the Eleven Plus because
he had missed so much instruction. Thus he initially attended, not a grammar
school, but Ashfield Boys' Secondary School, recently built about a hundred yards
from the Parker family home. The teachers at Ashfield were young and idealistic,
and Parker regarded the two years he spent there as 'the most productive of my
whole education'. Stewart found a mentor in John Malone, the English teacher and
vice-principal, eulogized by the adult Parker as 'an enthusiast who responded with
warmth and delight to the enthusiasms of others, and in particular to those of his
pupils'. Malone—a soft-spoken, bespectacled, courteous man with impeccable
Methodist College and Cambridge credentials—was a genuine radical who believed
fervently that schools should participate in the work of social reconstruction. As
such, he campaigned for 'the opportunity for equality' in addition to 'equal opportunity'. An early advocate of comprehensive education, Malone thought it immoral
as well as misguided to steer children at the age of 11 into academic grooves that
would determine their lot in life. He also feared (presciently) that the use of the
qualifying exam would subvert the egalitarian impulse behind the original legislation and end up reinforcing social stratification. At Ashfield, and later at Orangefield Boys' School (where he was headmaster), Malone challenged his students
to excel, regardless of the fact that the system had already branded them as failures.
'[I]f I had to write a Morality play around him,' Parker declared in 1986,

> I would probably select from amongst all the possible names with which to character-
> ise him—Integrity, Commitment, Service, and so on—the allegorical name of Zeal.
> He was a true zealot for the emancipation of the mind and imagination, and for an
> educational system which would afford the greatest nurture to the least naturally
> endowed child in the most wretched environment in the land. It was a zeal which
> drew its force from such diverse traditions as Northern Irish Protestant radicalism, a
> particular brand of Christian socialism, and a Cambridge Leavisite aesthetic. It was a
> quietly crusading zeal which instinctively fixed on anything and everything within its
> ken as a potential learning resource: drama included.[32]

Parker credited John Malone with introducing him to the theatre. In 1955,
Ashfield mounted its first school play, with Malone as director and producer. He
chose the fifteenth-century allegorical drama *Everyman* and cast Stewart, who had
never read a play or entered a theatre, as Everyman. On another occasion, Malone
encouraged Stewart to bring in the conjuring set he got for Christmas and perform
magic tricks for the class, whereby his pupil 'experienced for the first time that
heady and highly addictive sensation of putting one over on an audience'.[33]

As important as his fostering was to Stewart, Malone knew his pupil belonged in a grammar school, and with the help of the head of Ashfield, A. C. Stanley, he made sure Stewart got into one. A review exam children could sit after proving themselves at their secondary schools allowed for some mobility between levels for the more academically gifted of those passed over at the Eleven Plus. Stewart was transferred to Sullivan Upper School in this manner, but (thanks to a friendship between Stanley and the vice-principal and soon-to-be headmaster of Sullivan, John Frost) he came to Sullivan early, in May 1955, and was an 'academically invisible' pupil there for the summer term; he remained officially on the Ashfield roll for a time, with the formal review and transfer taking place months later. By dint of what James Hawthorne, then a maths teacher at Sullivan, calls this 'unusual and illegal manoeuvre', Stewart had the opportunity to get used to his new school before the other transferees.[34]

At Sullivan, Stewart received special tuition to help him make up the ground he had lost in some academic subjects. May Neill, one of his English teachers, explains that many educators at both secondary and grammar schools opposed the two-tier system of post-primary education and thus had a vested interest in the success of so-called 'review' pupils. In Stewart's case, sundry adults at Ashfield and Sullivan bent the rules to enable him to be where he was, in 'a drama that was taking place far above his level', but Stewart himself, as Hawthorne puts it, 'seemed unaware that he was at least part of the cast'. From his point of view, Parker recalled ruefully, 'My status reverted from star to clod.'[35]

Other factors also conspired to make the transition difficult. Sullivan Upper School was in Holywood, a British Army garrison town to the north-east of Sydenham. Though only about five miles from his home (Stewart cycled to school), Holywood was clearly *outside* Belfast. In class terms, too, Sullivan presented an alien world. It was not, in those days, an exclusive grammar school, but rather unfashionable compared to the likes of Campbell College, Methodist College, and the Royal Belfast Academical Institution. Unfortunately, Sullivan's peripheral status made the school administration neurotically anxious about its image. Regulations regarding school uniform were enforced to the smallest particular, and 'individual genius', in the words of May Neill, was distrusted as 'being too out of line with bourgeois respectability'. Stewart did not play rugby, which further marginalized him in the school's culture. Having finally encountered pedagogy that inspired him at Ashfield, he found the move to Sullivan wrenching:

> I had two and a half years of Latin, French, History, Snobbery and Conformity to catch up on, just when I was on the verge of striking poses on the utmost rock and wrenching white hot poems from my steaming heart. The social stuffiness and intellectual drudgery combined to make me resentful, morose, wretched and inwardly priggish and arrogant: in short, adolescent, but with a vengeance.

At one point Frost, undoubtedly with the best intentions, summoned Stewart to his office to suggest that he try to modify his east Belfast accent. That 'really got up his nose', Stewart's sister recalls. Similar scenes were being played out in headmasters' studies throughout Northern Ireland around this time, but not every pupil so exhorted rejected the advice with the same disdain.[36]

Received Pronunciation represented social capital. Positions of advantage and authority in Northern Ireland were still filled to an extraordinary degree by middle-class English people—or, at any rate, people from other parts of the Empire with something approximating the proper accent. They dominated the university, the BBC, the world of 'culture', and the bureaucracy. Local, indigenous, and, especially, working-class experience was devalued. In 1976, Parker recalled the subtle humiliations of those days, writing that 'We were supposed to be British, but when you visited "the mainland" (an insult in itself) they took you for a Canadian or a Scot.... We didn't have any country, we just had a Province. A very, very provincial Province—politically corrupt, culturally bankrupt, full of aggressive inferiority, sectarian, self-obsessed, and unutterably dreary.' This cultural cringe was particularly evident in schools, where the literary texts studied were invariably the classics of the English nation, with perhaps a nod to William Butler Yeats. Michael Longley, educated in Belfast around the same time as Parker, remembers that 'At primary school (and later at grammar school) there was little on the curriculum to suggest that we were living in Ireland: no Irish history except when it impinged on the grand parade of English monarchs; no Irish literature; no Irish art; no Irish music.' C. S. Lewis's birthplace was within walking distance of Parker's own; Louis MacNeice had been raised nearby; Philip Larkin spent five years in the early 1950s as a librarian at Queen's; and Northern Irish writers such as Michael McLaverty and Sam Hanna Bell were living and working in the city. Yet, according to Seamus Heaney and critic John Wilson Foster, Belfast's youth were not encouraged to think of literature as being written by people like them.[37]

Nor had the sexual revolution hit Northern Ireland yet. Wherever several hundred teenagers are gathered together there will be sexual tension, and at co-educational Sullivan Upper School students did pair off. But fear of the consequences of sexual activity in those pre-pill days, combined with the evangelical Christian ethos endemic to Sullivan, made for an atmosphere of sexual repression (there were, for example, no school dances).[38] Stewart in those days worshipped girls from afar. At Sullivan he fixated on the prettiest girl in the school, who barely acknowledged his existence—Bob Granleese remembers hitch-hiking to the youth hostel in Cushendall with Stewart when they were both sixth-formers because the Sullivan Geographic Society, to which the girl belonged, was there on a field trip. Another time they hitch-hiked to Portrush because Stewart had a crush on a girl working as a waitress there for the summer. With half a crown between them, they survived the weekend sleeping tentless on the freezing strand.[39] Despite such efforts, Stewart's frustration regarding the opposite sex remained well-nigh total throughout his school years.

Stewart's teachers at Sullivan remember him variously as 'affable and positive', albeit 'shy and "respectful"' (Hawthorne); 'a lonely, rather bleak sort of figure.... shy, even sullen, and certainly not an easy social mixer' (Neill); 'competent if not outstanding' in his studies (Frost); 'a decent, hard-working boy' (Charles Grime); and 'highly individual' and a bit 'arrogant' (Charles Burrowes). To Terence Brown, three years behind Stewart at Sullivan, he already seemed to have an inside track on a more interesting world. In his younger contemporary's eyes, Stewart stood out as an aesthete in a philistine place, a loner who somehow conveyed a sense of style and self-assurance. He was not happy there; in later life, Parker often talked about Ashfield and John Malone but rarely mentioned Sullivan by name. When he did discuss his grammar school career, it was usually in a slighting or dismissive manner, although he conceded in an interview for the Queen's student newspaper in 1961 that 'It wouldn't have mattered what school I went to, it probably would have been worse anywhere else, I just hated it.'[40]

Stewart's innate individuality no doubt would have made his teen years, with their attendant pressure to conform, difficult under any circumstances. This pressure was exaggerated in British grammar schools of the time, and the resistance to it of Parker and others like him had its basis in class antagonism, as well as the normal teenage distrust of authority. Novelist Deirdre Wilson writes that the grammar schools were 'seen by some as Jacob's ladders allowing bright young chaps to climb out of nowhere. To some bright chaps they were more like colonies, with their school caps, house teams, Latin mottoes, distant echoes of the Eton Boating Song. Irony seemed too weak a reaction.' On the other hand, even as Stewart's sense of working-class solidarity grew in opposition to the social environment at school, it became increasingly obvious that he did not fit in easily at home either. The attraction of intellectual life drew him irrevocably away from his familiar world; objectionable though it might be in many ways, grammar school remained the place where people talked about Shakespeare and John Donne. The same stubborn independence that made Sullivan seem absurd also alienated him from the Belfast working-class culture he felt increasingly nostalgic about, where the street resembled an extended family. In finishing at Sullivan and aiming at university, Stewart followed a path that none of his relatives had travelled before him, and the usual adolescent angst was compounded, in his case, by the anxiety of the unknown.[41]

There were some consolations. Stewart belonged to the tennis club, the music society, and the debating society, then discussing such motions as 'This House considers that the banning of Rock 'n' Roll films is in the best interests of today's youth' (defeated overwhelmingly), 'This House considers that girls should be trained for marriage and not for other careers' (another defeat by a large majority), and 'In the opinion of this House the Scout Movement is out-of-date' (resoundingly defeated). He was especially active with the Dramatic Society, known for its highly regarded annual productions of Shakespeare plays directed by English teacher Charles Grime. Grime took Stewart under his wing, casting him as Polonius in *Hamlet*, the Earl of Gloucester in *King Lear*, and King Henry IV in *Henry IV, Part I*.[42]

Privately, Stewart was already consumed by another abiding passion. *Everyman* had been, as he put it later, 'the first work of literature to flood my mind with light'. He began writing around age 13, and at 15 he suddenly decided he wanted to make a living at it. This was an extraordinary ambition for a working-class boy in the mid-1950s—in Belfast, of all places, where the announcement that one aspired to be an author was apt to provoke the cryptic response '*You're* the boy', delivered in a tone that conveyed simultaneously amusement, bemusement, and a touch of contempt. His family attributes Stewart's career choice to the influence of John Malone. He would not have picked up the idea at home. 'There was no literary tradition in my family and none in Sydenham either where we lived', Parker remembered; 'There was no trace of any interest in the arts at all in my family.' Growing up, he recalled, 'I'd never read any children's books, and very little fiction of any kind; instead, I'd read books I found around the house, like an account of a transatlantic crossing in a small boat and the autobiography of a man who'd lost both arms in the war.'[43]

The dullness of Stewart's contributions to the Sullivan magazine drove Miss Neill to despair.[44] Unbeknownst to her, though, he was, as he quipped in 1987, 'A teenage poet. Writing all about how desperately unfair life had been, only to me. What a lonely soul I was. All this unrequited love—the passionate focus and desperate infatuations I had with all the little blonde-haired blue-eyed little girls who were in a class above me...' This description misrepresents his younger self. The concerns of his adolescent poetry were more existential than lovelorn. In an analysis of his earliest work which he probably wrote as an undergraduate, he reflected that 'The first big influence which imposed a thread of continuous subject-matter on my poetry was the realisation of the lack of a reason for life.' The question of what to do with this insight 'absorbed my whole life and thinking for two years. I discarded it unanswered, but satisfied.'[45]

Like many a budding writer before him, Stewart derived some sense of meaning and purpose from the act of writing itself. The epigraph he chose for his first poetry notebook came from 'Third Elegy' by Alex Comfort: 'Teach me to live/a speaking fountain for the tongueless faces', and he clearly already saw himself as a representative voice of his generation, of adolescents in general, and of the Belfast working class.[46] Small wonder that he often felt like 'a changeling' growing up in his family.[47]

Stewart's parents and siblings regarded him as a quiet, 'placid' child (though he himself would probably have used the word 'stoic'). His absent-mindedness, legendary in the Parker household, rendered him capable of riding his bicycle to the butcher's shop to pick up meat for his mother and walking home with the package under his arm, having forgotten his bike—or of reaching the shops and forgetting why he had been sent. In a family full of engineers, he stuck out by virtue of his inaptitude for anything mechanical. (His brother George remembers him trying to fix a puncture on his bicycle tyre by patching the outside of it without mending the inner tube.) A photograph of Stewart at the age of about 14 shows a boy with a thin, unformed face, round spectacles, and a serious expression, posing self-consciously with a book. There is no hint in it of the *joie de vivre* for which he would be beloved by his many friends in years to come. His Scout's Own paper on the subject of Time, written around the same period, similarly reveals scant trace of the humour that would distinguish his mature work:

> Coming back to this business of human life, I would like you to ask yourself, 'Is a human life really that long'? Of course an average man's life is 70 years, but think how many of these are lost. The first five are not really profitable, and in fact most of these

years are completely lost to memory. The last five or ten are also more or less lost, as it is then that old age necessitates the losing of time. So we can narrow the real years of human life down to only a few dozen. And the most important part of those years are the very ones we are going through now, that is, the teens. So remember that now, above all times, is the time not to lose.[48]

In the Parker family circle, Stewart's mother, not Stewart, was the life of the party.

Belle Parker was a tiny woman (five feet tall) with a big personality, an accomplished and enthusiastic storyteller who, in the words of her husband, 'would have talked the leg off a stool'. She delighted in being the centre of attention and held court daily for a devoted circle of neighbourhood women. A connoisseur of gossip, her irreverent wit and blunt, outspoken manner made her extremely popular. Living with her could be trying, however. She was highly protective of her children, especially Stewart—'the child', the delicate one. Perhaps she clung to him more possessively because she felt she had lost touch with her elder son during the war, when he lived with his grandparents in Larne for five years. She 'coddled' Stewart, according to his father, but had little patience with his wool-gathering.[49] For his part, Stewart compared himself unfavourably to his handsome, athletic, and practical brother and felt destined to disappoint her.

A woman of extreme emotions, Belle did not hesitate to express them. Stewart, despite his fascination with drama, disliked emotional scenes off-stage but was subjected to frequent histrionics by his mother, whose outbursts he could try to ignore but could not prevent. Poor health intensified her emotional highs and lows. When Stewart was about 13, she put her back out trying to move a heavy piece of furniture; arthritis set in, and in later years she traced her health problems (which included hip-replacement surgery and years as an invalid) to that incident. She spent extended periods in hospital during Stewart's teens, which felt to him at first like a desertion and later like a liberation. As a young man, he dedicated a poem to her in which he imaged their relationship in terms of a war in which he was now prepared to call a truce:

> Even having me twisted your spine.
> The war was on, everywhere.
> You suckled me in an air-raid shelter,
> Flak lodged in your nerves,
> It gritted deeper, inflamed
> As the years went.
> . . . .
> They dragged you into a Home and I was free.
> Every Sunday, I went to see
> You; small, crowled and ugly with grief.
> You snorted wetly into your handkerchief,
> Often jammed it between your teeth
> To keep from screaming.
>
> Mother, it seems that always
> We have been visiting each other.

You're back in your real home now.
The doctors give us 'a new start'.
Twenty-one years since they cut us apart,
Mother, the war is over.[50]

Stewart apparently believed that his mother would not object to his publishing this peace offering. However, when the poem appeared in the *Kilkenny Magazine* in 1966, she felt betrayed and outraged, and afterwards he was much more circumspect in his public references to her.

Stewart always felt more affinity with his father, a quiet, mild, and ingenious man happy to support his youngest child's eccentric interests, whether this entailed making a costume for him to wear on stage as Everyman or waking up at 2 a.m. to drive him to Kinnegar to listen to birdsong all day. When, at the age of 14 or 15, his attention shifted from wild birds to budgerigars, his father built an outdoor aviary of wood and wire netting, with a de luxe birdhouse and a tree for Stewart's eight or nine budgies to sit on. Parker believed that his childhood ended in this aviary. For a while he 'lavished attention and affection' on the birds, but by then he had transferred to Sullivan and spent most of his time studying. Gradually,

> I began to feel that dread secret ebbing of interest which I wouldn't even confess to myself. I got increasingly careless about cleaning out the aviary and filling their seed bowl. One morning the aviary was quiet. The birds were a gaudy heap of corpses. . . . I had neglected them and they were dead. I filled up with remorse until my joints actually ached. It was the last time I wept, the tears slowly tearing themselves one by one through the seared eyeballs. Speechlessly I got some twigs and cord to make crosses, dug a grave and buried the bundle of little albatrosses. The remorse went grinding on for days.

Parker remembered this horrific experience as 'a form of birth trauma, an awakening to the terrible burden of being a free agent'.[51] It was not the last time he would be torn between the bonds of affection and the demands of intellectual work.

2

Queen's University

As a 'fresher' at Queen's University Belfast in 1959, Stewart Parker threw himself into student life with the enthusiasm of someone released from prison—a sentiment he shared with many of his contemporaries. In Northern Irish grammar schools of the time rigorous academic demands were coupled with strict discipline and attempts at social control. Parker had never been comfortable at Sullivan, despite—or perhaps because of—extra attention from teachers and administrators. At university he found less pressure to conform and more opportunity to meet people with similar interests. A loner at Sullivan, at Queen's Parker revealed a talent for friendship, moving in a number of circles. By his third year, he was well-known enough on campus to be profiled in the student newspaper, *Gown*; the writer remarked that 'The range of his friends and the levels of these friendships is continually surprising.' Parker himself observed that his ability to divide his time and attention gave him 'a desirable anonymity'. Tall and thin, with a diffident manner, wavy hair reaching to his collar (long by the standards of the day), a ready smile, and intense and protuberant blue eyes, Parker had an energizing quality that attracted others. Those who got to know him found him forthright and wryly funny.[1]

Parker could not have chosen a better time than the early 1960s to be an undergraduate in Northern Ireland. Although the region still suffered from higher unemployment than the rest of the United Kingdom, anyone with a university degree (a small elite within the population) could confidently expect a good job after graduation. Students' resulting sense of security contributed to an easygoing university environment in which extra-curricular activities were at least as important as formal studies to many. Nevertheless, Parker's first two years at Queen's were marked by little that could be called student activism, leading one writer in *Gown* to wonder in May 1960 why the sort of student demonstrations occurring in Third World countries were so 'improbable' in the US and the UK.[2]

As yet the only degree-granting university in Northern Ireland, Queen's represented both a microcosm of the society and an indicator of its future, since changes in the social structure manifested themselves there first. The effects of the 1947 Northern Ireland Education Act had begun to show by the time Parker arrived. For one thing, more students were attending university than ever before. Parker's year consisted of 900 members; in 1948, the entering cohort included only 620.[3] The social background of the incoming students also diverged from that of earlier student generations. Before the education reforms, few working-class families had possessed both the money and the will required to send their offspring to the grammar schools that could prepare them for university. The Act enabled working-class men and women to obtain higher education at public expense. Moreover, because Catholics were routinely discriminated against (and thus tended to be poorer), the Act benefited them disproportionately.

Since its founding in 1845, Queen's had been an oasis of religious toleration. Local Protestant clergy and the Roman Catholic hierarchy agreed, as unfortunately they did not regarding secondary education, on the principle of 'united secular and separate religious instruction'. Catholic students accordingly had long made up a significant proportion of the student body.[4] The difference between these earlier Catholic contingents and the one entering Queen's around the same time as Parker was that the latter contained a noticeable concentration of students from disadvantaged backgrounds. These had every reason to blame their misfortunes on a corrupt Northern Irish state, and within a decade, as their confidence caught up with their abilities, Catholic students would make their presence felt in novel ways.

In 1959, though, open protest remained almost unthinkable. Most students, Protestant and Catholic alike, instead revelled in the liberal atmosphere of the university, where they discovered they were not as different as they had thought. While their closest friendships tended to be with people from the same side of the sectarian divide, being at Queen's allowed them to meet and talk with people from the 'other' side in a relatively relaxed setting, an opportunity unprecedented for many. Lecturers from elsewhere were sometimes struck by the seeming determination of Queen's students to segregate themselves by religion, but the students themselves perceived the university experience as vastly liberating and found the general atmosphere the most open and tolerant that they had encountered in Northern Ireland. Maintaining the smooth surface of the time required considerable circumspection and even repression. 'After all,' Seamus Heaney reflects, 'the very words Catholic and Protestant defined the no-go areas; they were like buoys marking out the position of toxic dumping grounds within the Northern Irish psyche.' The optimism was real, though. Most students who considered the issue believed their generation would be the one to transcend the brutal Northern Irish past and saw no reason why the necessary social transformation could not be accomplished in a peaceful and reasonable manner. The inaugural debate at the Queen's Literific Society during Parker's first year considered the motion 'That this house has confidence in the Rising Generation'.[5]

Parker and most of his friends at Queen's saw themselves on the left politically. In those days, this meant supporting the Campaign for Nuclear Disarmament and following the civil rights movement in the US. (News and first-hand accounts of sit-ins at segregated lunch counters in Atlanta, the Freedom Rides aimed at desegregating transportation, and the activities of Martin Luther King, Jr appeared in *Gown* during Parker's time at Queen's.)[6] Not coincidentally, one of the strongholds of left-leaning student opinion was the Jazz Club, to which Parker belonged; members met weekly to listen to music they knew stemmed from African-American roots. (For Christmas one year, Parker gave a girlfriend a recording of Ray Charles's 'Georgia On My Mind', and when Louis Armstrong played in Belfast a large group from Queen's attended.)[7]

If these young people focused less on the Catholic/Protestant division within Northern Ireland, it was partly because they considered it irrelevant and partly because they had been conditioned by 'such thorough-going apartheid' that they barely noticed it. The Dramatic Society ('Dramsoc') was a consciously, or self-consciously, non-sectarian club, although Protestant members vastly outnumbered Catholic ones. Its parties, where sing-songs alternated between nationalist and loyalist tunes and one might even hear 'The Sash My Father Wore' sung in Irish, drew students from around the university, including those who had nothing to do with productions. Queen's students lionized Sam Thompson, the local dramatist whose play *Over the Bridge*, first produced in January 1960, called attention to sectarianism in the shipyards; and *Gown*, proclaiming itself 'the only independent newspaper now publishing in Belfast', printed an exposé in December 1960 of the Reverend Ian Paisley's acknowledged though unofficial links with Ulster Protestant Action (an organization 'pledged to the maintenance of Protestant supremacy in Ulster').[8] Few, however, regarded sectarianism as anything to do with them.

Parker admired Sam Thompson and talked about his own desire to be politically engaged. In this he was not unusual. Patrick Grant, a slightly younger contemporary who, as the product of a 'mixed' marriage, was more sensitive than most to the nuances of religious prejudice on both sides, says that what distinguished Parker from other students on the left was his view of sectarianism as a 'malicious blight' and, in itself, perhaps the worst problem Northern Ireland faced. Many students, especially those who owed their places to the Education Act, were less conscious of religious than of class differences at the university. The majority of Queen's students still came from middle-class homes, with accents and attitudes alien to the new wave. Parker impressed working-class friends with his evident pride in his background and refusal to change his accent, to attempt to pass as middle-class, or to be cowed by subtle social distinctions. His egalitarian outlook complemented his anti-sectarianism, since he deplored the way religious bigotry divided the working class in Northern Ireland.[9]

In the late 1950s and early 1960s, though, surveying the wider world seemed more progressive than political introspection. Queen's belonged to a British imperial system of higher education, which gave it a remarkably cosmopolitan aura. Michael Grant, who became Vice-Chancellor in 1959, had previously been at the University of Khartoum (and before that at the University of Edinburgh).[10] Although most of the students were Northern Irish, professors and lecturers were at least as likely to come from Britain or English-speaking countries overseas as they were to hail from any part of Ireland. Philip Hobsbaum, an Englishman who arrived at Queen's as an assistant lecturer in 1962, enjoyed the 'ecumenical' flavour of the university, recollecting that 'if there was a bias, it was towards the foreign and the exotic'.[11] This had a salutary impact on students whose experience had often been limited to the provincial.

Middle-class Queen's students generally enrolled in professional courses like law, medicine, and engineering; working-class (especially Catholic) beneficiaries of the Education Act, whose expectations remained modest, were more apt to choose arts subjects. Arts students could do a three-year 'pass' degree in general studies or a four-year Honours course in one subject. All students began with three subjects in their first year. Honours students took two subjects in the second year and concentrated in the final two years on their major subject. Parker was one of about a dozen students in his year to undertake the English Honours course, and his Queen's transcript records that he studied Spanish and Modern History along with English during his first year and Philosophy as a subsidiary subject in his second year.[12]

Professor Peter Butter, a genteel Anglo-Scotsman, headed the English Department in Parker's time. Vague, kindly, and unfailingly polite, he invited the Honours students to his home on the Malone Road for formal sherry parties. Old and Middle English were taught by another Scotsman, John Braidwood, friendly and fair despite his military bearing and brisk manner. Parker liked Braidwood but was more directly influenced by two rising stars in the department, Gamini Salgado and Laurence Lerner. Brilliant and charismatic, Salgado came from Ceylon. His lectures on Elizabethan and Jacobean drama were performances in themselves, and he also took an interest in modern theatre, producing Bertolt Brecht's *Galileo* at Queen's in December 1962. Lerner, a South African who shared Salgado's love of theatre, marvelled at the parallels between Northern Ireland and South Africa and at his students' professed ability to tell Protestants from Catholics on sight. He taught mainly seventeenth-century poetry, but he wrote poetry, too, and promoted modern poetry and drama. Lerner spent the 1960/61 academic year in the US and thus became a magnet for students interested in American literature as well (though he did not care for most of it himself). A man of formidable intellect, impatient and challenging, Lerner injected a note of relevance into a conservative curriculum, bringing, in Seamus Deane's words, 'the streets of Belfast and the poems and novels we read into contact with one another'.[13]

The course of study then included little twentieth-century literature. According to what Butter terms the 'Oxford ethos' that predominated, students were thought capable of reading the literature of their own era without assistance, requiring their teachers' 'superior knowledge' to help them with earlier works. Irish literature, as such, did not feature in the curriculum, though George Bernard Shaw and Edmund Burke were studied as English authors. Seamus Heaney (a conscientious student) recalls only one scholarly discussion of W. B. Yeats as an Irish writer, 'a slightly negative lecture' by Professor Butter 'about the dreaminess of Yeats's early style'. George Watson, who began the Honours course in 1960, confirms Heaney's account and adds that James Joyce was not taught formally at Queen's until Philip Hobsbaum included *Ulysses* in a special option on the twentieth-century novel around 1963. To note these omissions is not to imply there was deliberate discrimination against the Irish dimension of literature in English, but it illustrates the extent to which Queen's saw itself in a British rather than an Irish context.[14]

Though contemporary literature did not appear on the English Honours syllabus, it was hardly unknown to Queen's students. The members of a small but active literary subculture at the university kept each other informed of developments in poetry, fiction, drama, film, philosophy, psychology, and music. These budding aesthetes were not exclusively English, or even arts, students.[15] They congregated in

Dramsoc and on the staffs of student publications. Along with these activities, they shared the assumption that a university education was not limited to formal instruction but extended into their interactions with each other and the world outside Queen's.

Parker and his arty contemporaries regarded their official studies as incomplete and their teachers as largely incapable of shedding light on the essential questions. They saw the plight of their generation as unique in human experience: they were the first people to have grown up under the threat of nuclear annihilation, and this often seemed the most salient fact of their existence. Reviewing the previous half-century, they saw one catastrophe after another: two devastating World Wars, a global Depression, the insane excesses of fascism, the betrayal of the communist ideal, the abrupt collapse of the British Empire, the Cold War. Norman Mailer summed up their dilemma in his 1957 essay 'The White Negro', a text Parker and his friends read with interest, writing that

> we will never be able to determine the psychic havoc of the concentration camps and the atom bomb upon the unconscious mind of almost everyone alive in these years.... [I]n the middle of an economic civilization founded upon the confidence that time could indeed be subjected to our will, our psyche was subjected to the intolerable anxiety that death being causeless, life was causeless as well, and time deprived of cause and effect had come to a stop.[16]

For perspectives on how to live in a world stripped of certainty and security, Parker and others turned to the works of writers ten to twenty years older than themselves who had begun publishing in the 1950s. In British terms, this meant the Angry Young Men; on the other side of the Atlantic, the Beats. Both the Beats and the Angry Young Men had been influenced by French existentialism, and writers like Jean-Paul Sartre were also much read and discussed at Queen's in those days.[17]

In his assessment of the new British writers of the 1950s, *The Angry Decade* (1958), Kenneth Allsop argued that a more accurate description of the current mood would be 'dissentient'. This contrariness came in several varieties: revolutionary and emotional (exemplified by playwright John Osborne), cynically neutral (like novelist Kingsley Amis), and philosophical (a stance represented by Colin Wilson, existentialist author of *The Outsider*). Despite their differences, Allsop maintained, these writers were alike in disagreeing 'with majority sentiments and opinions'. The difference between their post-war angst and the American version was the difference between Britain and the US—in short, class consciousness. The archetypal Angry Young Man is Jimmy Porter, protagonist of Osborne's 1956 play *Look Back in Anger*, which dramatizes the conflict between a university-educated but underemployed man from a working-class background and his middle-class wife in a dreary provincial town. Allsop described 'the new dissentients' as a 'rootless, faithless, classless class'.[18] These writers and the characters they depicted were alienated from British society partly because they felt excluded from taking their rightful place in it.

The American Beats (more appealing to the Queen's littérateurs) went further. Rather than rebelling against their society, they dropped out of it. Theirs was an art of 'disengagement', according to Kenneth Rexroth, an older ally. Another poet and critic, Lawrence Lipton, referred to the 'disaffiliation' of the younger generation, and Mailer described the 'hipster', or 'American existentialist', in similar terms: '... if the fate of twentieth century man is to live with death from adolescence to premature senescence, why then the only life-giving answer is to accept the terms of death, to live with death as immediate danger, to divorce oneself from society, to exist without roots, to set out on that uncharted journey into the rebellious imperatives of the self'.[19]

Jack Kerouac, who named the movement ('Beat' was short for 'beatific') and whose book *On the Road* did much to popularize it, saw the impulse driving the Beats as essentially religious—they were finding God through finding themselves. Mailer agreed that 'to be with it is to have grace ... for you are then nearer to that God which every hipster believes is located in the senses of his body ... not the God of the churches but the unachievable whisper of mystery within the sex, the paradise of limitless energy and perception just beyond the next wave of the next orgasm'.[20] Sex was not the only path towards enlightenment: drugs, alcohol, jazz music, and meditation were other means advocated by the Beats for achieving an enlarged state of consciousness, and one can easily understand the attraction of their philosophy for men in their late teens and early twenties.

An associate of Parker's at the time recalls that they also loved the idea of being 'on the move, to be on the road, to be going ... it didn't matter where you were going as long as there was somewhere to go'. To read Kerouac, Allen Ginsberg, Gregory Corso, and Lawrence Ferlinghetti was to enter into the America they conjured up: vast, anarchic, diverse, infinitely more interesting than Belfast. The Beats employed colloquial American speech, familiar to Queen's students from films and popular songs. One of the bohemian crowd made a trip to the US and brought back recordings of some of the Beat poets reading their works, and Parker and his friends listened to these repeatedly. Their 'Bible' was the *Evergreen Review*, a quarterly literary and cultural journal based in New York City which published the Beats along with more established American and European writers. They all dreamed of going to the US, the place where 'everything was happening'.[21]

Younger writers in Britain and America differed in many ways, then, but they shared certain attitudes and approaches. Among them were a consciousness of themselves as a new generation with new problems, a preoccupation with death and an accompanying determination to live fully in the moment, an awareness of the self as essentially isolated, an alienation from other individuals and society, a commitment to self-exploration and non-conformity, a use of language that mimicked speech, and a distrust of women often bordering on misogyny. Presumably these were the things that attracted disciples at Queen's; student writing of the time displays many of the same characteristics. The list of plays produced by Dramsoc from 1959 to 1961, the years of Parker's most active involvement with it, likewise yields examples of 'dissentience' in all its forms, as well as evidence of an obsession with the US. In addition to plays by Shaw and T. S. Eliot, Dramsoc performed *Huis Clos* and *The Flies* by Sartre, *Look Back in Anger*, *The Lesson* by Eugene Ionesco, two one-acts by William Saroyan, *The Crucible* by Arthur Miller, and Edward Albee's *The Zoo Story*.[22]

The British and American influences are clear, as is the lack of specifically Irish influences. Beckett mattered to Parker and his friends, but Beckett published in the *Evergreen Review*. Parker also admired Joyce, but, like Beckett, he could be seen as belonging at least as much to Europe as to Ireland.[23] If one narrowed the focus to Northern Ireland, the contemporary cultural landscape looked even more barren. In drama there was working-class playwright Sam Thompson, and Parker also respected Stewart Love, who had had several plays on television.[24] For the most part, though, the professional theatres appeared to him to be 'playing each other off for the best Belfast kitchen comedies and farces, best being synonymous with cheapest, crudest and most money-spinning'. The situation did not look any better in the other literary arts. In an article written for a student magazine in 1962, Parker bemoaned the fact that 'Ulster is famous for unemployment, pubs, and Field Marshals. How many famous Ulster writers do you know of? Louis Macneice [*sic*] and C. S. Lewis are English-educated and English-minded. Brian Moore's in Canada. Kenneth Martin's in London. Who the hell could thrive in the creative climate that prevails here?'[25] Many years later he recalled that Northern Ireland seemed 'like the back end of nowhere and we all felt really out of it....We were terribly wet behind the ears—and kind of craven in our deference to everything happening elsewhere.'[26]

One positive by-product of this sense of operating in a cultural vacuum was the freedom it gave young writers. Since they did not see themselves as working within a thriving literary tradition, they could create their own from examples that inspired them. Several Queen's University magazines—including *Q*, *Interest* (founded by Parker in 1960), and the English Society's *Gorgon*—published short stories and poems by students. There was also a vogue for original plays, to the extent that a commentator in *Gown* observed that 'If Dramatic Society members continue writing plays at their present rate, they will soon have more playwrights than actors.'[27] Literary undergraduates read and reviewed each other's work—always seriously, sometimes savagely. Student writers at Queen's with Parker included, among others, Seamus Heaney, David Farrell, Seamus Deane, John Hamilton, Jim Caffrey, Bill Morrison, Ian Hill, Don Carleton, Alan Gabbey, and George McWhirter; many of them became professional creative writers, academics, journalists, and theatre practitioners.[28]

Most of these writers did not confine themselves to any one genre, dabbling in poetry, fiction, journalism, criticism, even cartooning. Parker himself wrote poems, short stories, a novel, songs, essays, reviews, and plays as an undergraduate. In this atmosphere young writers at Queen's learned from and influenced each other. John Hamilton, the most respected student playwright at Queen's, introduced his friends to the 'theatre of the absurd', especially Ionesco, pushing them away from the naturalistic forms Northern Irish writing had typically taken.[29] Even more obviously an arbiter of taste, Ian Hill was instrumental in nearly every publishing and cultural enterprise at Queen's, specializing in journalism and criticism rather than creative writing. One of the first of the Queen's beatniks, Hill matriculated in

1956 and—because he was doing an especially long course (dentistry)—did not leave the university until the spring of 1962. Bill Morrison remembers Hill as 'the ubiquitous man' and 'a great promoter'.[30]

These young writers regarded themselves and each other as the future of Northern Irish literature, and with reason. Queen's served as the focus for most innovation in the local arts. People who had been active in student societies often haunted the university after they graduated, returning to direct plays, give readings of their work, or publish in Queen's magazines. The Belfast Festival—which over time would become a city-wide showcase for music, visual art, theatre, film, writing, and dance, attracting international artists to Northern Ireland—began in 1961 as a student-run arts festival featuring mainly undergraduate performances and publications. It was natural, then, for Hill, surveying the sorry state of 'Writing in Ulster' for *Gown*, to feel confident that Queen's students would soon play an important role in that larger arena, opining, for instance, that 'Parker is certainly the best poet we have at the moment, with Seamus Deane an interesting second'.[31] Parker expressed similar ideas in martial terms in the autumn of 1962: 'Queen's is not an oasis, but it is a powder-store, and if enough people light matches, we can blast our way out of this cultural siege and then start the war in earnest.'[32]

Many students were shocked upon reaching the university to discover how much unstructured time they had. A focal point of Queen's social life for male undergraduates was the Student Union building at the corner of University Square and Botanic Avenue, and students thronged its steps and entrance hall to meet friends, sell magazines, promote causes, and read the notices posted there. (Women, greatly outnumbered in this period and overshadowed in most student organizations, had their own Women Students' Hall in a house on University Square.) The Union housed McMordie Hall, home of the Literific Society, as well as a Fiction Library with comfortable armchairs, a liberal smoking policy, and a collection that included 'scandalous' books like D. H. Lawrence's *Lady Chatterley's Lover*. Upstairs were smoking and games rooms regarded as the domain of engineers and mathematicians; students interested in the arts congregated in the dining hall alongside the Union building. There, as Niki Hill writes, 'the cigarette smoke hung in the coloured light that streamed through the stained glass windows and a cup of coffee could be made to last a morning, an afternoon'. At the unofficial Dramsoc table, Parker and his friends would talk for hours about plays and playwrights. Discussions begun there might continue in one of the student-frequented pubs around the university. What with one thing and another, a friend from the time reflects, 'We didn't do much studying.'[33]

From the moment he arrived at Queen's, Parker had been determined to make his mark on the place. The high-profile Dramatic Society had traditionally been the preserve of the plummiest English accents around the university. By the time he matriculated in 1959, Dramsoc had become less intimidatingly elitist, but among the first batches of Education Act students were many aspiring thespians who attended one meeting or audition and were put off or rejected. Some never came back; others eventually returned to become leading lights in the society. Roy Alcorn, one of the latter, left Queen's in 1957 but remained in Belfast to teach and continued to direct for Dramsoc. Jovial and down-to-earth, Alcorn was famed for his Elvis Presley imitation and punning humour. He auditioned Parker for Dramsoc's Christmas production, Shaw's *Saint Joan*, and—impressed by this newcomer from Sullivan, a school renowned for its Shakespeare productions—gave him the substantial role of the Dauphin.[34]

While it was flattering to receive a large part in a major Dramsoc production and to play opposite Nonie Devine—one of the most popular women at Queen's—as Joan, Shaw describes the Dauphin as 'a poor creature physically'.[35] Moreover, Alcorn had decided he should be played as a 'babbling sort of a person' and 'imposed' on Parker 'the longest pause that you have ever heard in any play in your life' at the moment when he is 'hypnotized' by Joan. The student reviewer, Ian Hill, called Alcorn's direction overly dramatic or melodramatic, 'part Shakespeare and part Tomelty', and 'Mr Parker's Dauphin…an unfortunate choice'. This initial experience with Dramsoc may have been responsible for Parker's abiding distaste for Shaw, but it did not end his undergraduate acting career. Because of it, he was by the end of his first term a person of note on the Queen's campus, whose name had already been mentioned several times in *Gown*'s 'Faces in the Crowd' column.[36]

Parker had also begun to establish a reputation as a writer, though his first attempt in this arena also met with derision. He submitted to *Gorgon* a revision of a poem written at Sullivan, a sad piece about a shipyard worker who leads a life of quiet desperation, finally closing 'his forty-six/Inarticulate years of vague despair/With a poem written on the river'. David Jenkins, an editor of the Queen's literary magazine *Q*, reviewed *Gorgon* for *Gown*, condemning Parker's poem: ' "Suicide", by Stewart Parker…should not have been published. It can be of value to no one and harmful to the purpose of the magazine if…everything is indiscriminately accepted by the editor.' Parker did not allow this rebuff to deter him from trying again, and the next term he had a short story accepted by *Q*. 'Johnny's Story' captures the frustration of a young man whose 'attempts to catalogue life, and death, and God, are swamped by [his] craving for a girl'—a girl who, although she has been dating him for five weeks, is 'going steady' with someone else. This time, the anonymous *Gown* reviewer proclaimed that 'in the author of "Johnny's Story" "Q" has found a new writer with some idea of what a short story can do'.[37]

In the spring of Parker's freshman year he played the First Priest in Eliot's *Murder in the Cathedral*—Dramsoc's festival production, which it entered in the full-length division of amateur and university drama competitions around Ireland. The play won awards in Ballymoney, Portadown, and Newry, and carried off top prizes for best production and best producer at the Universities' Drama Association Festival in Dublin, where the three priests were highly commended. Bill Morrison also attended this last festival, directing and acting in Dramsoc's one-act entry, N. F. Simpson's *The Hole* (this won no prizes, but a writer in *Gown* believed Queen's had struck a blow 'for the cause of modern drama in this philistine island' by producing it).[38] Parker and Morrison probably became friendly on this trip to Dublin.

Morrison had joined Dramsoc the previous year and was now its secretary. A *Gown* profile published during his final year at Queen's gives a vivid picture of him:

'An anaemic, slightly haggard face above a squat, powerful body; crouched shoulders combined with a studied fastidiousness of gesture and movement—Bill Morrison is an enigma squeezed into the tightest of tight trousers. To some he is a mixed-up hipster. To others he is a bum acting the part of a mixed-up hipster. To most he is either mildly or violently antipathetic.' Morrison spent his academic career at Queen's trying unsuccessfully to flunk out of his law course because he had already decided that his future lay in the theatre, though he was not yet sure whether he wanted to be an actor or a playwright. Self-consciously theatrical, he dressed in black, rolled his own cigarettes, and saw himself as Ulster's answer to Marlon Brando. Although he came from a middle-class background (his father was headmaster of a primary school in Ballymoney), Morrison adopted an Angry Young Man persona and liked to write in a working-class voice. Parker would certainly have encountered him around the Dramsoc 'hut' (a pre-fabricated metal-sided building between Fitzwilliam and Camden Streets, where the society performed all but its biggest productions) but may not previously have had the opportunity to get to know him well. Authoritative, egotistical, articulate, and opinionated, Morrison held a fascination for Parker, a year behind him at the university. With shared interests in theatre, writing, jazz, and Americana, they would be close companions and collaborators for the next few years before the competition always latent in their friendship got the upper hand. Less remarkable than the association's ending is the fact that it lasted as long and as intensely as it did, since in many ways their personalities were diametrically opposed. Stewart, friends agreed, was the 'gentle' one; Bill, by his own admission, was 'aggressive' and 'offensive'. Bill was forceful; Stewart gave at least the impression of being easygoing. Bill used people; Stewart, though also ambitious, was not manipulative. Bill was relentlessly macho; Stewart even then hated the cruder forms of male sociability. Stewart was universally liked, while Bill was almost as universally loathed.[39]

One of the first fruits of their oddly assorted friendship was a production of *Sweeney Agonistes* with a largely fresher cast for Dramsoc's Annual General Meeting in October 1960. Morrison directed Eliot's strange, fragmentary playlet whose title character sums life up in the words 'Birth, and copulation, and death'. Parker composed and performed music for the play. Together—'risking pretension', as Ian Hill observed—they wrote and recited a prologue for the piece. Its tone may be surmised from the review in *Gown*, which identifies Sweeney as 'the outsider, the beat, the intellectual schizophrenic of the thirties' who 'rejects society because it does not communicate with him and he knows he can never communicate with it—though he must always go on trying'.[40]

Sweeney was presented as half of a double-bill with a one-act by William Saroyan called *The Hungerers*, which Parker directed. This play, an allegory about different types of hunger—for food, for love, for fame—also dates from the 1930s. It takes place in the room of an unpublished writer whose work is continually interrupted by the people who shelter there from the rain. A stagehand (identified in Parker's production as Death, and played by Morrison) keeps rearranging the furniture, and the rest of the characters die and come back to life repeatedly. In a lengthy introduction Saroyan explains that 'The hunger of these hungerers is.... a hunger for immortality. The simple immortality that comes about when human beings rid themselves of all world-imposed absurdities and know the foolishness of pride.... When they know love. When they know there can be no death if there is love.'[41]

Parker acquired his own first practical experience of love as a result of this Dramsoc production. One of the cast members of *Sweeney Agonistes* was Elizabeth (Liz) Davidson, a first-year student in the English Department. She and Stewart, she recalls, 'became very close', indeed 'inseparable', for that academic year. Liz was his first real girlfriend, and they spent vast amounts of time working together on Dramsoc projects. She remembers him as 'very serious', though with a 'thorough-going sense of humour—black at times, cynical for one so young'. They declared their love for one another, but he gave her to understand that he could not experience emotion freely and fully like other people. Colin Wilson's book *The Outsider*, which presented alienation as concomitant with genius, had made a strong impression on Stewart, and the difficulty of genuine communication obsessed him. He was also in the process of growing away from his roots, despite the fact that (like 60 per cent of Queen's students at the time) he still lived at home with his family and travelled to and from Queen's by bus, bicycle, or on foot. His rapport with his father had suffered because Stewart no longer felt able to talk with him about his academic and extra-curricular pursuits, and he suspected that both his parents thought he should be working, as his brother and sister were. Liz recollects that the 'dislocation between home and university troubled Stewart', perhaps accounting in part for the 'sense of detachment' which he regarded as 'a necessary (but not comfortable) part of being a writer'.[42]

This 'sense of detachment' is much in evidence in 'The Decision', a short story Parker published in *Q* later that first term of his second year. Like the narrator of 'Johnny's Story', the central character both wants and fears connection with other people. As the story opens, the unnamed protagonist walks home, bracing himself for the coming encounter. He meets his weeping mother in the sitting-room and asks how his father is, receiving no reply. He then goes to the back bedroom where his father lies ill. The father tries to put a brave face on his suffering, while the son observes that his condition has deteriorated and struggles to keep his feelings in check, offering words of consolation he does not believe. He walks into the back garden, alternately berating himself for and rationalizing his wish to cut himself off from his family:

> I'm a callous bastard, he thought; I am, but it's no use, it[']s the only way. You unchain yourself and make a bond with somebody, and then it happens, and they're suffering, and you can't comfort them, and your inadequacy kills you.
>
> The sound of his father's coughing fell out of the house.
>
> No, no, no, I can't I won't, don't claim me father, don't claim my compassion, my love, I have none for you, I have none. Pity is suffering and love is suffering and you can only cut yourself off, you can only be neutral, it's no use joining in the fist-fight, you can only climb above it and look on....
>
> You can only climb above. I am a reporter. I will observe. I will never weep for anyone in pain, and when I am in pain no-one will ever weep for me. It is the only way.

Readers are informed that 'He made the decision [quickly]', a statement followed by the protagonist asking his mother for money for clothes, taking one last look at his father and being overcome by an emotion he identifies as 'revulsion', and running into the night. Perhaps he has decided to escape for good, never to return—or maybe the 'decision' is simply one about what attitude (neutrality) to take towards the unpleasant circumstances of his home life.[43]

The obscurity of this piece likely indicates how close its themes then were to Parker. Regarded in terms of influences, the story reflects the literature he had been reading and thinking about. The alienation, acceptance of individual isolation, and impulse towards autonomy at its core come straight out of a young man's intoxication with the Beats. On another level, the story deals with the universal problem of adolescence: the separation of one's sense of self from the constructions of one's family.

The father's illness, however, adds a complicating twist to an otherwise unremarkable coming-of-age story. How does a young man make the break into adulthood if his parents start needing him before he stops needing them? Probably at the cost of intense guilt, if he is sensitive. This story likely contains a significant autobiographical element, although its superficial details differ from Parker's own. In his family, it was his mother rather than his father who suffered from mysterious and incapacitating ailments and for whom his feelings oscillated between resentment and lacerating pity. In 'The Decision' he tries out one possible resolution to his dilemma, as his protagonist accepts neutrality as a necessary condition of his continued functioning. This refusal to feel Parker tried to justify to himself as essential for a writer's dispassionate observation, but it may equally have been an attempt to evade emotions that threatened to overwhelm him. In vowing to 'climb above' his father's pain, the protagonist of this story chooses to observe rather than to live.

Although the negotiation between home and university preoccupied him, Parker never spoke about his family with most of his friends. Instead, he immersed himself in his university life. In his second year, around the time he was working on the double-bill and starting to go out with Liz Davidson, he launched a project that would demand much of his time and energy. Queen's, he noted, had a good student newspaper and a literary magazine, it had 'a dustbin full of duplicated, stapled, distinctly amateurish society productions' (*Gorgon* was one of these), but it did not have 'a regular serious magazine comparable to those of other universities...a literary platform of all-important topics like politics and religion...a collective voice'. With the help of 'a heterogeneous and slightly odd collection of students', mainly friends from Sullivan and Dramsoc, Parker resolved 'to work like hell in order to provide undergraduates in Ulster with the privilege of freedom of speech'.[44] The result was *Interest*, a student magazine launched in November 1960 with an eclectic list of contents, including a short story, a few poems, a couple of political articles, a political cartoon, articles on Albert Einstein and Marty Wilde, a film review, and a survey of books on French poetry.

After an initial £50 grant from the Queen's administration, *Interest* had to support itself through sales and advertising. Thus it was, as Parker emphasized, 'an independent University magazine', and he made a special appeal in the first issue for students who endorsed the idea to contribute pieces to it: 'particularly if you are an engineer or a scientist (or, incidentally, a Unionist—as usual the minority cause is always the most articulate)'. Morrison explains that the word 'independent' in the magazine's subtitle signalled *Interest*'s non-partisan and non-sectarian stance, implying 'that we were at least agnostics'. He interviewed Stewart about the concept behind the magazine for *Interest*'s inaugural issue, and Parker took the opportunity to state explicitly that 'I myself, claim no bias in any sphere. The basis of my whole personal philosophy is tolerance—no, I think neutrality is a better word—neutrality.'[45] Over successive issues the magazine demonstrated the range of its editor's interests, with features on a wide variety of topics—from John F. Kennedy to student drinking, James Joyce to quantum mechanics, eugenics to existentialism, the Common Market to the daily routine of a research student, and much besides—together with creative writing by students and lecturers, cartoons, and reviews. (Ian Hill was simultaneously broadening the focus of *Q*, which he renamed *The Q Review*, beyond literature to culture generally. The *Evergreen Review*, with its heterogeneous contents, probably inspired both young men.)

From its first appearance, *Interest* compared well with other student publications at Queen's. Production values were of an almost professional standard, and Parker kept the contributions on a high plane by drawing on his wide-ranging acquaintance at the university. He stayed on as editor through the autumn of 1961, then handed the reins to Nan Shearan, an original member of staff. Freed from editorial duties, Parker could write more for the magazine. By the autumn of 1962, *Interest* had become an established part of Queen's student culture, regularly selling out its print run of 1,000 copies (as many as *Q* or *Gown*).[46]

In the autumn of 1960, Morrison (now president of Dramsoc) had also enlisted Parker's help with an audacious undertaking of his own. Each year the British National Union of Students (NUS) sponsored a drama festival and competition in association with the *Sunday Times*. Universities could enter productions in both full-length and one-act categories. Adjudicators visited campuses throughout the UK and chose a few plays in each category to travel to the festival, which took place in a different location each year, and compete for the prizes. Morrison had decided that Queen's should enter a student-written play in the one-act category, something that had not been done before. He decreed that Dramsoc would have its own mini-festival of original one-acts open to anyone who cared to write one. Lecturers from the English Department would choose one play to nominate for the NUS competition. Dramsoc produced six plays: two by Jim Caffrey, two by John Hamilton, one by Roy Alcorn, and one by Morrison. According to Liz Davidson, these 'owed much to Pinter, Beckett, and Ionesco, in their lack of discernible plot, and desperate pessimism'. Parker directed two of the plays and acted and played the guitar in Morrison's. Morrison's play, *A Kind of Nothing*, was chosen to represent Queen's in the competition, and the NUS adjudicators invited Dramsoc to bring it to the 1961 festival, held in Leeds in early January. Caffrey designed the set, Parker composed the music, Hill debuted as a director, and a large delegation from Queen's made the trek to Yorkshire over the winter recess. *A Kind of*

Nothing did not take a prize, but the trip offered an intense unifying experience for the young thespians.[47]

Not to be outdone by Morrison, Parker wrote his own first play around the same time: *Duet for Laughing Men*, a 'Tragi-comedy in One Act' commissioned by the Student Christian Movement in Queen's University and Stranmillis Training College and performed at Stranmillis in early December 1960 under Parker's direction. The idea for the piece had come to him as 'an image of two men walking backwards onto a stage laughing'—the play began with their collision. Only a brief description survives, but it gives a sense of its flavour: 'An Old Man is seen stretching back to fading days gone by while the Young Man reaches forward to the warmth and excitement of life. The damning fact is "a tragic and ignoble combination of the sublime and the ridiculous": both are celebrating their fifty-and-a-halfth birthday.' By 19, then, Parker was writing as well as performing in and directing plays, although it would be a long time before he took the activity as anything more than an entertaining way to pass the time.[48]

For his twenty-first birthday in 1961, Morrison received a 'portable' reel-to-reel tape recorder. Both he and Parker were interested in the influence of new technologies on writing, and the two decided to write a play together by recording improvised scenes and tinkering with the result. 'It had quite a lot of laughs in it', Morrison says: 'Stewart's part was much better than mine, I definitely remember that.'[49] Dramsoc produced *The Way It Had To Be* in March 1961, with Hill directing and a cast that included Parker, Morrison, and Morrison's girlfriend Valerie Lilley. Set in a 'Pinter-shambles' room, the play centred on two flatmates who both lust after the same girl. Caffrey summarized the plot in a disgusted review for *Gown*:

> The realist Joe, or should I say Bill Morrison, is looking for something out of life—he thinks it's sex—he doesn't know. The dreamer Benny, played superbly by Mr. Parker (I have never seen him give such a good performance) is searching for something, perhaps just another dream, but at least he is looking for it; and in the process he goes mad, kills his friend in a childish game, and then subjects 'the girl upstairs'...to a similar, unseen, fate, and that's it.

As in Morrison's earlier play, John Osborne-type confrontation featured prominently, along with bizarre actions.[50]

The following month, Dramsoc entered *The Way It Had To Be* in the one-act section of the Universities' Drama Association Festival, held in Galway that year. Parker and Morrison's play made little impression. Years later, Hill's then-girlfriend recalled the trip: 'We piled into one of those cars that doesn't keep death off the roads and headed to Galway. I cannot remember how the play went, only that all the way home Stewart was in excruciating pain in one leg and we kept telling him he should go to the doctor about it.'[51] Parker did not know it, but his university career would soon be bifurcated in an extraordinary and unexpected fashion.

3

Intimations of Mortality

It started with a strange sensation in his foot that quickly ran up his leg, accompanied by a faint red line. Parker ignored this mystery as long as he could, although he began to complain to friends about it. The inexplicable soreness, not incapacitating at first, gradually grew. After a few months, as the pain intensified and localized under his left knee, he sought medical advice.[1]

The first doctor Parker saw diagnosed rheumatism and prescribed a liniment and pain-killers. Some time later, his sister Joan woke in the middle of the night and went downstairs to find him sitting alone, his face contorted in pain, sweat rolling down his cheeks, 'in agony'. The liniment had obviously not worked, and he soon returned to the doctor's surgery. This time, he was sent to Belfast's Royal Victoria Hospital so that an orthopaedic surgeon could examine the leg. The surgeon surprised Parker by asking that a bone chip be taken for inspection then and there. By the end of that day he lay in a hospital bed, dimly sensing that a new phase of his existence was about to begin.[2]

This exploratory surgery revealed something far worse than it would occur to most 19-year-olds to worry about: Parker had a bone cancer known as Ewing's Tumour. At the time, the only effective treatment for such a tumour was amputation of the diseased limb before the cancer spread. Parker had expected to remain in hospital at least a week but did not learn immediately what would happen to him. His parents, however, were consulted within hours of the diagnosis and agreed that his leg should be removed at mid-thigh to make sure of eliminating all the cancerous cells; although an amputation below the knee would afford Parker more freedom of movement, the doctors thought it too risky in his case. Then, for days afterwards, his family had to conceal the reality of his plight from him.[3]

Parker was not told about the amputation until the eve of it. He describes that fateful announcement in *Hopdance*, an autobiographical novel written in the early 1970s. The surgeon blandly informs the protagonist, Tosh, that he has 'a species of tumour on the femur' which could 'spread fairly rapidly'. His only chance is 'immediate surgery':

—I'm afraid we'll have to take your leg off, said the surgeon.

It seemed too simple a way to put it. Tosh's heart was like a fish trying to jump out of his chest.

—You mean—amputation? he said foolishly.

—Yes, said the surgeon, in the same *sotto voce*, —I think the sooner the better. We were planning on tomorrow morning, if you agree to that....

Lunatic phrases were flashing into Tosh's mind. He wanted to say something ruefully ironic which would make the surgeon smile and calm the blood thundering
between his ears. He almost said What the hell, at least I won't have to play football
again. But he couldn't trust his voice not to crack and ruin it.
—Is there no other way? he said.[4]

In the novel, Tosh feels 'a fake theatricality taking him over to keep things operational' during the encounters with his family that follow this revelation. Parker likewise exhibited an iron self-control in the presence of other people, choosing to
protect them insofar as he could over expressing the emotions that threatened to
swamp him. When his sister Joan remarked sympathetically that the news of his
impending amputation 'must have been a dreadful shock for you', he responded, 'It
must have been a dreadful shock for you, too.' He did tell his family it was just as
well that he had never aspired to football stardom, and he observed that if he had to
have an amputation, it had happened at the best possible time: if he had been
younger, he would have had to have a new leg made for him every year to keep up
with his growth; if he had been older, it would have been harder for him to accept.[5]

Only alone could Parker look squarely at his predicament. According to his own
testimony in *Hopdance*, he experienced a surprising calm the night before the
operation:

> There was an almost inhuman clarity in his mind, his head felt rinsed, he was imbued
> with a limpid serenity. Unknown was the only word for what was facing him. It might
> be death. Whatever that meant. It would certainly be some form of death. He pushed
> back the bedclothes and placed his left leg on top of them. He wouldn't be the same
> person after they took it away. A quarter of him would have disappeared. He studied
> the leg intently, memorising it. From thigh to ankle it looked sick and defeated, with
> its wasted muscles and white hairlessness and the six inch vertical scar down the front,
> crossed at intervals by stitch-marks, like a cartographers' railway line. But the foot
> clearly wanted to live. It was forlornly expressive like an eager dog staring into the
> muzzle of its master's shotgun. Its nails were slightly yellowed and needed trimming.
> An ancient fossilised corn rounded out the smallest toe. It was obvious why feet had
> never ranked high in the aesthetics of the human anatomy, they were its faintly comic
> antipodes, its point of contact with the soil. For all that there was a harmony of line
> and proportion at which Tosh marvelled.

Throughout the novel Tosh grapples with the question of who he really is—or, as
he puts it at one point, 'Where does I end?' He does not feel truly represented by
his interactions with other people, since he is different with every person he
encounters. Where, then, can he locate his essential self? Is it the voice in his head,
the articulator of his consciousness? But what about that consciousness itself,
which has recently centred itself on a throbbing pain? Surely the 'I' exists in the
body, too—is at least 'Voice immersed in body.' But if this is the case, Tosh reflects,
then what will losing a piece of himself as significant as a leg mean to him?

It strikes Tosh more than once that facing death would be easier if he had
some system of belief to make sense of it, but his lost religious faith does not come
rushing back in his time of need. As much as he would like to, he cannot lean for

support on anything apart from himself. On this dark night, his chief terror is of losing his ability to represent the experience to himself:

> The only resource he was aware of was the voice in his head itself, the fact of his own consciousness, and it was telling him that tomorrow when the knife and the saw went in, it itself would be drowned in gristle and blood and then he would have no resources at all. The fear created by such a prospect was an experience which entirely transcended the familiar everyday emotion which had frequently loosened his bowels and dried his mouth. It was a state of emotional refrigeration which had created the almost preternatural calm in which his thoughts were ordering themselves so composedly.

Even as Tosh recognizes his overpowering emotion as one of fear, however, 'He was aware of taking conscious pleasure in the rational processes of his mind for the first time in his life, just as he had perceived the shapeliness of the human foot for the first time. He would be deprived of both of these attributes tomorrow morning.' His leg would be gone for ever, but his rationality eventually might be recovered. Tosh is already coming to the realization that, in the absence of what he had earlier referred to as the longed-for 'foolproof system', he will have to create for himself any positive meaning that his ordeal is going to have for him. If he survives, he vows, he will assume ownership of his life in a new way:

> His life had been remarkable to nobody but himself up to this point, and to him it had been a fretted, directionless affair, crowded with other people whom he could never know, who rose and fell like skittles in their unhappy dealings with one another and with him. That existence was at its solitary climax now for him, and for them it was already over, if they ever saw him again he would not be the same person. He had a powerful sense of having reached the end of his growing. The growth was cankered. If the canker could be excised he would have arrived at last at the unknown life which he was destined to live. It would be his own life and he would have to live it with whatever resources were available. In the meantime a wave as tall as a ship was creeping soundlessly towards him over the dark water.

Stewart Parker's left leg was amputated on 17 May 1961, after which he remained in the Royal Victoria Hospital for three months. The first stage of convalescence from an amputation involves allowing the stump to heal and shrink, since only when its size has stabilized can a person be fitted with an artificial limb. During his confinement, Parker initially spent most of his time in bed with the stump under a cage to prevent the bedclothes from sticking to the bloody bandages. His sensations alternated between physical agony and a morphine haze. At times he was plagued by phantom pain—feeling, for example, a cramp in his missing foot. Like Tosh, for the first few days he remained 'in a new dimension beyond messages'.[6]

Soon enough, he received a steady stream of visitors: family members, friends from Queen's, former teachers, the family minister. Mostly he tried to put them at ease (and distract himself from his private delirium) by making conversation as if nothing terrible were wrong. He had his family bring him his guitar and started entertaining the other occupants of his ward as soon as he could focus on anything besides his wound. Two of his aunts were relieved to find him playing it on the balcony, 'as happy as if nothing had happened'. Few people saw him without his social mask. One who did was a cousin, David Dickson, taken by their grandfather to see Parker shortly after the operation. About 14 at the time, Dickson was too awed by the enormity of his cousin's misfortune to say anything to him. He just sat and stared, and Parker, obviously in great pain for the duration of the visit, pulled himself into a sitting position with the help of a bar hanging above the bed and stared back. Later, Parker told his grandfather that 'David Dickson was the only one who showed me any respect.'[7]

Parker felt most comfortable with his fellow patients, mainly victims of accidents. With them, he explored a range of human sensibility beyond the normal reach. His siblings remember him being particularly friendly with a rough-edged man from the Markets area of Belfast; the two of them joked together and played tricks on the nurses. He may or may not have been the same man who, as Parker later explained to a friend, suffered from a gangrenous toe. The toe's condition gradually deteriorated, until one day it fell off. This provoked gales of laughter from Parker and the toe's owner: 'at the time that seemed the funniest thing that either one of them had ever experienced'.[8] The grotesque element in hospital humour bore affinities to a comic strain which attracted Parker to certain kinds of literature. He believed laughter to be 'the most complicated human response of all...to my mind, the only characteristically human response.... The kind of laughing that Pinter elicits, or Ionesco, or Joseph Heller, is exceedingly profound and very enjoyable....It is a highly sophisticated and fundamentally human response to a vision of life which you recognise as peculiarly valid in our state of mortescence.'[9]

As he began to feel more himself, Parker looked ahead to the coming academic year. He had missed his second-year exams and would have to sit them in September, so he asked his friends and teachers to bring him books and notes so he could study. He also had to work at regaining his mobility. For the first few months, all he had were crutches and an empty space where the leg had been. He remained on crutches when he finally left hospital. While recovering at home during the last part of the summer, he was fitted for his first artificial leg. This 'pylon limb'—a crude, temporary affair—consisted of two bare metal bars, a joint that had to be manually levered to bend the leg, two more bars below this 'knee', and a piece of wood at the bottom to stand on. The limb attached to his body by means of a belt and a shoulder harness and had a socket at the top that the stump fitted into. Parker wore this leg to find his balance and learn to walk again. It would be another several months before he would be fitted for a flesh-coloured 'articulated leg' whose knee-lever was not worked by hand.[10]

Parker quickly came to appreciate the professionalism of people who worked at limb-fitting centres, places he would come to know well in the various cities in which he lived because prostheses do not last for ever and must be repaired, replaced, and adjusted for weight loss or gain. Like hospitals, these were thronged with survivors of various sorts of disaster, and the characters he met in them fascinated him.[11] In *Hopdance*, Parker depicts Tosh's first visit to the limb-fitting centre and his dawning realization that he himself is a 'case', 'badged for life' by his experience. Sitting in the waiting room,

> He scanned the line of feet opposite. One foot of each pair sat cocked on its heel at an odd angle; in two cases, a shiny brown patch of leg visible above the top of the sock contrasted oddly with the hairy whiteness of the corresponding patch alongside it. By these signs shall we be known. Tosh raised his eyes discreetly and scrutinised the faces: a young red-haired country boy, a heavyset man with hair in his nostrils, a thin old man with violet strings of veins across the backs of his hands. It had not occurred to him till now that he was a member of a freemasonry. A novice arrived for initiation.

In the company of this new fraternity, there was no need to pretend.

Dealing with the rest of the world proved harder. If *Hopdance* accurately portrays his emotional life at the time, Parker kept most people at a distance with an imitation of nonchalance. In the novel, when a girl Tosh used to fancy visits him while he is still on crutches, he answers her polite 'How are you?' with the words 'I'm alive but not exactly kicking.' The text continues, 'His mouth spoke this line like a volunteer from the audience reading in for an actor who has met with an accident, he had written it down in all his letters, it was a line from a script which served him now in lieu of conversation, a shoddy anthology of clichés and bad jokes. When he listened to other people talking, they all seemed to be drawing on similar scripts.' More upsetting to Tosh, though, are people who will not be fobbed off with such repartee. Honest conversation would open up too many subjects he cannot bear to consider closely. He shuts himself off from his girlfriend, Prudence, whose concern grates on him:

> He didn't want to be on his own with her or anybody. He didn't want to 'talk'. That talking in particular had been done enough times already; so had all talking in general as a valuable activity. Two voices were grinding him to the point of breakdown, one at the red mouth of his severed thigh and the old one in his head. Their endless vituperation was all the dialogue he could contain.

At some point during that endless summer, Parker broke off his relationship with Liz Davidson. She speculates that 'Perhaps he couldn't cope with my emotions as well as his own, or (more likely) it would have ended about then anyway.'[12] Even before his illness he had been uneasy with extravagant displays of emotion, and when Liz first came to see him in hospital after his surgery she had become almost hysterical and had to be taken from the room. His mother, always highly strung, also had trouble accepting the amputation. Bob Granleese, one of Parker's childhood friends, recollects that she appeared to age quickly then and that Parker sought excuses to get out of the house.[13] Judging from the *Hopdance* manuscript, he believed that his sanity depended on keeping his own feelings firmly repressed, which led him to avoid people he saw as potentially destabilizing.

Granleese remembers that the only time Parker seemed close to falling apart was when he believed the same pain had begun to affect his remaining leg. (Fortunately, this fear turned out to be groundless.) Parker provides a revealing description of Tosh's reaction to a similar suspicion:

He was in terror now, for the first time, of his consciousness. For three days he had felt the controls slithering, a groundswell of hysterical irrationality rising up to engulf him. Now he knew that this was the thing he feared most. That was why Prudence's compulsive obsessiveness, his mother's long shrill quarrel with her life, even Harrison's surly barracking, had maddened him and at the same time provoked a stolid refusal to respond. He had shunned their claims on him, had refused to entertain claims, because their goaded unrestrainable hearts had clawed at the passions in his own, and he was afraid to acknowledge or unleash them. He was emotionally as well as physically halt. He had been an emotional coward, and the feelings he had shrunk most sharply away from were his own because their power appalled him. Now they were rising up to dominate him.[14]

Whether or not this passage reflects Parker's conscious thoughts at the time, it almost certainly represents his mature analysis of his younger self's coping mechanisms.

Parker returned to Queen's that autumn with a carefully contrived public image projecting an extraordinary sang-froid. Later he looked with irony on his re-entry to student life ('"And what did *you* do during the summer?" "I had my leg amputated…"'), but at the time he wished to appear unaffected by his loss. Because his cancer had been diagnosed late in the academic year, and his long hospital stay had taken place over the summer holidays, it seemed to students who did not know him well that he was there one day with two legs and back again the next with one. Many believed, as one acquaintance remembers, that 'he lost it in a car crash after a wild weekend at Portrush, the local seaside resort, the only seaside resort where the Northern Ireland youth could escape the tight confines of strait-laced disapproving adults'. (In a novel, *Combo*, that Parker was then writing, one of the characters loses a leg in such a comparatively romantic fashion.) When Seamus Deane mustered the courage to ask Parker about the 'accident' directly, he replied that there had, indeed, been an accident, but 'an accident *in* the body rather than *through* the body'.[15]

The amputation made Parker something of a celebrity on campus, and on 6 October 1961 the student newspaper, *Gown*, ran a profile of him that offers a snapshot of his interests and attitudes at a crucial stage in his development. The writer reported that Parker 'had his left leg amputated in May and gives the impression of being curious about it' and quoted him as saying, 'It's just a minor irritation physically. Pain was a fascinating experience. In many ways I'm glad it happened, it steadied me a lot.' Parker summed up his personal philosophy, which he divulged owed a great deal to the works of Aldous Huxley, in the sentence 'You've got to realise you're a bastard first, then you can get somewhere.' In other words, the writer explained, 'He believes that one must realise one's insignificance in order to achieve an ultimate state of humility.' In this, Parker felt, losing his leg was actually a help, a 'reminder'. Queried about his tastes in music, he mentioned Miles Davis, the Modern Jazz Quartet, and various jazz guitarists. Parker identified his favourite poet as John Donne, expressing 'contempt' for the 'contemporary movement'. He favoured Harold Pinter among present-day playwrights and thought J. D. Salinger's *The Catcher in the Rye* the best novel of the previous decade. Parker still saw poetry as his chosen literary medium, and he declared that 'Poetry to me is the greatest, the purest form of expression. I believe I haven't written a line of poetry yet. A lot of verse but no poetry.' He also wrote prose (because, he said, he found it easier) and had written 'plays in collaboration on the principle that two heads are better than one but plays are not as important to him as a vehicle of expression. His interest in theatre is great.' The interviewer emphasized 'the calmness and certainty of his reactions to the most extreme situations'. Towards the end of the article, Parker is quoted as insisting, 'You must say that really I'm a very happy person.'[16]

There was a certain bravado in such a declaration at such a time, but it indicates Parker's determination not to wallow in self-pity. A friend from Queen's who later became a professional psychologist recalls that Parker took comfort in his conviction that writers should suffer and used it to adopt a 'philosophical' approach to the loss of his leg. Facing death himself also cast new light on the literature that had engaged his attention during his first undergraduate years, as the urgency of living in the moment became ever clearer to him. It was not only the American Beats who had emphasized the arbitrary and fleeting nature of life. Well before Parker's cancer was discovered, he had shared with Liz Davidson his enthusiasm for 'Tichborne's Elegy', written in 1586 shortly before the poet's execution. In it, the repeated line 'And now I live, and now my life is done' underlines the simultanity of life and death.[17]

While the amputation restricted Parker's freedom in some respects, it also, paradoxically, conferred on him greater autonomy. With the excuse that his false limb made it awkward for him to clamber on and off buses, he and Bill Morrison convinced his family that it would make more sense for him to rent a flat near the university than to continue to live at home. Thus the two became flatmates, but they had left the housing search rather late. The only flat they could find belonged to a self-styled 'naturopath' who resembled Chico Marx. Morrison remembers him as 'a man of intense theories', one being that Parker had brought on his cancer by eating too much fried food. Most of this odd healer's income derived from properties he owned around the university. The ground-floor flat on Magdala Street that Parker and Morrison rented from him, then being converted, was effectively a building site, with cement floors and exposed brick and mortar walls. It consisted of two rooms plus the kitchen and an unfinished but usable bathroom. The place, though damp and expensive, was convenient and in such bad shape to begin with that the landlord did not much care what they did to it. Very little housekeeping or cooking got done there, but plenty of late-night talking, drinking, and partying, since the flat rapidly acquired the reputation of an open house for the bohemian crowd.[18]

Parker's friends rallied to give him physical and emotional support, though few realized how badly he needed it. Ian Hill recollects that 'people were initially astonished that he wasn't downcast. He may have been inside, but he generally didn't seem downcast at all.... [H]e was as amusing and laconic, witty, as he'd always been—on the surface anyway.' The main change, from Hill's perspective, was that Parker seemed more focused, more intent on getting things done, since 'He knew that he wasn't clear forever, that he would have to go back for tests and there was a very good chance that he wouldn't last very long. . . . He had to do things, couldn't laze about.'[19] This aura of concentrated purpose attached to Parker for the rest of his life.

Bill Morrison saw more of the anguish Parker endured. The pylon limb chafed the stump until the skin was raw and tender, even bleeding at times, and there were mornings when he could not bear to put it on. On these occasions, Morrison would half-carry Parker (the leg tucked underneath his arm) to the university, where he would sit through a few classes—after which, with luck, the pain would have eased enough for him to strap on the leg and stagger home.[20] This first, acute, phase of adjustment did not last long, fortunately. What followed was a determined attempt by both of them to resume their old activities as if nothing had changed. Parker was still editing and writing for *Interest*, the magazine he had founded. He also renewed his involvement in Dramsoc, directing *The Glass Menagerie* by Tennessee Williams in the autumn of 1961.

That December, Parker, Morrison, and several other Queen's writers and actors put together a satirical revue for the first Queen's Festival, presenting it for one night only in the basement of Whitla Hall. *Beyond the Fridge* took inspiration from *Beyond the Fringe*, a cabaret by Dudley Moore, Peter Cook, Jonathan Miller, and Alan Bennett (students at Oxford and Cambridge) which had scored a popular success at a recent Edinburgh Festival before going on to London and New York. The Queen's version consisted of skits and funny songs. These were mostly innocent enough, though Morrison recalls one sketch comprising the unabridged official record of a meeting of a Stormont subcommittee, the members of which droned on in a series of non sequiturs: 'We didn't have to alter a line . . . we just did it as it was but nobody had done anything like that before. We had never dared to stand up and say there's a lot of old idiots about doing awful things here.'[21]

The Festival as a whole, mainly a coordinated fortnight of student society functions that would have taken place over the course of the autumn term anyway, received a jaded review in *Gown*. The revue, however, garnered praise as 'original, adventurous and enterprising and—to everyone's surprise, hilariously funny'. Morrison remembers the night as a triumph, but it marked the end of Parker's acting career. Years later he told Niki Hill that 'I had lost my bottle, standing there on one leg.'[22] In his description of the revue that Tosh and his friend Harrison write in *Hopdance*, Parker explains that Tosh 'could sense already the failure of a previously hidden nerve—he would never again be able to get up before an audience and perform with an unconscious faith in the easy security of his own stage presence. The world no longer offered security of any sort whatsoever.'

Chronically short of funds, Parker and Morrison lived off the land as much as possible. Students from wealthy families often hosted parties out of town, and the two would be invited to provide entertainment. They evolved an 'existential cabaret act' in which Parker played his guitar and sang while Morrison made the rounds of the party insulting people in what he took to be a witty fashion. They would return from these forays with all the food they could carry and perhaps a bottle or two as payment. On other occasions, they received free tickets to Queen's formal dances in exchange for performing during the interval when the band took a break.

Afterwards, back in the flat, a small group of friends would stay up late, talking and joking. One endlessly fascinating subject of speculation was the cause of Parker's illness. Their favourite theory was propounded in a book by an American professor who explained the high incidence of cancer in Northern Ireland by arguing that it had received a disproportionate percentage of fallout from nuclear tests in the United States. Believing this allowed them to think of him as a war victim, which appealed to their anti-bomb sensibilities.[23] Later still, Parker and Morrison probably continued their conversations as Tosh and Harrison do in *Hopdance*: 'Sometimes in the early hours, the flat finally empty, they would lie each in his bed in the dark talking through the open doors of their rooms, listening to jazz from a foreign station on the new radio that Tosh's brother had given him in hospital.'[24]

Despite this non-stop activity and relentless sociability, Parker's inner experience of the time was of unbearable loneliness. Dissatisfied with the quality of his old relationships, he longed for stronger connections to other people. Parker's most enduring close friendship dates from the period shortly after his return to university. Sam Fannin, an older cousin of Bill Morrison's, had never learned to mask and repress his feelings. Because he had rebelled at school by not performing to the level of his abilities, his father apprenticed him to a chemist at 18. He filled prescriptions during the day and studied pharmacy at night, but he hated being confined to a shop. When the opportunity arose to become a representative for a pharmaceutical company, he leapt at it. The job required travel throughout Ireland, and its perks included a decent salary, a lunch allowance, the use of a company car, and a flexible schedule. The occupation of travelling salesman suited him mainly because it left him plenty of free time. Fannin could usually finish his work by 12:30 or so, leaving him the afternoon and evening to pursue his manifold other interests. His job did not engage his intellect, so he was drawn to creative people. They, in turn, appreciated his openness, curiosity, native intelligence, storytelling ability, and varied contacts. He consorted easily with all types of people: doctors and chemists he met in the course of his professional life; businessmen; BBC producers, for whom he did some freelance reporting and broadcasting; jazz musicians, with whom he played saxophone and then drums in various showbands; members of the Northern Ireland Labour Party; Northern Irish artists, theatre practitioners, and writers; and, through his cousin, bohemian Queen's students. He impressed this last group with his instinctive understanding of how the world worked and the way in which he seemed to embody the Beat ideal of perpetual motion. As Morrison puts it, on the inside Sam Fannin was Charlie Parker, on the outside a man in a suit.[25]

One of Fannin's first impressions of Parker was of him struggling to walk with his new artificial leg on snow that had melted and then frozen again. Poor bastard, he thought, but admiration for the humour and strength of character with which Parker handled his disability soon eclipsed any pity Fannin felt for him. Although Fannin was eight years older, the two became fast friends. They shared a passion for jazz and an enthusiasm for the arts generally and were intrigued by each other's divergent modes of life. Despite their differences, they could talk about almost anything and remained in close contact until Parker's death.[26]

Parker also made a deeper commitment to his vocation after the amputation. Although he had wanted to be a writer since age 15, losing a leg focused him on his writing in a more intense and disciplined fashion. In part, this concentration on a sedentary art served as compensation for his loss of physical powers. More positively, having faced and survived the most fearful prospect human beings *can* face, he felt he had gained insights worth sharing into both himself and the general human condition. Though hardly obvious from a superficial examination of Parker's later work, often humorous, ontological shock propelled his creativity. Attempting in 1986 to explain why he wrote plays, Parker stated that 'I am much obsessed by death; and by the spiritual void from which many of us have to confront it. Images present themselves to me in this regard which are beyond rationality, dragged on to the stage from the very borders of consciousness, powerfully charged for me in a way I cannot define.' The amputation may also have been liberating for Parker in seeming to vitiate any expectation he might have had for himself of material success. A few years afterwards, he confided to a friend that, before the discovery of his cancer, the only amputees he had ever noticed were beggars. Thus, when he learned he would be going through life with one leg, he became convinced he would also be poor.[27] This might sound like a depressing prospect, but deciding that poverty would be his fate reinforced Parker's dedication to an utterly impractical career choice.

Parker began writing his first novel during his convalescence. *Combo* is structured like a jazz number; according to his preliminary notes, he wanted 'to make the music indistinguishable from the plot'. The four main characters are associated with different instruments. After an opening section to set the scene, they take turns delivering 'solos', each describing the events of one day of a four-day Easter weekend in 'Hexley' (a seaside resort modelled on Portrush) and all expressing similar ideas and emotions. The four middle sections are followed by a concluding section, set later in time and reflecting on their shared experience.[28]

Alan, an intellectual university student and Angry Young Man who plays the guitar, is paired with Walt, a rootless Beat who plays the tenor saxophone. After jamming together in a jazz club, the two establish a close bond. Their developing relationship has a peculiar intensity, probably because they represent aspects of the young author himself. Alan and Walt personify different strands of the literary and intellectual influences that had captured Parker's imagination during his first undergraduate years, and his notes indicate that his biggest challenge in writing the novel lay in keeping these characters distinct from one another. He even drew himself a chart, listing under the headings of 'Alan' and 'Walt' the associations evoked by each: under 'Alan' roots, objectivity, cynicism, cool, cerebral, sex, spiritual beauty, belief in experience, past and future, Northern, and the early Eliot and under 'Walt' impermanence, subjectivity, despair, passionate, sensual, love, physical beauty, belief in the moment, present, Southern, and the early Ginsberg. The friendship between them enacts a dialectic between their philosophies, with each learning from the other. The other central characters, who do not play the instruments with which they are identified, are paired romantically. Ann (the piano) appears at first to be a wholly stereotypical female, but her self-awareness redeems her. Johnny (the trumpet) is a motorbike king who differs from his companions by virtue of his greater understanding that his behaviour is self-destructive. The friends accompanying the major characters represent, in Parker's schema, 'Our rhythm section, bass and drums. The tempo of bloody monotony.'

Johnny, Ann, Walt, and Alan share an acute sense of isolation. Although all confess to extreme loneliness, they fear the disappointment that might result from reaching out only to discover that those they wish to commune with do not live up to their expectations. Parker uses the imagery of pilgrimage to explain the obscure impulse that brings his characters to Hexley, where they will meet. Approaching the town, Walt ruminates, 'Surprising how paganism lives on. Corporate fertility rites. The pilgrims trek to the sacred place, to worship at the shrine of sex, and pay their homage. Bathe in the sacred waters. Perform strange ritualistic dances. Rejoice with alcoholic stimulants. . . . The Druids would have loved it.' The pagan pilgrimage motif helps Parker illuminate the plight of young people cut adrift from the consoling certainties of their parents. His youthful protagonists have rebelled against older norms of behaviour but still seek other sources of meaning for their lives. As the novel opens, they exist unsatisfactorily in a vacuum in which orthodox religious belief has been replaced by empty hedonism.

The failure of traditional religion to answer their needs is only one symptom of what Parker referred to in his notes as the 'gulf of generations'. He saw himself and his contemporaries as the products of a set of circumstances dividing them from the values and assumptions of their elders. This damaged generation owed its distinctive identity to the Second World War (its atrocities, stresses, and stringencies), the over-shadowing fact of The Bomb (what Parker termed 'the greatest factor'), secondary and higher education that severed them from their roots without fully integrating them into the old establishment, and the 'new culture' (mass-based and market-driven, built of what he called 'little scraps of acquired knowledge'). Although the growing intimacy between the pairs of characters is a step towards a more life-affirming existence for each of them, it takes violence to make those who survive it accept that what they do matters, if only to themselves. Returning from Hexley on Monday night, the car with Alan and Walt in it and the motorbike that Johnny and Ann are riding collide around a tight corner. Johnny dies instantly; Ann and Walt end up in hospital (where Walt loses a leg); only Alan returns more or less unscathed to his old life at university. In a letter to Alan, Walt (the character who had most thoroughly 'surrendered' before the weekend in Hexley, convinced that 'since nothing could be permanent everything was to be discarded') reflects positively on his gruelling experience: 'Let's say that you have to be experientially equipped for living, and that it's fifteen times harder now than it ever was before. We had a baptism by fire in the war. Maybe making it involves having a confirmation by fire as well.'[29]

Combo never made it into print, but work Parker published in the two years following his amputation also takes up themes of generational angst, individual isolation, and the redemptive power of suffering. George Watson, a fellow English Honours student friendly with Parker at this time, remembers being unimpressed by his poetry, the 'apocalyptic' nature of which seemed to him at odds with its apparently easygoing author.[30] In a young man who had recently undergone the trauma of an amputation, however, thoughts of death and deformity and the enforced solitude that might accompany the latter are hardly surprising. More remarkable is the fact that Parker appeared to almost everyone who knew him undaunted by his harrowing experience.

An intensified focus on creative writing helped Parker cultivate a new serenity during his final years at Queen's. Poems first published in 1962 and 1963 indicate that he had adopted an attitude akin to Walt's towards his disablement. Rather than viewing the loss of his leg solely as a physical handicap, he chose to regard his 'confirmation by fire' as a spiritual gain. In 'The Broken Lives', for example, the 21-year-old poet drew on the biographies of famous writers to suggest that there is a link between suffering and creativity, some artistic compensation to be wrung from human misfortune:

> I learn the broken lives.
> ....
> They spring from the living page to learn me bend my spine to the already-
> begun breaking.
> The only whole lives are the broken lives.[31]

By the time 'The Broken Lives' appeared, Parker's own life had become markedly more 'whole'. At the end of his first year as an amputee, at a party thrown by fellow Dramsoc member Denis Payne, he met a woman with whom he would achieve the kind of intimacy he had hitherto only dreamed about. Kate Ireland was petite and striking, with porcelain white skin and long dark hair. Four years Stewart's senior, she had left Queen's with a first-class degree in English literature shortly before he arrived there. She spent about two years teaching at a girls' school in England before returning to Belfast after her father died. When she met Stewart, she was a research student at Queen's, working on a Master's thesis entitled 'The Rise of the Citizen in Elizabethan Domestic Drama'. Soft-spoken and reserved, Kate was an only child whose parents had hoped she would pursue an academic career. Her intellect undoubtedly attracted him; she had an enormously retentive memory and could supply a literary allusion for any occasion. In company she found congenial Kate was vivacious and witty, and she had considerable talent as an actor. Perhaps because she had lost a parent, she understood and related to Stewart's serious side. On the other hand, she shared his sense of humour, and people who saw them together early on remember them constantly holding hands, whispering, and giggling. Like Stewart, she was an individualist, but they could communicate on a profound level. Best of all, she accepted him exactly as he was, artificial leg and all, and buttressed his sense of himself as a desirable man. Kate did not warm to many of Stewart's friends, apart from Sam Fannin; his involvement with her restricted his social life, since she preferred to be alone with him. In return for the attention she demanded, however, she offered passionate commitment and an implicit faith in his abilities as a writer. With Kate, he believed, he could finally throw every aspect of his being into a relationship with another person.[32]

Soon after they began going out, Stewart and Kate spent a summer together in England. Queen's students often sought summer jobs abroad; after Stewart's first year, for example, he had worked at a pea canning factory near Cambridge. In this summer of 1962, he got a job working for Sellotape in London, and Kate found an excuse to be there too. They maintained separate addresses in London—he at a flat he was ostensibly sharing with his friend Roy Nimmons and several other young men, and she at a room in a house on Oakley Street in Chelsea. In practice, after a few nights at the flat—where, Nimmons complains, they 'laughed the time away disturbing everyone's sleep'—the lovers 'retired in isolation' to the rented room. This was barely big enough for one person, let alone two, but in it they could cohabit far from the watchful eyes of parents and the rest of Belfast.[33]

At the Oakley Street house they made a valuable contact. Ed Barrett, the occupant of the master bedroom, taught in the English department at Hamilton College, a small men's college in upstate New York, and delighted in meeting two 'very sweet' young people with interests similar to his. They began to spend a considerable amount of time together and eventually, at Barrett's suggestion, kept a joint household, with himself providing the meat for their evening meals and Stewart and Kate the vegetables. Later in the summer, when Austin and Margaret Briggs (another Hamilton professor and his wife) passed through London, the five had dinner together. All the Americans were charmed—particularly by Kate, who impressed them as a brilliant conversationalist. By the end of their stay in Chelsea, Barrett had planted in Stewart's mind the idea of applying for a visiting lectureship at Hamilton.[34]

Parker's relationship with Kate probably influenced his decision to stay on at Queen's to pursue a Master's after finishing the English Honours course with a 2.1 degree in spring 1963.[35] He did not embark on his postgraduate career with any burning desire to devote his life to academic research. He wanted to be a creative writer and viewed the acquisition of higher degrees as a means to that end. Working on a Master's allowed him to remain on scholarship at Queen's, the most tolerable place for him to be in Belfast. Possession of the degree would, he hoped, make him employable in the US. Its size and anonymity attracted him, as did its music and the sense he had of the freedom of movement possible there. George Watson recalls that Parker dreamed of driving down Route 66 and loved the songs of Chuck Berry and others who celebrated speed and mobility. During heated discussions in the English Honours Library, where advanced undergraduates and research students gathered, Parker would listen without saying much himself, humming and tapping out tunes on his false leg. He also sang while walking, keeping time with his steps: 'Long distance information, get me Memphis, Tennessee...' (but, he would add, Boulder, Colorado, would do as a substitute).[36]

With nothing more than a vague idea that he wanted to do his Master's research on an American topic, Parker arrived for his first meeting with his supervisor in October 1963. Philip Hobsbaum had been hired the previous autumn to replace Laurence Lerner, who had left Queen's for the University of Sussex. He already knew Parker by name, sight, and reputation, but they had not yet made one another's acquaintance. His first distinct impression of Parker on this occasion was a heavy 'clump, clump, clump...up the stairs'—'like a ghost in galoshes'. His second was of a baby-faced young man with 'a very resonant, clear voice'. 'I took to him very much', Hobsbaum later recalled, forthwith inviting Parker to become one of the founding members of the Belfast Writers' Group he was organizing.[37]

Hobsbaum impressed himself upon Queen's students as a forceful personality and electrifying lecturer who would stride to the front of a class, strip off his overcoat, shake his umbrella, and launch without pausing into a disquisition beginning with a long passage of verse quoted from memory. He did not merely teach literature, he lived it. He took his students' education seriously and would lose his temper with those who had the temerity to come to class unprepared, but this exactingness signified the respect with which he regarded them. Only 30 years old when he arrived in Belfast, Hobsbaum was on a first-name basis with those he taught. He invited students to informal gatherings at his home and spent long hours in the pubs with them, holding forth with the volubility that one interlocutor has described as 'words rattled out as from a Bofors gun, sprayed in arcs of honesty in answer to the most mundane of questions'. Hobsbaum possessed a capacious memory for names, anecdotes, quotations, and songs, and his conversation abounded in digressions, strong opinions, and arcane literary and historical asides. Dead writers of the distant past and the most illustrious of contemporaries were subjects alike of gossip and character-dissection, making him irresistible company for young writers, despite his tendency to be inspiring and infuriating by turns.[38]

Hobsbaum based the procedures of the Belfast Group on those he had evolved in other writers' groups he had helped to found in Cambridge and London. Meetings took place at his house weekly during term, on a weeknight, and members were admitted solely at his discretion; he invited people based on his assessment of their promise as well as their achievement. The Group was conceived less as a workshop for work-in-progress than as a forum for sharing pieces writers regarded as finished. For each meeting, one member would be designated to present his or her recent writing (several poems, a short story, part of a novel or play, or a translation). The 'Group sheet' for the week would be typed, duplicated, and distributed to members before the meeting, so that discussion of the writing could be based on reflection rather than snap judgements. At the meeting itself, the writer would read the work aloud, after which everyone else would talk about it as if they were encountering it in an English literature seminar. Thus writers learned (sometimes the hard way) whether or not the meanings they had intended were coming through. After about an hour there would be a break for coffee, followed by an opportunity for anyone present to read aloud any literary work he or she wished to share. This could be something by a classic or a modern writer, or perhaps a recent composition by the reader. The Group provided its members with a community of people who valued literature, an incentive to write, and the sense of an attentive and supportive readership.[39]

Hobsbaum encouraged Group members to write about what they knew, to 'use Belfast'—a novel concept for some, who had been used to thinking of Northern Ireland as the antithesis of poetry. Hobsbaum urged the writers to have confidence in themselves and their own, unique experience. Seamus Heaney's later reflections on the Belfast Group record his gratitude for that advice especially; Hobsbaum, he recalled, insisted 'that the social and political exacerbations of our place should irrupt and disrupt the decorums of literature'. Derek Mahon, who attended Group meetings only once or twice when he happened to be visiting Belfast, nevertheless observed in 1970 that 'The Hobsbaum seminar . . . was probably first to [crystallize] the sense of a new Northern poetry. Here was this man from London, people thought, whose name and whose friends' names appeared in leading journals, and he's actually taking us *seriously*.' Hobsbaum's wide-ranging literary connections, as well as his contacts with the local media, helped to make Group writers feel part of something noteworthy. In May 1964, for example, Parker—along with Heaney, Joan Watton, Hugh Bredin, and John Bond—read at the Irish PEN meeting, held in Belfast; that February, Parker had presented a programme on 'Poetry in the University' for the BBC Northern Ireland radio series *The Arts in Ulster* as part of the 1964 Queen's Festival.[40]

Heaney remembers that, at the Group's first meeting, 'Stewart Parker read his poems and was the first—and last—writer to stand up as he did so.' Parker was obviously 'encumbered' by his artificial leg. 'In spite of this,' Heaney writes, 'he lurched formally and significantly to his feet, a move which in retrospect gains great symbolic power. It was a signal of personal victory, of the triumph of artistic utterance over demeaning circumstances, of the possibility of genial spirits in the face of destructive events.' From the beginning, Hobsbaum regarded Parker and Heaney, only slightly acquainted before, as his stars. Fortunately, both were mature enough to handle such expectations without attracting as much jealousy as others might have done in a similar position. They also had a sincere regard for each other, which occasional moments of tension between them did not dispel. Their differences were largely cultural and aesthetic. Jack Pakenham, whom Michael Longley (a later member of the Group) recalls 'rather disapproved of what everyone else was producing, and . . . backed up his often outspoken criticism with his own free-wheeling surrealist verse', explains that because Heaney was one of the strongest writers in the Group, his pastoral poems tended to set the tone. Pakenham and others felt they were being pushed in a certain 'English' direction, towards solid, 'prosaic' poems about country things: 'weasals, stoats, mad uncles'. Parker and Pakenham himself, on the other hand, were much more interested in American poetry at that time, especially Beat poets like Allen Ginsberg, Lawrence Ferling-hetti, and Gregory Corso. As city boys, they also had trouble identifying with the Ireland evoked by Heaney's poetry. *Their* Ireland was populated by window cleaners and bus conductors, rather than by thatchers, cattle breeders, and small farmers.[41]

Parker's first Group sheet consisted of six poems reflecting his personal preoccupations: 'Valediction for Hammy' (John Hamilton, who left Belfast in the autumn of 1963 to do a postgraduate certificate in drama at the University of Bristol), 'Paddy Dies', 'Inside a Home for the Old' (about the residents of a nursing home, forgotten 'crazed sages'), 'The Broken Lives', 'Postscript', and 'Coming Out'. In this last poem, the speaker describes his release from hospital after the amputation of his leg in terms that relate his private trauma to the social upheaval of war. As he and his father exit to the street, he concludes by implying that he has left one hospital—an avowed gathering place for the sick and injured—for another,

unacknowledged one: 'Only the clocks have changed./And a massive familiar surgeon is at my elbow,/To welcome me back home into the hospital.'[42]

Parker's subsequent contributions to the Group in the first year of its existence
also seemed to Hobsbaum to illustrate Charles Baudelaire's dictum that the world
is one great hospital. Presented in two separate Group sheets, they comprised mini-
chapters from his second 'novel' (later entitled *The Jest-Book of ST Toile.*) These are
set in a grammar school more distinctly of a time (the mid-to-late 1950s) than of
a place and populated by students and teachers who are all, as one of them puts it,
'freaks'. Archie is 'worried about his Weltanschauung'; Shrink's hobby is 'collecting
irony; any old irony'; Lecompte speaks in ominous free verse that must be interpreted by a pompous friend; Crutch (named after the enormous crutch he carries)
is 'Games Captain, House Captain, Head Prefect, fly-half of the First Fifteen, crack
bat of the First Eleven . . . eldest son of one of the Governors' and—though he does
not realize it—'the loneliest, unhappiest, most hated, most pitied, most unfortunate boy in the school'; Art sees his life as an 'enormous joke' that unfortunately is
'almost never funny'. Many of the fragments presented to the Group were character sketches, and Hobsbaum read them all as 'nightmare versions' of Parker himself: the cripple unable to inspire affection in anyone, the spouter of fake poetry,
the 'comedian whose jokes go wrong'.[43]

At the same time that Parker was adopting a more disciplined approach to writing with the support of the Group, he also made his first foray into post-Dramsoc
theatre. Bill Morrison had graduated from Queen's in spring 1962, and he and
Parker had returned to the homes of their respective families and lost touch for a
while. Morrison had gone to work as a trainee manager at Shorts, but he hated his
job and still hankered after a theatrical career. In spring 1963 he directed a full-
length version of *The Way It Had To Be*, the play he had written with Parker, as
Queen's University's entry for several amateur drama festivals. The adjudicator of
the festival in Bangor turned out to be the director of the Belfast Arts Theatre, and
he offered Morrison an acting job. By May, Morrison had thrown over middle-
class respectability and returned to the bohemian life. With his girlfriend Valerie
Lilley, John Hamilton, and Sam Fannin, he moved into a flat in Hope House (on
College Park behind the university) which had once belonged to the painter Colin
Middleton and that quickly became an upscale version of the Magdala Street flat.
Since most of the occupants no longer subsisted on student budgets, they could
afford to throw elaborate parties at which a wide cross-section of the Belfast artistic
community would regularly appear. Parker was naturally invited to attend and
provide music for these, and he and Morrison became friendly again. Over the
summer, Stewart and Kate, both living with parents, used Hope House for their
trysts, and when Hamilton moved to Bristol that autumn Parker more or less took
over his room.[44]

Around then, Parker conceived the idea of starting a 'stage club' to present experimental drama, revues, music, poetry readings, and new work by local dramatists
whose plays were not being produced by the strictly commercial or amateur companies in town. He enlisted the assistance of Morrison and Fannin (who became the
enterprise's business manager), and the New Stage Club was born. They aimed, as

Parker explained in an article for *Gown*, to create 'a place where people can go every week to watch drama, and to discuss it over coffee with actors, producers, set-designers, authors even' and 'a stage on which new ideas in presentation can be tried out'. The organizers raised a little capital through a founder-member scheme and decided to mount three programmes in December 1963 to test the market for such a venture in Belfast before planning a full season. They secured a draughty hall with seating for about 100 in the Maritime Hotel at 36 College Square North, near the Royal Belfast Academical Institution and the technical college. This auditorium already had a reputation as a young people's entertainment venue, being used on Monday and Tuesday nights by the International Cinema Club and on Friday and Saturday nights by Van Morrison and his blues band. The New Stage Club, for a nominal rent, had the run of the place on Wednesdays and Thursdays.[45]

During the three weeks of its trial operation, the New Stage Club presented three one-act plays by John Hamilton, a double-bill consisting of *The Sugar Cubes* by Stewart Love and *The Way It Had To Be* by Parker and Morrison (which starred in the 'Stewart' role a Queen's undergraduate named Graham Rea, later better known as Stephen Rea), and André Obey's *Frost at Midnight*, a French Christmas play that Roy Alcorn transposed to an Ulster market town so effectively that many in the audience mistook it for a new Northern Irish drama. John Boyd and Ronald Mason, prominent BBC producers, offered the group moral support, as did Parker's hero, playwright Sam Thompson; the Opera House let them borrow flood- and spotlights; and each of the programmes attracted substantial audiences and sympathetic reviews in the local newspapers. In short, almost everyone involved with theatre and the media in Belfast encouraged the New Stage Club and desired its success. Nevertheless, the club had a short lifespan. It collapsed mainly because of a falling-out between Parker and Morrison, who proved annoyingly eager to lord it over his colleagues by flaunting his new professional theatre credentials, attempting to overrule Parker on matters of policy and looking down his nose at the 'amateur' actors and directors participating in the club's productions. After a particularly acrimonious row in Hope House, Parker vowed to Fannin that he would never work with Morrison again. Even had there not been such friction between its organizers, the considerable financial and time demands of the project would likely, as Morrison speculates, have quickly outstripped their resources. At the time, though, the self-destruction of the New Stage Club, with its ambitious goal of providing a venue and an audience for indigenous and innovative Northern Irish drama, threw Parker into 'a fit of depression' and probably contributed to his decision to leave Belfast the following spring.[46]

Meanwhile, a distant fourth in priority behind Kate, the Group, and the New Stage Club, there remained the Master's thesis he was supposed to be writing. Hobsbaum had urged Parker to tie his research to his own passions. Parker told him that he wrote, that he had been involved in theatre, and that he aspired to write a 'poetic drama'. Hobsbaum accordingly suggested that he should write his thesis on people who had tried to do the same in the twentieth century, and Parker eventually narrowed his topic to unrelated attempts by three poets to create a 'new' theatre by incorporating non-naturalistic elements in their plays. He intended to complete the thesis during the 1963/64 academic year, but he secured a temporary job in the US and moved there before finishing. It would be the summer of 1966 before he finally submitted 'The Modern Poet as Dramatist: Some Aspects of Non-Realistic Drama, with Special Reference to Eliot, Yeats and Cummings' for examination. By then, as he informed Hobsbaum, he felt he had 'learnt a little about the nature of drama, and more about my own makeup and capacities'.[47]

Although Parker's work on his MA thesis may have been largely against his grain, it is a solid piece of scholarship that reveals flashes of its author's personality. Eliot was an obvious choice (Parker himself had acted in two of his plays), Yeats probably appealed partly because he was Irish, and these two writers were not only towering figures in modern poetry but also highly committed to their work in the theatre over a long period. The inclusion of E. E. Cummings, who wrote only one full-length play, reflected Parker's enthusiasms most purely. The chapters on Eliot and Yeats are dutiful if characteristically idiosyncratic. Parker takes Eliot to task for the way his plays often veer between naturalistic and symbolic levels, faulting his inconsistent use of the chorus in *Murder in the Cathedral* and his failure fully to exploit the physical stage in his four full-length plays in a contemporary setting, and labels the fragment *Sweeney Agonistes* Eliot's most successful work for the stage. In the Yeats section, Parker traces the sources of one of the poet's character-types in an effort to show 'how entirely Irish the Yeatsian Fool is', maintaining that Yeats's drama 'remains even at its most esoteric, an expression of Ireland'. As in his discussion of Eliot, Parker singles out what had been regarded as a bizarre and confusing work for special praise, comparing *The Herne's Egg* to the Theatre of the Absurd and arguing that the play 'presents to mid-twentieth-century man a powerful image of his inmost life'.[48]

The most interesting part of the thesis from a biographical standpoint is the chapter on Cummings's *Him* (1927). Explicating it scene by scene, showing how each fits into the pattern of the work and reinforces its meaning, Parker defends the play against the charges of incoherence and obscurity that had been laid against it. Cummings's subject matter, the 'difficulties which confront and frustrate the modern playwright', urgently concerned Parker, who describes *Him* as 'a frustrated poet/ dramatist's case history'. In Parker's reading of the play, the main character (Him) is a neurotic, at odds with his society, his occupation, his sexuality, and his culture, with its materialism and disregard for non-commercial art. Limited by the versions of popular theatre available to him in the 1920s, he turns to the circus as a type of performance art involving the audience more directly. But his deepest-rooted problem is his estrangement from himself and from his lover, Me, whose pregnancy he fails to notice through most of the play. Him, Parker suggests, fears mortality so much that he has cut himself off from birth and life, too—indeed, from anything entailing change. He seeks permanence and transcendence through art, keeping his artist-self inviolable from Me and their relationship at a superficial level. But this self-protective approach produces neither personal nor professional satisfaction, because an artist alienated from 'his life-source, the man…withers into an esoteric hermit'. 'We can see', Parker writes, 'that the libido and his aspirations as an artist are precisely the things which Him needs to equate with one another.' Him's intimate life and his writing, which he had regarded as competing with one another, must be integrated in order for him to become a whole person and a successful artist.[49]

This message Parker read into the play spoke to many of the issues he had been trying for years to resolve for himself: balancing the demands of life and art, deciding whether detachment or commitment better served an artist, coming to terms with death. He was also impressed by the formal devices Cummings employed to convey his points, which included a box set that seemed to revolve; a non-chronological structure; the introduction of modern Fates (gossipy old ladies representing the background noise of a consumer culture) who view and comment obliquely on the action; the expressionist inclusion of a circus freak show at the climax of the play; and the significant casting of a single actor in numerous roles.

Parker interprets the middle section of the play, a succession of seemingly unrelated scenes, as a representation of Him's efforts to write popular drama, with each scene parodying a different form, from sex comedy to detective-thriller. He surmises further that the nine scenes of this play-within-the-play (like the nine circus freaks appearing towards the end of the play) correspond to the nine months of Me's pregnancy, and that the drums Him and Me hear at various points in the drama represent her labour pains. Probably in response to Hobsbaum's criticism, Parker tempers his admiration for the play in his concluding remarks on it, allowing that it 'is exceedingly demanding and peculiarly exasperating' and acknowledging that 'a great deal more of the play's meaning will emerge from painstaking analysis in the study than from experiencing it in the theatre'. He insists that 'audiences today, schooled in the plays of the Theatre of the Absurd, are more prepared to meet the demands of *Him* than the original audiences were' but also calls attention to the play's bewildering lack of exposition and to the self-indulgent length of the parody scenes.[50] Nevertheless, Parker makes it clear that he comprehends and approves of Cummings's experimental techniques, even if these are too subtle to be obvious in performance. Although he argues in his thesis that Yeats ultimately produced the most satisfying drama, Cummings's play proved a more abiding influence on his own work for the stage.[51]

Parker's analysis of *Him* also confirmed some of his personal decisions. At the beginning of the play, Him introduces himself as 'Everyman', suggesting to Parker that he must 'make a spiritual journey towards some kind of reckoning'. He needs to learn, Parker believes, that 'aliveness can only be achieved through other people. By giving to them, we relieve ourselves of the burden of individual spiritual death. It is in the nature of things that this act of giving should itself be tainted with death, but that is a matter for the recipient to resolve afresh. The main point is that this act of giving, which is a mortal act, sanctifies life and thus recreates it; in this sense, self-fulfillment comes by *affirming* mortality, not by denying it.'[52] In the soul-searching that followed his cancer diagnosis, Parker had reached similar conclusions about the necessity of reaching out to others and allowing himself to become attached to them in defiance of loss and death. Only human ties, he came to believe, could give life meaning. His developing relationship with Kate Ireland reinforced him in that view.

In the spring of 1964, Parker applied for teaching jobs at a number of American colleges and universities. Hobsbaum hoped his protégé would pursue a doctorate, but Parker was more interested in living in the US than in extending his student career. He accepted an offer from an institution that would allow him to teach on the expectation of a Master's degree—Hamilton College. The decision to emigrate forced other decisions, and Stewart and Kate made plans to marry. His sister Joan was the first family member he informed of his intentions, and he asked her anxiously how she supposed their mother would react. 'She'll go berserk', Joan predicted confidently, and so she did. Belle Parker had always been possessive of her youngest child, and the fact of his marrying a woman she felt she barely knew combined with his announcement that he intended to move across the Atlantic was a double blow. (Bob Granleese, who would visit the Parker family to hear his friend's news after Stewart left for the US, got the 'funny feeling' that his mother had basically disowned him at that point.) Stewart's father and siblings were more understanding. His brother George would have liked to try living in America himself, and Herbie Parker felt it stood to reason that his son should go where the work was. From the security of a teaching position, he reasoned, Stewart could do his creative writing on the side if he wished. Thus, not without drama, Stewart and Kate were married on 26 August 1964 (Kate's mother's wedding anniversary) and left Belfast immediately to begin their new life in the new world.[53]

4

'Calling Myself a Writer'

Stewart and Kate Parker spent their wedding night in a succession of planes and airports, passing through Dublin, Shannon, Newfoundland, and Boston before reaching New York City, where they were met by Stewart's new colleagues Ed Barrett and Austin Briggs and their wives and conveyed to Hamilton College in Clinton, about 250 miles away. Parker had come in search of the cutting edge of art and culture, but his new surroundings exuded an aura of fixed tradition. Hamilton, chartered in 1812, is one of the oldest colleges in the US. The town of Clinton dates from the late eighteenth century and boasts a number of buildings from that era. All this must have been remote from the images conjured by the words 'New York' to an untravelled 22-year-old from Belfast. Years later, Parker told a Northern Irish friend that he had a stronger sense of history in North America than he did at home, since even in New York State there remained tracts of farmland where people might live in a house their grandparents had built 'with their bare hands'. In contrast to the ambience of upstate New York, Belfast as Parker knew it seemed a modern nineteenth-century city.[1]

Hamilton rivalled Clinton in size and represented a world unto itself for those who studied and taught there, albeit a small one. In 1964, Hamilton comprised about eight hundred students and ninety-five faculty members in all ranks. The all-male student body remained remarkably homogeneous in other ways as well. Despite active recruitment, there were only about half a dozen black students on campus at any given time; similarly, most Hamilton students came from privileged backgrounds, and jackets and ties were still compulsory at dinner. Classes met six days a week, and underclassmen had to document attendance at 'a religious service or meeting of their own choosing once a week'. In their free time, students relieved the tension created by hard work and regimentation through excessive drinking.[2]

Faculty social life displayed the incestuous quality captured by Edward Albee in *Who's Afraid of Virginia Woolf?* (1962). Professors and instructors socialized among themselves, mainly at dinner parties, with little distinction by age or department. Those interested in the arts also focused on the Hamilton student dramatic society, the Charlatans, which usually produced two full-length plays a year, along with one-act plays by students, dramatic readings, and other short works. Performances took place in the Minor Theater, a state-of-the-art facility new when Parker arrived; in an early letter to Philip Hobsbaum, he named 'their beautiful theatre' as one of the 'insidious pressures' he anticipated would distract him from writing at Hamilton. (The chapel could also be converted to a theatrical venue by removing the altar and erecting a curtain, and occasionally the dining hall served in this capacity as well.) Women for the female roles came from the ranks of faculty wives and the local high school, and faculty members directed, attended, and sometimes acted in the productions. Theatre represented a key form of entertainment at the college, since even seeing a film required a car trip to neighbouring Utica.[3]

In the self-contained universe of Hamilton, Stewart and Kate made an instant and favourable impression. Their innocence and openness charmed the faculty set, while younger friends admired their cosmopolitan style. They were young, in love, enthusiastic, intelligent, and creative, with the added appeal of exoticism. Kate struck people as the dominant partner in those days; more forceful and outgoing than Stewart, she radiated vitality and dressed in outrageous London mod fashions. Her pixie-ish manner did not conceal her intellect, and she seemed more genteel and worldly than her husband. Indeed, it surprised some that Stewart, not she, wrote. She read, for hours on end, and quickly began acting with the Charlatans. Her sense of theatricality extended to social situations in which she performed the role of faculty wife, at first with aplomb and later with increasing impatience. In contrast to Kate, with her mercurial wit, Stewart won people over with quiet humour and warmth. He seemed shy and anxious at first and took his work, both teaching and writing, seriously. He also demonstrated that he knew how to have fun, though, and his distinctive laugh and 'eccentric genius hat' were personal trademarks.[4]

Parker fulfilled one of his American dreams immediately. After taking driving lessons and acquiring a licence, he purchased a used Studebaker for $635. With his cumbersome prosthesis, Parker found it difficult to walk long distances; owning and operating a car conferred a degree of personal freedom unknown to him before. Other ambitions took longer to achieve. The summer after his second year at Hamilton, in July 1966, he attended the Newport Jazz Festival in Rhode Island. The Dave Brubeck Quartet, the John Coltrane Quintet, Stan Getz, Thelonious Monk, Duke Ellington, Ella Fitzgerald, Dizzy Gillespie, Miles Davis, Count Basie, and others performed, and Parker remembered the experience later as one of the highlights of his time in the US. Shorter trips to New York City to attend satirical revues at Upstairs at the Downstairs or, on one occasion, a burlesque show, and jaunts to Stratford, Ontario, and Burlington, Vermont, for Shakespeare festivals in the summer of 1965 provided fodder for letters home and helped Parker feel closer to the action than he usually did in Clinton.[5]

Despite his quaint surroundings, Parker soon discovered that the life of a small college teacher is one of unremitting labour. As an instructor, his course assignments at first consisted entirely of freshman English classes. 'They grind their academics into the ground here', Parker wrote despairingly to Hobsbaum, adding that he gave twelve lectures and marked fifty-five essays a week. Making matters worse, a number of his classes met at 8 a.m., never an hour when he shone. Despite Hobsbaum's repeated advice to put instruction third after his creative writing and research, Parker had concluded by the autumn of his second year at Hamilton that 'teaching involves me too much: I get very concerned about it, and sit up to all hours of the night working on essays and worrying about methods of presenting the material. This is a suicidal approach, but I can't change it; not here, at any rate.'

Scarcely older than his students, Parker had an excellent rapport with them but probably felt the need to be over-prepared for class sessions. With his Buddy Holly glasses, passion for popular music, and rollicking gait, he stuck out among the Hamilton faculty. Some of his students even had trouble understanding him, and he told his sister about his effort to develop a 'mid-Atlantic' accent to alleviate the problem (according to Ed Barrett, he never succeeded in this endeavour).[6]

Not all Parker's teaching at Hamilton took place in classrooms. He applied much of his energy to practical experiments in theatre. Likely attracted by their status as early examples of popular, vernacular drama combining instruction with entertainment, he directed productions of five medieval mystery plays. He also dabbled in verse drama, a carry-over from his Dramsoc days and the work on his MA thesis (still in progress during most of his Hamilton sojourn). In December 1964, he directed *The Second Shepherd's Play* by the Wakefield Master; in January 1966 he mounted productions of *Herod the Great* and another Wakefield mystery play; in November 1966 he took the part of the First Voice in a Charlatans staged reading of Dylan Thomas's *Under Milk Wood*; and in December 1966, shortly before leaving Hamilton, he directed *The Salutation* and *The First Shepherd's Play* from the Wakefield cycle, along with Eliot's *Sweeney Agonistes*. Peter Kingsley, a student who acted in one of Parker's mystery play productions, remembers him as a 'terrific, supportive' director. Gerard Moses, a friend who became a professional theatre director, expresses no surprise that Parker eventually devoted his career to drama, although he showed no particular interest in writing for the stage in the early 1960s. Moses, who took the key role of Mak in *The Second Shepherd's Play*, also found him a 'wonderful director' who understood that theatrical language consists of gestures as well as words. Despite Parker's limp, Moses recalls him as someone whose mind expressed itself physically; indeed, one of his first impressions of Parker consisted of the sense that he could be 'a great actor'. In addition to his theatre work, Parker seized other opportunities to perform, giving poetry readings and presenting an evening of traditional Scottish, Irish, and American ballads.[7]

Parker's less structured free-time activities also contained large elements of play-acting. He and Kate preferred to entertain informally, and they and whichever of their friends had dropped by would read aloud to one another or hold in-house play readings. Sometimes they played dictionary games, charades, or 'the Parker game', in which players built up to a punch line punning on a well-known phrase. Parker also played his guitar and sang from a repertoire that included Lonnie Donegan's 'Does Your Chewing Gum Lose Its Flavour?' along with pieces by Cole Porter and fellow Tin Pan Alley composers, Irish and American folk songs, Beatles tunes, and other rock and roll numbers. He sang or hummed much of the time, encouraging guests to sing too. There were hours of conversation as well, about literature, theatre, and life. Endowed with a home of her own, Kate introduced Stewart to gracious living on a budget. Her cooking, which he had first enjoyed when they lived together in London, continued to inspire his devotion; she was 'an alchemist in the kitchen', Parker's niece recalls. Friends in New York State remembered decades later Kate's creative twists on old favourites, such as Irish stew with cranberries in it, like 'little time bombs'. Over-all, the Parkers impressed people as a couple able to amuse themselves without spending money and to find joy even in pedestrian moments.[8]

Over the course of the two and a half years that Parker taught at Hamilton, he and Kate spent progressively less time with the faculty members who had first befriended them and more with people closer to their own age. This proved a source of hurt, especially to the Barretts and Briggses, and it may have reflected the Parkers' desire to escape the supervision of people who had taken an almost paren-tal interest in them. Then again, perhaps their shift of allegiance demonstrated nothing more than a wish to cultivate relationships with people with whom they had more in common. Those who knew Stewart and Kate most intimately during the Hamilton years were either students or younger faculty members who had recently graduated from Hamilton themselves. This orientation was unusual in those hierarchical days, when at a college like Hamilton students and professors saw a great deal of each other but rarely socialized, and Austin Briggs, for one, regarded Parker as immature because of it. Younger friends, in contrast, saw his disregard of the conventions of student–teacher interaction as evidence of his egali-tarian nature.[9]

Parker's closest friend during his first years at Hamilton, John Paul, shared his sense of the seriousness of life. Paul was an upperclassman at Hamilton and a poet. Their mutual interest in writing brought them together, and their commitment to the social and spiritual reform of their respective societies drew them closer. Just before Parker's arrival, Paul had volunteered during the 'Freedom Summer' of 1964, a civil rights push orchestrated by the Council of Federated Organizations, chiefly the Student Nonviolent Coordinating Committee and the Congress of Racial Equality, to register black voters in Mississippi. During the brief training in non-violent resistance that volunteers received before heading south, Paul got to know Michael Schwerner and Andrew Goodman. These volunteers, from New York State like Paul himself, left for Mississippi before him, and by the time he arrived they and a black colleague, James Chaney, had gone missing (they were later found dead). On Paul's first day in Mississippi, men with shotguns surrounded him and ordered him to leave, which he refused to do. He survived three months in the state, marvelling at the spiritual wealth of people who lived in physical pov-erty, and at the religious faith, strength, and dignity of the black community. After this experience of idealism in action, Paul no longer fitted in at Hamilton and felt an affinity with Parker, another outsider who had also come close to death as a young man. The two talked at length about everything, including writing, Parker's amputation (a subject off-limits to most people), and sectarian division in North-ern Ireland, which Parker compared to the racial divide in the US.[10]

Other early intimates got to know the Parkers through a shared love of theatre. Peter Kingsley, a mainstay of the Charlatans who later acted professionally, appeared with Kate in numerous productions. Though as lighthearted and carefree as John Paul was earnest and concerned, he and Stewart appreciated each other's talents despite their different outlooks on life. Gerard Moses, an instructor in the Public Speaking Department, worked with the Charlatans as an adviser, director, and actor and remembers Kate as a 'stunning' actor able to reveal the turbulence beneath apparent repose. He spent many hours at the Parkers' apartment before leaving Hamilton in the autumn of 1965.[11]

Successive academic years brought new companions into the Parkers' lives. Ken Mealy, a significant arrival, taught French in the Department of Romance Languages and became fast friends with them. Distinguished by his energy, flair, boisterous laugh, fine tenor voice, and good looks, he dressed like an Edwardian dandy and had expensive tastes that, unlike the Parkers, he could afford to indulge. Everything Mealy owned was first-class, including a stereo system that Stewart likely coveted, and his taste in music ranged from hard rock to opera. At his apartment, impromptu parties formed to listen to the new Jimi Hendrix or Incredible String Band album.[12]

Another addition to the Parkers' circle in 1966 was a freshman named Terry Keenan, with a mother from Dublin, paternal grandparents from Belfast, and aspirations as a poet. Naturally, he and Stewart fell in with each other after their initial encounter at a poetry reading. Hamilton had begun by now to feel the revolutionary effects of the 1960s, and Keenan stood out as the most readily identifiable representative of the counter-culture, with his long hair, bright red pin-striped trousers, and knee-high fringed boots. He acted too, taking part in the Charlatans' staged reading of *Under Milk Wood* and playing an angel in Parker's production of *The First Shepherd's Play*.[13]

Throughout his time at Hamilton, Parker's creative writing competed, generally unsuccessfully, with his teaching and extra-curricular activities. His lack of productivity frustrated him, although he managed to complete a few projects. The first, a long poem entitled 'The Casualty Meditates Upon His Journey', he finished in December 1964 after mulling it over for seven or eight months. Parker's amputation inspired the poem, but his personal experience is channelled into a post-war reflection in which the speaker's personal ordeal is mirrored by the devastation of his city:

> Open or closed, my eyes see
> traction: pulleys and joists to support broken limbs
> in their white casing, like cranes supporting girders;
> the city's landscape is littered with cranes,
> the poking broken fingers of some vast wreckage,
> of some smashed fuselage;
> the streets must be teeming with images.

Lying, it seems, in his hospital bed, the Casualty listens to the sounds of the city which float up through an open window from the street below and remembers the world outside. He describes the rubbish dump where he played as a child, filled with the charred remains of 'yesterday's fires' and mounds of discarded books which he compares to 'the Auschwitz piles'.

Images of overt destruction give way in section two of the poem to snapshots of the crass materialism characterizing much of modern, disposable Western culture. As if in recoil, the mind's eye of the speaker glides in cinematic fashion away from the bland artifice of the storefronts to the bus-stop where ranks of girls returning from the dance halls, 'harpies and muses all', 'coax', 'invite', and 'torture' the Casualty with their unattainable charms. The third and final section of the poem abounds in references to Proverbs, chapter seven. These biblical verses, attributed to Solomon (himself a famous womanizer), warn against adultery and the wiles of the harlot. The inter-textual relationship with Proverbs lends ambiguity to the poem's ending, as the moon speaks the words attributed to the temptress in the Bible, with a blank line emphasizing the provisional nature of the solace offered:

> silently, night's morphine fades,
> into the window swims the ancient moon.
> He knows he is benign, and impregnates the city
> with his fire, and makes the cranes stand up
> to tent the hymen of the sky, and says:
> Come let us take our fill of love
>
> until the morning.[14]

In a letter to Hobsbaum, Parker explained that 'The ending has given me hell because, although it is the only "true" experience in the poem, it sounds very self-consciously literary.'[15]

Parker still thought of himself primarily as a poet in the mid-1960s, but it would be over a year before he wrote another poem. Probably self-disgust, as much as anything else, caused him to reply shortly when Terry Keenan asked in the autumn of 1966 about current Irish poetry: 'There are no poets in Ireland.' Stranded in Clinton, New York, it seemed to Parker that he had exiled himself from Belfast just as, perversely, things were starting to happen there. News had reached him in the summer of 1965 that Seamus Heaney had signed a deal with Faber and Faber for a first volume of poetry, and he wrote to Hobsbaum that this accomplishment by a fellow Group member represented 'a personal triumph, a triumph for the university, and most of all, a triumph for Belfast'.[16] Nevertheless, his genuine pride in Heaney must have been mixed with envy when the latter's *Death of a Naturalist* appeared the following year to favourable reviews.

'I feel completely cut off from Belfast here', Parker complained to Hobsbaum, but his Northern Irish connections helped him obtain what publications he had in this period. Managing a Belfast-based literary career from upstate New York presented problems, however, in those days before e-mail, fax machines, and inexpensive long-distance phone calls. In spring 1965, the *Northern Review*, edited by Paddy Lynch and Michael Mitchell, published a collection of the 'fragments' set at a grammar school that Parker had shared with the Group in 1963/64, 'The Preambles of S T Toile', in its first issue. The journal published 'The Casualty Meditates Upon His Journey' in its second issue, later that year. Parker was impressed by the *Northern Review*'s production values but irritated by the editors' treatment of him, since in neither case did they inform him that his work would be included, seek his permission to publish, or send him a complimentary copy in a timely fashion. Moreover, the 'Preambles' were printed in the wrong order and improperly laid out. 'They will have to tighten up their organisation if the magazine is not going to be just another Belfast artistic shambles', he observed prophetically to Hobsbaum.[17]

Around the same time, Parker received what he referred to as 'virtually my first "professional" printing': the inclusion of three of his works in *Young Commonwealth Poets '65*, an anthology published by Heinemann in association with the Cardiff Commonwealth Arts Festival.[18] The following summer, the *Kilkenny Magazine* published two of his early poems. More significant, in spring 1966, was the publication of Parker's first collection of poetry, a pamphlet entitled *The Casualty's Meditation*. This appeared in conjunction with the Queen's Festival in a series that included pamphlets by Michael Longley, Seamus Heaney, Derek Mahon, Arthur Terry, Joan Watton, Philip Hobsbaum, James Simmons, and Seamus Deane. Most of the poems contained in *The Casualty's Meditation* ('The Casualty Meditates Upon His Journey', 'Coming Out', 'Postscript', 'Paddy Dies', 'The Broken Lives', and 'Health') had been published before, but together they made a unified statement, reached a wider audience, and shared in the attention accorded the series as a whole.[19]

Several of Parker's contemporaries were achieving a measure of recognition beyond the North. In an article for the *Spectator* in August 1966, Hobsbaum noted that four young Northern Irish poets—James Simmons, Michael Longley, Derek Mahon, and Seamus Heaney—had recently won 'substantial awards' in London and claimed for Northern Ireland 'a most extraordinary revival in literature and the theatre'. He generously devoted an entire paragraph to 'Stewart Parker, a poet who has won no awards and few publications', calling 'The Casualty Meditates Upon His Journey' 'one of the most remarkable productions of our time'. Such propaganda efforts on his behalf, though undoubtedly heartening, heightened Parker's sense of resting on his laurels. Even before the *Spectator* piece appeared, Parker had written to Hobsbaum expressing appreciation for 'the plugging that you have done for me at home' and adding, 'I'm afraid and ashamed to say that my achievement doesn't deserve it.'[20]

Parker's day-to-day activities as an instructor continued to monopolize his attention, a situation that made him increasingly unhappy. A journal entry from 1 April 1966 reflects his resolve to start making his creative writing a priority: 'Old lesson, learned yet again for April Fool's Day—in order to write you have to write. You can't fast for a year and then sit down to a hearty masterpiece. For the first time in my life that I can remember, I've worked steadily for five consecutive days, about 2–6 hours a day. The gain is extraordinary. Must persevere in same.' On 29 April, however, he bid 'Goodbye to exactly four weeks of silence—April-fooled again' and reflected glumly that 'Teaching employs one-tenth of my mind. If you do not breath [sic] deeply, the usable space in your lungs contracts: if you do not eat much, your stomach shrinks; if you are a writer and you teach, your mind silts up—nine-tenths of it.'

Parker must have suspected early on that academic life did not suit him, but he found it so hard to renounce the security of a teaching position that for a time he tried to convince himself that Hamilton College was the real problem. Parker and his favourite students and colleagues found Hamilton's approach to the teaching of literature unbearably stodgy, which heightened his dissatisfaction with teaching in general. The study of English there remained largely historical: Austin Briggs's Modern British Literature class was the only course offering to concentrate entirely on twentieth-century literature. Ezra Pound had attended Hamilton, but his poetry was not taught there; there was no contemporary drama class. As early as the autumn of 1965, Parker dreamed of returning to the British Isles, and he applied for assistant lectureships at Essex, East Anglia, Warwick, and Kent; a lectureship at Hull College of Education; a job as Curator to Yeats's Tower; and a position as Research Associate in Richard Hoggart's Centre for Contemporary Cultural Studies in Birmingham. None of these applications succeeded—just as well, since he really wanted to live in London, doing whatever work he could find to pay the bills and focusing on his writing. Finally, promised a chance to teach the creative writing class (offered only in alternate years), he agreed to stay at Hamilton through the 1966 autumn semester.[21]

Having resigned themselves to extending their stay in Clinton, Stewart and Kate splurged that summer on what he described to Hobsbaum at the outset as 'a grand-slam, six-week train bash right around the Continent' and in retrospect as 'an 8½ thousand-mile oddyssey [*sic*] around America...journeying through over twenty states and confronting the greatness and the hellishness which inform this country'.[22] At last, he was going to see the America depicted in the Hollywood movies of his childhood and the Jack Kerouac books and Allen Ginsberg poems of his Queen's days. He and Kate flew to Chicago on 1 August and travelled overland around the US before flying back to New York from Kentucky on 5 September. They first visited Minneapolis, where they attended several plays at Irish director Tyrone Guthrie's new theatre. The next phase of the trip took them in search of the Wild West: Cheyenne, Wyoming; Shoshone and Hailey, Idaho (birthplace of Ezra Pound); and Salt Lake City, Utah (where Parker encountered the Story of Mormonism presented throughout the city).

Everywhere they went, Parker delighted in recognizing such familiar types as a fellow passenger who reminded him of a 'grizzly prospector'; a sheriff complete with 'high heel boots, white Stetson, denims—and bone handled gun slung loose in black holster'; and a waitress who looked 'like woman travelling West to be a school mistress'. At one point, watching a Western in a cinema in Shoshone, a cowboy walked in and sat in front of them, and Parker experienced a '[b]izarre confusion of illusion and reality'.[23] They made a pilgrimage to San Francisco, staying for ten days and spotting Lawrence Ferlinghetti at the City Lights Bookstore, then returned to the road for visits to Los Angeles, the Grand Canyon, and Santa Fe.

The US was finally meeting Parker's expectations. On the evening of 30 August, after a deliriously long day of travel, he wrote in his journal, 'Evening—coasting out of New Mexico to strains of a delightful flute solo. Herbie Mann. Two boys (one Mexican) behind with portable gramophone. In my left ear, rich strains of Houston negro accent. I am in America.' Three days in New Orleans, a jazz mecca, rounded out the trip, apart from a last train ride through Alabama, Tennessee, and Kentucky. Parker bought an 8mm camera before the trip, and by the end of the journey he had shot ten four-minute movie reels that he hoped to edit into a thirty-minute film 'when I can afford a splicer'. His 'newest ambition', he wrote Hobsbaum, was to attend film school and learn camera technique. Meanwhile, he planned to use the film and his journal to help him write a book about the trip, 'maybe a poem, maybe a collection of prose bits, dialogue, anything'.[24] Whatever came of his 'oddyssey', at least now he could not be accused of leaving the US without having seen it.

His Master's thesis finally behind him, Parker attempted some creative writing again, completing a short story that same summer. 'The Recipient' records the feelings of helplessness and uncertainty washing over a young man whose girlfriend thinks she might be pregnant. During a visit to the dentist, he frets over his options: 'A cheap abortion, never. Living in sin. That would be the brave thing, the principled thing to do. But to do it you would have to be brave and principled, you would have to be James Joyce or somebody.' Nevertheless, he reasons, he himself 'would do it like a shot'; the problem is that he cannot imagine asking it of Charly, his girlfriend, because 'Women are your true-born bourgeoisie...under the skin, even the wildest of them. A showy wedding, a shiny well-stocked kitchen, a large dream house with a well trained hubby to promote, which of them would not trade her guitar and jeans, or her right to vote, and probably her right arm, for all of that?' He reminds himself that Charly is not like that, 'but she wasn't like him either'. His fear of losing his freedom leads him into resentment of women in general, intensified by the accident that in his regular dentist's absence he is seen by a female one. When he returns to his flat, half-resigned to a middle-class marriage and career, he finds a note from his girlfriend saying the scare has passed—news that leaves him feeling strangely let down. Parker regarded the story as more conventional than most of the short fiction he had been writing, but he submitted it to a magazine for young adults called *Discern*. Its acceptance mitigated Parker's disappointment over Faber and Faber's rejection of some of his 'fragments' for a planned prose anthology, which had probably confirmed his suspicion that the latest of his ST Toile pieces were 'a lot more contrived and self-conscious than the earlier ones'.[25]

Another project begun in the summer of 1966 was a radio play initially entitled *Victor, Son of Sam*, later renamed *Headcase*, and eventually called *Speaking of Red Indians*.[26] Set on the Wednesday before the Saturday wedding of Victor and 'The Girl', it reworks the biblical story of Samson and Delilah (the Philistine harlot who betrays him by learning that his superhuman strength resides in his hair and shearing him). The Girl is cutting Victor's hair; he suspects that he will not be happy with the result. *Speaking of Red Indians* resembles 'The Recipient' in its depiction of passive male suffering at female hands; Victor even compares getting his hair cut to going to the dentist and declares his dislike of both.

The first half of the script showcases The Girl's role-playing; Victor even suggests that he does not know who she really is, crying in exasperation at one point, 'You never *stop* pretending.'[27] Among the personae she assumes with Victor are those of schoolmistress and mother of a recalcitrant small boy, speaking to him sternly or in a baby talk that unnerves him. He obviously worries about how marriage will change him, her, and their relationship, and she wilfully exacerbates his misgivings by withholding sexual favours and treating him like a child. Her cutting of his hair symbolizes her psychological domination of him, his emasculation, the stripping-away of his former identity.

Victor's subconscious fears are brought to the surface by a visit from his best mate, Marshall, who delivers the gag wedding gift of a stuffed and mounted moose head. The fact that The Girl dislikes Victor's friends is alluded to more than once, and Marshall says he himself will not marry, 'unless I really lose my head'. During his call, Marshall discourses at length on losing body parts—fingernails and toe-nails, appendix, teeth—unmistakably implying that Victor risks losing one or two more important appendages. Marshall insists that hair has a special 'significance', citing the poet John Donne, who 'used to wear a lock of his wife's hair on his wrist, handcuff-style'. He returns to the subject later in a seeming non sequitur after Victor loses his temper with him: 'Speaking of Red Indians . . . their attitude to hair is very striking. The way they used to collect the scalps of their victims. . . . Apparently they believed the soul was in the hair. . . . The daughters in certain tribes presented human scalps as a dowry. You know, before they got married.' This speech recalls Victor's earlier admonition to The Girl, 'Don't scalp me now', and again before the end of the play he will tell her that 'I don't want to look scalped.'[28]

Animating both 'The Recipient' and *Speaking of Red Indians* is the main male characters' visceral apprehension about the ways in which committing themselves to a particular woman might change their priorities and limit them. Since Parker himself had been married only about two years when he conceived these pieces, it is natural to wonder whether or not they were informed by his own experience of being a husband. Peter Kingsley recollects that he often heard 'half-jocular banter' similar to that of Victor and The Girl between Stewart and Kate, although Stewart appeared to 'relish' her humour. Moreover, like the protagonist of 'The Recipient', Parker might have considered marrying tantamount to compromising his bohe-mian principles. His decision to wed had been made under some duress, since his potential employers had given him to understand that it would not do for him to live openly in Clinton with a woman not his wife.[29] Certainly immigration restric-tions made Kate's tenure in the US simpler as Stewart's spouse. Although people close to the Parkers at the time agree that they were generally very happy with each other, there were also persistent hints that, as Ed Barrett later put it, the marriage was always 'more difficult' than most of their friends realized.[30]

As early as January 1965, Parker commented obliquely in a letter to Hobsbaum on the challenges of adjusting to his new circumstances, writing that for a while the previous autumn he 'had all but decided that the pressures of married life and a frenetic job in a frenetic country had smothered for good any frail creative organ-ism I might have had'. The nature of those 'pressures' had much to do with Kate's temperament. Margaret Briggs remembers Barrett saying that Parker had sought his advice, confiding that Kate had crying fits in the middle of the night and con-fessing that he did not know how to react. Margaret herself concluded that Kate's mysterious unhappiness was something Stewart had to try to assuage in private, while she 'sparkled' in company: 'everybody loved to be with her'. Because few people saw the troubled aspect of Kate, her rare public displays of neurosis seemed shockingly uncharacteristic. Austin Briggs recalls one particularly 'frightening' episode after one of Kate's triumphant theatrical performances when, surrounded by friends eager to congratulate her, she suffered something like an attack of claustrophobia: 'I remember Stewart suddenly having to *get Kate home*...something was decidedly wrong, and she was right on the edge of hysteria, with no particular trigger that I knew.' After observing similar scenes on other occasions, he came to see her as almost a split personality: 'There was a Kate who was endlessly smiling and happy, and there was another Kate whom I eventually decided really had some quite severe psychological problems.'[31]

John Paul describes Kate as 'a person of some extremes' who had become adept at handling her dark, brooding side. Often, he believes, her bold public face masked pain and turmoil. In other instances, she would 'get kind of black around the eyes and withdraw'. Over time, her intensely private nature alienated her from the gossipy faculty wives' circle, and she found life in Clinton more and more isolating.[32] If, as seems likely, she took Stewart alone into her confidence, then the burden of helping her manage her moodiness and anxiety fell squarely on him—and his habitual response of baffled sympathy and stoic endurance of her emotional storms probably did neither of them much good.

In late 1966, the Parkers decided to return to Belfast for at least the first half of 1967. Perhaps homesickness led Stewart to choose Belfast over London as the place to launch his full-time writing career, or maybe he thought residence there would help him secure a grant from the Arts Council of Northern Ireland.[33] In Belfast he could likely get enough work from BBC Northern Ireland to live on, and his literary connections might help him earn more artistic commissions. The transition would be easier in a familiar city, so he could concentrate on writing.

Another factor in Parker's decision to return to Belfast, instead of striking out in London, might have been a related determination to come back to the US for another stint of teaching, this time at a larger and more exciting place than Hamilton. In the autumn of 1966, James McConkey, a novelist and professor of creative writing at Cornell University, came to Hamilton to give a reading; he sat in on one of Parker's creative writing classes and formed a high opinion of him. Stewart and Kate spent a weekend at McConkey's farm outside Ithaca and met some of his colleagues informally. After this visit, McConkey encouraged Parker to apply for an instructorship in creative writing for the 1967/68 academic year. Before Parker left Clinton at the end of January 1967, he had been offered a job teaching in the creative writing and Freshman Humanities programmes at Cornell, renewable for up to three years.[34]

Making these arrangements to return to the US after six or seven months in Belfast must have helped Parker face the homecoming, since he would now be visiting en route to the next phase of a plausible career rather than crawling back to his roots in defeat. Writing in his journal shortly before his campus interview, he had looked forward to the impending move with both trepidation and hope, willing himself to make the most of his time away from teaching: 'Just over two weeks till we're off back to Belfast. I keep setting myself these tests. I failed the Clinton Test (would write non-stop: would not return home till I had bargaining power in the form of RECOGNITION: etc.). Will I really settle down and grind out my vision on paper this time? Do I know by now what a fool I am? The two questions seem to be connected—if I can say yes to the second, I will be able to say yes to the first.' The list of projects in various stages of composition that he hoped to complete by the end of the summer included three plays, a novel, and a long poem: 'Also more stories, but if I can finish off this lot in six months, I'll be prepared to acquiesce in the universe.'[35]

In Belfast, Stewart and Kate visited each of their families often and met up frequently with Stewart's best friend, Sam Fannin, and Kate's best friend, Brenda Callaghan, and their respective spouses. Stewart also saw Queen's literary associates John Hamilton and Joan Newmann (formerly Watton) on a regular basis. Occasionally he got together with other old friends (Ian Hill, Seamus Heaney, Roy Alcorn, Roy Nimmons, even Bill Morrison) or with poets he had not known personally before, such as Derek Mahon and Michael Longley, but he did not want literary gossip and politics to distract him from the actual business of writing.

Parker's primary goal for his time in Belfast was to live by his pen, so he made contact during his first week home with BBC producer John Boyd.[36] The BBC through the 1940s and 1950s had been an outpost of Empire in Northern Ireland, with most important jobs filled by English people and local voices largely unheard. By the late 1960s, the efforts of men like Boyd and features producer Sam Hanna Bell had changed much of that. Announcers still needed middle-class English accents, but people from the North had more power behind the scenes, and more programming focused on local topics. The Northern Irish producers were overwhelmingly Protestant, but many were liberals committed to opening the institution to the diversity of the region. In this time of decreased sectarian tension and political thawing between Northern Ireland and the Republic of Ireland, BBC Northern Ireland was coming into its own as a 'free society' within the North.[37]

Freelancing for the BBC was nice work if you could get it. Interested parties presented themselves at Broadcasting House and auditioned. If they could strike the right tone (correct, communicative, and casual), they were issued recording equipment and sent to interview someone or investigate something. To complete an assignment, these citizen-reporters wrote and recorded their own stories. Capable ones would be called repeatedly.[38] With his acting experience, university education, and writing ability, Parker took easily to this kind of journalism. He auditioned as an interviewer on 13 March and got work the next day. Before leaving on 1 September, he reported seven or eight news stories. Also in March, with the backing of Northern Ireland's drama producer, David Turner, the BBC accepted *Speaking of Red Indians*. It was rehearsed and recorded in mid-July, with Bill Morrison in the role of Victor, and Parker had taken the first step towards becoming a professional playwright as well as a professional writer.

By now, feeling productive and stimulated again, Parker had begun to think of his move to the US as a mistake and to regret that he would return there at the end of the summer. In his journal, he reflected on the relief of being at home again and the perils of being away:

Six weeks back. Looking over them, they are rich with incident. Really alive again. The last two and a half years seem more and more like a bite out of my life, neatly bitten and swallowed as quick as half a biscuit. A lightning jump from 22 to 25: those priceless years gone for good. But I'm making it, hanging on, fending off those Institutions that threaten to take you over and process you into hygienic social gadgets, one after the other. Life for the Resident Alien, the Refugee, is precarious, at all times. What the hell will I have turned into, *been* turned into, in five years? But here and now, here today, I'm free.[39]

Discovering how to stay connected to Belfast wherever he might be physically would be one of the challenges facing Parker later that year.

His mentor John Malone could help him in that quest. In 1957, Malone had moved from the vice-principalship at Ashfield to the position of head at the new Orangefield Boys' School, where he continued his innovative work with pupils who had not shone on the Eleven Plus exam. To help make the case for comprehensive education, Malone ran Orangefield along the lines of a grammar school. In addition to the vocational education considered the proper business of secondary schools, he stressed theatre, art, music, politics, and athletics and sought to make Orangefield a focus for its largely working-class community. Eventually, in defiance of the Northern Irish educational system, he instituted A-level classes to prepare his students for university.[40]

Among the qualities that made the unassuming Malone a dynamic leader were his keen eye for talent and ability to take 'ordinary individuals and make them extraordinary'. Robert Crone, an Orangefield graduate who worked as Malone's assistant on later projects, recalls his 'genius' for taking 'disparate individuals' and making them part of a grander scheme, the outlines of which they themselves might sense only dimly. Wherever he went, he looked for people who could advance his vision of a more egalitarian society, and over his lifetime he built a vast network of gifted friends and supporters. Stewart Parker was one of these. About a month after returning to Belfast, Parker attended a play at Orangefield; the following week, Malone invited him to visit during school hours; the week after that, he came to teach a class. Malone soon introduced him to David Hammond and Douglas Carson, former Orangefield English and history teachers respectively, then producing the radio programmes of the Schools Department of BBC Northern Ireland.[41]

The BBC's charter included an educational mission, and a central Schools Department in London produced programmes on history, literature, science, and even physical education which were broadcast weekly in a format aimed at the classrooms of the UK. Each region also had slots it could fill with its own programming. Not until 1960, however, roughly forty years after the other regions, did Northern Ireland acquire its own Schools Department to produce programmes of mainly local interest. The delay had been political: Unionist officials resisted the creation of a broadcasting entity intended to focus on 'Irish' subjects, associated in their minds with republican views; Nationalists, for their part, regarded with suspicion the offerings of a Broadcasting Corporation with the prefix 'British' attached to its name. The formation of the Northern Irish Schools Department thus reflected the détente of the time. It began as a one-man show under the direction of James Hawthorne, Parker's maths teacher from Sullivan. When a television service was added to the department, Hawthorne went to run that, and Hammond came on, with Carson joining him about a year later. These teachers turned producers were responsible for several series of programmes annually on Irish history, Irish geography, Irish writing, and Northern Irish history and culture.[42]

This project dovetailed with one of the central tenets of Malone's educational philosophy. People needed, he believed, to perceive the relevance to their own lives of what they were learning. Thus, he advocated for local studies, courses that encouraged young people to investigate their own area and, through this exploration, develop skills in the various disciplines. The ethos of the Northern Irish Schools Department also chimed with the social and political currents that had enabled the creation of the Ulster Folk Museum, established by law in 1958 and opened to the public in embryonic form in the summer of 1964. This complex of exhibition galleries, archives, and reconstructed buildings from around Ulster was the brainchild of Estyn Evans, Professor of Geography at Queen's University, whose researches had revealed a material culture and oral tradition largely shared by Northern Protestants and Catholics. He imagined the Ulster Folk Museum as 'a composite picture of the cultural landscape' which could focus the attention of all Northern Ireland's factions on the elements of history that united rather than divided them. The local Schools producers had a similar conception of their own mission. Their broadcasts were enjoyed by the general population, as well as by the captive audiences in classrooms, and those who tuned in had a chance, in the anonymous space provided by radio, to enrich their understanding of Northern Ireland and its complex relationship with the rest of Ireland, Britain, Europe, and the world.[43]

The liberal ideology of the Schools Department would not have been the only thing to recommend it to Parker in 1967. One of the most important employers of creative writers in Northern Ireland, Schools produced well over a hundred programme segments each year, a much larger output than the Drama Department. In addition to the programmes themselves, Schools produced publications for use as study guides in conjunction with the broadcasts. The list of Irish writers who wrote for BBC Schools Northern Ireland includes, among others, Seamus Heaney, Michael Longley, Paul Muldoon, John Montague, Brian Friel, Maurice Leitch, Stewart Love, Derek Mahon, John McGahern, Benedict Kiely, and Bernard MacLaverty. Most Northern Irish actors of note likewise worked for Schools; Liam Neeson got his start there, and the department also provided employment for the actors of the Ulster Group Theatre.[44]

Parker and many of the other aspiring novelists and poets who wrote for Schools regarded the work mainly as a source of income, but it also provided a useful apprenticeship, especially for a budding playwright. Involvement with the BBC fostered a professional attitude. Accuracy was paramount, and writers had to work to a deadline; they usually had about a month to draft a script, which would then undergo (sometimes extensive) revision before being sent to the studio for recording and editing. Moreover, most Schools programmes adopted a semi-dramatized format, with a narrator and actors, and were treated by the producers and technical support people as serious radio drama. The use of Ulster dialect distinguished BBC Schools Northern Ireland productions, and, because most programmes were only twenty minutes long, writing for them honed skills of selection, exposition, clarity, and concision.[45] Parker wrote several Schools scripts that spring and summer of 1967 and forged a working relationship with the local producers which would resume when he moved back to Belfast in 1969. Throughout his subsequent career, his on-the-job training as a Schools writer would leave its mark on his interests, strategies, and craftsmanship as a playwright.

At the time, though, Parker fretted about his scant progress on the novel, poems, and plays he had intended to write in Belfast, observing in his journal at the beginning of May that he was 'getting a hell of a lot of commercial work, not spending enough time (no time, actually) on ART'. A week later, as if in response, Michael Emmerson offered him a literary commission. Emmerson, a slightly younger contemporary of Parker's at Queen's, had been an impresario even as an undergraduate. In the summer of 1962, he brought a production of John Hamilton's one-act play *The Jesus Revolution* to the Edinburgh Festival. The piece depicted God as a stern father and Jesus as a rebellious son who exceeds his brief on earth by setting up a new 'brotherhood', and Emmerson daringly cast a black actor in the latter role. He did not know, however, about a blasphemy law prohibiting the representation of God and Christ on the public stage, and the Lord Chamberlain banned the play. This only added to the notoriety of the occasion, especially when the Belfast newspapers got wind of the story.[46]

The first two Queen's Arts Festivals, in 1961 and 1962, had been arranged largely by and for students and run by a committee comprising representatives from all participating university societies. This system proved unwieldy, and in 1963 the Students' Representative Council appointed a director to improve the event's organization. The first appointee resigned, and Emmerson became the director of the third Festival, which took place in the spring of 1964. From the start he planned to increase the 'thematic and artistic order' of the programme and to broaden its scope to make it more popular (around this time, the word 'Arts' was dropped from the title). Emmerson's first Festival went so well that he was asked to stay on as Professional Director after graduation, and for the next several years he pursued his dream of a more professional, even international, Belfast Festival at Queen's, subsidized by the university but not limited to it. Financial constraints and conflict with university officials over his desire to bring the celebration ever more outside Queen's finally prompted Emmerson to resign before the 1971 Festival.[47]

In 1967, though, Emmerson was in his heyday as Festival director, full of ideas to make the annual event (now held in the autumn) a means of sparking creative endeavour and cultural appreciation throughout the year—the pamphlet series that included Parker's *The Casualty's Meditation* being one such initiative. A highly strung, flamboyant Englishman, Emmerson possessed both ambition and the ability to make others share his vision. Philip Hobsbaum describes him as an entrepreneur with 'the cheek of a devil'. Now Emmerson sought Parker's help with a special project for the coming Festival. Because 1967 marked the tercentenary of Jonathan Swift's birth, Emmerson intended to commemorate him with a series of lectures. He also wanted Dramsoc to present a stage production based on Swift's life and career and thought he could persuade Tyrone Guthrie, the internationally renowned theatre director who had been elected to the honorary position of Chancellor of Queen's University in 1963, to direct it. As a model, Emmerson suggested John Barton's 1962 work *The Hollow Crown; An entertainment by and about the kings and queens of England: music, poetry, speeches, letters and other writings from the chronicles, from plays, and in the monarch's own words, also music concerning them and by them*, which had been performed at the 1964 Festival. The project would entail not so much play-writing as selecting and arranging passages from the writings of Swift and his associates, but Emmerson wanted someone with theatrical and writing experience to shape the whole for the stage. He offered Parker £75 for a ninety-minute script, but the possibility of working with Guthrie represented a bigger inducement. When Emmerson showed Parker a letter from Guthrie stating that he would be 'proud' to direct such a work, Parker assented to the proposal; as he wrote later, it then seemed to him like 'the biggest single stroke of good fortune' that had come his way 'in ten years of writing'.[48]

Parker researched and wrote his 'entertainment', *The Yahoos' Overthrow*, between mid-May and early August. Describing his effort later, he maintained that he had read through 'the whole of Swift's literary remains', over forty volumes of fiction, verse, journals, essays, letters, and biography. He worked 'arduously', he recalled, 'to incorporate into the work only words written by Swift and his contemporaries', even though it would have been 'easier and quicker to write a play *about* Swift'. The script bears out Parker's suspicion that he might have taken his assignment too literally. Drawn entirely from primary sources, it contains little signposting to help an audience follow the story. Perhaps because it reminded him of his own frustrated yearning for fame and success, Parker devoted a disproportionate amount of the piece to Swift's unrewarding angling for patronage and advancement in England. In comparison, Swift's literary career surfaces only intermittently, making *The Yahoos' Overthrow* more confusing than enlightening for a reader not already knowledgeable about Swift's biography. Parker delivered the script with what he termed in retrospect 'trepidation', expecting Guthrie to demand revisions, but also with a feeling of accomplishment at a job completed in a workmanlike spirit.[49]

While compiling the Swift piece, Parker completed two other projects in an intense burst of productivity. One was a full-length stage play (his first) based on the story of Deirdre from the ancient Ulster saga of tales. Parker had been planning it for several months, but a visit from his erstwhile friend and rival Bill Morrison in mid-June provided the impetus to start writing. Morrison was working on a play for a drama contest sponsored by Irish Life, an insurance company, which he mentioned in teasing fashion to Parker; the deadline was less than two weeks away. Parker decided to write his Deirdre play in time to submit it to the competition also. He finished it in one week flat, posting the script to Dublin a few days later.[50]

Parker probably first encountered the story of Deirdre, a young woman of whom it is predicted that her devastating beauty will bring disaster to Ulster, through the plays of W. B. Yeats and J. M. Synge. Conchobor, the King of Ulster, orders the child taken from her parents and raised as his fosterling, intending to marry her when she comes of age. Deirdre, however, runs away with Noisiu and his two brothers, the sweet-singing sons of Uisliu, to a safe haven in Scotland. Some time later they are persuaded to return to Ulster by Conchobor's friend Fergus, who assures them the King will pardon them. Fergus has been deceived, and the brothers and Deirdre walk into a trap, resulting in the death of the men and civil war in the province, as Fergus burns Emain Macha to the ground in retaliation for Conchobor's treachery. Conchobor holds Deirdre captive, and most versions of the story end with her killing herself to escape from him.

Parker was surely conscious of working within an *Irish* literary and theatrical tradition in choosing this subject. He might even have felt he had a better right to Deirdre's story than Yeats and Synge, since it came from his part of the island, not theirs. As if to emphasize this connection, he made *The Sensational Real-life Drama of Deirdre Porter* a quintessentially Belfast play. Following Synge's lead in *Deirdre of the Sorrows*, Parker wrote in the vernacular—that of working-class east Belfast. As Yeats had done in *Deirdre*, Parker included songs in his play, mostly variants on Belfast children's songs. Parker's Deirdre, like Parker himself, hails from Belfast's shipyard district. Like him, she longs for a freer, more stimulating existence and seeks it in North America; also like him, she feels compelled to return.[51]

Parker did not write a costume drama about Deirdre, like Yeats and Synge, but, as Joyce did in *Ulysses*, made the myth the skeleton for a modern story. An article that had appeared in the Belfast *News Letter* the previous September, about a 37-year-old man convicted of manslaughter for killing his unfaithful 19-year-old wife, had fused with Deirdre's story in Parker's mind, and he aimed for a gritty social realism.[52] Deirdre (identified only as the 'Young Girl' in the script—perhaps to underline her archetypal nature, perhaps because 'Deirdre' is not a name common among Ulster Protestants) is presented as a victim of her circumstances, a potential artist constricted both by her working-class background and by the limited roles available to women in her Belfast. At 17 she seduces and marries a man twenty-one years her senior, hoping he will take her to his boyhood Dublin home. When he does not, she grows restless and runs away with a younger man who leads a showband and dreams of commercial success in the US. Her new lover also fails to satisfy her inchoate longing for an artistic life, and she seems incapable of imagining a way to achieve it on her own. She wants to go home, so, when her husband (the 'Older Man') sends word that he will grant her a divorce if she returns to Belfast, she and the 'Young Man' come back. Upon their arrival, the police, acting on a tip from the Older Man, arrest the Young Man and his brothers for drug-dealing. When the Young Girl confronts her husband about this betrayal and taunts him by saying she still prefers her younger lover, he strikes and accidentally kills her. Throughout the play, parallels between the story of Deirdre and that of the Young Girl are made explicit by the clumsy device of alternating scenes involving the latter with scenes in which a chorus of children read and act out a verse translation of the legend. Though an apprentice piece, *Deirdre Porter* introduces elements and themes that recur in Parker's later plays and demonstrates his intention, fulfilled in his mature work, to write about present-day Belfast.[53]

The last project Parker finished in Belfast was a radio play called *Sam Todd For God* that he entered for a drama contest organized by the BBC.[54] This absurdist piece focuses on a suburban couple, Gregg and Doreen Dregg (i.e. 'the dregs'), who discover that a dwarf lives in their garage. The dwarf is, we infer, Sam Todd, but we never know his reason for being there or anything about him. The other characters see him variously as a saint, a mental patient, an incognito actor, a philosopher, and a fraud; Gregg esteems him as a person of wisdom and eloquence, but every time he is about to speak the scene ends. Often, though, the parrot he gives the Dreggs seems to talk for him, uttering cryptic comments like 'Sam Todd For God!'

Throughout, Parker plays in post-modern fashion with the conventions of radio and with the blurring between life and entertainment typical of the age of mass communication. He frames his play as an episode in a series called *This Is Your Life In Their Hands*, 'a suburban story of everyday folk', which has its own theme music and is interrupted at regular intervals by commercial breaks and canned laughter and applause.[55] Within the play, Gregg watches a television programme, also called *This Is Your Life In Their Hands*, with a compère played by the same actor who plays the radio announcer at the beginning. This, however, is described as 'a weekly documentary magazine of the spooky and the kooky, of the tricks and kicks of this stranger-than-fiction world of ours, a television bazaar of the bizarre'. 'Shocks are our business', the compère explains unabashedly when he arrives to investigate the Dreggs' mysterious lodger, and he seems disappointed to hear that Sam's main activities are singing, talking, and thinking.[56]

Parker adds another layer of self-referentiality near the end, when Gregg turns on the radio in search of some music and we overhear part of an arts discussion in which the three participants appear to analyse Parker's play itself. One speaker argues that 'he' is 'purely and simply an emblem of the artist. He has his muse, appropriately a bird, I think, but he's without roots, he's pitifully shrunken, he's alienated from his environment, nobody listens to him, and, to come to the point... he is entirely powerless.' Another suggests that 'multiple levels of meaning are intended', including 'the problem of evil as it manifests itself in our society': 'it appears without warning, seemingly from nowhere, inexplicably', but 'its recipients' are 'so cocooned in the sterility of their material well-being, they face this immemorial hazard with an entire lack of feeling'. The third speaker protests, 'I consider this to be an only mildly diverting piece of dramatic philosophising, which is specious as allegory, simply because it is confused and confusing. It would be instructive indeed to find out how many people listened in to it, and how many of those had the least idea of what it was all about.' None of this makes any impression on the audience within the play. As the speakers launch into a debate on the appropriateness of introducing the question of a work's reception into the critical discourse, Gregg abruptly switches off the radio. When Doreen asks if he has been listening to anything good, he replies, 'Just some culture programme.' Art, Parker implies, has become another commodity, one more element in the background noise of our lives.[57]

About two-thirds of the way through the play, Gregg informs Doreen that he and Sam plan to embark on a journey. Possibly to prevent this, Doreen seduces Sam, telling her husband that the dwarf attacked her, and Gregg chases him away and strangles the parrot. In the last scene Doreen announces she is pregnant. We are obviously meant to conclude that the baby is Sam's—not that this brings us any closer to a logical interpretation of the play, which seems designed to resist such analysis. If *Deirdre Porter* anticipates Parker's later dramatic work, *Sam Todd For God* looks back to the preoccupations of his undergraduate days.

Reviewing the seven months in Belfast as he prepared to return to the US, Parker took pride in his accomplishments. In his journal he made a neat list: *Speaking of Red Indians*, *The Sensational Real-life Drama of Deirdre Porter*, *Sam Todd For God*, and *The Yahoos' Overthrow*. Underneath it he wrote,

> Just over two weeks to go till the Cornell test. I've completed the above, and am happy to have done so. It remains to be seen how good they are. But I now have at least justified calling myself a writer. . . . I've liked it here this time—the flat, the talk, the pubs, the coal fire, the solitary life late at night, the earning my keep at the typewriter. This is a way to live if I could make it somehow permanent.[58]

Finding a way to do just that would be the puzzle remaining after 'the Cornell test'.

5

Talking About (Cultural) Revolution

The buoyant optimism regarding his writing career which Parker felt towards the end of his time in Belfast dissipated within a few weeks of his return to the United States. As one piece of bad news after another reached him, he grew increasingly discouraged but did not abandon his ambition to live by his writing. The disappointments and humiliations of his two years in Ithaca did, however, prompt him to focus more on what he had to say and less on who might be listening. Simultaneously, the supercharged atmosphere of the US during the turbulent years from 1967 to 1969 sharpened Parker's sense of the political potential of creative writing. As the anti-war and civil rights movements convulsed Cornell University, along with other campuses, Parker was caught up in events both as a participant and as an observer already starting to apply his American experience to an analysis of his native place.

In October 1967, Parker learned that neither *The Sensational Real-life Drama of Deirdre Porter* nor *Sam Todd For God* had won their respective contests. The adjudicators for the Irish Life Drama Award placed the former in a 'very encouraging' category but did not short-list it for the prize, remarking that it read like a short story dramatized and lacked substance for three acts. *Sam Todd For God* also struck the judges of the BBC Prize Play contest as demonstrating talent, but, as David Turner explained in a letter to Parker, they found it obscure: 'The trouble I think with your writing is that you have the well-bred diffidence of the poet and not enough of the vulgar self-importance of the dramatist. . . . One cannot write the kind of play that you seem bent on writing without making a firmer and more definite commitment to what precisely it is you want to say.' Two months later, Turner wrote again to tell Parker that *Speaking of Red Indians* had finally been broadcast, 'And nobody said nothing.' Meanwhile, Parker discovered that *Discern*, the magazine that had accepted his story 'The Recipient', had evidently not got off the ground (he noted in his journal that it 'appears not to exist'), and, when he tried again to sell the story, he received rejections from 'about seven different magazines'.[1]

More devastating to Parker than any of this, a letter he received in late September from Michael Emmerson informed him that Tyrone Guthrie's rehearsal schedule at the National Theatre in London had been rearranged, making it impossible for him to direct Parker's Swift piece for Festival 67. Emmerson insisted that it had been 'one of my particularly favourite items all along' and asked Parker to 'imagine how very upset I am about this'. Emmerson's distress did not compare with that of Parker, who assumed that something less innocuous than a new rehearsal schedule lay behind Guthrie's inability to direct his script and spent much of the autumn brooding about what had happened. The bitter nature of his reflections may be inferred from a journal entry on 28 September:

> Guthrie has decided *The Yahoos' Overthrow* smells bad, and has decided against directing it, despite his contracting by letter to do so.... The shamefulness of the situation is this: he has decided, not against me, but against Swift. My brief was to create a *Hollow Crown* style of entertainment i.e. a collage of letters, journal entries, poems and songs etc. I'm convinced I selected all the most dramatic passages.... If Guthrie dislikes it, then he dislikes Swift, which is more than enough to condemn his sensibility to the lower reaches of Hell.... I think I would have had enough humility to have accepted his suggestions for re-ordering the structure of the thing: but he didn't quarrel with the structure, he simply rejected the whole work outright. So he is a man of drastically limited perception, and I feel disappointed: I had taken him for an ally and a champion. Apparently there is no such phenomenon as a good great man.

Nevertheless, Parker wrote to Guthrie requesting an assessment of the work. When he had not received a reply several weeks later, he concluded that 'Guthrie has apparently decided that not even my letters are worth reading.' Taking stock the day after his twenty-sixth birthday, it appeared to Parker that 'After 10 years of earnest writing, I have moved almost nowhere', and he conceded that, at times, 'the failure crushes me': 'A human being is not all machinery, and I have more than the average lust for widespread recognition and comprehension and (say it) acclaim.'[2]

Parker kept his fuming mostly to himself until early December, when his family sent him a Belfast newspaper containing a preview of Festival events; these included a staged reading, directed by Guthrie, of a play entitled *Swift* by established play-wright Eugene McCabe. At this point, and with no expectation of a reply, Parker poured out his hurt feelings in a long letter to Guthrie that laid out the facts from his point of view and asked for 'the story'. The letter ended with a challenge to the eminent director: 'Convince me that you're *not* a major theatrical genius of the twentieth century who is also a major shit.' To his chagrin, Parker received a letter from Guthrie a few weeks later that began with the assertion that he had written to Parker months earlier explaining his side of the story, but his letter had been returned to him with the addressee marked 'UNKNOWN'. Guthrie stated that he had never promised to direct the piece, since he never agreed to direct anything with-out reading it first. He *had* read the completed script and found it 'undramatic', but, even if he had liked it better, he would not have been able to fit rehearsing it in Belfast into his schedule (the McCabe reading had been rehearsed in spare moments at the National). In short, Guthrie suggested, Parker had been the victim of a misrepresentation by Emmerson; he regretted the misunderstanding, but made no apologies.[3]

Parker replied the same day Guthrie's note arrived, thanking him for helping to clear up 'the frustrations that have been in my mind...for the last four months' and allowing that 'I was extraordinarily naive to believe that a man of your stature would agree to direct an unseen (and at that stage unwritten) script.'

However, he admitted, 'It is a heavy blow that you disliked it so entirely. I have read your books; I have made my pilgrimages to Stratford, Ontario and Minneapolis; when, therefore, you say that the cursed thing is undramatic, I believe you. But I can't for the life of me figure out how else it could have been done.' The letter ended on a diplomatic note: 'I deeply regret this shambles.... I hope very much that some day I will be in a position to convince you that I am not entirely a clod.'[4]

During that wretched autumn of 1967, the one bright spot professionally was the publication of Parker's second Festival pamphlet, *Maw: A Journey*, in a series with pamphlets by Ted Hughes, Iain Crichton Smith, George Mackay Brown, and James Simmons.[5] This collection had been inspired by Parker's trip around the US in 1966. A biographical note describes him as 'a Resident Alien in the United States', and the eight poems, which play on the double meaning of 'maw' as both the mouth or stomach of a voracious animal and as a slang word for 'mother', reflect that point of view. The first, 'Chicago Allegory', makes an overweight policeman a metaphor for the authoritarian yet self-indulgent culture of the US. Another poem exploring the latent violence of the all-American way of life is devoted to Charles Whitman, the University of Texas student who shot and killed fourteen people and injured thirty from the top of the university's twenty-seven-storey administration building in the summer of 1966. This rapping reflection on the psychology of a mass murderer ends with the speaker's admission that

> times I get mad
> times I envy Whitman
> he grabbed his slice of power
> in that ivory tower

Other poems focus on those outcast from the American Dream, such as demented and destitute people in San Francisco and a Black woman encountered on the train, who, Parker had noted in his journal, 'Hadn't heard of Grand Canyon (& maybe not of Ireland).'[6]

Despite the dominant tone of critical detachment, the longest poem in the pamphlet, 'Railroad Ode', captures Parker's delight in his American adventures and in the storied expanse of his temporary abode. It is also a love song to trains,

> beginning with the entrance of the Burlington Morning Zephyr
> august and irresistible as an ocean roller
> amongst the fussy dusty commuter trains
> her one white eye in the forehead
> and the steady clang of her voice
> and her airbrakes like the calf muscles
> of a prima ballerina, easing her
> to a dead
> halt.

The poem proceeds through a travelogue recited from the perspective of a train passenger, concluding with the declaration

> I am pretending that this is the Rock Island Line
> and that Poor Paddy, Railroad Bill and Casey Jones
> are at my elbow;
>
> and they are.

Seamus Heaney, who read *Maw* before it was printed, responded with an 'impulse fan mail' that must have lifted Parker's spirits: 'if I was talking to you I'd grunt "Smashing" and leave it at that. For what it's worth, I think they're some of the best poems I've read to have appeared in the last few years. The jealousy test applies.'[7]

Meanwhile, Parker struggled to finish *The Jest-Book of ST Toile*, designed to challenge what he saw as two of the most cherished novelistic conventions. In notes dated 21 January 1968, he mused that most literature attempts to enlighten the reader by presenting character developing through chronological incidents to a climactic realization: 'Even writers like Joyce and Conrad, who liquefied the time-sequence, adhered to the traditional concept of character growth to ultimate awareness in which the reader shares.' Parker acknowledged some linear development in his own life but felt increasingly aware of what he termed the 'much more powerful force' of simultaneity. For example, his entire education might exist in his mind as 'one suspended moment': 'The crucial revelation emanates from this simultaneous happening of many events which may have no linear connection with one another at all.' In brief, Parker had decided, 'Life is largely lived, not in the present tense, but in the continuous past tense.'

While the past remained vivid in the mind and might thus metamorphose continually, Parker doubted that most people changed fundamentally over time. Instead, he thought, people equipped themselves early with 'a viable character-type' from which they seldom deviated. Parker conceived of the *Jest-Book* as a rejection of the novel as he knew it. In it, he aimed to capture the truth of 'simultaneity of event and stasis of character...pitted against an alarmingly unpredictable universe'. He believed this insight animated not only the *Jest-Book* but all his work.

Parker based his novel, or anti-novel, in part on the prose fragments with a grammar school setting that he had presented to the Belfast Writers' Group in 1963/64. Since then, he had added sketches and expanded the scope of the book.[8] Flann O'Brien's *At Swim-Two-Birds* (1939) probably influenced its form. As in O'Brien's novel, stories about an eccentric group of characters alternate with passages of self-conscious first-person reflection on the part of a narrator purportedly the author of the whole.

ST Toile (saint and scholar) is a bored university student scribbling 'jests' in a jotter. He spends much of his time hiding in the wardrobe of his bedroom to evade detection by the young woman living across the street, on whom he spies with binoculars. 'ST Toile' inverts 'T. S. Eliot', and Parker borrows the associations of formal experimentation, 'modern' sensibility, and morbid introspection. Modernist art, he suggests, often serves the artist as a substitute for life. Toile's existence is cramped and limited; he has no desire to know the young woman as a person in her own right. She exists for him only as the object of his fascination and fodder for his writing. At the end of the book, though, she reveals herself to be smarter than he is when she waves at him to show she has been aware of his attention all along.

The three main characters in Toile's (and Parker's) book are close friends both at school and university. Most of the *Jest-Book* consists of episodes from their lives, interspersed with vignettes of their mutual acquaintances. Sometimes one character appears alone; at other times he interacts with one or both of the others. These passages are arranged non-chronologically, with scenes from university mixed with scenes from school, but the basic characters of the boys remain constant. All of them, along with Toile himself, project aspects of Parker's own personality or situation. Art invents songs, stories, and poems; he is an artist, a wise-cracking orphan, 'a Resident Alien who speaks the language well'. Shrink, 'a casualty meditating and diminishing', is an amputee and a philosophical collector of irony. Archie is a hapless victim of circumstance, repeatedly overwhelmed and betrayed by life.[9]

Events do take place—Shrink's amputation and sudden death, for example, or Archie's brief possession of the woman of his dreams (who ends up marrying his best friend, Art)—but plot does not drive the *Jest-Book*. Its unity derives from its theme that people are freaks and any order in the universe is a perverse one. As Art muses, 'It was all a very perplexing big joke, and he found it hard to postulate a sense of humour warped enough to perpetrate it.' Archie entertains more alarming possibilities, asking, 'do you ever get the feeling that somehow there's been a horrendous unspeakable mistake? A bloody enormous sort of universal gaffe?' The one-legged Shrink sees life as 'a struggle to stay upright' and tells a nurse that his private symbol is 'Stilts. We're all on stilts. Walking over fire, earth, air and water at their most fractious. The vagaries of fate are when you fall.' This, he continues, would be bad enough, but life's difficulty is compounded by the fact that other people are also trying to knock you over: 'You'd think that we'd have realised by this time, lamented Shrink. About pain. The only enemy. And stopped putting the boot in. And concentrated on staying upright.' Shrink speaks directly for Parker here, but, immediately after the scene in which he expresses these views, Toile comments, 'Shrink will clearly have to go, he talks too damm [*sic*] much.' For him, everything comes down to the sex instinct, from which he sometimes yearns to be liberated.[10]

All these notions converge midway through the book in Art's retelling of the story of Genesis. In his version, there is no serpent and no forbidden fruit. Adam and Eve stumble upon the mystery of sex accidentally when Adam happens to stroke Eve's left nipple. Her arousal so terrifies him that he runs and hides underground for two days. Eve, miffed, seduces God Himself, who is similarly unnerved. Unsure what to do, He equips himself with binoculars and decides to wait and watch. Adam, meanwhile, emerges from his hiding place to comfort the despondent Eve. He invents various kinds of art and even builds her a house to try to distract her, but she only wants his sexual attention, which she finally obtains. God is 'at once furious and oddly enchanted': angry with Eve, jealous of Adam, and proud. Nevertheless, their discovery causes Him to withdraw: '. . . they had started this whole thing themselves, and they could damm [*sic*] well carry on with it themselves, and if he felt like playing the odd joke on them, he would damm [*sic*] well do it, and for a start he was leaving them in darkness—no more trips down there to keep an eye on things, no thank you.' Life as we know it is both a mistake *and* a joke; complications arise from a combination of fate and human will; God is as baffled by it as we are; and sex is at the root of most of the confusion.[11]

Parker completed *The Jest-Book of ST Toile* in the summer of 1968 and posted it in mid-September to a London-based literary agent who had expressed an interest three years earlier in the extracts published in the *Northern Review*. Parker soon received a reply from him, declining to handle the book because it struck him as too much of a private joke to be marketable. 'I must now begin the dreary round of publishing houses', Parker complained in his journal; 'I thought I had finished something, but it seems that I've merely started something less rewarding.'[12] (He would have been even more dejected had he known how this story would end. Twelve different publishers rejected the *Jest-Book* between 1968 and 1972 before Parker gave up on it.)

Probably around this time, Parker made one of the biggest mistakes of his life. While he taught at Cornell, Kate continued to act in theatrical productions at Hamilton College (about one hundred miles distant), and she often spent a week or more away from home. During one of her absences, Stewart had a sexual encounter with another woman. Opportunities for casual intercourse abounded in the permissive atmosphere of most major American universities in the late 1960s.[13] Stewart's transgression, the result of momentary attraction and curiosity, was the act of a young man who had been almost wholly inexperienced sexually when he met Kate, and he regretted it immediately. After consulting his friend John Paul, then working in the library at Cornell, he decided he owed it to Kate to confess the incident. They both valued honesty, and Stewart did not wish to begin concealing things from her now. He also wanted Kate to understand that what had happened was no reflection on her, because he loved her and sought to preserve their relationship.[14]

Both men expected Kate to be upset, but neither anticipated the depth of her hurt. 'The very fundament of trust between them felt shattered to her', Paul remembers. Stewart's revelation reduced Kate to despair, and she seriously considered ending their marriage. They stayed together, and relations between them gradually normalized, but Paul speculates that thereafter the marriage might have seemed more vulnerable from Kate's perspective. Stewart's infidelity, without significance in itself, represented a 'critical blow' to Kate which 'became a factor in the relationship afterwards'. After Stewart told her about it, Kate's 'darkness' was increasingly evident in public; people became more aware of the 'weight' of her presence, and sometimes she would burst into tears and disappear. Parker and Paul referred to the months after Stewart's confession as Kate's 'black period', and Stewart had both to endure the guilt for his actions and to witness the suffering his thoughtlessness had caused the person he loved most.[15]

The end of December found Parker in a reflective mood. He summed up 1968 as 'in many ways a regrettable year, but not a forgettable one unfortunately. Worst since 65, and much worse—more seriously awful—than that was.' Much as he might wish that certain things had never happened, he looked towards the future rather than the past, formulating two New Year resolutions with significance for both his personal and professional lives:

1. To cultivate quietness.
2. To strengthen the capacity for self-honesty till it swallows up the craving to be published. To write for the sake of my own truth instead of for the sake of getting into print.[16]

Despite his marital problems and the early disappointments over the *Jest-Book*, Parker was determined to keep writing. In the autumn of 1968 he had three priorities: a revision of *Deirdre Porter*, notes towards another work of experimental fiction (never completed) about a trickster figure called Kilroy, and research for a play he planned to write about Henry Joy McCracken.[17] This last project had been at the back of his mind since at least September or October 1967, likely inspired by his time in Belfast earlier that year. Writing for BBC Schools Northern Ireland and regularly visiting John Malone, Parker had developed an interest in local history. McCracken had been one of the most radical leaders of the United Irishmen, Irish republicans who instigated an unsuccessful rebellion against British rule in 1798. One of their great, though fleeting, achievements had been to bring Protestants, Catholics, and Dissenters together in the common name of Irishmen. In the late 1960s, when Parker began reading about that period of Irish history, the 1790s presented an attractive alternative to the stultification of the status quo, in which most Northern Irish Protestants resisted any identification with Catholics or the Republic of Ireland. For a liberal Protestant like Parker, it was exhilarating to discover that, in 1798, Belfast Presbyterians had been at the forefront of the movement for Irish autonomy from England. McCracken particularly appealed to Parker because, although he came from a middle-class background, his outlook had been egalitarian as well as non-sectarian.[18] In addition to the specifically Northern Irish significance of the story, Parker saw the United Irishmen in the larger context of cultural and political divisions between people: notes he made in the summer of 1968 draw parallels with rifts between, for example, Flemings and Walloons in Belgium, and Arabs and Jews in the Middle East. He also used his thinking about the play as a focus for consideration of general issues of political commitment.

Events in the US and at Cornell University gave Parker much to ponder throughout the 1968/69 academic year. The Vietnam War, for one, loomed ever larger in the minds of young people across the country. In 1965, the US had initiated a sustained bombing campaign against North Vietnam and sent its first ground troops to the war; each year since, the conflict had intensified. More American servicemen died in Vietnam in 1967 than had in all the previous years of the war, with no end in sight.[19]

Against this background, on 17 May 1968, nine anti-war protesters entered the office of the Selective Service System in Catonsville, Maryland, filled two wastebins with draft records, and set them ablaze with homemade napalm. All the demonstrators were practising Catholics; two were priests. Philip and Daniel Berrigan, who joked about their Irish heritage when asked how they came to be such 'troublemakers', had focused their respective ministries on poverty and racial discrimination but had come to feel that no progress could be made on domestic social issues unless the US withdrew from Vietnam. Disillusioned by the scant effect that lectures, meetings with Congressmen, and marches seemed to have on US foreign policy, they turned to more emphatic methods. Philip had already been convicted for an earlier act of theatrical protest, in which he and three others destroyed draft records by pouring blood over them. He was due to be sentenced for this offence on 27 May—hence the timing of the raid on Catonsville.[20]

The trial of the 'Catonsville Nine' took place in a Baltimore federal court in early October 1968. Parker followed it avidly, fascinated by the spectacle of reform-minded individuals driven by their spiritual and social convictions to illegal acts. The trial held special interest for people in Ithaca because, at the time of the incident, Daniel Berrigan worked at Cornell. University officials announced that students would not be penalized for missing classes to attend it, and hundreds did. Parker drove to Baltimore with John Paul for the opening of the trial, where, Paul remembers, they sat next to Dorothy Day, founder of the Catholic Worker movement. The defendants were ultimately found guilty on three counts: destruction of US property, destruction of Selective Service records, and interference with the Selective Service Act of 1967.[21]

In the month between the trial and the sentencing, Daniel Berrigan returned to Cornell, and on 24 October he and the defence counsel, Harrop Freeman (a Cornell professor), spoke at a public meeting. Parker attended and found the occasion profoundly moving, reflecting in his journal,

> A few weeks ago, I had a nightmare in which I was facing a long jail sentence and the full horror of it made itself real to me—of being disallowed your humanity until you're forty-seven years old or whatever. Even if the Nine get six years each, the least they can expect, Berrigan will be in his fifties—the younger ones will lose for ever their twenties and early thirties. To me it's nightmare, to them it's fact.
>
> Given that, how can anybody fail to support what they did, the seriousness of their conviction? How can people dismiss them as 'martyrs'? Or why has that word suddenly taken on a pejorative ring? They *are* martyrs. Martyrs can be proud, wrong-headed. Martyrs are paradoxical, even inexplicable. Berrigan is in some ways a dangerous martyr, maybe a self-deluding one. But there is one inexorable truth about martyrs—that they suffer on behalf of the rest of humanity. The Catonsville Nine surrendered to martyrdom in behalf of every human being injured in body, mind or soul by the war.

Parker left the gathering ashamed of ever having been 'indifferent to all of this' and with a resolution for the future: 'Bruce Detweiler, the best SDS [Students for a Democratic Society] speaker, suggested that the cultural revolutionaries are far in advance of the purely political revolutionaries. This is true, and I have to live that truth.'[22]

A few months later, Parker increased his personal involvement with the anti-war effort. About a three-and-a-half-hour drive from Ithaca lay Allenwood Prison Camp, a minimum-security facility connected with Lewisburg Federal Penitentiary, where a number of draft resisters had been incarcerated. Several Cornell professors decided to demonstrate their support by holding classes in the prison, aimed at the political prisoners but open to any.[23] Parker and his English Department colleague Neil Hertz taught a fortnightly writing class there from February to July 1969. To their surprise, 'ordinary' prisoners attended in greater numbers than the draft resisters. Moreover, since many who came were poor and Black, the experience constituted, for Parker, a crash course in American race relations. The 'passionate political commitment' of the Black prisoners impressed him; as he wrote later, 'no matter how the classes started out, they nearly always resolved into a noisy, volatile debate about Black oppression'.[24]

The subject was timely in 1969. The civil rights movement had recently entered a militant phase centred less on the South than on Northern cities transformed by a wave of Black internal emigration dating from about 1940. The March on Washington of August 1963 had marked the high point of the influence of Martin Luther King, Jr and his philosophy of non-violent resistance. Subsequent events— such as the 1965 voting rights march King led from Selma to Montgomery, Alabama, provoking a savage backlash—convinced a younger generation of Black leaders that it made no sense to hold themselves to a policy of non-violence when their enemies refused to do the same. By 1966, the Student Nonviolent Coordinating Committee had begun calling for 'Black Power' and the revolutionary Black Panther party had been formed. Meanwhile, violence engulfed Black communities around the US. Starting in 1964, the country endured successive summers of ghetto riots. There were forty-three race riots in 1966, and in 1967 the ghettos resembled war zones, with riots breaking out in 114 cities in thirty-two states and a death toll of at least eighty-eight. King, who saw the Vietnam War as the biggest obstacle to racial progress, was killed on 4 April 1968. The assassination two months later of Robert Kennedy, who had campaigned against the war and on behalf of the poor, added to the impression of chaos.[25]

Small wonder the Black inmates Parker encountered at Allenwood were in a bellicose mood. Whatever white prisoners wrote about, Black members of the group contended that their works meant nothing to Black people and took over the class with an argument among themselves. This divide both intrigued and stymied Parker, who found his American partner no better equipped to deal with it than himself. Although he hardly ever wrote in his journal about his university classes, Parker analysed the group dynamics of every prison session in this private record. A particular problem, he recollected a year later, was presented by one of the older Black prisoners, a con man who 'took the view that all Black politicians, policemen, bourgeoisie, businessmen and teachers should be shot as traitors to their people: how the revolution should proceed thereafter was cloudy'. Parker 'Didn't want to stop this in authoritarian manner, couldn't control it, tried unsuccessfully to direct discussion onto organization, style, vocabulary, rhetoric: which, naturally, was impossible.'[26]

Parker hoped the impasse could be broken if the inmates would write about prison, 'the one thing they have in common'. Although this rarely happened, the experience proved absorbing and rewarding for him. He and Hertz especially admired autobiographical works by two Black prisoners which reminded them of

Eldridge Cleaver's *Soul on Ice*, a best seller in 1968. One of the men, 'a natural writer', 'described writing in the dark, not being able even to see the paper' and, 'when in solitary confinement in Oklahoma, writing stuff and flushing it down the lavatory'.[27] They encouraged both inmates, due for release, to move to Ithaca and enrol at Cornell through the university's innovative COSEP (Committee on Special Education Projects) programme, launched in 1963 to increase the number of minority students on campus—from eight to 250 by 1968/69. Unfortunately, neither made a smooth transition.[28]

They were hardly alone among the COSEP students in experiencing culture shock. Indeed, the dissatisfaction of many Black students with Cornell had grown over the past few years as the harassment they sometimes experienced on a predominantly white campus made them receptive to the separatist Black power ideology gaining ascendancy in the country at large. An increasingly radical Afro-American Society (AAS) led a protest in March and April 1968 that culminated in the takeover of the Economics Department, holding the chairman hostage for several hours. Partly as a result, the university and Black students reached an understanding that Cornell would develop courses on the African-American experience with the goal of establishing a Black studies programme, though the two parties disagreed on what this should look like. Some AAS leaders wanted 'a completely autonomous program, open only to black students and staffed only by black professors'. University administrators did not think students should dictate academic policy, and many of the older liberals on the faculty found the idea of a distinct degree-granting Black college at Cornell objectionable on civil rights grounds.[29]

At 2 a.m. on 18 April 1969 (days after the Cornell Board of Trustees voted to establish and fund an Afro-American studies centre), the Student-Faculty Board on Student Conduct issued reprimands to three Black students charged with Student Code violations. The AAS retaliated at 5:45 a.m. on 19 April by occupying Willard Straight Hall, the student union, whose guest rooms were filled with visitors for Parents Weekend.[30] Cornell in 1969 had the third-largest SDS chapter in the country, and members of this group, forewarned, immediately formed a cordon around the building to protect the hundred or so Black students inside and publicize their grievances. Despite their efforts, white fraternity members charged the Straight and fought with Black students inside before being repulsed, prompting the Black students to smuggle in guns to defend themselves. At this point, university administrators, fearing both the students and the several hundred state troopers preparing to storm the campus, acceded to most of the students' demands (including amnesty for the takeover and nullification of the reprimands). At 4:10 the next afternoon, AAS members exited the building, waving rifles and raising their fists in Black power salutes.[31]

Parker's experiences at Allenwood had primed him for something like this, and he participated in the drama of the next few days. The administrators' deal with the students had to be ratified by the whole faculty, which, in a tense meeting on 21 April, voted to retain the reprimands as a gesture of resistance to coercion. Parker attached himself to a group called Concerned Faculty, consisting mainly of self-consciously 'radical' professors who sympathized with the Black students and believed the faculty vote should be overturned. On 22 April he spent the entire afternoon at meetings of the Concerned Faculty and Arts College Faculty before attending an SDS meeting in Barton Hall that evening which turned into a rally involving thousands of students and a number of faculty members. Parker and about 2,000 others stayed in the building all night in a show of support for the AAS, and, at a Concerned Faculty meeting the next morning, he signed a 'pledge to sit-in, encircle, or join students in occupation of a building if Faculty once again fails to nullify'.[32]

This pledge was never called in. At noon, the full faculty rescinded its earlier decision. The immediate crisis averted, rival groups on campus channelled their energy into teach-ins and meetings, which Parker attended for several days before his attention reverted to mundane matters. The incident made a lasting impression on him, however, as his play *Pentecost*, set during the Ulster Workers' Council Strike of 1974, attests. One character compares the state of emergency in Belfast with campus unrest at an unnamed American university:

> it's not as if I'm unfamiliar with tense situations. Six years ago, I was standing in a human chain encircling a building. It was in America...a university. Black students had seized the building and smuggled in guns, the police were lined up in their hundreds, ready to storm it. Me and a fewscore of other white liberals had put our bodies in between, holding hands with each other, armed blacks behind us and armed cops in front...it was scary as hell, but there was playacting involved too, a big American psychodrama, the college president and the blacks' leader were up on a stage together at the end, hugging each other, I don't quite see that happening here.[33]

This passage hints at the cultural obstacles Parker encountered in trying to apply his American insights to Northern Ireland. Nevertheless, he was making such connections by the late 1960s.

Apart from a burst of reading and research over the 1968/69 Christmas vacation, Parker had not managed much work on his 1798 play. It and its protagonist were in his thoughts, however, and Parker likely projected onto Henry Joy McCracken some of his feelings about his own political experiences in the late 1960s. Friends from Cornell remember Parker as passionately interested in, yet critically detached from, US issues of the time. With a foreigner's diffidence, he stayed on the margins of the action, and a colleague noted both Parker's commitment to radical goals and the ironic edge to his involvement with political causes. A note in Parker's journal from June 1969 suggests the impact his personal observations were having on his perception of McCracken's plight and decisions. He saw McCracken as

> a man of compassion and altruism in a company of ideologues: Tone the Republican, Hope the Socialist, the Orange Monarchists, the Dublin Oligarchs, the Belfast Capitalists. He has no dogma, only the thrust of an imaginative and understanding character. But he cannot find a way to work outside the struggle for power between the dogmas, and he is drawn in and destroyed.

Palpable in this is Parker's sense of the danger posed to a thoughtful person by any kind of extremism. His nature was that of the artist rather than the activist. Despite his conviction of the necessity for political commitment, he would always struggle to maintain his ability to see opposing sides of any controversy. Another expression of this disposition was his stated desire, near the end of 1968, 'to become a stateless person, if it's possible and at all practical'.[34]

Parker remained in Ithaca until mid-August 1969, teaching summer school at Cornell. He also reconnected with the stage by helping with Cornell Summer Theatre's production of Brendan Behan's *The Hostage*, about a British soldier held by the Irish Republican Army in Dublin in an unsuccessful attempt to prevent the execution of an IRA volunteer in Belfast gaol. Set in 1960, the play pokes fun at the supposedly anachronistic fanaticism of the so-called New IRA, which carries on as if the War of Independence (1919–21) and the Irish Civil War (1922/3) were still raging. The prisoner is kept in a boarding house owned by an eccentric Anglo-Irishman and managed by his comrade from the 1916 Rising, who supplements the dwindling proceeds from republicans on the run by letting prostitutes work on site. The inhabitants of the house sympathize with the English soldier, but ultimately he is shot during a police raid—though whether by the IRA or by the Irish authorities is never entirely clear.

Parker, as Cornell's resident Irish theatre expert, assisted the production as an accent coach, while Kate played a whore in the cast. As a result of their involvement they made a new friend: Alfred Gingold, who played the hostage. Gingold remembers them as a great couple, in concert with each other 'like a hand in a glove', and he savoured their contrasting senses of humour: Stewart's hearty, Kate's sly and whimsical. The three spent many happy hours talking and drinking whiskey. Despite this intimacy, Gingold did not even wonder, in 1969, whether his friends were Catholics or Protestants, nor did he understand what the IRA wanted. From an American perspective, such matters seemed of historical interest only. Parker, on the other hand, spoke of the setting of the play—a twilight zone of the Troubles of the 1920s—as a condition he lived in as an Irish person. All such violent outbreaks in Ireland were, for him, part of a continuum, flare-ups of ever-present tension.[35]

With mingled regret and relief, Stewart and Kate made plans to leave Ithaca and return to Ireland. Parker could have renewed his contract as an instructor for one more year, but by now he wanted to go home. On 8 August, he taught his last summer school class and noted his exhaustion in his journal, adding, 'May never teach again, unless out of financial desperation.' A mere two days later, however, in a letter to the chairman of Cornell's English Department, Parker asked to be considered as an instructor for future summer school sessions, since 'This would be a means of revisiting the campus, and it might also allow us to retain our Resident Alien status.'[36]

The Parkers departed on 14 August, fulfilling a longstanding dream of Stewart's by travelling on the *Queen Elizabeth II* in homage to his paternal great-grandfather, an engineer on a paddle-wheel ship.[37] The only 'discordant note' was sounded by disturbing news from Northern Ireland, where sectarian rioting in Derry and Belfast, which had begun in earnest on 12 August, had resulted, by the time they set sail, in the deployment of British troops in the province to help the Northern

Ireland government contain the situation. 'The Troubles' were flaring up yet again. Parker read the headlines every morning in the ship's computerized *Daily Telegraph* and recorded his sense of foreboding:

> Shadows of gunmen in the streets of Belfast, 8 people shot dead and many more wounded[,] 4,000 homeless, streets of houses and shops and factories burnt out, terror and vicious hatred rampant, refugee centres in the South, hospitals just over the border, the whole brutal historical nightmare of 1641 and 1798 and 1916 lurching through the streets again and across the breezy countryside. Approaching it with a deep sense of dread.[38]

6

Back to Belfast

In returning to Belfast in 1969, Stewart Parker sought to achieve self-sufficiency as a writer and to reclaim his native ground as material for his work. At the time, he stood out among Northern Irish writers in attempting to earn his keep solely by writing.[1] He cobbled together a living through myriad projects, making barely enough money to support himself and Kate. The necessity of writing what people would pay him to write, rather than what he wanted to write, tried his patience, but his varied forays into journalism, editing, broadcasting, and education during his first few years back home deepened his understanding of Belfast's history and cultures and forced him to develop the attitudes and work habits of a conscientious craftsman rather than a temperamental artist. Parker's commitment to writing as a form of political action and desire to help make Belfast a better place, instead of seeking to escape from it, had been strengthened while he observed social upheavals in the United States. As the Troubles heated up over the ensuing years, they tested and solidified his resolve.

The violence that came to a head in August 1969 emerged gradually. Since its founding in 1967, the Northern Ireland Civil Rights Association (NICRA) had been calling for electoral and police reform, protection of civil liberties, and equitable distribution of housing and local government jobs. Unfortunately, the fact that NICRA chose to operate within a constitutional framework was lost on the Unionist establishment, which regarded any significant movement involving the Catholic minority as a plot to subvert the state. Much of the bloodshed of the following decades might have been avoided if the local authority had responded promptly and imaginatively to the protesters' grievances. As a character in Parker's play *Pentecost* puts it, 'there was no need for any of it, they held all the cards, they only needed to be marginally generous'.[2] Generosity, however, proved beyond the Northern Ireland government. Captain Terence O'Neill, prime minister from March 1963 until April 1969, showed some willingness to make changes, but the right wing of his own Unionist Party stymied him.

Unionist inflexibility was one source of increasing tension in the North; another was the progressively more militant tactics pursued by civil rights campaigners. Borrowing from the American civil rights and anti-war movements, leaders organized peaceful but sizeable meetings, marches, and sit-downs. As Jonathan Bardon points out, however, the peculiar history and divided demographic of Northern Ireland ensured that this sort of protest did not take place on neutral ground. Instead, 'parades and demonstrations were bound to be regarded as assertions of, or challenges to, the territorial imperative of one side or the other'. The first such rally, an August 1968 march from Coalisland to Dungannon to draw attention to the unfair allocation of public housing, involved 2,500 people without violence, though the marchers were met by an angry loyalist counter-demonstration and forcibly prevented by police from following their planned route. A civil rights march in Derry on 5 October 1968 ended less happily. The Northern Ireland government had banned it after the loyalist Apprentice Boys of Derry declared their intention to march over the same route on the same day, but civil rights parade planners decided to proceed regardless. Police beat marchers as they attempted to move towards the centre of Derry or sat down singing 'We Shall Overcome'. Two days of rioting, quelled by police, ensued. Most significantly for the future of Northern Ireland, scenes of police using their batons on unarmed marchers and bystanders were televised world-wide, attracting the sympathy of people, including British politicians, who had previously taken scant interest in the North. The incident and its aftermath also resulted in the growth and radicalization of the civil rights movement itself. Instead of the four hundred or so who had turned out on 5 October, subsequent civil rights protests in Derry drew thousands of participants. A historian of the civil rights movement argues, however, that it was on its way to failure at the moment of its greatest success. The violence visited on protesters in 1968 helped create a mass movement, but many of the new adherents were drawn more by anger than by a commitment to the non-sectarian and non-violent ethos of the original civil rights leaders. Meanwhile, the old fault lines between Protestants and Catholics were opening up again. Ultimately, the movement created 'hopes which could not be fulfilled on one side and fears which could not be assuaged on the other'.[3]

The People's Democracy (PD), a left-wing student group, formed spontaneously right after the 5 October march and was soon dominated by its most radical members, including Eamonn McCann, Bernadette Devlin, and Michael Farrell, who advocated a policy of deliberate provocation in an attempt to expose the bigotry of the Unionist government and force Westminster to intervene in the internal affairs of Northern Ireland. The leaders of PD, who (like Parker) were or had been Queen's students during the détente of the 1960s, had little or no idea of the depth and virulence of sectarian feeling still lurking beneath the surface of Northern Ireland. At the beginning of 1969, and against the advice of more moderate civil rights leaders, members of the group set out on a 75-mile march from Belfast to Derry inspired by the one led by Martin Luther King, Jr from Selma to Montgomery in 1965. Like King's voting rights march, the PD trek galvanized their opponents. Loyalists harassed the marchers all along their route, and, as the young people neared their destination on 4 January, attacked them at Burntollet Bridge with stones, bottles, pieces of wood, and iron bars. The policemen assigned to protect the marchers were unwilling or unable to do their job, and the attackers included off-duty members of the auxiliary police, known as B Specials.

After this, a peaceful resolution of the political crisis became impossible and three main elements of the contemporary Troubles—Unionist resistance to change, a roused and mobilized Catholic population, and the brutal and embittered forces of extreme Protestant reaction—were firmly in place. A fourth element, a confused and cautious British government, remained inactive until mid-August 1969. At the height of Northern Ireland's summer 'marching season', during which loyalists commemorate historic Protestant victories and celebrate their continued ascendancy over Northern Ireland's Catholics, the Stormont government, now led by James Chichester-Clark, declared itself unable to contain sectarian disturbances and asked London to send troops into Derry and Belfast. The Westminster government reluctantly complied with the request on 14 August and, in the short term, restored some kind of order. The British Army received welcome at the time as the protector of Catholics from the Royal Ulster Constabulary (RUC), Northern Ireland's often-undisciplined police force, and its auxiliary, as well as loyalist gangs. In the longer term, however, the decision to send troops without also taking over civil authority from Stormont was a mistake that would bedevil British policy in Northern Ireland for decades. Instead of capitalizing on the opportunity to act as an impartial arbiter of the situation, the British government (and its Army) were, in effect, propping up the Protestant monopoly there. The violence of the preceding two months had left ten people dead, over nine hundred injured, £8 million worth of damage (over 80 per cent of it to Catholic-owned or occupied premises), and 3 per cent of Belfast's Catholic households displaced.[4]

Parker arrived home at this point, on 21 August 1969. The split in republican ranks occasioned by the disappointment of certain Belfast hard-liners at the organization's failure to protect Catholics during the 1969 riots had already begun, but it would be almost another year before the Provisional IRA engaged in its first sustained military action. Thus, on the heels of his American experiences, it seemed clear to Parker that the fault in the situation lay mostly on the Protestant/unionist side. One of his oldest friends in Belfast, Sam Fannin, who met his ship and briefed him on recent developments, encouraged this view. Fannin, a Protestant by birth like Parker, approved the goals of the civil rights movement and felt mortified by his relatives' terrified and hostile reaction to it. With him, Parker visited unfamiliar parts of Belfast, including a folk music club on the Falls Road. Transgressing a traditional boundary of Northern Irish life, the two enrolled in Irish language classes offered by Queen's University's Extramural Department. (They abandoned an earlier attempt to join an Irish for Beginners class purportedly being offered at the Rupert Stanley College of Further Education in east Belfast when loyalist demonstrators threatened to incorporate Fannin's car into the barricade they were busily erecting across the end of the street to keep out the 'popeheads'.)[5]

Parker also investigated the political landscape for himself, studying Belfast like an outsider. He toured loyalist and republican strongholds on the Shankill and Falls Roads, listened to pirate radio broadcasts emanating from both sides, and attended a few PD meetings. The outlines of his own fundamental political beliefs may be discerned in a series of journalistic pieces published in the first half of 1970. He produced four of the most significant for the *Irish Times*, which had invited young writers to submit sample articles. 'Buntus Belfast' dissected Parker's reasons for wanting to learn Irish; 'An Ulster Volunteer' attempted to place the life of his maternal grandfather in political and historical context; 'School for Revolution' described his experience of teaching at Allenwood Prison Camp; and 'The

Tribe and Thompson' made a case for the importance of the recently deceased Protestant playwright Sam Thompson.[6]

One tenet of Parker's thinking at this time (and throughout his career) was that the Protestant 'tribe' of Northern Ireland 'is now in the centre of the Irish arena. Its actions and feelings will crucially affect the future course of the country's history.' Parker acknowledged his own implication in the neurosis of the tribe, 'the atavistic panic of the Northern prod…that still crawls around in there underneath the weighty luggage of my education', although what he saw as his people's irrationality and inarticulateness embarrassed him. He described the envy he felt listening to pirate radio broadcasts and comparing the Catholic and Protestant efforts: 'from Free Belfast, eloquent political homilies full of wit and passion alternating with passionate witty folk-songs full of eloquence; from Orange Lil and Roaring Meg, tongue-snared bluster alternating with The Sash and God Save the Queen, repeated and repeated like an incurable stammer'. Nevertheless, despite his decision to study 'the Fenian's tongue', he declared that he did not want to do anything as clichéd as change sides:

> That is what most Northern prod writers and intellectuals have done in the past. Their theory has been cultural homogeneity, but their reality has been a sense of inferiority to the 'real' Ireland, a hatred of Belfast, a wistful reverence for the mountainy folk. However, my problem is that I feel an almost Oedipal obsession with Belfast. The city has stuck to me like a burr on my sleeve that no amount of flapping will dislodge. I cannot sink my identity in Dublin, nor in New York or Toronto, or London or Glasgow either, for it is skulking somewhere in the fierce, drab, absurd streets of Belfast which was once Beal Feirste, and that's why I'm learning Irish.

Parker clearly took a cultural interest in things 'Irish' in addition to things 'British' (and American). Unlike many unionists, he also had no problem conceiving of himself as Irish. Rather than simply turning republican, however, Parker wanted to look in as well as out, reserving the right that Sam Thompson had claimed for himself with the words 'a writer like me may criticise his own people because he likes them very well'.[7]

Parker saw Northern Protestants' confusion about who they were as a basic problem. He reported the complaint of one of his aunts that 'nobody understands us' and admitted, 'I couldn't find the callousness or courage to point out that we don't understand ourselves, that we have no words to define the schisms that splinter every corner of our lives.' Facing the future bravely and sensibly would necessitate a real effort to understand the past, he thought. This idea, he knew, conflicted with the attitude of many forward-thinking people. Introducing the article about his grandfather, Parker wrote:

> Nearly every day now in the North, the plea goes out to 'forget the past'. Such advice is both impracticable and pernicious. On the one hand, you can't forget a nightmare while you are still dreaming it. On the other, it is survival through comprehension that is healthy, not survival through amnesia. Besides, the past is not a dead letter. The past is explosive cargo in everybody's family dresser. Your grandfather is the past.[8]

Parker's grandfather, James Lynas, had signed the Ulster Solemn League and Covenant of 1912 to oppose Home Rule in Ireland and, as a member of the original

Ulster Volunteer Force, participated in gun-running in 1914 as a prelude, if it came to that, to using force to ensure that the province remained an integral part of the United Kingdom. (Years later, Parker remarked that the Theatre of the Absurd had always seemed 'realistic' to him, since he had been 'weaned on the myths of the old Ulster Volunteer Force, who smuggled guns into Northern Ireland with the express intention of taking on the British Army to prove and assert the UVF's own British-ness'.) In the event, the First World War interrupted the Home Rule debate, and, instead of fighting the British Army, Parker's grandfather joined it, along with tens of thousands of other Ulstermen. Their sacrifices in the trenches gave another ironic twist to Northern Irish history. Parker noted the conjunction of the Battle of the Boyne and the Battle of the Somme in 'Shankill Road folklore' and commented, 'How a battle fought against Germany in alliance with France became an item in the historical crusade against Papists is part of the cruel joke that fate and politics played on my grandfather and his like-minded contemporaries.' In political terms, Parker saw his grandfather as a classic example of 'the honest Protestant working man, deluded and exploited by the Orange and Tory gentry and their military-industrial complex', but, he added, 'it isn't easy to think politically of your grandfather':

> He is a small man, spry and upright, but forced to shuffle a little by the enormous wounds in his thighs and calves. He chuckles a lot, says "ospital' and 'threevin'' for 'dreaming'; he is shy, proud and alone. And all his life he has thought of Roman Catholics as a feared and deadly enemy....As far as I can tell, my grandfather only hated the Germans in the way that St. George hated the dragon. Were his feelings towards Catholics of the same ilk? The subject is taboo.[9]

Parker reiterated the notion of sectarianism being encouraged by imperial elites for reasons of their own in a letter he wrote to the editor of the *New York Times* in July 1970 objecting to the comment in a recent column that 'All Irish, whether they favor Green or Orange, enjoy a fight.' According to Parker,

> This convenient stereotype has served the English well for 700 years. The recurrent outbreaks of violence on their neighboring island could be dismissed as merely the lovable but feckless Irish being unruly again. There was no need to recognize the agony of a people pillaged, humiliated and finally halved in numbers under an English mili-tary autocracy.
> The first large-scale resistance to this repression was organized and led by Irish Prot-estants in 1798. After it had been crushed, the English and the landed gentry pursued their classic policy of divide-and-conquer. They exploited religious differences until sectarianism became the lifeblood of Irish politics and of Irish life.

The contemporary riots, Parker argued, were only the latest phase in this ongoing drama, and, as a 'citizen of Belfast', he assured the author of the offending column that those who lived in that city were 'not enjoying their terror, confusion or fren-zied hatreds'.[10]

Parker's willingness to indict Britain, even at this early stage of the Troubles, indicates a nationalist tinge to his understanding of history. This did not mean he saw unionists as irrelevant. He resented the landed and business interests of

Northern Ireland, who had manipulated the British connection in order to oppress Catholics, and he almost preferred the open bigotry of Ian Paisley to what he regarded as the hypocrisy of mainstream unionism.[11] Parker parted company with nationalists, however, in viewing partition as a symptom of the problem rather than as the problem itself. He regarded communal distrust and hostility as the real issues that would have to be resolved independent of any new constitutional arrangement. Both Catholics and Protestants, he believed, had much to learn from and about each other. Catholics might look hopefully towards the Republic, while Protestants cherished their attachment to the UK, 'but they both know secretly that their corporate soul is out there somewhere in No Man's Land. Until it is located and defined, talk of the reunification of Ireland is empty. Not until the North can put words to its sense of selfhood will the island become united again, whether the Border goes or stays.'[12]

The image of no man's land recurs in Parker's commentary on Northern Ireland, and it epitomizes how he saw himself in relation to his native place. He belonged to the North, he readily admitted, yet the very nature of his belonging ensured that, emotionally, he would always be an outsider. No man's land was his own precarious 'home': unclaimed ground between two warring sides, riddled with ambiguity. This elusive middle ground was a place of possibility and uncertainty that he embraced by temperament, but he would insist in 1987 that his affinity with it also stemmed from his upbringing:

> Growing up in Belfast as a working class Protestant, I had access to all sorts but did not feel a part of any of them. You're led to believe you're British, yet the English don't recognise you as such. On the other hand, you're Irish because you're born in Ireland, but the people in the Free State don't recognise you as such. The working class element adds another dimension, because you are alienated from the Unionist establishment. You feel conversant with all of those things, but not obliged to any of them. In a sense you inhabit no-man's land.

Although the crisis of identity experienced by working-class Protestants in Northern Ireland frequently manifested itself in 'destructive' ways, Parker maintained that it could be remarkably fruitful for a writer, since 'You've got a hell of a lot to explore.'[13]

In the early 1970s, however, there were few writers from Parker's background to whom he could look as models—apart from Sam Thompson, whose socialist convictions and willingness to confront the sectarianism he saw as Ireland's greatest problem Parker memorably described in 1970: 'In Northern Ireland we have neither religion nor politics, but only a kind of fog of religi-otics which seeps in everywhere. To be a writer is to be a public figure, up there in the trenches with the captains and the clergymen. Sam Thompson fully accepted this and he roamed about fearlessly in no-man's-land waving a red flag.'[14]

Born in Belfast in 1916, Thompson went to work at age 14, being employed first in the shipyard and later as a painter for Belfast Corporation. He served as a shop steward in his union, becoming a writer by chance in middle age, when BBC producer and author Sam Hanna Bell overheard him telling shipyard stories and encouraged him to write them down. Thompson made Irish theatre history with his first full-length play, *Over the Bridge*, written between 1955 and 1957 and based on events he remembered from the shipyard. It depicts a trade union weakened by personal ambition, self-interest, lack of faith in union values, evangelical religion, and, above all, sectarianism. Parker found the play's message straightforward: 'there were sectarian pogroms in the shipyard in 1920–22 and in 1935; all their elements are thriving still; here's how it could happen again'.[15]

Thompson had offered the script to James Ellis, the new director of productions of the Ulster Group Theatre, who accepted it despite Thompson's prediction that he 'would not touch [it] with a barge-pole'. Rehearsals for *Over the Bridge* had already begun when Ritchie McKee, chairman of the Group's board of directors, read it, deemed it inflammatory, and, when Thompson refused to make requested changes, persuaded a majority of the board that it should be withdrawn in May 1959. In what Parker termed a 'staggering repudiation of drama as a serious art form', the board proclaimed its determination 'not to mount any play which would offend or affront the religious or political beliefs or sensibilities of the man in the street of any denomination or class in the community and which would give rise to sectarian or political controversy of an extreme nature'. The scandal over the board's action resulted directly or indirectly in the resignation of half the board and all the acting members of the company, marking the effective end of the old Group Theatre. Meanwhile, Ellis and Thompson formed an independent production company and arranged to stage the play at the Empire Theatre, a venue owned by a Dublin family and associated with light entertainment.[16]

Over the Bridge, featuring many former Group actors, opened on 26 January 1960 and played to full houses for six weeks, attracting a total of 42,000 people—many of them shipyard workers who had never before attended a play but who knew, as Parker put it, 'the reality of [Thompson's] fictions'. Thompson's challenge to his peers is unmistakable, and surely it is not fanciful to suggest, as Parker did in 1970, that 'his work contributed to that extraordinary mass meeting in the shipyard of 15 August 1969, at which the 8,000 workers, brought together by their shop stewards in the midst of renewed civil anarchy and bloodshed, voted in favour of maintaining "peace and goodwill in the yard and throughout the province"'. Indeed, Sandy Scott, the shop steward chiefly responsible for that meeting, spoke approvingly of the play.[17]

The original audience for *Over the Bridge* included Parker, then in his first year at Queen's, and his uncle Edwin Jobes, a shipwright. This marked the first time, Parker commented later, that he had seen working-class people realistically portrayed on stage, and he experienced the shock of 'recognition'. Parker recalled the occasion in his *Irish Times* piece about Thompson:

> We were like members of a lost tribe, thrust before a mirror for the first time, scared and yet delighted by our images, sensing even then that they were much more than a mere reflection. And the mirror was no missionary trinket, but the work of a dues-paying member of the tribe, a man with the plain prod name of Sam Thompson.[18]

Thompson wrote two more stage plays: *The Evangelist* (1963) and *The Masquer-ade*, an unproduced exploration of fascism. The BBC broadcast his television play, *Cemented with Love*, in April 1965. Thompson himself had died two months ear-lier at age 49, succumbing to heart disease and overwork in the offices of the Northern Ireland Labour Party, for which he had waged, in 1964, a quixotic cam-paign to be elected MP for the rural district of South Down. In his three produced plays, Parker argued, he had conveyed 'his complete diagnosis of Ulster's disease': '*Over the Bridge* shows sectarianism worming its way through people's working lives, *The Evangelist* uncovers the fanaticism and hypocrisy deforming their reli-gion, and *Cemented with Love* the appalling corruption of their traditional political parties, Unionist and Nationalist.' Parker felt Thompson's untimely demise as 'a grievous loss to Irish drama' and to Northern Ireland: 'He has never been needed more than in the dark days since his death. The painful missing factor in the whole Ulster equation is a sane and compassionate leader for the Protestant working class. There is no knowing how Sam Thompson would have fared in this perhaps impossible position, but he remains the nearest thing to such a man that we have yet seen.'[19]

By the time Parker wrote these words he had become a semi-official advocate for Thompson in addition to an admirer of his work, having been approached in October 1969 by Brian Garrett, an acquaintance from Queen's then a solicitor, a Northern Ireland Labour Party activist, and Thompson's literary executor. Garrett needed someone to organize the playwright's papers, left in an appalling state at his sudden death. Thompson had tossed handwritten scraps, pages of typescript, let-ters, press clippings, and other memorabilia into two large tea chests. In some cases, he had not even kept a copy of a produced script, and actors had to be tracked down in the hope that somebody had saved one. Putting this archive in order would be no small job, but Garrett sought to ensure the future availability of Thompson's work. He thought the project would allow Parker to earn a bit of money and feel his way back into Belfast, and he suspected (correctly) that Parker would sense an affinity with Thompson.[20]

The 'Sam Thompson Project', as Parker called it, evolved in several directions over a period of about three years. One product was the December 1970 publica-tion of *Over the Bridge* by the Dublin imprint Gill and Macmillan, with what publisher Michael Gill lauded as a 'superb and exciting' introduction by Parker. In phase two of the project, Parker prepared the Sam Thompson archive for the Belfast Central Library, which had bought Thompson's papers at Garrett's instiga-tion. In a grant application to the Arts Council of Northern Ireland, Parker explained that, in addition to cataloguing Thompson's papers, he would edit Thompson's remaining plays to provide clean acting scripts for drama groups wishing to perform them. The organization of the archive represented a few months' full-time work that ended up taking several times longer since Parker could concentrate on it for only an hour or two at a time amid the press of his other professional obligations. He earned small sums from the Arts Council, Gill and Macmillan, and the Belfast Corporation, but regarded the project primarily as, 'a labour of love'.[21]

Though Parker's later work for the stage does not resemble Thompson's in any obvious way, his predecessor remained an enduring influence. Thompson's independence, outspokenness, vision, and fidelity to his roots all resonated with Parker, who articulated his view of the older man's importance to the 'tribe' of working-class Northern Irish Protestants:

> Paisley is the cry of its blood and of the dark side of its mind, where race memories snout blindly around and psychic wounds cry like a child for succour. But Sam Thompson was the voice of the [tribe's] heart and its head, the voice of all that is civilised and decent in Belfast working-class life, the embodiment of its impassioned commonsense and derisive good nature.... All through his work flows a swift deep current of love for his people and a conviction of their giant potential, thwarted though it has been down the years.

Thompson, Parker wrote, 'saw right from the start that poverty and sectarian violence were root and branch of the one ugly tree', and in embodying that insight his work eerily predicted the resurgence of the Troubles while laying the foundation for a serious, engaged Northern Irish drama. Thompson's sense of the political potential of theatre inspired Parker, who insisted that plays like *Over the Bridge* 'do not "express" despair or hatred, they involve you in attitudes to those emotions. They conquer by defining them.' In a situation like the Troubles, 'The "real thing" (and the newsreels of it) is chaotic flux, overwhelmingly meaningless. Drama rescues us from the chaos by giving it a shape and a pattern, affording us insights and a saving chance to contemplate them.' The most social of art forms could serve a vital social purpose.[22]

Parker also considered the social function of drama in the context of BBC Northern Ireland's Schools Department, one of his main employers throughout the early 1970s. Parker had worked for Schools in the spring of 1967, and he renewed contact with the producers within a fortnight of his return to Belfast in 1969. Tony McAuley, a folk singer, broadcaster, and writer who had been teaching English at St Patrick's Secondary School in Belfast, had recently joined David Hammond and Douglas Carson, and Parker researched and wrote for all three. Conceived in a time of optimism, Schools, in Carson's words, became an 'emergency service' after the outbreak of open hostilities.[23]

At first the unit seemed uncertain how to handle this new responsibility. One script Parker wrote for McAuley, 'Your Neighbours', depicts a group of Protestant teenagers who decide to do something to improve their run-down neighbourhood. They apply to the Voluntary Service Bureau (VSB), an agency recruiting volunteers for service projects, and are matched with an elderly disabled man who needs his house redecorated. Some of their parents object because the old man is 'of the other persuasion', but the young people do the job, expressing their hope that the idea 'might catch on'.[24] The piece essentially advertised the VSB, and an edict from further up in the BBC had forbidden allusions to the violence. As a result, McAuley remembers,

> The script dodged and fudged the real issue of sectarian bigotry. It was a cop out, but this place was full of fear and tension in those days, and the BBC was as usual afraid

to stick its head above the parapet. The 'neighbours' script was part of a series which was designed ... to promote a message of good will etc at a time when we all knew a shooting war was about to erupt. The BBC management were among the few who couldn't see the writing on the wall, and since all scripts were vetted by a senior management determined to offend no one, every programme ended up 'saying nothing'. Not even Stewart could rock the proverbial boat.[25]

Prohibited from dealing directly with the Troubles, the Schools producers quickly decided to play to their strengths by focusing on the North's history and culture. They aspired to reach a diverse mass audience, and they aimed, through a more consistent and coherent treatment of Irish subjects than that provided by any other BBC department in the region, to give people new ways to think about the contemporary turmoil. One of the oldest and most popular Schools productions was the radio miscellany *Today and Yesterday in Northern Ireland*, inaugurated in 1961 and intended to be understood by 11-year-olds. It drew on a rich variety of materials, including history, legend, folklore, social geography, storytelling, and music. For example, 'The Narrow Seas', one *Today and Yesterday* series to which Parker made substantial contributions in 1969/70, demonstrated the many ways in which Ireland and Scotland (separated at one point by only twelve miles of water) had interacted over the centuries. Hardly limited to people bent on conquest or plantation, the two-way traffic also included migrant workers, missionaries, sailors, and folk artists. The series revealed no clear-cut division between 'British' and 'Irish' culture; Northern Ireland itself functioned as the dynamic crossroads where elements of both constantly combined and evolved.[26]

Topics Parker treated for Schools in the early 1970s encompassed historical subjects like the Battle of the Somme; biographical studies of famous Irishmen like Jonathan Swift, or local celebrities such as Sam Thompson; and investigations of Northern occupations and institutions. These projects often entailed personal interviews as well as library research and allowed Parker to draw on his expertise in certain fields while developing new interests in local studies. A detailed description of one script Parker wrote in 1971 for a *Today and Yesterday* series on 'Five Men of the Eighteenth Century', produced by McAuley, illustrates the challenges Parker faced in his Schools writing and some of the strategies he used to overcome them.

The accomplishments of this piece's subject, Hugh O'Donnell, the first parish priest in Belfast and founder of the oldest Catholic chapel in the city, would in themselves have alienated many Protestant listeners. On the other hand, most children hearing the segment in school would be learning about him for the first time, so Parker had to find a way into O'Donnell's story which would allow him to fill in the necessary background. The script, however, must not read like a lecture. Schools scripts relied on a mixture of narration and dramatization to pull listeners into the story and allow them to identify with the characters, many of whom spoke in a familiar Northern Irish vernacular. The main objective—communicating accurate information in the span of twenty minutes—required Parker to select representative incidents that both epitomized the broader issues surrounding O'Donnell's life and lent themselves to being dramatized. But Parker and McAuley also had a liberal political purpose in telling this story, one that could not appear too obvious or preachy: they wanted to show that relations between Catholics and Protestants in Belfast had not always been as tense and antagonistic as they happened to be in 1971.

Parker balanced these competing claims by means of a structure perfectly suited to his needs. Instead of telling O'Donnell's story in linear fashion, beginning with his birth in 1739, Parker opens in 1814 with O'Donnell's funeral. The narrated part of the script consists of a conversation between a Belfast shopkeeper and a visiting Dubliner who wants to know what all the fuss is about. The shopkeeper emphasizes that the dead man, although a Catholic in a largely Protestant and unionist city, was respected by all, and he explains why in a series of flashback scenes depicting various phases of O'Donnell's life through dialogue read by actors: his early education by a fugitive priest in the days of the penal laws aimed at Catholics and dissenters; his priestly training in Spain; his posting to Belfast in 1768; his dream of opening 'proper chapels' in the city; his decision to test the law prohibiting Catholics from holding religious services.

Parker's narrator, the shopkeeper, not only relates these events but displays a clear attitude towards them. He tells his interlocutor that he was a Belfast Volunteer, one of those who lobbied for reforms from 'that upper-class men's club in Dublin they used to call a Parliament'. The Volunteers, mainly Presbyterians, had agitated for the Irish parliament to become independent from the English parliament and for the repeal of the penal laws; thus (though it probably seemed odd to Parker's primary school audience) O'Donnell regarded Belfast's Presbyterians as the strongest allies of its Catholics, with a common cause. The shopkeeper proceeds to describe the opening of St Mary's in 1784, informing the astonished Dubliner that Protestants helped Catholics raise the money to pay for it. Sadly, the new spirit of cooperation did not last long. With the unsuccessful 1798 rebellion against English rule came violence that turned former friends against each other. The shopkeeper expresses no personal opinion about the rebellion, but he makes it clear that O'Donnell, along with most other Catholic priests in Ireland, opposed it (a flashback presents him worrying that the progress he has achieved through 'caution and prudence' is being undone by the resort to force). As the segment ends where it began, with O'Donnell's funeral, the shopkeeper mourns both the man and 'the spirit of brotherhood that breathed through everyone who lived in those days'.[27]

Later in his career, Parker would write a number of plays based on actual people and events, including *Joyce in June*, a television play featuring James Joyce; *Northern Star*, a stage play centred on Henry Joy McCracken and the United Irishmen; and *Heavenly Bodies*, a stage biography of playwright Dion Boucicault. These demonstrate how deeply Parker absorbed the lessons of his Schools apprenticeship. Many of the hallmarks of his mature writing—meticulous research and attention to detail, skilful handling of exposition, non-linear structure, a penchant for commenting on the present by way of the past, and a subtle political agenda—derive from techniques he sharpened in the 1970s to cope with the unique demands of BBC Schools.

Parker also worked on another curricular project with John Malone, seconded from the headship of Orangefield Boys' School in January 1970 to lead the Schools

Project in Community Relations, a Ministry of Education investigation into ways that schools might work to forge links between Northern Ireland's factions. Throughout 1970 and 1971, Malone focused on three main spheres of activity: fostering communication among teachers, pupils, and parents from Protestant and Catholic schools; enhancing the educational experience of pupils in areas of acute 'social need' through new facilities and mentoring programmes; and finding ways to integrate moral education and local studies into the secondary school curriculum. Parker assisted Malone in 1971 with the General Studies (Northern Ireland) Project, which sought to provide teachers with units of primary source material on a range of local subjects for use in various classes. Though mindful of global contexts, Malone agreed with Estyn Evans that 'a solution to the community's problem lies in the discovery of a common cultural heritage'. Parker helped with the literary offerings, compiling and introducing collections of Irish short stories and Ulster poetry.[28]

From his perspective as a jobbing writer, Parker looked askance at the current state of the literary genres. He met regularly with Michael Foley, then co-editor of the Northern Irish journal *The Honest Ulsterman*, for drinks and literary argument, and one of the few things they agreed upon was what they saw as the moribund state of Irish writing, particularly the 'humourless', 'pious', and 'dull' local variety. The view further afield offered little more to their taste. Parker still wrote poetry and even attended the occasional Group meeting, but he dismissed current poetry in May 1970 as 'Annotations to an Insight'. Around the same time, in a negative review of Colin Wilson's *The Killer*, he expressed the view that 'like most serious contemporary writers' the author had 'lost faith in the novel'. Worst of all was drama, since the most avant-garde theatre practitioners appeared to have abjured writing. In the 'new expressionism',

> Writers are shunned as wordbound, reactionary, stiff-limbed, and totalitarian: all of which they mostly are. So the actors overthrow their old dictator, and set up a groovy commune, because, actors are hip to where it's at, and with such pitifully limited equipment they create a similarly limited Statement about War and Sex. Bodies and nerves are unsheathed on stage and in the audience, to no particular avail. Far from being liberated, everybody gets more uptight, the whole exercise being more closely akin to current experiments in group therapy than to anything you might call art.

Nevertheless, despite Parker's admission that 'I would rather do almost anything than go to the theatre these days' and his understanding of theatre as 'the most volatile and the least perfectible of all the arts', he obviously regarded the challenges presented by it as especially compelling. In order for theatre to begin to live up to its potential again, he concluded, 'writers will need to reconstruct the theatre from scratch. Locked out by both the establishment and the anti-establishment, they will have to begin from their own bodies, their own voices and friends.... [I]n so doing, they may rediscover the sources of their poetry and their fictions.'[29]

The BBC provided a potential market for Parker's early drama. In addition to his work for Schools, he also wrote radio drama aimed at adults. One early abortive effort was *Hurra! My Boys, For Freedom*, a ninety-minute radio script Parker proposed to write as a means of feeling his way into the Henry Joy McCracken play he had been contemplating since the autumn of 1967. In March 1970, he submitted a synopsis and sample scene to Roger Pine, who had just taken over from David Turner as BBC Northern Ireland's radio drama producer for a year. In his description of the play, Parker focused on the dynamic by which pleas for reform, if repressed, give way to calls for revolution. In McCracken's Ireland, 'republicanism gains prominence over equality' as the radicals become convinced that justice will not be achieved until the connection with England is broken. McCracken himself, whom Parker saw as fundamentally apolitical, 'was driven into taking the republican oath out of a sense of desperation at the futility of peaceful and legal methods'. A similar dynamic had been transforming the Northern Irish civil rights movement in Parker's own time, and he acknowledged this parallel with a quotation from one of McCracken's fellow revolutionaries which he termed 'a perennial truism': "'The present state of Ireland bears so strongly on the past, that in delineating the one we seem to portray the character of both.'" Nevertheless, Parker insisted, 'my concerns in this play extend beyond the Irish situation':

> I conceived the play while living in America and engaging in the struggle against the Vietnam war and for Black liberation. I saw that Henry Joy McCracken was a man of compassion and altruism in a company of ideologues.... The ideologies squabbled away, while the great mass of apolitical, impoverished, suffering humanity struggled on in the background. When the squabbling turned to violence, the peasantry bore the brunt of it.

Pine was interested in *Hurra! My Boys, For Freedom*, but in those days radio drama was commissioned on a national, rather than a regional, basis. Whereas in the past it had been possible to produce drama for the local market, now all drama ideas had to be sold to the whole BBC network. 'London' rejected Parker's proposal without explanation, and the McCracken idea retreated to the back of his mind.[30]

One project that did come to fruition was called *Minnie and Maisie and Lily Freed*. Parker had originally conceived of this as a short story, decided to try writing it for radio, submitted the idea once for television, and finally got it accepted as radio drama. The £137.50 the BBC paid for the play probably made it the biggest commission he had received to date.[31] Parker wrote most of the play in October and November 1969, though he revised it several times after that. It was recorded and edited in July 1971 and transmitted that August on Radio 4.[32]

Minnie and Maisie and Lily Freed centres on three elderly Belfast ladies (played in the BBC production by Elizabeth Begley, Margaret D'Arcy, and Catherine Gibson, all veterans of the Ulster Group Theatre) who attend weddings the way other people might go to see films or plays. They scan the newspapers looking for likely prospects and show up at the churches where weddings are taking place as part of the 'congregation'. Hardly a week goes by without their witnessing some couple's nuptials, and they refer to them by name ('Toner and Gibson', 'Friers and Rolston'), rating and comparing the scenery, costumes, musical accompaniment, and artistes.[33]

Most of the piece's humour stems from the fact that none of them has any experience of marital bliss. Sisters Minnie and Maisie are spinsters, though both cherish the memory of a long-ago suitor named Mr Baskett—each believes she heroically renounced him for her sister. Lily is married to a drunken lout who beats and berates her. Moreover, the wedding the women attend in the course of the play does not encourage the audience to assume that her experience is atypical: the bride is pregnant, and the resentful groom is chatting up the bridesmaid before the wedding party even leaves the church.

Minnie and Maisie and Lily Freed marks an important stage in Parker's development as a playwright, though it relies more upon a comic concept than a fully realized plot. Since the idea for the play dated from at least 1967, Parker made no attempt to engage with the Troubles, even as a backdrop, but its focus on working-class Belfast characters and speech reflects his growing determination to draw directly on his surroundings in his dramatic writing. The anachronistic flavour of the dialogue and music in the scenes between the two sisters and Mr Baskett anticipates the flashback scenes in *Spokesong*, and the 'mannish' character of Maisie, who claims she 'chose to be an only woman', resembles in some respects the suffragette Kitty in the later play. In addition to the use of incidental music, one of the conventions of radio drama, Parker embeds excerpts from at least six songs (including 'Daisy Bell', or 'A Bicycle Built for Two', which also features prominently in *Spokesong*) in this forty-five-minute play. The inclusion of quirky characters, sometimes seemingly for their own sake, further foreshadows his future work. The production of *Minnie and Maisie and Lily Freed* did not fully satisfy Parker, but he later acknowledged its value as an apprentice piece.[34]

Minnie and Maisie and Lily Freed represented a rare opportunity in these years for Parker to be paid for doing his 'own' work, writing he would have tried to do whether he were paid for it or not. Most of the time he felt, as he put it at the end of 1969, that he was 'allowing commercial necessity to keep Art out in the darkness'. He supported himself largely by acting as an intellectual for hire, appearing frequently on local BBC arts discussion programmes and reviewing books regularly for the *Irish Press* and *Irish Times*. In 1970, Parker convinced the *Irish Times* to engage him to write a fortnightly column on current popular music, that newspaper's first such feature. For years he had maintained that singer-songwriters such as Joni Mitchell and Randy Newman were producing the finest poetry being written, and he also believed that 'the best rock music is the most dynamic of our lively arts'. At the same time, Parker had few illusions about the music industry. He understood the temptation to appeal to the lowest common denominator, and he felt that the objections of those who professed to hate pop music were founded on over-exposure to bad examples of the genre ('pap') and lack of knowledge of the good (musically complicated and verbally witty). *High Pop*, as he entitled the feature, might convert some of these sceptics to an appreciation of what could be done within the popular format. Parker also aimed to treat the artists with respect and help them counter the 'dangers' faced by 'all artists working in a popular milieu', as he outlined them in his first column:

> To the entrepreneurs they are merely another saleable product, to be beatified while the public wants them, and thrown in the bin when they're no longer selling. The

artistic establishment, on the other hand, is either disdainful or patronising. Thus deprived of a healthy critical atmosphere, their work is vulnerable to diseases: in particular to commercialism, pretentiousness and repetitiveness.

Parker took the work more seriously than he took himself as a critic, offering unabashedly subjective opinions, informed yet humorous, of the music and books about music that he liked and did not like.[35]

Parker's signal quality as a music critic was one familiar to his friends: an eagerness to share the things that excited him personally. He enjoyed a wide range of popular music, from folk-influenced bands like Dr Strangely Strange and The Incredible String Band to soul singer Tina Turner. He loved James Taylor, the Grateful Dead, Van Morrison, Crosby Stills Nash and Young, The Band, some Bob Dylan, and the Beatles (he thought the second side of *Abbey Road* 'possibly the finest achievement in rock music'), along with such now-forgotten groups as the 'innovative' and cerebral Soft Machine. When review records were late to arrive or failed to show up, he might discourse for entire columns on topics like the blues roots of pop music or the media's handling of it. For over six years, from April 1970 to August 1976, Parker celebrated the achievements of musicians who managed to meld the 'international medium' of pop music with their own 'idiosyncratic sense of reality'. He did this for fun, for the review copies of albums (which he could either keep or sell to Dougie Knight, who ran a second-hand record business in Belfast that had started as a sideline to his bicycle shop), and, most of all, for the six guineas the *Irish Times* paid him for each column. This was, remarkably, the only steady pay cheque he received in the early 1970s.[36]

Another BBC commission from 1970/1 gave Parker the chance to apply his critical faculty to a topic that, like most introspective people, he had pondered extensively in private: himself. Producer John Boyd requested an autobiographical script from Parker in late August 1970 and approved his synopsis about a month later. Parker wrote the piece in November and December 1970 and recorded it in the summer of 1971. *Self Portrait*, with Parker (introduced as an 'Ulster poet') narrating, was transmitted in Northern Ireland on 3 October 1971.[37] The talk's original title, *The Green Light*, reflects its unifying theme of Parker's quest for the 'mystery and romance...that every human being craves as much as he craves lunch': 'Years later I was to find the supreme expression of this unnameable hunger in Scott Fitzgerald's novel *The Great Gatsby*. I was tantalised by a sense of wonder, an intimation of perfection, as Gatsby is by the green light across the bay from his estate.'[38]

Parker begins his story with the bombing of east Belfast by the Germans in spring 1941, before his birth, in order to underline his consciousness of himself and his contemporaries as 'the children of the new age'. He goes on to recount key events of his childhood and adolescence in roughly chronological order, emphasizing, with a keen sense of what works on radio, the various sounds that surrounded and engaged him. Throughout, he presents himself both as a product of a particular place and people and as someone in instinctive rebellion against them. His discussion of his education provides a typical example. For the BBC production

Parker had to cut most of a graphic description of his hated primary school, but he was allowed to excoriate the 'behaviourist' pedagogy he encountered there. Nevertheless, he confesses, 'I learnt to play the system, even to the point of winning that ultimate Honour Card, a university degree, for having a combed mind and tidy memory. Now I'm busy trying to unlearn that very skill, to gear my mind to some healthier system.'[39]

Parker touches only obliquely on politics and again highlights his individuality:

> Which brings me to all those fashionable Ulster incidents: the time I got beat up by a Catholic gang, the love affair with a sweet Papist girl brutally crushed by intolerant parents, and so on. I haven't mentioned these yet because they never happened to me.... The Twelfth was fairly exciting, what with collecting wood for the bonfire and waving at my Uncle and Grandfather in the procession. All in all, my self-centredness was almost impregnable. At the same time, the accompanying introspection made me aware of the poison in the Ulster system and saved me from growing up to be that palsied surgeon, the liberal Unionist.[40]

Rather than finding a personal outlet in organized religion or political parties, Parker yearned for a purer form of self-expression. Amongst a flurry of adolescent experimentation, he writes, 'there was one activity stealthily creeping up on me, a driving force that would brook no rival as ingenuous as a hobby. It was the single mouth for all my hungers. It was not content to be a vocation, it insisted on being a job too, and finally a way of life. It was writing.'[41]

Parker credits his poor health with reinforcing his natural inclinations, musing, 'Illnesses are presumably accidents and yet it amazes me how they seem to have woven themselves symmetrically into the design of my growing up. Maybe I would have been a celebrated trick cyclist or an Olympic harrier if I hadn't had such a sickly constitution, but I doubt it.' Hospitals, he came to believe, 'hold the secret of the human condition', and Belfast (in an image cut from the final version) 'often seems like one vast clinic, all dark windy corridors and huddled queues, and no doctors'. At the end of his self-portrait, Parker points to his amputation as a crucial factor in the shaping of his mature personality:

> My adolescence ended, almost too neatly, after I had made the great escape to university. It was as if all the frustrations, the spiritual oppression and drudgery had culminated in a physical canker. A bone tumour developed in my left leg, and the leg was amputated. I was maimed. But the process of coping with that reality developed or uncovered a stability and a serenity that I had desperately wanted for as long as I could remember.

Remaining from his previous life was 'the desire to penetrate the heart of all mystery'.[42]

Self Portrait painted a picture that would have been unrecognizable to many of Parker's acquaintances, who tended to forget (if indeed they ever noticed) his physical disability and who generally underestimated his seriousness of purpose. The most abiding impression many of his friends have of Parker is of his unrestrained and infectious laugh, which seemed an outpouring of his benign nature. 'Cheerful', 'jovial', 'positive', and 'light-hearted' are words that recur in descriptions of

Parker by those who spent time with him in the early 1970s, from people who knew him only casually or professionally to his most intimate friends. He was 'always in a good mood', his sparring partner Michael Foley recalls, and seemed to have no 'negative emotions'.[43]

Parker's 'happy energy' buoyed those around him, drawing out their best. Possessed of a self-confidence that never manifested itself in arrogance, he encouraged his friends to believe in themselves too. Gregarious by nature, Parker socialized often, mostly in small groups or one-on-one. As he had done at university, he established relationships with a vast range of people. He compartmentalized his social life, however, meeting separately with individuals or groups who were often unaware of each other's existence, and refusing to confine himself to any one clique.[44]

'Stickin' out', a general term of approbation Parker used at the time, sums up his presence for Foley. Freshly returned from the US, he struck many in Belfast as 'exotic'. He wore granny glasses like John Lennon; his long, fair hair wound in corkscrew curls around his face; and he dressed in what Tom McLaughlin, who met him regularly along with Foley, refers to as an 'alternative' fashion, favouring seersucker trousers, flowered waistcoats, striped shirts, and long scarves, all probably acquired at the Oxfam shop. People who had never spoken to him noticed the extraordinary figure Parker cut, with his odd gait, clothes that would not have looked out of place on 'a bookie's runner', and habit of humming wherever he went. Ronald Mason, then head of programming for BBC Northern Ireland, describes him as a 'man of his time'—an apt appraisal, since even people like Brian Garrett, only a few years older than Parker, saw him as a member of a distinct generation. The openness to fresh perspectives that made him seem 'younger than his age' showed in Parker's predilection for the company of people considerably younger than himself. Foley and McLaughlin, for example, were seven or eight years Parker's junior, and they felt 'cynical' and 'worldly wise' compared to him.[45]

In this and other ways, Parker's wife served as a foil to him. His marriage reflected his private, serious side, an aspect of him that many of his acquaintances never saw, just as they rarely saw Kate. David Evans, who shared a house with the Parkers in the early 1970s, found them fascinating as a couple because their differences seemed complementary. Stewart fastened on the modern, wanting to know what was happening 'the day after tomorrow', while Kate struck him as nearly 'Victorian', hardly deigning to read anything written later than the mid-nineteenth century. If Kate was 'Victorian', though, she was Victorian in the mode of Jane Eyre. Compared with Stewart, she came across as 'reserved', even 'unsociable'. McLaughlin, who recollects that Kate rarely went out with Stewart, did not imagine that she minded staying at home since she impressed him as 'self-possessed', 'opinionated', and not at all 'deferential': 'He did his own thing, and she must have done her own thing.' Kate's moodiness contrasted with Stewart's even temper, and she remained prone to a 'darkness' he did not display. Individualistic like him, this characteristic in her took the form of eccentricity rather than exuberance. Her difference had a 'fey' quality; she inhabited a separate reality from other people and thus preferred quiet to social situations. Only her closest friends saw her in anything like a relaxed mode. Others often found it difficult to connect with her. Tony McAuley, who met Kate a few times, formed the impression of someone 'protective' of both herself and Stewart, likening her to a snail that never quite came out of its shell.[46]

Despite their surface incompatibilities, Stewart and Kate were an uncommonly close couple, living together in one room through much of the 1970s. An intensely intellectual woman, Kate was ideally suited in many respects to be the wife of a struggling writer. Her passionate devotion to both literature and theatre and her faith in Stewart's vocation expressed themselves in her willingness to make sacrifices so he could devote himself to writing. For a married man, Parker retained views on marriage as an institution that seemed strangely bohemian to Michael Foley. He felt strongly that writers should not have conventional jobs or families because these would distract them from their work. His favourite cautionary example was John Hamilton, his friend from Queen's: the most talented writer he had ever known, he said, who gave it up when he got married. He and Kate, in contrast, appeared to Foley to have a 'pact' to remain childless, making them the only young couple Foley knew who did not want a family.[47]

The Parkers lived from hand to mouth in these days, surviving on less than seemed possible to those who knew them. (Sam Fannin, who often joined Stewart and Kate for lunch, made a point of bringing the food because they never had any in the house.) Kate wore their poverty like a badge of honour. She understood how much Stewart valued being able to write, and she did not pressure him to find a steady job. Nor, pleading fragile nerves, did she look for a regular pay cheque herself, although she had taught before she met Stewart. She tutored a bit to help pay the bills, but mostly she directed her efforts to making what little they had go as far as possible—she 'could make a home out of a cardboard box', one friend recalls—and providing physical and emotional support to her husband. In this division of labour their 'bohemian' relationship remained quite traditional, but Kate made a deliberate choice to devote her own energy to Stewart's career because she believed in his talent. 'You can't talk to your wife,' Parker told Foley, relaxing into an evening of male companionship at the Club Bar, but in fact he did talk to Kate constantly. She was the only person he would discuss his work in progress with in any detail, and he drew on her encyclopaedic reading and prodigious memory in countless ways.[48]

In some specifics, the account Parker gave of himself in his radio self-portrait is corroborated by his friends. He really had, according to Foley, escaped the 'worst aspects' of the Irish character: bigotry, puritanism, resentment. Most 'un-Irish' of all, he had apparently 'purged' himself of all tribal attachments. The combination in Parker of a 'light' nature and an 'impassioned' commitment to his writing also impressed Foley as unusual. Most Irish writers he knew lacked confidence and took a 'furtive', almost 'hangdog', approach to their work. Foley, like Parker himself, attributed many of Parker's distinctive qualities to his early brush with death. Most could be interpreted as signs of a determination to live in the moment. Petty jealousy and anger wasted precious time. Work, though important, should not consume life. Money, when you had it, should be spent rather than saved (Parker's 'hedonism', on those rare occasions when he had any money to spend, both shocked and delighted Foley). Life, in short, should be enjoyed as much as possible.[49] Throughout his adult life, Parker's gift for giving his full attention to the present moment made him attractive to all kinds of people; they might or might not understand the dark reason for his lightness, but they responded to his *presence*.

Upon arriving in Belfast in 1969, the Parkers stayed with Kate's mother on Hillsborough Drive in east Belfast. By mid-September, though, they had migrated to the university district. Until the end of the year, they occupied the top floor of a house in Chlorine Gardens owned by Kate's closest friend from university, Brenda Callaghan, and her husband, Sydney, a Methodist minister and social activist who had helped found the Belfast Samaritans in 1962. While they lived there, Stewart sometimes took telephone calls for the Samaritans if Sydney was out and the caller especially wanted to speak to a man, as women often did. With his sympathetic and inviting demeanour, Brenda also sometimes asked him to help entertain the various 'oddballs' who came to see Sydney.[50] In January 1970, the couple moved once again, into a flat in College Green House, on College Green behind Queen's. This, too, perhaps because of the expense, proved a temporary arrangement; they stayed there only until June of that year.[51]

Since their return, Stewart and Kate had been looking for a cottage to buy or rent in the Mourne Mountains, just across the border from the Republic and a little over an hour by car south of Belfast. Stewart's parents had recently begun renting a holiday cottage near Rostrevor, after having been introduced to the village by a friend of theirs who worked as a travelling salesman. Herbie and Belle Parker went down almost every weekend, bringing some of Herbie's home brew and a jug of wine, and held open house for the locals. Soon Stewart's brother and his family had also rented a cottage there, where they spent many weekends and longer periods at Easter and in the summer, and all the Parkers were well-known and well-liked by the villagers. Herbie often sang in a pub at weekends and could move the crowd to laughter or tears. Although the district, like most country border regions, skewed strongly nationalist, the extended Parker family fitted into the community, helping every year with the haymaking (then still done by hand) and other farming tasks. (Parker's niece remembers her mother assisting with the delivery of piglets and her father helping a farmer fix his old tractor.) When Parker made arrangements in May 1970 to rent a cottage near Rostrevor, he thus followed his family's lead.[52]

Unlike the rest of his family, however, Stewart intended to make his cottage, which he and Kate called Awltlekeltie, his main residence. There were good reasons why most Belfast visitors came down only in the summer. In the early 1970s, the concept of self-catering cottages was new to the area, and they tended to be primitive, to say the least. Parker's sister-in-law recalls that most of the weekend cottages were simply old buildings, often abandoned houses, that farmers were no longer using. They typically lacked (as Stewart and Kate's did) indoor plumbing, electricity, and running water.[53]

For these reasons, and business ones, it was not practical to stay at the cottage all the time. Stewart and Kate commuted between Rostrevor and Belfast in the early

1970s, living in Rostrevor from Thursday until Sunday or Monday, and staying with Kate's mother or with friends in Belfast on the other nights of the week. This arrangement, facilitated by Parker's purchase of a used Volkswagen automatic in 1970, enabled them to take advantage of the best of both urban and rural worlds and helped to balance Stewart's craving for company and stimulation with Kate's preference for peace and privacy.[54] Parker revelled in his increased proximity to the land and to the pagan and early Christian Irish past, savouring the beauty of the surrounding landscapes, exploring the region thoroughly, and making a point of learning the local history.[55]

Precarious finances probably constituted their main motive for spending so much time in the country, however. The rent was minimal, on the condition that they handle any needed repairs. Stewart and Kate, who started moving into the cottage in August 1970, spent most of their long weekends for the first several months making it habitable: setting up their 'bathroom' with a chemical toilet, jug, and basin; whitewashing; painting; laying carpet; waging war against the rats perpetually at their food box; trying to stop the roof from leaking; digging ditches; cementing walls; and otherwise attempting to hold back the elements. Awltlekeltie was long and narrow, shaped like a streetcar and only a bit wider, with big rooms on either end of a corridor containing the two bedrooms. Oil lamps provided light, and Kate cooked over the fire or on a two-burner gas stove. Long after they were settled, the cottage remained draughty, damp, and cold.[56]

Despite the physical hardships of their life in Rostrevor, Stewart and Kate loved it. The relative isolation of the cottage gave Stewart the quiet he needed to concentrate on his writing, while allowing him to keep up his characteristically hectic pace while they were in Belfast. He spent his time in the country working on whatever projects he had in progress, reading, writing letters, chopping wood, listening to the radio, playing his guitar or flute, visiting neighbours or entertaining friends, reading aloud with Kate, playing Scrabble and Monopoly, walking, taking scenic drives, or going to a nearby town for a meal or a film. Sundays were devoted to drinking tea and a ceremonious reading of several Sunday newspapers. Stewart would return to Belfast refreshed and ready for a bath and a round of appointments with friends and employers.[57]

Parker's weekly routine fell into a predictable pattern through 1970 and 1971. During the days he ran errands or worked. In the evenings he went out almost every night he spent in the city. In 1976, he included 'the pubs' on a list of things he had missed most about Belfast when living in the US, and meeting friends for a drink was a staple of his social life. Though not a heavy drinker by Irish standards—Michael Foley, for one, never saw him drunk—Parker enjoyed drinking and the give and take of pub banter (another thing he had missed about Belfast was the way 'every conversation gets handled like a one-act play'). He met Foley and McLaughlin about once a week, usually on a Monday night. Tuesday nights were for Irish classes, if they were in session, and drinking with Sam Fannin afterwards. On other nights, Parker might meet up with other friends, either at a pub or at the friends' homes; watch television; or go to a play or, more often, a film, usually at the Queen's Film Theatre (he was 'obsessed with acting', Foley recalls).[58]

Throughout the early 1970s, Parker's ties to the US remained strong. Unlike many Irish people who had spent time there, Brian Garrett remarks, Parker did not come back with a phoney American accent, but he seemed to have absorbed America on such a deep level that it had become a part of him. Other friends recall that he relished the energy and enthusiasm, the extrovert personality, of the US, and that he approved of the way Americans appreciated success. American literature continued to excite him—particular favourites at the time were Richard Brautigan's *Trout Fishing in America* and *The Hawkline Monster*—and the communication he maintained with friends in New York State knowledgeable about popular music enabled him to 'discover' many new artists for his *High Pop* column.[59]

Parker had returned to Belfast because, despite its attractions, he missed something in the US. Living there, for him, seemed too much like being on a 'permanent holiday'. In Belfast, he told Foley, 'You're hearing things every day that go straight into your work.' Nevertheless, Parker sought to keep his American connections fresh. In 1970, 1971, 1972, and 1974, he taught summer school at Cornell University. His classes included Modern Drama and Modern Irish Literature, the work paid well, there were few students and no snow, and he and Kate could catch up with friends. An *Irish Times* article published in December 1971 described Parker as living 'half the year in Belfast and half in New York, where he has a summer lectureship in English'.[60] Someone had exaggerated, but the opportunity to teach during the summer session, when he got it, did allow him and Kate to escape from Belfast for six or eight weeks in the summer, missing most of the 'marching season' with its heightened political tension. This means of relieving the pressures of daily existence became increasingly important to them as the Troubles intensified.

7

Living in Interesting Times

On Stewart Parker's return from Ithaca in mid-August 1971, he found the situation in Belfast fundamentally altered by the introduction of internment without trial of suspected terrorists. This drastic measure represented a desperate reaction to a year of intensifying violence on all sides and worsening relations between Catholics and the British Army (whose relations with Protestants had been strained from the outset). Far from reversing this negative trend, however, internment ushered in levels of ferocity that made the previous two years of unrest pale in comparison. Over the next several years (and the quarter-century that followed) the people of Northern Ireland gradually accepted the possibility that their problems would not admit of any quick, straightforward political solution. The excitement many had felt in 1968/9 yielded to the realization that the current Troubles were, like the Northern climate, something they would have to cope with indefinitely. As the 'crisis' extended itself from year to year, the pressure on writers to 'respond' to it increased. Most of the best ones did, though often with reluctance and a keen awareness of the danger of exploiting such material for its sensationalism. Parker himself eventually answered the call for writing with relevance to the current state of Northern Ireland. He maintained in the early 1970s, however, that it was too soon to expect artists to have detached themselves sufficiently from the rush of events to evolve forms capable of making sense of them.

Most of Parker's writing then consisted of what he would have described as hack work for the BBC and assorted newspapers and journals. In addition, he laboured to support himself at several other jobs that had little or nothing, in his view, to do with art. He did not even keep a diary through most of 1972, and his daily record for 1973 and 1974 consists of the barest notations of his doings. Consequently, one can rarely say with authority what he made of events as they unfolded. Like other people in the North, he followed the daily drama of the Troubles and focused on survival. He also, however, observed and participated in the projects of various friends and associates bent on tackling the underlying social problems that had given rise to the political violence. Whether or not Parker was directly involved in any particular such enterprise, his friends brought him their stories. His appreciative faculty was such, one intimate recalls, that people felt compelled to share their experiences, drawn to him 'like courtiers'.[1] Consciously or not, Parker in these years stored up impressions of Belfast at the height of the Troubles that he would draw on in plays written throughout his subsequent career as a dramatist. *Spokesong*; *Catchpenny Twist*; *I'm a Dreamer Montreal*; *Iris in the Traffic, Ruby in the Rain*;

Northern Star, *Lost Belongings*, and *Pentecost* all bear the marks of his personal and vicarious immersion in a multiplicity of facets of Belfast life at this surreal time. Some knowledge of events in the city in the 1970s is thus essential to an understanding of Parker's mature achievement.

The 'honeymoon' between the Army and Northern Ireland's Catholics had proved a short one. The Provisional IRA, which in December 1969 had split from the 'Official' IRA (now publicly committed to parliamentary politics), encouraged friction between Catholic civilians and British soldiers.[2] Moreover, it remained unclear exactly which 'civil power' the Army ultimately served: the British government or Stormont. On 18 June 1970, barely ten weeks after the first major conflict, in Ballymurphy, between the Army and Catholic rioters, a Westminster general election brought to power the Conservative government of Edward Heath. Heath's victory ousted Labour Home Secretary James Callaghan, who had finally concluded that direct rule of Northern Ireland from London was needed and only awaited an opportunity to impose it.[3] It would be almost another two years before the British government stripped Stormont of its authority. By then, the era of goodwill between the Army and Northern Ireland's Catholic population seemed long ago and fantastic.

Events through the summer of 1970 hastened this estrangement. The new British government ignored warnings to ban provocative Protestant marches, and the Provisional IRA fought its first big gun battles on 27 June against Protestant rioters in Ardoyne and the Short Strand, isolated Catholic enclaves. The Lower Falls curfew of 3–5 July, which restricted people to their homes while the Army conducted a house-to-house search for weapons, prompted the Official IRA to re-enter the war against the British Army, and recruitment to the Provisionals went 'dizzily fast' through the last half of 1970.[4]

The Provisionals carried on a bombing campaign that summer, but most of the explosions (100 by mid-September) were small, as Jonathan Bardon recounts, 'merely a foretaste of what was to come'. Promised local government reforms had not materialized, and, in October 1970, the Civil Rights Association indicated its readiness to return to the streets. The Provos' bombing campaign continued into 1971; on 9 February, for example, two BBC engineers and three construction workers were killed by a landmine in County Tyrone which had wrecked a BBC transmitter, deaths noted by Parker in his journal. Riots lasting for days were common in both Protestant and Catholic areas. On 20 March, Northern Ireland's Prime Minister James Chichester-Clark resigned after the British government offered him only 1,300 of 3,000 additional troops he had requested. He was succeeded by Brian Faulkner, who had long been a proponent of internment, convinced that it had helped the Stormont government contain the IRA during its last major campaign from 1956 to 1962. The upsurge in Provisional IRA bombing activity during his first months in office helped him make his case to the British government: thirty-seven explosions in April, forty-seven in May, fifty in June, ninety-one in July. Faulkner got what he wanted, not because others thought internment would work, but because the British government felt the need to do something and no one could think of anything better to do.[5]

Soldiers, accompanied by RUC Special Branch officers, fanned out across Northern Ireland shortly after 4 a.m. on 9 August 1971, intent on arresting 452 suspects. Of the 342 picked up, 105 were released after two days; the rest were imprisoned. Bardon notes internment's 'entirely one-sided' nature. In addition to being a political disaster because of its partisan application, internment yielded no military benefit. Out-of-date police intelligence ensured that few of those interned were active in the Provisional IRA. Instead, Official IRA members, many uninvolved, made up the majority of those arrested. Even more striking than the policy's failure was its social cost. In the three weeks following the introduction of internment, over one in every hundred families in Belfast moved house, many destroying their homes as they left, to prevent 'the other side' from living in them. Rioting was rampant, and the Provisionals intensified their military activity aimed at wrecking Northern Ireland's economy and driving the British government to withdraw. There were 131 bombings during August 1971, 196 in September, and 117 in October. In 1971 as a whole, 34 people had died as a result of the Troubles before the start of internment, but 140 were killed in the remaining months.[6]

Long before these grim statistics could be compiled, Parker regarded internment as 'a grave mistake'. In late September, he cited to a friend 'several cases...where Protestants have been found with arms hoards or suspected of bombing, yet those Protestants are not interned'. Not only was internment clearly not working, Parker said, but it could not work, 'because it's impossible to win a guerilla war'. Ominously, the Provisional offensive spurred the organization of loyalist forces in reaction. During September 1971, a number of Protestant 'vigilante and paramilitary groups' combined in the Ulster Defence Association. (The UDA, military and working-class in its outlook, would boast forty to fifty thousand members at its peak in 1972.) The same month, Ian Paisley announced the formation of the Democratic Unionist Party (DUP) to represent Protestants who regarded the existing Unionist government as weak.[7]

Much as Parker deplored the unfairness of the internment policy and regretted the increased militancy of working-class unionists, it was hard for a Northern Protestant not to feel embattled as Provisional IRA attacks resulted in ever more disruption and civilian casualties. People living in relatively safe areas of Belfast who had previously watched the Troubles on television, along with the rest of the world, found their daily routines affected. In early September, bombs damaged Bedford House, where the BBC producers who regularly employed Parker had their offices. Traffic jams caused by bomb fires or car searches became a fact of life in the city. Out walking before or after an evening in the pub with Michael Foley and Tom McLaughlin, Parker might be frisked by soldiers, the more so because his artificial leg made it look as if he had a rifle concealed in his trousers. A Catholic neighbour in Rostrevor was warned she would be burned out if she sold a parcel of land to a Protestant. When Stewart and Kate attempted to take Stewart's brother and sister-in-law out to dinner in October, they avoided the city centre because their guests were 'apprehensive about explosions', choosing instead a restaurant on Botanic Avenue, near Queen's. No sooner had they been seated, Parker wrote, than a large bomb went off nearby, clearing the restaurant 'except for us'. They stayed and ate, but all anyone really wanted was to get home safely. Further explosions 'punctuate[d] the conversation' later that evening and continued as Stewart and Kate lay in bed that night. (The first, large detonation turned out to have been in a favourite bookshop.)[8]

About three weeks later, Parker read and judged 'excellent' a speech by Conor Cruise O'Brien, a Labour Party member of Dáil Éireann (the lower house of the Irish parliament). O'Brien made the remarks, published in their entirety in the *Irish Times*, in the context of a debate at University College, Dublin between himself and Tomás Mac Giolla, president of (Official) Sinn Féin. O'Brien began by challenging the basis of Mac Giolla's authority, since 'Sinn Féin is the open, civilian, legal expression of a secret and illegal army.' Rather than abiding by the will of a majority of the people, expressed through their votes, Sinn Féin 'reserves to itself—or rather to the army which it serves—the right to set aside as invalid any decisions of the people, or its elected representatives, which the private army does not like'. Any similarities between the Labour Party's programme and the stated goals of Sinn Féin were overshadowed by this basic difference in the parties' attitudes towards the democratic process, O'Brien asserted. The Officials had been trying for months to distinguish their own activities from the Provisionals' blatantly sectarian attacks, but O'Brien pointed out the absurdity of such a distinction: 'it doesn't matter much to Protestants who are killed or injured, or to their friends, which particular Catholic private army did which particular job'. Protestants in the North, he asserted, saw the IRA, 'in all its varieties', as 'a cruel and deadly enemy' and 'the expression of the hostility of the Catholic community towards Protestants'. Not only was the IRA offensive unjustifiable morally or democratically, O'Brien concluded, but it could not achieve its objective: 'The Northern Catholic Bishops have asked the appropriate question: "Who in their sane senses wants to bomb a million Protestants into a United Ireland?" Who wants to—and also, who in their sane senses thinks they can do it? The attempt can not result in unity.' Impressed by O'Brien's framing of the issues, Parker wrote him a letter in response. O'Brien's arguments chimed with his own view that the paramilitaries on both sides were parasites on their respective communities and his vehement opposition to violence as a means to any political end.[9]

The author of an *Irish Times* leader commenting approvingly on O'Brien's speech remarked, 'How many on the Provisional side will see that, even if their aim is not to provoke retaliation from the Protestant side in the North, the logical result of their actions may be to do exactly that?' In a year dominated by the Provisional offensive, one of the most appalling events was the December explosion in McGurk's Bar in North Queen Street, Belfast, of a bomb planted by the modern-day Ulster Volunteer Force, a group Parker had earlier called 'a kind of Harold Pinter invention, men with sticks of gelignite playing blind man's bluff'. The blast left sixteen people dead and twelve others injured, making it responsible, at the time, for the greatest loss of civilian life in one incident in the conflict.[10]

People were realizing by now that there were no 'civilians' in this conflict. The first year or two of upheaval, Sam Fannin recalls, had been exciting, almost 'fun', with violence formalized in set-piece gun battles between the police and Army and various factions of the IRA. Soon, however, the carnage grew more arbitrary, as pubs, restaurants, shops—anywhere people gathered—became targets.[11] 'Bloody Sunday' on 30 January 1972 marked a major turning-point. At the end of a huge anti-internment rally in Derry, arranged by the Civil Rights Association in defiance of a ban on demonstrations, troops from the British Parachute Regiment fired into the crowd of ten thousand or more, killing thirteen immediately and seriously injuring at least an equal number, one of whom died later. The soldiers claimed to have been fired upon first, but those on the march had a starkly different perception; none of the men killed could be proved to have been holding a gun or a bomb. The event had a devastating impact on mainstream Catholic opinion. John Hume, a local civil rights leader, reported that many in Derry's Bogside now demanded 'a united Ireland or nothing'. Anti-British feeling ran high in the Republic as well as in Northern Ireland. The Irish government recalled its ambassador in London, and on 2 February an angry crowd burned down the British Embassy in Dublin.[12]

The extreme wing of unionism met Catholic outrage in kind. On 9 February, William Craig, hard-line former Northern Ireland Minister for Home Affairs, founded Ulster Vanguard as a forum for disaffected loyalists. At a meeting on 18 March attended by sixty thousand or more people, Craig declaimed, 'We must build up a dossier of the men and women who are a menace to this country, because if and when the politicians fail us, it may be our job to liquidate the enemy.' Such views gained ground in response to even more horrific attacks by the IRA in the wake of Bloody Sunday. On 4 March 1972, for example, a bomb in the Abercorn Restaurant in Belfast, packed with Saturday morning shoppers, exploded with no warning. Two women died instantly; four other people lost both their legs; at least 130 were injured. Certainly Parker, as an amputee, did not need to have the costs—to those maimed as well as to the families and friends of those killed outright—spelled out for him. A few weeks later, a 100-pound Provisional bomb detonated in Lower Donegall Street in Belfast, killing six people and injuring more than a hundred. Not only was there no warning, but a hoax call led people towards the bomb.[13]

The British government had let the Stormont government take the lead on security policy since August 1971; now Heath found the arrangement untenable. He informed Faulkner on 24 March that Westminster would assume law and order powers. As expected, Faulkner and his ministers resigned in protest, and Heath announced that the Stormont government would be suspended for a year, during which Northern Ireland would be administered by a British Secretary of State for Northern Ireland through a new British government department, the Northern Ireland Office. Little did anyone suspect at the time that, apart from a few months in 1974, direct rule from London would last for over twenty-five years. Unfortunately, any hopes that the political changes might lead to a reduction in the level of violence swiftly faded.[14]

In particular, a Provisional car bombing campaign, initiated early in 1972 with the aim of making Northern Ireland prohibitively expensive for the British government to administer, gathered momentum and added to the sense of random terror.

The mere sight of a parked car could arouse suspicion, so leaving one's vehicle on the street in central Belfast might result in its being blown up by the security forces. As civilian casualties mounted, support for the IRA in the Catholic community declined. In response to the uproar over its 'execution' of a British soldier who also happened to be a Derry Catholic home on leave, the Official IRA ended its military activities for good on 29 May 1972. The Provisionals, however, continued fighting.[15]

On 21 July 1972, Parker was teaching summer school at Cornell University. Back in Belfast, Sam Fannin and his daughter sat in a traffic jam, wondering what had caused it. They found out as they drew level with the Oxford Street bus station where, as Alf McCreary describes the scene, 'firemen and rescue workers [were] scraping up the remains of human beings into plastic bags, like lumps of red, jellied meat from the pavement'. Fatalities included people who had been waiting in traffic alongside the station; Fannin remembers thinking that he and his daughter could easily have been among them. They witnessed one part of what rapidly became known as 'Bloody Friday': the Provisionals had detonated twenty bombs within sixty-five minutes in central Belfast, killing nine people and injuring a further 130. Targets included bus and train stations, a taxi office, a hotel, and a shopping centre. Ten days later, the British government took advantage of the reaction against the Provos to launch Operation Motorman, the largest British military operation since the Suez crisis of 1956, to dismantle the barricades marking the boundaries of both republican and loyalist 'no-go' areas and bring the ghettos back under some semblance of Army control.[16]

Although the Provisional IRA had been most obviously on the offensive through the spring and summer of 1972, loyalists had not been quiescent. On 13 May, over sixty people were hurt by a bomb planted in a west Belfast pub, and gun battles between Catholics and Protestants marked May and June. More disturbing to those professing no interest in politics was a sectarian assassination campaign undertaken in retaliation for indiscriminate Provisional bombings. Beginning in April 1972, loyalist 'murder gangs' trawled the streets for Catholics to torture and kill, making no effort to target people actually involved in republican activity. The notorious 'Shankill Butchers', one of the best-known of these gangs, is believed to have committed its first murder right after Bloody Friday. Tom McLaughlin recalls that stepping out at night on any errand became a terrifying experience. An approaching car might contain people bent on killing one, for no other reason than that one happened to be in the wrong place at the wrong time. Although he lived next to Queen's University, where the illusion of safety could usually be maintained, a man had been murdered on Cromwell Road, a few streets away.[17]

All in all, 1972 remains the bloodiest year of the modern Troubles, with 467 people dying as a result of them. There were 10,628 documented shootings and over 1,800 bombs planted. This mayhem had profound social and psychological effects on the population of Northern Ireland. A close friend of Parker's found himself in the summer of 1972 more easily angered than usual, reflecting in his journal, 'When I hear that something has been blown up, I feel so bad inside—like someone[']s taken something from me. THEY HAVE.' Nicholas Round, a member with Parker of the original Belfast Writers' Group, mourned the passing of the vibrancy and sense of possibility that had characterized Belfast, and especially Queen's, in the early 1960s. Local politics became the major topic of conversation, and it grew difficult to get around the city. People left Belfast, and outsiders stopped coming in. Michael Foley departed, starting a job in London that September. Parker pronounced this 'A Good Thing'—he encouraged his friends to get out of Belfast, if only for a while. Foley did not think himself in danger, although the house on Botanic Avenue containing his office had been badly damaged by a car bomb. McLaughlin, also living in London by 1973, felt more urgency about his own decision to leave. His College Green flat had been broken into and 'Fenians get out' written on the wall. He and his wife derived no reassurance from the opinion of the police that the message was not meant 'personally'.[18]

Kate Parker, too, would have preferred to emigrate; friends knew about her wish to live in the US for more than a couple of months a year. She had regretted their return to Belfast in August 1971, and, as the violence worsened, so did her dissatisfaction.[19] Stewart, for his part, did not imagine himself ever leaving Belfast permanently; he found it 'comfortable', he said, 'like an old coat'. Rationalizing in the autumn of 1971 his decision to remain, although it would have been fairly easy for him to go elsewhere, he explained, as a friend recorded, that 'your friends and relations are still here and you'd be worrying about them, it's better to stay on and know things aren't as bad as the papers have them'.[20]

The notion that newspapers might be exaggerating the difficulties faced by ordinary citizens of Belfast must have seemed quaint by the end of 1972, as the violence grew ever more senseless and sickening. Anxiety touched everyone. Sam Fannin, who played the drums in a showband fronted by Derry musician Gay McIntyre, had to be on the road at 2 or 3 a.m. after gigs, an increasingly stressful experience. He would often be stopped by the police or Army, McIntyre 'starting in on the Hail Marys' in the passenger seat beside him. One soldier or policeman would question Fannin and examine his licence, but there would be ten others in the dark that he could not see, although he heard the click of their rifles. Moreover, when someone flagged him down, he could never be sure whom he would encounter when his car came to a halt. Most likely he would find the security forces, but it might also turn out to be one of the paramilitaries. Once, when Fannin was in the country returning to Belfast after a show, two men stepped in front of his car. They opened the passenger door, and he saw they had a gun. Because he could tell they were young and nervous, Fannin pretended not to notice it and asked in a friendly manner if they needed a lift, offering to take them anywhere they wanted. They settled in the back seat, putting away the gun. He left his original passenger, a singer with the band, at her home in north Belfast, and hinted to the hitch-hikers that they, too, might wish to get out at this point. But, no, Fannin had to drive them through narrow back streets to the heart of the Falls district, where they finally asked to be dropped off. He thought they would steal his (company) car, but instead they asked politely if he wanted a fare. Fannin said that would not be necessary but requested some cigarettes, which they gave him. Things like that, he stresses, could happen at any time without warning.[21]

To live their lives, city dwellers cultivated an attitude of fatalism, almost indifference. One surgeon, interviewed by Alf McCreary for his book about the effects of the violence on people, recalled seeing a man, after an explosion, sweeping soot off the carpet in his house as if he 'had done this every day'. Another man, watching a riot near the Grosvenor Road, observed a passerby stop, light his cigarette from the same match that had just been used to ignite a petrol bomb, thank the bomber, and walk on. A friend of Parker's described a gun battle at a housing estate, 'as shown on ... T.V.': 'Pictures of estate show man cutting his grass with push lawnmower right in the middle of the battle. Woman whose house is completely full of bullet holes says, "I'll not leave ... but you know it scares the children a wee bit".' Parker himself commented in his journal in October 1971 that he had 'Lunched in lounge of pub blown up some weeks ago & woman killed—McGlades. V. congenial lounge, excellent sandwiches.'[22]

People kept their 'antennae always working' and became adept at avoiding potential trouble. Survival involved developing a sixth sense about explosions. A friend of Parker's recalls being on Rugby Road, behind Queen's, when he suddenly ducked for no apparent reason. An instant later, a huge bomb went off on Botanic Avenue. He speculated that invisible shock waves must have reached him before the sound did.[23]

Even people who could muster the stoicism necessary to continue going to work or school, doing the grocery shopping, and running essential errands (and not everybody could do this much) curtailed their activity according to the dictates of prudence. There were places one did not go, and other places one did not go at night. One avoided fringe areas, where paramilitaries or murder gangs might be waiting to shoot people they did not recognize. The commercial centre, traditionally shared territory, became a dangerous place because it was so frequently bombed in the early 1970s. People stayed close to home, especially after the Abercorn Restaurant bombing. Tony McAuley, whose work at the BBC often kept him in central Belfast well into the evening, recollects that after about 6 p.m. it would be deserted, like a ghost town. The nightlife of the city took place 'behind the barricades', inside the ghettos. People's mental lives tended to be similarly circumscribed. Although Belfast ran on gossip, one talked freely only with a few friends. Fannin remembers destroying republican pamphlets in his possession, just in case loyalists broke into his flat.[24]

This shutting down of normal social activity in Belfast must have been particularly frustrating for Parker, who enjoyed meeting and talking with a variety of people and maintained ties with a large network of friends. The bombing campaign drove people inward on themselves and their immediate circles. Instead of going out at night, they entertained themselves at home or called at each other's houses. People still went to pubs, but they chose them carefully. Parker met Fannin a couple of times weekly at the Eglantine Inn, which in an effort to bolster security had closed off one of its two entrances, so that access to their favourite bar could now be gained only through the gents toilet. Cinemas, too, continued to do good business, and Parker saw a great many films in the 1970s.[25]

Fortunately for his sanity, he had also developed a new group of friends by 1971, a wildly creative set of Queen's students and recent graduates adept at making their own fun. After spending much time in their company that year, in November Stewart and Kate moved into a shared house with them at 7 Rugby Road.[26] As the Troubles closed in, it was as if Parker surveyed his acquaintances and decided whom he wished to be marooned with. In his unproduced play *Deirdre Porter*, the protagonist Deirdre had daydreamed about people who 'don't scrabble all day in the dirt for money like everybody else does—they live on the bare essentials, and they enjoy most of all each other's company, walking about, sitting drinking, singing to each other and talking and listening'. At No. 7, Parker found such a community, and, like Deirdre, his impulse was 'to join them and then slam shut the door on the whole festering universe'.[27]

The linchpins of the group were John Gilbert and Marcus Patton, friends since their schooldays at Campbell College, one of the most exclusive and conservative public schools in Northern Ireland. As boarders they felt keenly their incarceration, but they found relief from the rugby-dominated ethos of the place in the formation, with a few friends, of 'a rather anarchic literary group' specializing in 'surreal and very tongue-in-cheek material'. Patton spent two or three hours a day in the music practice rooms, playing the piano and developing tastes ranging from early music to avant-garde compositions. Gilbert devised extravagant displays of what he would later learn to call concrete poetry, once filling his study with crumpled newspaper from floor to ceiling and escaping via the window. Both did A-level art and proceeded to Queen's in 1966 to study architecture, finishing their undergraduate course in 1970 and staying on until 1972 to work on Master's degrees (they moved into the Rugby Road flat in 1970). In the spirit of the time, they regarded university as an opportunity to do pretty much what they wanted: painting, drawing, photographing, writing, and organizing exhibits. They helped revive the student magazine *Interest*, founded by Parker in 1960. Gilbert also started a new one, *Crab Grass*, focusing on short poems largely of the fake-serious variety; the endeavour was more about providing excuses for illustrations than about the poetry itself. He and Patton produced five issues between 1969 and 1972, each more elaborate than the last, with special inserts, musical supplements, and foldout pages. This eccentric publication first brought Parker to the door of No. 7, answering the editor's call for 'Projections, communications, visitations, free samples, tenders, correspondence, and contributions'. Parker invited Gilbert to participate in an edition of the arts programme he was compiling and introducing for the BBC. They met in person on the day of the recording, 24 January 1971, and hit it off immediately. 'Your poetry is crap!', Gilbert remembers Parker saying, and he recognized a kindred spirit.[28]

The household at Rugby Road consisted of a floating population of up to about ten people, most artistically inclined. Residents at various times during Parker's tenure included Gerry Thompson (then an architecture student and bicycle enthusiast, later a humour writer and shiatsu expert), David Evans (a practising architect then launching a second career as a painter), and Patrick O'Connor (an Englishman of Irish descent working to establish a community arts centre in the working-class Protestant enclave of Sandy Row). Other friends who visited but did not live there included Brian McKibbin, another architect, and his wife, Nancy, an arts administrator, whose London flat made a handy base for Rugby Road residents visiting the capital. Another member of the group, Joanna Mules, would become a painter and teacher but was then working in a bookstore near Queen's. Stewart persuaded her to retake her A-levels, and Kate tutored her for them.[29] Often around in later years was Gina Leishman, a musician who carried on a long-distance love affair with Gilbert through much of the 1970s.[30] Stewart and Kate were the sole married couple in the house and significantly older than the other residents, apart from Evans, and they quickly became the fulcrum of the community, looked to as role models by most of their younger friends. Evans believes they served almost as hip surrogate parents. Gilbert, in particular, full of urgency and mid-twenties angst and uncertainty, regarded Stewart as a mentor as well as a friend.[31]

These and other creative people contributed to the social activities of the house. Kate regularly visited the War on Want store and bought all the old sheet music she could find from the 1890s through the Second World War period, and she and Patton would accompany the singing for long musical evenings. Gilbert's Victorian magic lantern set provided another form of entertainment. He picked up slides in second-hand shops around Belfast, but rarely got a complete set; the challenge would be to concoct a story that could connect, say, half a set of Great War images and half a set of *Jack and the Beanstalk*. Dramatic readings, charades, and communal meals lasting for hours also passed the time pleasantly.[32]

The friends collaborated on more formal artistic projects too. Parker played his flute as a member of an early music consort organized by Patton to present a concert of medieval carols for the Queen's Music Society in December 1971. Less than a week later, members of the household featured in a lunchtime concert at the other end of the musical spectrum, with Patton's performances of a percussion piece by John Cage and his and Gilbert's modern 'Tomato Sonata'. Gilbert had constructed an inflatable tomato eight feet in diameter out of red plastic bags. This sat alongside the musicians, spitting polystyrene seeds through the first part of the piece; as the music reached a climax, the tomato exploded, and Gilbert stepped out wearing fighter pilot garb with a tomato insignia. The tomato enjoyed a second life as Gilbert's entry in a concrete poetry contest sponsored by the Ulster Museum and Guinness. 'Tomato Road Block', which won a £50 prize, parodied the road blocks that so-called community defence associations were erecting around Belfast. It consisted of the tomato and a road sign with a picture of a tomato on it indicating a tomato ahead. In the summer of 1972, Gilbert put the tomato in the middle of Rugby Road with the road sign next to it, to see how people would react. Everyone seemed to like it; even policemen from a passing Land-Rover simply hopped out and looked at it, laughed, and drove away without demanding that it be taken down.[33]

The Rugby Road social calendar peaked with the annual New Year's Eve banquet, an intensified version of the sort of things that happened there all the time. The nominal host of these extravaganzas was Sir Henry Tonk, a papier-mâché mannequin constructed by Patton in 1970 after he had bought an antique over-sized piano made by an Ernest A. Tonk of New York. Speculating that Tonk pianos had been used in the production of 'honky-tonk' music, he and Gilbert invented a convoluted history for the entire Tonk family, including Henry, Ernest's brother, who ended up in Belfast after a series of melodramatic adventures. (Michael Foley, visiting No. 7, discovered with surprise that Henry Tonk had his own room, with a brass nameplate on the door and a picture of his love, Louisa Nightingale, on the wall.) Ushering in the New Year took the entire day, with a large event in the morning attended by all and sundry and the more select banquet starting in the evening and often lasting until five or six the following morning. Each banquet had a theme reflected in the food (or at least the titles of the courses) and featured 'entertainments'. In 1974, for example, it was Tonk-Oil (celebrating Henry's discovery of oil in the front garden: the menu included such delights as petroleum pâté, oil leeks, and oil things bright and beautiful). Parker frequently closed these gatherings, and similar ones, with his rendition of Frank Sinatra's 'One for My Baby (And One More for the Road)', a song he performed while pretending to get drunker and drunker.[34]

The décor of the house reflected the eclectic interests and aesthetic senses of its inhabitants. Foley recalls specimens of conceptual art, such as a huge, ornate gilt picture frame with a tiny pair of red Y-fronts suspended in the middle. An aviary at the top of the stairs, created by attaching a mesh-covered wooden frame to the cupola, held at one point four birds whose squawking echoed below. Gilbert, who contemplated becoming a professional photographer, had a darkroom in the attic. He and Patton, both lovers of Victoriana and inveterate collectors, constantly brought home bits and pieces of Belfast, readily available because of all the demolition going on. Victorian shop signs and posters vied for attention with a mounted stag's head and stuffed birds, along with objets d'art crafted by the housemates (including an elaborate lampshade fashioned from coat hangers and a gigantic slice of cake made of hardboard and fabric which surmounted the roof of the garage). In the autumn of 1971, Gilbert painted the front door bright red, with the door frame fading out to white in five shades of purple. The gate he painted gold, and the gateposts white with mauve diamonds. Over the door of the house, in red Irish gothic lettering, Gilbert wrote 'La Grande Palace Mysterieuse' (one of many complaints 'the Palace' received from its staider neighbours was that from the Queen's French Department about this 'bad French'.) As Tony McAuley remarks, the flamboyant decoration made 'a statement' at a time when almost everyone else in Belfast was lying low.[35]

The residents of No. 7 never voted on this 'statement', but it concerned non-conformity and the importance of aesthetics in daily life. It expressed their desire to brighten Belfast and not to let themselves be engrossed by the Troubles to the exclusion of everything else. It sought to provoke people passing the house to wonder what was going on inside. The inhabitants of the Palace deplored the increasing isolation of people—in suburbs, cars, and in front of television sets—a trend accelerated in Northern Ireland by the violence. Their ethos was populist and anti-institutional. They hated mass consumer culture and advocated positive individual and community action in the face of the prevailing negativity. As Marcus Patton recalls, 'we weren't just burying our heads in the sand but were very concerned about what was happening to Belfast and places and buildings and people we loved', only 'our reaction was not to mope about it or to take sides in a battle we certainly didn't want, but to look outside (geographically to America or England, historically to the middle ages or Victoriana, to books and music and creativity) for ideas and ideals and humour'.[36] In *Lost Belongings*, Parker based his character Lenny Harrigan's living arrangements on the Rugby Road household.

Not surprisingly, the Palace attracted a great deal of attention. It was robbed at least twice, searched by the Army, and eyed by the drug squad. One of the most memorable of the Palace's uninvited guests, a woman named Margaret wearing a long white evening gown and a red plastic rose, turned up in July 1972 after walking all the way from Aldergrove airport. She said God had sent her over from her home in Southend-on-Sea to solve Northern Ireland's problem, and Christ had directed her to this very door. Gerry Thompson and John Gilbert were alone in the house at the time, and, after she had cooked them omelettes and cleaned the kitchen from top to bottom, they offered her Patton's unoccupied room for the night. She insisted on sleeping in Thompson's room instead. (She wanted to sleep *with* Thompson, but he politely declined.) Bursting into his room next morning, she informed a terrified Gilbert that Christ would allow her to take off her clothes and join him in bed, but only if he wished her to do so. He did not. The young men eventually got her to divulge the name and number of one of her friends; the unfazed woman on the other end of the line promised to have money for a return ticket waiting for Margaret at Aldergrove. Thompson escorted her to the bus terminal, where, getting on the bus, she told the driver, 'Jesus sent me', and he replied, 'Did Jesus give you money for the fare?' Parker imported this incident wholesale into the fourth of his *Lost Belongings* films, 'Lenny Leaps In'. In his retelling, though, an English journalist, unlike Gilbert and Thompson, succumbs to the woman in white's blandishments.[37]

Thompson left Belfast for Nottingham shortly after this episode. Patton, too, departed in the summer of 1972, to take up a conservation job in Edinburgh. By the end of the year he had bought a flat in Edinburgh which quickly developed into a Palace annex. He took in lodgers to help with the mortgage, including Gina Leishman and a librarian named Steph Pickering who soon became a staple at Tonk banquets with her Marlene Dietrich impersonation. The exodus from No. 7 mirrored a larger pattern of emigration from Northern Ireland by middle-class professionals. Gilbert recalls that most people from his year at Queen's left after completing their courses; the violence exacerbated a pre-existing tendency for people with higher educational qualifications to seek wider prospects. This meant that people like Gilbert and Parker, who remained, made a point of doing so, but it also meant they spent a fair amount of time wondering why they were staying and if they should.[38]

Parker's uncertainties centred on his career, since the need to earn money to live on largely dictated what writing he did. He still worked regularly for the Schools Department of BBC Northern Ireland, despite the constraints imposed by the unit's 'miserly' budgets as BBC management shifted more resources to news coverage of the Troubles. He continued to write his *High Pop* column for the *Irish Times*, and he reviewed books for the *Irish Times* and *Irish Press*. He also worked frequently for BBC Northern Ireland's Arts Programmes Department, which (like Schools but unlike the Radio Drama Department) could make programmes specifically for Northern Ireland, although it also produced pieces for the national network. Beginning in 1972 or 1973, Parker contributed often to *Saturday Review*, a radio programme presented by Tony McAuley's sister Róisín, critiquing books, plays, records, and cultural phenomena. Starting in April 1974, he also featured monthly on another BBC arts programme called *Bookends*. Parker and three other reviewers engaged in spontaneous chat about three or four books of current interest, including but not limited to new fiction; their conversation was recorded and edited for broadcast. He would, on occasion, serialize books for broadcast by the BBC, dividing them into sections of precisely the right length—such efforts, in 1971/2, included a detective novel entitled *May You Die in Ireland*. Like Lenny in *Lost Belongings*, Parker was your man for 'reviews, previews, interviews, overviews, whatever you care to name, pal'.[39]

He also continued to work as an educator in various capacities. In 1972 and 1973, he put a great deal of time and thought into another project for John Malone: a collection of original short stories aimed at teenaged boys who could not read well, lacked interest in school, and came from areas of social deprivation. *The Bus Stories* utilize almost a comic book format, with colourful illustrations by Marcus Patton. Each tale is told from the perspective of an adolescent boy, and all take place on city buses. Parker saw riding a bus as a universal experience, at least for people without much money, and situations unfolding on buses could thus engage boys from both sides of the sectarian divide. The stories consist mainly of the narrator's descriptions of other passengers, including a drunk man trying to manoeuvre a 24-inch television set down the bus aisle, a child who sticks his head out the window and cannot get it back in, a learning-impaired classmate the narrator fights with against his better instincts, and a haggard bus driver who snaps and drives out of the city to the seaside. The deeper significance of the sketches lies in the narrator's reactions to the events he witnesses and takes part in and the hints offered about his family difficulties and negative self-image. As the author of a glowing review in the *Education Times* noted, the stories 'don't offer a "moral" . . . but they may contribute to moral education by helping young people towards a keener awareness of themselves and of other people'. In addition to the function of *The Bus Stories* as a classroom text, David Hammond televised several of them in November 1973 for BBC Schools.[40]

Another educational undertaking that involved Parker in the early 1970s was Interplay, a theatre group established by the Arts Council of Northern Ireland in 1972 to tour secondary and grammar schools, performing classic and documentary plays. One purpose of the company was to provide employment for Northern actors robbed of their livelihood by the public's growing inclination to stay at home in the evenings. These included well-known locals like Stella McCusker, J. J. Murphy, and Catherine Gibson. Hubert and Dorothy Wilmot, whose Arts Theatre had closed its doors on 14 October 1971 as a result of the civil unrest, managed Interplay. The artistic director, Denis Smyth, had just returned to Belfast after fellowship studies abroad. He brought enthusiasm about the 'Joan Littlewood approach' (integrating projections, song, and mime with the drama) to the enterprise, along with a commitment to hire local writers. Parker wrote two hour-long pieces on commission for the company: *The Trial of Mr. Pickwick*, a stage adaptation of Charles Dickens's *The Pickwick Papers*, in 1973 and *The Blue and the Grey*, a play about the American Civil War, in 1975. These scripts paid modestly, but Interplay productions were seen by a great many young people throughout Northern Ireland, a likely source of satisfaction for the playwright.[41]

Parker engaged directly in instruction as well. In September 1970 he had been offered, and declined, a tutorial post at Queen's. Two years later, however, he accepted an invitation from Louis Muinzer to teach for the Queen's Extramural Department, 'The People's Department'. This continuing education programme offered university-level courses to people who wanted to study simply for the love of learning rather than for degrees. Muinzer liked to recruit local writers as instructors because he thought they should have contact with their immediate audience. Parker taught weekly classes in Irish literature in the autumns of 1972 and 1973 and the winters of 1973 and 1974. These were 'imaginatively conceived', Muinzer recalls, covering material ranging from the ancient Irish saga *Táin Bó Cuailnge* to the work of Parker's contemporaries and lavishing particular attention on Parker's favourite writers (Swift, Beckett, Joyce) and on twentieth-century Irish drama. One of his students remembers him as a 'wonderful', 'inspirational' teacher. He always brought a box of books to class to lend students, and afterwards he would go to a pub with them or bring them back to Rugby Road to listen to records.[42]

Amid all this activity, Parker's 'own' work had to be fitted into spare moments. Despite his profound reservations about contemporary poetry, he remained for a time ambitious for his own, partly because, as he later remarked, 'In Irish culture, poetry is still the supreme form.' In November 1971, he received a £300 bursary from the Arts Council of Northern Ireland. These awards were intended to relieve financial pressure on writers so they could devote more time to creative work. Parker then described his current projects as 'a radio play based on the theme of Deirdre and the Sons of Usna, but in the context of Belfast today', a 'translation into modern verse of the 9th century Irish work, "The Voyage of St. Brendan"', and 'a long sequence of poems'.[43] None of these projects came to fruition in the 1970s—a circumstance that may have had something to do with Parker's future difficulty coaxing funds out of the Arts Council.

John Scotney, then radio drama producer for BBC Northern Ireland, had invited Parker to adapt his Deirdre play for radio, but he expressed doubt about whether or not he would be able to sell the script to the national network, a necessary prelude to production. Probably this offered insufficient incentive for Parker to invest his limited time in the rewrite; anyway, Scotney left Belfast shortly after issuing the invitation.[44] Parker's interest in the Brendan story burned more intensely in 1971; he and Kate travelled in September to sites associated with the seafaring saint in counties Kerry, Clare, and Galway. Parker also read numerous books on Brendan and, armed with his schoolboy Latin and a Latin dictionary, was indeed working on a verse translation (never completed) of the Hiberno-Latin voyage narrative *Navigatio Sancti Brendani Abbatis*.[45]

Parker came closest to finishing the sequence of poems he called 'Parker's Fitts'. This had been mentioned in his journal as early as the spring of 1969, and, at the end of that year, Parker had included it on a list of projects lying 'in abeyance' owing to 'commercial necessity'. He worked on individual poems through 1970 and 1971, and by December 1971 he had fifteen in a more or less final state. An undated list of first lines includes twenty-six numbered poems, at least nineteen of which were published or broadcast in 1972 and 1973.[46] The Fitts are untitled short poems of irregular length and form. Though touted as 'love poems' in a reading Parker did for BBC Scotland in early 1973, they abound in violent and surreal imagery. In one, the speaker compares his 'ecstasy' to 'a jackdaw crashing down the chimney' with 'soiled demented wings'; in another, hounds tear a hare into 'wriggling stumps'; others mention blood, bombs, and 'ambulances/sliding by with unspeakable cargo'.[47] Oblique references to Parker's amputation and to the Northern Irish Troubles pervade the sequence.

Several of the poems share an implied protagonist (Parker's alter ego), a modern incarnation of Thomas Rhymer, hero of a medieval border ballad depicting his abduction by the queen of Elfland; he is required to serve her for seven years, after which she returns him to the world and rewards him with the power of prophecy. This ballad was one of Parker's five 'sacred texts'. In undated notes made perhaps years later, he enumerated and explicated them thus:

> Jacob & the Angel—my condition (lame)
> Thomas Rhymer (border ballad)—my calling
> Sleeping Beauty—my poetic soul
> Brendan the Navigator—my aspiration
> The Ancient Mariner—my fate

Allusions to any of these in a Parker work generally carry deep private significance, and the Fitts contain several. In addition to the references to Thomas, one of the poems (originally dedicated to Kate) ends with an allusion to the biblical story of Jacob, crippled in wrestling all night with a 'man' (popularly taken to be an angel) from whom he ultimately extracts a blessing and acquires the new name of Israel. Parker incorporates this idea of simultaneous wounding and sanctifying in an image of communion painful as well as sustaining: 'there's no salve,/no being saved, except we bless/our angel wrestlers up every street/and down again. I love you.' Brendan does not appear explicitly, but the poetic persona of the Fitts is, like him, a traveller. Instead of sailing in a curragh, however, he rides on a city bus; the first Fitt begins with the line 'Here's the bus now. All aboard please.'[48] (In undated typed notes, Parker had advanced a 'definition' of poetry as 'a bus ride from the suburb to…City Hall. Or rather the red bus itself, in which you sit', poet and reader passing 'objects without relationships, disjointed images' among which the poet begins to make 'correspondences' so that 'when the reader finally steps off at the terminus, he will know that he has reached the heart of an organism like a rose'.) Despite their personal meaning, however, and the years Parker evidently spent thinking about and writing them, the Fitts were not published in book form in his lifetime.[49]

Thus, by the mid-1970s, it might have appeared that all these purportedly major projects had come to nothing. Nevertheless, they laid the groundwork for notable achievements in years to come. These three examples illustrate the strikingly retentive quality of Parker's mind and the tenacity with which he held on to and reworked ideas once they grasped his imagination. The Deirdre story ultimately served as the framework for *Lost Belongings*, which encapsulated much of his experience of living in Northern Ireland through the 1970s. Parker's fascination with St Brendan found its eventual expression in his stage play *Pratt's Fall*, about the discovery of a map that might—or might not—prove that Irish monks beat Columbus to the New World. And Parker explored the literary and psychological resonances of his 'sacred texts' (and the implacable reality of death) more fully than in the Fitts in his expressionist play *Nightshade* and his autobiographical novel *Hopdance*.

Hopdance was arguably the most significant, though least-discussed, of Parker's literary endeavours of the early 1970s. For nearly ten years after his amputation, Parker lived with the constant fear that his cancer would recur. In his late twenties, he decided to confront the 'longer term psychological effects' of the fact that 'a big bit of my body was gone to the grave'. In one of the Fitts, the speaker asks, 'Do you ever take pity on your own lost face?/A fragile convalescent face,/scarcely a vestige, pale spectral/flotsam afloat in the fluid gloaming.' *Hopdance*, discussed in the third chapter of this book in the context of Parker's amputation, takes a sustained look at Parker's younger self just before, during, and after his bout with cancer. The protagonist's name, Tosh, signifies his callowness before this ordeal, and the novel depicts his initiation, through unspeakable pain, into a more authentic relationship with the world and with those around him.[50]

Parker held that 'the worst experience a writer can have is one that is far beyond the reach of language, as pain is'. The physical dimension of his loss had overwhelmed any other response in the immediate aftermath of his surgery; for some time following his release from hospital, he remembered, 'I was in terrible pain, I was in a stupor.... I was drifting through life in a dream.' He came to believe that he had been in a state of shock, 'so preoccupied with trying to survive that there [was] no time for thinking about anything else'. After the shock faded, a resolute determination to resume his life as if the amputation were merely a minor inconvenience helped Parker smother his knowledge that it might be 'seven or eight years' before he could assume the amputation had removed all cancerous cells from his body. In February 1970, he suddenly felt the urge to treat his story more directly than he could in his poetry, as a form of catharsis. In the manuscript, Tosh, trying to sell the Productions Committee of the Dramatic Society on his idea for a play based on 'The Rime of the Ancient Mariner', identifies the 'artistic impulse' as a kind of 'confessional fever': 'It's the obsessive need to rehearse your memory of hell. If you don't enact it from time to time, it'll rend out your heart.'[51]

In addition to this compulsion to relive an excruciating time in his life, one he rarely discussed even with his closest friends, Parker also sought to endow the experience with meaning in light of what came before and after it. Before his cancer diagnosis, Tosh is afflicted with a 'canker' of loneliness; by the end of the novel, he is reaching out to other people, convinced that 'it's only through each other that we exist at all'. In the last scene of the manuscript, Tosh shares his story with a one-legged beggar and finds, in that exchange, a measure of freedom and peace. Like Stephen Dedalus, the protagonist of Joyce's *A Portrait of the Artist as a Young Man* (which surely influenced Parker in the telling of his own story), Tosh in a moment of crisis sets the vocational course of his life. Both young artists reject tacit expectations on them to achieve 'success' in a manner that would appear sensible to their respective families and societies, in order to devote themselves to the more uncertain fortunes of creative writing. This theme in *Hopdance* is sometimes obscured by the vivid details of Tosh's gruelling experience, but Parker foreshadows his future direction near the end of the scene immediately before the amputation. Tosh spends his last hours before the pre-operative drugs make him incapable of coherent thought writing 'a fairsized essay on the state of poetry in contemporary society'.[52]

Parker originally entitled the piece *Caution in the Traffic, Prudence in the Rain*, and at first he envisaged it as a screenplay, which may account in part for its episodic nature.[53] The psychological subject-matter lent itself more readily to novelistic treatment, but Parker retained a structure of non-chronological vignettes. He worked on it sporadically in 1970 and 1971 and more steadily through 1972 and 1973, finishing a draft on 24 September 1973. He began tinkering with the order of the scenes and typing a final draft, but by early 1975 he acknowledged to himself that he had lost interest in the project; he had needed to write the book but could not summon the energy to polish and revise it. 'I've spent too long considering it,' he observed in his journal, 'I don't know what it's trying to be anymore. Only thing that's certain is, it's too short for publishers.' Uncharacteristically, Parker made no attempt to get this novel, or any excerpts from it, into print. Instead, as he told an interviewer in 1977, he put the manuscript aside, convinced it had served a private, therapeutic purpose for him.[54]

Hopdance also helped Parker to evolve work habits that would enable him to write the things he cared about even amid the pressures of paid work with more immediate deadlines. Possibly as the result of a New Year resolution, he recorded on 10 January 1972 the completion of his 'first daily chore of 300 words'. The discipline enforced by having a production goal proved useful to Parker, and he adapted this system for most of his creative work thereafter. By the mid-1980s, with a more ambitious quota of three handwritten pages, he pursued this mode of writing almost fetishistically, refusing to let even moving house disrupt his established work habits and not stopping on any given day until he had produced his three pages.[55]

In the early 1970s, however, there were too many competing demands on Parker's time to allow him the luxury of total concentration. In addition to the teaching and reviewing that paid the bills, he assisted his friends with some of their projects. John Gilbert, especially, spurred him to idealistic action. Like most socially concerned young architects of the late 1960s and early 1970s, Gilbert took an interest in urban planning. While politics in Northern Ireland tended to fixate on the national question, two interlocking planning initiatives being implemented at this time would have farther-reaching effects than the bombers on the future shape of Belfast. Redevelopment and the Belfast Urban Motorway had both been mooted shortly after the Second World War, but the Unionist regime did not focus on them until the 1960s. With declining shipbuilding and linen industries, Northern Ireland needed to attract new manufacturers. Belfast, however, was overcrowded, with insufficient housing and expensive land. The Stormont government accordingly hoped to lure industry to 'growth areas' near Belfast, rather than to the capital itself. A 'stop line' established a green belt around Belfast, limiting building to inside the existing city limits or well outside them. Government planners sought to relieve congestion in the city by encouraging people to leave for the growth areas, where they would provide labour for the projected new industries, and considered a modern motorway system essential to transport goods and raw materials between the areas earmarked for industrial development and the docks in Belfast and Larne.[56]

Little of this grand scheme took shape according to plan, although Belfast clearly required some sort of redevelopment. As late as 1974, a House Condition Survey exposed almost 25 per cent of all dwellings in the Belfast urban area as 'statutorily unfit'. In the inner city west of the Lagan, this figure approached 50 per cent; nearly a quarter of the houses there had been built before 1870, and about one-third lacked basic amenities like washbasins and indoor toilets. Gilbert knew well the substandard living conditions endured by many of Belfast's poorer residents, having first observed them in early 1968 when he took photographs in Sandy Row, a loyalist neighbourhood near Queen's, to illustrate an article for *Interest* written by another undergraduate. This introduction to working-class culture led to 'further walkabouts' with a camera, in the course of which Gilbert encountered Divis Flats under construction. This high- and medium-rise complex, like nearby Unity Flats, represented a late-1960s response to the fact that Catholics, in particular, hesitated to move out to the predominantly Protestant growth areas. The stop line limited the land available for new houses, so the Belfast Corporation tried building up instead. Residents, desperate to stay in the area, at first welcomed the initiative, but even before their completion the flats were plagued by problems common to large low-income housing projects around the world. The Northern Ireland Housing Executive, which took control of public housing away from local councils in 1971 to ensure a fairer allocation of resources, soon abandoned the multi-storey model, but much damage had already been done. Gilbert dates his passion for social housing from his first visit to the Divis Flats site, remembering his shock at 'the inhumane process by which people were rehoused and the conditions that they had to live in' and noting, '[t]he values and cohesion of the community seemed to count for nothing'. One tour of the area, he maintains, 'changed my life': 'From then on I have been interested in working with communities to help them improve housing conditions on their own grounds.'[57]

Partly because of the Troubles, which politicized people while simultaneously contributing to a breakdown in city services, the number of active community

groups in Belfast had increased exponentially after 1971, with some 300 in existence by 1973. Gilbert worked with such groups on both sides of the sectarian
divide. He began by volunteering with the Sandy Row Redevelopment Association, producing their newsletter and providing drawings in support of their campaign for new terraced housing instead of flats. Later, Gilbert became an ad hoc
member of the Markets Redevelopment Association. Members feared the imminent destruction of their neighbourhood, since the planners had recommended
replacing the houses with flats and doubling the width of Cromac Street, bisecting
the community. The association distributed a questionnaire to every household in
the Catholic district, which garnered a 97 per cent response rate and helped them
make their successful case for new terraced housing to the authorities. Gilbert
attended the group's meetings to take notes and translate the tenants' ideas to
paper. After these weekly gatherings, which typically lasted for hours, he and a
couple of other members of the association would repair to Rugby Road and talk
until 2 or 3 a.m., frequently joined by Parker.[58]

Gilbert and others involved in community advocacy at this time quickly came
to see plans for the Belfast Urban Motorway, or BUM, as one of the biggest threats
to the integrity of working-class districts of the city.[59] Traffic consultants commissioned in 1965 had advised the construction of three ring roads. The innermost,
running through central Belfast, was to be an elevated motorway six lanes wide
and 30 feet high. The first phase of this construction, joining the M1 and M2
through west Belfast, had been approved in 1969 with little controversy. Owing to
the Troubles, however, work had not begun in earnest. Meanwhile, some people
were starting to question the wisdom of a transportation plan biased towards cars.
Damage to the environment, more traffic fatalities, a decline in the quality and
quantity of public transport, and the cost of building and maintaining an upgraded
road system were mentioned as negative consequences of an urban motorway.

In Belfast, where roads and badly needed public housing competed for the same
land and resources, there were other objections. The motorway was slated to run
through redevelopment districts, since land was cheaper in these areas and easier to
obtain. This meant that working-class people who would benefit least from the
motorway would suffer most because of it. The motorway as envisaged would
consume 300 acres of land and require the demolition of 7,000 houses. These
gigantic roads would slice through neighbourhoods, in some cases destroying large
parts of them. In Sandy Row, for instance, the original plans would have entailed
790 of the 2,400 houses being torn down and another 500 made unfit for
habitation.

Even on paper, the motorway wreaked havoc on Belfast's poor. The mere suggestion that it could be built in a particular area accelerated urban blight, since landlords
stopped putting money into properties they might have to sell at any moment and
the housing authorities delayed redevelopment projects pending decisions on the
motorway's route. Moreover, in addition to the motorway itself, the transportation
plan recommended 'improvements' to major radial roads to enable them to carry
more traffic faster. These streets had been the hearts of their respective communities,
and opponents of the motorway predicted that making them less pedestrian-oriented

would reduce people's sense of identity with their neighbourhoods. Liberals also noticed disapprovingly that the motorway was routed to create a permanent barrier between Protestant and Catholic ghettos in parts of west Belfast.

As the volume of criticism increased, authorities responded with a new public inquiry into the Belfast Urban Area Plan. The inspector heard thirty-three days of submissions in February, March, and April 1972, the most exhaustive critique being offered by the Sandy Row Redevelopment Association, aided by Gilbert. The official report on the inquiry also records among the witnesses '**Mr. Stewart Parker and Mr. John Gilbert** both of 7 Rugby Road Belfast': 'Mr. Parker represented people's emotional feelings about the City so aptly described in Mr. Brett's book "Buildings of Belfast 1700–1914". Mr. Gilbert shared Mr. Parker's views and they were concerned lest the city would suffer if given over to the motor-car and become an inhuman and sterile environment.' Gerry Thompson recalls that Parker spoke eloquently about Belfast as a radial city; one could look up any of its main arteries and see green hills, but an inner ring road would spoil this effect. In addition to such aesthetic considerations and their solidarity with the working-class people who would be most negatively affected by the already-approved phase one of the inner ring road, the members of the Rugby Road household felt directly threatened by the larger plans. Phase two of the project would run through the heart of the university district, cutting Queen's off from the city centre.[60]

Wishing to influence policy but recognizing that their testimony as individuals would not be taken seriously, the residents of the Palace and some friends constituted themselves in May 1973 as the Belfast Urban Study Group (BUS). With Parker as honorary secretary, the group argued that 'the Belfast Urban Motorway should be abandoned and an alternative transportation plan produced for the city'. Using the example of Nottingham, a city about the size of Belfast which had traded its urban motorway plans for a comprehensive public transportation scheme, BUS urged the politicians to reassert control over a process dominated by an administrative inertia in which 'each past decision is being used to justify the next'. BUS followed the motorway debate, issuing communiqués at regular intervals and summarizing the case against it in two booklets, *The B. U. S. Report on the Belfast Urban Motorway* (1973) and *The Off-White Elephant* (1974), designed to provide community groups fighting the motorway with ammunition. The group lobbied politicians—including representatives of the Social Democratic and Labour Party (the mainstream nationalist party), Alliance (a bi-communal liberal unionist party), and the Unionist Party—and staged a teach-in on the motorway on 6 October 1973.[61]

As part of this public relations campaign, Parker wrote a radio feature produced by Brian Barfield of Arts Programmes and broadcast on 2 October 1973. *Safe as Houses: The Great Belfast Urban Motorway Show* takes a satirical look at the rising costs and declining quality of life accompanying the motorway's development as seen through the eyes of a long-suffering working-class couple, Bertie and Bridget Polarity. Barfield recalls that the piece 'caused enormous political problems' for him, having to be vetted by the BBC Controller of Northern Ireland himself. The Controller stipulated a 'right of reply' for the builders of the ring road, so a substantive discussion of the issues followed Parker's feature. The following month, the script of *Safe as Houses* appeared in the Northern Irish news magazine *Fortnight*.[62]

The biggest triumph of the anti-motorway forces came in October 1973, when the new Belfast Council, which replaced the Belfast Corporation as part of local government reform that year, endorsed a motion calling on the government (under direct rule, Westminster rather than Stormont) to reconsider if a ring road were needed. David Cook, an Alliance councillor, proposed the motion, and a councillor from the Shankill, Fred Proctor, explained his vote for it thus, 'The plans will harm our people. The SDLP are also against them for what they will do to their people, and on this I think they are right.' Eddie Meehan, secretary of the Lower Falls Residents' Association, was quoted in the *Observer* as saying, 'UDA, UVF—I don't care who they are when they're trying to stop the motorway.' As an English journalist covering the story commented, the controversy was 'showing the opposing sectarian groups that they have at least some things in common'. Unfortunately, as a result of the reorganization, district councils had lost all power over roads and planning, so the Belfast Council's recommendations were purely advisory. Nevertheless, BUS and others could now point out that elected officials as well as community groups opposed the ring road. Shortly afterwards, Parker and Gilbert were featured discussing their crusade in the *Irish Times*. 'The days of the car are numbered', Parker declared. 'You have only to go into an American city to see how devastating it is to concentrate on the car. The heart of the city decays, housing is run down, the whites have fled to the suburbs, leaving the centre to the blacks. It is all strangled by roads.' 'If the motorway were carried through,' according to Parker, 'Belfast would be much more drastically altered than it has been by the bombing. . . . It is a sorry look out when you are blown up on the one hand and on the other pulled down by the redevelopers.'[63]

Ultimately, BUS did not achieve its goal of persuading the government to adopt 'a totally new transport policy for Belfast which involves scrapping not only the Motorway but the majority of the other road improvements at present being carried out'. The Belfast Council, after much arm-twisting by the Ministry of Development, reversed its earlier vote in July 1974, and construction of phase one of the motorway proceeded, along with the upgrading of major arteries in the city. From John Gilbert's perspective, the effort had failed. Phases two and three, however, were 'postponed' indefinitely, and BUS deserves some credit for that.[64]

In the spring of 1973, Gilbert had initiated another project: the restoration of 9 Rugby Road. This house—like No. 7, owned by Queen's—had stood empty as long as Gilbert and Marcus Patton could remember. They suspected the university administration of waiting until the lease on No. 7 ran out to demolish both large Victorian dwellings to use the land for something else. Preservationists at heart, they hated the thought of this. Even after Patton moved to Edinburgh, Gilbert continued to wonder how to save No. 9. He conceived the idea of approaching Queen's with a creative proposal, convincing the administration to let them renovate the house, providing all supplies and labour themselves, in exchange for five years' rent-free occupancy once the work was done. He secretly hoped Queen's would not destroy it once it had been restored to its glory. Meanwhile, the Palace's occupants would be allowed to extend their lease on No. 7 until No. 9 became habitable.[65]

The task was immense. Parker pitched in willingly, but his artificial leg kept him from some jobs and he lacked skill at others. He devoted long hours to No. 9 while in Belfast, but never enough to satisfy Gilbert. Madeleine Stewart, who moved into No. 7 in the summer of 1973, provided Gilbert with significant financial and practical support, but he did most of the work. He later calculated that he spent 1,874 hours on the project between late June 1973 and October 1974, when he, the Parkers, and Madeleine finally moved into No. 9. Gina Leishman remembers him as 'fanatical' about it, fired by a vision of the restored house with a happy household in it. Gilbert himself worried that he was using the renovation to hide from the 'battles of the world' but also understood implicitly the psychological need the project satisfied for him; he worked, he observed in his journal, 'as if I'm piecing together all the broken pieces'. The restoration gave rise to much tension among the housemates, but the 'Nouvelle Palace' justified for a time the effort that went into it.[66]

John Fairleigh, an urbane acquaintance from university days who taught psychology at Queen's, also had designs on Parker's time and energy. Recently returned from several years abroad on the Continent and in the US, he lived across the Botanic Gardens from Rugby Road at 11 Colenso Parade. There he entertained people from an extraordinary range of Belfast networks. Among his manifold interests, Fairleigh belonged to groups advocating more constructive treatment of offenders, and he sympathized with the plight of internees and political prisoners from a general position in favour of educational services for the incarcerated. As a member of a board of visitors to Long Kesh prison camp, Fairleigh discovered there was almost nothing for inmates to do and convinced the authorities to allow instructors in to teach classes if he could find qualified people to do so voluntarily. He recruited thirty or forty teachers to offer classes at Long Kesh at least once a week, though he recalls that prison administrators, citing security concerns, treated the operation with 'suspicion and a certain amount of obstructiveness'.[67]

In the *Irish Times* piece he had written about his teaching stint at Allenwood Prison Camp in New York State, Parker had opined that 'it is in the prisons and not in the courthouses that part of the destiny of the country is being spun'. No doubt he believed the same applied in Northern Ireland. He volunteered to teach a creative writing class at Long Kesh, which met from July to December 1973. In addition to writing, he exposed the inmates to drama, often of a political nature (Sam Thompson's *Over the Bridge*, Brendan Behan's *The Quare Fellow*, Bertolt Brecht's *Galileo*). His introduction to Long Kesh left him 'Unstrung', but over the course of his seventeen visits he developed a great rapport with his students. Parker regarded the young Provisional IRA leader Gerry Adams as one of the brightest of these, though he had difficulty reconciling Adams's obvious intelligence with his defence of physical force as a political tactic. Voluntary teaching was a pastime Parker could ill afford, especially with lengthy security checks added on either side of a two-hour class, but the Long Kesh sessions offered him a fascinating glimpse of a side of Northern Irish life shrouded from public view. He remarked to John Gilbert at one point that the prisoners seemed to be looking with unusual interest at a chair he sat on while leading his classes—eventually he learned they had been digging a tunnel beneath it. Later, Parker heard with an insider's understanding the story of a visiting lecturer kidnapped by his class and made to disrobe so that an inmate who looked like him could don his clothes and leave the prison openly; he got as far as the final exit door before being noticed and apprehended.[68] Parker would use the tale in the third of his *Lost Belongings* films, 'A Wanted Man', only in his version the prisoner's escape attempt succeeds. In 1973, however, Parker did not rush to incorporate this experience into his creative writing.

The first of Parker's literary works conceived with the Troubles in mind was a dramatic poem called 'Requiem' commissioned by Radio 3, written in the summer of 1973, produced by Brian Barfield, and aired as part of the BBC Northern Ireland arts anthology programme *Causeway* on 18 August 1973. He composed the piece specifically for radio (part of their brief, Barfield recalls, was to do something in the medium that could not be done in any other); integral to it are sound effects, a protagonist's voice on two separate tracks, and interpolations by two other voices, all woven into one kaleidoscopic whole.[69] Parker sought to recreate the aftermath of a pub bombing, and the piece opens with pub noise cut suddenly by the sound of a detonation fading to a low roar as the first voice track picks up. 'I always knew this would happen', the voice of a middle-aged man intones calmly; the same voice, more excited, exclaims shortly afterwards on track two, 'I never thought this would happen.' The speaker on track one regrets not leaving Belfast when he had the chance, and he remembers on track two his youthful failure to return to a fish trap he left set in a river and declares himself haunted by the thought of the fish his action might have condemned to death.

The pub noise shifts to church noise, and a minister discourses on the city, become 'as a widow'. 'Blood on the kerbs./Ghost town', the minister concludes, and a female voice with a piercing working-class Belfast accent comes up in the middle of a sentence:

> . . . . we're
> taking a deputation
> she says, I'm
> leading a delegation
> down the town, never
> mind your deputation,
> I says, if you'd take
> a delegation into
> your hearts it'd serve
> you better, if you'd
> make a few demands
> there, and that's the
> God's honest truth . . .

This voice, which contrasts sharply with what comes before and after it, locates the root of the violence in sectarian animosity.

The protagonist, who takes over again immediately after this, is more concerned with its results. At the end of the piece his voice on the two separate tracks chants in unison: 'The streets are full of our ghosts/There's a legion in the streets now./The streets are teeming with us now.' After a brief pause, the voice on the first track continues alone with a repetition of the minister's words, 'Blood on the kerbs. Ghost/town', followed after another pause by the sound of an automatic weapon firing. 'Requiem' closes quietly with the voice on track one in prayer: 'Holy God./ Give me peace./Give us birth./Give us birth.' This piece—read by Denys Hawthorne, Graeme Roberts, and Catherine Gibson—closed the *Causeway* programme. Its treatment of the bloodshed, unusually direct in Parker's *oeuvre*, signalled the importance that ghosts would have for him throughout his writing career.[70]

Meanwhile, the paramilitaries showed no signs of suspending their operations. Two incidents in the summer and early autumn of 1973 hit uncomfortably close to Rugby Road. First, a popular social worker named Sean Armstrong, a contemporary of Parker at Queen's, was killed by what Seamus Heaney, in an elegy for him, called a 'pointblank teatime bullet'. It was unclear which side had done it, but someone had apparently suspected him of being a police informer. Community workers existed, again in Heaney's words, '[d]angerously out between' the opposing factions; in the early years of the Troubles, the security forces courted public opinion by providing food, equipment, and entertainment for play schemes, so social workers could easily look suspicious. The murder of Armstrong, well-known and well-liked, sent shock waves through the network of social activists. Parker's house-mate Patrick O'Connor departed Belfast for good within a month of it, and John Gilbert could not bring himself to write anything about it in his journal, 'save that those living must somehow live a fuller life to make up for it'.[71]

A few months later, another friend received paramilitary threats. Ron Wiener, active in BUS as a volunteer community planner in the Shankill Road district, left the city temporarily after a story in the Provisionals' newspaper accused him and his colleagues of being British 'academic spies'. Wiener, an English social psychologist funded by the Cadbury and Rowntree Trusts to study ways in which social scientists might help working-class communities, ran the Northern Ireland Research Institute. Though his own work focused mainly on loyalists, another researcher had been carrying out surveys in the Catholic housing estate Andersonstown which drew the ire of the Provos and prompted the allegation that information gathered was 'passed straight to the British Army for repression and to the British Government for policy formation'. The *Sunday Times* highlighted the episode in a front-page story on 23 September 1973, reporting that 'The researchers had spent several days preparing a detailed rebuttal of similar IRA rumours but they stopped work immediately [after the article appeared in *Republican News*], fearing that their own lives and those of anyone associating with them might be in danger.' Gilbert perceived the Provisionals' real target: 'the "reformists" who help people to channel their energies in community activities like planning instead of letting them go out and kill somebody in the cause of the "real" (bullet in the head) marxist revolutionaries'. Gilbert knew himself to be vulnerable to such charges owing to his involvement with the Markets Redevelopment Association; on one level, he reflected, it all seemed like a game, only 'it's not exciting, it's bloody harrowing'.[72]

The pervasive stress also affected writers and writing. As one of the participants in a radio investigation of 'The Artist's Conflict in Ulster', prepared by John Fairleigh for the BBC World Service that June, Parker had insisted it was too early for lasting works of art to be emerging from the Troubles. 'You'll find', he said, 'that in most historical periods where there has been great social unrest and change, writers and artists in general have not been able to respond whilst they—the thing was happening to them. They've needed time to detach themselves from it, to meditate upon it, and to work up... forms to cope with it.' For the Northern Irish artist, the 'situation' was 'bred into one's bones', so 'one is not simply affected by the last four years of actual warfare. One is affected by the last, in my case, thirty-one years of social tension: in the family, in the community, in school and university, and so on.' This tension could not be adequately comprehended by 'writing plays, or poems, or stories about street fighting'. Such surface realism would never, he believed, capture the truth of the times. 'It seems to me,' Parker declared, 'that what is needed is a development of some kind of surrealistic form. If one reads a daily newspaper or watches a television broadcast here, this is what strikes one: the kind of crazy insanity of the juxtaposition of events. And so far nobody has managed to evolve a style or a form of writing that will adequately contain that. And this is something that I personally am involved in seeking.'[73] Much, if not most, of Parker's subsequent career as a writer may be usefully viewed in the context of this search for forms whose complexity would match the intricacies of Northern Irish life.

8

A Professional Playwright

Through 1974 and 1975, encouraged by commissions from the BBC and stimulating professional collaborations, Parker committed himself to one literary genre: drama. This decision reflected the fact that he was finally producing work that measured up to his own rigorous artistic standards, as well as receiving his first acclaim as a writer. Parker's choice to dedicate his talents to the most social of art forms also mirrored his determination to start exploring the subject of the Troubles. 'Requiem' had been one small attempt to capture the thoughts and emotions of this time; henceforth, almost everything he wrote could be read as commenting on the political and social upheavals he had witnessed in Belfast. Parker eschewed direct treatments of the violence, however. He preferred to take a longer view, situating the stuff of daily news broadcasts in the context of the history of the relationship between Britain and Ireland, believing that this approach would prove more illuminating and enduring. He focused most sympathetically on the plight of people whose political outlook, if they had any political impulse, was not sectarian but who were forced, nevertheless, to live amid the detritus of Ireland's colonial past. As he explained in 1976, 'The thing that obsesses me is the link between the past and the present. How do you cope with the present when the past is still unfinished?'[1]

Ironically, as Parker embraced Belfast more fully in his writing, he grew less attached to it in his person. He had been eager to return in 1969, but five years of penurious struggle and an atmosphere of personal danger and constricted activity had taken their toll. Parker was writing about Belfast for an imagined audience of Belfast people, but he had also begun to envisage a different sort of life for himself elsewhere. His increasing disillusionment with the city stemmed from what he perceived as a lack of local support for and interest in his work, compounded by the grim political outlook. The Ulster Workers' Council Strike of May 1974, which smashed people's hopes for a negotiated settlement of the Troubles, inaugurated twenty years of political stagnation. Parker later remembered those fateful two weeks as '[o]ne of the bleakest, most negative times' in recent Northern Irish history. After the strike, although they had no idea how long-lasting its effects would be, Parker and many of his closest friends no longer wondered whether or not to leave Belfast, but when, how, and where to go.[2]

The Troubles had claimed over 900 lives by the end of 1973. There were, though, signs during that year that a political resolution might be possible. The violence had abated almost by half from the atrocious levels of 1972, and the basis of the national debate had shifted as the British and Irish governments moved towards closer cooperation. Nearer to home, Parker and his friends knew that Protestant and Catholic neighbourhood associations and even paramilitaries in west Belfast had made common cause against the Belfast Urban Motorway, and they hoped that wider agreement might be cultivated on other issues.[3] Moreover, the British government clearly did not want to continue the direct rule of Northern Ireland indefinitely. Westminster sought to devolve most domestic powers to a reconstituted Northern Irish government but would not countenance a return to the Stormont system of Unionist monopoly. In March 1973, a British government White Paper endorsed a governmental framework designed to accommodate the Catholic minority within a Northern Irish state. Key elements included a Northern Ireland Assembly elected via proportional representation, a 'power-sharing' executive committee comprised of elected leaders from both communities, and a Council of Ireland to coordinate policies among Dublin, Belfast, and London on such matters as tourism and transport. In Northern Ireland, the British proposal was seconded enthusiastically by the small, centrist Alliance Party, more guardedly by the nationalist Social Democratic and Labour Party (SDLP), and reluctantly by the Ulster Unionist Party (UUP).

Prospects hinged on whether or not Brian Faulkner, who had tacitly accepted the White Paper, could carry enough unionists with him to make the plan workable. William Craig immediately left the UUP to found the Vanguard Unionist Progressive Party, notable for its ties to the loyalist paramilitary Ulster Defence Association (UDA) and for its willingness to consider a future for Northern Ireland outside the union if the British government insisted on including nationalists. Less equivocal about the union but also opposed to the British blueprint was Ian Paisley's Democratic Unionist Party (DUP). Local government elections in May and elections for the new Northern Ireland Assembly in June showed unionist parties opposed to power-sharing gaining ground. Faulkner's Unionist Party split, with 'Official Unionists' supporting him and 'Unionists' (or the 'unpledged') on record against the White Paper. Even many Official Unionists were ambivalent about the constitutional proposals. Of the seventy-eight seats in the Assembly, the Official Unionists held twenty-four, unionists opposed to power-sharing won twenty-six, the SDLP got nineteen, and the Alliance Party eight. The Northern Ireland Labour Party, which Parker habitually supported, elected only one member.

Starting in October, Secretary of State for Northern Ireland William Whitelaw chaired talks between the amenable parties on the formation of the Northern Ireland executive, an economic and social programme, and contentious law and order issues. By late November, it was announced that the executive would consist of eleven members (six Faulknerite Unionists, four SDLP, and one Alliance), with Faulkner as Chief Executive and Gerry Fitt of the SDLP as Deputy Chief Executive. Loyalists and republicans instantly denounced this breakthrough.

The last major issue to be resolved before devolution concerned the Irish dimension of the settlement. High-level negotiations among representatives of the Northern Ireland executive and the British and Irish governments took place in early December 1973 at Sunningdale, the civil service staff college in Berkshire, to determine the make-up and functions of the Council of Ireland. The British Prime Minister, Edward Heath, attended throughout, as did his counterpart from the Irish Republic, Liam Cosgrave. Heath betrayed his incomprehension of the delicacy of the proceedings, however, in reassigning Whitelaw, the one British official with an intimate understanding of Northern Irish politics, a few days before the conference began.

Anti-power-sharing unionists, excluded from the Sunningdale talks, were furious. 'Unpledged' Unionists, led by Harry West, had already founded the Ulster Unionist Assembly Party; moreover, five of the seven Unionist Members of Parliament at Westminster announced they would follow West instead of Faulkner. On 6 December, the United Ulster Unionist Council (UUUC)— consisting of Vanguard, the DUP, and members of the Unionist Party and the Orange Order—was formed specifically to oppose power-sharing; a few days later, several loyalist paramilitaries, including the UDA and the Ulster Volunteer Force (UVF), similarly banded together and promised to support politicians opposing the Council of Ireland, seen both by them and by the SDLP as the first step towards a united Ireland. Faulkner remained the leader of the Unionist Party, and a power-sharing majority still existed in the Northern Ireland Assembly, but these circumstances obscured the actual erosion of support among unionists for the British government's plan. Heath worried more about securing the SDLP's participation, thereby marginalizing the Provisionals on the nationalist side, than about loyalist sensitivities.

Faulkner regarded the Council as 'necessary nonsense'. The SDLP leadership tried to sell the agreement to its members by emphasizing the importance of the Council as a prelude to fuller integration—an interpretation that sounded plausible to loyalists, at any rate. The British government remained diplomatically vague as to what exactly the Council of Ireland would do, wittingly or not reinforcing both unwarranted hopes and exaggerated fears.[4]

The Northern Ireland executive took office on 1 January 1974. Within a week, the governing body of the Unionist Party rejected the parts of the Sunningdale Agreement dealing with the Council of Ireland, and West replaced Faulkner as party leader. This shuffle put Faulkner in the odd position of being 'a "prime minister" without a party'.[5] The legitimacy of the power-sharing executive was thus disputed from the outset, with loyalists questioning Faulkner's claim to represent mainstream unionist opinion. And, once again, decisions made in London for unrelated reasons exacerbated a tenuous situation in Northern Ireland.

In early February (over the objections of the Secretary of State for Northern Ireland), Heath called a general election for the end of the month. Loyalists mobilized to turn the election in Northern Ireland into a referendum on Sunningdale. Unionist, Vanguard, and DUP leaders agreed upon one UUUC candidate for each constituency; the pro-Sunningdale forces, less cannily, fielded two, three, or even four candidates for the same seats at Westminster. Predictably, the UUUC won by a landslide, garnering eleven of the twelve seats (with 51.1 per cent of the votes). On the national level, Heath failed to put together a new ruling coalition, and a minority Labour government took over, with Harold Wilson as Prime Minister.

Wilson appointed Merlyn Rees Secretary of State for Northern Ireland, but Rees would have little time to feel his way into the job before facing a crisis.

The general election made it obvious that the coalition in charge at Stormont commanded a majority only in the Assembly itself. In late March, the Ulster Workers' Council (UWC) called for new Assembly elections, a demand it repeated with increasing urgency over the coming weeks. This group had developed from one formed in the shipyards in 1969; by 1974 it consisted of a committee made up of representatives from Northern Irish industries with a predominantly Protestant workforce, including Harland & Wolff, Short Brothers, the power stations, and other manufacturing and engineering works. The UWC threatened crippling industrial action if not given its way, but few took the organization seriously at first. The British and Northern Ireland governments had no idea how well-organized the workers were and for how long—since at least December—they had been planning a strike to make Northern Ireland ungovernable. (Loyalist politicians had actually been working behind the scenes to slow movement in this direction, since they knew a strike would not initially have public support.)[6] On 14 May, after the Assembly rejected a motion condemning power-sharing and the Council of Ireland, the UWC announced a strike: electricity would be the first industry affected, with power production to be cut almost in half. The next day, the UWC called for a general strike, forcing several large firms to close.

Once the strike began, political and paramilitary leaders jumped on the UWC bandwagon. The involvement of the paramilitaries enhanced its effectiveness, since they did not hesitate to apply force, or the spectre of it, in 'advising' businesses to send workers home. By 15 May, four-hour power cuts affected much of Northern Ireland, and the ferry from Larne to Scotland had been prevented from leaving. The strike gained momentum through the week, with so many Belfast buses seized for barricades that the bus service suspended entire routes. Tensions rose dramatically on 17 May, when car bombs exploded in Dublin and Monaghan, in the Republic, killing twenty-seven people and injuring over 120 others. No one claimed responsibility, but Sammy Smyth, a UDA member and press officer for the strike coordinating committee, proclaimed, 'I am very happy about the bombings in Dublin. There is a war with the Free State and now we are laughing at them.' Craig denounced Rees for refusing to negotiate with the UWC and warned that vital services were in jeopardy. From his Rugby Road vantage-point, John Gilbert recorded in his journal that 'it looks like as of tomorrow there will be absolutely no electricity whatsoever. The general atmosphere is one of impending war.'[7]

This dire prediction went unfulfilled, although by the following day the blackouts were lasting for up to six hours and dairies and bakeries had shut down. On 19 May, Rees declared a state of emergency. That night, a Sunday, the UWC ordered the construction of nearly a hundred road-blocks to isolate Belfast from the surrounding countryside. Parker, who had escaped to Rostrevor for the weekend, barely made it back to Rugby Road. The next day he delivered a script to the BBC, full, he recalled later, of 'liberal determination that these people were not going to stop me doing my work. I ... set out with great determination to stand up to these bully boys.' His progress to the city centre went unchallenged, but he found a surreal scene: 'The BBC in darkness. All these producers sitting in rooms, with candles. Petrol stations being taken over by hooded men with guns and a kind of vision of Armageddon being promulgated over the radio, the feeling that the whole structure of society had broken down. It was quite frightening.' Robert Fisk, a reporter who covered the UWC Strike for *The Times* and later wrote a book about it, recounts that, by the morning of 20 May, 'there was no tangible sign, either in the city or in its outskirts, that the elected politicians had any power'. Still, the Northern Ireland executive laboured under the naive impression that 'support for the strike was based on a false understanding of Sunningdale' and that 'Once this had been removed by a clear agreed statement from the executive support for the strikers would diminish.' Gilbert, less sanguinely, confided to his journal his belief that 'the workers council are precipitating the disastrous, and that the British Gov are making good use of it as an excuse to get out'.[8]

Though the British government condemned the strike, it seemed disinclined to do anything to stop it. Both the police and the Army refrained from intervening as they watched barricades being erected and vehicles being hijacked.[9] Gilbert noted glumly: 'Westminster has re-affirmed that it will have nothing to do with the workers council. That's OK for those at Westminster. The situation worsens with the threat to cut off oil and petrol supplies. It really looks like they might form a provisional government. God help us.... We've all been thinking of where we should be going if it gets much worse.' The next day, in a local bookstore, Gilbert encountered a UWC notice forbidding the purchase of any newspaper except the Belfast *News Letter*. He defiantly bought the *Irish Times*, observing, 'The English news give second place to us. They still call it a strike, when really it's a coup.' 'The tension is quite unbearable', he commented, adding, 'Stew got through a good bottle of whiskey today.'[10]

A story in the *Irish Times* on 21 May quoted a conversation between a soldier and a Belfast man about the UWC and its motives. 'Why are they doing it?' asked the soldier. 'To stay British', the local replied. 'But they aren't f—ing British' was the soldier's bemused response. His puzzlement appeared to be shared by people on the 'mainland' who should have known better. On 25 May, Wilson made a national television and radio broadcast about the strike. After reiterating his position that 'the Northern Ireland Assembly and the Northern Ireland executive provide the only basis for peace, the only basis for order and good government in Northern Ireland', he continued in words that still stung in the North decades later:

> The people on this side of the water—British parents—have seen their sons vilified and spat upon and murdered. British taxpayers have seen the taxes they have poured out, almost without regard to cost... going into Northern Ireland. They see property destroyed by evil violence and are asked to pick up the bill for rebuilding it. Yet people who benefit from all this now viciously defy Westminster, purporting to act as though they were an elected government; people who spend their lives sponging on Westminster and British democracy and then systematically assault democratic methods. Who do these people think they are?

Unionists, whether or not they supported the strike, were outraged; they thought they were British, but apparently their own government regarded them as special category citizens.[11]

The reaction of John Gilbert, certainly no UWC supporter, was typical. He complained in his journal, 'Wilson gave a speech which he said was to the Nation but turned out to be addressed solely to the English.... He seems to think that the strikers are a minority.' The future appeared terrifying to him: 'I can't predict, but it looks like the strike will continue—eventually the army will have to be called in—> trouble or, strike continues—executive crumbles—> takeover. I am apprehensive. How many will die in the coming week?'[12]

On 27 May, the Army took over twenty-one petrol stations across Northern Ireland. The UWC responded by ordering the power supply reduced even further, to 10 per cent of capacity, and an extension of the strike to 'essential' workers. For nearly a week now, the people of Northern Ireland had been experiencing power cuts lasting up to twelve hours. Food supplies in towns dwindled; social services were in chaos; telephones and the post had become unreliable; schools had closed; gravediggers had stopped burying the dead; the gas was cut off; and the water and sewage systems were threatened. 'Yes', Gilbert reflected, 'it all seemed like doomsday, living for the hour of the next broadcast.'[13]

Faulkner, faced with the imminent prospect of large parts of Belfast being flooded with raw sewage, decided the time had come to talk with the UWC about ending the strike but could not convince his SDLP colleagues on the executive of this. When Rees, too, refused to meet the strikers, Faulkner tendered his resignation, bringing down the Northern Ireland government. Direct rule by the British government resumed, and the Northern Ireland Assembly was prorogued indefinitely. With the executive gone and the Sunningdale Agreement rendered unworkable, most loyalists felt that the work stoppage had achieved its aims and returned to their jobs on 29 May; the strike's organizers officially ended it later that day.[14] Thus, anti-climactically, the drama concluded. The world had not ended, only an experiment in self-government.

The UWC Strike did, however, mark the end of serious political initiatives in the North for a long time to come. The SDLP blamed the British government for not reacting more forcefully to the start of the strike and focused more exclusively on the goal of a united Ireland. Loyalists were more likely now to subscribe to a form of Ulster nationalism, rejecting both the British and the Irish governments. In yet another general election, in October 1974, candidates fielded by the UUUC won ten of the twelve Northern Irish seats at Westminster and raised their share of the vote to 58.1 per cent; a new pro-power-sharing unionist party, led by Faulkner, earned only 2.9 per cent of the vote and no seats. The British government, meanwhile, had proposed a Constitutional Convention to draw a blueprint for a new government in Northern Ireland. It stipulated several conditions: any plan must include power-sharing, be acceptable to the United Kingdom as a whole, and recognize Northern Ireland's 'special relationship' with the Republic of Ireland. One could hardly blame the Provisional IRA for suspecting that the entire exercise was intended only to allow the British to exit Northern Ireland with dignity when the Convention inevitably failed to produce recommendations acceptable to them.[15]

Parker's reactions to the tumultuous events of May 1974 would find their fullest expression in *Pentecost*, written nearly thirteen years later. For now, he tried to work despite the prevailing air of hopelessness. Indeed, the collapse of the most promising political initiative since the Troubles began reinforced his sense of the social relevance of the writer's vocation. With the politicians, as he put it in 1986, 'withdrawing into their sectarian stockades', Northern Ireland's artists were left 'to construct a working model of wholeness by means of which this society can begin to hold up its head in the world'.[16] Drama, of all the literary genres, struck him as having perhaps the most political potential. Experienced in a communal setting and shared in the moment, theatre could touch groups of people with special immediacy.

Radio offered a proving ground for Parker's early professional forays into dramatic writing. By 1973, he had developed a close relationship with BBC Northern Ireland's Arts Programmes Department, under the leadership of senior Arts producer Brian Barfield. Many of the features produced by Arts Programmes were dramatic in nature; the main difference between a feature and straight drama was that the former alternated narration and dramatized sequences, while the latter did not employ a narrator. In fact, Arts features resembled the scripts Parker continued to turn out for BBC Schools, in which he usually dealt with Irish history. One feature he wrote in late 1973 and early 1974 approached the topic on an adult level. Parker based *Clotworthy*, a two-part 'pantomime', on a volume of historical documents compiled and annotated by A. P. W. Malcolmson to present the life and deeds of an eccentric Earl of Massereene. He used rhymed narrative passages to establish settings and sketch the background to scenes illustrating representative moments in his subject's career, with transitions effected by period music.[17]

Born in 1743, Clotworthy never quite recovers after falling off a horse at age 14. Rash and gullible, he sets out as a young man to repair through gambling and farfetched business ventures the fortune depleted by his father. Soon he is imprisoned in Paris, a fate he chooses over returning to Antrim and putting his business dealings in the hands of his mother's agent. He tells his French lover, a woman of obscure and dubious origin, that the Irish are one step away from savagery, incapable of managing their affairs and thus dependent on the 'wise and benevolent' guidance of people like himself. She finds this attitude peculiar in an Irish lord, but he explains that he thinks of himself as 'an Englishman'. Throughout his life, Clotworthy spends more time in debtors' prisons in France and England than he does in Ireland, although he returns there to live in 1797, just in time to oppose the 1798 rebellion. After the rebels' defeat, he drafts a petition to the Lord Lieutenant asking to be made governor of the North of Ireland, 'a just and fitting role for one such as I'. Clotworthy dies in 1805, leaving the bulk of his estate to his wife, a former skivvy. His will is overturned when his family convinces a jury he was 'weak in his mind'.[18]

Clotworthy's biography attracted Parker with the opportunities it presented for comic scenes. However, *Clotworthy* also demonstrates his ease with the idiom and context of the Irish eighteenth century and his tendency to use historical figures to comment on the present state of Ireland, as he would do most memorably with Henry Joy McCracken in *Northern Star*. In dramatizing the story of the insane earl, Parker made the serious point that, for much of its modern history, Ireland had been governed by absentee landlords who felt little connection to the place and were even less capable of administering it effectively. Clotworthy, with his ridiculous name and more ridiculous life, showed the absurdity both of hereditary aristocracy and of 'English' control of Ireland. In some ways, Edward Heath and Harold Wilson were his ignominious heirs.

The production of *Clotworthy* established a useful connection for Parker, since Barfield induced London-based Northern Irish actor Allan McClelland to play the lead. McClelland, a flamboyantly gay man from a strict Ulster Presbyterian background, began his career as an actor with the Ulster Group Theatre but shook the dust of the province from his shoes when he moved to the metropolis. He found steady employment as a character actor in London; among other claims to fame, he had spent two years in the original West End cast of Agatha Christie's play *The Mousetrap*. McClelland performed the part of Clotworthy with aplomb and encouraged the young playwright. Parker would trade on McClelland's name and professional credentials the following year in an effort to raise money to produce a stage play.[19]

An even more formative experience for Parker was BBC Radio Drama's commissioning and production of his play *The Iceberg*. He had conceived and researched it in August 1973 and been informed that September that it would be produced by BBC Northern Ireland for Radio 3. Parker worked on the script from October until the following May, and the play was recorded in December 1974 and transmitted on 7 January 1975.[20] In *The Iceberg* he tells a story about *Titanic* that does not focus on its sinking on 15 April 1912. Everyone knows that happened, and Parker plays on the audience's knowledge throughout in a textbook application of dramatic irony, but the action centres on Hugh and Danny, workers from the Belfast shipyard that built what was, at the time of its launch, 'the largest movable object ever made by man'.[21]

The audience does not even have the usual suspense of wondering whether the protagonists will live or die, because they are already dead—ghosts haunting the ship on its maiden voyage. Parker got the idea for the play, he later recalled, from the words of Irish socialist James Connolly, who pointed out that, while people around the world mourned the deaths of millionaires on board *Titanic*, no one seemed to give a thought to the seventeen Belfast shipyard workers killed during its construction.[22] People can see and hear Hugh and Danny, and the two men feel emotions and sensations, but they are beyond harm. The destiny of the other passengers, though, has yet to be decided. In the closing moments of the play, as the ship approaches and hits the iceberg, Hugh and Danny's description of the scene echoes the language they used earlier to describe the instant of their own accident. Parker suggests in this way that what is about to happen to the ship is no worse than what happened individually to the shipyard workers. By writing the play, he rescued their deaths from inconsequence.

Parker also noted the coincidence in time between the shipwreck and the debate in the House of Commons on the Third Irish Home Rule Bill. Organized unionist resistance to the idea of Home Rule for the whole of Ireland would result directly in partition and indirectly in the Troubles experienced by Parker and his contemporaries. In *The Iceberg*, Parker makes the doomed ship a metaphor for the equally ill-fated statelet of Northern Ireland. Its grand main staircase and first-class dining saloon are designed and decorated 'in the style of the time of William and Mary', the very time when Protestants were solidifying their control of Ulster, and it represents the province's 'proudest offering—to the Empire—and to the world'. What had been regarded as a monument to Belfast ingenuity, however, would be remembered as a tragic vessel whose short career was marred by the hubris that allowed it to set sail with 2,201 people and only twenty lifeboats on board. Indeed, John Wilson Foster posits, the disaster represented, for unionists, a 'collective trauma' whose effects continued to be felt generations later: 'the loss of *Titanic* has come to symbolise unconsciously the thwarted nationhood of Ulster Protestants'. When Hugh and Danny read in the ship's newspaper about protests against the Home Rule Bill in Belfast and German plans to build an even bigger ocean liner than *Titanic*, Parker is pointing out that Belfast's fate is being decided in the context of imperial competition that has little to do with its best interests (four years later, 5,500 men of the Ulster Division would be killed or wounded during the first two days of the Battle of the Somme). Danny is crestfallen but sure that 'Harland's 'ill build a bigger one again.' 'Certainly they will,' Hugh agrees facetiously, 'they'll put a slipway under Belfast and launch the whole cursed city into the river—after the people have all been shot by the Army—for refusing to obey orders and abandon ship.'[23]

Parker's reworking of a bit of *Titanic* lore develops Hugh's assessment of Northern Ireland's disadvantage vis-à-vis England. Those familiar with the *Titanic* legend know the story of a diabolical stoker whose head was seen sticking out of the top of a funnel as the ship left Queenstown, the harbour in County Cork where it stopped briefly to load mail and passengers. This same man, supposedly, tried to steal the first Marconi operator's lifebelt while the ship was sinking but was prevented from doing so by the second Marconi operator. Foster explains that in contemporary accounts he was portrayed as ' "a grimy stoker of gigantic proportions" ' and, eventually, by the 'racist logic' of the time, ' "a negro stoker" '. In *The Iceberg*, Hugh and Danny see him looking down from the funnel and at first take him for 'the bogey man' but soon realize that the rear funnel he has ascended is a dummy one used as a ventilation shaft. They meet the stoker below decks later in the play and discover he is a bigoted Englishman. When he asks them if they are Irish, Danny replies defensively that they 'come from the shipyard', but the man makes no distinction between them and the other 'paddies' he has persecuted over the years.[24]

Danny comes across as more intellectual, but more politically naive, than Hugh. Although he spouts clichés about the Southern Irish, he obviously feels more at home with third-class Cork passengers Molly and Rosaleen than with anyone else they encounter on the ship, and he cites Thomas Moore and Shakespeare with equal facility. Hugh, who believes he himself was 'only fit to drive rivets', is never-theless feeling his way towards a radical critique of the interlocked systems of capi-talism, imperialism, and political unionism, seeing a common interest among working men of all sorts. 'If you've four or five thousand men building a ship,' Danny argues, 'it stands to reason some of them'll have accidents. There's men killed on every ship.' 'Why? For what?' asks Hugh. His questions hang unanswered over the end of the play, but perhaps the meeting of ship and iceberg is what the two have expected all along, the 'something' that will 'happen to clear it all up'. For if *Titanic* is the ship of state, a microcosm of an unjust society, then all the wealthy passengers can see is the tip of the iceberg, and sooner or later the vessel is doomed to founder on the submerged aspirations of the mass of the population.[25]

A reviewer for the *Listener* declared *The Iceberg* 'a most successful play', and the *Guardian*'s critic found it 'worth hearing again'. Much of the credit belonged to its producer, Michael Heffernan, for whom Parker quickly 'developed a lot of affec-tion and respect'. Heffernan had arrived in Belfast in 1973 to head BBC Northern Ireland's Radio Drama Department, which despite a distinguished pedigree (Tyrone Guthrie, Denis Johnston, and Ronald Mason had all been BBC Northern Ireland Radio Drama producers) had been in danger of extinction for a while. David Turner's departure in early 1970 led to a succession of producers, none of whom stayed longer than a year and a half. Mason, Head of Programming for Northern Ireland by 1973, fought to save the department from BBC higher-ups who wanted to eliminate it on the grounds that there were no good writers in Northern Ireland. Originally from Ballymena, Mason had worked for several years as a radio drama producer in London. On his return, he strove to open the local BBC to new voices and ways of doing things. He wanted the national BBC to value what Belfast had to offer, but he also wanted BBC Northern Ireland to shake off its parochialism and achieve the highest production standards. An expansive man who adored drinking and gossiping, Mason excelled at spotting talent. He found Barfield and Róisín McAuley in the Presentation Department and let them start producing features when they were both still announcers. He engaged Paul Muldoon as an Arts producer straight from university, and he brought Heffernan over from London. Mason believed in hiring intelligent, creative people and giving them encouragement and a free hand. His conception of the role of a drama pro-ducer was similar: to discover, nurture, and develop writing talent in a region.[26]

Heffernan, whose job description included commissioning, directing, and pro-ducing radio plays, shared Mason's vision. Born in the Republic of Ireland in 1947, he grew up mainly in Nottingham and studied philosophy at Cambridge Univer-sity. After joining the BBC on a graduate trainee scheme, he tried out a number of different departments in London before coming to Belfast. In radio drama he found the intellectual companionship he sought. A perfectionist with chronic dif-ficulty finishing things, Heffernan made extensive use of multi-tracking, recording actors and sounds on separate tracks and then fiddling endlessly in post-produc-tion. He thought analytically about the medium of radio and what he called 'psy-cho acoustics', the art of using sound to evoke feelings. He loved collaborating with writers and composers, and his best work used a great deal of music.[27]

Heffernan was the first of Parker's professional associates to become an intimate friend as well, and their shared affinity for music helped to draw them together. Heffernan played piano and possessed a fine singing voice; his tastes were wide-ranging and indiscriminate. He could sight-read or reproduce music by ear with ease, and his talents enlivened many a musical evening at Rugby Road. Another characteristic they had in common was a sense of humour, though Heffernan's tended towards the dryly witty, mock-serious variety. Parker told an American friend that 'He does a one-man version of Handel's *Messiah*, singing all the parts and the orchestra, which renders me a helpless fool.' Although a Catholic and an Irish nationalist, who prided himself on never having carried a British passport, Heffernan initially struck most Irish people as being stereotypically English, with what Parker termed his '*very* posh accent and full-blown Cambridge/BBC style'. This almost seemed a role he played, as Parker explained: 'He's the English son of Irish expatriate parents, and I mean English—just like in the moving pictures, curling lips, languid knuckles, really *limey*.' Heffernan regarded himself as an Irish-man who loved his country enough to criticize its provinciality. He favoured a united Ireland but hated the IRA, and many of his closest friends were, like Parker, Protestants. In his own career he aspired to produce work that transcended narrow nationality.[28]

Parker appreciated Heffernan's formidable intellect and fierce resistance to medi-ocrity. Perhaps their most important shared quality was a zest for life derived from a hard-earned sense of its fleetingness. Born with a congenital heart defect, Heffernan remained frail; the BBC hired him on the condition that he stick to radio production, since his superiors considered television work too stressful for him. Heffernan fully expected to die young and so resolved to make the most of what-ever time he had. The experience of having faced death early united him with Parker.[29] They revelled in each other's company, chatting vivaciously about 'phi-losophy & morality & pluralistic values' or 'life and drama'. Parker, who believed that Heffernan had fully realized *The Iceberg* in production, trusted his critical judgement implicitly, turning to him for specific script advice in the future and accepting most of it without question.[30]

Like Brian Barfield, but unlike most other BBC Northern Ireland producers, Heffernan often brought London-based Northern Irish actors to Belfast for pro-ductions, a predilection that did not endear him to locally based actors. Thus the recording of *The Iceberg* allowed Parker to reconnect with a friend from university. Graham Rea had travelled a long way from the New Stage Club. At Parker's sug-gestion, he had abandoned his studies and become a professional actor, changing his first name to Stephen. Although he came from a working-class Protestant back-ground, the main effect of university on Rea had been to confirm him in a repub-lican stance towards Irish politics. He bypassed the Dramatic Society at Queen's, devoting himself instead to a self-consciously nationalistic group he founded called the Young Irish Theatre Company. In the late 1960s, desiring closer contact with the soul of the Irish nation, he moved to Dublin to study and work at the Abbey Theatre. There he found what seemed to him a decadent tradition, in which plays were produced with no attention to their political or intellectual content. He left in disgust and gravitated towards London, where at least he could count on a climate of high professional standards. After several years of working in experimental theatre groups on 'the fringe' and honing a more physical style of acting, Rea had begun to achieve some recognition—including a stint in the company at the Royal Court, the premier London theatre for new writing since its 1956 production of John Osborne's *Look Back in Anger*.[31]

Rea's involvement, with his connection to the cutting edge of the English stage, gave an added frisson of excitement to Parker's *Iceberg* experience. For his part, Rea, who played Danny, savoured the chance to do a Belfast play after his time in London and noted Parker's sympathy for working people and ability to write in dialect without patronizing his characters. The two discovered they had more in common than ever, talking for hours about theatre and their wish to do ambitious stage work in Northern Ireland. A few months later, Rea returned to Belfast to act in another radio drama, this time staying at Rugby Road. Struck anew by the actor's eagerness to work in the North, Parker observed in his journal that Rea would be 'a natural actor for almost anything I want to write—like a sad-faced horse, long and lean, in a circus comedy routine'.[32]

Parker had begun 1975 with a sense of momentousness and sharpened purpose, writing in his diary on 1 January: 'I am 33. Age of Christ at the crucifixion. Dante in the dark wood. The most crucial year of life.' Some time earlier, he had repeated to Michael Foley the advice of Philip Hobsbaum, who warned against dabbling in too many genres; people who tried to do everything, Hobsbaum maintained, often accomplished little in any genre. Now, after much literary experimentation, Parker took this dictum to heart himself. *The Iceberg* convinced him that drama was his *métier*, and from the beginning of 1975 Parker followed a plan laid down for himself on 6 January to 'concentrate on plays'.[33]

His determination to leave his mark as a writer, as well as his long-standing interest in theatre, had been rekindled the previous summer, in Ithaca, where he taught classes on James Joyce and modern drama at Cornell. He and Kate rented a flat in the home of a woman named Bea MacLeod, who had a Master's degree in directing from the Yale School of Drama and, in the past, had run a Black theatre company in Montreal. She worked at the Telluride Institute, an honours programme at Cornell, but continued to follow theatrical developments, and she and Parker enjoyed discussing them. MacLeod encouraged his writing, confiding that Vladimir Nabokov, who had rented her house for a year, had written *Lolita* there. That same summer, Parker's friend Nancy Cole directed a staged version of *The Iceberg* in a black box theatre at Cornell, with Parker reading the part of Danny. They presented it as a visual enactment of the recording of a radio play, with the audience sitting on three sides around the cast, members of which were equipped with old-fashioned microphones. A sound man performed the effects live, and various stage business provided visual interest.[34]

In Ithaca, Parker began researching what he called in his journal the 'Bicycle play'. This, like *The Iceberg*, would hinge on a bit of local lore connected to the larger history of transportation: the fact that John Boyd Dunlop, a Scottish veterinarian, invented the pneumatic tyre in 1887 while living in Belfast.[35] Parker planned to combine this story with a modern one, also linked to the theme of transportation and inspired by John Gilbert's fight to inject a more humane spirit into the public discourse on redevelopment and the Belfast Urban Motorway. He had started writing the play by the end of 1974, and in January 1975 he settled on a title: *Spokesong; or The Common Wheel.* Now Parker had a professional goal and a stage project in hand, but, apart from the difficulties any unproven dramatist must expect in trying to get work produced, one huge problem remained: no professional theatre company then operating in Northern Ireland was committed to producing new local writing that aspired to anything more than entertainment.[36]

During Parker's lifetime, the Ulster Group Theatre had been renowned for its popular productions of new plays by Northern writers and for effective ensemble acting. However, the company had disintegrated in 1959 as a result of the furore about Sam Thompson's *Over the Bridge.* From 1960 to 1971, the theatre, under the management of comedian James Young (who publicly renounced 'arty-crafty nonsense'), concentrated on long, profitable runs of Ulster comedies. With the worsening of the Troubles, however, even this activity ceased.[37]

The Arts Theatre had also suspended its operations in 1971, citing the bombs that deterred people from attending performances. Managed by Hubert and Dorothy Wilmot since its founding in the 1940s, the Arts operated in several locations around Belfast before opening a purpose-built 450-seat theatre on Botanic Avenue in 1961. The Wilmots, who in the smaller venues specialized in the production of avant-garde world drama, abandoned this policy during the 1960s in favour of musicals, comedies, and thrillers.[38] Thus, even if the Arts Theatre had been producing plays in 1975, it would have been unlikely to mount a new drama by an unknown playwright.

This left the Lyric Players Theatre, which by 1975 was the only theatre in Belfast to have remained open throughout the disturbances.[39] The Lyric began in 1951 as an amateur group performing for an invited audience in the house of its founder and director, Mary O'Malley. She had grown up near Cork and lived in Dublin in the 1930s and 1940s, where she volunteered at the Abbey, frequented the Gate Theatre, and was involved with a socialist theatre company called the New Theatre Group. In 1947 she married Pearse O'Malley, a psychiatrist from south Armagh then establishing the Department of Neurology and Psychiatry at the Mater Hospital in Belfast. The couple settled in the city, where they would remain for the next thirty years. Mary—a middle-class, convent-educated member of the anti-partition Irish Labour Party—felt terribly isolated in the North. The Lyric Players brought her into close collaboration with local artists, musicians, and dancers, as well as many of Belfast's legal, medical, and teaching professionals: people united by their love of theatre. Those close to the couple speculated that Pearse encouraged Mary in her theatrical hobby to keep her occupied because the prospect of Mary with nothing to do frightened him. Their courtship, she records, had revolved around Pearse's generous contributions to her many causes, and this pattern continued with his total subsidy of the Lyric from its founding until 1960. At this point, the O'Malleys decided that 'we could not continue financing it for ever' and established the Lyric as a non-profit-making association under the nominal control

of seven trustees and with the stated aims of building or obtaining a theatre building in or near Belfast in which to present dramatic work of 'cultural and educational value' from world theatre, including at least one W. B. Yeats play each year
and with 'special consideration' to be given to 'Irish poets, writers, and dramatists'.[40] This policy enshrined the Lyric's existing practice, since it focused primarily
on the works of Yeats and other writers of the Irish Revival, Shakespeare plays and
other world classics, and plays from the contemporary Dublin repertoire. Meanwhile, Mary O'Malley kept adding ancillary activities to the Lyric's purview,
including, at various times, a drama school, an art gallery, a music academy, an
Irish handcrafts shop, and a literary magazine called *Threshold*. She regarded herself
as a missionary, bringing the benefits of high culture and Irish national spirit (for
her these amounted to much the same thing) to a place she found lacking in
worthwhile culture of its own.

For the next eight years, while raising money for the new theatre, the Lyric continued to operate from the O'Malleys' home on Derryvolgie Avenue (part of which
had been converted into an auditorium seating fifty), with expenses met by the
O'Malleys as before. Mary continued to choose and direct the vast majority of the
plays presented and to hone the Lyric's 'house style', characterized by attention to
diction and the text and a stylized, anti-realistic form of movement. Parker likely
became aware of the Lyric while a student at Queen's in the early 1960s, but,
despite his interest in theatre, it probably did not impinge much on his consciousness. He socialized with members of the Circle Theatre, a rival amateur organization that produced current world drama and the occasional new play by a Northern
Irish writer, including one by Parker's friend John Hamilton.[41] The O'Malleys
moved in circles far removed from his own. The idea of insinuating himself into a
private house off the Malone Road for the purpose of attending a coterie production of plays by Yeats, if it occurred to him, would have held little appeal.

In the lead-up to the building of the new Lyric Theatre and the conversion of
the Lyric Players from an amateur to a professional theatre company, Mary
O'Malley arranged public performances in larger venues of plays by Sean O'Casey
and other writers she felt had general appeal, while still producing the more esoteric plays at Derryvolgie Avenue. Parker's first documented encounter with the
Lyric came in 1967, when he reviewed a bill comprised of three Yeats plays for the
BBC. As if determined to prove he was no Belfast philistine, he recklessly set
himself up as O'Malley's nemesis. Speaking as one who had given Yeats pride of
place in an MA thesis on poetic drama, Parker began by saying, 'I was dismayed
that Mary O'Malley presented these three fine plays in the reverse order of their
composition', proceeding to a scholarly analysis of the scripts combined with
frank criticism of the production. Worse, from O'Malley's perspective, he singled
out for negative attention precisely those aspects of the staging she generally
prided herself on most. The actors in *A Full Moon in March*, the most allegorical
play, Parker argued, 'spoke the words with too much psychological fervour'; the
set for *The Words Upon the Window Pane*, 'gnarled and grey and impressionistic',
should have been 'realistic down to the last detail, to set off the spiritual terror of
the play itself'; *Deirdre* 'needs acting in the grand style, and it doesn't get it'. The

BBC producer—likely John Boyd—cut Parker's final paragraph, but it sums up his attitude:

> Mary O'Malley has to be admired for producing Yeats plays at all. But it would be a disservice to the company to be blindly uncritical on this score; and I have to say that these productions are not what they could be. There is not enough evidence in them that Yeats' intentions and theories have been considered. There's not enough of an attempt to evolve an appropriate ensemble style of acting. Attention to detail is lacking.[42]

Even without this final damnation, Parker's assessment must have infuriated O'Malley.

Nevertheless, with youthful arrogance, Parker sent the Lyric his play *The Sensational Real-life Drama of Deirdre Porter*, written the same week as his review, and apparently expected the company to produce it. This gesture indicates how little he knew about Mary O'Malley at the time. She ran the Lyric Players without any of the sectarian prejudice that underlay much of social life in Belfast, welcoming Protestants and Catholics alike on the basis of their dedication and what she perceived as their talent. She would work with anyone willing to do her bidding, but people defied her at their peril. Dark and dramatic-looking, with a commanding and intense manner, O'Malley characterized herself as 'an all or nothing woman'. People not altogether for her were apt to be regarded as being against her. In retrospect, it is hardly surprising that, after Parker submitted his script, 'There was no response whatever for two years.'[43]

More remarkable is the fact that, two years later, the Lyric did show interest in the play. The company's 1968 transition to its new home, a 300-seat theatre on Ridgeway Street, had not gone smoothly. The Lyric had begun to receive a substantial operational subsidy from the Arts Council, but this did not cover its new expenses. Internal strife compounded the stress put on the budget and the artistic policy by shortage of money. The O'Malleys had no patience for the 'whatever you say, say nothing' style of Northern discourse. Their prominent involvement, some of the plays produced, and the fact that the Lyric performed on Sunday contributed to the theatre's 'green' reputation. Ian Hill, a friend of Parker's from Queen's then working as a journalist in Belfast, precipitated a crisis right before the new theatre's opening by mischievously asking if the Lyric would be playing the (British) national anthem at the end of its performances, as was customary in public venues in the North. Obviously the O'Malleys had no intention of doing any such thing, but, to avoid alienating a hefty sector of their potential audience, they accepted a compromise that the anthem could be played on 'special official and public occasions'. Tension also existed between the O'Malleys and the theatre professionals starting to be more involved at the Lyric. Mary O'Malley had announced her retirement from day-to-day theatre duties in August 1968, but she remained on the scene. Christopher Fitz-Simon was brought up from Dublin to assume the post of director of productions (O'Malley did not dignify such employees with the title of artistic director, lest it give them delusions of grandeur). They quarrelled almost immediately over the season's programme, since Fitz-Simon questioned

O'Malley's belief that Yeats could be made popular, and O'Malley's will prevailed. Fitz-Simon quickly realized that he would not even be allowed to cast productions without interference from the founder, and within a few months he had resigned.[44] After a brief period early in 1969 when the theatre closed for reorganization, Lyric stalwart Denis Smyth stepped into the breach as director of productions, and Parker approached him about his Deirdre script.

Smyth wanted the Lyric, as Northern Ireland's sole publicly funded theatre, to become a centre for new writing, although Mary O'Malley had hitherto shown scant interest in Northern Irish drama. He planned to open the 1969/70 season with *Over the Bridge*, in order to arouse enthusiasm about local material, and to follow that with Parker's play. Smyth believes he was thinking in terms of a foyer production or staged reading, but Parker in 1985 recalled 'discussions…about casting, design and rewrites'. Whatever the plan, it never came to fruition. *Over the Bridge* was supposed to go into rehearsal in August; when the sectarian rioting began, members of the cast (several of whom had belonged to the Group Theatre back in 1959) warned Smyth off Thompson's play. Given their experience, they feared it might be incendiary: that there was a literal danger of the new theatre being burnt down. Smyth, a cautious man, hastily substituted *The Field* by John B. Keane. This eliminated the rationale for doing Parker's play, the production of which was consequently scuttled, or at least postponed indefinitely. Meanwhile, Smyth himself received a fellowship to study and observe theatre in London, and programme planning reverted to those with no regard for local playwrights.[45]

Parker tried, without much hope, to salvage the situation by delivering a copy of the script to the new director of productions, Peter Jackson, who was, he noted in his journal, 'snide about it'. As it happened, Mary O'Malley also found Jackson 'totally unsatisfactory' and banished him within three weeks. This move brought no comfort to Parker, however, since O'Malley herself resumed overt control of the Lyric's programme and artistic policy. Although she was not on the Lyric's payroll and had no formal theatrical training or professional experience, she would act, in essence, as artistic director until 1976. Her unwillingness, or inability, to let go had an immense impact on the cultural landscape in Belfast, especially after 1971 when she held an effective monopoly on theatre production in the city. As Lyric historian Roy Connolly mildly puts it, 'the legacy of the amateur past' proved 'the defining influence' on its development. O'Malley favoured actors and directors who had been involved with the company in the Derryvolgie Avenue days, even when they were not available to work full-time, and she clashed repeatedly with those who tried to instil a more professional ethos, seeing herself as the guardian of a hallowed tradition. All this contributed to the perception voiced by local drama critic J. D. Stewart in 1973 that the Lyric was 'a personal institute run on public funds'.[46]

Parker, too, worked as a drama critic in the early 1970s. He did a bit of reviewing for the *Honest Ulsterman* in 1970—as did Kate, who had auditioned unsuccessfully for the Lyric on more than one occasion in 1969.[47] Frank Ormsby, then one of the journal's editors, recalls that these reviews 'did not go down well' with the Lyric management, and Parker believed that, partly because of them, he would never get a play put on in Belfast. BBC Arts producer Brian Barfield, who notes that 'candour' in theatre reviews had been unusual in Belfast, appreciated Parker's 'critical edge', hiring him to critique theatre productions for the radio programme *Saturday Review*. Barfield considered the fact that Parker was 'not part of the Ulster arts establishment' to be an asset to him as a critic. Although his reviews were not uniformly negative, Parker's impolitic honesty must have done much to confirm his status as an outsider.[48]

By 1975, though, Parker no longer cared what 'Hail, Mary, full of Yeats' thought of him.[49] His grudge against her for not producing his Deirdre play had been superseded by years of observing the theatre's activities, and his dissatisfaction now transcended any sense of personal slight. He objected to the Lyric because it did not, in his view, mount productions worthy of a professional theatre; remembering the early 1970s, he would assert bluntly in 1985 that 'The work it was doing was execrable, and continued to be so till some years later.' He also resented the way Northern Irish writers were given short shrift in the Lyric's repertoire—the occasional production of a Brian Friel play being about as far as Mary O'Malley was prepared to go as a concession to local taste. In particular, the Lyric hardly ever produced new writing in its early years as a professional company. In its first seven seasons at Ridgeway Street, from autumn 1968 through the spring of 1975, the Lyric premièred only three new Northern Irish plays: all of them by John Boyd, who, around the time he retired from the BBC, became the theatre's literary adviser in 1971 (a position he would hold until 1994).[50]

This neglect frustrated Parker, especially since the reception of Boyd's play *The Flats* (1971) had demonstrated the hunger of Belfast audiences for dramatic work that spoke to their current predicament. Inspired by a real-life loyalist siege of the Catholic Unity Flats and by the work of Sean O'Casey, the play makes a thinly veiled socialist plea for victims of the violence on both sides; the original production proved popular enough to merit revival before the end of the season. Unfortunately, happy as he might have been to see the Lyric starting to engage with local writing, Parker found the play itself atrocious.[51] He was hugely entertained the following year by Ormsby's satirical 'Write-An-Ulster-Play Kit', a facetious commentary on the hackneyed characters, themes, and symbols employed by writers of 'Troubles' plays like Boyd and Wilson John Haire, whose melodramatic depiction of the disintegration of a mixed marriage, *Within Two Shadows*, the Lyric produced in 1972 after it had been done at the Royal Court.[52]

Thus, Parker did not even think of offering *Spokesong* to the Lyric, Northern Ireland's only subsidized theatre. Mindful of the precedent set by *Over the Bridge*, which had been mounted triumphantly by a coalition of actors and directors when the Group's board refused to produce it as Thompson had written it, he felt instead that 'its only hope resided in being presented in the right way—which meant an independent production'. He and Michael Heffernan (who had agreed to direct *Spokesong*) formulated the plan of opening the play in Belfast in the summer and then taking it to the Edinburgh Festival Fringe in August.[53] In late January 1975, they applied to the Arts Council of Northern Ireland for funding, suggesting tactfully that 'the play and its style of presentation would not fit easily into the production policy of the Lyric Theatre' and describing the project as 'part of a theatrical movement seeking new directions in local playwriting and production'.[54] The Arts Council deferred a final decision on their last-minute request until mid-April and also told them it could not provide money for presentation of the play outside Northern Ireland. Parker and Heffernan consequently decided to apply also to the Belfast District Council for a subvention towards the Edinburgh trip, and at the end of February Parker travelled to Edinburgh and confidently booked a hall. In pursuing sources of funding, the two called themselves Ixion Productions. They probably meant the name to allude subtly to the play's subject-matter, but it carried ominous connotations: Ixion, a denizen of the Graeco-Roman underworld, was punished by being fastened for eternity around the circumference of a constantly turning wheel. The moniker probably came to seem sinisterly appropriate as they endured a series of setbacks to their aims and made new plans, only to encounter fresh obstacles.

Heffernan's health worried them almost from the beginning. Within a few weeks of their application to the Arts Council, he learned that he needed major heart surgery in early April which would have to be followed by three months' convalescence. This would make it difficult, if not impossible, for him to direct *Spokesong* for a summer opening in Belfast. By mid-March, though, after Parker had recruited Stephen Rea to play the main part of Frank Stock, a modern-day Belfast bicycle salesman, Heffernan convinced himself that he might be able to direct the play if they opened in Edinburgh in late August. Around the same time, Parker and Heffernan persuaded Allan McClelland to join the cast as Frank Stock's grandfather and Hubert Wilmot to promise the Arts Theatre building for a Belfast run in the autumn. By the end of March, when Heffernan headed to Nottingham for his operation, arrangements appeared to be well in hand.

Parker's solicitor friend Brian Garrett, 'crackling w/energy and busily optimistic' about the prospect of interesting local businesses in the project, agreed to help raise money for Edinburgh. He got trades unionist Sandy Scott, actor/director James Ellis, and Olympic pentathlon winner Mary Peters to join him in commending *Spokesong* to the attention of the Belfast District Council and the Dunlop Rubber Company, which he hoped might provide 'a substantial degree of support'. When this latter hope proved unfounded, Garrett, undeterred, proceeded at the end of April on another tack of trying to recruit twenty 'programme sponsors' from a list of companies with Northern Irish connections, each of which would be asked to contribute £75 towards the production in return for an advertisement in the programme. This appeal yielded only one positive response. The application to the Belfast District Council had also been denied, so, on 10 May, Parker and Garrett reluctantly concluded that 'Edinburgh was definitely out'.[55]

Now the possibility of any production at all hinged on the decision of the Arts Council, which Parker had been lobbying throughout April. In the middle of that month he had found a set and lighting designer. Michael Poynor, who specialized in large musicals and other shows with complex technical requirements, had been deputy artistic director of the Lyric Theatre since 1973, acting as director of productions during most of the 1974/5 season when Mary O'Malley took a 'sabbatical'. He had been meeting some friction in his attempts to make the Lyric's work 'more visually stimulating' and 'physical' and planned to leave the theatre within weeks, but he expressed a willingness to return to Belfast to help with Parker's production. Poynor drew up a bare-bones budget for *Spokesong* which Parker included as part of the final application to the Arts Council; he estimated the show could be produced for £3,000 if expenses were carefully monitored. Early in April, Parker had also given a copy of the first draft of the script to Michael Barnes, director of the Queen's Festival since 1973. Barnes wanted the play for November but emphasized that the Festival could not sponsor the production without an Arts Council subsidy. Parker wrote to the Arts Council on 16 April, the day before it was due to decide on his and Heffernan's original application for a subvention, describing all developments since the end of January and offering to take any Belfast production of *Spokesong* on a tour of Northern Ireland.[56] Then he anxiously awaited a reply.

Late that month, the Arts Council's Assistant Director for Drama, Frank Murphy, assured Parker that *Spokesong* would 'almost certainly get Arts Council backing', as part of the Festival or outside it, 'barring some drastic development'. On 13 May, however, the day after he withdrew his play from the Edinburgh Festival Fringe programme, Parker phoned Murphy yet again and learned that, since the Arts Council would be receiving less money from the British government than it had expected, there would be no funds for 'special' projects such as *Spokesong*. Barnes maintained that a Festival production remained a 'distinct possibility', but not on Ixion's costing: they could expect no more than £2,000, probably less. Parker noted despairingly that 'We seem to be on a slide towards a dramatised reading by the Mother's [sic] Union Drama Society.'[57]

The next evening Parker attended the first performance of Patrick Galvin's new play *We Do It for Love* at the Lyric. Galvin, a poet from Cork and a friend of Mary O'Malley, had been drawn to Belfast by the Troubles. This was his third offering to the theatre since becoming its writer-in-residence in 1973 under a scheme supported by the Leverhulme Trust. *We Do It for Love* originated in a conversation with O'Malley in which she urged him to 'go into the ghettos, imbibe the atmosphere and collect the ballads'. Less a play than 'an entertainment...in eighteen scenes', the form of *We Do It for Love* recalled music hall, with sketches of people coping in different ways with the violence and revue-style musical numbers (popular songs to which Galvin had set new words—an undertaker, for example, singing a version of 'Happy Days are Here Again'). The character of Moses Docker, who plies a makeshift merry-go-round (a metaphor for the Irish Troubles, which come and go with new 'riders'), provided a unifying element. Galvin's was, as Roy Connolly observes, 'an outsider's perspective on Northern Ireland, not hamstrung by sensitivity to the complex nature of local issues'. *We Do It for Love* 'lampooned those responsible for violence, reducing terrorists, army, and civilians alike to stereotypes, in an effort to unite the community in condemnation', but, 'in ridiculing all parties in the Northern Irish conflict', Galvin 'by implication ridiculed all the people of Northern Ireland'. Nevertheless, the show scored one of the biggest commercial successes the Lyric ever had: booking 108 per cent during its initial run, touring the British Isles, and being revived as a finale to the following season.[58]

Parker, there on opening night as a theatre critic, found it a 'stale, third-hand, vulgar and soft-centred farrago of cheap stunts'. He wrote in his journal that the experience of watching it

> Got me very angry and pent up. Rushed to the bar for a large whiskey at interval, and wd. have proceeded to the street had I not to review the thing. Endured the second-half, w/ the audience mindlessly swallowing every last hammed-up, tasteless trick of a sterile sensibility, and clapping for more. Left the theatre wanting to take it apart with my bare hands.

Even after 'a bath and a pill', he 'still had trouble calming down enough to sleep'. The next day, he begged Brian Barfield to find someone else to review the play. In the end, they agreed that he could 'simply describe the thing without comment' and 'let it condemn itself'.[59]

The timing of this incident, amid Parker's increasingly futile attempts to get *Spokesong* the sort of professional production that could begin to do justice to his script, surely contributed to his choler. Galvin's variety show was getting the production money and attention that properly belonged to *him*; that was *his* audience laughing itself silly at the Lyric (and could an audience that approved Galvin's effort be expected to appreciate what made his own play superior?). Worse yet, Parker could not help but notice superficial similarities between *We Do It for Love* and *Spokesong*, including the integration of songs, an unexpectedly comic approach to serious subject-matter, and the use of a central 'cyclical' symbol. It would have mortified him to imagine that people might assume he had been influenced by a show he thought crude and offensive. Insult was added to injury the day after the Galvin première, when Parker watched *The Dandelion Clock*, a television play by Wilson John Haire that 'turned out to be an almost total disaster'.[60]

A phone call a few days later from Barnes—informing Parker that, since the Festival would receive no extra money for drama from the Arts Council, it would probably not be presenting *Spokesong*—did not improve his mood. 'End of the line', he noted glumly in his journal. He described Michael Heffernan as 'consumed with anger' but called his own response 'quite measured': 'a part of me fully expected this, and wd. have been disturbed if it *hadn't* happened. But more important, I'm facing the usual defeat and frustration this time with a few precious allies. That makes a big difference. Fight to the death.' Nevertheless, for the short term, the initiative had stalled. In Nottingham, where Heffernan was still recovering, he and Parker met Stephen Rea and Allan McClelland to discuss the situation, and that, Parker recalled ten years later, 'was effectively the end of Ixion Productions'. Repeated delays had meant the loss of Poynor and Rea to other projects and the dissolution of the original *Spokesong* coalition.[61]

Even before this meeting, Parker, at Heffernan's suggestion, had begun exploring the possibility of getting the play onto the programme of the Dublin Theatre Festival in October. Their contact was Godfrey Quigley, an actor with the Irish Theatre Company. He and Donal Donnelly, another actor, ran an organization called the World Theatre Company—'more or less', Parker later remembered, 'from the glove compartment of Godfrey's car'. Quigley and Donnelly decided they wanted to produce *Spokesong*, and the Dublin Theatre Festival accepted their proposal on 22 July. This development struck Parker as 'Simply immense', but the deal nearly fell apart at the last moment when they had difficulty finding a suitable venue. Fighting a feeling of 'complete desolation', Parker travelled to Dublin to look for one himself; he found the John Player Theatre, which he described in his journal as a 'V. well-appointed modern 300-seater house, w/practicable stage.' His subsequent recollection paints a less rosy picture of 'a venue unique in Ireland, and possibly the world. It is a constituent part of the Player-Wills cigarette factory, and is consequently permeated with the smell of tobacco whilst being entirely devoid of a liquor licence. It also has a flat oblong floor facing a flat end-stage. Many of the entrances and exits in *Spokesong* have to be accomplished on bicycles....the omens were not propitious.'[62] At the time, however, all that mattered was that the show had finally been slated for production.

Still Parker could not relax. No sooner had serious discussions about casting and budget got underway than Heffernan began to feel ill again and feared his new heart valve was being rejected. On a day in mid-August when Heffernan had taken to his bed with a severe headache, Parker ran into Ronald Mason at the BBC. Mason told Parker that he thought it 'madness' for Heffernan to try to direct a stage play in his condition. This encounter must have thrown Parker into a moral quandary, since he desperately wanted Heffernan to direct *Spokesong*, which Heffernan himself wished to do, but he surely doubted the advisability of subjecting his friend to any stress. Parker fled to Edinburgh for the Festival, remaining over two weeks and returning at the beginning of September to tackle 'the responsibilities of the play' only with reluctance.[63]

Meanwhile, through the tribulations of the previous eight months, Parker had been working on the script of *Spokesong*, hardly more than an idea when he and Heffernan filed their first Arts Council application in January. Then, Parker had explained that the play would be set in a Belfast bicycle shop run by Frank Stock, 'who sees the bicycle as the answer to the city's traffic problems, its security crisis and the profound spiritual malaise underlying both'. It would also tell the story of Frank's paternal grandfather, Francis, who founded the shop in 1895 after being the first cyclist to test Dunlop's pneumatic tyre in a race. Parker asserted that

> By ranging freely back and forth across the last eighty years, the play offers an unexpected and entertaining perspective on the historical processes which have led up to our current public nightmare. It seeks to offer hope in a time of gloom and despair by celebrating the qualities of common humanity which have survived the storm—qualities summed up in the nature of the bicycle itself.[64]

The present-day and flashback scenes would complement and comment on each other, as Francis and Frank each wooed and won his true love (hard-headed, pragmatic women with the deceptively delicate names of Kitty and Daisy). Dramatic tension in the modern story would be provided by competition for Daisy's affections from Julian, a photographer visiting from England, and the Troubles themselves, which tempt her to leave Northern Ireland and Frank.

Parker vowed not to write 'the 473d version of "Juno and the Paycock"', preferring to try to depict 'the reality' of contemporary Belfast as he had experienced it. For an emblem of faith in the future in the midst of chaos, he seized on the anti-motorway campaign—as Daisy points out to Julian, there is a good story in 'grown men earnestly discussing the pros and cons of a road system . . . in a city that's being blasted asunder all round them'.[65] John Gilbert (who, ironically, was coming to the agonizing decision to leave Belfast while Parker was writing *Spokesong*) served as a model for Frank's idealism, public spirit, and rootedness. Daisy's down-to-earth manner and blunt speech were based on a friend of Gilbert's named Julie MacRae, who sometimes called round to the Rugby Road household. Parker did not know her well at the time, but he found her 'attractively full-blooded' and identified her with a certain type of tough Belfast woman. Kitty likely owed something to Parker's friend Joanna Mules, with whom she shared red hair, a father in the British military, advanced feminist views, and an emphatic way of speaking; her surname, Carberry, also recalls Anna Johnston MacManus, a Northern writer, editor, and nationalist activist who published under the name Ethna Carbery.[66]

Frank leads his community association, trying to keep it from being co-opted by Daisy's father, Duncan, the local paramilitary leader. In a threatening encounter after Frank has declined to make a 'wee contribution' to Duncan's organization, the older man confronts him with the question 'have you no belief in law and order?' Frank replies, 'Not when you phrase it in the abstract like that, no.' He focuses on the concrete difficulties faced by citizens of Belfast caught between the bureaucrats with their Urban Area Redevelopment Plan and the 'freelance redevelopment' perpetrated by the terrorists. Gilbert and Parker's Belfast Urban Study Group (BUS) had used the bus as a symbol of community and advocated the upgrading of public transportation as an alternative to the building of an inner ring road. Frank, for his part, advances a master plan built around the bicycle, a symbol of individual autonomy. People would be happier and the city safer, he argues, if Belfast banned cars from the city centre and established a civic fleet of 50,000 free bicycles.[67]

Parker conceived the last major element of the play in early February, when he came up with the idea for a character called the Trick Cyclist. In his MA thesis, he had praised the way E. E. Cummings developed a theme by using one character in multiple roles in his play *Him*. More recently, he had loved both the stage and screen versions of the musical *Cabaret*, in which the nightclub's Master of Ceremonies incarnates the decadence of Berlin between the world wars and sings songs counterpointing the dramatic action. The Trick Cyclist serves a similar purpose in *Spokesong*: mediating between past and present, presiding over the action on stage, taking a number of parts, and singing songs that reinforce the audience's sense of the play's taking place 'during the early 1970's [*sic*] and the eighty years preceding them' by parodying a succession of musical styles. In dress and deportment he recalls the variety-act, a popular form of working-class entertainment in late Victorian and early twentieth-century Belfast. In the course of his first turn, as the inspector at the public inquiry where Frank makes his case for 'the bicycle solution', the Trick Cyclist tells the audience, 'I am up here in fact to represent you', and Parker imagined the character as a 'Chorus figure' embodying 'the spirit of Belfast'.[68] This 'spirit' is often repressive; the Trick Cyclist even undercuts the play's happy ending by helping Julian rob the till while Frank and Daisy pedal off stage on a bicycle built for two. On a positive note, he represents the playfulness and delight in language for its own sake which Parker also perceived in Belfast culture.

Parker began his work on *Spokesong* by reading books on cycling, and the play is, on one level, 'about' the history of the bicycle. For Frank, the story of the bicycle is more important than the kind of history Daisy teaches at the secondary school where she works, being emblematic of 'all the things that ordinary people do with their time'. Unlike the car, which can harbour a bomb, the bicycle, he maintains, is an inherently peaceful machine that 'hides nothing and threatens nothing'. The link between bicycles and personal freedom is another element of Frank's philosophy, and this aspect of the subject also inspired Parker, as it had the Victorians who first commented on the bicycle phenomenon. In some of his earliest notes for the play, he characterized the invention of the bicycle and the pneumatic tyre as a 'blow for human liberty'. According to Frank, much of the beauty of the bicycle comes down to 'control over your own life'. 'So far as personal transport goes—' he elaborates, 'the bicycle was the last advance in technology that everybody understands.' Modern men and women are 'unhinged', he suggests, because 'our lives are at the mercy of alien machines, mysteries for other people to solve'.[69]

Parker called bicycles the 'conceit' upon which he based *Spokesong*. Declaring in 1985 that he took it 'as a given that the tribal, sectarian malevolence in [Northern Irish] society is the deepest, most enduring and least tractable evil in our inheritance', he claimed to have chosen a 'unifying image' for *Spokesong* 'precisely on the basis of its incongruity: a decrepit bicycle shop'. 'One of my strategies', he confided,

> was to try to write a play about violence which would ambush the audience with pleasure, and there are few subjects more pleasurable than the history of the bicycle. Then again, it is an aspect of social history which runs (I can put it no other way) in tandem with the political history of the Unionist/Nationalist ideological divide, in an uncanny and provocative fashion. The period from Dunlop's 1888 invention of the pneumatic tyre in Belfast, to the ecology movement bike-revival of the early 1970's [*sic*], encompasses the end of Parnellism, Randolph Churchill and the Orange Card, the Home Rule Bills, the Great War, Partition, and so on, right up to Bloody Sunday and Bloody Friday.

Parker offered the romance between Francis and Kitty as an image of inclusiveness, since they are 'Victorian idealists of wildly conflicting hues—she a Maud-Gonne-style Nationalist, he an Empire Loyalist' who have only one thing in common: 'a passionate love of the bicycle, which is a form of love for humanity itself'.[70]

Despite his clarity of purpose, Parker found writing *Spokesong* a challenge—partly because, simultaneously, he had to master the craft of stage writing, wrestling for the first time since his university days with knotty 'problems of construction, getting bodies on and off, keeping plot going, at the same time as working out what the people say to each other'. Possibly because of the unsettled political context, it proved easier to establish a situation than to resolve it. Consequently, Act I was easier to write than Act II. Parker completed a first version of the script by the end of March 1975, in haste because Stephen Rea had interested the Royal Court's Theatre Upstairs in the play but needed to show them a full draft as soon as possible. In a letter accompanying this 'rough draft' to the Royal Court, Parker acknowledged its flaws: 'There are a lot of awkwardnesses here (set speeches, crudely informative dialogue, incomplete characterization, etc.) which ought to have disappeared by the final draft.'[71]

The Theatre Upstairs declined to add *Spokesong* to its season on the strength of this script. Of more immediate importance to Parker was Michael Heffernan's dissatisfaction with it. He had liked Act I but informed Parker in early May that he did not care for Act II in its present form. 'Most of what he says I agree with', Parker admitted in his journal.[72] Later that month, in Nottingham, Heffernan offered specific advice on reworking the second act, and Parker revised the entire play in June, sharpening its focus. He cut several of the Trick Cyclist's roles (Horse-loving Lady, Belfast Corporation Official, and Army Public Relations Officer), probably to streamline the structure and avoid overwhelming the audience with characters and concepts, and reordered some of the scenes in Act II.

Apart from such polishing, the major changes between the original draft of *Spokesong* and subsequent versions of it centre on the character of Julian. In the early draft, he was not related to Frank but merely stayed with him for the five months he spent in Belfast. He was not conniving or hostile; indeed, near the end of the play he encouraged Frank by asserting that his ideas, though eccentric, were valuable because the *values* in them were good. His observations about Belfast, coming from a bona fide outsider, allowed Parker to convey to a general audience some unusual features of daily life during the Troubles. Although Daisy went with Julian to London and stayed at his flat for the four months that elapsed between the acts in this version of the script, there was no romantic relationship between them, and the suggestion that she should accompany him reportedly came from her. Because the fact that Daisy was considering leaving Belfast was not signalled in Act I, the news that she had gone came as a shock in Act II. Her decision to return was equally unmotivated, and the ending, with Frank and Daisy riding off on a tandem, was unadulterated by any shadow of the complications the play had evoked. Too much of the critical action took place offstage, so that audience members heard conversations about things that had happened instead of seeing them happening and drawing their own conclusions.

Perhaps Parker decided the play as first written lacked an adequate antagonist for Frank. He may have had second thoughts, too, about making Frank's epiphany result from a conversation with an Englishman. Revision transformed *Spokesong* when Parker turned Julian into Frank's adopted brother, a bitter émigré who would welcome the total destruction of Belfast. In notes towards the rewrite, Parker reminded himself of 'the question to be posed: what is the right and best way to deal with the past?' He knew he needed to '[k]eep that central', and the new take on Julian helped him to do that. Julian questions Frank's romantic view of their dead grandparents, who bequeathed him the building and Frank the business (making the shop a metaphor for Northern Ireland's divided heritage). He ridicules Frank for clinging to his memories, calling history 'the accumulated turds of human endeavour', and tries to force him 'into the future' by selling the building to Duncan Bell for a headquarters. Frank, in contrast, argues that it is not so easy to leave the past behind because 'You *are* your own past....Hate it and you hate yourself.' In order to survive, you must 'master' it.[73]

One of Heffernan's persistent objections to the script had been that Frank 'needs to *do* something instead of just have things happen to him'. Parker attempted to redress this criticism in a reworking of the ending which the Dublin production company had also requested. He added a climactic speech for Frank, in which he grapples before the audience with the central issue of the play. This scene comes after Daisy informs him that she will be leaving with Julian and Julian tells him he has sold the shop. Frank has vainly sought comfort in thoughts of Francis and Kitty with their belief in bicycles, and he finally admits he is 'lost', since 'I don't see any future for an advocate of cycling in this town.' After a brief absence, he drunkenly reappears with the Trick Cyclist, who helps him 'extinguish' Francis and Kitty and serves as the mute witness to the crumbling of Frank's faith in humanity. Resigned now to the loss of his 'former existence', Frank is left with a perplexing question:

> your past...the past, I'm talking about...the air's full of it...you have to breathe it...but you can't grab hold of it...you see what I'm saying...it's everywhere but you can't locate it...you see where I'm driving...how can something that's fundamental...be irrecoverable...and uncontrollable...answer me that...you take the point...how are you supposed to live?[74]

Frank cannot answer the question he so gropingly poses. It is left to Daisy—who had earlier advised him, 'Try riding your damn bike out into the real world'—to indicate a way forward. In another scene added towards the end of composition, Daisy confronts Julian after learning he has sold the shop to her father and angrily informs him that his cynicism equips him with as partial a view of the human condition as Frank's optimism. Torn earlier between Frank's impractical idealism and Julian's witty nihilism, Daisy has decided that, bleak as the present is, the future will be worse if people stop appealing to the best qualities in each other. *Both* Frank and Julian, she declares, have some growing up to do. Belfast will change for the better only when people start dealing with others the way they 'really are', in their 'depravity' *and* their 'sweet reason'. 'There'll be no fresh start with a nice clean sheet', Daisy concludes, implying that despair on that account would be self-indulgent. In the final scene, she reveals that she is buying the shop, having threatened to turn her father in to the police if he did not let her have it, and *Spokesong* ends with the prospect of her and Frank embarking on a life together, though she insists there will be 'No wedding bells'.[75]

Music by Jimmy Kennedy was another late addition to the play. Parker had always intended to use songs in *Spokesong*, but, although he planned to write the lyrics for at least some of these himself, he had not found a composer by the time he completed the second draft. Around this time, he learned that Kennedy, a composer and lyricist from the North who had found his way to America's Tin Pan Alley via the British equivalent, Denmark Street, had retired to Ireland in 1971. Parker was still writing *High Pop* (his popular music review column for the *Irish Times*, which had recently switched to an 'enlarged and broadened' weekly format), and he located and interviewed Kennedy. Parker marvelled at the length and breadth of Kennedy's career, in the course of which he had weathered numerous changes in musical taste while producing such standards as 'The Teddy Bears' Picnic', 'The Cokey-Cokey', 'Isle of Capri', 'Red Sails in the Sunset', '(We're Gonna Hang Out) The Washing on the Siegfried Line', 'South of the Border (Down Mexico Way)', and 'Down the Trail of Aching Hearts'. The two men hit it off, and Kennedy wrote to Parker the day the *High Pop* piece appeared to thank him for his article ('easily the best that has been written about me'). It then occurred to Parker that Kennedy would be 'the perfect man' to write the music for *Spokesong*, since 'his career practically spans the period covered in the play'. The day after the play was approved for inclusion in the Dublin Theatre Festival, Parker wrote to Kennedy and asked if he might find any 'fun or pleasure' in setting half a dozen or so of Parker's lyrics to music. After assuring himself that the production would really happen, Kennedy agreed to the proposal and graciously declined to accept a fee for his work. Parker requested, and received from Kennedy, a Cocktail Song, a Parlour Song, a Music-Hall Song, an Army Song, and a Cowboy Song, among others. He also included Harry Dacre's vintage 'Daisy Bell' several times in the play, despite Kennedy's regret that they would not have a 'love-theme' of their own and thus audiences would leave the theatre humming Dacre's song instead of one of theirs.[76]

With the challenges of writing and selling met at last, the challenges of production began. Luckily, Allan McClelland was still available for Francis, but the other parts remained to be cast. After asking if he thought he could handle singing and riding a unicycle, Parker and Heffernan engaged Pitt Wilkinson, an English actor working at the Lyric, to play the Trick Cyclist. Although an unpredictable alcoholic, he had the right combination of humour and menace for the role. The rest of the actors were based in Dublin: Máire Ní Ghráinne and Raymond Hardie, both working at the Abbey, were cast as Kitty and Frank; Barry McGovern agreed to play Julian; and Ruth Hegarty got the part of Daisy. Hardie especially pleased Parker, since he came from the North, had been a protégé of Parker's old friend Roy Alcorn and a neighbour of John Hamilton, and had attended the New Stage Club.[77]

Rehearsals began on 15 September 1975, three weeks to the day before *Spokesong*'s scheduled opening. Heffernan, who had done little stage directing, was tense and nervous; McClelland, bossy and egotistical, never hesitated to voice an opinion or vaunt his metropolitan theatre experience; Wilkinson, on at least one occasion, showed up drunk first thing in the morning. Parker haunted the theatre, taking every opportunity that presented itself to talk to the actors about their characters. 'World Theatre Productions', as he informed Alfred Gingold, 'turned out to be little more than a letter-heading', so Parker himself handled all the publicity. He could also 'be found at various times supervising costume hire, fetching accessories from the Irish Raleigh factory, and painting the bicycle ramp we had built, from the side aisle up on to the stage, an hour before the first-night audience was due to appear'.[78]

Lacking money, Parker fortunately had devoted friends. John Malone provided paper, stencils, and a secretary's help to duplicate scripts. Kate typed the master to Parker's dictation. John Gilbert, with no theatre experience, designed and built the set, basing it on a bicycle shop in Cromac Square run by the Stone family, as well as making the posters and borrowing spotlights for the production. Along with Ken and June Lambla, an American couple working with him at the Northern Ireland Housing Executive who had moved into 9 Rugby Road in July (bringing the household's first refrigerator), Gilbert stayed up all night on 4 October to fit up the stage.[79]

Parker's anxiety grew to such a pitch that Heffernan briefly banned him from rehearsals. Opening night he found 'like your own execution', an opinion of openings he would hold throughout his career. He slipped into the back of the theatre half-way through the first act to watch the proceedings in agony, noting every small mistake, and escaped before the intermission to drink whiskey in his car—whence Kate had to retrieve him to be introduced to Cearbhall Ó Dálaigh, the President of Ireland and a bicycle enthusiast. The audience seemed unresponsive to him, reacting with only '[m]odified rapture' at the end. After drinking until 5 a.m., Parker, Heffernan, and McClelland picked up the morning papers to read the first reviews: an 'unqualified rave' from the *Irish Times*, a 'vitriolic panning' from the *Irish Independent*, and an ambivalent response from the *Irish Press*. Not until that evening, when the *Evening Press* and *Evening Herald* had weighed in favourably, did Parker believe the trend was positive. The English critics, who saw the show later in the week, were even more laudatory, with John Peter of the *Sunday Times* calling *Spokesong* 'the best stage debut I have seen for years and the finest thing at this year's Festival' and praising the writing as 'both tough and poetic' and John Barber describing it in the *Daily Telegraph* as a 'small miracle of spinning wheels and shifting moods'. By the end of the six-day run, it was standing-room only.[80]

Given Parker's political aims, he especially appreciated a '[s]plendid' review of *Spokesong* in *Hibernia*. Its author, Niall Stokes, saw the play as 'genuinely entertaining but also the most insightful comment on the [Northern] situation that we have been treated to in a theatre over the past five years', praising its intelligent dialogue and 'straightforward ideas and argument'. He regarded Parker as representative of a 'new voice in Northern politics':

one which mouths neither the clichés of the hard-line extremists of every shade on the one hand nor at the other the tired pleas of the gormless moderates caught up in the middle of a historical inevitability which they refuse to recognise. It is the voice of those who have developed the depth of vision to seek potential solutions through reference to factors which seem only tangental [*sic*], who are radical enough to look into the 'beyond capitalism' that lies ahead and to find there what Ivan Illich has called 'feasible utopias' which are applicable to the present.

Parker, who would continue to be frustrated by the apparent inability of most theatre critics to penetrate *Spokesong*'s endearing surface, felt his efforts vindicated by this assessment.[81]

On 10 October, Parker and Heffernan 'agreed to let Belfast drop—if they want the play, they can ask for it—no more striving to arouse their interest'. Parker commented in his journal that 'We're concentrating on London from now on.' Upon his return to Belfast, he was courted by the Lyric (Dublin acclaim ever being, for Mary O'Malley, the *sine qua non* of a play's worth). Poet John Hewitt, one of the theatre's trustees, phoned on 13 October to offer Parker the writer-in-residence position after Patrick Galvin's departure. Parker turned it down, as he recorded, with the 'awful thought... that I might have accepted it five years ago'. Not easily deterred from something she wanted, O'Malley next approached Heffernan to offer to buy an option on *Spokesong*, to be directed by him with the Lyric company: 'Godawful thought', Parker remarked in his diary. Finally, on 16 October, John Boyd called to make sure Parker knew all the details of the fellowship offer. 'Just in case I might change my mind', Parker noted. 'Courteously, I declined so to do.' (Boyd's own recollection is that Parker rejected the proffered post 'with disdain'.)[82]

Acceptance in Northern Ireland seemed less important to Parker now that the world appeared to be opening up to him. For a heady few days after its Festival run ended, it looked like *Spokesong* might transfer to the Abbey's Peacock Theatre, but this opportunity was lost through lack of money. Meanwhile, largely because of the continued efforts of Stephen Rea on Parker's behalf, the Royal Court Theatre had taken an interest in *Spokesong*; in November, they bought a twelve-month option on the show, with the expressed intent of producing it the following May or June. The Kings Head, one of London's premier fringe venues, had made an offer at the same time, and a letter in mid-October from a German man who wanted to translate the play provided a hint of things to come. Also thanks to Rea, Max Stafford-Clark and his Joint Stock Company, British pioneers in the workshop development of plays, wished to commission Parker and were soliciting ideas from him. At a meeting in London in mid-December, Stafford-Clark and Parker discussed several possibilities, and Parker left with the impression that, although nothing had been concluded, there were 'strong chances' of the collaboration taking place.[83]

Parker finally had an agent now. Hugh Alexander represented one of the actors in the *Spokesong* cast and had agreed to negotiate a contract for Parker with the Dublin Theatre Festival. On a trip to London in late October, Parker lunched with Alexander, who greatly impressed him, as that day's journal entry attests: 'Splendid man, v. showbiz. Told me all about the agency & himself & stood me the best (& biggest) steak I've ever eaten. Turns out I'm the only playwright on his books—it's me & 27 actors, from Milo O'Shea on down.' This last detail should have been cause for alarm, but Parker, though a mature writer, remained naive when it came to the business side of his work. He did not yet realize that the expertise required to be an actor's agent differed from that needed by a dramatist's agent. For the moment, it was enough to be taken seriously by someone who seemed at home in the world he aspired to enter.[84]

On his thirty-fourth birthday, Parker decided the time had come to adjust his persona to fit such an adult age. A haircut and new herringbone overcoat helped him look the part of an up-and-coming playwright. He also realized he needed to write another play, and fast. He had begun preliminary work on a script about a song-writing team, provisionally called *Catchpenny*, and other stage play ideas crowded his mind. In addition to Henry Joy McCracken, whose story he had been contemplating since 1967 and would eventually treat in *Northern Star* (1984), references in his journal and a notebook he kept around this time indicate that by the end of 1975 the seeds for *Nightshade* (1980) and *Pratt's Fall* (1983) had already been planted, and Parker toyed with the notion of a stage version of *The Iceberg*. Not all his dramatic works were conceived with stage production in mind, however. A story line inspired by Joyce's *Ulysses*, about Molly Bloom's Ulster concert tour, was imagined from the beginning (in 1974) as a television play and would be produced as such in 1982's *Joyce in June*.

The excitement over *Spokesong* in 1975 largely overshadowed other projects. Parker had worked on this play in a more concentrated fashion, and over a longer period, than he had worked on anything before, but he still had to do all kinds of other writing to support himself. He consequently fell into the habit of doing his most serious composition late at night and into the wee hours of the morning, a mode of working he never abandoned. During the day, he attended to more mundane commitments, which in 1975 included *High Pop* and contributions to productions of the Arts Programmes Department of BBC Northern Ireland such as *Bookends* and *Saturday Review* (on which Parker featured regularly as a critic and frequently filled in as the presenter). He also guest presented in 1974 and 1975 such music programmes as *Speaking Personally* (a Northern Irish version of *Desert Island Discs*, with local celebrities talking about and playing records of their favourite music) and *Variations* (a similar programme, which included records from several different musical genres).[85]

Arts Programmes also commissioned occasional features. For example, *The Joyous Wheel*, a musical documentary on the history of the bicycle which Parker wrote in September 1975, absorbed some of the excess research he had done for *Spokesong*. Recorded in an RTÉ studio during the Dublin run of the play, it used several members of the *Spokesong* cast. BBC Northern Ireland later sold this programme to the national network, and Parker also mined it for a feature on Dunlop he wrote for the BBC World Service.[86] The Radio Drama Department offered more lucrative opportunities, and at the end of 1975 he had a project in hand for Heffernan called *I'm a Dreamer Montreal*, a radio play based on the Irish showband milieu familiar to Parker from Sam Fannin's stories.

Parker's first television piece was also produced and transmitted in 1975. This had grown, obliquely, out of a five-minute story Parker had written in April and May 1971 at the request of Gerry McCrudden, one of BBC Northern Ireland's first television producers. 'I'm a Wallflower, You're a Weed', which Denys Hawthorne read for television as a 'talking head', later appeared in the *Honest Ulsterman*. It depicts patients in a hospital (one a teenager, one a doctor) awaiting the arrival of visitors; the younger one comments on the 'terrible hidden antagonism between visitors and patients' and observes that 'suffering', like 'love', is 'entirely self-centred'. In March 1974, McCrudden invited Parker to write a thirty-minute television script based on the short story.[87] The play, which Parker delivered in May, underwent two changes of title (called *Rock of Ages*, *Hearts and Minds*, and, finally, *Private Grounds*) and multiple revisions before production commenced over a year later. The main continuity between it and the original short story is Parker's exploration of the tensions inherent in encounters between the sick and the healthy.

The play depicts an encounter between the members of a family—Joe (evidently some sort of paramilitary officer), Doris, and their teenaged daughter, Phyllis—and Murf, a man in a wheelchair who approaches them as they prepare a picnic on the private grounds of the title. He tells them that these belong to a hospital, where he is a patient. When Phyllis asks if he were hurt as a result of the Troubles, Murf allows that he was. In response to her continued questions, he shares a long story about getting shot while saving his employer from a fire started by a petrol bomb. Other stories he tells fail to add up, however, and gradually members of the family (first Joe, then the others) start to suspect him of fabricating them. Any doubts the audience might share on this score are confirmed near the end of the play when he jumps to his feet to protect Phyllis during an argument with her father. He runs away, and she runs after him—only to discover that he is sick, but not owing to the Troubles: he has pleurisy. When she asks why he lied, he replies, 'It was what you wanted to hear, wasn't it?...It's what everybody wants to hear.'[88] The slim plot resembles Synge's *The Playboy of the Western World*, with the women enthralled by a lie they have prompted, then turning on the storyteller when his tale is exposed as fiction.

Private Grounds, one of the first BBC Northern Ireland television plays shot on location, was recorded on videotape in July on the grounds of a Big House near Portaferry called Quintin Castle. Parker had been unusually ambivalent during the writing process; several times he considered abandoning the play, or wished the BBC would, persisting with it mainly because it paid well. His belief in the play grew during the week or so devoted to rehearsing and recording it, however. The script was well served by the actors (Joe McPartland, who had played Hugh in *The Iceberg*, as Joe; Catherine Gibson, a veteran of several of Parker's radio pieces, as Doris; Kate Thompson as Phyllis; and John Hewitt—the actor, not the poet—as Murf), and Parker felt 'relieved' that even the read-through sounded 'fine'. 'One encouraging feature of this little play', he noted, 'is that the dialogue is speakable and utterly convincing as realistic speech.' The actors, he added, had been complimenting him on 'how easy they find it to learn'. In *Spokesong* he had aimed at a more self-consciously literary effect (a 'contemporary version' of William Congreve's dialogue) as opposed to naturalism, but he understood that the requirements of a television script were different. Parker also enjoyed being involved in the business of television production and learning about some of its technical aspects.[89]

Private Grounds was aired on 21 November 1975, and once again Parker 'felt relieved that it came over O.K.'. When he visited his parents a few days later, though, their negative reaction confirmed his lingering uncertainty about its worth. They had been proud of his theatre debut and the attention *Spokesong* had garnered, but 'They didn't like the television play & were fairly blunt about it', repeating to him disparaging comments made by others. Their touchiness on the subject came as a shock, since the responses he had heard up to that point—from Brian Barfield and Michael Heffernan, as well as from members of Kate's mother's church who told her how much they had liked it—had been affirming.[90]

Probably Stewart's parents interpreted the play more personally than others who watched it, finding offence where none was intended or being painfully reminded of things they would rather forget. He himself had suffered from pleurisy as a child, and his missing leg must often have prompted people to wonder, morbidly, if he had been caught in sectarian crossfire. The world of hospitals, which Parker believed contained the essence of the human condition, likely held no such positive associations for his parents. They might even have taken Joe's grumbling that Phyllis should never have been allowed to attend 'that school' (presumably a grammar school) and that she should be out 'earning her keep' as a critical comment on them: although they had always supported their younger son's educational aspirations, they had trouble understanding why someone with a university degree should always be on the verge of pennilessness. Then, again, maybe they simply disliked the play, which *is* rather odd and inconclusive (why is Murf in a wheelchair? are any of the stories he tells true? is the hospital a mental hospital? what exactly is Joe's involvement in the violence?). Whatever the reason for it, his parents' rejection of *Private Grounds* depressed Parker, partly because he had been hoping, through television, to touch people like them and their friends. They had not liked it, and Parker concluded from this that the play was a failure.[91] Significantly, he expunged *Private Grounds* from his record as a writer, omitting it from any list of his works that he compiled in the future, although he continued to claim much earlier radio plays, such as *Speaking of Red Indians* and *Minnie and Maisie and Lily Freed*. This incident might also have reinforced Parker's lack of interest in finding a publisher for *Hopdance*, the autobiographical novel about his amputation. He was 34 years old and living a life his parents could not begin to imagine, but clearly their good opinion still mattered to him.

Parker's final project in 1975, *Herod the Great*, adapted the medieval mystery play of the same name which tells the story of Herod's slaughter of the innocents in a vain attempt to kill Jesus in infancy. The Arts Programmes Department commissioned the piece, produced by Paul Muldoon. Parker wrote the script in November, and the play was transmitted in Northern Ireland on 27 December. The work took him back to his beginnings as a writer, since the medieval morality play *Everyman*, in which he starred as a 13-year-old, had been the first piece of literature to make a deep impression on him. Later, as an instructor at Hamilton College, he had directed student productions of several mystery plays, including *Herod the Great*. For the radio version, Parker stayed close to the text of the Wakefield Cycle but shortened it and updated the language, as well as 'translating' it into Northern Irish vernacular. The effect is sometimes startlingly topical, with a peculiarly appropriate resonance in the North. In the final speech of the play, for example, Herod praises his henchmen for their efficiency in killing all children under two years of age in his realm before issuing the standard disclaimer of guilt:

> It's regrettable that innocent blood should be shed
> I mourn as much as any man for the dead.
> But if people have permitted themselves to be swayed
> By dangerous ideas, what else, I'm afraid,
> Can you expect?
> Some poor souls may perish.
> Still, you can't be too squeamish
> When you're trying to establish
> Regularity and respect.[92]

Faithful to the sense of the medieval text, Parker's version echoes the public pronouncements of the perpetrators of violence on all sides of Northern Ireland's conflict, who typically expressed regret before asserting that their ends justified any means necessary to achieve them.

The year ended on a high note at Rugby Road, with the biggest and best Henry Tonk banquet to date, Tonkerama. The film industry provided the theme, with the afternoon entertainment consisting of the 'première' of a silent screen melodrama enacted with the aid of a strobe light and featuring Henry as the leading man. Ken Lambla erected a pink and white awning in front of the Nouvelle Palace, and guests, dressed in their gala best, walked through the front door on a red carpet. Henry arrived in a limousine. On the roof, residents perched a giant King Kong head with paw outstretched, and revellers overheard two elderly ladies passing by complain that the place was becoming a middle-class slum. The banquet consisted of dishes alluding to famous movies: along with Parker's Moby Duck, highlights included John Gilbert's Earthquake, with a crème brûlée earth's crust and a silver foil volcano that spewed custard, and June Lambla and Steph Pickering's Follow the Yellow Brick Road to the Gizzard of Oz, with yellow corn 'bricks' and broccoli trees leading up to a pot of beef stew with a green gelatine castle moulded around it. None of the diners dropped out during the evening, as usually happened. Instead, Parker recorded, 'Everybody kept very lively, and bed was not attained to until after 7.30 A.M. A worthy finale to what has probably been the best year of my life to date.'[93]

9

Suddenly Somebody

The enthusiastic reception of *Spokesong* transformed Stewart Parker's life. The play was produced in at least ten countries in the years immediately following its première at the Dublin Theatre Festival in 1975, and Parker followed it in person to London, Belgium, Canada, and the United States between the autumn of 1976 and the spring of 1978. Building on *Spokesong*'s success, he focused exclusively on play-writing, giving up most of the other work that had supported him during the first half of the decade. By the beginning of 1977, he even started saving money. Not all the changes wrought by this career breakthrough were positive, however. In particular, his new stature put an increasing strain on his marriage. Stewart spent much time outside Northern Ireland, attending to business in London and else-where. Consequently, ever more people in his life, especially in his professional life, knew him alone rather than as one of a pair. Moreover, the fact that Kate had no intellectual work that absorbed her as writing plays engaged him became a prob-lem for them as Stewart grew more passionately invested in his theatrical endeav-ours. Changes in the Rugby Road household and in the physical and mental health of Kate's mother put added pressure on the union.

Of all the possibilities presented by the Dublin production of *Spokesong*, Parker most relished the prospect of working with Joint Stock. This theatre collective had, since its first production in January 1974, brought the approach of the Fringe into the British theatrical establishment and involved such highly regarded figures as Max Stafford-Clark, David Hare, David Aukin, and William Gaskill. In the pre-ferred Joint Stock method, actors, writer, and director cooperated in the creation of a script, playing with an idea for several weeks in workshop sessions before the writer withdrew to compose a draft. The company favoured historical and political themes, and the time devoted to research, acting exercises, and improvisation gave the playwright a factual base from which to work, as well as a sense of the person-alities and abilities of the actors who would incarnate the characters and a 'physical vocabulary' upon which to draw. The script would be fine-tuned during rehearsals and perhaps reworked after the first public performances. Parker—whose experi-ence with the BBC had accustomed him to working in a documentary mode, who liked creating characters with specific actors in mind, and who enjoyed collabora-tion—was well suited for the Joint Stock style of theatre.[1]

At Stafford-Clark's invitation, Parker had proposed a project in early November 1975 based on Joyce Marlow's book *Captain Boycott and the Irish*. This details events of the autumn of 1880, when members of the Land League discovered the power of ostracism in dealing with landlords who evicted tenants from their farms or charged unjustly high rents. Captain Charles Boycott, the English agent for Lord Erne's estate in County Mayo, complained of such treatment in a letter to *The Times* and received aid from Ulster Conservatives who sent an armed group of Orangemen south to harvest his crops when locals refused to work for him. Boycott's corn and potatoes were saved, but it was a 'pyrrhic victory', as Jonathan Bardon notes, since it had cost £10,000 to do it. Meanwhile, the word 'boycott' entered the language.[2]

Both the incident and the 'conflicting perceptions of the same reality' that it illustrated intrigued Parker. Borrowing a concept from Dutch philosopher of history Johan Huizinga, whose book *Homo Ludens* he had read in February 1975, Parker viewed the entire episode as 'a form of play'. Boycott's story, he believed, still had much to say 'about typical English and Irish attitudes'. It would lend itself to the Joint Stock treatment because of 'its intrinsic theatrical values, its peculiar suitability to group creation, and the major social issues which it raises for exploration and debate'. Parker saw as chief among these 'the issue of political violence and its alternatives'. The boycott movement represented a short-lived compromise between the constitutional and physical force wings of Irish nationalism, and 'the search for ways of effecting radical change which stop short of violence is a universal and continuing one'.[3]

After meeting with Stafford-Clark in mid-December, Parker prepared a detailed outline of the Boycott script. He aimed 'to concentrate on the experiences and reactions of the ordinary people caught up in the affair'. To that end, he had selected 'a series of moments when each of the groups in turn [Boycott's household, the tenantry, the Ulster Relief Force, the British cabinet, the Land League leaders] is at play', since 'People are perhaps at their most characteristic when playing' and 'reveal most about their group loyalties'. These scenes, he thought, should be 'quite distinct set pieces' to reflect the fact that the groups had little interaction with each other: 'Continuity is provided by the unfolding narrative and by the fact that the same actors are reappearing in the various scenes.'[4] He posted his synopsis to Joint Stock in mid-January 1976. Less than a week later, he received a letter from Stafford-Clark implicitly accepting his proposal and suggesting that, rather than Parker travelling to London, the company should come to Ireland in late June for the workshop portion of the project—a notion of which Parker wholeheartedly approved.

With the Joint Stock script on the back burner, Parker turned to a radio play he had pitched to the BBC in February 1975. He had learned it would be commissioned by the network that April and had received the first half of his fee for it in May. Now he had to write it. The idea for *I'm a Dreamer Montreal* had come to him after a Christmas visit to his family in 1973 during which his brother, in response to Stewart's customary request for stories about anything 'funny' that anyone at his work had said or done, entertained him with anecdotes about a colleague who loved to sing but always got the words wrong. The man rendered a Fairy Liquid commercial ('hands that do dishes can be soft as your face') as 'my hands are judicious and they're soft as my face', and he sang 'I'm a Dreamer Montreal' instead of 'I'm a Dreamer, Aren't We All?'.[5]

Parker imagined a showband singer named Nelson Glover with the same problem, allowing him to incorporate stories told to him by Sam Fannin, who played the drums in Gay McIntyre's showband. This, Fannin reminisces, was 'the type of dance band that played in hotels, golf clubs, annual conferences, drinking clubs', a 'group of 4–6 musicians who could play country & western, jazz, traditional music, some pop'—the kind of band that 'has largely disappeared beneath the rock steam roller'. Showbands played covers of popular songs; their performances gave Irish people access to live popular music in the days before international pop stars added Ireland to their tours. McIntyre, hailed in his youth as 'the Irish Charlie Parker', was an accomplished musician whom homesickness had brought back from London to his native Derry. Fannin could not match him musically, but McIntyre kept him on because he tended towards hypochondria (like the band leader in Parker's play) and believed Fannin's job as a pharmaceutical rep (and the fact that his brother was a neurosurgeon) gave him medical insight. Throughout the worst of the Troubles, this band played a regular Saturday night dance at the Dunadry Hotel, between Belfast and Antrim, along with assorted down-market gigs elsewhere.[6]

According to Fannin, musicians in bands frequently grew so tired of the songs they had to play repeatedly that they would invent new words for them: 'Help Me Make It Through the Night', for example, might become 'Help Me Make It Through Your Tights'. Nelson Glover's faulty renditions, in contrast, are not premeditated; he simply cannot remember the lyrics and fails to see why it should matter. In his view, 'the singer has a certain leeway. A poetic licence.' 'It's yourself you put across', he advises an aspiring singer: 'You just express your own personality.'[7] Nelson is a genuine innocent in a place and time when such innocence could be fatal. His political naiveté is symbolized by his inability to keep the words of songs straight and his unwillingness to try to do so. Living for his art and believing in the artist's ability to reshape reality, he hardly notices that the Troubles exist until they affect him directly.

Parker drew specifically on two of Fannin's many memorable experiences in *I'm a Dreamer Montreal*. Once, Fannin recounts, McIntyre arranged for them to play at a private function on the Whiterock Road, off the Falls Road, in Belfast. The Troubles were at their height and the area in question '150 per cent republican'. Nevertheless, off they went in Fannin's company car to a school hall packed with a rowdy crowd, members of which had been drinking heavily. Before long, some in the audience began brawling. Two men joined the band on stage, stood to attention, and told the party-goers they were ashamed of them. That was when the musicians learned that the IRA, not the civil rights movement as they had thought, had sponsored the event. The organizers commanded the band to play 'the anthem'. A performance of 'The Soldier's Song' briefly quelled the disturbance, but then it resumed. Around 1 a.m., the band members said they would have to be going and were paid in cash, but a gun battle outside trapped them there until things calmed down enough for them to leave with an IRA escort.[8] Nelson has a similar brush with the IRA in the play, but, rather than escaping unscathed, he is picked up (with a suspicious amount of cash) outside the hall by an army patrol and kept overnight for questioning.

In the course of his interrogation, Nelson is asked to prove his claim to be a singer by performing the Beatles song 'Help', the words of which he mangles. A military policeman returning from patrol takes Nelson for a terrorist and plays mind games with him. Seeing a photo Nelson has been carrying around with him of the young woman he admires, the MP tells him she has been caught in cross-fire and killed. As soon as he is released from custody, Nelson goes to the morgue to look for her body and is frisked by a soldier who thinks he might be there to try to steal 'a couple of high security stiffs' before they can be identified. Here, again, his experience mirrors that of Fannin, who once went to the morgue in search of the body of an elderly relative who had died suddenly. The night before there had been a serious gun battle between the IRA and the British Army, and the bodies of two IRA men were in the morgue. British soldiers were hanging about the building, waiting to harass family members of the volunteers. Mistaking Fannin for one of these, they pushed him around, prodded him with rifles, and insulted him.[9]

Nelson's unworldliness survives these encounters, and the bombing of the music library where he works, but it is shattered in the penultimate scene, when he learns that the 'health club' where Sandra, the girl of his dreams, works is actually a massage parlour (in Belfast at the time synonymous with a brothel). Not only that, but he spots among the patrons a cross-section of Northern Irish society: the organizer of the republican dance, the detective who questioned him, his boss from the library, even his uncle. It is a sadder but a wiser Nelson who informs a bus conductor at the end of the play that the words to the song the man is singing are 'I'm a dreamer, aren't we all?' and not 'I'm a dreamer Montreal'. Listeners can infer that his new respect for lyrics coincides with a more acute awareness of his surroundings.

Parker had trouble concentrating on *I'm a Dreamer Montreal*, he wrote, 'because my mind keeps straining at the leash to get into another stage play'. With the Royal Court holding an option on *Spokesong* and Joint Stock eager to work with him on devising a script, his sights were set higher than radio drama. Now he aspired unreservedly to theatrical success in London. This ambition received a boost in early February, when he learned that the National Theatre of Belgium would produce *Spokesong* in French that autumn. He felt 'bowled over' by this news, since he had 'never even been on the continent of *Europe*'. Moreover, the Belgian version would be directed by Bernard Goss, a reputable London director whose recent production of Tom Stoppard's *Rosencrantz and Guildenstern Are Dead* had won acclaim at the Young Vic.[10]

With such enticing prospects, Parker was already beginning to feel (and speak) as if he no longer lived in Belfast. Interviewed in late February by Michael Barnes and Brian Barfield for a radio discussion of 'Theatre in Ulster Today', Parker did not mince words. After describing his strenuous efforts to get *Spokesong* produced in Belfast, he expressed the opinion that 'the play may very well circumnavigate the globe before it is seen in the city in which it was written and about which it was written and to some degree *for* which it was written, if indeed it is ever seen here'. He dismissed the Lyric Players Theatre as irrelevant, arguing that it had started out inheriting the Abbey Theatre's tradition of 'bourgeois nationalism...a tradition, in my opinion, which is now utterly bankrupt'. Later, finding itself 'the only game in town', the Lyric 'took on the aegis of a kind of civic theatre, doing plays from the world repertory'. These two functions, Parker believed, had not 'coalesced', and 'production values at the Lyric have suffered enormously because of that hybrid position'. The Lyric, therefore, was 'not the theatre to look to for genuine new departures or for exciting and stimulating work.... this is demonstrated by the fact that nothing has ever really come out of the Lyric, in terms of acting or writing, that has been permanently important or that has made any kind of impact—of the kind that has been made in the past by writers like Sam Thompson, by *all* of the actors who came out of the Group tradition, Colin Blakely on back'. Listening to the programme on air several days later, Parker heard with satisfaction the 'Lyric being assailed from all sides' and 'Felt more than ever the power of the theatre to liberate the soul, mind—and probably body, in the end—from Lilliput.'[11]

Parker burned more bridges, less deliberately, in early March, when one of the journal's editors asked him to contribute to an *Honest Ulsterman* symposium on Philip Hobsbaum's Belfast Writers' Group. He responded by writing 'a brief parody-memoir on the spot':

> Great days—Belfast before the war—I knew them all, the one with the beard and guitar, and the other famous one, the bog person. How well I remember those Tuesday nights, or Mondays was it, the intense waggling of pencils, the big generous plate of biscuits, the fine acrid tang of the Nescafe, God yes. The air blue with repressed curses and Silk Cut smoke! What did we find to talk about so interminably, you're probably wondering—why, the world was young, poetry was under every stone, just waiting to crawl out and be mimeographed. Poetry! God how we craved it, molested it, exalted it, lived it—but above all explicated it! All gone, long gone. These days, for a long time now, I'm allergic to contemporary verse. Every time I pick it up, a strange sudden profound lethargy overwhelms me, I have to drop it immediately, unread, to avoid a catatonic stupor. Alas, the other muse, the sleazy voluptuous one of those boyish days, has me under wedlock and key; it's the New Stage Club I really remember well.

Though probably not calculated to offend, these flippant comments were wounding to those who did not share Parker's boredom with modern poetry. Joan Newmann, a fellow founding member of the Belfast Writers' Group, recollects that this piece also upset Parker's former colleagues because he sounded as if he did not even remember their names.[12]

Having given up on poetry, Parker eagerly sought to prove himself in his new career of playwright. In the spring of 1975, he had begun making notes (mainly a list of possible song titles) towards a stage play about a team of songwriters. His work on *Spokesong* had reminded him how much he liked writing lyrics, and he wanted to produce more of them. In addition, as he explained later, he felt the subject would speak with particular force to people his age and younger, who remembered 'the landmarks in their lives by means of hit records'. 'And', he added, 'everybody who came up with Lennon and McCartney sees a songwriting partnership as the choicest form of heroism.'[13] Parker's songwriters, though, would not be artist-heroes. More than five years of writing his *High Pop* column for the *Irish Times* had honed his interest in the music business as well as in music itself, and he had, on occasion, reviewed books about the packaging and selling of pop music.[14] Early in his thinking about the play, he had decided that 'catchpenny' would be part of the title; he meant *Catchpenny Twist*, the name he finally settled on, to evoke the pernicious effect of commercialism on pop culture. 'Money', he wrote, 'is often lavished upon movies, television series, songs, all of them full of energy and promise for much of their length. Then, at a crucial moment, there is a sickly lurch away from the issues that have been raised and towards the box-office returns—the moment of sell-out: the catchpenny twist.'[15]

Two public events in the summer of 1975 helped shape the play in Parker's mind. On 5 June, Northern Ireland participated in a British referendum on whether or not the United Kingdom should remain a member of the European Economic Community. The measure passed in the North, but Parker remained sceptical about the then-common notion that the EEC might make Northern Ireland's divisions irrelevant. In a notebook entry probably from mid-February 1976, Parker envisaged his songwriter play as 'A critique of the assumption that Ireland will be liberated from her past by Common Market cosmopolitanism.' *Spokesong* had posed the question of how to cope with the Irish past. The past also featured in *Catchpenny Twist*, Parker noted, represented by 'the decay of both Unionism and Republicanism, which are in their death throes'. In this play, though, he explicitly contrasted it with 'a modern technological society' he found 'murderous also, in its own inviting way'. The conflict between the two was 'savagely focussed' for Parker on 31 July 1975 when members of the Dublin-based Miami Showband driving home after a gig were ambushed and killed by the loyalist Ulster Volunteer Force just north of the border. This atrocity seemed especially senseless to many because the band included Protestants and Catholics, who had grown up on both sides of the border. 'The Miami Showband musicians', Parker acknowledged, 'died because of where they lived, not because of what they did for a living. But even so, the blood-shed derived a horrific added force from the sense that ancient and modern had taken flesh, the one to wreak a blind atavistic revenge on the other.'[16]

Parker's songwriters, Roy Fletcher and Martyn Semple, 'indulge a cosmopolitan fantasy of Success, as a mode of escape from the past'. They cannot be said to have sold out artistically, since their sole ambition is to make money. They do, however, compromise their principles in pursuit of financial gain after being fired from their teaching jobs. Although both insist the Troubles have nothing to do with them, they unwisely launch their career in Belfast by writing, on the one hand, republican martyr-ballads to order for Martyn's ex-wife, Marie Kyle, an IRA activist, and, on the other, comic songs for Roy's cousin in the 'Protestant gestapo'. Soon the pair must leave Belfast with unseemly haste after receiving two live bullets in the post. They flee to Dublin, where they meet up with another former teacher and friend from university days, Monagh Cahoon, who has been working in a run-down cabaret. Roy, who is in love with her, suggests that the three of them should team up and 'co-ordinate everything—writing, singing, clothes, records, marketing, promotion'. Monagh accedes to this proposal, although she thinks their songs are drivel and her romantic energy remains fixed on her married lover, Ian Playfair, a Belfast-based television broadcaster.[17]

Just as the trio begins to achieve some recognition, Roy and Martyn have to move again after learning they are being sought by paramilitaries on both sides who, having discovered that they were supplying songs to both loyalists and republicans, suspect them of being British spies. They settle in London and start courting record companies there. One executive offers encouragement but advises them to 'lose the lady' ('Too old, too ordinary, and twopence a dozen'). Their willingness to cut Monagh loose is the real 'catchpenny twist' in the play, but first the three compete at an international song festival in Luxembourg which is a scaled-down version of the Eurovision Song Contest. As a pop music critic, Parker could hardly ignore that annual spectacle of popular music catering to the lowest common denominator. In February 1976 he had even served on a panel to choose the British entry (the song with 'the most intense degree of cheerful imbecility won', he noted in his journal). Such pan-European contests favoured songs with inane lyrics, since they had to appeal across myriad language barriers. Parker's 'The Zig-Zag Song' parodies the typical Eurovision winner, with a chorus consisting mainly of 'LA-LA' and verses like 'NOW YOU KNOW THE ZIG ZAG SONG/ALL JOIN IN THE ZIG ZAG SONG/TO AND FRO THE ZIG ZAG SONG/ALL BEGIN THE ZIG ZAG SONG'. Roy and Martyn do not fare well with their own entry, 'Crybaby', largely because Monagh is suffering a nervous breakdown in response to the news that Playfair has been shot and killed while filming.[18]

Parker subtitled *Catchpenny Twist* 'A Charade in Two Acts'. In a note to the published script, he explained that the play

> tries to keep one foot in real life while the other steps into a realm of...well, nothing as grand as myth or allegory or even parable. I ended up employing the humble word 'charade'. It seemed apt for the goings-on in my native city.
>
> The play is a comedy for most of the time, which some people might think distasteful. Yet how else do you write about a situation which is desperate but not serious?[19]

Audiences are less likely to react negatively to the comic elements of *Catchpenny Twist* than to the fact that Parker does not keep the play in a comic mode. The murder of Playfair indicates that the characters are not invulnerable. This point is emphasized in the play's final scene, immediately following the hilarity of the song contest. Roy, Martyn, and Monagh (the latter virtually comatose from the pills she has taken to deaden her pain) are sitting in the airport lounge in Luxembourg waiting for their plane out. Roy and Martyn read a newspaper account of their early career that blows their cover, discuss Martyn's suggestion that they should return to their (Irish) 'roots', and decide to drop Monagh now that she has publicly disgraced herself. During this dialogue, they open congratulatory telegrams. The end of the play abruptly departs from realism, as Martyn unwraps a package he has also been holding:

> (*He rips the tape off the package. Simultaneously—Blackout.*
> *Explosion. A noisy drum intro. The band strikes up. A red spot comes on, showing* MONAGH *on her feet, smiling brightly, with a hand mike.* ROY *and* MARTYNS' *seats are toppled over. In the red glow, we see them on their knees, hands and faces covered in blood, groping about blindly.*)

The last words the audience hears are the lyrics to 'Crybaby', as Monagh sings, 'DON'T BE A CRYBABY/IF YOU WANNA BE MY BABY...'. Even those Northern Irish people who wish most strenuously to ignore politics, Parker suggests, cannot escape the legacy of the past. And artists, whose insight into the situation might be presumed to be greater than the average person's, have no business even trying to avoid it. This startling ending represents Parker's refusal of the 'catchpenny twist', a confounding of audience expectations that veers *away* from easy popularity and charm.[20]

Parker worked intensely on *Catchpenny Twist* in spring 1976, writing the first draft between mid-March and mid-May. Near the end of this period, he received bad news regarding the Joint Stock project. In late January, Max Stafford-Clark had stated his intention of applying to the Arts Council of Northern Ireland for funds to conduct a two-week workshop on Parker's *Boycott* idea in Northern Ireland. This would involve Parker, four Joint Stock actors and a director, and two local actors in improvisation and research. In mid-April, Joint Stock finally made a formal application, requesting £1,335 and offering to tour Northern Ireland with the play.[21] Parker was immediately summoned to the Arts Council to discuss Joint Stock's request. He heard nothing more until 5 May, when he learned the Arts Council had rejected the application on the grounds that it would prefer to give the money to local artists.

Coming so soon after the *Spokesong* denials, this decision demoralized Parker. Michael Heffernan urged him to protest, but his energy for righteous indignation had been drained. 'I see no point in persevering here', he observed tersely in his journal. 'Nothing is ever going to change in any sphere of life.' Instead, he worked doggedly on *Catchpenny Twist*, redoubling his usual efforts until he finished a draft. He tried to put the Arts Council's refusal of support from his mind, but he never forgot or stopped feeling bitter about it. A friend close to Parker at the end of his life recalls that 'He continued to feel...that this episode was the point in his career when he could have had an association with a vibrant company of some excellence which would have helped him to grow theatrically and given him a platform for his work. And that for little more than a thousand pounds this chance was lost and was never to come again.'[22]

Scarcely a week after Parker heard about the Arts Council's decision, as Kate finished typing *Catchpenny Twist* to his dictation, Parker's agent Hugh Alexander informed him that the Royal Court had dropped its option on *Spokesong*, citing 'financial difficulties'—a reason Parker rejected. Luckily, the Kings Head Theatre Club in Islington still wanted the play.[23] Parker had already planned a trip to London, leaving the next day, to shop *Catchpenny Twist* around to directors and producers, meet with Bernard Goss to discuss the latter's production of *Spokesong* for the Belgian National Theatre, and see Stephen Rea perform in Samuel Beckett's *Endgame* at the Royal Court. While there, he visited the Kings Head.

About six years previously, Dan Crawford, a New Yorker, had turned a billiard room at the back of the Kings Head pub into a theatre club (it cost twenty-five pence a year to join) with seats for 125 people, although a few more could be accommodated at a pinch. Crawford's idiosyncratic tastes determined the programme; a typical Kings Head play, he explains, took a humanistic, even sentimental, view of its subject and usually included music. The 'theatre' was outfitted with wooden tables and chairs, and patrons could order dinner before the show and drinks during it. Open fires provided the only heat. In the mid-1970s, though, the Kings Head's reputation transcended its rudimentary facilities. Productions at this fringe venue were attended by media and theatre professionals and reviewed by top London critics. In 1975, the Kings Head's production of Robert Patrick's *Kennedy's Children* had transferred to the West End, where it ran for nine months after a six-month run in Islington. There were many reasons, then, for Parker to take heart in this theatre's interest in his work, and the space gave him a 'Good feeling.' Crawford brimmed over with plans for the production and had chosen a director, Robert Gillespie. He treated the whole thing, Parker noticed, 'as a fait accompli', and his enthusiasm transferred itself to Parker.[24] By the time a contract was finalized between the Kings Head and Parker's agent, Parker had already met Crawford and Gillespie to discuss casting and other production issues, and by mid-June they had agreed that the play would open in early September.

Meanwhile, with *Catchpenny Twist* presentable and a London production of *Spokesong* launched, Parker wanted to begin work on another play. One idea he had was a dramatic treatment of the life of Dion Boucicault, the Victorian Irish playwright famous for his melodramas. Parker had borrowed a volume of his plays from the library in early April and been enthralled by the biographical introduction, quickly deciding that Boucicault's life (every bit as improbable and excessive as any of his plays) would make a good television series or stage play. In the months that followed, he read several of Boucicault's plays and took whatever opportunities presented themselves to see any of them performed.[25] When Parker visited Dublin in early June, composer Jimmy Kennedy piqued his interest in another Victorian compatriot, 'the Irish singing clown' Johnny Patterson. Kennedy and his agent wanted Parker to write the book for a musical about Patterson for which Kennedy had already written five original songs. Parker liked the story but worried that his treatment of it would not mesh with theirs. Nevertheless, he thought he would 'have a crack at the Johnny Patterson material', although he declined to commit himself to Kennedy's project at this point.[26] Although neither play idea achieved final form in the 1970s, Parker later combined them in *Heavenly Bodies*.

Parker felt most ready to tackle the script for a play he had been contemplating since December 1975, depicting an undertaker as a businessman developing a monopoly over burial. By the end of May 1976, he had decided that the undertaker should also be an amateur magician whose daughter helps him with his tricks and that another character would be his ambitious assistant.[27] In August, after a couple of months spent working on other things, Parker began researching the play, which he had decided to call *Nightshade*, obtaining copies of Colin Parkes's *Bereavement: Studies of Grief in Adult Life*, Jessica Mitford's *The American Way of Death*, and Geoffrey Gorer's *Death, Grief, and Mourning*. Thoughts of the play dominated what little quiet time he had, but it would be quite a while before Parker could focus on writing it.

He also devoted time in June and July 1976 to revisions of *Catchpenny Twist* and a reworking of *The Iceberg* as a stage play that would not rely on the device of convincing the audience that it was watching the recording of a radio play (as the staged version in Ithaca in the summer of 1974 had done). To spare the set designer from having to rebuild *Titanic* on stage, Parker abandoned naturalistic conventions. The main characters, Hugh and Danny, are presented realistically, but the rest of the named parts are played by members of the ship's band, all of whom are dressed in evening clothes and white face make-up. The setting is similarly stylized, a series of rostra 'at different levels, and connected by steps and ladders', which merely implies a luxury liner with a central 'palm court arrangement' and, at the highest point, a davit with the suggestion of a lifeboat suspended from it.[28] Once Parker reconceived the play in this mode, few other revisions were required, and the dialogue and action remain much as in the radio version.

Throughout the first half of 1976, Parker still had to do plenty of more prosaic work for the BBC and the *Irish Times* to make ends meet. Although he had achieved a measure of critical success, this had not yet been translated into financial security. Among his assignments in 1976 were a television script on St Patrick; a treatment for a radio feature on Sean O'Casey's *The Silver Tassie*; interviewing and consulting for a *Gallery* television programme on Jimmy Kennedy; a television script based on his *Bus Stories* for the central BBC; occasional reviewing for *Bookends* (though Parker no longer participated regularly); reviewing rock music for and sometimes presenting *Saturday Review*; and the weekly *High Pop* column (often written about the same albums he reviewed for radio). One especially time-consuming project involved helping the Arts Programmes Department of BBC Northern Ireland develop a new Friday night radio arts programme, *Friday Supplement*, which Parker presented several times that autumn. He made a bold decision regarding this kind of work, though, on 4 August 1976. The *Irish Times* had asked him to write a long article on 'popular music today', and when he sent his copy to the newspaper he included a note saying that he would like to quit writing *High Pop* by October. 'Is this a mistake?' he wondered in his journal. 'It does bring in £500 a year, which is more than 1/4 of my total earnings. Plus the records. But it's a constant treadmill. I think the time has come to make a total commitment to playwriting.' Thanks to Michael Heffernan, who had read the play in May, the BBC network wanted to buy *Catchpenny Twist* for a television play, a prospect that thrilled Parker: 'Apart from reaching the massive audience, maybe at last I'll make a little money out of a play.'[29] Knowledge of this interest no doubt stiffened his resolution to concentrate on drama. He wrote his final *High Pop* column at the end of August.

Parker knew where he wanted his career to go, and, remarkably, it seemed to be moving in the right direction. The same could not be said of his personal life, then being tugged by disturbing undercurrents. After the February discovery that their cottage in Rostrevor had been broken into, he and Kate rarely spent long weekends there any more, going down mainly for the occasional Sunday and leaving only a few possessions there. Kate, especially, missed the quiet and fresh air and the opportunity to spend time alone with her husband. Another underlying source of tension in their marriage surfaced emphatically that summer. Kate understood that Stewart wished to move to London—and sooner rather than later, since most of his potential work was based there. In late June, a consideration of holiday plans triggered in her 'an anxiety attack about the possibility of moving to London'. Her 'emotional storm' brewed until the couple faced the issue directly with a serious discussion of the subject, which concluded with the decision that Stewart should commute instead during the next six months or so.[30]

The matter had not been settled, however, and Kate remained out of sorts during a July trip to London. The thought of having to live in the city, which she found overwhelming, made her literally sick. Stewart finally persuaded her to talk about what was bothering her and learned that she feared London and would have preferred an 'intimate holiday in Scotland'. Likely more important than either of these was her admission that she had been, as Stewart recorded in his journal, 'feeling that my work was all I was really interested in'. He added contritely: 'The whole holiday has been poisoned by a classic misunderstanding. Plus my obtuseness.' The two of them cut short their trip to return to Belfast.[31]

Kate's distress intensified when they arrived home and discovered that her mother had been ill in their absence. Kate, who every week spent at least one night at her mother's house, arranged to stay with her for several days. On 30 July she shared with Stewart her concern over her mother's 'worrying mental wanderings' and 'erratic behaviour'. The opinion of some of her relatives that it was her duty to move into her mother's house and take care of her compounded her anxiety.[32] Stewart tried to calm her, but Kate remained so tense that he was greatly relieved to escape to London for the second week of *Spokesong* rehearsals at the Kings Head.

In Edinburgh for its annual Festival at the end of August, Stewart once again broached with Kate the subject of 'her continuing bad state of mind'. Later the same day, they talked with Marcus Patton about the possibility of her getting involved with the second-hand bookshop that he and another friend, Steph Pickering, were planning to open in Edinburgh. Patton endorsed the idea, and, probably at this time, Stewart and Kate came to the understanding that they would move to Edinburgh as soon as they had managed to save enough money.[33] Edinburgh represented a compromise destination: away from Belfast, but relatively close to it, and a mere train ride from London. Because of the existence of the Rugby Road 'annexe' at Patton's flat in Edinburgh, the city, which they knew only from visits, seemed almost an extension of Belfast to them and had been the setting for many happy memories of Festivals and feasts. Returning to Belfast after the previous year's Festival, in the immediate aftermath of the Miami Showband massacre, Parker had been engulfed by 'the sense that the war is coming to a head' and wondered if the next time they came to Edinburgh it would be 'as refugees'.[34] The city seemed a haven, and the prospect of a career for Kate made it even more attractive.

London still exerted a magnetic pull on Stewart, however, and he would spend more and more time there, often alone, as his play-writing career developed. His first foothold in the capital was the Kings Head production of *Spokesong*, and he approached the collaboration with eager expectation. On his first extended visit, he stayed in a 'grotty' room over the pub: 'The dream of the dipsomaniac Irishman', he quipped, 'living above a pub theatre.' He liked the cast, though he had initially questioned the choice of Robert Bridges, an actor weighing over 20 stone, to play the Trick Cyclist (Dan Crawford allows that Bridges turned out to be a 'variable' performer). The actors who played Frank, Daisy, and Francis—Niall Buggy, Annabel Leventon, and Patrick Waldron—most consistently pleased Parker. A relaxed atmosphere prevailed at rehearsals, with the cast quickly accustomed to Parker's presence and willing to take notes from him, and Crawford showed genuine interest in him and his work. A warm sense of homecoming suffused Parker. At the end of his second day monitoring rehearsals, he and Crawford stayed up late counting the pub's takings, drinking beer, and talking. The conversation ended with Crawford asking if he would like to apply for a play-writing residency at the Kings Head. 'Said I would', Parker recorded, with a self-consciously Joycean echo, 'Yes.'[35]

Crawford scheduled *Spokesong*'s opening night after consulting an astrologer armed with Parker's date of birth. Despite such expert advice, the first preview, on 7 September, seemed 'A horrible mess' from Parker's point of view. He smothered his 'anguish' as best he could by getting 'extremely drunk'. Some of this can be discounted as reflecting an author's hyper-sensitivity. John Gilbert, who saw the production on the same night, thought the cast much stronger than in Dublin and believed that the songs, and even the accents, were better. He noted in his journal, though, that Parker felt the actors were playing the script for laughs and 'confusing' the audience. The next day, Parker confronted the director and discovered that he did not understand a number of elements of the play, including the role of the Trick Cyclist. Parker regretted that they had not had this conversation at the beginning of the rehearsal period, but he cheered up after finding the show 'Immeasurably better' that night: 'Having had an audience to play to at last, the cast are pulling the production up.'[36]

This improvement continued throughout the preview week, so that by the night of the press opening, 14 September, Parker felt 'fairly calm', despite a packed house and the presence of all the critics at an adjacent table. As soon as the play got underway, he wrote in his journal, 'I knew it was going to be OK.' An enthusiastic audience summoned the cast back for two curtain calls, filling Parker with 'relief and thankfulness'. He had even more to be thankful for when he read the reviews. He first saw B. A. Young's 'unqualified rave' in the *Financial Times*: 'I can't recommend it too highly', Young concluded. The *Daily Telegraph*'s John Barber hailed Parker as 'a brilliant new writer', while Michael Billington in the *Guardian* lauded the show's 'freewheeling lightness and gaiety'. *Time Out*'s critic, Ann McFerran, urged readers not to miss 'this brilliantly funny, deeply moving play', and Milton Shulman in the *Evening Standard* wrote that Parker had 'brought to the appalling beastliness of the Irish dilemma a gentle irony and a generous comic spirit that makes this one of the truly amusing plays of the year'. By then even Parker had begun 'to feel that the play may be a success'. Reviewers from *The Times*, *Observer*, *Sunday Telegraph*, and *Spectator* joined in the chorus of praise. Writing to Bea MacLeod at the end of the month, Parker speculated that the London critics 'must be grateful for a laugh, since they have to sit through so many gloomy plays'.[37]

Privately, Parker believed none of the critics had 'penetrated the play's surface', and he hated 'the way *Spokesong* is treated as a lighthearted frolic'. He could not complain about the results of these reviews, however. The Kings Head saw its fortunes reversed overnight. The pub's telephone service was cut off for lack of payment the day after the reviews started to appear, but Crawford collected everyone's spare change and got it restored within hours. He needed a working phone to handle this 'flat out hit'. The Saturday after the opening, the theatre had to turn away 300 people; Crawford immediately extended the play's run until Christmas, and he had already begun taking reservations for the end of October and talking about a possible transfer to the West End. Meanwhile, Parker had returned home to Belfast, after three and a half weeks away, with two gifts from Crawford: a 'House Full' sign and a £100 advance from the safe. He plunged back into the grind of BBC work, helping producers Paul Muldoon and Martin Dillon plan the new *Friday Supplement* programme, due to go on air at the beginning of October. No wonder he suffered from 'the post-baby blues'.[38]

Parker soon found out, though, that good reviews had the power to do more than pack a theatre every night. 'Life has changed a bit', he reported to Alfred Gingold: 'Suddenly people are ringing *me*.' Within a month of *Spokesong*'s first performances in London, Parker received letters from three authorities at Thames Television—a script executive and two producers (one of whom, Andrew Brown, had produced a television series beloved by Parker, *Rock Follies*)—all praising *Spokesong* and expressing interest in his future work. He also had a letter from a BBC script editor in Birmingham, requesting a copy of the *Spokesong* script, and one from David Aukin, a founder of Joint Stock, then administrator at the Hampstead Theatre, one of the few London theatres that produced new work, offering to commission a play.[39]

The Thames Television interest paid dividends even before Parker had the chance to meet any of his new fans. A few days after he got the first letter, Cecil Taylor, BBC Head of Programmes Northern Ireland, having heard through the grapevine that Thames wanted a Parker play for television, rang him to say he wished to finalize the purchase of *Catchpenny Twist*, pending for nearly two months. A morning of telephone calls between BBC authorities in Belfast and London and Parker's agent resulted in a deal allowing the BBC to commission the script for a seventy-five-minute *Play for Today* at a fee of £1,650, almost certainly the most Parker had ever earned for one piece of writing. *Play for Today* was then 'the most prestigious slot on television for a writer'. The subjects of the plays varied, but the programme had a reputation for presenting 'political and socially agitating' work.[40] *Catchpenny Twist* would make history as the first full-length television play made in Belfast, which at the time did not have a television drama department. Michael Heffernan would act as script editor, but the producer/director would have to be brought over from London.[41]

The day after the *Catchpenny Twist* deal was made, Stewart and Kate headed up the Antrim coast for a two-day holiday in celebration. Ominously, what they intended as a restful getaway became the occasion for another series of 'soul-searching' discussions. Their interactions repeatedly ended in 'Anguished self-analytic talk' until they proceeded home again, 'a point of tension & weariness reached'. That night, an attack of spasms in the stump of his amputated leg disturbed Parker's sleep, always a sign that he was under tremendous stress.[42]

As he generally did, Parker took refuge from emotional turmoil in his work. The first royalty cheque from the Kings Head and the news that *Plays and Players* magazine planned to publish *Spokesong* as its December/January play text heartened him considerably. He also had the timely distraction of a week-long trip to London in mid-October to check up on the show, talk about transfer possibilities with Crawford, meet with people at Thames Television and the BBC, and try to arouse theatrical interest in *Catchpenny Twist*. By this time, the bohemian hospitality of the Kings Head (where he was invited to sleep on a 'bare bed w/ a pile of dusty drapes, hessian & old coats for bedding') had lost its initial appeal.[43] He soon opted for the superior comfort of the flat occupied by John Gilbert's architect friend, Brian McKibbin, his wife Nancy, and their daughter Laura. This was where he and Kate usually stayed when they came to London, and from now until the McKibbins moved to Canada in June 1977 it would be Parker's base on solitary trips as well. The warmth of their welcome made London feel like a second home; because they shared so many friends, Nancy always arranged reunions with the London-based ones. This time, Parker got to see Ken and June Lambla, who had moved out of 9 Rugby Road on 10 October and were stopping briefly in London on their way back to the US.

Parker's meetings at Thames Television resulted in the company's commissioning a treatment from him for a series of television plays based on the life of Dion Boucicault. (He wrote this synopsis about a month later, but Thames ultimately decided against making the series.) The Thames executives also talked about wanting to film *Spokesong*, as did the BBC Birmingham script editor Parker lunched with a couple of days later, but these proposals also came to nought—probably just as well, since much of *Spokesong*'s power stems from its theatrical form and would have been diluted on film. Nevertheless, Parker had made some important contacts and influential allies at Thames. One lasting friendship also came out of these encounters, since Andrew Brown introduced Parker to Howard Schuman, the American writer of *Rock Follies*. The two dramatists would remain in close contact until Parker's death. A meeting at the Hampstead Theatre, where *Catchpenny Twist* had already been read and rejected, went less well: 'Like walking into a shooting gallery & finding yourself the target', Parker observed.[44]

Parker returned to Belfast in time for his birthday on 20 October, pleased to find the domestic air considerably cleared. In his absence, Kate had devoted herself to writing a dramatic entertainment for him entitled *The Courtship of Lady Mary*, based on an idea she had told him about years before. Encouraged by this initiative on her part, Parker took the script to Brian Barfield at the BBC in early November. A couple of months later, Kate herself met with Barfield to discuss the possibility of writing features for him, though nothing came of this.[45]

A few weeks after *Spokesong* opened, Parker had begun working on another play of his own. *The Actress and the Bishop*, written in September and October 1976, was a forty-minute one-act designed to be performed by the *Spokesong* leads (Niall Buggy and Annabel Leventon) at lunchtime in the Kings Head. 'Lunchtime theatre is quite a thing in London fringe theatres', Parker explained to an American friend, 'and gets a fair amount of coverage.' *The Actress and the Bishop* derives from a British joke formula, which Parker explicated thus: 'it's when an unwitting double entendre is uttered and somebody ripostes "... as the actress said to the bishop"'—he and Sam Fannin frequently entertained one another with such knowing humour. 'Any show...with this title', Fannin comments, 'would be bound to pull in the punters.'[46]

The idea of making a play out of a compromising situation involving an actress and a bishop dated from 1972. Teaching a play-writing course for Cornell University's summer session, Parker had written a skit called *The Actress and the Bishop* for the class. This resembled a cross between a sex farce and a political drama. A Catholic actress and Protestant bishop wake up together in the Bishop's Palace after a one-night stand. Gunfire keeps them there for a time, and they argue about the ways in which each other's latent attitudes sustain the Troubles. 'Couldn't make up my mind what kind of play it was meant to be, so it's ended up a weird mongrel', Parker wrote to John Gilbert: 'The students think it's good, which just goes to show how little I've taught them.' Nevertheless, Denys Hawthorne, acting Radio Drama producer for BBC Northern Ireland, attempted, unsuccessfully, to sell a proposal based on the script to the network.[47]

About the only thing *The Actress and the Bishop* shares with the earlier sketch is a theory about the similarities between theatre and religion. Parker made this comparison obliquely in a few lines in the play's original version. In the text as performed, comparing the two and speculating about their common origin in magic are major themes both of conversation between the actress and the bishop and of the long sermon the bishop rehearses in the second half of the play. The Troubles are not mentioned; instead, the context is comic and the characters rounded and sympathetic. A young bishop has arranged for the performance in his cathedral of a rock musical called *Sodom's Lot*, and he and the actress playing Lot's wife become friendly. They go bird-watching together (an occasion for jokes about Great Tits and Night-jars) and then strike up a relationship. Their romance is blighted, however, because the actress is married (although she has not seen her actor husband in three years) and the bishop fears becoming the butt of smutty humour. As he attempts to explain to his lover why they cannot go on seeing each other, the text reaches a crescendo of risqué double meanings:

> I know it's hard to grasp, I mean I don't know how to put it to you...Oh, my God...I mean put yourself in my position...oh no...I can't get on top of it, I mean look at it my way, I mean it's very hard, I mean I can't get it straight, when you get right down to it, nothing will fit, Oh Jesus, I've lost my grip, it won't come out right, I mean I don't know how to get out of it!

'Well...thank you for coming', he lamely concludes. 'Thank you for having me', she replies.[48]

Dan Crawford liked the play and let Parker direct it himself. The actors were ambivalent (rehearsing or performing during the day and again in the evening left little time for anything else) but assented to a nine-performance run opening on 9 December 1976. The show attracted healthy crowds for a lunchtime slot and earned favourable reviews from the *Daily Telegraph* and the *Guardian*. Parker believed the production achieved his own objectives, as he described them to Alfred Gingold: 'It had the desired effect of injecting new life into the *Spokesong* run, and it allowed me to dabble in the shallow end of directing without getting drowned.'[49]

Rehearsals for *The Actress and the Bishop* were briefly interrupted in November by a short trip Parker took to Belgium for the final rehearsals and first public performance (in Louvain) of the Belgian National Theatre's *Spokesong*. He judged this production 'lively & clever but Gallic and rather humourless'. Opening night, which began inauspiciously with the Trick Cyclist tumbling off his unicycle on his first entrance, confirmed Parker's initial impression, with the audience 'bemused & finally bored'. Six weeks later Parker returned to Belgium, with Kate, for the gala opening in Brussels. He found the show 'Tightened up w/cuts since November, to more audience response, but still a long way from *Spokesong*.' The critics were equally unimpressed, one characterizing the play as 'une pièce inexportable'. 'Possibly a combination of bicycles and urban violence would not appeal to the Belgian national character in any guise,' Parker ruefully speculated to Gingold, 'but the contributions of an aged and humourless academic translator and a non-French speaking English director didn't help much.' However, he added philosophically, he and Kate had enjoyed a 'marvellous holiday'.[50]

Fortunately, the Kings Head production of *Spokesong* remained a source of pride. At the beginning of December, Parker won a play-writing bursary sponsored by Thames Television. He would be paid £1,750 to be on 'attachment' to the Kings Head for the next twelve months. Although Parker would remain in Belfast, the money would allow him to make frequent visits to London. His main obligation would be to write a play for the Kings Head.[51]

Less than two weeks later, Parker learned he had received the *Evening Standard*'s Most Promising Playwright Award for 1976. He confided to his journal his 'Strange feeling of having some unaccountable magic power—everything I touch turning up trumps.' Kate, he noted in the same entry, was 'having a crisis', though he chose to focus instead on a phone call from Crawford announcing that he had arranged for *Spokesong* to transfer to the Arts Theatre Club in the West End on 2 February: the same day Parker would collect his statuette at the Savoy. 'The wheel of fortune has become positively embarrassing', he wrote to Bea MacLeod. Almost as if to bring himself down a bit, Parker spent some time in the second half of December researching and making notes towards his planned undertaker play. Even the falling-through of the transfer deal at the end of the month, however, could not dampen his spirits. Crawford assured him that, after a two-week break, the *Spokesong* cast would return to the Kings Head to continue the run until mid-February at least, and Parker pronounced this 'satisfying news' on which to end 'the most important year in my life'.[52]

The new year began on a forward-looking note. In January 1977, Parker opened an account at the Halifax Building Society to start saving for a flat in Edinburgh. Meanwhile, he struggled to begin writing the undertaker play, distracted by snatches of news about another possible *Spokesong* transfer and by looming trouble with Jimmy Kennedy. The latter had composed the music for *Spokesong* as a favour to Parker and had not, in 1975, requested a stake in the script. The international interest in the play, about which Parker and his agent, Hugh Alexander, had kept Kennedy apprised, took him by surprise, and he had begun to regret his generosity. In late January, having heard from Alexander about various European agreements for the play, Kennedy phoned Parker, 'indignant that he wasn't to get a royalty'. 'These are uncomfortable, uneasy days', Parker remarked in his journal. 'So hard to sift out what's important and sustain a flow of energy into it. Constantly edgy & unsettled.' This mood intensified during rocky contract talks between Crawford and Alexander (finally resolved to enable a transfer to the Vaudeville Theatre in the West End to proceed in February) and Alexander and Kennedy. Kennedy rejected Parker's offer of 10 per cent of his royalties and by mid-February was demanding 25 per cent of Parker's earnings to date, plus at least 20 per cent of his future royalties. These payments to Kennedy, plus percentages owed to the Dublin Theatre Festival (40 per cent) and Alexander (10 per cent), meant that Parker would be allowed to keep only 25–30 per cent of his own royalties. Moreover, in the short term, his income from the play would be drastically reduced as he paid past royalties to Kennedy. 'Intensely dispiriting', Parker commented in his journal. 'A wealthy septuagenarian ripping me off. Resolve to have nothing more to do with him.'[53] The *Evening Standard* award ceremony offered a welcome diversion, topped off nicely by a taxi ride back to the McKibbins' flat past the Vaudeville, with Parker's name in lights out front.

Spokesong opened in the West End on 16 February 1977, and several of the critics (along with Parker himself) regarded it as diminished by the change of venue. As one reviewer commented, 'it seems trapped somewhat by the confining shape of a conventional stage'.[54] The lead-up to the opening saw the cast in open rebellion against the director, Robert Gillespie, and the crew at the Vaudeville refusing both to help the Kings Head designer adapt the old set to the new space and to let anyone else help him. The first preview performance took place before the director, cast, and crew had made it through a complete dress rehearsal, with predictable technical difficulties. Parker reported to John Gilbert a few days after the opening that 'the great West End is exactly the same as the Dublin Theatre Festival, only worse':

> We had two weeks to effect the transfer from the back-room of a pub to a red-plush proscenium arch theatre with two balconies, seating 559. There was no designer (not provided for in the budget). The director had taken a job in TV and wasn't available till 2 days before opening. The cast were performing in the King's [*sic*] Head each evening also up to 2 days before opening, and two of them had taken afternoon jobs. A publicity budget of £3,000 was given to a crony of the producer's, who appeared to spend it on nothing except commercials on Capital Radio—virtually no posters, no newspaper ads, not even a display of quotes outside the theatre.

Nevertheless, Parker claimed, he had enjoyed himself—'up until the dreaded opening night'. This impressed upon him the difference between a Kings Head audience and a West End one: 'a collection of stuffed shirts, half of them in the terminal stages of consumption, coughing their lungs up, and the other half concentrating very hard on unwrapping their Quality Street. I sat in a box, where I couldn't see the stage, and drank a bottle of brandy.' Still, Parker marvelled, 'I've got a play in the West End.' He reminded Gilbert that the last Belfast play to reach that exalted height, *Over the Bridge* in 1960, had lasted only a week. 'I think we might make it to four weeks', he predicted. 'It would have been nice to have another long run, but the play has already done far, far more than I ever dreamed it could, and I'm more than satisfied. I'm ecstatic!'[55]

In the event, *Spokesong* lasted four and a half weeks at the Vaudeville. Crawford hoped to the last that some miracle would intervene to save the production. The Dunlop Rubber Company had put £10,000 into the transfer, and he thought the firm might be persuaded to contribute £10,000 more, but Dunlop prudently cut its losses. Mediocre box office could not sustain the show despite some decent reviews. These were not raves on the magnitude of those *Spokesong* had received at the Kings Head, but the performances of Leventon and Buggy were universally praised, and most of the critics spoke warmly about the play itself.[56] The Vaudeville *Spokesong* closed on 19 March 1977, ending what the playwright already nostalgically called 'the London *Spokesong* era'.[57]

Parker was spared depression over *Spokesong*'s demise by the news, which had reached him in late February, that the Abbey Theatre would produce *Catchpenny Twist* on its experimental Peacock stage. He had been trying to interest theatre managements in the play since the previous May, approaching the Royal Court, the National, the Dublin Theatre Festival, the Royal Shakespeare Company, and the Hampstead in addition to the Abbey. Pat Laffan wanted to direct it that summer, along with *The Actress and the Bishop* as a lunchtime show, so preparation would begin almost immediately. 'No time for regrets', Parker observed, 'No need.'[58]

Meanwhile, plans for the television version of *Catchpenny Twist* were proceeding. The day after confirming that there would indeed be a stage production, Parker met Michael Heffernan and Rob Knights, the London-based producer/director, to review the script and talk about adapting it for television. Within days, Parker had begun doing rewrites. He also confronted the now-urgent task of finding someone to compose music to go with his lyrics. He decided to approach Shaun Davey, a Northern-born composer living in Dublin whose light rock album he had reviewed for *High Pop*. After arranging to meet Davey, he remembered that he had heard about him from Marcus Patton and John Gilbert. All three had attended Campbell College, where, as part of a tiny band of artistically inclined pupils, they dabbled in music, visual art, and creative writing. Parker visited Davey early in March and listened to some of his tapes. 'He's been dividing his time between teaching Hist. of Art, & writing, arranging & producing songs, jingles & incidental music. In short, he's ideal', Parker proclaimed in his journal, adding that he had given Davey the play to read.[59] The younger man liked it, inaugurating their partnership.

Around the same time, frustrated by repeated postponements of the recording of his radio play *I'm a Dreamer Montreal*, Parker tried his hand at an 'instant adaptation' of that script for television, which he completed in three days in late February. Now he had something to show television producers interested in his work. Thames Television purchased an option on the television version of the play that summer, and in autumn Parker learned that a new drama producer there, Rob Buckler, wanted to make it and that Thames therefore would commission it for £1,260. Meanwhile, BBC Northern Ireland finally produced the radio version in April and May 1977. The cast included actors featured in previous BBC productions of Parker plays—notably John Hewitt as Nelson Glover and Joe McPartland as the band leader, Gaye—as well as a young Liam Neeson in a tiny part as the morgue attendant. Listening to a playback of the piece later, Parker felt it worked 'reasonably well', although much of the production failed 'to achieve what I had envisaged'. A gulf seemed to have opened up between himself and Heffernan, who may have been jealous that Parker's career was surging ahead at the very moment when he believed his own had stalled because of his continuing poor health—or maybe he felt, like Kate, that Parker's work now absorbed his energies to the exclusion of everything else. Whatever the reason, Parker had noticed in January an 'Odd feeling of constraint now between us', although he had no idea what had happened to create it. Heffernan had moved into 9 Rugby Road in mid-October 1976, but he moved out again by mid-January 1977.[60] By August he would leave Belfast for a new job with the BBC in London. *I'm a Dreamer Montreal* was aired in the meantime on the afternoon of 20 July, disappointing Parker by producing little critical or popular response.

The middle of March found Parker trying to generate an idea for a 'chamber musical' for the Kings Head. An earnings statement he received near the end of the month shattered his concentration, however. As he recorded in his journal, royalties from the Vaudeville and an advance from Australia for *Spokesong*, Kings Head royalties for *The Actress and the Bishop*, and payments from a couple of television programmes that had included excerpts from these plays, 'minus commission, VAT and Jimmy Kennedy's payoff, leaves me with £5.87. Unbelievable. I'm virtually broke again.' After shifting £200 from his building society account to the bank, Parker wrote to Kennedy—ostensibly to inform him that he was definitely not interested in collaborating on Kennedy's Johnny Patterson musical, but really to let him know about the bite his demands were taking out of Parker's earnings ('Incidentally, I got a statement of income yesterday, for the period December '76 to March '77, with a cheque for £5.87.... So I'm not in any danger just yet of being corrupted by success!').[61]

The same day, Parker felt himself coming down with the flu: 'the fourth virus I've caught since early January, each one more severe. Can only put it down to stress of the last six months. I suppose I'll have to ease up on the worrying.' Time in bed put him in a reflective mood: 'This illness is telling me to straighten out the priorities. The work and the ideas in the work are what matter. Let the rest look after itself.' He applied this philosophical attitude to a delicate exchange of letters with Kennedy, who had been genuinely shocked to hear about the precarious state of Parker's finances. When Kennedy offered to split his 'final payment' of £116 with the playwright, Parker, who had a better grasp of *Spokesong*'s earnings potential, replied coolly: 'Of course I can't possibly accept your cheque: the £116 is your due entitlement according to the terms agreed with Hugh Alexander and me, as was the preceding £285, which was what really wiped out my income for the past three months. We were obligated to meet these demands at the time, and it would be most unbusinesslike for any money to be informally returned to me at this stage.' Kennedy, now acutely 'embarrassed', protested that had he had 'any inkling' that the terms agreed would be 'onerous' for Parker, he would not have insisted upon them. Parker used this concession to press for a renegotiation of the contract 'to cover any future income I may earn from the play'. He suggested that Kennedy might 'moderate' his demand on the play's earnings from 25 per cent to 10 per cent; Kennedy countered with 12½ per cent, and the matter was settled.[62]

In early May 1977, a political crisis eclipsed Parker's personal concerns. Several loyalist groups, led by Ian Paisley, had demanded a return to majority rule in the North and a stronger offensive against the Provisional IRA. On 25 April, Paisley announced that he would call a strike in May to protest against the British government's handling of Northern Ireland's affairs. Like other Belfast residents, Parker spent the next several days stockpiling coal, petrol, and provisions to withstand a lengthy siege. People feared a repeat of the 1974 Ulster Workers' Council Strike, certainly what Paisley intended. The strike began on 3 May and shut down many parts of the city, although most of the shops closest to Rugby Road remained open. Factories operated, but there were reports of high absenteeism and intimidation of workers.

It soon became clear that this stoppage would not follow the same course as the UWC Strike, however, mainly because Protestants did not unite in support of it. The Ulster Unionist Party, Vanguard, and the Orange Order criticized the strike, and the workers themselves disagreed about its wisdom. By 5 May most had returned to work. Crucially, the Ballylumford power station workers stayed on the job; they had been essential to the success of the 1974 strike, and without their participation other businesses were enabled to keep running. As the strike wore on without making any headway, the strikers grew desperate. A bus driver was shot and killed, shutting down bus services in Belfast; a petrol station attendant was murdered; and Paisley was arrested after blockading himself in Ballymena. No publicity stunt, however, could disguise the fact that the majority of the province's workers did not wish to follow him this time. On 13 May, the strike ended without the strikers' demands being met. This 'Wonderful' result seemed to Parker to vindicate the judgement of ordinary people.[63]

During the strike, Parker began work on his play for the Kings Head. Over a year earlier, he had watched a television documentary that included a segment about the Black Irish of the Caribbean island of Montserrat. One of the Leeward Islands, Montserrat had been settled in 1632 by Irish Catholics fleeing religious persecution in other British colonies in the New World. At least six of the island's seventeenth-century governors were Irishmen, and in 1678, the year of the colony's first census, the Irish made up a majority of the population. That changed in the late seventeenth and early eighteenth centuries, as Montserrat's planters (some Irish, others English) switched from small-scale tobacco farming to sugar planting, meeting their increased need for labour with African slaves; these quickly outnumbered the Irish indentured servants and small tradesmen who had previously comprised most of the work-force of the island. Many Irish left for other colonies, but enough remained to intermarry gradually with their Black neighbours (finally released from slavery in 1834), producing offspring with names like Wendell O'Flaherty. In 1977, Montserrat, with its overwhelmingly Black population, remained a British Crown Colony with a governor appointed by Queen Elizabeth II. The Irish legacy lingered in place-names, surnames (both those acquired through intermarriage and those taken from former masters at the time of emancipation), and cultural traditions. On this 'Emerald Isle of the Caribbean', a shamrock decorated the front of the British Governor's house and served as the immigration stamp.[64]

In early May, having already received two instalments of his Thames bursary, Parker visited a friend recently returned from Montserrat and started reading up on the island, sure that here he had 'the substance of some sort of entertainment'.[65] Intrigued by the musical possibilities of an Irish–Caribbean fusion, which also excited Shaun Davey, Parker began writing what he had tentatively entitled *Jubilo*. On the surface, this piece seemed worlds away from the simultaneous political events in Northern Ireland, but the abortive loyalist strike had a decisive influence on the script. Parker wanted to highlight the power of average people to prevent bad things being done in their name, and to do so he proposed to transport a microcosm of Northern Ireland to the sunny Caribbean. The action of the play would be set on a fictional island named Macalla (the Irish word for 'echo'), modelled on Montserrat but differing from it in crucial respects. Unlike Montserrat, where the vast majority of the roughly 13,000 inhabitants were content as British subjects, Macalla would have a nationalist movement plotting the overthrow of the colonial administration, and the salient divisions on Parker's island would be political rather than racial.

Parker made *Jubilo* his main writing project through the summer of 1977—to the relief of Dan Crawford, who wanted to mount the show in November. What he had intended as a light-hearted frolic, however, proved unexpectedly difficult to produce. An original idea and setting were no use without a plot and convincing characters, and here Parker found himself uncharacteristically inhibited. The end of May saw him 'battling to get a style established'; by 7 June he had managed to eke out only fifteen 'fruitless' pages and feared he would have to start over; only in mid-June did he begin to sense 'a glimmer of possibility'. Parker was still struggling with writer's block in early July. 'My problem', he explained in a letter to Alfred Gingold, 'is to write a book and lyrics for a combined Irish and black West Indian cast. Never having touched down in the [Caribbean], I feel a little nervous of the task. I'm trying to cover myself by filing it under Fantasy, but how others will perceive it is something else.'[66]

Interspersed with Parker's increasingly frantic efforts to write *Jubilo* were a number of other personal and professional concerns. His mother, diagnosed with an arthritic hip in January 1977, spent 9 May to 6 July in hospital, first to be put into traction and then for a hip joint operation. In May, the Long Wharf Theatre in New Haven, Connecticut, made an offer for *Spokesong*, news that Parker had been waiting and hoping for since they had requested a script in January; in September he learned that their production would open in February 1978.

Meanwhile, in July, an actor friend of John Fairleigh's named Richard Kay performed, with Sheila Reid, *The Actress and the Bishop* at the Oxford Playhouse and later at the Young Vic studio in London (a production that failed to please either Parker or the critics over-much).[67]

The Peacock production of *Catchpenny Twist*, which went into rehearsal in late July, constituted Parker's most significant non-writing commitment that summer. He liked the cast, which included Deirdre Donnelly as Monagh, Raymond Hardie (the original Frank Stock) as Roy, and Desmond Cave as Martyn. Parker shuttled between Belfast and Dublin in August, seeing roughly half the rehearsals. A preview on 24 August sold out, with twenty people standing, and left him feeling 'pleased & hopeful'. The opening on the following night provoked the usual 'dark night of the soul', but the audience responded favourably.[68] Parker dared to hope for another hit.

The reviews, however, struck him as 'demoralising and anguishing'. All the critics praised the acting of the three protagonists (and of Des Keogh, who played several bit parts), although some expressed doubts about Donnelly's singing. The play itself inspired more ambivalent reactions. David Nowlan of the *Irish Times* began his critique by observing that 'The trouble with plays about bores is that they tend to be boring. The risk in musicals about unsuccessful song-writers is that the songs may be indifferent. When the singer of those songs is supposed to be a bad singer the hazard is, predictably, multiplied.' *Catchpenny Twist*, he suggested, 'runs the full gamut of these risks and problems'. Con Houlihan panned the music in the *Irish Press* and called the play 'a rickety vehicle for jokes and gags', a disappointment after *Spokesong*, before urging readers, inexplicably, not to miss it. The *Irish Independent's* critic, Desmond Rushe, enjoyed the play, although he complained about being 'punished by the decibel level' and unable to understand the words of the songs. Reviews in the *Sunday Press* and *Evening Press* were more positive, largely because the reviewers evidently had more tolerance for pop music, but Gus Smith of the *Sunday Independent* voiced the weariness of many in the Republic with the subject of the Troubles when he complained that 'the North no longer amuses me'.[69] Parker, devastated, spent the better part of two afternoons in bed drinking Pernod.

If *Catchpenny Twist* did not achieve success of *Spokesong* dimensions, it hardly flopped. By early September the show averaged 75 per cent business (about a hundred people in the audience each night). This figure dropped off precipitately towards the middle of the month, but *Catchpenny Twist* received a boost near the end of its run when *The Actress and the Bishop* opened in the lunchtime slot, with Des Keogh and Billie Morton (who played multiple small female parts in *Catchpenny*) in the title roles. The one-act broke the Peacock's lunchtime attendance records, earned glowing reviews, and had its run extended by popular demand. The last three days of *Catchpenny Twist's* run coincided with the start of the Dublin Theatre Festival, and these performances were packed. Parker attended the final one on 8 October and judged the acting 'first-rate & well-received'. Unfortunately, the London critics had not yet arrived in town, so this Festival did not result in metropolitan exposure for the playwright.[70]

Upon returning to Belfast after the Dublin opening of *Catchpenny Twist*, Parker had resumed the dispiriting task of trying to finish his script for the Kings Head. This he found even harder now, with his 'confidence gone to pieces'. On 9 September, he flew to London to deliver a rough draft of the script to Dan Crawford and to meet Tony Tanner, the New York-based director Crawford had engaged for the production. Parker took an instant liking to Tanner, who felt the script still needed a great deal of work and made useful suggestions regarding revisions. Back in Belfast, Parker ground away at a second draft, changing the name of the play from *Jubilo* to *Kingdom Come*. On 21 September he posted copies of the revised Act I to Crawford and Tanner. Crawford accepted it with the caveat that it seemed a bit short, but Tanner phoned from New York to say that it did not seem to him to have enough plot. As Parker summarized their conversation, Tanner argued that 'Nothing happens. Feels that we must either get another director, or postpone opening till I draw out the full potential of the script.' Parker 'Felt a little shell-shocked. Another in an apparently endless series of traumas. But after thinking it over, began to feel calmer. Liberated, even. There's no longer any great need for the show to open this year—and I can finish it at my leisure, instead of in another blind rush.'[71]

Crawford and Davey agreed to a postponement, and Parker returned to the script. Three weeks later, he confessed to 'floundering around' with 'this damned musical': 'It's one of those psychic monster things, which started out as a pleasant jeu d'esprit, the plaything of an idle hour, and has gradually grown into a massive neurosis, a blight on the landscape, a plague in the midst of famine. Three more weeks I'll give it—then I quit.'[72] Tanner's enthusiastic approval of the new and improved Act I in late October gave Parker the motivation to carry on with the rewriting, which he finally finished on 10 November, exhausted. Crawford now planned to start rehearsals in mid-December, for a mid-January opening.

The writing of *Kingdom Come* was not the only thing preying on Parker in the late summer and early autumn of 1977. Kate's state of mind still worried him. A variety of considerations had conspired to keep her on edge since the previous summer. Anxiety about moving, concern about her mother, uncertainty about what she should pursue in the way of satisfying work now that Stewart's career so engrossed him, and dissatisfaction about finding herself on the margins of his professional life were some of these. The angst flowing from these sources and from the fact that Kate and Stewart enjoyed less time alone together was compounded by changes in the Rugby Road household, which in its heyday had been like a family to her. Its cohesiveness had been threatened after the departure of John Gilbert in the autumn of 1975 and effectively dissolved when Ken and June Lambla moved out in October 1976. Parker informed Gilbert in January 1977 that 'The palace is more of a transients' dormitory than a bourgeois commune these days. . . . there's no cooking schedule or other regular house get-togethers, which is sad.' Madeleine Stewart remained a resident but spent much of her time out. Michael Heffernan had lasted only a few months before moving back to his own house. Julie MacRae lived there but was kept so busy with her work as a counselling psychologist that she was seldom seen. A historian named Brian Walker had stayed at Rugby Road part of the week during the 1976/7 academic year before leaving for a year in Liverpool; his room had been taken by a recent university graduate, Angélique Day, who worked at the Public Records Office. Other residents at various times included an Irish language specialist named Eugene McKendry and Madeleine's cousin Charlie, a surveyor.[73] The rooms were full, but the spirit of the beehive had departed. Kate was well aware that the life she had known in Belfast was ending, but she did not know what would replace it. Her uncertainty resulted in a generalized psychic disturbance that manifested itself at times in mysterious physical symptoms: a sore back in August, for example, and a ringing in her ear that persisted for months before being diagnosed as a circulatory problem exacerbated by nervous stress (and the caffeine and cigarettes Kate used to help her cope).

Relations between Stewart and Kate had been strained in mid-August, when she joined him in Dublin during the *Catchpenny Twist* rehearsals and made no effort to socialize with his professional associates there. Angered by her 'Graceless, stiff and neurotic' demeanour, he remarked in his journal, 'This behaviour defeats me.' The drive home the next day was tense, with Kate in tears for much of it. Circumstances brought the couple closer at the end of the month; Stewart's despondency about *Catchpenny Twist*'s reception gave Kate a chance to play the supportive role, one at which she excelled and in which she felt comfortable. A month later, though, the marriage was fraught once again. Stewart and Kate travelled to Edinburgh in late September to visit Marcus Patton, Steph Pickering, and other friends there and to do some preliminary house-hunting. Stewart visited Patton and Pickering's bookshop, West Port Books, which had opened for business in January and which Kate had seen and he had not. He pronounced it as 'handsome & congenial' as she had described it and left her there to help out for the afternoon. That night, without warning, Kate broke down, wailing that she wished she had never been born. This nonplussed Stewart, since Kate's official position on the planned move to Edinburgh had been that she could hardly wait to be settled there. The next day he felt frankly 'desperate', his stump so sore he could barely walk. The two of them drove round areas they might want to live in and looked at houses but saw nothing they both liked and could afford.[74]

Back in Belfast a few days later, Stewart awoke from a nightmare at 7 a.m., well before his customary hour of rising. The tension had been wearing on him, and when Kate returned from a visit to her mother that afternoon he intercepted more 'Awful vibes'. He had reached his breaking point and told her so. He could not, he said, 'go on sustaining the pressures of my work and her neuroses as well, not after fifteen months of it. I feel as if I'll crack up if it goes on like this.'[75] Kate insisted she would be fine if the doctors could get to the bottom of her ear complaint, and they got drunk with Julie MacRae in an attempt to defuse the situation. (Both Stewart and Kate tended to use alcohol as a crutch in times of stress, and he at least had been drinking more heavily than usual of late.) Encouraged by the fact that they had at last talked openly about their problems, he allowed himself to believe that Kate might be all right now.

Work prevented him from dwelling on his personal difficulties. One project then coming to a head was the television production of *Catchpenny Twist*. This had nearly been scuttled back in April when Cecil Taylor, BBC Head of Programmes Northern Ireland, realized the play would be presented on stage at the Peacock several months before it was aired as a *Play for Today*. Worried that this would pre-empt the television production, he had sent out a memo proposing that the BBC should 'seriously consider' cancelling its *Catchpenny Twist* if the Peacock production went ahead. Heffernan negotiated with the authorities in London, who agreed that a Peacock production would be acceptable, but not a transfer to the Abbey main stage or any London production. Hugh Alexander arranged this with the Abbey, and plans for the television play proceeded, but Parker resented the BBC dictating such conditions at this late stage.[76]

The television version of *Catchpenny Twist* does not differ substantially from the stage one; most of Parker's changes consisted of streamlining the action to fit the same material into a shorter timespan. He cut three songs and the first scene (in which Roy, Martyn, and Monagh are fired from their teaching jobs), plunging the audience into a song-writing scene at once. Ian Playfair, Monagh's lover, is a bigger presence throughout, mentioned repeatedly and shown waving to Monagh in a scene on a Belfast street that takes place before the opening credits. Near the end of the play, the audience sees Monagh reacting as she hears a radio report about Playfair's death, but nowhere in the script are Roy and Martyn made aware of it. There is more ambiguity in the television version about exactly how bad Monagh's performance in Luxembourg is (and thus how justified Roy and Martyn might be in dropping her from the team), plus the added suggestion that *she* actually wrote their best song. Throughout, Parker added locations and showed things that would have been impossible or unwieldy to present on stage. He made one significant change to the ending of the play, since the stage version's peculiar mix of realism and surrealism would have been awkward on television—both too realistic and not realistic enough. Rather than showing a bloodied Roy and Martyn groping about on the floor of the airport lounge, Parker froze the action on Martyn opening the package and continued with sound alone: first the sound of a letter-bomb going off and then the sound of Monagh singing her song, a hard-driving rock number called 'Steeplejack' introduced earlier in the play. In such ways, Parker preserved the essence of *Catchpenny Twist* while presenting it in a format more amenable to television.

Parker watched the filming at the end of September and beginning of October and worried about the compatibility of his style with that of the director, Rob Knights. At the run-through, the play seemed to him 'very downbeat & muted & rather English', with little of the humour getting through. He continued to fret during the week that the television *Catchpenny Twist* would turn out 'muted & glossy', even 'semi-lobotomised'. In London for the editing of the piece in November, Parker was reassured to find it looking 'rawer & tougher' in that context. He delighted anew in Shaun Davey's songs and backing tracks and approved of two of the three main actors (Frances Tomelty as Monagh and Sam Dale as Martyn—Gerard Murphy as Roy struck him as less satisfactory). At a playback later that month, Parker felt 'overwhelmed' by the final product, and BBC insiders and journalists at a press showing a week later reacted almost equally warmly. *Time Out* and

Radio Times ran positive preview pieces on the play, making Parker optimistic about its prospects. *Catchpenny Twist* aired on 5 December, however, to sparse critical response. The BBC in Belfast did receive six complaints about it during the transmission, though: two about the language, one about the casting, one calling it 'inflammatory', one from a man who expressed his desire to blow up the BBC, and one from a woman who rang in tears to ask why it had been described as a comedy when it had such a tragic ending. Parker, who had earlier declared himself 'perfectly aware' that the chance of television 'saying something profound or offensive is very slim', should have been duly impressed.[77]

He was out of the country on transmission night, having been invited to Vancouver, Canada, for the final rehearsals and opening of a *Spokesong* production presented by City Stage and Carousel Theatre—its 'North American premiere'. Parker had acquired enough distance from his first play not to be overly upset by unevenness in the acting and accents, and he regarded the trip primarily as a holiday. He adored the city and many of the people he met there and got to see his friends Gina Leishman, who came to Vancouver from her new home in Oregon to meet him, and the McKibbins in Toronto on the return journey. He tore himself away from Canada with reluctance, feeling 'maudlin & forlorn' on the plane ride back.[78]

This sadness likely had more to do with what faced him upon his return than it did with his unwillingness to see an enjoyable experience end. He flew to London and spent a few days there observing *Kingdom Come* rehearsals before heading home. The metropolis looked 'filthy, sick, and choking to death' in comparison with 'ethereally beautiful' Vancouver. The show, developing well, proved the least of his worries. Kate was in Edinburgh, helping in the bookshop while he was away, and she had written to him at the Kings Head to complain of being ill and of having a terrible time. After a long telephone conversation with her on the night of his arrival, he reflected in his journal, 'I knew coming back would be bad but it was even worse.'[79]

During his absence, Parker's mother had been hospitalized for her back problems again. He took the overnight boat train to Belfast on 19 December but waited several days before stopping by his parents' house. To his relief, he discovered her in good spirits despite her pain, and everyone in his family 'v. civil indeed' about *Catchpenny Twist*. The seasonal festivities passed pleasantly, and Parker's end-of-year assessment, though less jubilant than in 1975 and 1976, concluded hopefully: 'Ending the year bruised, disturbed by many things, dismayed by some, but fundamentally feeling in luck and prepared to come out for the next round.'[80]

Final rehearsals, previews, and the opening of *Kingdom Come* dominated the first weeks of 1978. With book and lyrics by Parker and music by Shaun Davey, the musical is set on the fictional Caribbean island of Macalla, a remote outpost of the British Empire conquered 300 years ago by Anglo-Irish privateers under the aegis of the British crown and in which most of the population descends from Black slaves and early white settlers, including Irish indentured servants. The island was ruled for fifty years in the twentieth century by the British Union Party, pledged to the continuation of the link with Britain, and is now governed directly from

Westminster. In fact, the political configuration on the island bears an uncanny resemblance to that in Northern Ireland in 1978. Miss Dunwoody, an aristocratic unionist of the Anglo-Irish type, is in league with Wesley Gowan, a police chief representing the security forces. Father O'Prey, a Catholic priest, adheres to a separatism based on ethnicity and creed, while his ally, newspaperman Huey Lynch, espouses the secular republicanism that came to prominence in the North in the mid-1960s. Rosita Flanagan is a modern entrepreneur who deplores the disastrous impact of the island's strife on the tourist business and spies on both the unionist and nationalist factions on behalf of old Pycraft, Macalla's hapless English administrator. The final character, Teresa, seems without political views; she works as a serving girl at the Hotel Macalla, where the action of the play takes place. Rosita, Teresa, Lynch, and Gowan are black; Miss Dunwoody, Father O'Prey, and Pycraft are white; but race does not feature in the plot. The Caribbean setting merely allows Parker to draw a parallel between the situation in Northern Ireland and post-colonial animosities elsewhere.

Pycraft assembles this unlikely group to plan a pageant commemorating the three-hundredth anniversary of the island's settlement. The problem (one with relevance for Northern Ireland, where, in 1978, several such anniversaries loomed in the not-too-distant future) is how to commemorate something that half the population sees as a tragedy and the other half as a triumph. Gowan and Miss Dunwoody want to celebrate the accomplishments of the Anglo-Irish buccaneer who first acquired a lease to the island from the British crown. Rosita wishes to use the anniversary to refurbish the island's image. Lynch and O'Prey argue that the 'heroic event' that should be remembered is the Slave Uprising on St Patrick's Day, 1767.[81] They all agree to serve on the committee because most of them do not believe the pageant will take place. The unionists, led by Miss Dunwoody and Gowan, are planning a major strike for that day; Lynch and O'Prey are plotting an armed takeover of the government and the declaration of a republic. Teresa is forced to help further the schemes of both factions but manages to inform each one of the other's activities so that the unionists and nationalists neutralize one another. In the end she is called upon to bear the burden of the entertainment as well. Departing from the patriotic script Father O'Prey has written for her, Teresa sings a song of her own devising about taking charge of her own destiny. The play concludes with this celebration of the common sense of common people.

Casting *Kingdom Come* had been tricky, but Parker loved Glenna Forster-Jones as Rosita and thought Janet Bartley, who played Teresa, 'an exciting discovery'. Sonia Graham as Miss Dunwoody and Des Keogh (a hit in the Peacock's productions of *Catchpenny Twist* and *The Actress and the Bishop*) as Father O'Prey were both 'hilarious', in his opinion. The first preview, on 11 January, 'went like a dream', with 'excellent audience response'. By the final preview on 16 January, however, although the performance 'went like clockwork' it inspired 'No response at all'. 'I think people are mystified by it', Parker remarked in his journal.[82]

The reviews bore out his gloomy assessment, with the London critics hopelessly confused. The problem derived in part from the comic complications of the story. Parker later conceded that 'the attempt to do a send-up of an intrigue plot misfired.

It was too clever by half.' A more basic difficulty, however, lay in the critics' lack of familiarity with the prototype for Parker's fictional island: Northern Ireland. Several reviewers failed to grasp Britain's relationship with Macalla, bearing out Huey Lynch's description of the English as 'the charming dithering bungling deadly perpetrators of a crime they don't even know they've committed'. The *Guardian*'s Michael Billington regarded Macalla as an island colonized 300 years previously by the Irish and now mysteriously 'under the thumb of a British Governor-General', while Irving Wardle of *The Times* declared it 'as much of a shock to the spectators as it is to the characters when the royal yacht appears purposefully on the horizon; up to that point, one had taken Macalla for an Irish protectorate'. 'Perhaps', Wardle speculated, 'someone has taken the scissors to Mr Parker's book and snipped out [Pycraft's] credentials, together with explanations of all the other random alliances in this sunkissed Ulster.'[83]

The reviewers seemed unable to accept the fact that religion and political allegiance, not colour, are the salient identifying factors in Macalla. Parker likely intended to illustrate the arbitrariness of the signs people use to divide themselves from one another, but none of the critics recognized this. Keith Nurse referred in the *Daily Telegraph* to 'Protestant patriots' and 'Black republicans', and Michael Coveney wrote in the *Financial Times* that Father O'Prey, Miss Dunwoody, and Pycraft are the exponents of 'Anglo-Irish imperialism', while the 'voice of the people' sounds through Teresa's 'sung black power salute'. Billington complained, 'It is never clear why the black Macallans should be involved in the internal sectarian struggles of the whites and how Mr Parker reconciles his apolitical, plague-on-both-your-houses attitude to the Irish problem with his apparent endorsement of black political power.' He argued that 'in attempting to give us an Irish political allegory in the context of a Caribbean island's quest for identity, Mr Parker has managed to make a confusing situation almost wholly impenetrable'. Most of these reviews appeared the day after *Kingdom Come* opened, leading Parker to the unavoidable conclusion that 'We've flopped.' A number of the critics commented favourably on his lyrics, Davey's music, and several of the performances, but none of that consoled him. He spent half the day in bed, 'grieving', then returned to Belfast.[84]

Parker had little opportunity to dwell on his last opening; the time had come to think about the next one. On 22 January, he and Kate left for New York, on their way to New Haven, Connecticut, for the US première of *Spokesong*. They had not been to the US since the summer of 1974, and they revelled in the chance to see American friends again, joyfully phoning those they could not meet up with at once. The Long Wharf Theatre, producer of the show, was a regional theatre noted for introducing American audiences to modern British drama. Plays performed there were taken seriously by the New York critics, and several in recent memory had transferred to New York after their New Haven runs. The director of *Spokesong*, Kenneth Frankel, had assembled an impressive cast, all the members of which had Broadway credits: Joseph Maher as the Trick Cyclist, John Lithgow as Frank, Virginia Vestoff as Daisy, Josef Summer as Francis, Maria Tucci as Kitty, and John Horton as Julian. Parker, who observed two weeks of rehearsals and previews before the press opening, had concluded after a few days that 'this production is the most faithful to the script yet, and the one w/the all-round strongest cast'. 'I have been here before, however', he fretted: 'Again I have a certain premonition of puzzled audiences.'[85]

The memory of the *Kingdom Come* opening remained too fresh for Parker to feel sanguine about *Spokesong*'s prospects in the US. At the end of the month, though, he received news from London that enhanced his enjoyment of the work in New Haven. Conor Cruise O'Brien, then editor of the *Observer*, had taken the unusual step of offering a second opinion of *Kingdom Come* after that paper's regular critic gave the show a lukewarm review. O'Brien admitted to having attended the play in a sceptical mood, expecting 'a soon-fizzling joke, possibly accompanied by some dim message about the unity of the anti-imperialist struggle throughout the world'. However, 'The joke is brilliantly sustained....And the message is not dim but strong, valid and urgent....It is about the liberation of the people of Northern Ireland *from their supposed liberators*—the IRA in the case of the Catholics—and from their supposed defenders—the sectarian paramilitaries in the case of the Prot-estants.' O'Brien explicitly compared Teresa's 'escape from her embafflers' to the refusal of the majority of Protestant workers to heed Paisley's strike call in 1977. The play impressed him as a *tour de force*, but one the relation of which to North-ern Ireland might not be apparent to people who had never been there. 'By trans-posing Northern Ireland to another climate and to the key of comedy', Parker had 'liberated himself and his players, and his audience, from the emotional domi-nance of the rival fanatics'. Elated by O'Brien's intervention, Parker wrote to Shaun Davey from New Haven to call the piece to his attention: 'Suffice it to say that he understood entirely everything we were trying to do in the show.' Better still, according to Dan Crawford, *Kingdom Come* now played to full houses.[86]

Buoyed by these tidings, Parker renewed his focus on the *Spokesong* production. The dress rehearsal went badly, but the first previews well. David Pauker, a New York agent from The Lantz Office, came down to see one of them at the urging of Marc Berlin, an agent friend of Hugh Alexander's who had been helping him with some of Parker's contracts. Pauker praised the script and advised Parker to try to get Samuel French to publish it and make it available to theatre groups around the country. Parker liked the idea of having an agent in New York to look after his affairs in North America and rang Alexander to tell him about Pauker's interest.

On 6 February a blizzard blew up, developing into the worst storm in seventeen years by the end of the day. As a result, the Long Wharf cancelled the preview on 7 February, the last scheduled before the opening. The next morning, Ash Wednes-day, Stewart and Kate were awakened at 8 a.m. by a phone call from Belfast inform-ing them that Kate's mother had suffered a minor stroke, fallen into the fire, and burned one arm badly. Their Rugby Road housemate Julie MacRae had been stop-ping by Mrs Ireland's house each day to check on her, and she had discovered the accident. Now Mrs Ireland was undergoing surgery, and the surgeon thought Kate should be there. Kate, who had had to be persuaded to accompany Stewart to New Haven because she hesitated to leave her mother alone, was distraught. She and Stewart decided to book her a ticket to fly home the next evening—that way, at least, she could attend the opening and see Ken and June Lambla, who were driving cross-country to New Haven for it. Stewart would spend the weekend in Ithaca with friends as planned and fly back to Belfast early the following week. Only after making Kate's reservation did they learn the opening had been postponed until the following night.[87]

The next morning, Kate arose in 'awful shape, having finally assimilated the bad news'. Ken Lambla drove her to Kennedy Airport, accompanied by Stewart 'Feeling rotten & hopeless'. The two men then returned to New Haven, eating fast food in the car and getting to the theatre in time for the second act, which Stewart spent in the theatre office. As far as he could tell, the show was going well. Thus he experienced his long-awaited US première.[88]

Despite the pain and uncertainty shrouding his immediate future, or perhaps partly because of them, Parker contrived to enjoy the next few days. An 'idyllic drive' up to Ithaca with the Lamblas ended in a 'Joyous clamorous reunion' with the McKibbins, who had driven down from Canada, and Bea MacLeod, who promptly invited everyone to stay at her house for a long weekend. The next day, Richard Eder's review appeared in the *New York Times*. Parker, he wrote, had 'made art out of history' in 'a most funny and piercingly intelligent play that has opened in a marvelous production at the Long Wharf Theatre'. After describing the script and showering each actor with specific praise, Eder concluded that the Long Wharf's *Spokesong* offered 'a play and performances that give joy and hope to the theater'. A few days later, Clive Barnes seconded this assessment in the *New York Post*, calling *Spokesong* 'a dazzling play that combines warmth of sentiment with great emotional strength, and...intellectual playfulness' and adding, 'very few things this season have given me as much pleasure, and nothing has given me more'.[89] This conquest of the two most influential New York critics made a transfer appear certain, and, by mid-February, Edgar Rosenblum, the executive director of the Long Wharf, had already fielded numerous enquiries from New York producers.

Anguished communications from Kate in Belfast counterpointed Stewart's excitement over these developments. In a telephone call on 11 February, she said that her mother, though recovering physically, had deteriorated mentally. Nevertheless, she urged him to stay on for another week. Making what in hindsight looks like a fateful mistake, he let himself be talked into doing so. Upon arriving home on 18 February, he found a situation as dire as he had imagined, with Mrs Ireland's mind 'dulled and soured by the sclerosis' and Kate 'in bad shape, fighting to keep herself in control'. Moreover, *his* mother had returned to hospital to have the operation on her spine she had been waiting for, leaving his father 'confused and downcast'.[90] Worst of all, the events of the past ten days seemed to have confirmed Stewart and Kate's deepest suspicions about each other and their relationship. She had long believed he put his work before her in importance, and he had often felt she was more attached to her mother than to him. Now they would have to carry on somehow, with the question hanging over their heads of whether this latest adversity would eventually bring them closer or drive them further apart.

10

Dark Night of the Soul

Kate's mother's illness would shadow the next several years of Stewart Parker's life. Its unpredictable course greatly complicated the move to Edinburgh which Stewart and Kate had been planning to make for a year and a half already by early 1978. Caring for her mother exhausted Kate, and Stewart's frequent work-related absences became increasingly hard for her. Stewart had trouble sustaining momentum on new writing projects between the demands of the business and production sides of his work and the stress of his domestic life. In the relative isolation of Edinburgh, away from most of their friends and both separated from the subjects of most compelling interest to them, they found their marriage an uncertain source of comfort and strength. *Nightshade*, Parker's stage play of this period, reflects his prevailing state of mind in its preoccupation with loss and mourning.

In the two months after his return to Belfast from *Spokesong*'s triumphant opening in New Haven, Parker focused on two questions: that of when, or if, the production would transfer to New York City, and that of how to handle Mrs Ireland's obvious inability to continue living alone. Kate felt duty-bound to look after her mother herself, but Stewart thought her neither physically nor emotionally equipped for this task indefinitely. After weeks of agonized consideration, they decided that, upon Mrs Ireland's release from hospital, they would take her back to her own house to convalesce while they attempted to find a place for her in a residential care facility in Edinburgh. The experience of this transitional period conformed to Stewart's expectations, as he explained to their friend Bea MacLeod: 'By the end of three weeks [Kate's] mother was able to dress herself, get up and down stairs, and talk in a fairly coherent and sensible way, but Kate was having frequent fits of hysterics.' Having in the meantime determined that placing Mrs Ireland in a Scottish home would be prohibitively expensive, Stewart and other friends worked to convince Kate that her mother would do better in a home in Belfast, 'amongst familiar landmarks and people, with Kate making regular visits'. Armed with messages from the Long Wharf that he might be required in New York to help with a transfer as early as the end of March, Stewart persuaded Kate to put her mother into care for the few weeks that he expected to be away. To his relief, Mrs Ireland adjusted well to the move, and Kate 'came round to the view that it would be the best long-term solution for all concerned'. They consequently found her a permanent spot in Towell House, a home run by the Presbyterian church in her own area, and she moved into her room there in mid-April.[1]

The *Spokesong* transfer situation had a less satisfactory resolution. According to Parker's New York agent, the Long Wharf, which held an option on the play in the

United States, wanted to take *Spokesong* to Broadway and sought the New York producer who would offer them the best terms. The agent felt that Edgar Rosenblum, Long Wharf's executive director, had confused the issue by inviting multiple producers to consider the play, rather than picking one of those actively pursuing it and making a deal. Rosenblum finally settled on Lester Osterman, who had worked with the Long Wharf in the past and whose Morosco theatre would suit *Spokesong*, and the two men made a verbal agreement regarding the transfer. When Osterman was presented with a written contract, however, he found that Rosenblum had changed several key points, and, as a result, Osterman lost half his financing. They continued to negotiate, but in the meantime Osterman saw another Irish play, Hugh Leonard's *Da*, which his wife preferred to *Spokesong*, and he decided to put it into the Morosco instead. Meanwhile, Parker's agent had contacted another producer, Doris Abrahams, who wanted *Spokesong* but could not move fast enough to effect the transfer that spring. Any hope of an immediate transfer expired when two of the leading actors accepted other jobs. 'So that's it', Parker commented in his journal, 'I'm consigned to stay here. The dream's over.'[2]

Rosenblum and Arvin Brown, the Long Wharf's artistic director, visited London a few weeks later, and Parker met them there. They reiterated their hopes of reviving the *Spokesong* production in New York in the autumn; the cast members were all committed to doing it, and the Circle in the Square Theatre (where *Spokesong* director Kenneth Frankel served on the staff of the professional school) had offered to co-produce and host the play. 'So all is not lost after all', Parker wrote to MacLeod, though surely also mindful of his New York agent's disappointment that the Long Wharf had extended its option on the play (thus leaving delicate negotiations over its fate in Rosenblum's hands). He might have taken some comfort in composer Jimmy Kennedy's reminder that 'it takes a hell of a show to ride out the summer on Broadway' and in Frankel's opinion that deferring the transfer until the new season might allow them to make changes to the production that would improve its chances of a successful New York run.[3] Nevertheless, the dissolution of the original New York transfer deal disappointed him terribly after a particularly trying couple of months.

On 13 April, during a heavy snowstorm, Stewart and Kate moved into a room in Whigmaleerie, Marcus Patton's flat in Edinburgh. The next day, he began flat-hunting, and she went to work at West Port Books with Steph Pickering, who had bought out Patton's share of the business. The task of finding a place to live proved daunting, as Parker explained to Shaun Davey, 'due to high demand for flats, high prices for same, and great reluctance of Building Societies to loan money to impecunious playwrights'. Securing a mortgage required the expedient of presenting Stewart as an employee of his London agent, with an annual income of £6,000. Then he had to find a suitable property. After over a month of looking at neighbourhoods and buildings for a part of each day, Parker started applying himself to the task full-time. Even so, another month passed before he and Kate saw something both affordable and workable, got the building society to approve it, made a bid on it, and had their bid accepted. By the time this happened, they had forgotten what the place looked like.[4]

The first property they had ever owned, 103 Harrison Road, was small, a bit outside the area they had wanted to be in, and in need of extensive work. It was also, as Parker informed an American friend, 'a third-storey tenement…what you know as a fourth-floor walkup', accessed via numerous flights of stairs—far from ideal for a man with an artificial leg, though it featured a lovely view 'over picturesque Scottish hills at the front, and over playing-fields all the way to Edinburgh Castle at the back'. 'Now the time has come at last to settle into a daily chore', Parker wrote in his journal on 15 June, the day he learned the flat would be theirs. In reality it would be six months more before they were fully moved in, but they gradually turned it into a home like an 'eagle's nest', completely lined with books.[5]

The Parkers took possession of their flat in early July but remained at Whigmaleerie another month while the most urgent repairs were done. Patton had surprised his friends by accepting a job in Belfast with Hearth, a joint initiative of the Ulster Architectural Heritage Society and the National Trust to restore for use as housing 'modest dwellings of architectural significance' threatened with demolition. He returned to Northern Ireland mid-month, but the Parkers continued subletting their room from David and Karen Maxwell, Whigmaleerie residents who were buying it from Patton. The loss of one of their closest friends in Edinburgh would hinder the Parkers' adjustment to the city, but Stewart then confided to Bea MacLeod that he hoped Patton's departure would make Pickering 'very dependent on Kate': 'I think it'll be good medicine for her to be caught up in the demands of a job', he predicted confidently.[6]

Kate herself felt less enthusiasm about her new career as a second-hand bookseller. Pickering was open to the idea of taking Kate on as a partner and hence anxious to teach her about every aspect of running the shop. Kate, though, quickly made it clear that she did not seek anything more than a part-time job. She worked afternoons only because she wanted to keep the routine she and Stewart had of very late nights and late mornings, and she frequently arrived tardily (although she also often came in voluntarily to help on Saturdays). She had thought bookselling a genteel profession, and the 'grubbier' work took her aback. Pickering had to handle anything inherently stressful, like buying older books, since Kate's nerves were fragile 'at the best of times'. Kate knew a tremendous amount about books and enjoyed chatting with customers and ringing up their purchases, but the business side of the business did not appeal to her. Anyway, her effort to be a dutiful daughter preoccupied her, and she travelled to Belfast for a long weekend roughly every fortnight. Her mother's growing senility compounded the strain of these trips, since Mrs Ireland often had forgotten that Kate had just been over to see her and would complain that it had been 'an age' since her last visit. Such remarks inflamed the guilt Kate suffered over leaving her mother in a different city. Jennie Renton, a regular customer at West Port Books, noticed Kate's air of sadness and remembers her banging away at an old piano in the shop with enormous, pent-up emotion.[7]

Stewart, meanwhile, struggled to establish a regular work routine. He had finished one small task that spring. Rob Knights, producer/director of the television *Catchpenny Twist*, had expressed a desire in the summer of 1977 to make a film based on a piece in the *Guardian* about two 'opposite numbers' in British Army Intelligence and the Provisionals, and he wanted Parker to write it. Parker had since developed doubts about the compatibility of his style with that of Knights, but he knew his would-be collaborator to be 'quite a hot-shot in London', and the proposed film attracted him as 'a strong idea which I'd like very much to write'. He wondered if Knights would be able to raise money for it, though, and indeed he heard nothing about it for months.[8] Then, in mid-April 1978, Knights rang Parker to catch up, and they decided to try to revive the film project. By 16 May Parker had written a synopsis, entitled *Lost Belongings* and set in the summer of 1974.

Parker's version of the story begins with two additional characters—Simon Hunt, an English journalist, and Gretchen Reilly, an American graduate student in Celtic Studies—who meet on the Liverpool–Belfast ferry. He is going to Northern Ireland in search of stories to launch his career as a freelance writer and to visit a friend from Oxford, Riddel, a captain in the British Army with a desk job in Lisburn; she plans to see prehistoric monuments and (although she does not tell Hunt this) to make contact with her half-brother, Ducksy Boyle, a known IRA activist. It transpires that Riddel works undercover for Army Intelligence, spying on Boyle across the border. Hunt and Reilly see the two men meeting and talking, which raises the question of whether or not Boyle is an informer. Both Riddel and Boyle separately try to convince the others to leave, but before Reilly and Hunt do they witness the assassination of someone (probably Boyle) and are stranded on the side of the road in the rain. The synopsis ends with them staring into the fire at an itinerants' campsite. Knights evidently could not get the money together, because plans for their film proceeded no further at this time.[9]

Parker also worked fitfully on *Nightshade*, reading books like *The High Cost of Dying* by Ruth Mulvey Harmer and (an exciting discovery) a *Manual of Funeral Directing*. He played with lyrics for a 'Belfast song cycle' ('Purgatory' and 'Natural Son' were two of his titles) which he hoped Shaun Davey might set to music. He even began researching a radio play inspired in part by a Boy Scout troop reunion dinner that he had attended in March 1977 and found 'Pretty dire'. He had been, he recollected later, 'struck by how grown men revert to being boys on such occasions', and the play he contemplated would be 'a satire on masculine group behaviour'. The group in question, though, differed greatly from the 10th Belfast Scout Group. Parker had been annoyed by audiences' failure to grasp a joke near the beginning of *Catchpenny Twist* (Roy says they should have done 'the strip number' for the end-of-school assembly, and Monagh retorts, 'Oh certainly—with me flying kamikaze and you two on the ground crew'), so he decided to write a play centred on an annual get-together of Japanese men who had serviced kamikaze planes during the Second World War and, unlike the pilots who flew these suicide missions, survived to wax nostalgic about their wartime adventures. Parker shared his idea for *The Kamikaze Ground Staff Reunion Dinner* with Michael Heffernan in June 1978 and spent several days that month reading about the Japanese air force and modern Japanese history and writing a synopsis.[10]

Mostly, however, Parker experienced the spring and early summer of 1978—dominated by practical considerations regarding Kate's mother's living arrangements, real estate, and finances—as a 'void'. 'I want so much to work', he wrote desperately in his journal on 9 June, but nearly a fortnight later he remained in 'the doldrums, without any doubt'. Good reviews of his old rival Bill Morrison's play *Flying Blind* at the Royal Court left him feeling 'isolated and in trouble' at the end of the month. 'I'm out of key with the times', he confided to his journal. 'I fear the worst for *Nightshade*, before it's even written. I'm full of foreboding about the future. For a long time now, life has been nothing more than an endurance test. But what can I do, more than I'm doing now? Endure.' An outing next day to see Joseph Strick's film of Joyce's *A Portrait of the Artist as a Young Man* staved off utter depression; although he judged the film a 'terribly lame and insensitive treatment', he found it 'salutary to be challenged again, at this particular juncture, with the ideas of my guide and mentor'. In a contemporaneous letter to Shaun Davey, Parker analysed his strange state of mind:

> Edinburgh will probably be fine once I overcome the feeling of being in limbo; because moving is like a small death, you vanish from the lives of all the people you knew, and you turn into a stranger in another place. Coincidentally, a long hectic period of theatre involvement came to an end just as I made the move, so that the phone doesn't ring any more and there's rarely any mail. Limbo!

'At least', he conceded, 'you can do ordinary things here without the restrictions of Belfast—go to movies, eat out, walk round shops.'[11]

Two weeks later, Parker's spirits received a boost when he learned that the Hartford Stage Company in Connecticut would produce *Catchpenny Twist* that autumn and were willing to fly him out in mid-September and house him through the 6 October opening. He had met Irene Lewis, the 'youngish, shrewd and driving' associate director of the company, in January 1977 when she visited him in Belfast after seeing *Spokesong* at the Kings Head. She had stated an interest in *Catchpenny Twist* that August, but Parker's agent had refrained from telling his client about subsequent negotiations with the theatre until he finalized a deal, to spare him distress if an agreement could not be reached. As Parker informed Davey, 'Hartford is close to New York, and the HSC is very well thought of by the New York critics', so he expected the show would get 'a good deal of attention and coverage'.[12]

In July and August 1978, Parker polished the *Catchpenny Twist* script for its North American première and wrote a programme note putting the play's action into context for an American audience. He even flew to Hartford in late July for early production meetings. Excited by the chance to revisit the play, Parker proposed extensive restructuring, most of which Lewis talked him out of doing. He contented himself with making cuts, adding a scene to explain how Roy and Martyn began writing republican ballads, reordering a few existing scenes and intercutting others to present them simultaneously on different parts of the stage, and tinkering with some dialogue.[13]

Parker would return to Hartford less than two months later to help with rehearsals. Meanwhile, he and Kate were gradually moving into 103 Harrison Road. On a trip to Belfast in early August, they emptied Kate's mother's house, a 'mammoth task', and supervised the removal of their larger belongings from Rugby Road to

Edinburgh, and on 10 August they slept in their new home for the first time. Apart from helping John Gilbert celebrate his wedding to a Scottish woman, Rena McAllister, about a week later, and a holiday weekend on Arran in early September, he directed most of his energy between his two trips to Hartford towards unpacking, arranging furniture, assembling shelves and cupboards, and having appliances and utilities hooked up at the flat—tasks that bored and frustrated him. He also suffered for three weeks in August and September from a mysterious itch in his anus which disturbed his sleep unmercifully and was never adequately diagnosed. On 5 September he stayed in bed all day, 'Feeling at end of my rope (again).' When Kate arrived home from the bookshop complaining about the rush hour, he lashed out at her, articulating six months' worth of resentment over the turn their lives had taken: 'Bad bad feelings finally coming out. Murmured my feelings of having slaved for 6 months for her sake to no apparent end, but pointless. Just provoked the usual weeping, drunkenness, rhetoric.'[14] Over the next few days, the crisis passed; they were especially solicitous of each other, and Stewart finally saw a doctor who prescribed an anaesthetic ointment that at least quelled his symptoms before he flew to the US.

The *Catchpenny Twist* rehearsal period, though intense, seemed a welcome respite from domestic drudgery. The leading actors Irene Lewis had recruited for the production—Jarlath Conroy as Martyn, John Horn as Roy, and Patti LuPone as Monagh—all had Broadway credits, but at first they did not impress Parker. Lewis gave him 'terrific latitude...to talk through scenes & make suggestions', though. By the dress rehearsal, Parker thought the show had come together 'remarkably well'. Nevertheless, opening night loomed as 'Dark Night of the Soul time'. He could not bring himself to watch, but listened to the performance over the PA system with Lewis and a bottle of whiskey for support. It sounded 'reasonably OK'.[15]

The verdict of the critics, mostly from small Connecticut newspapers, proved similar. Reviewers mostly praised the acting and direction, although some felt the large stage overwhelmed the play and the naturalistic performance style did not match the material. Several writers noted wistfully *Catchpenny Twist*'s difference from *Spokesong*, a refrain familiar to Parker. Influential New York critic Clive Barnes reacted fairly typically. *Catchpenny Twist*, he wrote, 'has tremendous style, energy and interest. It is also uneven in structure, and uncertain in purpose. Nevertheless its writing alone confirms the suggestion of "Spokesong" that in Parker Ireland has found a new major playwright.' Sadly, owing to a New York newspaper strike, Barnes's assessment did not appear in print until after the show closed.[16]

Parker's New York agent felt good about the play's prospects in the US. Parker kept his own expectations in check, believing that *Catchpenny Twist*, unlike *Spokesong*, 'just doesn't have mass commercial appeal'.[17] After the opening, he shrugged off the ambivalent reviews and concentrated on enjoying the rest of his American stay. This time Kate had been present, and a few days later the two of them rented a Firebird and drove to Ithaca for a second (planned) house party with Bea MacLeod, the Lamblas, and the McKibbins.

Parker also took advantage of being in the US to attend to some *Spokesong* business. He had been informed that summer that Circle in the Square, a leading

Off-Broadway theatre with both uptown (Broadway) and downtown (Off-Broadway) venues, intended to mount *Spokesong* in its uptown theatre during the coming season. (His New York agent, David Pauker, explained that, technically, the production would be considered Off-Broadway but would be eligible for Broadway awards.) Circle in the Square had listed the play in early publicity for its upcoming season, but months had passed without a deal being signed. A week before Parker flew to Hartford for *Catchpenny Twist* rehearsals, Pauker shared the disquieting news that he had begun to doubt that the production would happen. Circle in the Square had not yet contacted him to discuss Parker's royalties, nor had they offered contracts to any of the actors. Pauker suspected Paul Libin, Circle in the Square's managing director, of stalling in the hope that Long Wharf's option on the play would expire, leaving him to make his own terms for the rights.[18]

Parker visited Circle in the Square in late September and met Libin and artistic director Theodore Mann, neither of whom appealed to him. Matters remained unresolved on 20 October, when Parker met Edgar Rosenblum at the Long Wharf in New Haven. Rosenblum and Libin had agreed money terms for the *Spokesong* transfer but were still debating about billing and artistic control. Rosenblum phoned Libin with Parker in the room and told the nervous playwright that Libin had ended their conversation by calling off the project. Parker, who flew out the next day, could hardly believe it when he heard on 1 November that a deal had actually been struck for the presentation of *Spokesong* at Circle in the Square in early spring 1979.

The matter most urgently requiring Parker's attention upon his return home was the filming of the television version of *I'm a Dreamer Montreal*. Thames Television had commissioned the piece in November 1977, but it had taken producer Rob Buckler nearly eight months to find a director for it. His eventual choice—Brian Farnham, who had directed some of *Rock Follies*—delighted Parker. The television script remained substantially the same as the radio script, apart from the adding of a Belfast street montage after Nelson's visit to the morgue and a rewriting of the ending that Buckler had requested. Instead of Nelson encountering Sandra working in a 'massage parlour', Parker set the crucial scene in a loyalist club where Nelson goes for a drink with his band mate Dickie. Here he discovers that Sandra is the 'fancy woman' of a gangster. Drunkenly oblivious to the danger he could be in, Nelson flirts with Sandra in front of her older lover, who carves his initials on Nelson's buttocks in revenge. Sandra callously grants her boyfriend's request for 'a wee song' ('The Green Grassy Slopes of the Boyne'), as Nelson pulls up his trousers and runs out the door. These changes made the scene both more realistic and more disturbing. As one television critic later put it, 'This is a strange little play by Stewart Parker with a first half all lightness and trivial nostalgic music, followed by a second half of horror, treachery and Northern Irish madness, which may well be an accurate summary of current affairs there but makes an oddly assorted entertainment.'[19]

Baby-faced Bryan Murray made a perfect Nelson, and the read-through in late October 'sounded good', Parker recorded in his journal, apart from some of the actors' Dublin accents. Still, he worried about 'the company's parsimony, which looks like preventing filming in Belfast & will wipe out any look of authenticity about the thing'. He was pleasantly surprised over the next fortnight of filming, though, by how like Belfast the locations, mainly in the East End, could be made to look. The studio days made an even bigger impact on him. He had always thought of stage plays as his 'real' work; writing to Bea MacLeod two years previously he had remarked that 'Apart from money, TV just feels second-best—and usually looks it too.' The making of *I'm a Dreamer Montreal* hit him with the force of a revelation. The first day of studio recording left him too keyed up to sleep, gushing in his journal about the 'enthralling, exhilarating, exciting day's work': 'This has to be television at its best, and it's more than good enough for me. For the first time, I feel in my heart that I can and shd. write for it.'[20]

His good experience with *I'm a Dreamer Montreal* kindled Parker's enthusiasm for another Thames project. Joan Rodker, a script executive at the company, had approached him shortly after *Kingdom Come* closed in March 1978 to invite him to consider ways to turn that show into a television series. In the throes of personal difficulties, Parker shrugged off the suggestion. Rodker had persisted, however, telling him at the end of October that she had been authorized to commission the pilot for a six-part series based on *Kingdom Come*. Parker would submit a fifty-minute script for one of the episodes, along with a descriptive list of the other five. If Thames approved the concept, it would commission the remaining scripts and produce the series. If not, it would drop the project but allow him to keep the half of the pilot fee paid on commission. Parker had agreed to meet her about the possibility, though he 'Felt no excitement, no elation, nothing. Except a groan at the decision to make, the work to do.'[21]

Parker met Rodker on 31 October, with an idea about how to proceed. As he reported to Shaun Davey, he told her that he did not think it possible to develop the stage script into a six-part series. He proposed revolving the series around a fictitious theatre group presenting the musical *Kingdom Come* on tour. The main characters would be the actors playing the seven roles in the play, plus other characters such as 'the Tony Tanner figure', 'the Dan Crawford figure', the playwright, and the composer. Each episode would focus on one or two of these, 'with flashbacks to their earlier lives', and would be set in a different city. 'During the tour,' Parker explained to Davey, 'tensions and allegiances spring up among the group and are juxtaposed with those in the stage show.' He envisaged that the series would incorporate all the songs they had written for the musical, as the television audience caught glimpses of the performances of the company, and that on top of that he and Davey would write many more songs (four to six per fifty-minute episode) about the characters' 'own feelings, their fantasies, their past lives, the places they're visiting, the people they encounter, their attitudes to each other'. While he waited to hear if Davey was willing to collaborate on the project, Parker began pondering the series as a whole. He soon encountered a problem, namely 'you can't write one line of a single episode till you've worked out structure & conventions of the entire six. Which may take forever.'[22]

By the time he returned to the work after the filming of *I'm a Dreamer Montreal*, he had received a long letter from Davey agreeing to participate, but only 'on the

1. Stewart Parker at about 14. Photo by Jack Chambers.

2. Stewart Parker (rear left) with other members of the 10th Belfast Scout Troop in 1956. Photo by John Cairns.

3. Stewart Parker in 1959. Photo by Jack Chambers.

4. Stewart Parker in 1961 with nurses from the Royal Victoria Hospital, Belfast, after the amputation of his left leg.

5. The Parker family in 1967. Herbie, Joan, Belle, Stewart, George (rear); Lynne and Julie (front). Photo by Margaret Parker.

6. Stewart and Kate Parker in August 1969.

7. Stewart Parker in Sydenham, early 1970s. Photo by John Gilbert.

8.
Stewart Parker on Botanic Avenue in Belfast in the summer of 1972. Photo by John Gilbert.

9.
The entrance to No. 7
Rugby Road.
Photo by John Gilbert.

10.
Sharing a meal at No. 9
Rugby Road (Madeleine
Stewart, Stewart Parker,
Kate Parker, June Lambla,
Ken Lambla).
Photo by John Gilbert.

11.
Michael Heffernan and
Kate Parker, mid-1970s.

12. Stephen Rea in Belfast, mid-1970s. Photo by John Gilbert.

13. Lesley Bruce, John Gilbert, and Stewart Parker, mid-1980s. Photo by Rena McAllister.

14 Lesley Bruce in 1986.
Photo by Stewart Parker.

15. Sam Fannin, late 1970s.
Photo by Stewart Parker.

16. Stewart Parker in Spain, April 1988. Photo by Lesley Bruce.

17. Marty Rea as the Trick Cyclist in the Rough Magic/Lyric Theatre production of *Spokesong*, directed by Lynne Parker, Belfast and Dublin, 2008. Photo by Chris Hill.

18. Eleanor Methven as Marian and Carol (Scanlan) Moore as Lily in the Rough Magic production of *Pentecost*, directed by Lynne Parker, Dublin, 1995. Photo by Amelia Stein.

basis that we work together closely and with an increased understanding of what each other is trying to do'. Davey had tired of being treated as the junior partner whose contribution was incidental to the finished drama. He worried, too, that Parker's proposed reworking of the material might cause them 'to lose the wonderfully absurd exotic quality of the original "Kingdom Come"…and at the same time make each episode too complicated, losing flow and directness'. Davey's reservations on this count were well-founded, though Parker brushed them off in his reply: 'All I can say is that I…will do my best to preserve a forward-driving narrative and clear and direct situations.' The 'basic concept' of the proposed series, he maintained, 'is the oldest one in the history of the musical: BACKSTAGE. The story couldn't be simpler: an acting company take a show around various cities, meeting with mixed fortunes on the way.' As for Davey's other query, Parker believed that 'the only way to preserve the "absurd exotic" quality which you mention *is* to branch out in a new direction. Thames may not agree. In which case they'll turn down the pilot and we'll call it quits. I'd rather do that and maybe have something potentially exciting to write than lumber myself with an enormous burden of grinding tedium and a series I didn't want my name attached to.'[23]

Davey wrote back pronouncing himself 'adjusted to the idea' but reiterating his desire 'to determine my own role within your work': 'For, much as I enjoy it, sending me song lyrics saying "this song is to occur here sung by so and so" is one thing, but allowing me a real constructive role in your work is another.' He suggested a procedure he would find more congenial. Instead of writing the lyrics as he wrote the script, Parker should write only the dialogue and send this to Davey, who would generate ideas about what aspects of the play might be fruitfully set to music. After meeting with Davey to discuss 'songs, who is to sing them, on or off screen, where they are to occur, whether music without words is also required etc', Parker would write the lyrics, which Davey would set to music as before, and together they would fine-tune the finished product. Davey hoped their exchange of letters would enable them to 'start a new phase of collaboration'. Parker himself felt a trifle uneasy about his partner's new assertiveness, remarking in his journal that Davey's proposed working method 'Sounds fine to me, but all this long-winded introspection is a bit disquieting. I hope we don't end up like Gilbert & Sullivan.'[24]

Parker wrote a detailed treatment for the series in early December, along with a letter to Rodker explaining that he wanted to achieve

a kind of television picaresque—adventures encountered by a group of rogues and vagabonds on their travels. The subject matter would be exactly the same as in the stage *Kingdom Come*—bigotry, fanaticism, myopia, xenophobia—the current state of these British islands. We would be viewing it at two levels—the fantasy level of the stage production and the more everyday level of the company's lives. All the ingredients of the stage musical would be there (including most of the show itself) but amplified, developed, and (I hope) enriched.

On 15 December, Rodker accepted the treatment. 'Thank God', Parker wrote in his journal, 'else my tv series would have died right after conception.'[25] He would make a small start on the pilot script the following month, although he would not get seriously into the writing until April 1979.

What with everything that still needed doing to the flat to make it comfortable now that the frigid weather had come, Parker had trouble settling to much of anything towards the end of 1978. In addition to dealing with the perennial car repairs, he kept busy ripping up old floor coverings and buying new ones, shopping for furniture, supervising workmen doing repairs, and cleaning up after them. 'What a waste of time all this is', he grumbled in his journal at the end of November. Less than two weeks later, after a botched central heating installation, he recorded feeling 'like a crushed vegetable'. That ordeal over, he still could not concentrate: 'My mind's been dry for so long. Sat in my new-fangled study for a bit, but too many distractions.' He longed 'to be writing a play again. You hate it while you're at it, pine for it when you're not.'[26]

The new year began with resolutions to be 'quietist' and 'stoic' contending against Parker's growing discontentment with Scotland, a 'Miserable country in the throes of snow, storms, & strikes. No bread in the shops. No grit on the roads. No petrol in the garages. And it's still only January 4th.' He remained sunk in gloom the next day, reflecting drearily, 'And here I am living quietly in Edinburgh. A life devoid of incident. Squandering time again. Remorseful about it again.' 'Another chance to try again', he added hopefully, but his depression got the last word: 'Five days since Hogmanay and we haven't been first-footed yet.' Later that month, after a couple of days spent filing manuscripts and sorting through old letters and contracts, he tried to look on the bright side: 'Extraordinary to be reminded how little I was paid for all that radio work and journalism. What wd. life have been if I'd never broken out of that? Show grateful, Stew. Remember what might have been, occasionally.' He strove also to keep in mind his new approach to life: 'Involved. Quietist. Stoic. Watchful. Adaptable. Calm, not passive. Choosing the decisive moment. Knowing when to commit everything.'[27]

As the date approached upon which he was supposed to fly to New York to help with the production of *Spokesong* on Broadway, Parker must have found it ever harder to remain detached. Part of him expected something to go wrong at the last moment, whether or not he actually knew that, as late as 10 January 1979, Circle in the Square had not secured signed contracts with any of the actors, nor with the designers, stage manager, vocal coach, or cycle coach. (As his US agent sternly informed Paul Libin, such dilatory behaviour raised 'serious questions about the commitment of Circle in the Square to this production'.)[28] Parker's agents did not direct him to purchase his plane ticket until four days before he left. After frantic preparations, he arrived in New York on 22 January.

Parker stayed for the first three and a half weeks in the empty flat of his friend Irene Lewis, then directing out of town. At first he kept busy with rewrites, rehearsals, visits to friends, and exploring the city (seeing his first Broadway shows, dining at Sardi's, people-watching in the Village), but by mid-February he acknowledged to himself that 'The work has now reached that pitch of boredom which indicates that I've nothing further to contribute for a while.' He attempted to spend some time writing, but instead found himself 'Puttering about, drinking too much again, watching TV, making long-distance phone calls.' He had never enjoyed spending much time alone, and on his own in a strange city he found it even harder than usual. 'Why', he wondered, 'do I indulge in these appalling bouts of self-pitying loneliness?'[29]

A few days in Ithaca with Bea MacLeod provided a timely break before Parker rejoined the *Spokesong* company, newly moved into the theatre for the final technical and dress rehearsals. Circle in the Square's long, narrow stage bore scant resemblance to the Long Wharf's, and the actors struggled to adjust. Two previews were cancelled, and at the first public performance, on 24 February, both the Trick Cyclist and Francis crashed into the audience on their initial entrances. The spectators, Parker noted, were 'silent as the grave', helping to make the show 'Purgatory to sit through'.[30] There ensued ten days of frenzied work and consideration by the management of desperate measures, including replacing one of the actors (an option rejected after vociferous objections from the rest of the cast).

The news that *I'm a Dreamer Montreal*, which was aired on 6 March, had been well-received offered Parker some satisfaction amid this turmoil. He had to try several times to reach Kate on the telephone to find out how it had gone because so many people were ringing their Edinburgh number to offer congratulations. The arrival of Kate herself a few days later supplied more tangible comfort. They were soon joined by Steph Pickering and her boyfriend Andy, Brian and Nancy McKibbin, Ken and June Lambla, John Fairleigh, and Gail and Danny Collins.[31] Surrounded by many of his closest friends—those who had travelled great distances to be with him, along with those such as Alfred Gingold, Irene Lewis, and Raymond and Judy Hardie who lived in New York—Parker could enjoy being in the city again.

Spokesong officially opened at Circle in the Square on 15 March 1979 and would run until 20 May. Parker could only bear to watch about twenty minutes of the opening night's performance. Mostly he haunted the foyer, where he mingled with audience members during the after-show party, for which the producers had laid on 'Irish' food and music. 'Which of the two was less authentic was a moot point, but the food had a nicer flavour', he reported to MacLeod:

> As soon as it was decent to do so, the gang slipped out and headed for Sardi's, where I had a table for 20 booked. . . . I remember stumbling into Sardi's in my white jacket and the people already at the table applauding. The rest of the night was sheer fun, the best (if not only) fun I've ever had at an opening. . . . It was the culmination of the 3½-year *Spokesong* saga, and if I never get another play on a stage, I'll count myself lucky indeed to have had the experience—and to have shared it with people I dearly love.

By the next day, Parker had satisfied himself that 'the notices, though not of the ecstatic Long Wharf variety, were nevertheless sound and respectable'.[32] He and Kate remained in New York to celebrate St Patrick's Day, then recuperated for a few days with the Lamblas at their home in Chicago. They arrived back in Edinburgh on 25 March and spent most of the following week in bed with 'exhaustion virus'.[33] Stewart had been away for over two months.

As soon as he could function, Parker began work on the pilot episode for the *Kingdom Come* series. In late April he submitted the first half of the script and a summary of the rest, and a few days later he left on another transatlantic voyage: to Canada, where he had been invited to speak at the annual meeting of the Canadian Association for Irish Studies. He flew into Toronto and visited the McKibbins before boarding a train west. The trip, reminiscent of the trek around the US that he and Kate had taken in the summer of 1966, took half a week, but Parker loved it. Apart from the varied scenery and the people he met en route, the leisurely pace enabled him to write his talk for the Vancouver conference.

This, delivered on 3 May, developed ideas about drama he had jotted down at the beginning of the year. The strengths of theatre in Ireland, he asserted, were in acting and writing, the weaknesses in directing and criticism. The reason for the latter, he speculated, was Irish theatre's lack 'of any intellectual or theoretical foundations'. Despite Yeats's esoteric theories, 'The national theatre movement found its mainstream in the great realist tragi-comedies of Synge and O'Casey.' Synge died young, and the Abbey rejected O'Casey's efforts to move towards a more socialist and experimental kind of play-writing. 'Even if the national theatre movement had developed a coherent and successful theatre ideology,' Parker contended, 'its politico-cultural motivation would have continued to dominate.' This 'nationalist idealism' had kept him 'at a distance' from the founders of the modern Irish theatre, since 'If you grow up an East Belfast Protestant, you scarcely acquire a clear sense of nationality, let alone nationalism. Both your Irishness and your Britishness are hedged about with ambivalence.'[34]

Only half-jokingly, Parker declared that he preferred to think of his own work for the stage as belonging 'in a venerable Anglo-Irish tradition of comedy of manners, stretching from Congreve and Farquhar through Sheridan and Goldsmith to Wilde and beyond—and that the national theatre movement was [merely] a temporary aberration in that stately progression'. At any rate, he argued, 'the Irish playwright today—or certainly the Northern Irish playwright—has to invent the theatre all over again'. As a start towards the kind of 'vital aesthetic rationale' he missed in current Irish theatre practice, Parker offered the ideas of Johan Huizinga's *Homo Ludens*: 'It seems to me very likely that Irish playwrights may have in common an unconscious impulse to express the most ancient element in playacting— the instinct for play itself.'[35]

This would make their enterprise a noble one, since Huizinga believed that, although both culture and civilization originated in play, 'the play-spirit began to wane in the eighteenth century and has been all but extinguished by the conditions of modern life'. 'If this is even partly true,' Parker continued, 'a quintessentially ludic theatre, celebrating and re-enacting the mystery of play, would perform a crucial function in our society.' Theatre, by his own definition, ranked 'amongst the most civilised and subtle of the public games that we play', with the audience a 'corporate player' licensing the playwright and actors to 'counterfeit reality': 'When the game is well played, the audience will be transported—but it has to be a transport of the head along with the heart.' Concluding, Parker called for Irish plays 'that confront the central issues of Western society, rather than those peculiar only to Crossmaglen or Connemara' and reminded his listeners that Yeats and Joyce had set the precedent of treating Ireland 'as a manageable microcosm of the whole Western culture'.[36]

Quite apart from his formal contribution to the proceedings, Parker had a marvellous time in Vancouver, getting together with old friends from City Stage and making new ones at the conference. 'Peace, it's wonderful', he observed in his journal. On the train back east he experienced a rush of nostalgia for his younger self ('I shd. take flute lessons. Read poetry again. Finish *Hopdance*'), and, summing up the fortnight at home, he wrote, 'Here endeth one of the best trips I've ever experienced.'[37]

Good and bad news greeted Parker upon his return: Joseph Maher, *Spokesong's* Trick Cyclist, had been nominated for a Tony Award, but Joan Rodker disliked his *Kingdom Come* pilot. Moreover, Rob Buckler, whom Parker had assumed would produce the series, had never agreed to do so and thought the pilot 'between-two-stools & not original enough'. Rodker wanted the three of them to meet and discuss the situation, but Parker told her 'there was no point, I couldn't see another way to do it, the meeting wd. be academic & we might as well abandon the thing'. 'I feel bad about the time wasted', he reflected in his journal. 'But at least I'm released for *Nightshade* & *Kamikaze*. Determined to wrap them up by summer's end.'[38]

After failing to gain any momentum on *Nightshade*, Parker turned to the other work-in-progress. He had submitted a synopsis of this radio play to the BBC in June 1978; the following month Michael Heffernan had told him Radio 3 would probably commission it, and the commission (for £500) had come through in early September. Parker wrote the script in May and June 1979 and revised it in July. *The Kamikaze Ground Staff Reunion Dinner* sends up British films of the immediate post-Second World War period, in which English veterans often reminisce about their war experiences. The joke, ideally suited to the non-visual medium of radio, is that the characters, while ostensibly Japanese, sound terribly English. As Colm Tóibín later put it, Parker '[called] into play modern British cliché-ridden, right-wing dialogue and [placed] it in the mouths of modern Japanese characters'. Robert Cooper, who had assumed Heffernan's position as head of radio drama in Belfast and would produce the play at the BBC studios in Edinburgh, recalls that Parker 'specified that, whilst the characters were obviously Japanese, they should be portrayed as their English social parallels'. This device made listeners 'feel a little uneasy. The attitudes expressed by the surviving heroes of the Kamikaze Special Attack Force seemed not dissimilar from those of "respectable" fighting men in more domestic surroundings. The mythologising of pain, grief, stupidity, defeat and human misery through a fog of time and booze is seen by us as both funny and ridiculous.'[39]

In a Northern Irish context, the play had another layer of resonance, since Parker's real targets were fanatical nationalism, hero worship, and the cult of blood sacrifice, all of which sustained the Troubles. He explained the serious theme behind his comedy by saying, 'There's nostalgia for war because life under it is simple and clear. Peace tends to be muddled and complicated. So a climate for a new war is established.'[40] The five main characters in *The Kamikaze Ground Staff Reunion Dinner* worked together during the war as mechanics servicing the planes flown by suicide bombers, and each year they meet to remember their glory days. This glory is reflected from the pilots who immolated themselves for the cause, but no less important to them for that. Now in their fifties, they represent a cross-section of modern 'Japanese' (i.e. English) society and a variety of nostalgic attitudes towards their wartime service.

Tokkotai, the most reactionary among them, has become an airline pilot. Despite his working-class origins, he has a patrician manner and inveighs against the Communist students whose protest at the airport delays his plane's landing in one of the play's opening segments. Irascible, elitist, racist, sexist, and jingoist, he laments the fact that the old imperial spirit seems lacking in modern youth. Shushin, a baker, similarly misses in peacetime qualities that he says abounded during the war. His business threatened by industrial action, he remembers the war as a time of harmony between workers and managers. Shimpu, younger and more lower-class than the others, drives a taxi. A repressed homosexual who pines for the all-male camaraderie of the base, he talks about killing himself to escape from his 'sluggish' wife and 'slob of a son' and complains that 'ever since the war ended I've had nothing strong and true and beautiful to live for'. Makoto, a bumbling dentist who admits he's 'never been any use with mechanical things', recalls the sense of common purpose people had during the war. Unlike Tokkotai and Shimpu, however, Makoto is not unhappy with his current life, and his toast 'to our departed friends' sounds the one note of genuine regret about the war during the after-dinner scene that makes up the bulk of the play. Most contented of all with his peacetime existence is Kamiwashi, a cheerfully vulgar insurance salesman, who creates a sensation at the end of the reunion party by calling for a toast 'to the kamikaze pilots who came home again'—'Because they didn't bloody feel like killing themselves and quite right too!'[41]

Kamiwashi's insistence that the suicide missions were nothing more than 'a tactic of defeat' and that the pilots were merely doing their jobs like everybody else precipitates the play's crisis, as an enraged Tokkotai calls on the others to join him in flying a 'kamikaze mission' to rescue 'the soul of Japan' from 'the ignominy and dishonour into which it has sunk'. He intends to commandeer a wide-bodied jet and 'dive-bomb it into the Communist revolutionaries who have seized the Departures Lounge'. Most of his companions dismiss his drunken ranting; only the suicidal Shimpu volunteers to help. In the event, the two can muster only a single-engine biplane. Mid-flight, Tokkotai suddenly remembers an important engagement the next day and tells Shimpu they must postpone the mission, but, before they can land, the plane runs out of fuel and crashes anyway. The final scene of the play depicts their loyal friends trying to figure out why, instead of hitting the Departures Lounge, they destroyed a mobile library van: this odd target must have some 'symbolic' significance. The newspapers report the incident as a tragic accident, but Makoto, Kamiwashi, and Shushin think they know better and plan to commemorate the event with a memorial dinner in their dead colleagues' honour.[42]

Robert Cooper assembled a first-rate cast for *The Kamikaze Ground Staff Reunion Dinner*, which included John Le Mesurier, well-known for his role in the classic British television comedy *Dad's Army*, as Makoto and Harry Towb, an actor from Belfast who had played a major role in the original *Over the Bridge* nearly twenty years previously, as Kamiwashi. Parker approved the production's 'crisp & full-blooded' effect. It was transmitted on Radio 3 on 16 December 1979, garnering glowing reviews in the *Guardian* and *Observer*. Even more important, it attracted the attention of the highest-ranking members of the BBC's radio drama hierarchy. Ronald Mason, by then head of radio drama for the whole network, termed the play 'a brilliant piece of writing...marvellously realised', and his assistant head, John Tydeman, called it 'one of the best radio plays I have heard in recent years.... pure and perfect radio, very, very funny and not unserious either'.[43]

Between the writing and the production of *The Kamikaze Ground Staff Reunion Dinner*, Parker made a change in his business affairs. He had come to realize that his agent Hugh Alexander's talents lay more in chatting people up than in negotiating performance rights and managing royalty accounts. Alexander himself knew he was out of his depth in dealing with these dramatist-related issues and had relied since at least 1977 on the advice and help of a dramatists' agent named Marc Berlin who worked in the same building, an informal arrangement that grew increasingly untenable as Berlin took over more and more of the actual work. In August 1979, Parker asked Alexander to enter into a 'formal association' with Berlin and expressed his desire 'to deal directly instead of indirectly with Marc on matters where he can be of particular service to me—as I have up to now in discussing the actual writing process with him'. The following month, Alexander effectively stepped aside. From then on, Berlin's agency, London Management, handled Parker's account, and Parker cemented a relationship with Berlin that included script editing as well as professional representation.[44]

Later in August, after a trip to Belfast for Marcus Patton's wedding to Joanna Mules, Parker turned to *Nightshade* once again. This play, which sprang from many of the same psychological sources as his novel *Hopdance*, developed from two separate ideas dating from 1975. In May of that year, after a night 'disturbed by stinging and twitching' in the stump of his amputated leg, the notion of writing a play based on the biblical story of Jacob wrestling with the angel seized Parker. He immediately read the story of Jacob's entire career in Genesis and then looked up four or five commentaries on that part of the Old Testament. He believed the episode would make 'a marvellous 30-min. television play': 'The situation is so magic, and so gravid with notions of conscience, and brotherhood.' Much of the imagery of *Nightshade* derived from this inspiration, though Parker used Jacob's story metaphorically rather than as the main focus of his plot, which came indirectly from Parker's second idea, in early December, to write a play about an undertaker, depicting him as a businessman developing a 'radical monopoly over burial'. (The title may have been suggested by Joseph Losey's 1970 film adaptation of L. P. Hartley's *The Go-Between*, which Parker greatly admired; the film shares thematic concerns with *Nightshade*, and, in it, deadly nightshade in an overgrown garden features as a central image.)[45]

Nightshade had been germinating for almost four years when Parker began grappling with the play in August 1979, and he had already worked most of it out in great detail. Over the years, his interest in the funeral business had become connected in his mind with many other issues. While the professional practices of funeral directors remained one thread in his tapestry, the play had turned into a wide-ranging meditation on how people confront—or fail to confront—loss and the fact of mortality. Parker later told an interviewer that *Nightshade* 'was a play in which I had to face up to monsters and phantoms in my mind—the realisation that you're going to die. I nearly died when I was 19 but it didn't enter my consciousness. In my 30s the fact that I was going to die hit me, and I wanted to deal with that.' In another, even more revealing, retrospective comment on the play, Parker said, 'I was trying to write about things I could barely articulate, to dredge up things from the unconscious mind that I still find it difficult to face. I set out to write about death, and I ended up writing about bereavement.'[46]

Parker's observation about E. E. Cummings's psycho-drama *Him* in his Master's thesis applies equally well to *Nightshade*: the playwright 'is not concerned to imitate a realistic action, but rather to reveal gradually an organic vision'.[47] In this highly theatrical play, Parker juggles private images and symbols, references to other texts, a realistic portrayal and social satire of the funeral industry, reflections on the inadequacy of modern institutions (including the Church, the medical profession, and schools) to enable humans to make sense of their ultimate demise, comedy and tragedy, naturalism and expressionism, music and magic tricks, and a psychological drama about the effect on a particular family of one member's disappearance and subsequent death. This fantasia on mourning and the refusal to mourn conveys a simple but crucial insight: death is an essential aspect of life. Dying, in fact, *is* living, and vice versa, and understanding this gives human existence its poignancy and meaning.

Psychiatrist Colin Parkes, in his book *Bereavement*—which Parker found 'very helpful' in planning *Nightshade*, emphasizes that 'grief is a process, not a state'. In what was likely an unconscious echo of this dictum, Parker in early notes for the play reminded himself that it should be '[n]ot a story, but a process'. For all the pyrotechnics of its staging, however, there *is* a human dilemma at the heart of *Nightshade*, and exploring it allows a coherent interpretation of the play.[48] John Quinn, the central character, is an undertaker who does conjuring tricks in his spare time. Funeral arranging gives him great pleasure, resembling as it does his avocation: he works to deny the reality of death by creating the illusion of peaceful sleep. Quinn rejects the title of 'undertaker' in favour of the more modern 'funeral director', which underlines the element of showmanship in his profession as well as aligning him with Parker himself, who compared the production of plays to sleight of hand.[49] Magic shows, theatre, and undertaking all involve the manipulation of appearances to create an alternate reality for spectators.

Although Quinn's detached approach to death may help him calm distraught clients, it is detrimental when it comes to handling his own grief. He is like a priest who does not believe in God: like his brother-in-law the Dean, in fact, who is rising quickly in the bureaucratic ranks of the Church but dismisses the Old

Testament as the primitive tales of a 'ragged band of desert nomads' and fails to engage his niece's religious doubts. Purveyors of comfort to others, they cannot partake of it themselves. The audience gradually learns that Quinn's wife, Agnes, had left him suddenly a year earlier, taking the firm's cash reserves. She acquired a lover, moved to another city, and died in a car accident. Quinn was notified and had her body cremated, but he has kept her death a secret from their teenaged daughter, Delia, on the dubious grounds that she is too vulnerable to handle the news. Relying on his 'professional status' in such matters, Quinn has borne his grief alone for the past six months. What he is really doing is denying the truth—out of his own unwillingness to face it at least as much as to shield his daughter.[50]

Denial is Quinn's usual approach to awkward facts that include not only his wife's desertion and death but Delia's behaviour problems, the dissatisfaction of his workers, and his firm's financial difficulties. His wilful blindness can seem like duplicity to the other characters, and it negatively affects their lives. Delia is denied the closure of knowing what happened to her mother. Her teacher, Miss Gault, is courted by Quinn but realizes when he tries to give her his wife's clothes that he will never accept her for herself but will want her to step, literally, into Agnes's shoes. Dr Dempster, a friend who dies halfway through the play, has her explicit instructions for a simple burial contravened by Quinn. A faithful employee, Albert Bell, loses his job because he continues to work at Quinn's command during a national labour action.

Despite the unintentional harm he does those close to him, Quinn himself is the biggest victim of his avoidance of anything potentially unpleasant. As a professional mortician, he understands death only as a physical phenomenon whose effects can and should be masked. His inability to incorporate the knowledge of his wife's death into his life paralyses him. Charming and cheerful, Quinn lacks the spiritual fortitude that comes from actively weathering pain and loss. He keeps a precarious grip on himself as long as Delia shares the illusion that Agnes remains alive, but from the moment she overhears him telling Miss Gault that his wife is actually dead, he begins to break down. Eventually he has to take a 'rest cure' and entrust the running of the business to the Dean, who delegates it to Vance, the assistant who has been scheming behind Quinn's back. Quinn's sudden decline puzzles Vance, but Delia regards the explanation as simple: 'He's come to grief, that's all. He's finally come to grief.'[51]

Delia is made of sterner stuff. Throughout *Nightshade* she plumbs the mystery of her mother's absence, preferring knowing the worst to the suspended animation Quinn cherishes. Delia wants not only to confront the truth herself but to force her father to face it too, and Parker's most theatrical devices illustrate the psychic show-down between them. The first scene, for example, takes place at the firm's holiday party, where Quinn and Delia perform a magic trick on what Parker describes in the opening stage direction as 'figuratively as well as literally' an 'inner stage'. Quinn has planned a variation on the cutting-a-lady-in-half routine, with Delia assisting. She steps into an empty 'magician's box', and, after turning it 360 degrees, Quinn 'takes a short plank, slots it into the side of the box, and pushes it through. Then a second and a third as the drum roll builds. He then holds up a large ornamental sword, slots it in, and pushes.' As the sword enters the box, 'There is a frightening scream from inside. Blood spurts out and runs down the front of the box. The music stops. Quinn suddenly tears the box open in a frenzy. Delia stands inside, clutching her stomach, face contorted in pain. Music starts again, very loud. She suddenly springs out with a dazzling smile, into a quick tap routine, and dances off.' After an awkward silence, Quinn regains his composure enough to pretend that he had intended this, and the party continues. At the time, the incident serves only to demonstrate that, as one employee puts it, Delia is 'a bit of a practical jester', or, in the words of another, 'Nutty as a fruitcake'. Looking back on this scene after seeing or reading the entire play, however, one realizes that it economically foreshadows the action of the whole.[52]

Delia repeatedly attempts to shock her father into acknowledging the inescapable reality of death, instead of taking refuge in 'magical' means of concealing it, and this primal scene replays itself in various guises at regular intervals. The end of Act I has the two of them once again performing in public. By now Quinn knows that Delia is aware of her mother's death, and he no longer has the excuse of protecting her to justify averting his eyes from the truth. The strain of staving off his own grief is starting to show on him, and Parker illustrates this with another 'inner stage' vignette. Quinn ushers Delia into the magic box, turns it around, and with the line 'No skeletons in our cupboard!' he opens it again to reveal—a skeleton. This much accords with his design. When he opens the box a second time, however, on Delia again, she is holding a prop dagger that she proceeds to stick into Quinn's heart before tap-dancing away.[53]

This moment symbolically encapsulates the action of Act II. Upon learning of Agnes's death, Delia feels an obscure need to follow in her mother's footsteps in an attempt to understand her. She re-enacts Agnes's flight, wearing her coat and hat, and traces her end to a 'grisly crematorium' in London. Having grieved thoroughly and emerged on the other side, Delia is now more determined than ever to help her father do the same. 'Let her go, Quinn', she urges him. 'Don't fight it. Loosen your grip. It's crippling you. She was what she was. We have to live.' Quinn keeps changing the subject, however, insisting that he is 'just a bit tired', and the play ends in an inconclusive and ambiguous fashion. Quinn is downstage one evening, trying to set a rat trap in the garden where he scattered Agnes's ashes, when Delia surprises him. Before we see her, though, the inner stage is flooded with light and her silhouette ('the figure of a woman in a hat and coat') appears in it. Quinn mistakes her for Agnes, springs the trap on his hand, and collapses. Delia and Vance diagnose his problem as 'heart failure.... One way or another' and prepare to call an ambulance, but Quinn does not revive before the end of the play. It remains an open question whether he will die or finally be ready to start living again.[54]

Delia believes in the redemptive value of suffering. Reading the story of Jacob, she is fascinated by the idea of a God who cripples before he blesses. She draws a similar moral from the story of Sleeping Beauty that her father used to tell her.[55] This tale appeals to Quinn for obvious reasons: sleeping for a hundred years before being awakened, still in the bloom of youth, is the fate he would wish for all his clients and the fantasy he constantly nurtures. Retelling the story in Act I at Delia's request, Quinn wants to highlight its supposedly happy ending. Delia, struggling to find some positive personal meaning in her mother's abrupt and still mysterious departure, expresses more interest in the metaphorical dimension of the princess's bizarre experience. 'The wound has to happen first', she explains to her father: 'There always has to be the wound. Before there can be the kiss.'[56]

Pain, Delia senses, is the price of mature awareness and love, but it must be consciously embraced before it can have a regenerative effect. Perhaps for this reason, the passive princess ceases to be the focus of the story in Delia's two subsequent allusions to it, which close Act I and Act II. After learning what became of her mother, Delia's attention shifts to the prince, a more active participant in his own fate. In context, Delia seems to identify the prince with herself and Sleeping Beauty with her father, still living in a dream. The ending of the story appears less blissful from the prince's point of view, since he has no way of knowing whether or not he can handle this 'stateless person', this 'unresolved chord in the waltz of time'. Emotional risk, Parker implies, is an essential condition of living fully, and there are no guarantees as to how such risk will pay off. Delia leaves her version of Sleeping Beauty as open-ended as the play itself, with the prince trying, tentatively and as yet unsuccessfully, to revive the sleeping princess and wondering, 'Did I get the year wrong? . . . Is this the right address?'[57]

Parker is more definite about the general human issues at stake in this case of bereavement than he is about the particular fates of his characters. Contemporary Western civilization, he suggests, accommodates so completely our wish to avoid contemplating the meaning of death that we have lost touch with the meaning of life. Delia, the wise child, articulates this idea most directly midway through Act II when she reads Miss Gault part of an essay she has written:

> we are the tribe which has lost the knowledge of how to die. In the boundless abundance of knowledge by which we act, this supreme skill has somehow been mislaid. Yet this one action—which we all dread—is the only one that's forced upon us all without exception. And we do it in shame and in confusion. Other tribes, who knew much less, at least knew this. They died with conviction and finesse. But we are entirely in the dark. And the black void of our ignorance spreads wider still. For a person begins to die at the moment of birth. So dying is an action that we perform throughout our lives. And so—at the heart's core—we are the tribe which has lost the knowledge of how to live.[58]

There can be little doubt that Delia in this pivotal speech expresses Parker's own understanding of death's relation to life.

Though there is a great deal of Parker in the character of Delia, he also identified with her father. Like Quinn, he preferred to focus on the fulfilling aspects of his life rather than on the intractable problems in it; he consistently demonstrated this propensity in his reactions to Kate's evident unhappiness. He typically weathered each emotional storm as it arose and then, persuading himself that things must get better because they could not get much worse, buried himself in his work. His immersion in stage and television production made him happiest, but it seemed only to feed Kate's distress. She loved theatre, but she hated show business and the brash, successful people who were a part of it (and whose company Stewart rather enjoyed). In *Nightshade*, significantly, Agnes disappeared only a few months after Quinn went into business for himself. Delia recalls that she 'couldn't stand the smell.... of white lilies and dark heavy clothes. Polished wood and sanctity and guilt and grief, the smog of the funeral industry', and Quinn himself allows that Agnes had '[t]oo much imagination' for the funeral business: 'The work put a strain on her, there's no doubt. She'd no professional objectivity. She suffered alongside every client. You can't afford to do that, any more than a doctor or a nurse.'[59]

Apart from the toll that Stewart's line of work, his intense commitment to his writing, and his frequent absences took on her, Kate suffered from a sense of inadequacy with roots deep in her own psyche and childhood. Every bit as intelligent as Stewart, she was not content to be a satellite of her husband but could not seem to find an outlet for her own considerable talents. Many of Parker's friends remember the serene belief he conveyed to them that they could change their lives for the better, but his wife defeated him. The support and encouragement he offered Kate were no match for her insecurity. Quinn experienced a similar frustration with Agnes, who was 'always at loggerheads' with herself. In terms that reverse the story of Jacob, he explains to Miss Gault that 'There was an element of the angel...trapped in her....As if it had flown too low. And some brute creature caught it by the heel. Wrestled it to the ground. Tore its wings. So that it was trapped in the earth. Pining for home.' He blames himself for the fact that his love for her did not suffice to make her happy: 'I never knew enough, never enough to comprehend her. She kept me forever on approval, she would never entirely give me her blessing. I could hear the sound of her crying from down there, in the summerhouse, for nothing was good enough, nothing free of pain, not with me, not with me....' Even after her death, the unresolved nature of their relationship haunts him; his last words before he collapses are 'Dear God, Agnes love, will you ever give my head peace!'[60]

Few of Parker's female characters resemble Kate. Agnes, who never appears on stage, comes closest to capturing her contradictory and mysterious nature. Monagh, the mercurial singer from *Catchpenny Twist*, also embodies some features of Kate's personality, including her sharp wit, enjoyment of performance, and emotionality. Both these plays probably represent Parker's subconscious expression of conflicting feelings about their relationship. In *Catchpenny Twist*, Roy and Martyn ostensibly die because of their foolish involvement with paramilitaries on both sides of Northern Ireland's sectarian divide. The emotional logic of the play is quite different, however. The two songwriters, making a pragmatic calculation about how best to advance their career, tacitly agree to drop the disintegrating Monagh from the team after her disastrous performance in Luxembourg, and their death by letter bomb comes immediately after they reach this decision to put business before love and friendship. Despite his recognition that Kate was becoming more of a liability than a helpmate to him with respect to his work, it seems that when Parker was writing *Catchpenny Twist* in 1976 he would have regarded leaving her as the basest form of treachery. By 1979, when he wrote *Nightshade*, her mother was institutionalized, Kate more dependent on him than ever, and severing the ties that bound them even more unthinkable. Under these circumstances, Quinn's situation in the play reads as a kind of wish fulfilment: Stewart could not abandon Kate, but what if *she* left *him*? 'Life was a torment to her', Quinn tells Miss Gault, so Agnes's death can be construed as 'a merciful release' both for her and for himself. Sadly for Quinn, though, he cannot maintain this attitude for long, and his indeterminate fate may reflect Parker's irresolution on the subject of his own marriage.[61]

Nightshade contained other private resonances. Like Delia's, Parker's mother had suffered a nervous breakdown when he was a teenager (in some early notes for the play, Agnes is not dead but in a mental hospital). In recent years she had become a chronic invalid whose back problems frequently sent her to hospital or confined her to bed. Parker, who had fought back from an amputation at the age of 19, believed that many of his mother's problems were psychosomatic. Having struggled to live fully himself despite his disability, it irritated him to see his mother resigned to and dwelling on her pain. Her vital energy, it seemed to him, had been directed towards death for a long time already; she was not living her life as she could and was keeping others from living theirs. It must occasionally have crossed his mind that her physical death would be easier to handle than this limbo. As Delia remarks to Vance in the play, 'there are many forms of dying and many degrees of deadness'.[62]

As a matter of self-preservation, Parker consciously resisted being pulled into his mother's orbit. The figure of the tyrannous invalid appears indirectly in *Nightshade*, however, in the form of Dr Dempster's father, who dies during the play after years of failing health. Dr Dempster had cared for him, but far from presenting this as a touching instance of filial devotion, Parker depicts their relationship as one that gave neither any pleasure. We learn that the doctor has been cheated by the terms of her father's will, and by the end of the play she herself has died from cirrhosis of the liver brought on by 'thirty-five years of solitary drinking'. She explains to the Dean:

> My father and I lived like wrestlers, always grappling for the upper hand. Though it was my mother's ghost in me that he was really wrestling with. At any rate it was a stupid waste of two lives. No sooner does he go down at last for the final time, than I'm pulled down directly after him. . . . I spend my whole life waiting for my father to die. And it's that very life—that life which I spent—that I'm now dying of in my turn.[63]

Parker, who had often noted the deleterious effect Kate and her mother had on each other, was almost certainly thinking of them when he introduced this topic into *Nightshade*. In worrying so extravagantly about her mother, Kate was jeopardizing not only their marriage but her own physical, mental, and emotional health.

Parker remarked in 1987 that *Nightshade* remained his favourite among his plays because he suffered most for it. This suffering had barely begun with the draining process of writing it. Shortly after completing the first draft, he read it aloud to Kate—their ritual practice when he finished something—and Gina Leishman, then visiting. Both women were 'rather shaken' by it, as he observed in his journal: 'Found it more powerful, less humorous, than I had anticipated.' Parker himself became 'quite emotional' while reading and had to take a sleeping pill that night. He later remembered that Kate, who usually read his scripts numerous times while they were in development, showed no further interest in reading *Nightshade*.[64]

Possibly Kate's negative reaction to the play stemmed from her uneasy recognition of personal referents in it. Others also found it hard to take, however. Chris Parr, artistic director of Edinburgh's Traverse Theatre Club, had written to Parker in April 1979 to express an interest in his work both for the stage and for television. Parr was then spending much of his time in Belfast, having been seconded from the Traverse to BBC Northern Ireland, where he worked as a script executive. Parker met him for lunch in early June and was invited to write a play for the Traverse. Parr, accordingly, received a copy of *Nightshade* as soon as Parker had one to show, but it struck him as 'unremittingly black', Parker recorded, admitting that Parr's assessment had cast him 'into the glooms. Feel certain I'll never get it onto a stage.'[65]

Other initial responses to the script were equally dispiriting. Parker had accepted an invitation to give a reading as part of a six-week celebration of Irish arts to take place in London early in 1980, and he wanted *Nightshade* to première in the capital during the festivities. He sent copies of the play to Peter Gill at the Riverside Studios, Hammersmith, and to Max Stafford-Clark at the Royal Court, but got nowhere. Gill informed Parker that his theatre was experiencing a period of financial retrenchment and thus not scheduling any new work. Stafford-Clark claimed to have enjoyed the writing but regarded the play as 'technically very hard and perhaps more suited to television', advising Parker to pursue any 'other possibilities' that might present themselves. Even Irene Lewis, the American director of *Catchpenny Twist*, confessed that she had not understood *Nightshade* and asked if he had written another draft.[66]

Two business trips helped Parker make it through the end of 1979 without succumbing entirely to despondency over his difficulty placing *Nightshade*. In October, he had been informed that the television version of *I'm a Dreamer Montreal* had won the Christopher Ewart-Biggs Memorial Award, established to commemorate the British Ambassador to Ireland murdered on 21 July 1976, twelve days after taking office. Ewart-Biggs had described his political views as 'liberal with a small "l"'; the prize had been established by his widow to recognize the writer whose recent work a panel of judges deemed did most to promote the late ambassador's ideals: 'peace and understanding in Ireland; the strengthening of the links between the peoples of Ireland and Britain; [and] closer co-operation between the partners of the European Community'. The award came with £1,500, but the honour meant as much to Parker, who admired both Ewart-Biggs and his wife.[67] The Irish Prime Minister, Jack Lynch, presented the award on 16 November, and Parker enjoyed a couple of days' carousing with Dublin theatre friends afterwards, followed by a jaunt to Belfast.

Ten days later, Parker found himself *in* Montreal, for a production of *Spokesong* at the Centaur Theatre there. He had been invited barely three weeks before, and the summons served as a 'fillip' at a melancholy time. He crammed the week he spent in Canada with new experiences, not least among them 'being able to watch show w/o a qualm or twinge—dispassionate calm, for the first ever time'. Parker regarded the holiday as far superior to the production, savouring the 'Gallic aspect' of the city and the many interesting people he met, including the 'v. approachable' Athol Fugard, whose *A Lesson from Aloes* was going into rehearsal at the same theatre.[68]

The year ended with the news that Dan Crawford would produce *Catchpenny Twist* at the Kings Head in a slot coinciding with the Irish arts festival. Parker pronounced it 'a wonderful way to conclude the decade' and agreed to Robert Gillespie as director, despite his less-than-perfect *Spokesong* performance, reasoning that at least Gillespie knew how to work the space and 'I'm older & less reticent now.'[69] Bryan Murray, so effective in *I'm a Dreamer Montreal*, was cast as the gentle lyricist, Martyn, and Tony Scannell as the acerbic composer, Roy; Nichola McAuliffe took the part of Monagh. Though less involved than he had been with the Kings Head's *Spokesong*, Parker attended several rehearsals and previews.

Catchpenny Twist opened at the Kings Head on 21 February 1980, the 'Easiest opening ever' for Parker because he did his reading for the Sense of Ireland Festival on the same night and so arrived only at the play's end. Everybody told him the show had gone well, and the reviews confirmed this report. The performances of the three leads earned praise, as did that of Tony Doyle, who played the smaller male parts. The English critics applauded Shaun Davey's clever musical parodies and Gillespie's well-paced direction. Best of all, they clearly understood Parker's message about the deadly reach of the Irish past. As Michael Billington of the *Guardian* wrote, 'far more effectively than many weightier works, it makes a good point about the long, inescapable shadow cast by the current Troubles'. The reviewers also highlighted the entertainment value of the piece, however. John Peter, for example, declared in the *Sunday Times*, 'The most appealing thing about Parker's work is the ease with which he blends lunatic humour with a gritty sense of reality. He's done it before in "Spokesong", and he does it again in this hard, ribald and hilarious little play.' The only negative review came from Michael Coveney of the *Financial Times*, who complained that the playwright 'is more interested in investigating the business of popular song writing than he is in writing a play about Ireland'. Parker found the first good reviews 'a pleasant surprise' but was thrilled with the positive consensus, exulting in his journal, '*Catchpenny* has definitely come into its inheritance!.... The play is at last vindicated, by its audiences more than anything. Never say die.'[70]

The London production of *Catchpenny Twist* capped an exceptionally promising two-month period in Parker's career. In late December 1979, a producer named June Roberts solicited a *Play for Today* idea from him. He had proposed reworking *The Kamikaze Ground Staff Reunion Dinner* for television. Although she doubted it would work without Japanese actors, she agreed to consider a treatment, which he submitted in mid-January. She then informed him that she did not have a studio slot available and asked him to write an original film for her instead. Parker decided to accept this project after Roberts promised to try to engage either Stephen Frears or Brian Farnham to direct.

Mulling over ideas for the film, Parker remembered a story his friend Julie Mac-Rae had told him while he was in Belfast for Christmas, about a remarkable sequence of events that had recently befallen her. As a social psychologist working extensively with both Catholic and Protestant community groups in 'flashpoint' areas around Belfast, she felt so overburdened and disillusioned that she now planned to emigrate to Canada. Aware that she had been 'affronted' upon learning that he had used her without her knowledge as a model for Daisy in *Spokesong*, Parker phoned MacRae, got her to recount the incident again in detail, and asked her permission to adapt her experience for television. She agreed, and the plot of *Iris in the Traffic, Ruby in the Rain* is based in its essentials on MacRae's story. Parker later described the film as one in which 'A girl and a woman, experiencing in the course of an evening family and personal crises, resolve them in the process of meeting each other.'[71] He had written the synopsis for it in the first half of February, Roberts had approved it, and Frears was interested in directing it, so Parker had every reason to be pleased with how things were proceeding on that front.

Independently, meanwhile, Chris Parr and producer Neil Zeiger had approached Parker in January with another television project. They wanted him to do a version of *The Kamikaze Ground Staff Reunion Dinner* as a *Play for Today*, to be made in Belfast. Parker handed the treatment he had written for Roberts to them, and by mid-February a contract promising him £2,700 had made its way through the BBC bureaucracy. His fortunes had improved to the extent that this commission did not strike him as 'vastly generous'.[72]

Most encouraging of all, a theatre production of *Nightshade* came into view by the end of February 1980. Parker had hoped the Traverse might mount it during the Edinburgh Festival, but Parr informed him in early January that this would not happen. He then sent the script to his New York agent with a long letter explaining how it could be streamlined in revision. Before that yielded any results, he received a positive response from Sean McCarthy, the Abbey Theatre's script editor and perhaps the first person to love the play on an initial reading, who had given *Nightshade* to the Abbey's artistic director, Joe Dowling. In early February, McCarthy phoned again to ask Parker to meet him and Dowling in London to discuss a production. Parker's elation subsided somewhat after their mid-February conference. The Abbey was not offering a main stage production, but one in the much smaller Peacock Theatre. Parker had imagined staging on a grand scale for this play, but in rethinking the script to present it to American producers he had already started to back away from his original conception, so he promised to consider it. A few days later, he met Colin Blakely, a well-known Northern Irish actor he wanted to play Quinn. Blakely had read the script Parker had sent him and seemed well-disposed towards it. Back in Edinburgh after the successful *Catchpenny Twist* opening, Parker broached the idea of directing *Nightshade* at the Abbey to Parr, who had warmed to the play on subsequent readings of it. Parr agreed to do it as long as he could work a Dublin production in around the Edinburgh Festival. Not only that, but a powerful New York producer named Doris Abrahams (one of those who had tried to obtain the *Spokesong* transfer rights) wanted to talk about *Nightshade* the next time Parker came to the US. With these hopeful developments in the background, Parker agreed in late February to a presentation of the play in the Peacock during the second week of the Dublin Theatre Festival in early October.

Any discordant notes at this time were sounded in Parker's personal life. Steph Pickering, one of their closest friends in Edinburgh, planned to leave the city (although she would not go until the end of the year). She had recently married, and her husband had been offered work overseas. She wanted to be free to join him wherever he went, so she took advantage of the expiration of her lease on the shop to sell the business. Kate had felt some pressure to buy out Pickering herself, but she resisted it because she, too, wished to remain mobile. She had been hurt the previous September by Pickering's decision not to make her a partner, though she had never shown much inclination to learn about the business side of the operation. Now the prospect of a new boss who might be less tolerant of her foibles as a worker inevitably provoked anxiety.

Kate still went to Belfast every few weeks to see her mother. Always depleting, these visits became exhausting when Mrs Ireland's condition took a turn for the worse. One such crisis occurred in mid-February 1980, when she made an unscheduled trip home after being told her mother was 'in bad spirits, staying in her room & acting hostile'. Kate described her to Stewart as 'back to worst of '78, incontinent & mad', news that filled him with foreboding.[73] This time, Mrs Ireland recovered quickly. The incident served, however, as a reminder of how fragile any peace of mind or sense of well-being he achieved could be.

Parker had completed about half of the *Kamikaze Ground Staff Reunion Dinner* television script when another trip to the US intervened. This time Kate came too, although they travelled separately so she could visit the McKibbins during the business portion of his stay. He went first to New York City, where his US agent had arranged a lunch for him on 12 March with Doris Abrahams and her partner. On this occasion, an astonished Parker inferred, 'the assumption seemed to be that they wd. produce it, Off-Broadway'. The following day, his agent phoned Abrahams and came to a verbal agreement with her that she would produce *Nightshade*, with a projected opening in mid-November.[74]

Next came a visit to Louisville, Kentucky, for the Actors Theatre of Louisville's annual Festival of New American Plays. This year, the company supplemented it with *The America Project*. Ten playwrights from other English-speaking countries had been asked to contribute ten-minute skits on the subject of America and Americans. Peter Shaffer, who shared a London agent with Parker, had been one of those invited, and, when he declined the offer, it was passed on to Parker. He had accepted the commission at the end of October and written and delivered his playlet in November 1979. *Tall Girls Have Everything*, which Parker described as a musical comedy, depicts the negotiation between Ivan, a Northern Irish piano teacher and aspiring composer innocently in love with American music and culture, and Faye, a tall, tanned, and imperious American academic thinking about renting a spare room in his flat. Peppered with snatches of popular songs evoked by Faye's comments and played and sung by Ivan, the skit ends with her deftly evading his sexual advances after agreeing to rent *his* room, not the spare one, for considerably less than the advertised price.[75]

Parker found the trip to Louisville a hugely enjoyable junket. The fun began on the flight from New York, 'hilarity incarnate' despite a three-and-a-half-hour snow delay. Alexandra Cann, who worked with Parker's London agent Marc Berlin on his account, introduced him to her live-in playwright boyfriend, Keith Dewhurst, initiating a lasting friendship. The performance of his skit, which did not please him, mattered little to Parker. The most successful ones, in his opinion, were Athol Fugard's and Brian Friel's, both singled out for praise, along with his, in Michael Billington's subsequent review of the proceedings.[76]

From Louisville, Parker proceeded to Chicago and a much-anticipated reunion with Ken and June Lambla and Brian and Nancy McKibbin, who had driven down from Canada with Kate. He arrived on St Patrick's Day, and there followed five happy days of excursions, shopping, eating, drinking, and talking. The strain in the Parkers' lives now became evident to their friends, however. Kate was often moody and sick during this visit, and it gradually dawned on the others that she must be drinking heavily, not only when they were together (they all did that) but secretly and alone. Steph Pickering had known this for some time. During the last months they worked in the shop together, she had noticed that Kate would periodically disappear into the storeroom and emerge smelling vaguely of alcohol and mouthwash. Stewart, who had never alluded to his wife's drinking before, once surprised Pickering by asking her point-blank if Kate drank at the shop, from which she surmised that this behaviour posed a problem at home as well.[77] Publicly, though, Stewart and Kate still for the most part kept their differences to themselves and presented a united front to the world.

Parker returned to Edinburgh via London, where he found the Kings Head sadly unable to capitalize on the success of *Catchpenny Twist*. The ceiling verged upon falling in, and a deluge of water poured into the theatre during performances whenever it rained.[78] A possible transfer to the Old Vic had come to nothing, largely because the Kings Head had no money to put into it. Seven performances had been cancelled owing to Bryan Murray's film commitments, and, since Murray remained in demand, Dan Crawford had been able to extend the run only by two weeks. Nevertheless, the show itself struck Parker as 'much improved. Tight & precise.'[79]

After all this gallivanting, Parker struggled to settle back into the solitary routine of writing. His working hours in the spring of 1980 were mostly devoted to rewriting *The Kamikaze Ground Staff Reunion Dinner* as a television play (much of this involved inserting songs, with lyrics by Parker and music by Dave Brown, musical director of the Kings Head production of *Catchpenny Twist*) and completing a second draft of *Nightshade*. The latter required 'refining the simplified & formalised staging' that Parker had decided to use. Progress was agonizingly slow; at one point, he recorded being 'Stuck on a single line for nigh two hours.' At first convinced that the play could be greatly improved by rewriting, he soon felt worn out with the effort, writing, 'I wrestle & wrestle, and end up leaving most of it unchanged.'[80]

Preparations for their respective productions distracted Parker from work on both scripts. It took from February to June for Neil Zeiger and Chris Parr to find a director for *Kamikaze*—they finally settled on Baz Taylor—and another three months to cast the show. Several first-class performers, including John Le Mesurier from the radio version, turned down roles because they did not think the play would work without Japanese-looking actors, and the cast remained incomplete until less than three weeks before the play went into production.

The news regarding *Nightshade* did not conduce to concentration either. The first blow came in early May, when Parker learned that Doris Abrahams had lost interest in the play. After his US trip, his London agents had decided to approach Max Stafford-Clark of the Royal Court again and try to get him to agree to a trans-atlantic co-production deal with Abrahams. This attempt engendered protracted negotiations over the terms of the UK option with the American producers, who gradually cooled on the project and withdrew. Parker tried to be philosophical about this development; in a letter to Bea MacLeod describing his lunch with Abrahams and her partner and the eventual collapse of the plans made that day, he remarked, 'I have learned enough by now to order the most expensive thing on the menu at these luncheons, since the chances are good that that's the extent of what you're going to get.'[81]

Meanwhile, plans for the Peacock production were going ahead, reminding Parker that completing a script to his satisfaction (which he had done by the end of May) only marked the beginning of an even more fraught process. Casting was extremely difficult, complicated by the fact that Joe Dowling wished to fill as many of the roles as possible with members of the Abbey company. Parker wanted a charming leading man to play Quinn, and when Colin Blakely proved unavailable, a search began that lasted from late April to mid-August, throwing the playwright into near-despair along the way. By late July, Parker had begun to wonder if they would 'ever get this show on the boards at all'. Mercifully, T. P. McKenna, initially 'mystified' by the *Nightshade* script, accepted the part after discussing it with Parker. Lise-Ann McLaughlin, from the Abbey company, had been cast as Delia in May. Other cast members included Michael Duffy as the Dean, Maureen Toal as Miss Gault, Colm Meaney as Vance, Kate Flynn as Dr Dempster, and Geoffrey Golden and Niall O'Brien as Quinn's employees Albert Bell and Vincent Kane.[82]

Parker travelled to Dublin in early September for the first rehearsals. There he was to share a flat with Chris Parr and his wife Terri, an uncomfortable arrange-ment for all. The couple's relationship was strained, and their tension fed into Parker's usual pre-production jitters (compounded in this case by the personal nature of the play's subject-matter). The first week of rehearsals went swimmingly, though, and Parr asked Parker to remain throughout the rehearsal period, leading rehearsals when Parr had to make day trips back to Edinburgh. Parker, flattered to be asked and enjoying the work, said he would consider it. A few hours later, how-ever, Terri burst in, announcing that 'she wasn't going to talk about the play because she hated it & it made her feel sick'. Her comments exacerbated Parker's own inse-curities about *Nightshade*, and he left the flat and 'walked about, in turmoil. Hear-ing the sound of people walking out of the theatre.' Too distressed to confront her again, he phoned his friend Noeleen Dowling and spent the night at her house.

Parker avoided Terri for the rest of the weekend and learned with relief on Monday that she had gone home and would not be back, even for opening night. Parr was 'mollifying & attentive' and Parker grateful to return to work, slightly the worse for wear. He did stay in Dublin for most of the rehearsal period, directing in Parr's absence. Better to be there than at home fretting: he spent the one week-long break he took in Edinburgh 'strained w/nervosity', drinking too much and attempting unsuccessfully to work on other writing projects.[83]

The first run-through went smoothly, but Parker found it 'Harrowing to watch', observing in his journal: 'The play packs a heavy punch, for me, anyway. I don't think audiences will be able to handle it.' Nearly two weeks before opening night, he confessed himself already 'In a shivery, manic state.' The final dress rehearsal did nothing to allay his anxiety, being so 'Ghastly' that Parr wanted to cancel that night's preview because the show had not yet settled in technically. Parker talked him out of this, since it would not help to resolve the problems, but that night at dinner with Kate, Noeleen, and her husband John he declared he had come to hate the play for its effect on him. The preview, fortunately, went surprisingly well. '[N]obody stormed out', although Parker felt himself 'Shaken by it.' Shaun Davey attended the performance and was startled to see him openly distraught. Parker called *Nightshade* his most 'personal' play, and he seemed to Davey almost 'fearful' of its being presented in public.[84]

'Nerves have now got me totally eaten away', Parker remarked in his journal the next day. He spent it helping with rehearsal, 'jollying' the cast along but dashing into Peacock administrator Douglas Kennedy's office for shots of whiskey between scenes. That night, he could not watch the play. On 9 October, opening night, after a day of nearly unbearable apprehension, he spent the entire performance in Kennedy's tiny office, drinking whiskey and listening to a cassette tape of Steely Dan's *Countdown to Ecstasy*. Parker made a point of getting drunk on opening nights, always excruciating for him, but he outdid himself this evening, solemnly introducing one of his agents, Alexandra Cann, to his friend Keith Dewhurst, having forgotten that they lived together. A party at the flat afterwards lasted until 4 a.m., but Parker stayed up even longer, alone.[85]

Knowing he could not face the press this time, he and Kate were on the road by 7 that morning, deliberately avoiding any newspapers that might contain reviews of *Nightshade*. His old friend Sam Fannin, who had left Belfast about the same time he had to take up a management position with his pharmaceutical company in England, had grown tired of the corporate world and had bought a small farm in Devon where he and his English wife, Ann, kept a few animals and offered bed and breakfast to holiday-makers.[86] Parker booked himself and Kate in for several days in mid-October and basked in the comfort of familiar companionship and rural peace. Parr phoned in news of the play's reception, better than Parker had expected.

There were critics who did not care for *Nightshade*, though the terms of their rejection baffled Parker. Michael Coveney of the *Financial Times*, for instance, called it 'an ingenious little play. . . . ambitious but ultimately inconsequential' and 'shot through with Mr. Parker's customary brand of irritating whimsy'. John Barber, whose notice in the *Daily Telegraph* Parker accidentally saw while in Devon, dismissed the play as 'an inconsequential drama about death in all its aspects' with too much 'graveyard humour', but saluted the playwright's 'ingenuity in devising a light, surrealist fantasy'. 'All this', Parker fumed in his journal, 'as a response to the most painful & gruelling experience of my artistic life.' Other reviewers, more predictably, complained that *Nightshade* was confusing, uneven, lacked a strong centre, or made too many demands on its audience (though this could also be construed as a virtue: as Michael Sheridan of the *Irish Press* put it, *Nightshade* was 'tough on the constitution', but so was *Ulysses*).[87]

Most critics praised the acting, though, and some reviews of the play were glowing. David McKenna, the critic for *In Dublin*, commented that *Nightshade* 'infiltrates the mind and the emotions, bringing unanswered questions and incomplete feelings. Because of this, it cannot be left in the theatre. It becomes, like any other truly lively force, a part of you.' Colm Tóibín in *Hibernia* pronounced the play 'a reviewer's nightmare and an audience's delight. ...there is no story that is told in sequence, no meaning that can be easily grasped. But as theatre it is superb.' Best of all, David Nowlan, in the *Irish Times*, judged *Nightshade* 'probably Stewart Parker's best play' and 'as original and as diverting a serious play as has been seen in Dublin for years'.[88]

Nightshade sold out its brief run at the Peacock. In what Parker called 'an ironic turn-up', Irish critics appreciated the play far more than did their English counterparts. He later saw this as evidence of a cultural difference: the English, unlike the Irish, were uncomfortable with writers treating humorously things they actually regarded with great gravity. The condescension of the London critics rankled with Parker, especially charges that he had interesting ideas but lacked discipline. 'The play was meticulously structured', he insisted. 'It had the structure of a dream, but it was all constructed like a piece of filigree, incredibly complex and delicate. There wasn't a colon or a semi-colon that wasn't worked out and balanced.' Whatever the justice or injustice of the critics' verdicts, Parker realized immediately that prospects for a London production in the near future were likely 'non-existent after these reviews'.[89]

He had no time to dwell on this disappointment, having been caught up within days of his return from Devon in details relating to the television production of *The Kamikaze Ground Staff Reunion Dinner*. He first met the cast in late October in London, and he made a second trip to the metropolis at the end of the month, checking in on rehearsals, which the director had reported were 'going like a dream'. He encountered, to his delight, 'funny & inventive work by all'.[90]

Between these two trips to London, Kate's mother was hospitalized after falling and breaking a bone at the base of her spine. Kate hurried to Northern Ireland, in 'a terrible state'. 'She's entirely at her mother's mercy', Parker commented in his journal. A few days later, she reported Mrs Ireland to be 'improving physically but mentally quite mad'. There was even some doubt about her ability to return to Towell House, a 'v. worrying' prospect for all concerned.[91]

Since the recording of *The Kamikaze Ground Staff Reunion Dinner* took place in Belfast, Stewart accompanied Kate on her next visit home, in early November. On their first full day in the city, Kate being 'prostrate all day w/nervous strain', Stewart went to visit Mrs Ireland alone. To him, she appeared to be 'making good progress, though you'd never know it from her alarmist kin'. He stopped by his parents' house, to find his own mother 'in bed, v. depressed & despairing, crying a lot'. Then he returned to John Fairleigh's house, their base in Belfast, where Kate remained 'tremulous'. 'It's going to be a testing week', he predicted.[92]

Professional satisfaction mitigated the personal rigours of this trip for Parker. Production of the television play was going well, and the Peacock brought *Nightshade* to the Belfast Festival this week. On 10 November, Parker 'devoured 6 double whiskies' before heading to the Arts Theatre for the opening. He managed to watch the first act, buoyed by a 'v. responsive & well-disposed' audience, but spent the second act in the office. 'Excellent buzz' following the show left him ecstatic. Parker might have been inclined to dismiss the first-night reaction as unrepresentative, heavily influenced by his friends in the audience, but *Nightshade* continued to draw appreciative crowds. Not only that, but the reviews were both excellent and perceptive. Martin O'Brien declared in the *Belfast Telegraph* that 'Mr. Parker has apparently intended that this colossal conundrum of a play should have no instantly recognisable message; instead the instantly recognisable odour of death. As a result it is all the more richer, the more stimulating and the more likely to seep into the consciousness of the viewer, rather than hit him direct.' The reviewer for the Belfast *News Letter* also wholeheartedly endorsed the show, asserting that 'this is a play to be seen, perhaps not once but two or three times to get [its] full implication'. And Ian Hill placed a rave review in the *Guardian*, in which he proclaimed *Nightshade* 'a play of major weight and importance'. Parker's amazement shows in a journal entry from the day after the opening: 'Good God, I have a hit in Belfast, and furthermore it's *Nightshade*, of all plays.' After the difficulty getting the project underway, the successful completion of the *Kamikaze* recording seemed almost as astonishing.[93]

Kate, who had gone back to Edinburgh for a few days, returned to Belfast for the final performance of *Nightshade* and to see her mother again. After she suffered what Stewart described as a '[f]it of hysteria' on her first night back, however, he persuaded her to take a day off from the hospital and called on Mrs Ireland by himself again. He discovered her 'sitting in a chair looking fully restored & sounding close to normality'. The next day he and Kate visited together, and Stewart observed anew the 'calamitous effect' she and her mother had on one another. Mrs Ireland would return to Towell House before the Parkers left for Edinburgh the following day, certainly a great relief to Stewart, but that night Kate once again succumbed to a bout of 'wild hysteria'. He thus had good reason to welcome their departure.[94]

Now Parker turned his attention to the television film June Roberts had commissioned in February. Somehow he had managed, in short bursts between other commitments, to write the script from April to August and revise it over the next two months. *Iris in the Traffic, Ruby in the Rain* tells the story of a rainy day in the lives of two Belfast women, Ruby Waring and Iris Mullan, whose paths almost cross several times in the course of it and who finally meet face to face at its end.

Ruby, based on Parker's friend Julie MacRae, is a 34-year-old social psychologist who works, as he explained in his synopsis for the film, 'designing and implementing programmes for a Community Development Unit sponsored by the government'. She is suffering from a bad cold and fed up with her job because most of her programmes are eviscerated by the Civil Service before they can take effect. Iris, an oblivious 19-year-old, spends the day being interviewed unsuccessfully for a job in a department store, listening to a friend's punk rock band perform, narrowly escaping a sexual assault, and attending a party.

Ruby leaves work early on this particular day and is driving home to bed when she spies a woman staggering along the footpath, blackened by fire from head to toe and with blood dripping from her hands. Taking her for the victim of a bombing, Ruby picks her up and discovers that her problems are of a different order. After locating the smoking ruins of the woman's house, Ruby learns that her name is Sadie and that she herself had set fire to the dwelling. Policemen on the scene ask Ruby to take the woman to the hospital, and she spends the rest of the afternoon and evening in a futile attempt to see that Sadie receives the mental health care she needs.

Late that night, when Ruby arrives at a neighbouring house to tell Sadie's children she has lost track of their mother, the audience finds out that Iris is Sadie's eldest daughter and that she has just had her mother committed to a mental institution. Iris knows the whole story of Ruby's efforts to help, and she fixes Ruby tea and sandwiches, brushes her hair, and paints her nails. Finally, Ruby is freed from her social worker role by allowing herself to be a woman cared for by other women. Parker wanted to make the point that 'People can be of assistance to each other, they can help each other, but usually in accidental, unlooked-for ways. And often the person who seems to be most passive and least together can offer support to one who seems, initially anyhow, least in need of it.'[95]

Parker later described *Iris in the Traffic, Ruby in the Rain* as 'a condensed female variant on the Dedalus-Bloom odyssey' in *Ulysses*.[96] As Joyce had done in that novel, Parker interweaves the activities of two characters of different ages, material circumstances, and temperaments who keep just missing each other through the events of one day and end their adventures together after a seemingly chance meeting. (In Parker's script, that meeting takes place in the home of a woman named Joyce, and he incorporated several references to the homecoming 'Ithaca' episode of *Ulysses* in the film's final sequence.) Like Leopold Bloom, the recently divorced Ruby is resourceful and down-to-earth, but weary and preoccupied by questions relating to her marital status. Iris, like Stephen Dedalus, is an impractical dreamer with a talent for survival, troubled by a lack of maternal support. Parker's comment in his synopsis that 'Ruby's story is the dominant one, but Iris's story is what gives it perspective' also reflects the structure of *Ulysses*.

Like Joyce's Dublin, Belfast is vividly evoked in *Iris in the Traffic, Ruby in the Rain*. Parker portrays a city beset by problems such as poverty, unemployment, alcoholism, mental illness, child abuse, spousal desertion, and sexual harassment—all heightened by the pressure of the Troubles, which divert attention and resources from these perennial social ills. Parker downplays sectarian issues, focusing instead on Iris and Ruby's origins in working-class Belfast, though Ruby has now ascended into the middle class and lives in the suburbs. (Part of the 'impact' the events she described to Parker had on Julie MacRae derived from the fact that the family she tried to assist lived on the same street in north Belfast where she had been born and brought up, and in the screenplay Parker specifies several shots of Ruby's family's now-derelict house across the street from that of the Mullans.) He explained to a potential director that

> Scenes 56 and 69 and 71 and 73…are specifically about the decay & disintegration of traditional working-class communities, all the values they enshrined, in the last twenty years. That's a process which has taken place in most cities in the British Isles. It has been exacerbated in Belfast by the battering of the Troubles. That's meant to be the point of the cutting back & forward between the living-room and the street, with the police jeep patrolling, and Ruby's birthplace a scarred and vandalised and bricked-up shell.[97]

'Will it ever change, do you think?' Iris asks Ruby. 'Not so long as the people go on putting up with it. All they have to do is get together, just once…', Ruby replies, but Iris concludes matter-of-factly that 'People are too scared.'[98] In its use of the terraced house as an emblem of working-class culture in Belfast, *Iris in the Traffic, Ruby in the Rain* movingly prefigures Parker's last stage play, *Pentecost*. As in *Pentecost*, female characters dominate this screenplay. Men are either absent or play minor or threatening roles. At the end of the film, the oasis of light and life created by the girls and women in Joyce's house is an image for the kind of community that might be possible in Northern Ireland if people could overcome their distrust of each other long enough to recognize their common interest.

From the film project's inception, June Roberts had hoped that Stephen Frears would direct it, and Parker had met Frears in February to discuss his plans for the script. After reading the finished screenplay, Frears still said he wanted to do it. When the two men met again in late November, however, it became apparent that they had utterly different ideas about what sort of film they would be making. Parker, who wanted as much of the action as possible filmed with local actors in Belfast, intended an unsentimental slice of Northern Irish life depicting the mundane realities of people's lives in the shadow of political violence rather than a British audience's stereotyped preconceptions about the place. Frears, on the other hand, struck Parker as wishing to use the script as 'a vehicle for the Great Stephen Frears Ulster Movie', full of epic and mythic overtones. In a letter to Frears drafted in early December 1980, Parker suggested various small ways in which they could underline the film's Belfast background—showing Iris and Ruby being searched as they enter shops and pubs, including a few shots of passing soldiers, and so forth—but also offered a spirited defence of the screenplay in its present form:

> If I were to bring the Troubles any further up front than I've indicated here, the very basis of the script would be undermined. I have in previous plays written about Protestants and Catholics, the relationship between England and Ireland, the historical roots of the present conflict, the consequences of a bombing, Dublin attitudes to the North, riots, shootings, letter bombs, the I. R. A., the U. D. A. and the whole damn

thing. Now I've come to the point where I can write a film about two women who live inside of all that, but who are preoccupied in their daily lives, like actual human beings, with their own emotional & social survival. The soldiers, the bombs, the political rhetoric, they take for granted, they've lived with it forever, it's like the traffic and the rain. You put up with it, you hardly notice it anymore. You wonder about your job or lack of it, or about your future, about your house, your marriage, your mother, about getting back to Ithaca.....[99]

Frears remained unconvinced, and in mid-December Parker heeded his exhortation to see action movies like John Ford's or Akira Kurosawa's by attending a showing of Kurosawa's *Kagemusha*, 'Chuckling throughout at Frears directing my attention to this apropos of *Iris & Ruby*. Like asking for a poem by Edward Thomas to be rewritten as *The Iliad*.' Later that night, after discussing the matter with Roberts, Parker phoned Frears and suggested they go their separate ways. Roberts offered the script to another director, who declined it, as Parker noted furiously in his journal, 'on the ground that it's unacceptable to film a story in Belfast, w/ what's happening there, which cd. equally well be taking place in Glasgow or Newcastle. Same old tyranny, same old director's wank.' A few days later, luckily, John Bruce, who had taken an interest in Northern Ireland since directing a television play by Wilson John Haire in the mid-1970s, agreed to direct the film, so 1980 saw that issue settled at least.[100]

One other major writing project had been simmering on the back burner for much of 1980. For years Parker had been interested both in St Brendan and in cartography, and he had been planning since at least the summer of 1976 to write a play about the discovery of a map that purportedly proves seafaring Irish monks reached America before Columbus.[101] In May, three days after the Feast of St Brendan, he sat down and wrote a synopsis of the play (*Pratt's Fall*) for his London agents in the hope that on the basis of it they could help him convince some London theatre management to commission it. The Royal Court declined to take the bait, but David Aukin at the Hampstead had offered Parker £1,000 in July to write the piece. By the end of 1980 he had researched and roughly outlined the whole play but had not started writing.

The year ended on a down beat. Kate having made up her mind not to go to Belfast for Christmas, Stewart went alone to visit their respective families for the holidays (as she had gone by herself at Easter while he finished a script). 'I do hate being on my own a lot', he remarked in his journal on 27 December. The two and a half years they had spent in Edinburgh so far had not been unproductive ones for Parker, but much of the fun had gone out of his life. As early as June 1979, he had wondered whether 'the slow and lacklustre nature of the work is due to my days being otherwise so empty. In the Palace I was constantly busy w/ hack work, cooking, talking to people, house events etc. And yet had a higher output per diem.' Like Bernard MacLaverty's before him, Parker's experience of moving from Belfast to Edinburgh had been 'like jumping out of the frying pan into the freezer'. In a travel piece he wrote for the *New York Times*, Parker described the city as 'the fiefdom of a high-bourgeois clan', and Sam Fannin comments that Parker was hardly alone in finding Edinburgh a 'tight wee place' culturally. In recent months his social life in the city had become even more barren: Noeleen Dowling and her husband John, close friends there, had moved to Dublin in May 1980, and Steph Pickering had left to join her husband in Dubai in late December. In July, Parker had acknowledged to himself a 'Profound dissatisfaction, for a long time now...with virtually every aspect of the life I'm led by', and this mood continued to predominate, although he had 'no idea what to do about it'.[102]

11

Leaps of Faith

On 17 May 1980, Stewart Parker noted in his journal the nineteenth anniversary of the amputation of his left leg. 'The same span led up to its loss—so I suppose I now begin a third life', he wrote: 'Here's good health to it.' His second life had begun abruptly with his cancer diagnosis, but in *Hopdance*, the novel he wrote about the experience, Parker presents this as preceded by a long period of dissatisfaction and inchoate longing, during which his alter ego suffers under the malign influence of an emotional 'canker'. Similarly, in the early 1980s, an upheaval in Parker's life followed a protracted period of discontent and nervous tension. As his marriage came to seem more an endurance test than a source of renewed strength and his home in Edinburgh less a haven than a proving ground, he seized on his work and the travel it necessitated as a means of escape and diversion. His frequent absences and periodic immersion in the exigencies of production allowed Parker to maintain (though barely at times) his patience with his wife's troubles and his own equilibrium. This delicate balance was upset, however, when he fell in love by imperceptible degrees with the wife of a collaborator. This unlooked-for development led to profound changes in Parker's life, and the theme of love's transforming power features prominently in two plays of the period, *Pratt's Fall* and *Joyce in June*.

After the strain of the previous year, 1981 began auspiciously with the news that the radio version of *The Kamikaze Ground Staff Reunion Dinner* had won a Giles Cooper Award as one of the four best radio plays transmitted by the BBC in 1980.[1] Recipients had been chosen from a field of nearly 500 original radio plays, and the panel of judges included the distinguished drama critic Martin Esslin. Sponsored jointly by the BBC and publisher Eyre Methuen, the award entailed, in lieu of a cash prize, publication in a volume with the other winners. Parker, always avid to have his plays in print, probably hoped his inclusion would give him leverage with Methuen's drama editor, Nick Hern, another of the judges. In any case, he felt proud to have collected 'the hat-trick of prizes—in theatre, TV & radio'.[2]

The television version of *Kamikaze* fared less well. Its transmission, in mid-February, confirmed the reservations of those who had passed on the project. Parker's producer friend Rob Buckler, for instance, returning a copy of the radio script to Parker in November 1979, had written, 'as I think you suggested from the outset, it isn't really suitable for film. . . . it really is an out-and-out radio play'.[3] Parker had been anxious to write for television again, however, at least in part for the sake of the comparatively large fees television work generated. When he got the chance to remake *Kamikaze*, he convinced himself of the aesthetic value of the endeavour.

He had enjoyed embellishing the script with songs and re-conceptualizing it for a visual medium, and he liked what the actors brought to it.

Radio, though, had allowed the characters to be *both* Japanese and English, while television forced awkward choices. Using Japanese actors was neither feasible nor desirable, since it would undermine the cartoonish quality of the characterizations and the unsettling effect of hearing English voices talking in patriotic terms about suicide bombers. So the producer and director opted for English actors while indicating the 'Japanese' nature of their roles by putting them in dark make-up. In other ways, as well, the production reveals that no one ever quite decided whether to treat it as a serious commentary on a specific historical phenomenon or a satirical take on war nostalgia in general. The stylized opening credits, for example, feature shots of ritual Japanese artefacts tumbled together with shells, gas masks, and other Second World War paraphernalia, setting a sententious tone promptly undermined by the play itself.[4] When the characters reminisce about the war, scenes in the television version flash back to it in a literal manner. Like *Dr Strangelove*, the piece ends with 'We'll Meet Again' playing behind the closing credits, but right before that the entire cast performs a ludicrously cheery number that does not even seem to belong to the same show as the opening.

Already at the first screening, Parker sensed '[t]he old inexorable despair' threatening to engulf him, and at the press showing the next day he felt 'nervous & wretched'. The play had been scheduled on the same night as a much bigger-name, bigger-money production, so hardly any critics saw it in advance. Parker noted that *Time Out* damned the play in its preview as 'disastrous, loud, stereotyped, etc.', and the writer of a preview in the *Observer* called it a 'shambles'. Subsequent reviews were few and mixed. Clive James recalled that the radio version of the play had 'instantly attracted wide attention, if only because of possessing the best title of any dramatic work since "Mourning Becomes Electra"'. The television production, in his opinion, 'revealed the piece to be pretty thin'. After watching *The Kamikaze Ground Staff Reunion Dinner* on television, Parker insisted that 'It just didn't look like any kind of disaster or shambles to me: on the contrary, it looked damned fine', but days later he conceded that his play had been 'outclassed' by other television offerings that week. 'I hope I'm not in the course of losing my nerve', he worried: 'Perhaps it's the start of the mid-life crisis.'[5]

From this blow to his ego, Parker moved straight into the production of his television film *Iris in the Traffic, Ruby in the Rain*. The previous month he had stayed in London with the energetic and sociable new director, John Bruce, his wife Lesley (herself a writer who had a television play in production with June Roberts), and their daughter Deborah, and the two men had discussed casting. This had since proceeded satisfactorily, with Parker's favourite Belfast actress, Frances Tomelty, cast as Ruby; Aingeal Grehan as Iris; Jake Burns, lead guitarist for the Belfast punk band Stiff Little Fingers (which, at Parker's suggestion, would provide most of the music for the film) as their mutual musician friend Ducksy; Bryan Murray as the student whose party Iris attends; Leila Webster as Iris's mother, Sadie; and Margaret D'Arcy as Ruby's mother. Producer June Roberts's agreement that most of the exterior scenes should be shot in Belfast also excited Parker, and he met the cast and crew there to begin filming in early March.[6]

The Belfast location afforded ample opportunities for verisimilitude, since locals, long accustomed to television cameras, seemed barely to notice the actors and crew on the streets and even joined in the action unselfconsciously. At Parker's urging, for instance, Bruce captured footage of a real-life demonstration led by Ian Paisley in the background of a shot of Iris walking past City Hall. Even the weather cooperated, with plenty of cloud cover and rain. At times when Parker struggled to gain traction on a script, as he was doing in early 1981 with *Pratt's Fall*, he found the all-encompassing nature of production work a welcome relief from the solitary slog of writing. While on location, he relished working day and night with his new film family and would stay up indefinitely after work ended, talking and drinking with the sturdiest of his colleagues. As long as the team's focus on the project remained intense, this routine energized rather than depleted Parker. Already by 4 March he declared, 'I love this work, more than any other I've done, I think', and by the end of the first week's filming he proclaimed himself to be 'feeling wonderful again'.[7]

Most of the interior scenes, and a few exterior ones, were shot in Liverpool during the second half of March, and here, too, Parker participated as an integral partner in the production. Not even an industrial dispute that threatened to rob the project of several members of the technical crew (and which twice halted work temporarily) could spoil his newly ebullient mood, which persisted until filming ended in late March. His sole weekend at home in Edinburgh during the filming, on the other hand, left him fighting for composure. Kate, whose aunt in Belfast fanned her guilt over having put her mother in care, had just received the latest in a series of letters reporting every difficulty her mother appeared to be having. She reacted in her usual overwrought manner, and Stewart, as he confided to his diary, 'Got profoundly depressed all over again, having succeeded in facing the *Iris & Ruby* situation w/ a degree of equanimity. All the efforts to organize the mother problem into normal proportions invariably come to nothing.'[8]

On one of his visits to London in February, Parker had lost his wedding ring—perhaps a subconscious expression of his feelings about the marriage at the time. Now Kate signalled her equal dissatisfaction with the status quo. She greeted him on his final return from Liverpool with the news that she had quit her job at the bookshop. 'What this forebodes, I can't say,' he reflected, 'but can't help feeling some trepidation.' Kate had never learned to drive, but the next day she abruptly asked for a chance behind the wheel. On the third day, according to him, the 'Subterranean processes of yesterday surfaced as discussion on the whole issue of work, dependence, disparity, whether we shd. split.....deadlocked as ever, leading later to tears as ever.'[9] They came to a truce rather than a resolution of the question, but it seemed obvious to both that there would have to be some changes if they were to stay together.

Stewart had long been advocating for a move to London, where most of his projects were based. If they lived there, he reasoned, he would not have to spend so much time away from home. Kate, however, hesitated to subject herself to the metropolis. On a joint visit to London in early April to view a rough assembly of

Iris in the Traffic, Ruby in the Rain, he showed her less built-up areas of the city like Greenwich and Blackheath, but she remained non-committal. After a reunion week at Sam Fannin's bed and breakfast in Devon with old friends from Rugby Road days, however, Kate announced suddenly on 23 April that she had decided they ought to move to London after all—in a year. Stewart clung to this promise of relocation like a lifeline through the abysmal Scottish spring of 1981, noting fervidly in his journal, 'I really long to leave this frigid photogenic town now, & be among friends.' Meanwhile, as he had observed several weeks earlier, he would have to 'tread warily to avoid the slough of despond'.[10]

Another development that spring, though, gave him renewed hope that Kate's unhappiness with her diminished role in his career might finally lead to her finding her own professional focus. In mid-June, he learned she had been making enquiries about freelance writing opportunities when a photographer from *Woman's Realm* rang asking for 'Liz Parker'. The magazine, it seemed, might want to publish an article Kate had described to them and wondered if she had any illustrations to go with it. This, he recorded, 'threw her into hysteria. She'd been keeping mum about it till she had [the] piece written' and now feared that because she had no pictures the magazine would lose interest. Stewart had to persuade her to see the query as an encouraging sign. In the event, the magazine bought Kate's article for £100. 'Best news for aeons', he declared. 'I really think she has a chance now to blaze a trail for herself.' Less than two weeks later, his optimism appeared vindicated by the publication of another of Kate's articles in the *Guardian*. This piece, about how few women used to shop at West Port Books, inspired several letters in response. 'All very re-invigorating', he noted approvingly.[11]

Parker's own writing had been a source mainly of frustration for him throughout the first half of the year. The play he fought to capture on paper, *Pratt's Fall*, had been commissioned by the Hampstead Theatre the previous July but had been on his mind for years before that. One of its elements, the story of St Brendan, had caught his imagination in early childhood. Like many other Irish monks of his time, Brendan, a sixth-century abbot, made missionary voyages throughout the British Isles. He became known as *the* seafarer thanks to the *Navigatio Sancti Brendani Abbatis*, a Latin poem dating from at least the ninth century which enjoyed immense popularity in medieval Europe. This *Voyage of St Brendan*, a Christian example of the Irish *imramm*, or voyage tale, relates how Brendan and a chosen crew of monks sailed the ocean for seven years in an ultimately successful quest for the Promised Land of the Saints. The romance of these journeys made a lasting impression on the young Parker, who attended the parish church of St Brendan the Navigator in Sydenham. 'I liked the pictures of him,' Parker recalled, 'sitting up in his curragh...in the middle of waves and leviathans.'[12]

As a modern translator of the *Navigatio* recounts, 'the tradition of Brendan's having not only voyaged, but discovered some western, fortunate, but lost island became in due course very persistent. The Island or Islands of Brendan feature on many a map, chart and globe between the thirteenth and sixteenth centuries and beyond.' Speculation about the real-world position of the Promised Land of the Saints continued to flourish. Much of this in Parker's lifetime centred on whether or not Irish monks could have reached North America centuries before either the Vikings or Christopher Columbus did. In 1967, for example, Parker wrote a radio feature on St Brendan for BBC Northern Ireland's Schools Department. As part of his research for the piece, he read *Land to the West* by Geoffrey Ashe, a book suggesting actual locales for the various places Brendan was said to have visited.[13]

The psychological dimension of the saint's religiously motivated wandering interested Parker at least as much as his nautical career, however. In late summer 1971, Parker talked at length with his friend John Paul about the intense faith it must have required to set out upon the uncharted ocean in an open leather boat, and in early September of that year he made a pilgrimage to places in Kerry, Clare, and Galway associated with St Brendan. Around this time, he researched the saint in preparation for writing an English verse translation of the *Navigatio*, which he worked on sporadically through at least December 1971 with the aid of a Middle English version of the poem and a Latin dictionary.[14] He never completed it, however; such an undertaking would have required far more time and concentrated attention than he could give it in those hand-to-mouth days, and probably his Latin proved unequal to the task in any case.

Two events in the mid-1970s likely revived Parker's interest in St Brendan. In 1976, John J. O'Meara published a modern English prose translation of the *Navigatio*. Around the same time, Tim Severin made his *Brendan* voyage. Severin, an adventurer and popular historian of exploration, decided to try to recreate the saint's legendary wanderings when his wife, a medievalist, observed that the *Navigatio*, in addition to its fantastic elements, contained a wealth of what sounded like practical detail about the construction of his curragh and the geography of the places he visited. With assorted helpers, Severin built a leather boat according to the specifications in the medieval text. Like Ashe, he believed that Brendan or other Irish monks might have reached North America by a route similar to the one used by the Norse several hundred years later, and he attempted to align places described in the *Navigatio* with plausible locales: the Hebrides, the Faroes, Iceland, and Newfoundland. Over the course of two separate trips in 1976 and 1977, he and a small crew crossed the Atlantic in their curragh *Brendan*. The project aroused great public interest, especially in Ireland, and Severin documented their journey in a film, which Parker watched on television in July 1978, and a book, *The Brendan Voyage*, that Parker read in July 1980.[15]

The 'discovery' of a map of part of the North American coastline, labelled '*Terra Repromissionis Sanctorum*', initiates the action in Parker's play. He had conceived *Pratt's Fall* when he decided to combine the Brendan material, long seeking an outlet, with another subject that fascinated him: old maps. The more experience Parker had as a dramatist, the more convinced he became that one needed at least two ideas for a play (by the end of his career he had elevated this belief into a fundamental principle of construction).[16] Probably some time in late summer 1976, Parker jotted in his notebook the germ of a play he then called *Cartography*: 'map controversy of the Brendan voyage, based on the Vinland story'.

The contentious debate over the so-called Vinland Map would have been remembered by the reading public in the mid-1970s and early 1980s, when Parker planned and wrote his play.[17] On 11 October 1965 (the day before Columbus Day), Yale University Press published a book entitled *The Vinland Map and the Tartar Relation* in conjunction with the announcement by Yale that it had purchased a manuscript world map depicting an uncannily accurate Greenland and an insular Vinland, a part of North America described in two saga accounts as having been visited by the Norse around 1000. Although the map did not 'prove' that the Vikings reached America before Columbus—experts generally believed that already—it created a sensation nevertheless. The 1440 date ascribed to the map on the basis of manuscript documents accompanying it would make it 150 years older than the earliest known map showing Norse contact with a land west of Greenland. Moreover, as one early commentator explained, an authenticated Vinland Map would be 'the only known map made prior to the voyage of Columbus showing clearly and unequivocally...the existence of America'.[18]

Claims made on the Vinland Map's behalf, however, met immediate opposition. The authors of the Yale volume—among them R. A. Skelton, superintendent of maps at the British Museum—were well-regarded in their respective fields, but none was an expert on medieval manuscript maps or Norse culture specifically. None knew the Scandinavian languages necessary to read the most recent scholarship on the medieval Norse, and the secrecy imposed by a publisher anxious to make as big a splash as possible with the volume describing the Vinland Map had precluded consultation with scholars who could have helped them. Indeed, it seemed to many at the time and later that they had been less intent on a rigorous examination of the evidence for and against the map than on building a case for its authenticity. This singleness of purpose had allowed them to gloss over difficulties that might otherwise have proved insurmountable, especially the lack of a known provenance, or place of origin, for the map.

The British Museum had declined to purchase the Vinland Map before Yale saw it, on the grounds of doubtful provenance and nineteenth-century-style handwriting, and much of the initial criticism of the Yale volume came from British scholars. In November 1966, the Smithsonian Institution in Washington, DC, hosted an international conference on the map at which both believers and sceptics had their say. Public questioning of the map began anew in 1974, when chemists in Chicago revealed that the map's ink contained an element not readily available until about 1923. This announcement provoked another round of stories in newspapers such as the *Observer* and the *Sunday Times*. Skelton had died in a car accident in 1970, but his former deputy Helen Wallis, inheritor of the title of superintendent of maps, convened a symposium at the Royal Geographical Society in February 1974, which again aired but did not allay doubts about the map.

Parker would have been familiar with these developments, both as someone with a keen amateur interest in cartography and as a devoted reader of the English Sunday papers. He probably wondered about the motivation of Skelton, an established scholar who, as Wallis told a reporter in 1974, 'began with doubts, but then decided [the map] was authentic'.[19] As much as someone in Skelton's position might have yearned for some spectacular discovery to crown his career, it seemed unlikely that he would deliberately mislead others. He must therefore have believed in the map himself, but what had induced him to thrust his normal caution aside in making historically improbable judgements that were bound to be challenged? Perhaps the desire to believe in something wonderful created its own irresistible momentum.

In writing *Pratt's Fall*, Parker incorporated many aspects of the Vinland Map controversy. In the play, a map of unknown provenance showing part of the North American coastline and containing a legend dating it to about 300 years after St Brendan's famous voyage is shown to the head of the map department at a major metropolitan library by a bearded adventurer who claims to have found it in the binding of a seventeenth-century printed edition of the *Navigatio*. Initially derisive, the scholar later persuades the library to buy the map, spends two years writing a book intended to convince people of its authenticity (published, provocatively, on Columbus Day), and presents her analysis at an international conference on the map. (In the course of his research, Parker read, in addition to books on cartography such as G. R. Crone's *Maps and Their Makers* and Charles Bricker's *Landmarks of Mapmaking*, the *Proceedings of the Vinland Map Conference*, from which he took many details.) *Pratt's Fall* ends more conclusively than the Vinland drama, however, with the map exposed as a fake.

Parker made another, more significant, change in transferring current events to the stage. He made his 'keeper of maps' female, introducing a motive other than academic hubris.[20] Victoria Pratt, the epitome of middle-class English womanhood, initially seems impervious to the charms of George Mahoney, a roughneck from Glasgow (with an Irish mother, no less). But Mahoney offers more than his dubious map. He provokes comparisons with Brendan by identifying himself as a seafarer, delivering yachts around the world for a living. A spiritual seeker, he also spent two years as a monk in County Kerry, though he is more reticent about this experience: 'It's like having a prison record. It makes people wonder about you.'[21]

Mahoney did not find what he sought in the monastery, however. In an early speech, he hints at what he feels himself to lack in his evocation of St Brendan's fabled journey, valuable to his mind precisely because it was undertaken without maps:

> Think of it fourteen hundred years ago. Those monks were living on the final precipice. The West coast of Ireland, the absolute edge of the known world. Every day lifting their eyes across a great grey heaving desert of a sea, stretching to the very rim of the earth itself. An unknown cosmic turbulence. Imagine what it meant to cast yourself into that. No map, no compass, in a shell of stretched cowhide. The boat you can maybe reconstruct... but not the state of being. Not the unconditional surrender to God's will. Not the wild surge of faith. Or the rapture of it, the blind leap into the dark. That class of a voyage is no longer in the sea's gift.

The seagoing monks, Mahoney asserts, were 'spiritual vagrants' who quested, not for a place, but for 'a state of grace'. Despite his intense appreciation of their belief in God, however, Mahoney does not share it. He left the religious life because he realized that he felt 'nostalgia for faith' rather than 'faith itself'.[22]

Victoria, at the beginning of the play, does not appear troubled by any such nostalgia. She prides herself on being an intellectual concerned solely with the preponderance of the evidence. Victoria's empirical and objective approach to life and scholarship contrasts with Mahoney's deployment of imagination and emotion in the search for his own kind of truth. Parker represents the temperamental difference between them in their varying attitudes towards 'the Brendan Map'. For her, it is 'a functional tool for people wanting to get from A to B'. For him, questions of the map's genuineness are secondary to its power to induce contemplation. Thus, rave reviews for Victoria's book defending the map depress Mahoney, who regrets its treatment as 'just another commodity' and declares himself 'half-inclined to disown it as a fake'.[23]

In his original synopsis of *Pratt's Fall*, Parker had explained that 'The play is the story of their mutual attraction, and the fundamental contest between their views of the world.' He had trouble finding a way into it, however. The problem lay in 'how to offer the material to the audience?' He arrived at an answer to this technical question when he decided, in December 1980, 'To tell the story through a feckless young man called Godfrey.'[24] The ironically named Godfrey Dudley is an English academic, director of a university Extramural Studies department. He meets Mahoney in that capacity, is present when the map comes to light, and introduces Mahoney to Victoria (with whom he attended university and for whom he harbours a secret lust).

With Godfrey acting as intermediary between the protagonists and the audience, it becomes clear that Mahoney and Victoria are more alike than different. Each hungers for absolute truth, though they have divergent ways of searching for it. In Godfrey's terms, both are 'true believers'.[25] He, on the other hand, is a 'congenital bystander' who represents the modern, secular tendency to question and qualify faith out of existence. Much given to doubts and fine distinctions, he envies the others' apparent certainty. Godfrey's fascinated response to Mahoney offers the audience a clue regarding his appeal to Victoria as well:

> old George had a way of making you wonder, if you weren't perhaps missing something deep down that you didn't even know you'd lost. All that talk of his, holy vagrancy and spiritual landfalls and so on. Not that you always caught his drift exactly. But it was the way he believed in belief itself, the [transcendency] of it. That was the thing. That's what was gripping.[26]

Victoria may tell herself and others that she makes her determination about the map on the basis of laboratory tests and evidence derived from the cartographical tradition, but less intellectual factors also influence her. One irony of the play is that Mahoney, who knows that his own attempted faith is merely a replica of the real thing (and that the map he has drawn is a hoax), induces actual faith in Victoria. She comes to believe passionately in the map, but also in Mahoney himself. In short, she falls in love with him. And love, Parker suggests, is the one leap of faith still routinely made in a secular society. The results, of course, do not always justify the risk, since love and faith are both proverbially blind.[27] Allowing herself to be seduced by the nostalgic allure of utter belief leads directly, in one sense, to Victoria's personal and professional ruin: a pratfall indeed.

But *Pratt's Fall* incorporates another level of irony that renders any such straightforward interpretation problematic and indicates Parker's own ambivalent attitudes towards love and faith at the time of the play's writing. Mahoney, who says he forged the map as a 'spiritual adventure', a 'calculated transgression of the moral law', and 'a satirical deception'—and who may have initiated his romantic conquest of Victoria in the same cynical spirit—ends up falling in love with her too. In perpetrating fraud, he finally discovers true emotion. At least this is what he claims, in a last scene between them set after he has spent several months in prison and she has quit her library job to work for a commercial map firm. He begs her for another chance, but she dismisses his entreaties as easily as she rejects his application for employment, having reverted to her narrow, empirical view of the world.[28]

Audience members must decide for themselves if Victoria is a 'prat' for believing Mahoney in the first place or for failing to believe him later. The play even holds out the small but tantalizing possibility that the map might be genuine after all: a 'lecturer in Wisconsin' theorizes that Mahoney lied about drawing it 'in a bid for notoriety', and the latter refuses to deny this. What we choose to believe, Parker implies, matters at least as much as 'the facts'. But do people who can believe without proof have something that other (perhaps wiser, more rational) people lack? Or does such implicit belief only expose them to ridicule?[29]

The fate of Parker's narrator provides a clue as to how the playwright might have answered that question. Godfrey prepares throughout *Pratt's Fall* for a wedding—his own. There are hints along the way that he might end up with Victoria. He obviously loves her, and they have been friends for years. Only in the final lines of the play does the audience learn that he is actually marrying Victoria's loud-mouthed sister, Serena, seemingly through no volition of his own. Godfrey does not 'fall' spectacularly like Victoria or Mahoney, and yet he seems deficient next to them. By the end of the play, Victoria has lost her newfound faith; Mahoney, overcome by love as he never was by belief in God, remains a victim of his own deception; but Godfrey, unable to believe in anything, is more pathetic than either of them. He has never reached out with passion for what he really wants (a large gin, Victoria) but sits back and watches the decisive people and takes what he is given (sherry, Serena). Indeed, when Parker began revising *Pratt's Fall* shortly before his death, he made one significant change in the portion he managed to finish: he changed his narrator's name to Godfrey Pratt. He may originally have intended the play as a dramatization of the siren call of 'nostalgia for faith', belief in belief itself, but its conclusion points up instead the possibly greater hazards of life in a spiritual vacuum.

'Oscillating feelings' about the worth of what he had written tempered Parker's joy in having finally finished the script when he sent it to his agents and to David Aukin at the Hampstead at the beginning of August 1981. He waited with more than his usual trepidation for Aukin's response, wondering if his silence indicated that he found the play 'an ill-considered trifle'. Nevertheless, Aukin's generally negative reading 'devastated' him. The Hampstead's director thought the play lacked 'dramatic impact': 'nothing actually ever happens, or rather anything that does happen, happens off-stage'. He complained about the dearth of 'real conflicts in the scenes' and stated that he did not care in the end 'whether or not the map was genuine'. Although Aukin did not reject the play outright, he did not feel he could produce it, 'at least in its present state', and asked if the script was 'meant to be a first draft' (it was not). He conceded, however, that he might have 'read it wrong' and invited Parker to talk about the play with him.[30]

Parker had a characteristically dual reaction to this dismissal, after over eight months of effort. On the one hand, he grieved and sought solace from those who would assure him that the failure of *Pratt's Fall* to impress Aukin must have as much to do with the difference between their sensibilities as with any problems in the script. Kate always gave Stewart unconditional support, but several other women close to Parker joined her in reassuring him at this time. His niece Lynne had come over with the Dublin University Players to present some plays at the Edinburgh Festival Fringe, and Parker confided in her. Though young, she already commanded his respect for her theatrical judgement. John Bruce's wife, Lesley, becoming a close friend in her own right, likewise proffered informed sympathy. She and Deborah were also in Edinburgh for the Festival when Parker received Aukin's letter, and he told her the whole story. Lesley read the play and declared that she loved it. Alexandra Cann, one of Parker's agents, chimed in soon after with the suggestion that if the Hampstead did not want it, they would look for a theatre management that did.[31]

While courting affirmations such as these, however, Parker brought himself around to the distasteful task of trying to convince both himself and Aukin that *Pratt's Fall* could be revised to answer the latter's objections. He listed scenes he could add to 'liven it up' and thought about ways to intensify the conflict between Victoria and Mahoney. Then he steeled himself for the meeting with Aukin, which was, from Parker's perspective, an unmitigated disaster. He went into it feeling anxious, and over lunch Aukin confirmed his worst fears. He 'pretty well condemned the play to outer darkness', Parker observed in his journal, '—narrow, dull, far too much research showing, Godfrey a mere device etc. I can't see how he cd. ever like it. But agreed to send another draft in 5–6 weeks. He has NO sense of humour. Depressing.'[32]

With no great expectations, Parker began another round of revisions, working on them from mid-September through to the end of November 1981. He brought characters on stage who had only been described in the earlier draft, assigning these cameos to a 'chorus' of several actors each playing multiple roles. In deference to the supposed impatience of audiences with technicalities, Parker cut some detail from the conference scene in which experts debate the merits of the Brendan Map, making the play leaner but less historically resonant. Finally, he heightened the tension between Mahoney and Victoria by emphasizing not only the temperamental differences between them but their national origins. Although this stereotyped distinction between national characters had been present in the original (with the Scots-Irish Mahoney representing the 'imaginative' Celt and the strait-laced Victoria embodying 'English' rationalism), it remained largely latent. In the revised draft, Parker underlined the element of national hostility in their relationship, even hinting that racial animus might have been part of Mahoney's motivation for faking the map. This emphasis provided more of the dramatic 'conflict' Aukin wanted, but it also made Mahoney's actions less mysterious and the oppositions in the play more obvious. If this reorientation of the action left the script a bit cruder, however, Parker also made local adjustments throughout that rendered the dialogue better and more precise, finding subtle ways to restate the themes of faith, lack of faith, and loss of faith.

Parker's prevailing mood at this time was tense and unhappy. He collapsed into physical illness in September and then dallied for nearly two weeks before he managed to make any changes to *Pratt's Fall.* 'Now seized by angst again, shaking w/ it', he remarked in his journal on 27 September: 'What the hell's the matter w/ me, I'm like a fearful child who can't cope w/ his homework.' Kate's edginess reinforced his own. Always easily discouraged, she had begun to receive rejection slips along with acceptances, and one article she had spent three weeks working on had to be shelved when the subject decided she did not want it published. Anxiety over wasted effort and the stress of current writing projects sent her to the doctor with severe insomnia in early October. Moreover, her mother's condition had deteriorated further. Mrs Ireland belonged in a geriatric ward by now, Kate was told during a trip to Belfast in late September, but it would probably be a year or two before she could be accommodated in one. Meanwhile, the staff of the home she lived in would cope as best they could.

Travel afforded Parker some relief, although he could not escape from himself. He had seen nothing of the Continent, apart from the brief trips to Belgium for the *Spokesong* production there, so he and Kate planned a holiday in Paris in October to mark his fortieth birthday. He found the city 'enchanting', but despite several days' worth of pleasant rambles and memorable meals he awoke on his birthday itself to 'bad thoughts'. These were dispelled temporarily in November by nearly three and a half weeks at Sam Fannin's farm in Devon, which he and Kate looked after while Fannin and his wife holidayed in Spain. Spending time in the countryside again proved healing, and they arranged with Fannin to pay for the renovation of an underused room at the farm as a 'country retreat'.[33] This plan was intended to allay Kate's reservations about the impending move to the capital; both sought to regain the balance between solitude and sociability they had enjoyed in the early 1970s when splitting their time between Belfast and Rostrevor.

Parker finished the *Pratt's Fall* rewrite in Devon, and the Bruces joined them for a weekend midway through the stay. The developing relationship with John, Lesley, and Deborah gave Parker much satisfaction in the second half of 1981; it seemed sure to outlive his professional association with John on *Iris in the Traffic, Ruby in the Rain*, and he counted it among the many reasons he looked forward to living in London. Since her August visit to Edinburgh, Lesley had become an even closer friend than John. Her sympathy about the *Pratt's Fall* setback had made her a confidante of Parker's. Apart from his friendships with Howard Schuman and Keith Dewhurst, he had no personal ties to speak of with other playwrights. Now, for the first time since university days, he was on intimate terms with a fellow dramatist, and he relished the opportunity to compare notes on shared experiences and discuss craft with someone engaged in similar work. He appreciated Lesley's serene and gracious manner, along with her sharply critical intelligence, sly sense of humour, demonstrated writing ability, and sincere interest in his work.

Lesley, like Parker himself, had discovered dramatic literature at age 13, when she saw Michael Redgrave play Hamlet with the Royal Shakespeare Company. She began reading Shakespeare on her own and, during school holidays, would go alone to the Old Vic to sit in a cheap seat in the gods and watch whatever was play-ing. Moreover, her father, a successful publicist first for the Rank Organization and then for a company within the new Independent Television network (ITV), would sometimes take her with him to the studio to see television plays being produced. She decided early that she wanted to write, and her parents, who did not see the value of university unless one planned to teach, encouraged her to acquire practical experience by working her way up through the ranks at the BBC. After a year at secretarial school, Lesley joined the BBC's African Service, where, although classi-fied as a secretary, she helped to train people who would be managing directors of radio networks in their African home countries. A year and a half later, Lesley moved over to BBC TV. Here she edged closer to her real love, television drama, and she did her secretarial work at night so she could watch rehearsals all day. Along the way, she met and married John. She left the BBC after six years when their daughter was born, since her long, unpredictable hours (coupled with John's frenetic schedule) did not mix well with new motherhood. When Deborah turned 3 and started attending play group, Lesley began working half-time on a degree in English and history through the Open University, finishing a year or so before meeting Parker. Acquiring the formal higher education she had felt herself to lack emboldened her to write television plays, which years spent helping to make them had well equipped her to do. Producer June Roberts had accepted the first one, a remarkable piece of luck since it had been written 'on spec'. Now Lesley hoped to establish herself as a television writer in more conventional channels, and she found friendship with the seasoned Parker affirming: she said she wanted to be a writer, and he told her she already was one.[34] Parker tried to encourage Kate, too, to believe in herself and her talent, and the example of Lesley's persistence and efforts to overcome her own doubts likely struck him as salutary. In addition, therefore, to enjoying her company himself, he hoped that Kate would develop an enabling friendship with Lesley, another woman launching a writing career in middle age.

The transmission of *Iris in the Traffic, Ruby in the Rain* the day after Parker returned to Edinburgh also helped make November 'by far the best month' of 1981 for him.[35] Though overshadowed by the seventh episode of a lavish serializa-tion of *Brideshead Revisited* which overlapped it in its time slot, Parker's television film earned favourable previews from critics, who praised it, in the words of one, as a '[w]arm and...splendidly understated study of two ordinary lives in Belfast.' Many noted that the city itself served mainly as a backdrop for the action; as a writer in the *Sunday Times* observed, 'the distant eee-aw sirens and the passing armoured cars make a host of points without ever labouring them'.[36] Reviews, though sparse, were generally positive. Parker was miffed by a 'silly' one in the *Listener* which singled out the scenes set in a punk club, filmed in Liverpool, as evidence of 'how much more depraved Belfast youth are than those of Liverpool or Glasgow', but on the whole he could not complain. '[I]t hasn't exactly been greeted as a television event', he acknowledged in his journal. Still, the enthusiasm of family and friends and 'reported praise from the houses, buses & hospital wards of Belfast' heartened him immensely. As the television critic for the *Belfast Telegraph* put it, 'Parker, in his use of the Troubles as an environment rather than a subject, is a writer one feels one can trust.'[37]

Parker's restored sense of well-being soon underwent another of the tests that recurred with discouraging regularity in this period. In early December, Kate received word that her mother had become so frail that she had to be fed; she was advised to visit her again as soon as possible. It came as a shock nevertheless when, two days later, she and Stewart were awakened by the news that her mother had just died, 'peacefully'. They travelled immediately to Belfast, and the next several days passed in a blur of funeral arrangements and other ritual formalities. Kate's relative calm impressed Stewart, who privately believed that 'She & her mother both have been released from a cruel torment.' Returning to Edinburgh, he reflected, 'The last five days seem like a dream. Too soon to know what the change will be.'[38] The removal from the equation of their marriage of a factor that had figured so hugely in it was, to say the least, disorienting.

'I feel a precious relaxation of spirit these days', Parker noted early in January: 'But the old fret is lurking.' Continued uncertainty about the status of *Pratt's Fall* at the Hampstead fed his underlying anxiety. David Aukin had written in mid-December to say that the new draft struck him as 'an enormous improvement' but also to express 'reservations' about producing the play. He promised to show the script to others at the theatre and to contact Parker early in 1982. His next letter, a month later, informed Parker that he had decided against production and released the Hampstead's rights in the play. 'So another theatre door bangs in my face', Parker observed desolately. 'I don't know what to do, other than what I'm doing. It seems impossible to break into the charmed circle. Or at any rate to stay there, after you've been shown round. If I could only get a theatre, a director, a company to show a little commitment. Maybe the move to London will achieve it. I can't go on feeding off fantasies.'[39]

'Self-important little messer' though he took Aukin to be, this final rejection prompted a new crisis of confidence for Parker. His domestic circumstances also felt particularly bleak that last January in Edinburgh, with no cash reserves and a host of household problems that included a water main frozen for ten days. On 15 January he summed these up in his journal: 'Still no running water, I'm itchy from lack of a bath, & there's freezing fog now over the snowy wastes. K. has cystitis, & the slater failed to show up early this morning to fix the roof.' 'So far,' he commented, 'this year is not living up to its promise.' Recognizing his proximity to the brink of depression, he strove to talk himself away from it: 'I have to somehow find from somewhere further faith, humility, humour, drive. I can't go back.' The *Irish Times* had recently invited Parker to write a weekly personal column, and he had been tempted to do so, if only for the money. But he had dedicated himself to the precarious life of a professional dramatist and was loath to accept any regular commitments that might interfere with that. He could not 'go back' to the past, either, though his professional difficulties spilled over into questions about his identity as a man. He lay awake most of one night later that week, 'Mind insisting on a haphazard review of my whole life, esp. the female connection, dredging up forgotten girlfriends from God knows where' (days later, he was still 'glooming'). And he never seriously considered going 'back' to Belfast, pinning his hopes on London instead.[40]

In early February, mindful that *Nightshade* had not yet received a British production, Parker was brought down by praise-filled reviews for a play about death and bereavement which had just premièred at the Hampstead. He was also jealously aware that Bill Morrison had a new play opening in Liverpool. Attention paid to other Northern Irish playwrights needled Parker on two levels. On one, he wondered if his own plays received a proportionate amount of press. On the other, he did not wish to be grouped with fellow Northern writers simply on the basis of shared provincial origins, and he disliked being compared with them, although he could not help making similar comparisons himself. He was consequently less than thrilled when the *Daily Mail* rang with the aim of including him, with Morrison and Graham Reid, in 'a piece on the Ulster school of Dramatists—a small and unremarkable Borstal', as Parker described it.[41]

The imminent transmission of Reid's first television play, *Too Late to Talk to Billy*, had occasioned the *Daily Mail* enquiry. Parker viewed this on 16 February and found it 'an old-fashioned homespun of family drama, w/extraneous sub-plots which shd. have been cut, dodgy studio work & acting by the veterans, & touching perfs. from the youngsters'. The British press, however, hailed Reid as the voice of Northern Ireland. '[E]ncomia' for this play, Parker remarked in his journal, did little to 'encourage me to persevere along my chosen thorny path'—'but what ever does?' he added ruefully, 'You poor creep.' After another sleep-deprived night, he vowed to quell his self-pity with the help of some new 'resolutions':

> to give up newspapers altogether, & television a lot, to read instead a lot, to withdraw into my own stockade and husband my own resources. The world is too much with me, in the wrong way. What matters is the work, & from this turning point of my forty years henceforth, to protect the work and my capacity for doing it. The press, public opinion, the stock exchange of value judgements, none of it matters. The drawing of an aesthetic groundplan, the body of work, literature, a mind in constant growth, letters to friends, sanity, health and happiness matter.[42]

As ever at times like this, Parker drew strength and inspiration from his favourite writer, James Joyce. A year earlier, the *Irish University Review* had invited him to contribute an essay to a Joyce centenary issue. In 'Me & Jim', written in late May 1981, Parker explained his feeling of affinity with Joyce. The experience of reading Joyce's work in his youth, along with Richard Ellmann's biography, had been, he wrote, 'a form of confirmation' of his vocation as a writer:

> In the tenacity of his emotional ties with Dublin, the possessive love mingled with the obsessive execration, the struggle over the years to [annex] the place to the realm of his own imagination, I saw mirrored my own whole tangled involvement with Belfast. In

his inexhaustible fascination with the idiosyncrasies of human character, I saw my own chief delight and preoccupation. In his waging of art as a battle towards an ultimate affirmation of that character, I saw my own highest aspiration.

Above all, Parker valued the 'decent generosity' of Joyce's vision, its 'inclusiveness'. In opposition to present-day Ireland's 'blind factions drunk with their own absolutism', it remained incumbent on writers 'to enfold human diversity and then to celebrate its wholeness in art', and Joyce offered a model for his own 'imaginative struggle' towards this elusive goal.[43]

Parker had wanted since 1974 to write a television piece focused on Molly Bloom's concert tour to Belfast in the company of Blazes Boylan (mentioned prospectively several times in *Ulysses*), thus drawing on his dual obsessions with Joyce and Belfast. He had shared the idea with his friend Michael Heffernan from the BBC, who encouraged him to submit a treatment of it at the beginning of 1980. In 1981, after accepting the assignment from the *Irish University Review* and before writing his article, it occurred to Parker that the Joyce centenary would provide the perfect occasion for his Molly Bloom play. He finally wrote a synopsis for Heffernan, who had moved from radio into television. Heffernan liked it and wanted to direct the play, but he felt it needed 'one additional element, an extra dimension, perhaps featuring Joyce himself'. Parker revised the synopsis, and Heffernan gave it to producer Terry Coles. Coles agreed in September to commission *Joyce in June*, although he did not think Heffernan was experienced enough to direct it, and, after some delicate negotiations with the Joyce estate over copyright issues, the project got a green light at the end of 1981. Parker immediately began background reading for the script: *Stephen Hero*, *Ulysses*, Stanislaus Joyce's diary and his book (*My Brother's Keeper*), and the Ellmann biography. His biggest challenge was to find 'some TV equivalent to Joycean method'. By 1 February, however, the day before Joyce's one-hundredth birthday, Parker had started writing, and this work engaged him at the low point of his morale later that month. He completed the script in early March, satisfied that he had crammed it 'with tasty morsels for those avid hunters of Joyceana'.[44]

In addition to the Molly-and-Blazes plot, Parker used *Joyce in June* to explore the complex interrelationship between life and art in the career of a creative writer. He took his cue from the first page of Ellmann's *James Joyce*:

> The life of an artist, but particularly that of Joyce, differs from the lives of other persons in that its events are becoming artistic sources even as they command his present attention. Instead of allowing each day... to lapse into imprecise memory, he shapes again the experiences which have shaped him.... In turn the process of reshaping experience becomes a part of his life, another of its recurrent events like rising or sleeping.[45]

Parker's play illustrates this conception of Joyce's creative process, through which events in his life are transformed and incorporated into whatever he is writing.

Joyce in June is divided into two parts. In the first, 'Artist As Young Man', Parker depicts incidents from Joyce's life in June 1904, the period Joyce later immortalized in *Ulysses* as a tribute to Nora Barnacle, whose enduring love affair with him began at this time: Joyce is courting Nora, dealing with financial problems, and working on *Stephen Hero*. In the second part of his play, Parker imagines another work that might have issued from the events of this phase of Joyce's life: a 'postscript to *Ulysses*' entitled 'Juanita, or the Rose of Castile' that could have described the aforementioned concert tour to Belfast. Parker wanted the two sections divided by a close-up of Joyce's face from the famous photograph his friend Constantine Curran took of him in 1904, and he proposed that the same actors be used in each part, with some 'real-life' characters appearing in both.[46] (A number of these doublings have thematic significance: Nora Barnacle is played by the same actress who plays Molly Bloom; Ted Keogh, one of Joyce's models for Blazes Boylan, is doubled with Boylan himself; and Joyce's sardonic brother Stanislaus is doubled with the company's drunken piano player, named McIntosh in allusion to the mystery man of the 'Hades' episode of *Ulysses*.) The second part of Parker's play can be imagined as passing through Joyce's mind in the moments that it takes Curran to photograph him. His chain of reflection is sparked by a chance remark from a passing acquaintance, Louis Werner, about a concert tour to the North aborted by the theft of train tickets, hotel bookings, and money. These 'facts' merge with Joyce's musings over the past few days to produce 'Juanita'.

In structuring his 'postscript to *Ulysses*', Parker demonstrated how thoroughly he had studied Joyce's techniques. Like Joyce, he used a myth and a work of art—the Don Juan legend and *Don Giovanni*—to frame his narrative. One scrap of information given in *Ulysses* about the Northern tour is that Molly Bloom and J. C. Doyle will be singing 'Là ci darem' from Mozart's opera. Blazes Boylan, moreover, makes a highly suitable 'provincial and petit-bourgeois' Don Juan.[47] As Joyce had done in *Ulysses*, Parker made characters and incidents in his work parallel similar but more exotic people and events in *Don Giovanni*. Molly Bloom, for example, is the Donna Elvira figure, whom Don Giovanni has abandoned and who seeks revenge on him, and Lucy Werner is Donna Anna, who resists his advances and whose father is killed by him in a duel (in 'Juanita', Boylan pushes Louis Werner from a moving train when the impresario threatens to remove him as tour manager). In the opera, Don Giovanni sarcastically invites the statue of the man he killed to supper, and the piece ends climactically with him being banished to Hell by the ghost of the Commendatore. 'Juanita' ends comically, when an irate Werner catches up with the concert party. Boylan, hearing that he is in Belfast, coolly invites him to dine and waits for him backstage while Molly and Doyle perform. When Werner arrives, Boylan hands him a brandy, which the older man disdainfully rejects, spilling the contents of the glass on Boylan's legs and feet as he proffers him a piece of paper detailing 'Assorted charges of embezzlement, fraud, assault and battery'.[48] Boylan defiantly puts a match to the summons and drops it on the floor, but his grand gesture sours when his trousers catch on fire, and the play ends with Blazes, alight, running across the stage of the Ulster Hall to the entertainment of the rest of the company.

Parker lays the groundwork for this use of *Don Giovanni* in the first part of *Joyce in June*. Stanislaus refers disparagingly to his brother as a 'Don Juan of the cakeshop', and Joyce, after coaxing a florin out of him, leaves singing 'Fin ch'an dal vino' from the opera. Later, in the pub, Joyce tells his friends that 'The brother has me pegged now as the Don Giovanni of Ringsend', at which they laugh and decide that Stanislaus himself must be the Don's 'misfortunate manservant' Leporello. Curran remarks, 'I saw the *Don Juan* of [Molière] in Paris, you know, a shocking piece of blasphemy altogether. It even scandalises the French. Now, there's a play you could translate, Jim, for the National Theatre Society' (Vincent Cosgrave quickly adds, 'Always providing you turned your man into a virgin Nationalist').[49]

Despite finding such comments amusing, Parker's Joyce resents the fact that those closest to him believe him capable only of carnal conquests, not 'true love'. As Cosgrave puts it, 'You're a queer bloody brilliant sort of a man, who's suddenly besotted with a country wench, who's only the first of many. . . . The enduring kind of love, which is spoken of in novels, is definitely not your mark'. Curran agrees that he would have expected the role of 'Don Giovanni, hounded by the rabblement' to appeal to him, but Joyce protests that he disapproves of the Don's 'chosen weapon': 'I'm a penman, not a cockman.' These sentiments reflect those of the actual Joyce, who despite his iconoclastic attitude towards marriage remained devoted to Nora until his death.[50]

Early in Parker's play, Nora comments favourably on the fashionable attire of Boylan's real-life model. This gives Joyce a motive to seek revenge on him in his fiction, and later, in 'Juanita', Boylan (the 'cockman') receives his come-uppance. His sexual shenanigans alienate Molly, who begins to think fondly of her husband. Leopold Bloom himself makes an appearance at the end of the play, waving at Molly from the balcony of the Ulster Hall, and Parker implies that he will take over the management of the tour from Boylan as well as reclaiming his rightful place in his wife's affections. Boylan, meanwhile, becomes a laughing-stock, his own ignominious version of Don Giovanni's Hell. Love ultimately triumphs over baser human impulses.

Parker channelled most of the levity of his spirit into his writing at the beginning of 1982. Reading *Joyce in June* or *Blue Money*, the last script Parker drafted in Edinburgh, someone who knew nothing about his life would assume he did not have a care in the world. The latter project dated from August 1981, when June Roberts told Parker she intended to form her own production company and asked him to submit an idea for a feature film. Regarded by some professional associates as intimidating, owing to her acid wit and insistence on setting the terms of her social interactions, Roberts was fiercely loyal to 'her' people. Parker regarded her as 'wacko', but agreeably so. Now she proposed to pay out of her own pocket for a script that would be produced only if she and her business partner, Jo Apted, managed to 'drum up finance for it'. A week after Roberts's invitation, Parker received a letter from an actor friend, Mike McCabe, suggesting that a current news story—about an Irish-born London mini-cab driver who had run off with a bag containing £241,590 left on the back seat of his car while his client ran an errand—would make a fine basis for a play or film. Parker agreed and soon convinced Roberts. ('Blue money' was underworld slang for cash unknown to the Inland Revenue.)[51] The chance of Roberts raising funds to make the film increased dramatically in

October 1981, when she showed Parker's synopsis to her friend Tim Curry, who expressed a desire to play the lead. Curry had achieved North American recognition for his part in the 1975 cult hit *The Rocky Horror Picture Show*, and Parker hoped he would have enough star power to attract investors. Nevertheless, production plans remained in the realm of fantasy when Parker wrote the bulk of the script in April 1982.

The driver whose exploit inspired *Blue Money* left an ex-wife and children in London, bought a car with cash immediately after absconding with a Nigerian businessman's hold all full of money, liked to sail, and was believed by police to have returned to Ireland after the robbery. Parker incorporated some version of these details in his screenplay, along with one mentioned in error in one of the newspaper articles McCabe sent him: that the driver was an amateur impressionist. He decided to build on this 'wonderfully suggestive' characteristic when he found out over dinner in a London restaurant that Tim Curry could do marvellous impressions himself. He refrained, however, from making any attempt to learn more about the 'real story', since 'I wanted to write something almost like a fairy-tale.'[52]

Larry Gormley, Parker's mini-cab driver, impersonates popular singers in clubs and bars and dreams of success in show business. He seems to be on the path to stardom when he auditions for a role in a West End musical that 'specifically calls for an Irish mimic who's a rock 'n roll freak'.[53] He gets the part, but the producer drops dead right after casting him, scuttling the production. Soon Larry, working out his notice after being laid off from his driving job, succumbs to temptation. One of his most unpleasant clients, a Colombian drug-dealer, leaves an unlocked briefcase full of money in Larry's car while he buys cigarettes. Larry drives away on impulse but quickly repents and tries to return the cash. His passenger, however, has disappeared, and Larry decides this is the break for which he has been waiting. With his girlfriend Pam, a Black Londoner and aspiring singer, he heads for Ireland, where he intends to open a club.

Most of the screenplay consists of their comic misadventures, as they are pursued by drug-runners, the British and Irish police, and petty thieves. Larry, never too busy to pause for a song, performs along the way numbers by artists ranging from Maurice Chevalier to Elvis Presley. As impractical as he is optimistic, he cannot capitalize on his heist, which had been for him 'a gesture. An act of defiance' against his fate. The money is misspent, stolen, lost, and destroyed. An 'executive member of the republican movement' offers to relieve him of it in Dublin, thus turning his crime into a 'political offence' and rendering him ineligible for extradition, but Larry refuses to allow it to be used to hurt people. He and Pam return to London, where they are promptly picked up by the British authorities. Because this is a fairy tale, the policemen who question him agree to release him without charge if he donates the remainder of the money to their Benevolent Fund. Not only that, but the director who had auditioned him for the musical has managed to find new production money, and Larry reaches his goal after all. Parker in his journal adjudged the script 'pure frivol', adding, 'I hope it proves commercial because it certainly isn't artistic.'[54]

The title and much of the background music for *Blue Money* come from a Van Morrison song of the same name, and around the time Parker was working on the screenplay (February to April 1982) he entertained the possibility of collaborating on a project with Morrison. A New York-based producer named Dick Fontaine saw a video of *Iris in the Traffic, Ruby in the Rain* and asked if Parker might like to write, with Morrison, a film musical set in Belfast. Parker, who admired Morrison's music, allowed himself to dream. He knew about Morrison's difficult reputation (a *Rolling Stone* piece Parker read while considering the offer 'firmly characterised him as undependable, unpredictable, moody, capricious and humourless'), but he pursued the matter anyway. In late March he attended a Morrison concert in London as the musician's guest and then met him to discuss scenarios for their proposed film. Parker suggested a musical based on the story of Deirdre of the Sorrows, but his potential collaborator seemed more inclined towards what Parker called 'rags-to-riches-to-disillusionment—the old tune'. The two men got on well, though, and agreed to talk again in a few weeks. The denouement, as Parker explained to Nancy and Brian McKibbin, had been foreseeable from the outset. After their three meetings in London, Morrison performed in Germany, proceeding 'to a nostalgic return to Belfast in the company of the producer. Evidently he hated the gigs, and was freaked by revisiting his old mates in Belfast, all with teenage kids and depressing stories; at any rate he bolted back to his hideaway in Marin County, leaving everything unresolved, the producer in a state of confusion, and myself confirmed in the original scepticism.'[55]

Equally inconclusive in this period were Parker's efforts to get *Pratt's Fall* produced. Since the Hampstead's final rejection in January—indeed, even before it—he had been sending the script to contacts on both sides of the Atlantic, including Irene Lewis (the American director of *Catchpenny Twist*), Peter Lichtenfels (new artistic director of Edinburgh's Traverse Theatre Club), and Sean McCarthy (script editor at the Abbey). Meanwhile, Parker's agents were showing it to London producers, but so far to no avail. When the tiny Traverse, which he had regarded as a last resort, turned the play down as insufficiently meaty, Parker nearly lost hope. Before this, however, he had given the script to his friend Marilyn Imrie, a radio drama producer at BBC Edinburgh. He asked if she might be persuaded to direct it; she said yes and promised to approach the Tron Theatre in Glasgow. Meanwhile, he had heard that Sean McCarthy regarded *Pratt's Fall* as a possible play for the Peacock Theatre, but when Parker reached him directly McCarthy told him that he and artistic director Joe Dowling had judged it 'too British to be done by the Abbey'. Imrie had suggested a Scots–Irish co-production between the Peacock and the Tron, a notion that appealed to Parker. McCarthy liked the idea, but Dowling did not, and so the matter rested by mid-May 1982. Parker believed the general lack of enthusiasm had everything to do with the fact that 'the piece is a light comedy set in London, the two main characters are English and Scots, and it has nothing whatsoever to do with the Northern Irish troubles. Since *Nightshade* hasn't been produced outside Ireland either, I can only assume that people want one kind of play and no other from me.'[56]

Personal annoyances compounded the professional ones. The Parkers' relocation to London could not take place until their Edinburgh flat had been sold, since nearly all their assets were tied up in the property. Perhaps because of his unhappy experience as a buyer, Stewart had at first felt confident that 103 Harrison Road would be snapped up instantly. It went on the market on 26 April, and he began paying rent on a flat in London on 1 May so the removal could take place as soon as a sale went through. After an initial flurry of interest, however, the number of people coming to view their flat dropped off markedly, and he started to fear it would be 'a long haul'. Because he had no urgent writing deadlines, he had nothing to do besides fret and help pack for a move that might or might not happen in the near future. Meanwhile, the malign Scottish climate treated him to one last spring snowstorm. Less than two weeks after the first showing, he already felt 'oppressed by the (in every sense) flat situation'.⁵⁷

The stress of being in limbo exacerbated the Parkers' marital difficulties, which had not been noticeably dispelled by the death of Kate's mother. As they came closer to making the change she dreaded and he longed for, underlying tensions rose to the surface. Their relationship reached a crisis on 10 May, when both allowed their private resentments into the open. In his journal he recorded being

> Wakened by a crash, which turned out to have been Kate falling off a table. She attacked me for not rushing to help. Which triggered off in me a furious outburst, engendered by the months & years of frustration, brought to a head by the impasse over the flat. Went on & on. Finally she went into town & came back w/ a pile of new clothes....Went for a drink, came back to find K. out & a note suggesting we separate. Got crocked....K. back at 11.00 & we blitzed on at each other till the early hours, falling into bed drunk & exhausted.

Soon Stewart would wish fervently that he had accepted Kate's suggestion that he go to London without her. At the time, though, they shared the impulse to salvage what they could of their life together. They 'Invalided along' through the next day, 'trying to reconstruct some kind of compatible truce'. The atmosphere between them remained 'oppressive', however, and they might not have managed to sustain their fragile cease-fire if the flat had not suddenly sold on 13 May—eighteen days after it went on the market, for more than the minimum asking price, and to the boyfriend of the first person who had viewed it. This seemed a wonderful stroke of good fortune, and Stewart and Kate threw their energies into getting ready to leave.⁵⁸

One week to the day later, Ascension Day, they supervised the removal of most of their belongings into storage and began driving south, reaching their destination on 21 May. They planned to spend the next few months in Golders Green, a Jewish area of London near Hampstead Heath which had, as a consequence of its Jewishness, a pleasantly 'American flavour' for Parker. The flat itself, 23A Waterlow Court, was let to him for a minimal rent by his friend Diana Purcell in Belfast. It had been bequeathed to her son by her estranged husband's late mother, and she suggested that Parker could use it over the summer (longer if necessary) as a base for house-hunting. As they had for much of their married life, Stewart and Kate would essentially live in one room, the guest room, since the flat remained crammed with the dead woman's possessions, most dating from the 1920s and 1930s. The entire block of flats had been designed on progressive lines as housing for single, educated women, and some of the original occupants were still *in situ*. The effect, as Parker noted, resembled 'rooms in college' in the middle of the suburbs, complete with quadrangle, gardens, and tennis courts. The spare bed was 'lumpy', the electrical outlets 'rudimentary & alarming', but the place had its compensations, being crowded with books reflecting the advanced tastes of their owner, including an early edition of *Ulysses*, too battered to be valuable to an actual collector, which Parker discovered with joy. (He later bought this holy relic and had a special box made for it.) Sam Fannin also believes that living there may have given Parker the initial idea for *Pentecost*, his stage play set in a house inhabited by the ghost of its late tenant, since the flat full of memorabilia fairly 'reeked' of Norah Purcell herself. Fannin recalls talking with Parker about the concept of a place preserving the 'vibes' of a dead person, and he adds that he spent one night alone there and found it 'scary'. In the event, Parker would stay in this 'haunted' flat until the end of 1982, sometimes scandalizing his elderly neighbours by flopping on his back in the quad to gaze at the stars in the wee hours of the morning.[59]

The weather, already hot, contrasted vividly with Edinburgh's, and Parker savoured the sensation that London finally belonged to him, making the rounds of friends and professional associates in a happy haze, exploring the area, and starting to look at houses. He had just enough of his favourite kind of work to do to make him feel usefully busy. *Joyce in June* had gone into production at last, after a series of delays and funding crises, and the producer, Terry Coles, and director, Donald McWhinnie, welcomed Parker's input at every stage. McWhinnie had directed Samuel Beckett's radio plays and the world première of Harold Pinter's stage play *The Caretaker*, among many acclaimed productions in his long career. Parker himself remembered a 'superb' *Endgame*, featuring Stephen Rea, which he had seen at the Royal Court in 1976. These accomplishments awed the playwright, as did McWhinnie's capacity for whiskey-drinking; lunches with him were boozy affairs, even by Parker's standards.[60]

Actor T. P. McKenna's son Kilian was cast as James Joyce, Gabriel Byrne as Ted Keogh/Blazes Boylan, Bridget De Courcy as Nora Barnacle/Molly Bloom, and Stephen Rea as Stanislaus Joyce/McIntosh. Rea was one of Parker's oldest friends in the business, but they had seen little of each other over the past five years or so. Their careers had gone into high gear around the same time, with Rea beginning to play starring roles in the most notable London theatres as Parker's play *Spokesong* took off in Dublin and London. Their planned collaboration on a Belfast/Edinburgh Festival production of *Spokesong* had failed to come to fruition, but Parker had hoped that Rea's insider status at the Royal Court and the National would help him get future plays mounted in these venues. And, naturally, he had anticipated that Rea would act in them. So far, this had not happened. In particular, Parker had been disappointed that Rea had declined an invitation to take a leading role in the Dublin production of *Catchpenny Twist*. Even so, Parker had believed he would at least take part in the television version of that play and was disagreeably surprised to learn that the actor had accepted a role in another television play which would preclude his participation without informing either Parker or Rob Knights, *Catchpenny Twist*'s director. This breach had such an 'alienating' effect on Parker that he began to suspect Rea of turning down parts in his plays on principle. Moreover, since 1980 Rea had been publicly involved with another Northern play-wright, Brian Friel, in the leadership of the Field Day Theatre Company, which toured annually in both Northern Ireland and the Republic and had as its mission the performance of challenging plays, to high professional standards and in a Northern voice, for a non-traditional audience. Given his long association with Rea and their shared vision of what Irish theatre needed, Parker could not help but feel pointedly excluded from this enterprise. Thus, his first response to McWhin-nie's suggestion that they offer Rea the role in *Joyce in June* had been 'But will he take it?' Take it he did, though, and the production afforded them the opportunity for such a thorough rapprochement that soon Parker once again began writing parts for Rea.[61]

Casting concluded, *Joyce in June* continued to go swimmingly. Parker, 'delirious' with pleasure after the read-through, enthused in his journal, 'This is the profession at its best & most rewarding.' McWhinnie sought his advice on making the script work, and Parker stood by to rewrite scenes as necessary throughout the rehearsal period. In the studio, in mid-July, the play 'went like a dream'. 'I think it may be the best television production I've ever had', Parker wrote to the McKibbins, '—but then I was permanently drunk for the whole five days.'[62]

This excess did not owe wholly, or even chiefly, to McWhinnie's influence. Like Joyce's in 1904, Parker's life had undergone a seismic disruption that June. At some point during the past year, he must have admitted to himself that Lesley Bruce occupied more than her proper share of space in his mind and heart. As far as he knew, though, she and John were happily married, and he still hoped his own mar-riage could be saved. Their friendship had developed in the context of their respec-tive families; anything more than friendship, she remembers, did not even seem 'possible' and was certainly never 'allowed or alluded to' by either of them. Indeed, Parker believed he had 'expunged' his secret love for her from his mind before the move to London.[63] Since then, though, he and Kate had seen a good deal of the Bruces, and his illicit feelings had come flooding back.

On 8 June, he accompanied John and Lesley to a birthday party for June Rob-erts. It was a large gathering, and Lesley recalls that after they arrived she did not see Stewart again until the end of the evening. He had had a lot to drink but seemed 'mellow' rather than drunk. Lesley sat down beside him, and, realizing that they could not be overheard, he 'recklessly' delivered 'a speech'. He had never meant to say it, he confided, but he loved her. Now, he worried, they would not be able to remain friends. He could hardly believe it when Lesley replied that she felt the same way and was glad he *had* 'said it'. Ten days later, he learned the whole story: her marriage had reached its own, unrelated, crisis point the previous autumn, and she and John had decided to separate. They were waiting until John found a flat within walking distance of their house to break the news to their daughter, at which point they would make their split public.[64]

From the moment he confessed his true feelings for her, Stewart and Lesley knew they would eventually be together. By 'firm mutual consent', however, they refrained from having 'an affair'. Knowing his love returned, he did not mind waiting as long as necessary to achieve their union. Surely he realized, too, that the happy resolution he desired would not be attained without a great deal of pain both for themselves and for people they loved. He thus felt no hurry to force the issue, but drifted through the unseasonably warm days in a 'blissful reverie'.[65] This ceased abruptly a few days before *Joyce in June* went into the studio. 'Around midnight, going to bed, K. asked me if I was in love w/ Lesley, and I told her all of it', he recorded in his journal on 9 July: 'And so the marriage came to a violent end.'

Parker described the immediate aftermath as 'a switchback ride of wild oscillating peril and joy'.[66] He and Kate had been together for twenty years; though their marriage had long been troubled, its demise caused him to remember and mourn for the whole of their joint life. In addition to his own grief and regret, the thought of her distress lacerated him. Simultaneously, however, he looked forward to his new partnership with Lesley. This would not be achieved quickly or easily, but he believed implicitly that being with her was not only what he wanted but what he needed. The last six months of 1982, during which he came to terms with the ending of one phase of his life and the beginning of another, were largely consumed by introspection.

Within thirty-six hours of Stewart's admission, Kate boarded a plane to California to stay with Ken and June Lambla, who had recently moved there: the first in a series of visits to old friends that would keep her on the move for about a year.[67] Stewart communicated with her frequently, by phone and letter, and his state of mind depended greatly on whether, at any given moment, Kate seemed to be adjusting well or badly. He confided in Ann Hasson, a young actor from the *Joyce in June* cast, and phoned her frequently to talk. Even if it had been possible, he would not have felt it right to move at once into a relationship with Lesley. First he had to grapple with his complicated feelings towards Kate, which included intense guilt over the way things had finally ended and worry about her future. He regretted more keenly than ever that she had chosen to invest herself in him and his career to the extent that the breakup of the marriage left her with little to call her own, and he suffered acutely over the pain she must be enduring.[68]

For the most part, Stewart kept his distance from their mutual friends during the first few months after he and Kate split up. He expected them to blame him for it—Kate certainly did—and he wanted her to have the full benefit of any support they could give her. In an exception to this policy, and not sure if they yet knew he and Kate had separated, he wrote a letter to Nancy and Brian McKibbin at the end of July to explain the situation from his point of view. Written on one of his relatively good days, it reflects his conviction that 'the decision to split was a positive one', especially since they had been on the brink of it for several years. He allowed that 'the combination of my obsession with my work and Kate's obsession with her mother was pretty fatal. We started to get unhappy all of six years ago, and it's been getting worse and worse, to the point where we were doing each other far more harm than good, and it was clearly never going to change.' Nevertheless, the actual parting had felt 'worse than a death, because the love has died, the twenty years of living together have died, but the other person is still there'. All the same, he hoped the rupture would afford them both the opportunity to achieve a fulfilment their marriage had ceased to give them:

> I know for certain that the end of the marriage is going to offer me the chance of a happiness which I haven't known for a very long time. But I honestly believe that the same applies to Kate. She certainly couldn't be any less happy than she's been in the past four years; but apart from that, she is now in a position where she *has* to take responsibility for her own life and her own destiny. If she can succeed in doing that, then she's going to know a kind of satisfaction and self-respect which the marriage never gave her—in fact it robbed her of them.
>
> The only thing I ever wanted for her was to make her happy, and I failed—but then how could I have succeeded? The only person who can make Kate truly happy, in her soul, is Kate herself. Now she has a real chance.[69]

Unfortunately, as her peregrinations continued, Kate grew increasingly unreconciled to what had happened, focusing her resentment on the events that had precipitated the separation rather than remembering how fraught her relationship with her husband had become long before he met Lesley. While in California she had seemed calm and reasonable, though she sounded 'slightly robot-like' to Stewart. As the months passed, she became more and more angry—with Stewart, but also with their friends. These were happy to help and sympathize with her, but they refused to take her side against him. One by one they re-established contact with him, and one by one she cut them off.[70] She remained in touch with Stewart himself for some time, but eventually even sporadic correspondence ceased. Any hope he might have held that their friendship could survive the death of their marriage proved unrealistic.

Throughout this angst-ridden interval, glimpses of the future he expected to share with Lesley sustained him: '...I know in my bones', he wrote to the McKibbins, 'that when we have endured the whole interminable nightmare, we're going to have an extraordinary life together, a kind of bond which very few people are lucky enough to be offered at this stage in their lives'. In late July they anticipated being united 'in 12–18 months' time'. Apart from their shared need to pick through the emotional detritus of their respective marriages, they were concerned about Lesley's daughter Deborah, then 12, who would have to assimilate in rapid succession the facts that her parents were separating and that Stewart had become a key figure in her mother's life. Stewart worried that she would think him responsible for her parents' divorce and hate him for it. Partly for this reason, he and Lesley carefully limited the amount of time they spent together at first. Instead of meeting, they wrote letters and talked on the telephone when they could. Stewart lived for these precious moments of communion, writing in his journal after one such conversation, 'Jesus, I absolutely love & need this extraordinary person. She's a drug in my bloodstream. More to me than my life, not that I'm paying any huge tribute in saying as much.'[71]

The closer Stewart felt to Lesley, though, the harder it seemed when he could not see or speak with her. A 'sense of the shortness of precious time together' shadowed their meetings in person, and when they were apart he felt himself to be in 'limbo'. He spent most of his time waiting, in desperate loneliness and various stages of anxiety, for the next opportunity to talk to or be with her. He knew his love to be fully reciprocated; nevertheless, he feared that something might yet happen to wrest happiness from his grasp. He could barely work, but luckily he had no major writing projects underway. Eventually it must have seemed to both of them that the risks of letting him go on like this outweighed the hazards of appearing to move too fast, and Stewart moved into Lesley and Deborah's home in Putney at the beginning of 1983, a few weeks after John moved out. Stewart found this arrangement uncomfortable, feeling himself to be 'an intruder', but it was the least disruptive way for himself and Lesley to be together in the short term. Once they were under the same roof, his emotions, high and low, became less extreme, and he could finally settle down to some writing again. 'I do want to work, devoutly', he remarked in his journal a few days after the move.[72] His third life had officially begun.

12

Fruition

The mid-1980s were phenomenally productive for Stewart Parker. Living in London, socializing with friends in the business, seeing films and plays, and being part of the metropolitan buzz he had previously experienced only as a visitor afforded him the kind of stimulation he had missed in Edinburgh, and he relished his changed circumstances. With domestic contentment came renewed energy and enthusiasm for his work, enabling him, for example, to complete *Northern Star*, a stage play about which he had been ruminating for years. Producers rated him among the best radio and television writers then working, he was commissioned to write a feature film, and even in the perpetually chancy world of the theatre it looked as though he might finally receive the recognition he deserved. 'This is the life I always wanted to live', Parker observed in his journal at the beginning of October 1984: 'I'm living it now, and I love it.'[1]

Parker's relationship with Lesley Bruce served as the corner-stone of his new happiness. Howard Schuman, who had known Parker since 1976, realized only in retrospect how difficult the preceding few years had been for his friend. Not given to complaint, always a person with immense zest for life, Parker took 'ebullience' to 'another level' when he and Lesley became a couple. They were 'meshed' emotionally and intellectually and together radiated 'something incredibly powerful', making theirs a union 'uplifting' to be around. Peter Farago, a director who worked extensively with Parker about this time, agrees that he and Lesley seemed 'tailor-made for each other'. Because both were playwrights, Sam Fannin remarks, they had 'an enormous amount in common', and their friendship, as well as their romance, was rooted in a shared commitment to their chosen vocation.[2]

Lesley recollects that she and Stewart, each emerging from a period of great 'emotional distress', felt they had 'saved each other's lives', and they took delight in the smallest events of every day. Stewart would run an errand and return with stories—living with him offered an education in seizing and savouring the moment. If she left the house during the day, she would feel 'excited' as she returned to think of Stewart there, warming their home like 'a fire'. A solitary worker herself, Lesley was startled at first by his predilection for writing in the living room, at the hub of the household's activity. Her gregarious teenaged daughter, Deborah, and her friends became used to his presence among them, pad of paper propped on the side of an enormous armchair. No matter how serious his intentions as a writer, he never wanted to be cut off from ordinary human interactions.[3]

By the time Parker moved in with Lesley and Deborah, he felt ready to resume his work routine. *Radio Pictures*, his script in progress in January 1983, had been commissioned the previous summer by Central TV. In June 1982, when offered a commission for a sixty-minute studio play, Parker had been 'in love with the world' and thought of the job as 'a jeu. To pay the mortgage.' When asked to produce a synopsis in August, however, his marriage had just broken up, leaving Parker so distraught that he could not manage even a one-sentence description, though this had not deterred Central. Since then, his confidence and excitement regarding television work had been further undermined by the indifferent reception of *Joyce in June*. Its transmission had come perilously close to being pushed into 1983, a possibility that enraged Parker because he had conceived the play explicitly as a centenary tribute to Joyce. It had finally been aired on 30 December 1982, in the dead zone between holidays. Not a soul had turned up for the press viewing, it had received just one (mixed) review, and only two friends had phoned to offer their congratulations on the night. 'I can't avoid a certain degree of despair', Parker remarked in his journal a few days before beginning work on the new script.[4] *Radio Pictures*, though, betrays little of the angst behind its composition. In this television play about the taping of a radio play, Parker comments wittily on both media, depicts the interplay between fictional and real people and worlds in the hothouse environment of a play's production, and presents a serious exchange of views on the purpose and worth of art, all with a deft lightness of touch.

The cast of characters of *Radio Pictures* includes the producer of the radio play, Glyn Bryce; its diffident writer, Rory Colquhon; the studio manager, Donna Melchett; the production secretary; three assistant studio managers (all named Jim); the four actors taking parts; and an announcer. At Cornell University in the summer of 1974, Parker and some of his friends had presented a stage production of one of his own radio plays, *The Iceberg*, which had created visual interest for the audience by exposing the artifice behind radio's creation of an alternate, purely aural universe.[5] *Radio Pictures* employs a similar strategy: showing actors flipping through magazines or knitting while others perform at the microphones, juxtaposing the actors' readings with candid commentary on them by the production team behind a soundproof window, and displaying the tactics used to make realistic sound effects. Through Rory, Parker dramatizes what must often have been his own feelings of irrelevance as the author of a piece in production; no one pays any attention to his reservations about the way things are going, and, although he is frequently asked for his opinions, no one listens to them.

Throughout, the play is amusingly self-referential. Glyn holds ideas similar to Parker's friend Michael Heffernan's about the creative freedom offered by radio, telling Rory that 'radio is very akin to film, except that radio is more visual. It's the distinction between your common or garden rabbit and its common or garden hutch, and the astounding bunny a magician pulls out of his topper, it's conjuring images out of the ether instead of merely approximating them on celluloid.' He dismisses television as 'a purely narcotic medium which atrophies the imaginative faculty', but Parker pokes gentle fun at Glyn's radio chauvinism, too, when he has him add, 'a genuine interchange of ideas like this one would never be allowed on to the screen'.[6]

In the play-within-the-play, Rory's *Mr. Deadman and Miss Goodbody*, Parker sends up his own youthful pretensions. This portentous allegory—along the lines of Parker's impenetrable and unproduced 1967 radio play *Sam Todd For God*—borrows its premise from his unpublished novel *The Jest-Book of ST Toile* (completed in 1968), the first-person narrator of which spends much of his time spying on a young woman across the street from the safety of his wardrobe. In *Radio Pictures*, the voyeur is a middle-aged dictionary compiler who takes compromising photos of his victim and uses words and images to keep the real world at bay. For Rory, Mr Deadman's fixation on Miss Goodbody symbolizes his yearning for 'a truth that remains in his control. A pure object of desire.' Near the end of the play she violates his sense of their proper relationship when she reveals that she knows he has been watching and photographing her and offers to pose for him, causing him to retreat in terror into the 'life of the mind'. Other characters in *Radio Pictures* have their own ideas about the play, if they think about it at all. Glyn sees a connection with 'the whole vexed issue of identity running through all your work'; Harry Tremlett, the actor playing Mr Deadman, thinks its action is 'all to do with non-communication', leading Donna to aver that, if he is correct, it is 'working a treat'; and Susanna Prine, Miss Goodbody herself, reads it as concealed autobiography.[7]

As he had wanted to do in his proposed television series about a travelling production of *Kingdom Come*, Parker alternates snatches of the play itself with more dramatic 'backstage' action mirroring the sexual frustration and repression of Rory's text. Harry lusts after Donna as Mr Deadman does after Miss Goodbody, but she prefers the Jim doing spot sound effects. Susanna fascinates Rory, and she plays with him like Miss Goodbody taunts *her* admirer. *Radio Pictures* builds to revelations that add a final layer of hilarity to the proceedings by highlighting the incestuous nature of the radio drama community. We learn, for example, that Glyn had fathered a stillborn child by Donna back in the days when she was his secretary, and that Harry and Susanna, who have treated each other with open hostility throughout the taping sessions while flirting with Donna and Rory, are actually a married couple.

Even in this comic piece, though, Parker could not escape the nagging moral questions that faced every Northern Irish writer of his generation. He injects them into *Radio Pictures* in a scene in which Susanna, who comes from the same town in County Down as Rory, accuses him of mere escapism. Earlier he had explained his theory that imagination 'annexes the future. The same way memory annexes the past. Memory and imagination are two edges of the same process.' Now he insists that 'imagination...goes its own way, it has to be let do that, Susanna, even when the city's burning. Otherwise the soul of man itself is burned out.' A heated exchange follows, and it is by no means clear who gets the better of the argument:

SUSANNA:	You're supposed to be an artist, you should be putting yourself at the service of your people. You're using your precious imagination as a substitute for reality.
COLQUHON:	But nurturing the imagination is a service, the only true service an artist can perform. Reality is meaningless until the imagination perceives it.
SUSANNA:	Is that so? Well, my sister's husband got shot in the head by the army. The bullet went clean through his imagination, without waiting for him to perceive it.
COLQUHON:	I'm sorry.
SUSANNA:	Is that the best you can say about it, Mr Playwright?
COLQUHON:	I'm afraid it's the best anybody can say about it. That's the point.

This conversation stands out vividly owing to its dissonance with the rest of the play. Self-division might even have had something to do with the odd elation Parker felt when he learned at the end of January 1983 that the production of *Radio Pictures* had been cancelled, so he 'was able to beat the deadline, & yet not have to face the test of an actual production'.[8]

In *Pratt's Fall*, too, Parker had tried to get away from the subject of the Troubles. Now, a year after the Hampstead rejected it, Parker's most recent stage play was finally in production at the Tron Theatre in Glasgow. The Glasgow Theatre Club had decided in September 1982 that it wanted to mount the play with or without the Abbey, and Parker, who had more or less given up on the piece, let them, despite some reservations which he listed for Bea MacLeod:

> The theatre is an 18th. century church building which has been adapted, and it's a very good space indeed for the show: but the people running it are well-intentioned novices, clueless about the nuts and bolts of actually doing plays. The budget is practically non-existent, nobody has yet been cast, and they're talking in terms of a 2-week rehearsal period...I hae me doots.[9]

These doubts were likely compounded by the fact that the play's director was John Bruce, who had read and loved the play shortly before his and Parker's marriages had ended. Marilyn Imrie, instigator of the Glasgow production, would not be available at the proper time to direct it, and Bruce expressed an interest. Recent events had strained their friendship, but both men believed they could still work together. Though Lesley suspected otherwise, she also thought it would be good for Deborah to see Stewart and her father cooperating on a project. Lesley recalls the collaboration as predictably 'difficult and stressful'. Casting, as always with a Parker play, proved challenging, and Imrie surmises that Bruce may have had trouble dealing with Scottish actors, who tended to be more confrontational towards directors than their English counterparts. Moreover, Bruce, a television director, had almost no theatre experience. Under more comfortable circumstances Parker could have helped a great deal, but he had much less involvement with the details of production than he usually did when one of his stage plays received its première. *Pratt's Fall* ran for two and a half weeks at the end of January and beginning of

February 1983, earning respectable reviews, although several of the critics commented on Bruce's 'timid' or 'irresolute' direction.[10]

Other theatrical developments in 1983 promised better. For a while, Parker had been receiving unaccustomed and welcome signs of interest in his stage plays from two theatres, the Birmingham Repertory Theatre and Belfast's Lyric Players Theatre. The blossoming of his connection with the Birmingham Repertory had begun the previous spring when Peter Farago, then an associate director with the theatre, arranged to meet Parker through the latter's agents. By August 1982, he had scheduled a spring 1983 production of *Nightshade* in the theatre's studio space. An intense Hungarian who had directed at a number of venues, including the Royal Court, Farago endeared himself to Parker with his enthusiasm for this particular work. His production, featuring Kenny Ireland as Quinn and Madeline Church as Delia, opened in Birmingham in June 1983 and received sympathetic reviews in *The Times* and the *Daily Telegraph*, reviving Parker's hopes that the play might yet attract the attention of London theatre managements and embark on a wider life. At the Birmingham Repertory, Farago had been concentrating on working with dramatists to produce new plays, and soon, probably by the end of the *Nightshade* run, Parker agreed to write for Birmingham a play he had been contemplating for some time about the Irish melodramatist Dion Boucicault.[11]

Parker's evolving relationship with the Lyric in Belfast came weighed down with historical baggage, since his political and aesthetic disagreements with the theatre's founders had made him since the mid-1970s as little inclined to work with them as they were to work with him. In October 1981, an actor friend relayed the news that a 'revolution' at the Lyric had ousted Mary and Pearse O'Malley from their positions of control. Their day-to-day involvement in the operations of the theatre had been waning for a while; in 1977, they had moved to County Wicklow in the Republic, motivated by concerns over Mary's health and weariness with the Troubles. Even removed from Belfast, however, they had maintained an inordinate influence over programming, casting, finances, and the like, largely through Pearse's role as secretary of the board of trustees. This position, by design, held executive authority between board meetings and allowed its holder to act more or less unilaterally. When Pearse decided a few years later to step down as secretary while remaining on the board, Ciaran McKeown was elected to the post on his recommendation. McKeown, a trustee since 1977, was a journalist and a friend of the O'Malleys, and they probably assumed he would keep them informed and follow their advice. Once in office, though, he proved less biddable than they had supposed. Despite his regard for what the O'Malleys had achieved in founding the Lyric, he soon came to believe that their continued dominance posed the greatest single obstacle to its growing into a truly professional and distinctively Northern Irish theatre. If the price of overseeing the Lyric in what McKeown regarded as a responsible way turned out to be the loss of their friendship, then he was willing to pay it. In successive showdowns through 1981 and 1982, McKeown led a board of trustees split four to three between reformers and O'Malley loyalists in asserting his own pre-eminence as secretary and establishing that senior staff members of the theatre should be empowered to wield authority in their respective fields.[12]

One result of this manoeuvring was that Leon Rubin, who became artistic director in 1981, had an unprecedented amount of control over the theatre's programme. At McKeown's suggestion, Rubin made a point of reaching out to
Northern Irish artists alienated from the Lyric in the past.[13] Northern playwrights
had suffered most from the Lyric's earlier exclusive policies, and Stewart Parker
seemed an obvious candidate for rehabilitation. In Belfast for Christmas in December 1981, Parker spent an evening with Rubin, who at the time wished to produce
Spokesong. Parker convinced him instead to mount *Kingdom Come*, never before
seen in Ireland. This production, directed and choreographed by Nona Shepphard
and featuring pop star Peter Straker in the role of Huey Lynch, scored a popular
success for the Lyric, which offered it as part of the Belfast Festival in November
1982.

Meanwhile, Rubin had expressed a willingness to commission the play about
Henry Joy McCracken, one of the Northern leaders of the 1798 rebellion, that
Parker had wanted to write since 1967. In a letter to Rubin in August 1982, Parker
described the play he envisaged. It would be set after the failure of the uprising, just
before McCracken's capture:

> In the course of the night, in the course of his dreams, both waking and sleeping, we
> will discover what his life has been—and what the life of his city will be in the decades
> stretching ahead up to the present day. I am primarily concerned with his human
> predicament, but then also with a critical moment in the course of Irish history, a
> moment which can encapsulate the quandaries and contradictions which continue to
> confound us.

'For obvious reasons', Parker concluded, 'I would very much like this play to open
in Belfast.' The prospect of commissioning a play on this topic written with such
an avowedly political aim threw the divided Lyric board into consternation. Moreover, since commissioning new work had never been a significant part of the theatre's culture, the £1,000 Rubin proposed to pay Parker for the script would have to
be shaved from the production budgets of already-scheduled plays. McKeown met
Parker to sound him out on his approach; impressed by the playwright's 'intimate
knowledge of the period', along with his sanity and intelligence, McKeown pledged
to devote his considerable energies to making sure that the collaboration took
place.[14]

Parker received his commission and began writing in August 1983. He
seized the opportunity to address Northern Irish people, delivering a Protestant, but not a unionist, critique of Irish republicanism and using the history
play format to deconstruct habits of mind that still nourished violence. Called
Northern Star, after the United Irishmen's newspaper, the play is set in 'Ireland,
the continuous past'. As Terence Brown has noted, this static conception of
history characterizes both communities in the North, with each side cherish-
ing totemic dates and images full of symbolic present-day significance. In
response to the remark that 'They forget nothing in this country, not ever',
Parker's McCracken replies bitterly, 'It's far worse than that. They misremem-
ber everything.'[15]

Northern Star focuses on the United Irishmen, the first modern revolutionaries to imagine a future for Ireland independent of Great Britain. The United Irishmen inspired, among others, the Young Irelanders of the 1840s, the Fenians, the Irish Republican Brotherhood, the IRA, and the Provisionals. In the elegant formulation of historian Kevin Whelan, the 1798 rebellion 'never passed into history, because it never passed out of politics'. Consequently, historical interpretations of the formative 1790s in Ireland have always themselves been deeply political.[16]

Parker sought to restore to popular memory the Belfast dimension of the 1798 rebellion. This centre of revolutionary thinking and activity had been eclipsed by long focus on Wexford and Dublin, especially in the Republic, but many of the most radical leaders of the United Irishmen—men like Samuel Neilson, Thomas Russell, James Hope, and Henry Joy McCracken—were Belfast-based. Theobald Wolfe Tone, the most celebrated of the United Irishmen, came from Dublin but had close ties with the Belfast wing of the movement. By placing the Belfast leaders centre stage, Parker indicated his dissatisfaction with the version of Irish history that had written Protestants out of the nation's story.

Parker clearly felt an affinity with McCracken, the protagonist of *Northern Star*. Apart from being a gifted mimic (a detail Parker treasured), McCracken embodied disinterested leadership, taking command of the entire Army of the North after the arrest or resignation of more senior leaders a mere three days before the rising was due to begin. With few men and little support, he performed creditably on the field of battle until, ironically, his reinforcements were routed by an enemy retreat, causing his own troops to flee in panic. He sympathized with the problems of working people, despite his middle-class background, and was apparently without sectarian prejudice. All this helped to make McCracken an ideal filter for Parker's own perspective on the United Irishmen, which was coloured by his socialist and secular politics.

In Parker's opinion, the truly radical contribution of the United Irishmen had been a new response to the question 'What did it mean to be Irish?' According to Parker's McCracken, 'It meant to be dispossessed, to live on ground that isn't ours, Protestant, Catholic, Dissenter, the whole motley crew of us, planted together in this soil to which we've no proper title.'[17] Before the 1790s, members of the Anglican Protestant Ascendancy had defined themselves as the Irish nation in a fashion that excluded both Catholics and Dissenters from the full privileges of citizenship. After the failure of the 1798 rebellion, Irish nationalism became almost indistinguishable from Catholic nationalism. The United Irishmen succeeded for a short time in de-coupling a sense of the Irish nation from sectarian allegiance. Looking back on them from the vantage-point of late twentieth-century Belfast, this seemed an extraordinary achievement.

Unfortunately, in Parker's view, the idealistic leaders of the United Irishmen in the North, mainly Presbyterians of the professional and mercantile classes living in the only region in Ireland where they constituted a majority of the population, never comprehended the depth of sectarian animosity in the rest of the country. In response to official persecution, the reformers-turned-revolutionaries augmented their numbers by enrolling tens of thousands of Catholic Defenders. Forging links between the two organizations was one of McCracken's signal achievements, but Parker regarded it with suspicion. To him, the rising of 1798 looked like two separate rebellions: in the North, an abortive assault on government troops by the rump of United Irishmen left after a Draconian government crackdown in 1797; in the South, particularly County Wexford, a more significant bloodbath involving the massacre of large numbers of Protestants. 'So much for the great revolution of United Irishmen', the defeated McCracken remarks: 'It comes out looking like just another Catholic riot.'[18] Events in Wexford cooled the ardour of liberal Protestants for Catholic emancipation and contributed to a reaction against the idea of an Irish nation that could contain all the separate strands of Irish society. The rising also solidified the British government's resolve to do away with the Irish Parliament through the Act of Union of 1800, which absorbed Ireland into the United Kingdom.

Parker, a modern-day Protestant sympathetic to the United Irishmen's original aim of 'a cordial union among *all the people of Ireland*', believed they had made two fatal mistakes. The first had been resorting to arms, the second allowing themselves to believe that an essentially sectarian force could be harnessed to achieve enlightened objectives. *Northern Star* holds out a double-edged message for Northern Protestants. To unionists, Parker says: you have a republican heritage, which you usually choose to deny. You, the Protestants of Northern Ireland, invented Irish republicanism. To those Protestants proudly aware of this heritage, he suggests that the United Irishmen were responsible not only for the ideal of republicanism, but also for its tradition of violence. In the anguished words of the disillusioned McCracken,

> all we've done … is to reinforce the locks, cram the cells fuller than ever of mangled bodies crawling round in their own shite and lunacy, and the cycle just goes on, playing out the same demented comedy of terrors from generation to generation, trapped in the same malignant legend, condemned to re-endure it as if the Anti-Christ who dreamed it up was driven astray in the wits by it and the entire pattern of depravity just goes spinning on out of control, on and on, round and round, till the day the world itself is burst asunder, that's the handsome birthright that we're handing on.[19]

Parker's most fundamental reconception of his McCracken play when he returned to it in 1983 was to set it in the aftermath of the rising. After the battle of Antrim, McCracken spent a month at large before being arrested. *Northern Star* takes place during one of his last nights as a free man. This enables McCracken in the play to look back on all his actions with the benefit of hindsight. Part of the historical McCracken's legend is that he intended to make a speech from the gallows, but, as an eyewitness recounted, 'Hoarse orders were given by the officers, the troops moved about, the people murmured, a horrible confusion ensued, and in a minute or so the manly, handsome figure on which the impression of nobility was stamped, was dangling at a rope's end.' In *Northern Star*, Parker imagines what McCracken would have said to the crowd had he been allowed to speak. In Parker's view, a man of McCracken's generous spirit could not have failed to see that his legacy might be malign, and his McCracken vigorously rejects the role of martyr for Irish freedom: 'A whore's pox then on the future! And I forgive it nothing, for there's nothing it will learn from those of us who swung for it, no peace to be got from it, for those of us who want nothing more now than to finish, a cat's flux on whatever holy picture they may fashion of me!'[20]

Because the United Irishmen were playing to posterity, *Northern Star* is filled with theatrical figures of speech, with McCracken as an actor rehearsing for his 'positively last appearance'. From the play's inception, Parker planned to avoid some of the pitfalls of historical drama by incorporating non-naturalistic elements. At first he intended to juxtapose scenes from the 1790s with modern commentary, and one page of early notes lists characters such as tourists, an American lecturer, and a folk singer. Another preliminary idea had been to write the historical passages in verse. The approach Parker finally settled on owes a great deal to James Joyce. The bulk of the script consists of seven flashback scenes of events leading up to the rising; each, in keeping with the theatrical metaphor, represents one of the ages of man: 'They have their exits and their entrances and one man in his time plays many parts, his acts being seven ages.' The United Irish movement lasted for seven years, and each scene depicts one stage in the rebels' progress from innocence through idealism, cleverness, dialectic, heroism, and compromise, to shame. In the Oxen of the Sun episode of *Ulysses*, which centres on childbirth, Joyce recapitulates the history of the English language to illustrate embryonic development. Parker, in this play about the 'birth' of a nation, modifies Joyce's device to reinforce the theatrical parallel, writing each of the seven scenes in the style of an earlier Irish playwright.[21]

Parker believed this strategy helped solve the problem of presenting the multi-layered nature of Irish experience. In a note written for the play's programme, he explained his logic:

> So how to write an Ulster history play?—since our past refuses to express itself as a linear, orderly narrative, in a convincing tone of voice? Tune into any given moment from it, and the wavelength soon grows crowded with a babble of voices from all the other moments, up to and including the present one. I have tried to accommodate this obstinate, crucial fact of life by eschewing any single style, and attempting instead a wide range of theatrical ventriloquism.

This way, too, Parker remarked, he 'could write a play set in 1798 which was speaking directly to people today. If I'd written it in a purely 18th century style it would have seemed remote and artificial. If I'd written it in a completely colloquial idiom of today it would have seemed unhistorical: people dressed up in fancy clothes talking as if they should be in jeans and T-shirts.'[22]

Although Parker imitates playwrights more or less in the order in which their own plays were written, the manner of expression chosen for each scene is appropriate to the matter being presented. For example, the Age of Compromise, 'of finally taking sides', portrays McCracken being sworn in as a member of the Defenders by a pair of sharps modelled on Sean O'Casey's Joxer and the Paycock. The dialect they speak comments playfully on unionist fears of 'Dublin' while making the serious point that McCracken is sacrificing ends to means. A passage about cultural renewal (the Age of Cleverness) is written in the epigrammatic mode of Oscar Wilde; a political debate between McCracken and the British officer who attempts to arrest him (the Age of Dialectic) is haunted by the ghost of George Bernard Shaw; the Age of Idealism, in which McCracken is shown 'uniting the rabble in a common love for his shining youthful ardour', is cast as a melodrama after the manner of Dion Bouci-cault; and a scene from the Heroic Age, in which McCracken and several of his friends first pledge themselves to 'the republic of United Irishmen', is presented in the inflated poetic language of John Millington Synge.[23]

This mimicry serves political as well as aesthetic ends. By imitating great Irish writers in turn, Parker intimates that he sees himself as their inheritor. Moreover, the Irish authors he invokes, like the republican revolutionaries the play is about, are overwhelmingly Protestant. In lines for McCracken, Parker voices the defen-siveness of liberal Protestants who consider themselves to be Irish but feel that identification to be subtly denied them:

> Look at me. My great-grandfather Joy was a French Huguenot, my great-grandfather McCracken was a Scottish Covenanter, persecuted, the pair of them, driven here from the shores of home, their home but not my home, because I'm Henry Joy McCracken and here to stay, a natural son of Belfast, as Irish a bastard as all the other incomers, blown into this port by the storm of history, Gaelic or Danish or Anglo-Norman, without distinction, it makes no odds, every mother's son of us children of nature on this sodden glorious patch of earth, unpossessed of deed or inheritance, without distinction.

The multiplicity of voices in the play underlines Parker's pluralistic vision of Irish identity while simultaneously commenting on the fact that the past and present in Ireland continue to shape each other. The technique of pastiche, he maintained, 'allowed me to march the play throughout the decades towards the present day and say to the audience, forget about historical veracity, forget about realism, I'm going to tell you a story about the origins of Republicanism and I'm going to offer you a point of view on what's gone wrong with it and why it's become corrupt and why it's now serving the opposite ends to what it set out to serve'. For Fintan O'Toole, the form of *Northern Star* reminds us that 'the events of 1798 are still being, liter-ally, played out': 'An extraordinary tension is created by the way the styles of writ-ing and performance move forward in time from the 18th century to the 20th. In terms of content, we are looking back on Henry Joy's tragic dilemmas. In terms of style, they are rushing forward to meet us.'[24]

The play's visual imagery also reinforces parallels between the past and present. McCracken is hiding in a burnt-out house, a common sight in Northern Ireland in the 1970s. The soldiers who burst in to search it at the end of Act I have black-ened faces, like their modern counterparts in the British Army. The prison scene, in which McCracken and his fellow inmates huddle wrapped in blankets and are ordered to 'muck out' their cell by a sadistic guard, is reminiscent of the protests and hunger strikes in the Maze Prison in the early 1980s. These echoes climax in the interrogation scene that takes place behind McCracken as he faces forward to deliver the last of the literary pastiches, a Beckettian monologue, straight to the audience. A lambeg drum is beaten as the signal for a blackout, after which a bright white light comes up slowly, directly overhead, to reveal the three actors who had been McCracken's cell mates in the previous scene '*standing facing the back wall, leaning on their fingertips, arms akimbo, against the wall, feet splayed out, with hoods over their heads*'. At the end of McCracken's speech, the prisoners howl as they are subjected to deafening white noise, and '*An INTERROGATOR bursts in carrying a baton. He pulls the first hooded prisoner away from the wall, throws him to the ground, and pinions him across the throat with the baton*'—demanding to know 'Who commanded the rebels in Down?'[25]

Parker intersperses the flashback scenes with dialogue in his own voice between McCracken and his lover Mary Bodle, sister Mary Ann, and comrade James Hope. (A schema of the play among Parker's notes divides its scenes into the 'Confessional' and the 'Rhetorical'.) In early plans for the play, a scene with Mary Bodle would have been just one of many. In the finished script, her critique of the heroic death wish represents the principal challenge to McCracken's point of view. Mary urges him to escape to America, where they can live with their child, arguing that what he regards as a noble intention to face the punishment for his actions is really a form of selfishness: 'The love of your family isn't enough. My love isn't enough. You want the love of the whole future world and heaven besides. All right, go ahead, let them love you to death, let them paint you in forty shades of green on some godforsaken gable-end!'[26]

James Hope similarly grew in importance as Parker pondered McCracken's story. He is 'banging on about his labouring classes' from the beginning of the play, even (anachronistically) before he would have been a member of the United Irishmen. In 1969, Parker had regarded Hope's proto-socialism as just one of the many dogmas McCracken had tried and failed to avoid. By the time he wrote *Northern Star*, however, he saw it as the only reasonable chance for the future and Hope himself as 'The steadfast light, the real Northern Star'. In a crucial conversation with Hope, 'a ghost from the future times', McCracken confesses to his working-class friend that he failed until far too late to recognize the material basis of the conflict: 'A field, with two men fighting over it. Cain and Abel. The bitterest fight in the history of man on this earth. We were city boys. What did we know about two men fighting over a field?' The aptly named Hope offers the consolation that the conflict might not be intractable if every man were equally rewarded for his labour, but McCracken wearily dismisses this optimism: 'Forget it, Jimmy. They won't listen. Have you ever known them to listen?'[27]

Parker shared both Hope's ultimate faith in the common man and McCracken's doubts regarding when the inhabitants of Belfast would come to their senses. The line 'Citizens of Belfast', repeated like a refrain throughout *Northern Star*, is aimed both at McCracken's imaginary audience, as he rehearses his 'famous last words', and at the real-life citizens of Belfast in the theatre audience. In McCracken's last long speech, love and longing mingle with apprehension regarding the future:

Why would one place break your heart, more than another? A place the like of that? Brain-damaged and dangerous, continuously violating itself, a place of perpetual

breakdown, incompatible voices, screeching obscenely away through the smoky dark wet. Burnt out and still burning. Nerve-damaged, pitiable. Frightening. As maddening and tiresome as any other pain-obsessed cripple.... we can't love it for what it is, only for what it might have been, if we'd got it right, if we'd made it whole. If. It's a ghost town now and always will be, angry and implacable ghosts. Me condemned to be one of their number. We never made a nation. Our brainchild. Stillborn. Our own fault. We botched the birth. So what if the English do bequeath us to one another some day? What then? When there's nobody else to blame except ourselves?[28]

The ending of the play holds out only as much hope as audience members can find in themselves and each other. McCracken mounts the platform one last time and places a noose around his neck. 'Citizens of Belfast...', he begins, but he gets no further before the beating of a lambeg drum (symbolic of twentieth-century unionist triumphalism) drowns out his words and the lights fade to black. Parker refuses any neat resolution to his drama, issuing instead a challenge to the audience to arrest the cycle of retribution.

Northern Star was but one of several projects Parker had underway in the second half of 1983, and he worked on it late at night when he concentrated best. Upon completing the first draft, he observed that he had been 'curiously detached from the writing of it':

> Two pages a night, Monday to Friday, without fail, but helped along by a lot of whiskey. The technical challenge and the whittling out of a coherent political statement probably combined together to make the process more cerebral than emotional. Also, living now at such a remove. I don't know if all that is detrimental, or if in fact it's worked to the play's advantage. Time will tell. At the top of its voice.

Rereading the script two months later, Parker declared himself 'Appalled by the rawness, gaucheness, the undiverting muddle of it.' He made no radical changes, however, focusing instead on 'the need to clarify, tighten up, signpost'.[29] By the middle of January 1984, he had finished rewriting the play and had posted it to Patrick Sandford, who had taken over from Leon Rubin as artistic director of the Lyric during 1983.

Meanwhile, *Pratt's Fall* had been produced in Ireland. Sean McCarthy, the Abbey's script editor since 1979, had grown tired of the conservatism of the National Theatre. He and Joe Dowling, artistic director since 1978, had done much to open the institution to a new generation of Irish playwrights, but lately they disagreed over the extent to which the theatre should commit itself to nurturing individual writers. McCarthy, for example, had been enthusiastic in 1982 about the idea of the Peacock co-producing *Pratt's Fall* with Glasgow's Tron Theatre, but he could not sell Dowling on the project—a difference of opinion (one of many at the time) that occasioned 'a big falling-out' between them. In 1983, McCarthy dropped to part-time at the Abbey to pursue an independent venture with Patrick Mason, a young resident director at the theatre who specialized in inventive productions of new work for the Peacock. Western Union, the touring company they founded and co-directed, had as its mission the presentation of contemporary drama outside theatrical centres. McCarthy had acted, directed, and managed a theatre company in Edinburgh for ten years in the late 1960s and 1970s before returning to his native Ireland, and he envisaged a large company that would tour the Republic, Northern Ireland, and Scotland, drawing actors and writers from all three places. *Pratt's Fall*, with its pan-British cast of characters, made a natural choice for the company, which produced it in repertoire with another play recently rejected by the Abbey. The first (and, as it turned out, the last) Western Union tour played Wexford, Limerick, Sligo, Belfast, and the Dublin Theatre Festival in the summer and early autumn of 1983. Parker had only minimal involvement with the show in rehearsal. He saw *Pratt's Fall* in Dublin and recorded his reactions: 'Production better than I had feared, superficial, but getting a lot of laughs. Audience responsive, but not a full house. Minor qualified success, of a familiar enough kind. But a remarkably angst-free evening.'[30]

Western Union had a less direct, though arguably more significant, impact on Parker's career by provoking communication between the playwright and the Field Day Theatre Company. When the *Pratt's Fall* production remained in the early planning stages, Julie Barber, Field Day's administrator, rang Parker to request a copy of the script, all the time insisting that Field Day had no intention of considering the play. The company's motives seemed transparent to Parker: 'They've heard a rumour that…Western Union are going to do it, & clearly want to check out the opposition. The hell w/ them', he decided, sending a programme from the Glasgow production instead. Less than three weeks later, he received a letter from Barber comprised of what he termed 'rude rhetorical questions' implying that Field Day *did*, in fact, want to consider *Pratt's Fall* for production. 'Are you interested in Field Day?' Barber concluded. Parker responded testily: 'Very interested. On the other hand, Field Day has not shown any interest in me during its three years of existence, until suddenly a new Irish touring company is on the verge of doing my work.…I don't think you'll do yourself any favours by alienating fellow artists.' Parker did not know that the members of Field Day's board of directors, at a meeting on 5 June, had rejected as unsuitable David Rudkin's play *The Saxon Shore*, which they had commissioned for the company's 1983 tour. This decision set them scrambling to make new tour plans in time to secure Arts Council funding and possibly had the collateral effect of transmuting idle curiosity about what Parker was doing into something more urgent.[31]

Field Day ended up substituting Athol Fugard's *Boesman and Lena* for the Rudkin play, but the possibility of collaborating with Parker had at least been brought to the fore. Parker sent a copy of his correspondence with Barber to his friend Stephen Rea, one of Field Day's founding members, and Rea responded several months later with an invitation to write something for the company: 'I think Field Day is the natural context for your writing, and I sense you feel that too. We're getting better at the business of theatre production, and our audience is the one you should be addressing.' Parker agreed with Rea but found the timing of the offer frustrating, complaining in his journal, 'They cd. have had *Pratt's Fall, Northern Star* or Boucicault. Now I can't do anything at all till '85, and no obvious idea suggests itself.' He would eventually accept a commission from Field Day, but for the moment he had more immediate concerns.[32]

One of these in October 1983 was the writing of his radio play *The Traveller*. The germ of this piece may be discerned in a note from the middle of Parker's 1971 journal for a 'Radio play on man travelling through a bleak birthday'. *The Traveller* dates more explicitly to the first months of 1980. A notebook in which Parker recorded ideas for a variety of writing projects from 1980 to 1988 contains this entry on its first page: 'A person is told a secret. Keeping this secret over the years costs him a lot. Then he finds that countless others were also told—that the bearer of the secret is no respecter of secrets.' The next entry, dated 17 February 1980, consists of a brief description of a film called *Travelling Man*: 'A travel writer. Becoming increasingly obsessive about his travelling as his relationships—wife, family, friends—wither away. And as the conviction grows within him that the world is soon about to blow itself away.' Parker then intended 'the Secret (or the Lie)' to be 'one trigger' for his journey and a friend belonging to a Survival Society to be another. He discussed the idea with Rob Buckler, producer of the television version of *I'm a Dreamer Montreal*. Buckler wanted to collaborate on such a film, but Parker was preoccupied at the time with other commitments (including, but not limited to, the original stage production of *Nightshade*, the television production of *The Kamikaze Ground Staff Reunion Dinner*, and the writing of *Iris in the Traffic, Ruby in the Rain* and *Pratt's Fall*). By January 1981, Parker was seeking to interest Buckler in yet another film project, content to leave his travel writer 'trundling round...in the mental outback' a while longer.[33]

An invitation from BBC Northern Ireland radio drama producer Robert Cooper changed Parker's focus on the traveller material. In July 1981, he offered Parker an 'open commission' to write a radio play on a subject of his choice. Parker's energies were then directed towards the stage and film, and he initially hesitated to accept more radio work. In September, however, he realized that *The Traveller* was 'quintessentially a radio piece' and decided to write it for Cooper. The following summer, the Central BBC in London commissioned the play for Radio 3. The single slot each week then devoted to drama on Radio 3 was the most prestigious for a radio play. Unlike the plays that aired on Radio 4, generally plot-driven and mainstream in subject matter, Radio 3 plays were supposed to be ambitious, even experimental. Dramatists coveted this slot because, in addition to its cachet, it did not stipulate a rigid duration; Parker's play could run from seventy-five to ninety minutes. (Those were 'Magical days', Lesley Bruce remembers, when BBC authorities still occasionally told a talented writer, 'here is a (half) fee for you to write us anything at all on any subject, whenever you can get it to us'.)[34]

By October 1983, when Parker began writing *The Traveller*, his vision for it had become less apocalyptic and more autobiographical. In 1980, when it first took shape in his imagination, he had been sunk in private despondency: isolated in an uncongenial city, helplessly watching his marriage disintegrate, and struggling to retain some vestige of faith in himself and his work. Looking back on this personal turmoil from the relative tranquillity of his new life in London, Parker intuited that his travel writer's mental state might be more compelling than anything he sees or hears on his journey. Two-thirds of the way through the play, the traveller begins to face up to the fact that he has been 'skating gracefully over the world's surface, I called it exploring but it wasn't, there's nowhere left to explore, apart from space. The space up there. Or the space between people. Or the space between your ears.'[35] *The Traveller* reflects Parker's apprehension that a writer can easily become a glorified voyeur; in the play, travelling serves the protagonist as a substitute for human engagement, which requires sustained effort and carries with it the potential for pain. Parker himself had often used the travel necessitated by his work as a playwright to distract himself from the problems in his life, and after the end of his marriage he had undergone his own period of tortured self-inspection. This had left him, at the beginning of 1983, 'On good days feeling like a pirate, on bad days like a stateless person.' His resultant musings on 'Homelessness, & the romany life' found their way into the radio play.[36]

The Traveller centres on the mid-life crisis of Thomas Merriman Sweeney, who once aspired to write poetry and novels but opted for travel writing instead. He has just turned 43 when he leaves home abruptly after learning that a secret he thought was shared by him and his wife, Vera, is known even to some of their casual acquaintances.[37] The secret itself is less important than the fact that Vera's ability to speak freely about something she had earlier considered shameful demonstrates that she has grown and changed in ways Sweeney has not noticed. He feels betrayed, but she argues without resentment that he barely knows her or their teenaged twins any more: 'Travelling's your real life. When you're back here you're just visiting.... It's how you've always wanted it.... So you can't expect at this stage to duck the consequences.'[38] Sweeney wrangles a commission to write a series on the present state of the United Kingdom and sets off on a trip around the country. Throughout the play, the misery and degradation he observes along his way mirror his own despair.

In order for his psychic wounds to begin to heal, Sweeney must come to terms with various aspects of his past. One of these is his discarded ambition to be a 'proper' writer. This abandoned artist-self speaks in the play with the voice of Sweeney's alter ego, Merriman. He accompanies Sweeney on his journey, forcing the sort of self-examination Sweeney resists and urging him to engage more fully with the people he meets. One realization Merriman nudges Sweeney towards is that his choices in life have had the effect of estranging him from those he cares about. A series of encounters with strangers and old friends culminates in a visit to Belfast, the city Sweeney is loath to call home and which he has avoided (apart from relatives' funerals) for the past twenty-one years.[39]

Like *Pratt's Fall*, *The Traveller* repeatedly poses the question of what, beyond their own inadequate selves, human beings can put their trust in. The play takes its title from Walter de la Mare's poem 'The Listeners', snatches of which are quoted throughout. Indeed, the first thing the audience hears is Sweeney reciting the opening: '"Is there anybody there?" said the Traveller,/Knocking on the moonlit door....' De la Mare's subject is the 'host of phantom listeners' who refuse to respond to 'that voice from the world of men', but Parker's attention remains squarely on the Traveller himself, whose attempts at honest communication resemble radio waves beamed into the void of space, or prayer in an age of doubt. Nevertheless, miraculously, at the end of the play human connection *does* appear possible, and human love makes it so.[40]

Parker's play is a modern, secular re-working of Dante Alighieri's theological quest poem *The Inferno*. As the poet Virgil escorts Dante through the underworld, Merriman serves as Sweeney's guide through his personal Hell: 'We're in the dark wood now, you and me', he remarks to Sweeney upon his first entrance, echoing Dante's famous opening lines ('Midway in our life's journey, I went astray/from the straight road and woke to find myself/alone in a dark wood'). As Sweeney delves deeper into his psyche, he descends further in his own inferno. Throughout the play, Parker establishes explicit parallels between the places and people Sweeney visits and Dante's nine circles of Hell and their inhabitants, and his protagonist's journey begins and ends on the Circle Line of London's Underground. Parker's metaphorical use of contemporary British locales and politics and his references to current events are also in the spirit of Dante, whose medieval mindset erected no artificial barriers between different spheres of human knowledge and experience. From beginning to end of *The Traveller*, Parker's imagery reinforces the Dantean parallels. Variations and synonyms of 'hell' crop up repeatedly, a character quotes briefly from *The Inferno*, and Sweeney even begins his first dispatch with the observation that the traveller through modern Britain feels himself to be in 'a banal secular travesty of Dante's Inferno'.[41] The play ends with Sweeney and Vera emerging from the Underground and looking up at the stars, just as Dante concludes his own tour of the underworld with a laborious climb back to the surface of the earth and a view of the heavens.

Parker delivered *The Traveller* to Robert Cooper, recently transferred to BBC Manchester, at the end of March 1984, and Cooper produced it that June, in what Parker approvingly termed a 'Strong, abrasive' fashion, with Donal McCann playing Sweeney, Derek Halligan as Merriman, and Carole Nimmons in the role of Vera. The BBC aired the play on 30 January 1985, to varied reviews. Gillian Reynolds opined in the *Daily Telegraph* that 'The scenes from national life had the bizarre edge of real life, grotesque as they were.' Mervyn Jones, on the other hand, argued in the *Listener* that the play's incidents 'made little logical sense' and declared that 'Stewart Parker's outstanding talent appears to be a quite frightening gift for sketching awful people.' Parker had so skilfully subordinated the detailed intertextual connections between *The Traveller* and *The Inferno* to his story that neither of these critics so much as mentioned (or noticed?) them. Cooper secretly thought *The Traveller* too private a play to be fully accessible to others, but BBC higher-ups liked it sufficiently to repeat it on 6 October 1985. Parker, dispirited though not especially perturbed by the general lack of understanding of the piece, intended to return to *The Traveller* someday and re-work it as a stage play.[42]

The fourteen months that elapsed between Parker's completion of the initial draft of *The Traveller* in November 1983 and its transmission were particularly eventful ones for him, replete with both high hopes and bitter disappointments. A production of *Nightshade* at the Kings Head early in 1984 was the first in a series of the latter. Peter Farago, who directed the play at the Birmingham Repertory in the spring of 1983, had initially spoken optimistically about the possibility of a co-production with the Royal Court or the Hampstead. After the play opened to good reviews in Birmingham, Parker himself had sent a copy of the script to the management of the Tricycle Theatre, Kilburn. Dan Crawford at the Kings Head had been the only London theatre manager to show any interest in *Nightshade*, however. Crawford had wanted to do the show since at least November 1981, though Parker did not think it could be done 'effectively' in that venue and had been almost relieved when a planned production had fallen through in early 1982. Farago directed the 1984 Kings Head production, which featured several of the actors he had used in Birmingham, and Parker likely hoped that the director's experience with the play would help to overcome the challenges presented by the lack of space and money he would have to work with in London. The critics disagreed. The first few reviews struck Parker as 'fair to middling', but he described the later ones as 'ghastly.... As bad as I've ever had.' These provoked the 'Usual crisis of faith, and chill inside.' A few months later, he assessed the experience more rationally, writing to his friend Nancy McKibbin that the Kings Head '—in spite of my continuing affection for it and for Dan Crawford—has run out of mileage. *Nightshade* didn't work there. The reviews ranged from respectful to terrible. And now the theatre is one of a dozen or more which is to lose its Arts Council grant, from next year.' This sad decline of the one London theatre that had consistently produced his work discouraged Parker immensely and made the thought of writing for the stage more daunting than ever.[43]

Parker's growing doubts about whether or not working in the theatre repaid the effort and forbearance it required were reinforced in the early months of 1984 by internal wrangles at the Lyric over *Northern Star*, a revised version of which he had submitted in mid-January. The theatre's artistic director, Patrick Sandford, originally intended it to open in April. Some board members, though, favoured an autumn date, and by the end of February the possibility of April had vanished and the debate had degenerated into one over 'when & if' the play would be done (Parker learned three suspense-filled weeks later that the Lyric would produce it in September or October). Parker's television play *Radio Pictures* remained similarly in limbo. In October 1983 he had been told that Central TV would finally produce it in spring 1984, but he learned in early February that *Radio Pictures* had been cancelled for the second time 'to allow the company to get caught up with one of its sitcoms'.[44]

'The house of cards is collapsing all round me', Parker commented: 'Thank God *Blue Money* is going so well and so enjoyably. I'd be suicidal otherwise.' Producers June Roberts and Jo Apted had intended this as a feature film and initially turned down co-production offers from television companies. After a number of unsuccessful approaches to film studios, however, they had agreed to co-produce the film with London Weekend Television (provider of content to the Independent Television network from Friday evening through Sunday), which put half a million pounds into the project. Rehearsals had begun in early January 1984 and filming a week later, with Parker present most of the time at locations in Dublin and Liverpool as well as London. Tim Curry played the lead, Larry, with gusto and flair (despite an 'Irish' accent that veered uncertainly between Belfast and Dublin); and Debby Bishop as his girlfriend, Dermot Crowley as his best mate, and Billy Connolly as a menacing hanger-on also admirably incarnated their characters. Director

Colin Bucksey performed his part with 'panache & flash', shooting the film in a mere five weeks: 'A hectic, headlong production', Parker commented in his journal, but 'Exciting & fun.' He thrived, as always, on the intense camaraderie of the cast and crew of a show in production, and the experience whetted his appetite for film work.[45]

Fortuitously, Parker received a phone call a month after the *Blue Money* filming ended from Peter Ormrod, who had directed an RTÉ/Channel 4 television series called *Caught in a Free State*. Now he wanted to direct a feature film based on the true story of a man in County Longford who, inspired by the Elvis Presley film *Roustabout*, had built a Wall of Death in his back garden. Parker's friend Sam Fannin recalls that Wall of Death spectaculars—in which a motorcyclist, aided by centrifugal force, climbed the inside of a huge drum while onlookers watched from above—were popular attractions at Irish fairs and amusement parks in his youth. These looked more dangerous than they were, he explains, 'being on a parallel with a pea rolling round a dish'. Ormrod had already made a documentary about the real-life builder of the Wall, and he had written two versions of a treatment, in short story form, for a fictionalized film: he wanted Parker to write it. The day after his first conversation with Ormrod, Parker talked on the phone with the producer of the proposed film, John Kelleher, a former Controller of Programmes for RTÉ 1 who now had his own production company. Although he had never before contracted to realize someone else's vision in a script, the project tempted Parker. He wanted to write films, and the basic Wall of Death story struck him as 'fascinating'.[46]

Parker met Kelleher and Ormrod at the beginning of April 1984. The former impressed him as 'affable, well-intentioned, not strong', the latter as 'slightly twitchy, odd, possibly shifty'. He told them he did not think the Wall of Death episode by itself would suffice to sustain a full-length film and suggested combining it with a story about smuggling on the border, which the president of the Irish Customs and Excise Union had described as 'a national scandal' in the mid-1980s. Petrol, alcohol, cigarettes, and electronic goods, all cheaper in Northern Ireland owing to its lower value added tax, were smuggled into the Republic in great quantities, depriving the Irish government's coffers of about 100 million Irish pounds in revenue annually; farm animals and grain were smuggled North and then 'legally' imported to the Republic, taking advantage of agricultural subsidies. The incorporation of this element would allow Parker to comment on corruption in Irish national life while exploring the law-evading culture of the border counties (a legacy of colonization); it would thicken the plot without rendering it incoherent, he believed, since smuggling and Wall of Death-building could both be construed as forms of risk-taking. Ormrod and Kelleher assented to the addition of a smuggling strand to the plot, and Parker agreed to write the screenplay for £15,000 against 3 per cent of the budget.[47]

Parker spent the better part of a week in Ireland, researching smuggling in the border counties. He then wrote his own treatment for the film, delivering it to Kelleher at the end of May 1984. The producer seemed 'enthusiastic' about Parker's outline. The director reacted less positively: when Parker met with him a week later to discuss the treatment, Ormrod 'raised objections to every element in it, bar the title and characters' names'. Parker left the meeting 'in a state of pent-up fury, exasperation, futility' and seriously considered quitting the enterprise. The next day, he told Kelleher he sensed 'a fundamental conflict of approach, of style, tone and the whole damned thing'. Parker found Ormrod's attitude to the script (that it should be regarded as a work-in-progress in which everything should remain 'fluid' and 'negotiable') 'entirely unacceptable'. Kelleher convinced Parker to remain on the team on condition that he himself would be actively involved and mediate meetings between Parker and Ormrod. Parker further stipulated, as he recorded in his journal, 'that the treatment stands, that two drafts of the screenplay is all he's going to get, and that if Ormrod fails to co-operate at that point, he'll get the elbow'. As Lesley reminded him, he had 'gone into the project knowing it would be thus', so 'the lesson should simply be assimilated, that you can't write something you care about, as a calculated, arm's-length exercise'.[48]

As inauspiciously as the project had begun, Parker's excitement about it grew as he worked on his screenplay, entitled *Eat the Peach* (a title appearing in one of his notebooks as early as 1981, in anticipation of an appropriate work to which to attach itself). The builder of the actual Wall of Death, Connie Kiernan, had been unable to articulate why he had done it. Parker had, accordingly, to supply his protagonist, Vinnie Galvin, with a plausible motive for undertaking such a wild scheme. He invented a character named Mrs Downing, a remnant of the Anglo-Irish gentry, who calls Vinnie to her house to make a repair. While he is there, she reads poetry to him, including some lines from T. S. Eliot's 'The Love Song of J. Alfred Prufrock' ('Shall I part my hair behind? Do I dare to eat a peach?'), which she explicates for Vinnie thus: 'The man in the poem is afraid of life, you see. He has never really lived. He feels like a bystander. Locked out of the feast of life. That's what the peach means to him. He lacks the courage to eat it.' Mrs Downing says it is too late for her to live the way she now wishes she had, but she urges Vinnie not to make the same mistake. She offers him a peach to eat and takes advantage of his bewilderment to seduce him. The encounter troubles Vinnie, both because he suspects Mrs Downing may be right about his letting life pass him by and because he loves his wife, Nora, and had no intention of being unfaithful to her. His unease reaches crisis proportions in the wee hours of the next morning, when, driving at speed around an abandoned quarry with his brother-in-law, Arthur, he discovers that Mrs Downing has killed herself when they happen upon her body. A couple of days later, he watches a videotape of *Roustabout*, in which Elvis plays a fairground hand who dreams of riding the Wall of Death. Suddenly it seems to Vinnie that he has found his purpose in life. He and Arthur start building their own Wall and take up smuggling to finance its completion when they run out of money. The rest of Parker's screenplay chronicles the struggle between the obsessed Vinnie and entities, including the village planning committee and the local clergy, who pressure him to settle down to a normal life. Images of death and entropy permeate Parker's screenplay, which presents Vinnie and his family as sparks of vitality in an otherwise moribund landscape. Nora, who at times seems to embody the forces of convention (walking out on Vinnie twice after he hatches the Wall plan), eventually understands what is driving him. The two reunite after the Wall is successfully finished and Vinnie finds out that no one (including, ultimately, himself) really cares about it. It is, after all, his wife and children who give his life meaning, and the screenplay concludes on this note, though with the implication that Vinnie will never again be ordinary: in the final scene, he and Arthur are building a helicopter.[49]

Parker wrote his *Eat the Peach* screenplay between the middle of June and the beginning of August 1984. He delivered the initial draft to Kelleher, who liked it although he said it would require significant cutting. Ten days later, Parker travelled to Dublin for a script meeting with Kelleher and Ormrod. Upon his arrival, he learned that Ormrod had made other plans without informing him, so he and Kelleher ended up scouting possible locations instead. Parker finally got to talk about his script with Ormrod early in September. Their meeting had been preceded by what Parker termed an 'infuriating wrangle' over whether or not Kelleher should be included in the discussion; Parker, 'seething', attempted to prove his willingness to cooperate by agreeing to see Ormrod alone. The conference itself, though, seemed 'low-key' after this build-up, and Parker departed from it reassured that, for all his truculence, Ormrod would be using '9/10 of the script'. He had every reason, therefore, to look forward confidently to the shooting of his first feature film, scheduled for the following spring, and by the end of October he had completed and delivered the second draft of his screenplay.[50]

In other ways, too, it appeared that Parker's luck had shifted back into positive channels by the autumn of 1984. More than a year earlier, he had given a copy of *Pratt's Fall* to a theatre director named Robert Chetwyn, his friend Howard Schuman's partner. Chetwyn wanted to direct it and had been approaching producers, at first without success. Then, on 25 September, he phoned Parker to report that Eddie Kulukundis had read the script after holding it for over four months and, amazingly, 'quite liked' it. Two days later, Parker and Chetwyn met Kulukundis and some of his associates. The producer talked about trying out the play in a short run outside London, with a view towards a transfer to the West End; he wanted an actress with star power for the part of Victoria ('Unreal', Parker marvelled in his journal). They decided to offer the leads to Helen Mirren and Bill Paterson, a Scottish actor Parker had already interested in the play. Mirren eventually turned down the role, but Paterson agreed to play Mahoney. By the end of January 1985, plans were firming up to rehearse the show from mid-October for a mid-November opening somewhere like the Oxford Playhouse, with the possibility of a transfer after Christmas. All depended on finding someone to play Victoria and an appropriate theatre to host the production, but both seemed entirely possible.[51]

The transmission of *Blue Money* on 7 October should have afforded Parker's ego another boost. This star vehicle for Tim Curry proved by far the most popular of the dramatist's works to date, attracting an audience of 11 million viewers (about 20 per cent of the then population of the UK). The critics shared the general enthusiasm, lauding Curry's versatile performance, the quality of the supporting actors, the 'rocking pace' of Colin Bucksey's direction, and the 'jauntily witty' script. All agreed that *Blue Money* put frivolity foremost, with Peter Ackroyd calling it in *The Times* 'escapist entertainment with a vengeance'. The irony of the fact that his least ambitious work was also his most 'successful' probably contributed to Parker's own ambivalent reaction to the film. The press screening left him unaccountably downcast, and when no one from outside the family or the production rang to congratulate him on transmission night, he 'Felt as let-down as after *Joyce in June*.'[52]

Parker had more exalted hopes for *Northern Star*. This play, he confided to Lesley, represented the best writing he was capable of doing. Now he tried to ensure that the Lyric's presentation showed it off to advantage. Peter Farago had been engaged to direct, at Parker's suggestion, and he consulted the playwright on every aspect of the production. Casting Henry Joy McCracken, who rarely leaves the stage, represented their first and biggest hurdle. Parker had imagined Liam Neeson in the role, but Neeson declined to commit to the production. Gerard McSorley, an actor from Omagh, County Tyrone, who had recently left the Abbey company and moved to London, accepted the part in early September, and Parker worked closely with him and Farago throughout the rehearsal period, most of which he spent in Belfast.[53]

Northern Star opened on 7 November 1984. Parker could not bring himself to watch, after a 'rough and wobbly' preview the night before, but he soon received ample reassurance that things had gone well. The critics praised McSorley's performance as McCracken, Farago's direction, Joe Vanek's striking set, the acting of various other cast members—and the play itself, the quality of which was readily apparent. The reviewer for the Belfast *News Letter* hailed *Northern Star* as 'nothing short of a classic—the best bit of drama to come to Belfast in years', while the *Belfast Telegraph*'s critic noted the play's 'lyrical quality' as well as its 'humour'. Critics from Dublin and London concurred. David Nowlan of the *Irish Times* began his review by commenting, 'It is good that Stewart Parker's first stage play to receive its premiere performance in his home town of Belfast should also be his best—by far.' He concluded, 'Seldom has Irish history been so provocatively or so entertainingly drawn on the stage. . . . "Northern Star" is not to be missed.' Ian Hill noted in the *Guardian* the appropriateness of the play's Belfast première but proclaimed that it 'also deserves a West End and a Broadway run', and John Peter declared in the *Sunday Times* that 'Only an Irishman could have written something like this: a freewheeling, lunatic sense of invention is harnessed to a cultivated, literary imagination and stoked up by moral outrage.' In one of the last, and most positive, reviews, Fintan O'Toole asserted in Dublin's *Sunday Tribune* that Parker's theatrical devices enhanced 'the sheer entertainment value of the play rather than bogging it down in its own cleverness' and pronounced *Northern Star* 'the best new Irish play of 1984'. Meanwhile, an *Irish Times* leader had cited the play, along with other offerings at the 1984 Belfast Festival, as evidence of 'Northern Vigour' challenging Dublin's cultural snobbishness.[54]

Parker liked the way *Northern Star* was attracting people who were not habitual theatre-goers and being discussed as a social document as well as a play. Barry White, a respected leader-writer for the *Belfast Telegraph*, for example, began a column by announcing that 'I've just returned from a play which everyone with the remotest interest in where Ulster is going and where it has been, should see. Stewart Parker's "Northern Star" at the Lyric is a classic, fit to live with—no, sur-passing—Brian Friel's "Translations".' He continued: '...the play crams in whole chapters of forgotten historical fact, in the most palatable form imaginable, and finds ways of opening up the arguments for and against violence.... Kitchen sink dramas of urban back-street life do their job, but Parker's play is on another plane entirely.'[55]

Parker invited political interpretations of *Northern Star* by making, in local interviews, statements carefully calculated to challenge unionist and nationalist sensibilities alike. David Simpson, in a profile for the establishment *Belfast Tele-graph*, quoted Parker as saying that it had been an 'extraordinary revelation' to him to discover in 1967 that 'Republicanism had been originated by middle-class Pres-byterians'. *Northern Star*, he averred, dealt with 'the birth of Republicanism which started as a movement to unite Catholics and Protestants, and by a process com-mon to all revolutionary movements lost its ideal and became identified with one side. It is a process which happened to the Civil Rights movement as well.' In an interview for the nationalist *Irish News*, Parker remarked that McCracken had often been accused of being a traitor to his Northern Protestant roots, but 'his radi-calism came out of the best traditions of Presbyterianism and he lived out the "protestant" concept of protesting against the establishment and the status quo': 'it is those who accuse him, the Paisleyites of this world, who, like the IRA, are the real betrayers of their own traditions'. While unionists might be affronted by Par-ker's emphasizing of the Protestant roots of Irish republicanism, nationalists could take issue with his assertion that the republican ideal had been corrupted by its association with political violence.[56]

Critics for both the *Belfast Telegraph* and the *Guardian* commented on the 'understated' or 'hushed' reception given *Northern Star* by an 'uneasy' first-night Belfast audience. Such disquiet accorded with Parker's intentions for the play, as he described them to the *Irish News*:

> I want audiences to appreciate that this is not an historical play. It may be set 200 years ago, but it is very much a play about today....
>
> McCracken had the perception to realise that the destiny of the North lay ulti-mately in the hands of the people of the North. In my view, the same principle applies today. Change cannot be imposed by distant governments in London or Dublin, it must come about as a result of consensus and compromise from all the people of our troubled little land. I hope that my play will hammer home that point and make the audience feel very uncomfortable indeed.[57]

Thrilled by what he later termed the 'electric' response to *Northern Star* in Belfast, Parker hand-delivered copies of the script to the Royal Court and the Hampstead Theatre Club a few days after the play opened and sent copies to the Royal Shake-speare Company, London's National Theatre, and the Abbey soon thereafter. Surely this time, he must have felt, his achievement as a dramatist would be recognized by the theatrical establishments of both his nations. He would wait hopefully during the ensuing several months for news of another production somewhere.[58]

Meanwhile, Parker had several other projects to keep him busy. One he had not counted on was the production of *Radio Pictures*, which took place in January and February 1985. The last he had heard of this piece had been the news, in February 1984, of its cancellation by Central TV. Since this was the second time Central had pulled it from production, he had been told to feel free to offer it elsewhere. Parker's agent had managed to sell it to the BBC in the interim, but Parker had no inkling of this fact until the director, Nick Renton, phoned on 14 January to tell him that the three studio days reserved for taping the play were in six weeks' time.[59]

Parker completed rewrites on the script over the ensuing two weeks, and Renton lined up a strong cast, including Geoffrey Palmer as the radio producer, Dinsdale Landen and Frances Tomelty as the leading actors, Dermot Crowley as the hapless dramatist, and Michael Bilton as an aged radio actor with a gift for imitating pigeons. Renton also complemented Parker's witty script with amusing visual touches, most of which involved the impassive sound effects man, who stood beside whichever actor happened to be at the microphone, clicking a camera, flapping an umbrella, even unzipping a dress he was wearing to capture the sound of the female protagonist undressing, all in full view of the television audience. Nevertheless, Parker experienced a 'Curious lack of excitement' in the studio: 'The pictures look so un-atmospheric & dull, and the system seems so cumbersome & antiquated.' Although one of the most fully realized of Parker's works for television, *Radio Pictures*, written as a nostalgic look at the conventions of radio drama, also represented his farewell to the genre of the television studio play. From now on, whether writing for television or the cinema, he would be thinking in terms of film.[60]

At the beginning of 1985, Lesley sold her house on Redgrave Road, and she and Stewart bought a house in Putney together, free of associations with her life before meeting him. The process took several months, occasioning some stress along the way, but by the end of April they had purchased a large terrace house on Chelverton Road, which reminded Stewart agreeably of the houses on Rugby Road in Belfast that he had shared with friends in the early 1970s. After the removal, on 10 May, Stewart felt, as he put it in his journal, 'exhausted, gratified, morose, . . . removed . . . stirred'. It would be a while before they were fully settled, but their life together had been formalized on a new level. Since neither wished to be married again, even to each other, choosing and furnishing their own house served as the outward symbol of their partnership. Finally, Stewart had a home that evoked an uncomplicated allegiance from him.

13

Show Business

The mid-1980s can be regarded as marking both the acme and the nadir of Stewart Parker's career as a dramatist. Happy in his personal life and at the height of his powers as a writer, he believed himself to be producing his best work to date. However, he bumped up repeatedly in these years against the limitations of drama as an art form. Whether applied in the theatre, in the television studio, or on the film set, drama is an art of the possible rather than the ideal, and a playwright depends on the good will, understanding, and professional skills of a host of other people to realize his vision. A gregarious person who genuinely enjoyed collaboration, Parker was also an exacting craftsman who craved greater control over his work than he could reasonably expect to have. Aspiring to write plays of lasting aesthetic value, he never came to terms with the compromises demanded of him in the process of putting his scripts before the public. The built-in conflict between art and practical and commercial considerations loomed ever larger for Parker as his ambitions in the realms of television and the cinema grew, and writing for the stage remained an endeavour as fraught with frustration as it always had been for him. In *Heavenly Bodies*, his stage play of this period, Parker used the cautionary story of Victorian dramatist Dion Boucicault to focus his own recurring questions about the price of popular success and the responsibility of a playwright to his own place, people, and perspective.

In January 1985, Parker embarked in earnest on what would be his most expansive and direct attempt to deal with the Northern Irish Troubles. *Lost Belongings* had a long and convoluted history, with roots in a film idea suggested to Parker in 1977 by director Rob Knights. In April 1978, Parker had written a synopsis for the film, about an English journalist and an American graduate student who have strange encounters with a Provisional IRA man and a British Army captain who are either spying on or colluding with each other. Knights had not sold the project, and it had lain dormant in Parker's mind until January 1981, when he watched a Thames Television series on Irish history, *The Troubles*, which he judged 'Grippingly & fairly done'. 'Horribly compulsive to view the newsreel of your own memories', Parker commented in his journal after seeing the fourth instalment, covering the period from 1966 to Bloody Sunday, adding that he had been 'Seized in bed by the idea of a film trilogy set in '70s Ulster.'[1]

Parker described his ideas for this trilogy in a letter the next day to producer Rob Buckler, explaining that 'The sort of antecedent I have in mind is the [Andrzej] Wajda trilogy about wartime Poland—*A Generation*, *Kanal* and *Ashes and Diamonds*.' The three films would have 'different characters, different milieus and tones of voice', but all would 'deal with individuals whose lives are affected by the large events in the midst of which they're trying to live. And taken together, they should present a composite picture of sorts, a summation of the Northern Irish seventies.' In addition to the original spy film, Parker discussed a story line about two working-class Protestant boys, Alec and Craig, growing up together in Belfast. Both would get involved with a loyalist paramilitary organization, but Alec would escape that life through his 'exceptional musical talent'. The third film—drawn, Parker insisted, 'straight from my own experience'—would centre on Lenny, who is living in a communal house in Belfast and 'hustling producers and feature editors for freelance work'. He is hired as a researcher for a television series about the history of the Troubles, with the task of finding 'articulate old people from both communities...particularly those with articulate sons and daughters and grandsons and grand-daughters' to give first-hand accounts of historical and more contemporary events, but he cannot find subjects who 'will behave in accordance with the concept of the series'.[2] Parker wrote a formal synopsis for the trilogy in late February 1981, and both Buckler and June Roberts, then producing *Iris in the Traffic, Ruby in the Rain*, attempted fruitlessly to interest television companies in the proposal. Once again, it receded to the back of Parker's mind.

In his initial letter to Buckler, Parker had expressed his conviction that 'a major phase of the troubles has come to an end, and a whole new chapter is about to begin'.[3] Developments in Northern Ireland over the rest of 1981 proved him remarkably prescient. Since 1976, when the British government abolished 'special category' status for paramilitary prisoners as part of an effort to define political terrorism as merely criminal activity, republican prisoners had been agitating to get it back. They wanted to be treated as prisoners of war and employed increasingly desperate means to secure that aim. The 'blanket' protest, 'no wash' protest, 'no slop-out' protest, and 'dirty' protest, all of which stemmed directly or indirectly from prisoners' refusal to wear prison clothing, were constituent parts of this campaign. In October 1980, the prisoners resorted to the tactic that had secured special category status for them in 1972: a hunger strike. They called off their strike in December, confident that their demands would be met, but they had underestimated the intransigence of British Prime Minister Margaret Thatcher. On 1 March 1981, Bobby Sands, the IRA leader in the Maze Prison, began another fast in pursuit of political status. This hunger strike would not end until 3 October 1981, and before it did ten prisoners, including Sands, were allowed to starve themselves to death.

The inmates never obtained special category status, but they won big victories in the propaganda war, according to political scientists Paul Bew and Gordon Gillespie, as 'republican prisoners appeared in the unwonted role of being prepared to accept suffering for their cause rather than simply inflicting suffering on its behalf'. Sinn Féin, the political arm of the republican movement, began contesting elections throughout Ireland and seemed to many at the time to pose a threat to the constitutional nationalist SDLP, long regarded as the voice of most Northern Catholics. Padraig O'Malley, author of a detailed study of the hunger strikes, notes that they did more than anything up to that point to polarize Northern Ireland: 'Within the Catholic community the hunger strikes cruelly exposed the ambiguous relationship between militant Republicanism and mainstream nationalism, between militant Republicanism and the Catholic Church.... Within the Protestant community they exposed the depth and intensity of Protestants' rage.... Their hatred of Republicanism became fused with their fear of Catholicism....' On 7 May 1981, when nearly 100,000 people attended Bobby Sands's funeral, Parker himself observed, 'The two communities are probably further apart now than at any time since '68.'[4]

Thus, with an even greater sense of urgency, Parker reconsidered *Lost Belongings* in September 1982, when a BBC producer named Guy Slater solicited an idea from him for a six-part series of television films. Parker's friend Howard Schuman, a television writer himself, explains that the chance to write a multi-part series represented the 'Holy Grail' for every serious television dramatist. Parker was especially pleased that Slater envisaged the project as a series of films, since the British television industry still produced many studio plays on videotape. In his proposal, he referred with unusual directness to his own political views, asserting that, while he had grown up in 'a Protestant Unionist family',

> I believe that there is no future for Ireland as a whole until the Protestants of the North come to acknowledge their own Irishness and arrive at an [accommodation] with the Catholic community by means of some confederal system, the logical and eventual outcome of which would be a unified Irish republic in a closer and more honest relationship with Britain. I believe that the Provisional I.R.A. campaign has set these prospects back by at least a generation. I also believe that there are fundamental ways in which the governments in Dublin and Belfast could enhance those prospects.[5]

Parker maintained, however, that he did not wish merely to 'expound such views': 'As a playwright, my overriding concern is to keep faith with the individual lives and aspirations of all my characters, and yet do equal justice to the big public events and historical forces which have been crucial in shaping their destinies', thus enabling an audience 'to perceive the thing in personal and human and entertaining terms rather than as a baffling muddle of irreconcilable abstractions'. The advantage of a multi-part series, Parker argued, was the 'inclusiveness' it would allow; he wanted it to 'contain the widest possible spread of religious and political attitudes in the Province, as well as ranging across the social classes, the generations, rural in addition to urban viewpoints, and some views from the outside world'.[6]

Because he believed the hunger strikes had caused a fundamental shift in attitudes across the political spectrum, Parker decided to confine himself to the period of the Troubles he knew from personal experience. As he explained later, 'each additional year away felt like another bandage wound around my writing hand.... At any rate, drama needs some measure of distance to achieve any kind of coherence. If the distance can't be emotional, then it has to be historical.'[7] In reconceiving *Lost Belongings* as a six-part series, Parker retained the three film ideas from the trilogy synopsis and added three more. One filled in the background of the IRA man, now named Hugh McBraill. The others set up and resolved a story running through the series.

This 'primary story' would be 'a modern version of one of the most ancient tales in Ulster Celtic mythology': the Exile of the Sons of Uisliu. This chronicle of youth betrayed by age had fascinated Parker since his early twenties; his first full-length stage play, never produced, had been a modern retelling of it. Writing that play in 1967, he had approached the tale through the dramatic works of Yeats and Synge. Since then, he had been even more forcibly struck by 'the brute power and lyrical intensity and wit' of the original Old Irish, which he encountered with the help of a Gaelic scholar during his time at Cornell University. Parker had never lost his resolve to find some way of making dramatic use of this story; in 1981 he had considered writing a musical based on it, and he had tried unsuccessfully to interest Van Morrison in the concept earlier in 1982. 'Although a modern audience would be unaware of the source,' he suggested in his proposal for the film series, '… stories as timeless as this one contain a universal resonance, which lends them infinitely more value than a merely anecdotal narrative'.[8]

For *Lost Belongings*, Parker imagined his teenaged protagonist Deirdre as the fruit of a union between a Protestant man and a married Catholic woman who both died in a house fire early in her childhood. She lives with her father's brother, a high-ranking Orangeman whose sexual desire for her makes her life miserable. Deirdre falls in love with Niall Ussher, a young Catholic man who leads a rock band comprised mainly of his brothers, and runs away with him to London. Eventually the young people return to Northern Ireland, where the band members are assaulted by her uncle's henchmen and Deirdre herself is taken captive by him. She manages to escape, more dead than alive, and the series would end with her 'suspended between life and death', a fitting image of the North itself. All the characters in the series would be connected to this story—Alec would be the son of Deirdre's uncle's neighbour, an RUC detective; Craig Deirdre's cousin; Lenny a friend of Niall's; Hugh McBraill Deirdre's half-brother (sacrificed by his mother when she eloped with Deirdre's father)—and their paths would cross throughout.[9]

A treatment, as Parker well knew, is 'a logical absurdity', a 'summary of and an evocation of and a commentary upon something which is entirely without existence: namely, a script'. Each time he described *Lost Belongings* for prospective backers, though, he became more excited about writing it, so it came as a terrible let-down when the initial response from BBC higher-ups, in January 1983, proved less than encouraging. Nevertheless, the BBC agreed to commission the pilot script, introducing Deirdre and her plight, and Parker produced a polished version of it between March and May of that year. Guy Slater passed it up the BBC hierarchy, only to learn that September that the BBC had already commissioned another major Ulster project, a six-part series on the army in Northern Ireland written by Graham Reid. This coincidence, as Parker noted in his journal, put his own series 'in grave peril, in spite of all so far concerned enthusing over the script'. At the very least, *Lost Belongings* would not soon go into production. The following February, Parker received the upsetting news that *Lost Belongings* had been definitively 'axed' by the BBC. Slater and Marc Berlin, Parker's agent, had ideas regarding other places to submit his treatment and pilot, but he himself believed 'it's finished for the foreseeable future'. 'I suppose I could always try it as a novel next', he commented.[10]

Parker had put this disappointment so thoroughly behind him that he could barely credit it when Berlin rang in August 1984 to say that he had interested another producer, David Elstein of Primetime Television, in *Lost Belongings*. The television production sector in the British Isles had mushroomed after the introduction of Channel Four in November 1982. This second non-BBC channel was intended to provide an outlet for less populist programmes on the independent network, fulfilling a function analogous to the one BBC2 was supposed to serve for the BBC. Existing ITV companies subsidized Channel Four's operations in exchange for the right to sell the new channel's advertising in their respective regions, but independent companies like Primetime supplied its 'product'. Channel Four acted as a 'virtual studio', bankrolling television programmes without making them itself. The arrangement appealed both to those who valued Channel Four's public service remit, which included the provision of 'matter calculated to appeal to tastes and interests not generally catered for by ITV' and promoting 'innovation and experiment in the form and content of programmes', and to the Thatcher government, which regarded free enterprise as a key tenet. The idea of working with Channel Four appealed to Parker, who approved of its politically progressive and artistically avant-garde ambitions, but he would have been happy for anyone to produce *Lost Belongings*. In mid-August he met Elstein, who impressed him as 'bright & direct'. Elstein believed he could interest Channel Four in the series and hoped to make it entirely on film and on location. 'A phoenix from the ashes', Parker marvelled: 'Scarcely dare believe in it.'[11]

Parker struggled to suspend his disbelief through negotiations between Primetime and Channel Four, which resulted in the latter putting up script development money, and between his agent and the other parties concerned, not fully succeeding until the first cheque arrived in mid-January 1985. Even then, he had difficulty settling down to write. The news that Jim Goddard might direct *Lost Belongings* offered a spur to productivity. Goddard's directing credits included inventive and popular crime drama serials for Euston Films (the film subsidiary of Thames Television), among them *The Sweeney*, a series which regularly ranked among the most-watched programmes on British television during four seasons between 1975 and 1978, the six-part serial *Out* (1978), and the thirteen-part serial *Fox* (1980). He had also directed Alan Bleasdale's single play *The Black Stuff*, aired by BBC2 in 1980, which spawned a successful five-part series, *Boys from the Blackstuff* (BBC2, 1982), directed by Philip Saville. Parker met Goddard at the end of January and found him 'Strong, direct, authoritative, down to earth.' Now, he reflected, 'it's up to me to deliver the goods. I cdn't. ask for better collaborators.'[12]

The development of *Lost Belongings* exemplifies the way in which multi-part serials were displacing single plays as the dominant form of 'authored drama' on British television in the early 1980s. Lez Cooke, author of a history of British television drama, explains that cost-conscious television companies regarded series and serial drama, or mini-series, as more economical than one-off plays because the costs of production could be spread over a number of episodes, actors required less rehearsal time since they built up familiarity with their characters, and audiences could be cultivated over the run of a programme. Companies frequently sought co-production money and distribution in English-speaking regions overseas, and the global market for multi-part television drama was more robust than for single plays. The end of the long-running BBC showcase for single plays, *Play for Today*, in 1984 was a sign of the times; the previous year, two other BBC anthology series of single plays, *Play of the Month* and *Playhouse*, had also ceased production. On the ITV network, such changes had come even earlier. Soon studio television plays like Parker's *Radio Pictures* would seem as anachronistic as the radio plays it celebrated. Ambitious television playwrights had two main choices in this climate: turn to screen writing for the fledgling British film industry or focus on longer-form serial drama.[13]

In this movement from single plays towards multi-part serials, Cooke sees *Boys from the Blackstuff* as 'transitional'. This series consisted of five single plays which could each stand alone, although they all used the same characters and concentrated on the same theme: the effects of Thatcher's economic policies on individuals. The protagonists of the series were unemployed men, formerly co-workers, in Liverpool. The first play introduced the main characters, and each of the remaining four centred on one of them. No one narrative spanned the five parts, but Bleasdale built up a compelling picture of a particular time and place through his presentation of specific characters and their problems. As Cooke notes, '*Boys from the Blackstuff* quickly became a television "event", tapping into the increasing public outcry about the social impact that Tory policies were having on working-class communities in the industrial heartlands of Britain.' Parker regarded *Boys from the Blackstuff* as inspirational, and it is easy to see why. Bleasdale's sympathetic and rounded portrayal of working-class characters, his use of humour to leaven grim subject-matter, his fidelity to a provincial region, and the way he approached politics through the lives of people all have their counterparts in Parker's own television drama. Structurally, too, Parker's original conception for *Lost Belongings*, in which each part would be self-contained but would gain from association with the others, resembled *Boys from the Blackstuff*. However, since Parker had completed a detailed treatment for his six-part series before the BBC aired Bleasdale's series, such similarities are more likely attributable to the writers' shared sensibilities than to any direct influence of Bleasdale on Parker.[14]

Lost Belongings, unlike *Boys from the Blackstuff*, had an overarching narrative, making it a more thoroughgoing serial drama. A continuous narrative thread had been present in Parker's vision of the work from the moment he decided to undergird it with the Deirdre legend, but Elstein and Goddard encouraged him to intertwine the six films even more as he wrote the last five scripts, which he did during December 1984 and the first seven months of 1985, and at the revision stage. Goddard, with his background in crime drama, promised to bring an edgy energy to Parker's project, but his work on *Out* and *Fox*, both complex narratives by Trevor Preston, had also equipped him with a theoretical interest in longer-form drama. He described *Fox* as 'an attempt... to say, OK the single play may be dead but we now see the possibility of starting something... called the television novel'. When Parker finished the first draft of the final script, he referred to it in his journal as the 'last chapter', and in later interviews he stated that, in *Lost Belongings*, he had tried to bring the complexity of the novel to television through, for example, the extensive use of flashbacks. 'We seem to be in a phase at the moment where individual writers are being given the chance to paint on a very large canvas', he remarked: 'Series like [Dennis Potter's] *The Singing Detective*, *Boys from the Blackstuff* and [Troy Kennedy Martin's] *Edge of Darkness* have the breadth and range of the finest fiction, but they are completely televisual, entering the national consciousness in the way literature doesn't any more.'[15]

The main plot of *Lost Belongings* and many of its characters derived from Parker's source material, the Deirdre legend. He was familiar both with the eighth- or ninth-century version of the Exile of the Sons of Uisliu preserved in the Book of Leinster and with the medieval retelling that had inspired treatments of the story by Lady Gregory, Yeats, and Synge in the early twentieth century. In the ancient story, a seer prophesies before Deirdre's birth that her beauty will bring civil war and destruction to Ulster. Conchobor, the king of Ulster, accordingly orders her raised in seclusion, with the intention of marrying her himself one day. When Deirdre approaches adulthood, however, she falls in love with Noisiu, one of the king's warriors, and runs away from Conchobor's kingdom with him and his brothers. Conchobor lures them back to Ulster with promises of forgiveness but has them attacked when they return. By the end of the saga account, Noisiu and the other sons of Uisliu are dead, the men of Ulster are divided against each other, Conchobor's capital has been destroyed, and Deirdre has killed herself.[16]

Throughout *Lost Belongings*, Parker draws parallels between people and situations from the Ulster Cycle of tales and their modern equivalents. The foreboding that attaches to Deirdre in the ancient story, for instance, is signalled in Parker's recasting of it by her mixed parentage: she is marked from the beginning as a misfit, accepted by neither side of her family or in her divided homeland. Deirdre's uncle, who represents King Conchobor, is a loyalist called Roy Connell who takes Deirdre in at his wife's behest a few years before she dies giving birth to twins (like the Macha of Irish mythology for whom Conchobor's royal seat, Emain Macha, is named). Roy's incestuous advances cause Deirdre to go into 'exile' with Niall and the family members in his band, whose musical endeavours mirror the sweet singing ascribed to Noisiu and his brothers in the old story. Roy's neighbour, a police officer named Harry Ferguson, stands in for the legendary Fergus, sent by the king to call Deirdre and the brothers home and betrayed along with the Sons of Uisliu when Conchobor makes a mockery of his pledge of safety. In some versions of the ancient story, Fergus has two sons, Illann the Fair, who dies defending Noisiu and his followers, and Buinne the Ruthless Red, who accepts a bribe to desert them. Their counterparts in *Lost Belongings* are Harry's daughter Carol (Deirdre's best friend), who works to discover what Roy has done to Deirdre and Niall, and Alec, whose middle-class, artistic life in west London is achieved at the cost of denying his Northern Irish roots.

Much of the imagery of *Lost Belongings* also comes from the Exile of the Sons of Uisliu. Near the beginning of the oldest extant version of the tale, Deirdre is compared to a flame, and fire features prominently in the rest of the story, which ends with Fergus torching Emain Macha in revenge for Conchobor's deception of him. Descriptions of burning are even more prevalent in the medieval elaboration on the legend, and Parker incorporates visual and verbal images of fire throughout his six films. In the second one, for example, he modulates between Alec grilling food in the garden of his London home and a horrific memory from his youth. A piece of fat flaring on the grill becomes a blazing truck tyre rolling down a Belfast street in 1968, as Alec recalls a time when he and Craig were threatened by a group of Catholic boys and escaped by pushing one of them onto the burning tyre. Fire also appears in less traumatic contexts: in a chemistry lab at Deirdre's school, in Deirdre's young cousin's talk of preparations for a 12 July bonfire, and so on. In a 1987 interview, Parker characterized fire as an image belonging to both Northern Irish Protestants and Catholics, signifying for him a kind of fever that could not be assuaged.[17]

Another recurring image in *Lost Belongings* is that of flowers and foliage. In the opening of the oldest version of Deirdre's story, the seer predicts that she will have cheeks like 'foxglove', and flowers appear repeatedly in Parker's descriptions. If fire represents the 'death wish' Parker saw as endemic to Irish culture, and the often-misdirected passion of Irish people, flowers symbolize the 'playful creativity' he believed to be the only force able to 'counter' it.[18] In *Lost Belongings*, the most powerful images combine the two, suggesting the dual possibilities inherent in Northern Ireland and its people: Niall's van is painted with 'branches of bright red flame'; Deirdre's father brings her mother into a house 'entirely bare of furniture and carpets, but with a fire burning in the grate, and flowers everywhere'; Alec and Craig do a hit on a florist's shop, shooting the shopkeeper. Like her ancient forebear, whose laments for Noisiu are famous set-pieces of Celtic literature, Deirdre is a poet, and the snatches of her poetry interspersed with the action underline the pattern of imagery pervading the scripts: '... a child of the fire, like a flower on a red branch, stretching out to gulp the air, burning whoever tries to pluck it. A white-hot flower on a red branch of fire. Flying up to claim the air. Burning whatever tries to quench it.'[19]

Parker did not expect his audience to notice all such correspondences, nor did he feel compelled to fit every aspect of his work into the mythological structure (many of the supporting characters, such as Lenny and the Provisional IRA leader Hugh McBraill, come out of Parker's own experience of Northern Ireland in the 1970s), but he indicates the importance of his source material in a scene about a third of the way through *Lost Belongings*. McBraill effects his escape from the Maze Prison by forcibly trading places with an English lecturer teaching a class like the ones Parker himself led at Long Kesh prison camp in 1973. That day's lesson hinges on the various uses to which the writers of the Irish literary revival put 'the same famous story from early Irish literature, the story known in folklore as Deirdre of the Sorrows'. The lecturer identifies four basic elements to the ancient Irish story—tragedy foreseen, love pitting youth against age, exile, and revenge—drawing

particular attention to the last two. It is, he says, worth examining such 'raw material of literature' to see 'what the writer has chosen to do with it, what sort of process
of refinement it has undergone in the workings of his or her imagination'.[20]

In Parker's hands, the theme of exile assumes central importance, but he puts
the emphasis less on separation from one's home than on a kind of internal exile he
regarded as the common inheritance of both communities in Northern Ireland.
Neither side feels securely at home in the North, he suggests, because both are too
neurotically preoccupied with possessing it materially to enjoy being in it. The title
Lost Belongings connotes both physical loss and this sense of spiritual homelessness.
If Protestants and Catholics would only recognize their shared ownership, both
groups would find their place—together. In a scene following one between McBraill
and the American academic Gretchen Reilly, in which he tells her that 'You can
learn the most from the teacher you least agree with', the English journalist Simon
Hunt and an officer in the British Army discuss the root cause of the Troubles. The
officer maintains complacently that sectarian divisions in the North will allow
England to hold Northern Ireland in the United Kingdom indefinitely, providing
what he sees as the 'buffer zone' necessary to keep their 'home' intact. Northern
Irish people, he argues,

> long ago lost their sense of belonging.... The Catholic lot lost it in 1921... their
> patriot comrades in Dublin had sold them out, done a deal with our chaps.... They
> were left to the mercy of the Protestant lot up here. Who of course never had any
> secure sense of belonging from the minute that they arrived.... of course they're all
> passionately attached to their blessed mountains and rivers and houses and streets... but
> they don't quite feel secure in the belief that it all belongs to them. Or they to it. What
> they really belong to is one another, actually.... If they were ever to acknowledge that,
> then we'd be finished here. They never will, though. They're too afraid to relax their
> grip in case they lose it altogether.[21]

Exchanges such as this substantiate Parker's assertion that 'the audience with
which I was first and foremost concerned [in *Lost Belongings*]... as in everything
else I have ever written, was my own people, the people of Northern Ireland'.
When intended audience is taken into account, the differences between the Deirdre
legend and Parker's treatment of it are as important as the similarities. For one
thing, Niall and the members of his band, unlike Noisiu and his brothers, are not
warriors. In the first film, Deirdre reacts with scorn when Carol Ferguson asks if he
might have been responsible for a petrol bomb thrown into Roy Connell's paint
store: 'Of course it frigging wasn't Niall, what are you talking about, you think just
because he's a Catholic he automatically throws petrol bombs?' Parker also presents
Deirdre more sympathetically, as a victim rather than a cause of Ulster's divisions.
She remains spirited and headstrong but is less wilfully self-destructive. At the end
of *Lost Belongings*, Deirdre does not kill herself. Instead, she goes mad, escapes
from her uncle's house, and wanders the city looking for Niall. The audience learns
in this episode that she is pregnant, and the series ends with her miscarrying her
baby, bleeding to death beneath the 'huge, ugly fluorescent cross' on the side of a
Belfast church. The final image, as Parker envisaged it, is of Deirdre looking straight

at the camera: 'It is a death of youth, love, hope and vision—staring us unforgivingly in the face.' Parker wrote of this scene: 'if classical tragedy is intended to purge its audience of pity and terror, this mongrel tragedy of the death of Deirdre Connell aims to provoke shame and rage, that she should be let die, like a hounded animal, outside the locked door of Ulster Christianity'.[22]

Parker worried explicitly while writing the last episode of *Lost Belongings* that it was 'coming out bleak & fatalistic, inducing resignation & hopelessness'. The night he finished the first draft of the screenplay, however, he realized that he 'could suddenly develop the minor figure of Carol Ferguson to inform the final tragic and horrifying images w/ a saeva indignatio, & show growth in counterpoint to Deirdre's death'. This insight resulted in a scene between Niall, who survived Roy Connell's attack and is recuperating in the Mater hospital, and Carol, as anxious as he to locate and help Deirdre. During their conversation, Carol acknowledges to herself that it is not only terrorists and overt bigots such as Deirdre's uncle who prolong the Troubles, but people who consider themselves uninvolved:

> CAROL: I've never set foot in this part of town before. I was scared of my life coming up here. I've never even talked to a Catholic this long before. Did you ever hear anything more ridiculous?
>
> NIALL: It's the place that's ridiculous, not you.
>
> CAROL: Oh, no, it's me all right. Me and you and everybody like us, we let it happen, we bloody vote for it. We've lost nearly everything that belongs to us now, everything that's human—every shred of human dignity, we don't even feel shame any more. All that counts is who's cock of the walk this week, cock of the dunghill more like.... [I]t's always the Brits to blame for everything, according to your crowd. According to our mob, it's Dublin is the root of all evil. What do the British really know or care about us? What does Dublin really know? We're the only ones that *know*. So why can we not even look each other straight in the face?

Niall's first reactions to Carol's self-accusation are dismissive or humorously evasive, but, as she prepares to leave to continue looking for Deirdre, he drops his habitual defences to offer her awkward thanks and encouragement: 'just...stick with it, I mean...if we all don't belong together, who does?...I mean, who the hell else would have us, any of us?...I really appreciate what you're doing.'[23] Even more than the romantic attachment between Deirdre and Niall, these tentative beginnings of communication, cooperation, and possibly friendship between Carol and Niall offer hope for Northern Ireland's future.

Parker delivered the last instalment of *Lost Belongings* at the end of July 1985. Now he could concentrate on other writing again. Even during the seven months of intense focus on his serial drama, it had hardly been the only thing on Parker's mind and agenda. The move to Chelverton Road, three film projects in various stages of development, the production and transmission of *Radio Pictures*, attempts to interest potential producers in *Northern Star*, the ongoing effort by Eddie

Kulukundis to mount a commercial production of *Pratt's Fall*, and plans for the Birmingham première of Parker's as-yet-unwritten play about Dion Boucicault (which he had decided to call *Heavenly Bodies*) also vied for his attention in the first half of 1985.

Blue Money, the Parker film starring Tim Curry which had proved such a hit on British television, had made its American debut at the Filmex Festival in Los Angeles on St Patrick's Day of that year. June Roberts, the producer, reported that it had received good reviews in the *Los Angeles Times* and the *Hollywood Reporter* and that the showing was sold out in advance and punctuated throughout by 'applause & laughter'. A few days later, she informed Parker that four major studios were seeking distribution rights. Within three weeks, however, they learned that nothing would come of this interest because the agent for London Weekend Television, obviously unprepared for the possibility of a cinematic release, had already 'disposed of' the video rights. The apex of *Blue Money*'s fortunes turned out to be the grand prize and a prize for best television film at the Banff Television Festival in Alberta, Canada, that June.[24]

Pre-production for *Eat the Peach* had meanwhile been moving ahead through the final months of 1984 and the first months of 1985. Parker had written the parts of Vinnie and Arthur with Gabriel Byrne and Stephen Rea in mind, and they had been cast in the roles at his suggestion. John Kelleher had secured development money from the Irish Film Board and the British National Film Development Fund and had pre-sold the UK television rights to Channel Four. In February 1985, Parker learned that Kelleher and another independent film producer named David Collins had joined forces in a new production and distribution venture, Strongbow, designed to take advantage of provisions of the Business Development Scheme of the Republic of Ireland's 1984 Finance Act which allowed individuals to write off large portions of their investments in certain high-risk manufacturing industries, including film-making. Strongbow, which pledged to approach each of its productions from 'a commercial perspective', eventually raised nearly half the production budget for *Eat the Peach* from individuals. Moreover, Strongbow used *Eat the Peach*, with its high-profile writer and lead actors, to spearhead a 'portfolio' consisting of four feature films and two television series, making the prospects of the company largely dependent upon its reception.[25]

Kelleher told Parker in early February that he expected filming to begin in June and also that the script had been 'undergoing structural changes & rewrites', news the dramatist tried to take philosophically, since 'I've known all along I wd. have to bite on that bullet'. Nothing, however, could have prepared Parker for the script, as revised by director Peter Ormrod, he received on 14 March. It 'turned out to be 60 per cent new material, all of it lumbering, badly written, disconnected dross, and 40 per cent my stuff rewritten and rearranged so that all the vitality, character & humour has been drained out of it'. The next day, Lesley having 'confirmed the worst', Parker made detailed notes pinpointing his objections to Ormrod's script and told his agent that he wanted his name taken off the project. Then, with his 'blood at boiling point', he attempted to write Kelleher a 'reasonably clinical and dispassionate' letter explaining what incensed him about the changes to *Eat the*

Peach. Chief among his objections was the failure of the revised script to tell 'a comprehensible and involving story'. It meandered through nearly half its length before introducing the Wall of Death theme, and, when the Wall of Death finally made an appearance, it seemed 'just one more jolly jape, as opposed to the rebellious gesture of a man who feels seriously trapped'. The treatment of the smuggling also struck him as both unrealistic and unenlightening about the place of smuggling in the local culture and its connection to a wider corruption in Irish life. The characters, similarly, had 'no emotional through-line, no consistency and no development'. In short, Parker found the revised script 'laboured, dull and confusing, a largely humourless exercise, often in the worst traditions of Irish showbusiness whimsy' and declared himself 'very sad and bitterly disappointed that the material has ended up like this'.[26]

Kelleher remained hopeful that Parker would 'become involved in further revisions', sending him yet another version of the script a couple of weeks later. This Parker judged 'a more orderly & coherent re-shaping of Ormrod's script, but as far removed as ever from the film I wanted to make'. By early April, both sides accepted that 'there was no bridging the gulf'. A month later, Parker noted with satisfaction that Stephen Rea had also left the project. Officially, Rea's decision had been prompted by Gabriel Byrne's defection to take a part in a Robert Altman film (Rea told a reporter that he had viewed *Eat the Peach* as a 'buddy movie' and, with Byrne gone, 'the chemistry essential to my conception of the film wasn't there any more'), but he had also been privy to Parker's anguish. 'At least', Parker reflected, the completed film would not be 'a botched compromise of my original scheme—it'll be a whole separate & distinct abortion'.[27]

Nearly five months of wrangling between Parker's agent and Strongbow ensued. Kelleher initially insisted both that Parker's name must appear on the screen and that he would not pay the second £15,000 owed on the script, due to Parker the day filming started. He eventually delivered on the money, but billing posed a more intractable problem. For a while, it looked like the parties would have to refer their dispute to arbitration. ('Extraordinary', Parker remarked: 'To have to go to the Writers' Guild & argue that your name be *removed* from a film's credits.') Finally, though, Kelleher agreed to Parker's terms.[28]

After the severing of his relationship with Strongbow, Parker continued to follow the progress of *Eat the Peach* from a distance. In January 1986, he learned indirectly that the character of Mrs Downing had been excised from the film, leaving him wondering how its makers would even be able to explain the title. Nevertheless, he felt no surprise when *Eat the Peach* opened to 'great acclaim' in Dublin that March. 'It seems to have come out as I expected', he wrote in his journal, '—shallow, fey, charming & commercial.' At least one reviewer shared Parker's opinion of the final product. Philip Molloy, writing in the *Irish Press*, commented that 'We don't know what motivates Vinny, or what he expects to get out of his wall of death. The publicity grandly tells us that it is an expression of his individuality, but the film doesn't.... [T]he finished film always looks like a "straightened" version of Parker's vision.... You get the feeling of the characters being held back from what is their potential.'[29]

Parker's outrage over the *Eat the Peach* débâcle centred on his erstwhile collaborators' apparent disregard for his professional status as a writer. As he told a reporter in September 1985, 'There's a different attitude to writing in films than in any other medium, a sort of feeling that a script is everybody's property. It's as if I was going down the mines and digging up raw material and they'd refine and process it.' Parker had been formed as a screenwriter in the sheltered environment of the BBC, where writers were treated with respect, and even in the independent television sector he had worked with directors and producers who appreciated what he wrote and considered it their business to realize his intentions. With *Eat the Peach*, for the first time, he encountered the more common cinematic notion of the writer as merely one cog in a much larger machine. Kelleher's partner, David Collins, presented the producers' point of view in a news story on the controversy, arguing that 'our purpose is not to make a film to illustrate a particular script, but to serve the director's ideas'. Parker would not abandon his ambition to write for the big screen, but he could never accept the ceding of artistic control that enterprise seemed to demand.[30]

Parker's third foray into film in 1985, which played itself out in roughly the same period as the unravelling of his association with *Eat the Peach*, thus represented the triumph of hope over experience. Back in March 1984 (less than three weeks before Ormrod made his initial contact with the playwright), Parker had read a story in the *Sunday Times* magazine about a bizarre Second World War prisoner of war camp at the Curragh military base near Dublin. The Irish Free State remained officially neutral during the war, so it offered similar—and extraordinarily liberal—treatment to fighters from both sides landing accidentally on its soil. The German and Allied airmen who made up the camp's population occupied identical compounds, and they could leave the camp during the day provided they stayed within a three-mile radius and signed forms promising, on their honour, to return. Many made friends with the locals and even had Irish girlfriends. They continued to receive their normal military pay and had good food, their own pub on the camp grounds, and freedom to follow their interests. The Germans, for the most part, accepted this idyll in the proper spirit of gratitude. The Allied airmen, however, who had only to cross the border with Northern Ireland to be in British territory, considered it their patriotic duty to try to escape—despite the exhortations of the British legation in Dublin, who told them they could do more for the war effort by staying put. (Behind the scenes, Ireland tacitly supported the Allies, and British officials did not wish to provoke the Irish government.) Allied prisoners made several escape attempts, as often as not thwarted by their own side, before the British and Irish governments agreed to have them secretly returned to their units. Parker decided immediately that the story of this camp would make a 'splendid film subject', but, shortly after this, he agreed to write *Eat the Peach* and filed the Curragh idea away for future reference.[31]

In January 1985, Parker received with mixed feelings his agent's report that a company called Network TV wanted him to write a feature film about the Second World War-era POWs in Ireland. Stretched to his limit with the writing of *Lost Belongings* and pre-production for *Radio Pictures* and *Eat the Peach*, and with the distinct possibility of a new *Pratt's Fall* production in the near future and the première of his Boucicault play (which he had not begun researching, let alone writing) little over a year away, he acknowledged to himself that 'I couldn't possibly get near it till early 1986, which is almost certainly too late for them.' Nevertheless, he lunched with the producers a few weeks later and found himself offering to deliver a synopsis by March and a completed script by the following January or February. He felt 'Insane to be entertaining another project at this juncture, but I really know this one belongs to me. Also, there is a curious weightlessness in this current flukey run of extraordinary good fortune.' Still, the abundance of opportunities that seemed open to Parker at this point in time bordered on being too much of a good thing. 'I'm not about to complain about being in work,' he confided to friends, 'but there is something malign in a fate which keeps you frustrated and outcast for years, and then overloads you with far more stuff than you could possibly hope to handle.'[32]

Exactly five weeks after this meeting came what Parker denoted in his journal as 'The day the sky fell in on *Eat the Peach*', when he read Ormrod's rewritten script and decided he could no longer work with him. Parker's subsequent withdrawal from that project did not create as much slack in his schedule as he might have wished, although it certainly should have increased his scepticism regarding film work. Despite any such qualms, he was torn in mid-April when he heard that Pat O'Connor, director of the film version of Bernard MacLaverty's novel *Cal*, might direct the POW film and that the producers still thought Parker the best person to write it. They insisted they would need the script by the end of the year at the latest, however, since they planned to begin shooting in the spring. Parker summed up his dilemma in his journal, writing, 'If I take it on, it'll crucify me, and if I turn it down, it'll cast a pall over me.' He agonized over this impossible choice for two weeks, finally deciding to make every effort to demonstrate his enthusiasm for the project. He did this so effectively that Ian McArthur, one of the producers, agreed to commission a treatment from Parker on the understanding that he would deliver the completed script by the end of February for filming in May and June. Parker's elation did not smother his awareness that 'It's still going to be a miracle if I manage to do it all.'[33]

Parker researched and wrote his treatment for the film, which he called *The Life of Rawley*, in August and September 1985. The facts regarding the Irish POW camp required no embellishment to make them entertaining, and Parker, as he usually did when dealing with the past, remained faithful to what had actually happened. His characters were fictional, but most of their exploits were rooted in reality. He incorporated particulars of all the escape attempts described in the magazine article he had read about the camp, along with most of the incidental details, using his imagination to flesh out their human elements. His Scottish protagonist, a young pilot named Ivan Rawley, is torn between his enjoyment of his incarceration in Ireland (including his love for a young Irish woman named Grania) and his uncomfortable sense that he ought to be doing everything he can to get back to fighting the war. Parker's treatment ends with the abrupt announcement that the Allied flyers are being released to rejoin their units, Rawley's realization that 'he may have seen Grania for the last time in his life', and a shot of him taking off in his bomber to 'an unknown fate'.[34]

McArthur initially responded positively to the treatment but later came to share O'Connor's doubts about its appeal to 'the money men'. In October, Parker accommodated the producers' request for 'a shorter, more fluid treatment' featuring the central character more prominently. He heard nothing more until March 1986, when he received a letter from McArthur with suggestions for ways to give the treatment more commercial potential internationally. These included, as Parker noted in his journal, 'making the American the hero, the RAF chap a reckless jack-the-lad, and so on: mid-Atlantic cliché all the way'. 'I fear it may be time to pull out', he concluded regretfully.[35] Thus his involvement with the POW film ended. Compared with the *Eat the Peach* fiasco, the negative effects on Parker were slight. Apart from the time he had spent writing and rewriting the treatment (time, in truth, that he could ill spare), he had invested little in the project. The main casualty in the affair was his dream of writing for the cinema, which had taken yet another beating.

Parker experienced other distractions from his writing-in-progress in 1985 and early 1986, some happier in nature than his disappointments with the film industry. One of these was the surprise success of *Radio Pictures*. The BBC aired this television play on 16 July 1985 to notices so 'rapturous' that, as Lesley Bruce informed a friend, they 'could scarcely have been improved upon if [Parker had] written them himself'. The critic for the *Evening Standard* called the play 'a delightful comedy', praising its script as 'intelligent and light as air'; the reviewer for the *Daily Express* pronounced *Radio Pictures* 'gloriously funny'; Sean Day-Lewis in the *Daily Telegraph* declared it 'a delight from beginning to end'; and an assessment in the *Listener* found the piece 'immaculate in all respects'. This critical consensus astonished Parker, who had assumed the play would 'only appeal to a small minority—people who enjoy being mentally teased'.[36]

In her review for *The Times*, Celia Brayfield remarked that 'It is tempting to wonder how the play would fare on stage, not least because it seemed to be finished too soon.' Her sentiments were echoed on high. Peter Hall, artistic director of the National Theatre, saw *Radio Pictures*, liked it, and suggested that Parker should have lunch with Nicholas Wright, the theatre's literary manager, to discuss the possibility of his adapting it as a stage play. This overture pleased and infuriated Parker in equal measure, as Lesley explained to Nancy McKibbin, since only about three weeks previously the theatre had returned *Northern Star* to the playwright 'with little more than a rejection slip'—'and there *was* a play fit for a National Theatre'. Parker met Wright, though, and agreed to undertake the adaptation if the National commissioned the work and seemed committed to producing it.[37]

The irony of the warm reception accorded a slight piece like *Radio Pictures* when he had been unable to interest any London management in *Northern Star*, his most ambitious as well as his most critically acclaimed stage play, rankled with Parker. Not only the National, but the RSC, the Hampstead, and the Royal Court had passed on the play, the literary manager of the last suggesting, condescendingly, that Parker should 'consider sending us a new play which is entirely of your own voice'.

Attempts to get *Northern Star* published had likewise come to nothing, with neither The Gallery Press in the Republic nor Blackstaff Press in the North showing any appreciable interest. The Lyric Players Theatre had abandoned plans for a spring tour of its production when the Northern Ireland Arts Council declined to fund it, but artistic director Patrick Sandford eventually arranged an autumn revival of the show, with a few cast substitutions (luckily Gerard McSorley was still available to play McCracken). This previewed in Sligo in mid-September before moving to the Olympia Theatre for the first week of the Dublin Theatre Festival, followed by a short tour of Northern Ireland.[38]

Parker thought the revived production even better than the original, and *Irish Times* critic David Nowlan judged it 'as fine a play as it was first time around': 'as cynically, as realistically and as sorrowfully true a picture of Irish political history as has ever been seen on the stage'. Gus Smith of the *Sunday Independent* wrote, 'Not since I first saw Brian Friel's "Translations" have I found a work so satisfying', and his colleague Desmond Rushe at the *Irish Independent* hailed 'theatre which is compelling at its best and never less than interesting at its worst'. Other Irish reviews were less wholeheartedly positive, but they were balanced by reactions from outside the island, with the reviewer from *The Times* proclaiming *Northern Star* 'a subtle and absorbing piece of theatre' and the *Observer*'s critic asserting that this 'remarkable virtuoso achievement...should be seen in England soon'. Best of all, a report on the Dublin Theatre Festival in *Time* magazine pointed to Parker's play as the 'high point'.[39]

Notwithstanding this good press, *Northern Star* played to half-full houses during its week in Dublin, and, as Parker learned from McSorley, the local newspapers labelled it 'the Festival's loss-maker'. 'So much for the sophistication & commitment of the Dublin audience', Parker griped in his journal, and Gus Smith observed that the poor attendance reflected 'what we down here think of Belfast and the North generally'. Parker could take some comfort in the fact that, at director Peter Farago's instigation, plans had been in place since February for a North American première at a studio venue in St Louis (attempts by American director Irene Lewis to arrange productions in other US locations had been met with the objection that the play was 'too Irish in its concerns'). In mid-November, however, Farago told him the St Louis theatre had cancelled its production ('Cold feet, basically'). This left Parker only the hope that Farago would, as he had intimated he might, produce *Northern Star* in Birmingham before staging *Heavenly Bodies* there. Farago had even mentioned the possibility of a co-production with London's Tricycle Theatre, then rapidly developing a reputation as a centre for new writing. The matter remained unresolved, though, when Farago left England at the beginning of December for a directing assignment abroad, and Parker inferred that '*Northern Star* is now w/out a future.'[40]

Two days later, 'as a defiant final throw', Parker wrote to the Tricycle's artistic director, Nicolas Kent, talking up *Northern Star* and enclosing the latest Dublin reviews. On 16 December, Parker met Kent at the Tricycle in Kilburn. He summed up their discussion in his journal as the 'Usual old codology. He thinks he might do the play as a co-production w/ Birmingham in the autumn, but only if his grant situation turns out to be favourable, in April. . . . He wonders if I'd accept a commission . . .'. After the meeting, Parker 'drove home, ragged, overstrung, the certainty seeping through me that my work is minor & peripheral'. That night, he spent three of the wee hours lying 'wide awake & in crisis'.[41]

Developments regarding *Pratt's Fall* also contributed to Parker's loss of confidence by the end of 1985. Throughout that year, Eddie Kulukundis's team had been trying to arrange a production of the play, either in the autumn of 1985 or early in 1986, which would try out in a good provincial theatre before, with luck, transferring into the West End. The challenges they faced included securing a suitable venue in which to open the play and signing a 'box-office' leading lady, while maintaining the availability and enthusiasm of those already committed to the project. Parker's periodic meetings with Knightsbridge Theatrical Productions left him taut with anticipation and frustration in turn. At various times, the *Pratt's Fall* group had a theatre and a plausible Victoria lined up, but never both simultaneously. Just before Christmas, Parker received word from Knightsbridge that they had decided to 'let the play go for the time being'. Though hardly surprising, the collapse of his West End prospects still hurt. 'All wasted, all for nothing,' he observed bleakly in his journal, 'the hustling, the praying, the meetings, the whole thirteen months and the three years preceding them. Apart from a further map of the inaccessible terrain.'[42]

Parker knew all too well that the production process for any of his plays inevitably involved, from his perspective, a fair amount of sitting around 'waiting for the house of cards to collapse'. No amount of experience induced him to accept this chronic uncertainty with equanimity, however—especially since the house of cards *did* collapse as often as not. Events concerning *Lost Belongings* in late 1985 and early 1986 forcibly reminded Parker of the precariousness of the dramatist's lot. Parker had drafted all six scripts by the end of July, and the Primetime Television producer, David Elstein, had pronounced himself 'delighted' with them. Representatives from Channel Four also appeared to be satisfied, and Jim Goddard still wanted to direct. Even before finishing the final script, however, Parker had received the 'slightly disquieting news' that RTÉ, which had been planning to co-produce the films with Primetime and Channel Four, might have trouble coming up with its share of the production money. Persistent doubts on this score had, by late August, caused the postponement of pre-production until October. This tentative start date was further revised in September, when Goddard informed his collaborators that he could not begin until the end of January. In December, however, on top of the ongoing budget crisis, Goddard's agent announced that he would not now be free until late summer. Parker knew at once this meant 'the end of that highly satisfactory arrangement', since filming would have to be underway by then in order to finish it before the days got prohibitively short. Now Elstein needed to find and hire another director capable of dealing with the intricacies of the scripts and their Northern Irish context and available at once to start work on a gigantic project that would take the better part of a year to complete.[43]

At least half a dozen directors turned down *Lost Belongings* in January and February 1986. The necessity of spending several months on location in Ireland did not strike most of them as an attractive part of the offer (the one director who did seem seriously tempted was forbidden by his wife to take the job). Parker found this search nerve-wracking but did not lose his composure until the end of January, when he learned that Elstein would be leaving Primetime to become Director of Programmes at Thames Television, effective April Fool's Day. 'So not only do I lack a director for *Lost Belongings*, I am now about to lose the producer', Parker noted hopelessly in his journal. Elstein promised to 'get a contract producer, seal the whole package before leaving', but Parker believed that 'the hazards have now grown huge & menacing'.[44]

Elstein proved as good as his word, though, hiring Barry Hanson to produce the films for Primetime. For over a decade, both at BBC Birmingham and at Thames, Hanson had been at the 'cutting edge' of British television drama, evincing a particular interest in regional and political writing and working on projects that challenged the naturalistic conventions and accepted subject-matter of ambitious television plays and films. Despite his new producer's appropriate credentials, Parker remained on tenterhooks through February and into March, as Hanson reported that 'every director in the country apparently is tied up' and shared his worries about Elstein's budget deal. After such conversations, Parker felt crippled with 'angst, & fears for the project's survival'.[45]

This suspense regarding *Lost Belongings* sapped Parker's energy and attention at a time when he badly needed to focus on the play about Dion Boucicault which he had contracted to provide for the Birmingham Repertory Theatre. Back in January 1985, director Peter Farago had scheduled *Heavenly Bodies* for April/May 1986. Owing to the press of other work, however, Parker did not begin researching the play until mid-September. He had been thinking about Boucicault since the spring of 1976, when he conceived the idea of treating the playwright's story dramatically, but now he felt compelled to find out all he could about his life and contexts. In the midst of all the research he thought necessary as a prelude to writing, Parker knew he must not lose sight of the central question, wondering in his journal, 'What is the play?'[46]

Boucicault had been creating controversy for nearly 150 years.[47] While he lived, his arrogance, extravagance, voracious sexual appetite, and vulgar success kept him well-supplied with enemies; since his death he had been slighted or reviled as often as celebrated. Having begun by writing comedies of manners like his first hit, *London Assurance* (1841), in the tradition of Restoration dramatists such as George Farquhar, he soon discerned that the audience of his day responded more favourably to coarser fare. During most of his half-century career, in the course of which he was responsible for over 150 works for the stage, starring in many of them, Boucicault squandered his considerable talent as a playwright to give the public what it wanted. He often adapted or pirated popular melodramas and farces, usually improving on what he borrowed—in this respect, if in no other, he deserved his appellation of 'The Irish Shakespeare'. In addition to stealing other people's plots, he plagiarized himself (as in *The Poor of New York*, *The Poor of Liverpool*, *The Poor of Leeds*, *The Streets of Manchester*, *The Streets of London*, and *The Streets of Dublin*, all variations on the same French melodrama, with local details changed). Most of Boucicault's original plays hinged more on special effects and sensation scenes than on subtle character development. He reigned supreme in the English-speaking theatre of the mid-nineteenth century, but theatre historians generally regard the Victorian era as a desert, and most of Boucicault's plays went out of fashion before he died in 1890.

Despite the derivative nature of most of his drama, though, Boucicault was a theatrical innovator who set precedents that continued to benefit twentieth-century playwrights like Parker. As a dramatist, he demanded, and won, a share of the theatre's gross receipts. As a manager, he challenged the predominance of the triple-bill, replacing it with one major play; helped end the custom of half-price admission after nine o'clock, which had made theatres into havens for the unrulier elements of society; inaugurated the practice of professional play-direction, sending well-prepared companies to perform his plays on tour; and introduced fire-proof scenery and other technical improvements. As an actor, he held advanced views, advising acting students to pay more attention to the proceedings on stage than to the audience.

For Parker and other Irish dramatists, his predecessor's achievement also had a local dimension. Boucicault was born in Dublin and, although he left Ireland in his youth and returned only occasionally, David Krause in the mid-1960s defended his claim to have 'invented the Irish drama'. The Anglo-Irish playwrights whose work Boucicault emulated in his first scripts had written within an English dramatic tradition for English audiences, setting their dramas in England with mostly English characters. Boucicault departed from this approach in his three most successful Irish plays—*The Colleen Bawn* (1860), *Arrah-na-Pogue* (1864), and *The Shaughraun* (1874)—which were set in Ireland, focused on Irish characters, and made liberal use of colloquial Irish speech. Parker regarded these three comedy-melodramas as 'full-blooded narratives in which the conventions of melodrama are simultaneously respected and subverted by a sly humour'. In them, he later wrote, 'Boucicault's few but precious original qualities as writer and actor joined forces with his (even fewer) admirable qualities as a man.... Like many Irish writers before and after him, he had tumbled headlong out of the country at an early age, only to find his imagination eventually returning there for its truest inspiration.' These works by Boucicault in turn inspired later Irish playwrights, such as Wilde, Shaw, Synge, and O'Casey, who acknowledged his theatrical power by imitating his stagecraft whether they respected him or not.[48]

Krause drew particular attention to Boucicault's revision of the hoary stereotype of the stage Irishman. This he revalued

> by making his Irishman the clever and attractive central character in a play set in Ireland, in which the absurd Englishman, or Anglo-Irishman, makes a fool of himself.... To be sure he is a blathering rogue, a cheerful liar with a powerful thirst, but he is also a liberated playboy who cavorts outside the ordinary restraints of society, a picaresque clown who ingeniously rights all wrongs with an instinctive sense of justice and bonhomie.[49]

For this reason, perhaps, Boucicault's Irish plays met with the approval of Irish audiences and critics in his time. As a celebrity, Boucicault became an increasingly outspoken Irish nationalist who used his popularity to put pressure on the British government for the release of Fenian prisoners, set *Arrah-na-Pogue* during the 1798 rebellion, made an escaped Fenian the hero of *The Shaughraun*, and, in *The Fireside Story of Ireland* (1881), described the English colonization with straightforward indignation.

Parker's initial interest in his forebear owed mainly to the preposterous 'plot' of Boucicault's life. Obscure origins; a play-writing career launched by a case of mistaken identity; early acclaim, followed by box-office failure, followed by a shameless pandering to mass tastes; a first wife dead under mysterious circumstances; an elopement; several fortunes (and theatrical empires) built and lost; innumerable affairs; a bigamous marriage in his sixties; and another shift in audience preferences that left him nearly forgotten long before his death—all this impressed Parker as drama in the raw. In a rejected proposal for a series of television plays about Boucicault which he submitted to Thames Television in November 1976, when *Spokesong* was still drawing crowds at the Kings Head, he had contended that 'few people are aware that Boucicault's life was as tumultuous, as full of comedy, pathos and improbability as the melodramas for which he became famous' and made a pitch for a television biography. Parker then envisaged six fifty-minute television plays, shot, for the most part, 'inside an actual large Victorian theatre', each 'called after a Boucicault play of the period in question' and alternating 'scenes from the life' with 'appropriate moments from the plays as they are being rehearsed or performed onstage: each commenting on the other, both stylistically and in content'.[50]

When Parker returned to Boucicault's story in the autumn of 1985, nine years had elapsed since the heady days of his own first hit in London. He could no longer regard Boucicault's career with any degree of complacency or treat it as an entertaining tale and nothing more. Examining his subject's life through the lens of his own, Parker fixed on three interconnected issues: Boucicault's relation to the dramatic tradition, to Ireland, and to the age in which he lived. Boucicault, as he put it in early notes towards the play, possessed the '[s]oul of an artist & a nationalist' but 'sold out to the show business: fame & wealth'. Parker had been struggling for years to remain true both to his artistic vision and to his country, and he had paid for his integrity. *Nightshade* and *Pratt's Fall* had never achieved the degree of exposure he wanted for them. *Northern Star*, which Parker regarded as his best play by far, had yet to be produced outside Ireland, and he acknowledged to himself the unlikelihood of its being adequately appreciated anywhere apart from Northern Ireland. Meanwhile, *Blue Money* and *Radio Pictures*, his least ambitious works for television, had brought him popularity unprecedented in his experience, and the unused screenplay he wrote for *Eat the Peach* (the idea for which had not originated with him) had earned Parker several times more money than *Northern Star* ever would. He also perceived a parallel between the materialism, sentimentality, and brutality of the Victorian period and the atmosphere of the 'Thatcherite eighties' in which he was living.[51] Boucicault's choices, amusingly remote no more, had come to seem painfully immediate.

As Parker began to think seriously about the form his play should take, he remained fond of his original conception of juxtaposing events from Boucicault's life with scenes from his plays. He felt overwhelmed, however, by the amount of material, from both the life and the work, from which he had to choose. As he had done in *I'm a Dreamer Montreal*, *Joyce in June*, and *Lost Belongings*, he wished to undergird Boucicault's story with a classical or mythological narrative, and he remained at an impasse until he decided which legend to use. The answer came to him in mid-September: Faust.[52] His Boucicault would be a talented playwright who had sold his soul into show business in exchange for worldly success. After doing some reading on early nineteenth-century theatre, Parker also decided that the play should be a burletta, or play with musical accompaniment, rather than a musical (as he and Farago had anticipated). He planned to include some songs, but sought to keep the feel of the piece authentically Victorian. It was probably at this juncture, as he thought about songs for the play and searched for a Mephistopheles character, that Parker recalled Johnny Patterson.

Patterson, billed as 'the Irish singing clown', was a popular circus performer who, though twenty years younger than Boucicault, died within a year of him.[53] Like Boucicault, he enjoyed a transatlantic reputation and received credit in his lifetime for improving the public opinion of Irishness, mixing colloquial expressions in Irish and English and dressing in a neat tweed costume with embroidered shamrocks on the sleeves and legs and a Celtic harp on the chest. He wrote all his own songs, some of which—'The Stone Outside Dan Murphy's Door', 'Bridget Donahue', 'The Hat My Father Wore' (adapted by the Orange Lodges as 'The Sash My Father Wore')—retained their popularity long after he had been forgotten. Parker had first heard about him in the spring of 1976, around the time he became interested in Boucicault, when Jimmy Kennedy, who had composed the music for *Spokesong*, suggested that they should collaborate on a musical about Patterson's life. He had passed on the project, and Kennedy had since died without completing it.

Parker had never forgotten Patterson's story, though, and adding it to Boucicault's provided just the catalyst he needed. The introduction of Patterson, who came from a rural Catholic background, allowed Parker to explore aspects of nineteenth-century Irish life alien to the urban Protestant Boucicault. His inclusion also serves to remind audiences that, as Krause points out, even the 'legitimate' theatre in which Boucicault began his career resembled 'a marathon variety show and three-ring circus'. Throughout his writing career, he had to contend with 'the taste of an audience…conditioned to triple-bill extravaganzas'. Patterson may have been a character in *Heavenly Bodies* before Parker decided to make him Boucicault's chief antagonist, but by the end of November Parker had determined that 'the play must be an impassioned debate between Patterson & Boucicault w/ the latter's place in posterity hinging on the outcome'.[54]

For his characterization of Patterson, Parker relied on the patchy information supplied to him by one of Kennedy's friends in 1977 and on his own imagination, using bits of the clown's story that suited his purposes and making no attempt to find out more about the historical Patterson. Parker knew of three differing accounts of Patterson's death, for instance. In one version, Patterson died of pneumonia after catching a bad cold; in the second he had a heart attack. In the third version, Patterson, having concluded that loyalists and nationalists should unite behind the Home Rule movement, composed a song entitled 'Do Your Best For One Another', which he performed with a miniature flag in each hand, one red with a crown on it and the other green with a harp. During Patterson's performance of this song one night in Tralee, a sectarian dispute broke out among audience members; in the ensuing riot he was struck over the head with an iron bar, and a few days later he died. Parker, naturally, favoured this variant.

The main action of *Heavenly Bodies* begins two days before Boucicault's death and opens on the stage of the Madison Square Theatre in New York City, where the ageing playwright is listening to a student declaim a speech from his own adaptation of the Faust legend. After Boucicault dismisses his acting class, another student reads Patterson's obituary to him. When the dramatist is left alone, Patterson's ghost appears from below the stage in a cloud of smoke, singing 'Do Your Best For One Another'. Expanding on the Faust motif, Patterson announces that he has come to collect on the devil's side of the bargain; Boucicault has reaped fame and fortune during his life, and now it is time for him to retire to the 'dark little limbo' reserved for him. Boucicault demands a review of his case, and the play consists largely of a series of flashbacks to Boucicault's career, with Patterson arguing that there is no essential difference between the two of them—they are both Irish clowns who belong together in a 'dark and dacent corner of obscurity'—while Boucicault maintains that he is a 'poet' deserving of a heavenly rest. In the course of the play, Boucicault must convince Patterson (and the audience) that *something* in his voluminous output partakes of the immortality of art. Throughout, Parker's Boucicault is a realistic portrayal of the historical figure, while Patterson (literally the devil's advocate) delivers speeches in a distinctly Parkeresque mode.[55]

Boucicault blames the Age for his failings, echoing the views of the real Boucicault, who suggested in 'The Decline of the Drama' (1877) that 'drama is the necessary product of the age in which it lives, and of which it is the moral, social, and physical expression'. Explaining why he gave up his dream of becoming a latter-day Farquhar, Parker's Boucicault cries, 'I was writing comedy of manners for a people who [had] passed beyond manners, beyond comedy. A New Age on the rise, oh yes...a New Dark Age of blood force...what entertainment does such an age demand, do you suppose?' The answer, of course, is melodrama, and Boucicault was kept busy honouring his bond to provide 'the beast' with 'lust, greed and sadism framed around with hearts and flowers'. Patterson allows that Boucicault is 'a walking testimonial to those values which have made our Victorian Age a golden one—plunder, greed, hypocrisy, cynicism, pious self-righteousness'.[56]

Throughout the play, the question of Boucicault's integrity is tied to that of his loyalty to his native country. The historical Boucicault largely left his Irishness behind in his drive for success. He was also, most likely, illegitimate, and Parker draws a dramatic parallel between Boucicault's ambiguous parentage and his ambivalent relationship with Ireland. Available evidence suggests that Boucicault's biological father was Dr Dionysius Lardner, a lecturer at Trinity College famous for his 134-volume *Cabinet Cyclopedia* and for his ludicrous public challenges to contemporary inventors and engineers. Dion Boucicault, who knew Lardner as his guardian, took after him in his libido, prolific output, and insatiable hunger for publicity. Sensitive on the subject of his paternity, however, Boucicault always regarded his mother's husband, wine merchant Samuel Smith Boursiquot, as his real father. Samuel Boursiquot ceased to live with his wife when Dion was about eight years old, and Parker draws an analogy in *Heavenly Bodies* between Boucicault's lost father and his lost Fatherland.[57]

Parker had learned from a conversation in late October 1985 with Boucicault's great-grandson, Christopher Calthrop, that Samuel Boursiquot played the violin. From this hint he created the Phantom Fiddler, who wanders on and off stage, providing melancholy musical accompaniment to moments of betrayal. The Phantom Fiddler represents not only Boucicault's 'legitimate' father but his own potent sense of dispossession. In Parker's notes for the play, he imagines Boucicault 'setting out to avenge himself on the world, for being illegitimate, for being Irish'. The problem with this, as Patterson points out, is that it is a purely selfish programme.

Boucicault spent the worst years of Ireland's Great Famine of the 1840s in Paris, looking for new plays to purloin for the London stage. Patterson calls him to account for this at the end of Act I, when he takes possession of the stage with a song from his own repertoire, 'The Garden Where the Praties Grow', which he intersperses with an account of the first time he performed the piece, before an audience of Famine exiles in England. The act ends with Patterson manhandling Boucicault onto the trap and the two descending together. He appears to have proved his point: Boucicault was a mere leech, 'a licensed song and dance man' of the British Empire that bled Ireland dry. Patterson implies that *his* ambition, more modest than Boucicault's, had been to entertain and comfort his own, Irish, people.[58]

After the interval, however, the audience discovers that the two men have returned for another round. The question that dominates Act II concerns the value of Boucicault's three famous Irish plays. Boucicault argues that he has done more for the Irish cause than Patterson has, citing his popularization of a rewritten version of 'The Wearing of the Green', his agitation and fund-raising on behalf of Fenian prisoners, and his frequent consultations with members of the Irish Party in Parliament, but Patterson dismisses these activities as bids for attention. 'I can understand your bitterness', Boucicault airily remarks; 'The same people who slaughtered you showered me with honours.' 'Sure, why wouldn't they?' Patterson retorts:

> You flattered the daylights out of them, with your silver-tongued charming peasant rascals, and all their winning, wheedling, conniving ways...you conjured up a never-never emerald island, fake heroics and mettlesome beauties and villains made of paste-board, outwitted through eternity by the bogus grinning peasant rogue as only you could play him—with the blather and codology and the gaslight moonshine.

'[W]ho the blazes are you to talk,' Boucicault bursts out; 'you offered them the same thing!' At this, a stage direction notes, 'PATTERSON *slowly smiles*'—Boucicault has inadvertently conceded his antagonist's major contention that there is no aesthetic distinction to be made between them.[59]

Now it truly seems that Boucicault has exhausted his case, but two days later, on his deathbed, he begs Patterson for one last scene: the wake from *The Shaughraun*, in which Conn attends his send-off by pretending to be dead. This scene, which Parker's Boucicault describes as 'the finest... of my career', is interrupted in *The Shaughraun* by the entrance of Captain Molineux, who informs the mourners that Conn's friend the Fenian prisoner has been pardoned, thus eliminating the need for Conn's masquerade. In *Heavenly Bodies*, the scene is played as Boucicault wrote it up to Molineux's entrance, at which point Parker rewrites his announcement: 'If any words could put life into him, I came here to speak them. A reprieve has been granted! A heavenly abode is prepared for him in spite of all!' 'I'm prepared to stretch a point', Patterson admits indulgently: 'It was a tidy little scene all right, that wake.'[60]

Heavenly Bodies ends with a spectacle Boucicault himself might have devised. An organ peals while the backdrop opens onto a vision of the night sky. Boucicault, bed and all, is drawn towards heaven, while the mourners from the wake fall on their knees and an angelic choir begins to sing. As music, singing, and bed approach their zenith, however, water suddenly pours in from the ceiling and Patterson gets the last word: 'Ah, holy God, isn't that just typical? The heavens open, and what happens?—the rain comes through the bloody roof!'[61]

Parker researched Boucicault's career and nineteenth-century theatre during September and most of October 1985. In addition to work in the London Library, his usual haunt, he spent several days examining and copying material held in Special Collections at the University of Kent in Canterbury. He read more than twenty of Boucicault's plays, along with *The Fireside Story of Ireland* and several of Boucicault's essays. He studied accounts of Boucicault by his contemporaries, as well as books on the playwright and his context by scholars, and he met Richard Fawkes, Boucicault's biographer, and Boucicault's great-grandson, who both supplied him with useful details. In 1968, Parker had expressed reservations regarding a play about Jonathan Swift which he believed took liberties with the facts. 'I feel rather strongly', he wrote, 'that historical plays (or novels) written today ought to be factually accurate—the interpretation of the facts is, of course, another matter.' Nothing in the intervening years had changed his views on this score. 'The horrible truth', he confessed, 'may be that I'm a pedant at heart.'[62]

One of the biggest challenges Parker faced in writing *Heavenly Bodies* involved selecting from this mass of material details that would convey the essence of Boucicault's life and times to an audience he could not assume knew anything of substance about either—and not just convey them, but comment upon them in a manner distinctively his own. The same task had faced him in the days when he wrote twenty-minute radio scripts for the Schools department of BBC Northern Ireland for programmes like *Today and Yesterday in Northern Ireland*, and he had undertaken similar processes of research, synthesis, analysis, and exposition more recently in plays such as *Joyce in June* and *Northern Star*. The difficulty of the enterprise seemed to be on an entirely different scale this time, though. Excessive in every way, Boucicault resisted confinement to one coherent narrative, and Parker felt honour-bound to incorporate the contradictions in his character. His desire to include passages from Boucicault's plays in counterpoint to the biographical elements of the play further complicated the job of writing it.

Personal factors also interfered with Parker's ability to muster the effort necessary to write this play. He had spent the first seven months of 1985 working flat-out on the scripts for *Lost Belongings*, and his energy reserves were dangerously depleted as a result. Moving house, the ruckus over *Eat the Peach*, the production and transmission of *Radio Pictures*, the writing of the POW treatment, the tour of *Northern Star*, and the protracted attempt to mount a commercial production of *Pratt's Fall*, which ended disappointingly around the time Parker finished drafting Act I of *Heavenly Bodies*, all took their toll, too. In early September, Parker's old friend Michael Heffernan had died of heart failure at the age of 38—a forceful reminder, as if he needed one, of his own mortality. Worn-out and despondent, he kept a wary eye on his mental and physical health as the year neared its end. 'Exhaustion is clearly not far away these days,' he observed in his journal on 4 November, 'and I'm terrified of being entirely overcome by it.' Already fighting what he termed in mid-December 'the low-ebb, irritable stasis which keeps recurring at intervals', Parker found his progress on the script of *Heavenly Bodies* threatened anew by the crisis over *Lost Belongings* in the early months of 1986.[63] Still he ploughed on, producing a first draft between the end of October 1985 and the beginning of February 1986.

During February and March, as director Peter Farago tried to put the rest of the production together, Parker rewrote the script. Heartened by the commitment of the Birmingham Repertory Theatre to producing the play in an appropriately extravagant manner and by the contributions of the composer, Jim Parker, and the set designer, Saul Radomsky, he reacted with mounting anxiety to Farago's reports of difficulties on the casting front. By the middle of March, Sam Dale (one of the leading actors from the television version of *Catchpenny Twist*) had agreed to play Patterson, to Parker's satisfaction. Casting Boucicault proved harder. Parker had hoped for Tim Curry; when Curry turned out to be unavailable, he approached Simon Callow, who declined the role. David Suchet liked the part but was not in a position to take it. About three weeks and three additional Boucicault prospects later, Parker had concluded that 'we have lost all possibility of the play being properly demonstrated, & of [its] having a larger life'.[64]

As a further half dozen actors, none of whom fitted Parker's image of Boucicault, were approached without success and the date that rehearsals should have begun came and went, Parker fought on with revisions to Act II. In his journal he labelled this 'One of those periods when you wonder why you go on doing it.' By St Patrick's Day the casting crisis had reached 'a very high level of blood pressure'— all too literally, as Parker discovered when he went to the doctor a few days later complaining of singing in his ears. Finally, on 21 March, Farago cast Timothy Spall as Boucicault. Parker thought Spall 'as wrong as possible' for the part but admitted to basing this impression 'on the slobbish parts I've seen him do on TV'. In any case, he could hardly object now to any warm-blooded actor. Two days later, he finished revising the script at last, ending that stage of this 'insane ordeal'. He had already 'lost faith in it'.[65]

Heavenly Bodies went into rehearsal the next day, and Parker shifted into production mode, quickly deciding that the potential existed for a good show, though the time to realize it had become 'perilously short'. He attended most of the rehearsals, in London and then in Birmingham, and Farago involved him fully, allowing him to give notes to the actors and even to direct on occasion. Upon closer acquaintance, he found Spall 'biddable', although he did not believe the actor ever figured out how to make Boucicault larger than life without tipping over into caricature. Dale came on 'great guns', and the ten actors playing the other fifty-seven parts 'hung on to everything' Farago and Parker gave them. The four weeks of rehearsal passed in a blur, with Parker feeling his usual total investment in the proceedings until the play opened on 22 April.[66]

The reviews, however, dropped him back into the 'Slough of despond.' Martin Cropper suggested in *The Times* that Parker had 'succumbed fatally to the equivocal charm of his subjects' and that the 'theatricality' of the piece remained 'self-conscious and rather flat, much in the manner of a run-of-the-mill showbiz story'. B. A. Young of the *Financial Times* puzzled over the fact that 'The real Johnny had nothing to do with Boucicault', informing readers that 'he is introduced as a commentary on Boucicault's Irish character, a reference perhaps clearer to the Irish than to me'. John Peter, absurdly, asserted in the *Sunday Times* that Boucicault's life had been inherently 'undramatic', but it was Michael Ratcliffe's review in the *Observer* ('a prizewinner for arrogance, omniscience, condescension') that tipped Parker over the edge of 'an abyss of fresh anguish, bewilderment, impotent rage'. Parker, Ratcliffe wrote, 'is even more interested in the way things are said than in anything he might have to say. His talents, instincts and intentions are at present at odds with themselves.' If Parker had 'a critical but sympathetic editor on his next play', he predicted, 'something good would emerge'.[67]

Parker wanted to believe that the indifferent reception of *Heavenly Bodies* could be explained by inadequacies in the acting that had caused 'the hacks' to miss out on 'the play's voice', but after attending a performance midway through the run he admitted to himself that 'the script needs a lot of work'. Part of the problem, Lesley Bruce recounts, was simply that the play had been written too close to being produced, so that Parker could not see trouble-spots clearly until it was too late to do anything about them. Nearly three hours long in performance, the script produced in Birmingham incorporated so many excerpts from Boucicault's own works for the stage that, as Ann FitzGerald observed in *The Stage and Television Today*, 'it felt occasionally as though we weren't spared any of them'. Parker ultimately found Cropper's assertion that the play 'could do with drastic trimming' hard to dispute, and he later revised his script to eliminate inessential characters and scenes, focus the action more tightly on the play's central question of Boucicault's enduring aesthetic worth, and streamline the dialogue.[68]

In the immediate aftermath of the *Heavenly Bodies* production, though, Parker was too overcome by a 'colossal sadness' even to consider undertaking any stage writing that he had not already promised to do. As he looked back over the past five years, his experience in the theatre appeared to him as a succession of 'catastrophes'. Less than three weeks after the final performance of the play in Birmingham, Nicolas Kent of the Tricycle Theatre told Parker that an autumn co-production of *Northern Star* looked less and less likely from his perspective but invited him to 'suggest ideas for a new play'. Parker responded in terms that afford insight into his state of mind: 'I feel, reluctantly, that it is probably more sensible and realistic if we don't enter into any agreement for a new play for 1987. The truth is that over the past month or two, I have been seriously mulling whether to give up play writing once my obligations to the National & Field Day are fulfilled—if not for good, then at least for a year or two.' Privately, he worried that more than his appetite for work might be at stake, confiding to his journal his fear that his 'equilibrium' remained 'dangerously frail' and his conviction that 'I have got to build a stronger, stable centre, somehow, otherwise I may destroy everything I value.'[69]

14

Last Words

In May 1986, after the production of *Heavenly Bodies* in Birmingham had 'come and gone like a brief, bad dream', Stewart Parker more or less decided to give up writing for the stage once he had fulfilled his outstanding commitments. '[L]ow in energy & spirits', he feared the loss of a sustaining sense of purpose. At this critical juncture, his mentor John Malone came to his rescue yet again, this time from beyond the grave. Malone, still hard at work directing the Schools Support Service (a staff and curriculum development project) from his office in the Department of Further Professional Studies in Education at Queen's University, had died of a coronary on 14 February 1982. Some of his friends and colleagues established a series of annual lectures in his memory and in July 1985 had invited Parker to deliver a lecture the following spring expounding 'some dimension' of his 'view of education'. Now, with the appointed date barely ten days away, he began working in earnest on his presentation. The completed lecture, entitled *Dramatis Personae*, is the fullest and most theoretical account Parker ever gave of his motivation and aims as a dramatist. The following year, he would apply the precepts laid out here in his last stage play, *Pentecost.*[1]

In preparation for the occasion, Parker recorded in a notebook his most vivid memories of Malone, reflecting in the lecture itself that 'I have no recollection whatsoever of John Malone's formal teaching of English during my two years at Ashfield.' Parker did remember, though, that Malone had cast him as Everyman in Ashfield's first school play and that he had once allowed him to perform magic tricks for his class-mates: 'In his openness and sensitivity to my own blind, gawky, fledgling creative impulses,' Parker declared, 'he succeeded in teaching me...that there is a necessary and vital polarity in drama: between *Everyman* and sleight of hand, between the Four Last Things and the three card trick, between poetry and patter, art and showbusiness.' Recalling Malone's attitude towards drama as 'the most natural form of education', a means of teaching every other school subject in addition to being an object of study itself, Parker said he concurred—'if for the word Drama we substitute the word Play'. Citing the Dutch philosopher Johan Huizinga's theory that 'civilization itself arises and unfolds in and as play', Parker argued that 'Play is how we test the world and register its realities. Play is how we experiment, imagine, invent, and move forward. Play is above all how we enjoy the earth and celebrate our life upon it.' He thought it no coincidence that 'this fundamental animal instinct, this self-sufficient force shaping the very evolution of human society, should share its name with those works of fiction which are presented by actors before an audience': 'the stage play, the screenplay, the radio and television play—these are merely particular and local forms of the play force, consciously shaped, fashioned by human imagination and usage into a highly sophisticated kind of game'.[2]

After speculating that Malone himself probably favoured didactic drama, Parker posed the rhetorical questions of whether or not plays should 'aim to instruct'—and, if so, how they could. In positing answers, he described twentieth-century drama as ranging between two poles: one represented by the 'Marxist missionary' Bertolt Brecht, the other by Samuel Beckett, 'an agnostic monk' whose 'work displays not the slightest inclination to teach or instruct anybody about anything'. Beckett and Brecht seem to share little in their approach to play-writing, but Parker identified a surprising commonality between them. Both believed in fun. Brecht wrote, 'From the first it has been the theatre's business to entertain people.... it needs no other passport than fun, but this it has got to have'. Parker saw Beckett's 'exercise of the play faculty' as even 'more thoroughgoing than Brecht's'. 'Beckett's vision', he contended, 'illumines our inner life, the life of the spirit in the nuclear age, and it does so by means of play. It exercises the very faculty in us which it dramatises in its characters', becoming thereby 'a civilising force'. Beckett's Theatre of the Absurd (which Parker would rename Theatre of the Ludicrous) could thus be 'characterised, in the broadest sense, as a form of education'.[3]

Brecht and Beckett, Parker believed, 'offer a formidable choice and challenge' to later playwrights. The influence of each remained inescapable, 'yet neither offers a clear road ahead'. In the final section of his lecture, Parker brought his musings home. 'What should drama be aiming to do in this society at this time?' he asked. 'Am I in any sense in the business of education?' He averred that his body of work constituted 'self-education for me rather than any kind of tutorial for the audience'. Nevertheless, 'my most fervent desire for them, once they're written, is that they give the audience a great night out, or in, as the case may be. They are in search of the truth and they aspire towards entertainment.' Considered together, his plays comprised a record of his 'personal quest for inclusiveness, for synthesis'.[4]

'A playwright', Parker continued, 'should aim to be a truth-teller, a sceptic in a credulous world, but there has to be also an element of the medium in his make-up':

> He becomes possessed by other voices, both divine and diabolic, and they must be given their say: voices generated by the energy emanating from an intense moment of conflict, in a time and place, though the time and place is always here and now during performance. All plays are ghost plays. They issue forth and take their shape from a conflict within the writer himself, often a wrestling match between the soothsayer and the medium, mind and intuition. The most shapely plays emerge when the antagonists wrestle each other to a draw.[5]

Northern Ireland had been throughout Parker's play-writing career a site of such conflict, and he acknowledged the 'traps and snares' of writing 'about and from within this particular place and time'—chief among these the fact that the 'raw material of drama is over-abundant here, easy pickings'. Mirroring life during the

Troubles without reflecting adequately upon it amounted, in Parker's opinion, to 'artistic abdication': 'Art amplifies and distorts, seeking to alter perceptions to a purpose. A play which reinforces complacent assumptions, which confirms lazy preconceptions, which fails to combine emotional honesty with coherent analysis, which goes in short for the easy answer, is in my view actually harmful.'[6]

Playwrights prepared to apply both intellect and imagination to the subject of the North, however, would find the work absorbing as well as challenging. The stakes were high because 'if ever a time and place cried out for the solace and rigour and passionate rejoinder of great drama, it is here and now. There is a whole culture to be achieved.' 'Drama', Parker argued,

> can contain the conflicts and contradictions, the cruelty and the killings, the implacable ghosts, the unending rancour, pettiness and meanness of spirit, the poverty of imagination and evasion of truth which unites our two communities in their compact of mutual impotence and sterility—all in a single image. Within that same single frame, it can demonstrate and celebrate a language as wholesome and nutritious as a wheaten farl, a stony wit and devious humour, an experiential vivacity and whole-heartedness, a true instinct for hospitality and generosity, which also and equally unite our two communities.[7]

Thinking of his own *Northern Star* and of Frank McGuinness's *Observe the Sons of Ulster Marching Towards the Somme*, which he had seen in Belfast in November 1985 and admired, Parker acknowledged that Ulster playwrights had already accomplished a 'certain amount': 'Alternative versions of the historical myths sacred to each of the communities have been staged: not in a spirit of mockery but in a spirit of realism, and out of a desire to substitute vibrant and authentic myths for the false and destructive ones on which we have been weaned.' The next step, he proposed, would be to 'cease the task of picking over the entrails of the past, and begin to hint at a vision of the future'. Contemplating, perhaps, the play he had yet to write for the Field Day Theatre Company, he postulated that the new responsibility of serious dramatists would be 'to find a belief in the future, and to express it with due defiance in the teeth of whatever gory chaos may meanwhile prevail'. Such work, 'neither didactic nor absurdist', would 'aim to inspire rather than to instruct, to offer ideas and attitudes in a spirit of critical enquiry', and 'to assert the primacy of the play-impulse over the deathwish'. 'For those of us who find ourselves writing from within a life-experience of this place, at this time,' he concluded, 'the demands could not be more formidable or more momentous.'[8]

Fortified by this return to fundamentals, Parker turned to the production of *Lost Belongings*, finally moving into high gear. In April, producer Barry Hanson had hired Tony Bicât to direct the series. Bicât, better known as a writer than as a director (although he always directed his own work), had been interested in the project even before Hanson agreed to take it on. The two men had worked together on Bicât's film *Christmas Present*, and Hanson mentioned in conversation that he might produce a film series by Stewart Parker. Bicât liked Parker's television work— 'plays where farce and tragedy existed only a breath apart'—and knew they shared an agent, so he asked Marc Berlin for a copy of *Lost Belongings* to read, mainly out of curiosity. Taken by the sweep and variety of the scripts, Bicât found himself, unexpectedly, yearning to direct them. Hanson tried to dissuade him, pointing out that the finance would probably fall through (which, in due course, much of it did), but Bicât's enthusiasm helped convince Hanson to commit himself to the enterprise. Bicât did not get the directing job, however, until the final director on the 'A-list' had turned it down.[9]

Bicât initially struck Parker as 'pleasant enough', but 'slow and waffly, & virtually characterless'. 'Tony's very quiet', he observed doubtfully to Berlin, finding him not at all 'like a Director'. Bicât spent two days at the beginning of the production process listening to Hanson and Parker read the scripts aloud at his request while he read the screen directions and made queries. 'Crackpot idea', Parker fumed in his journal, but Bicât's determination to understand at the outset what the playwright meant to convey signified his intention to treat *Lost Belongings* with the same respect as if he had written it. He had no ambition to express himself through the films or to change anything significant, seeking only to realize Parker's vision and confident that his own 'almost total ignorance of Ireland and "The Troubles"' would help him translate this to a general audience. A writer himself, Bicât considered Parker's desire to take part in the making of the series an asset, and the idea of having the playwright around during filming did not intimidate him. Parker might have wished at first for a director with a greater aura of authority, but he came to appreciate Bicât's four-square fidelity as a different sort of virtue, commenting after the fact that everyone involved with *Lost Belongings* had been 'making the same movie; a much rarer state of affairs than it may sound'.[10]

Throughout the winter and most of the spring of 1986, though, it appeared doubtful that anyone would be making any movie. RTÉ, which had pledged to provide one-third of the production money, turned out to be disturbingly reluctant to hand any of it over. Channel Four was not prepared to bear the whole financial burden of producing the series, and things remained at an impasse for months, with Hanson, unsure what sort of budget he would have, delaying hiring key personnel. Bicât demonstrated in this period that what he lacked in panache he made up for in persistence. Knowing they must begin filming by July to complete the shoot before the days became uneconomically short, he proceeded as if the start date were fixed, leaving the money worries to Hanson. He stayed in touch with Parker and shuttled busily between London, Belfast, and Dublin, assessing locations and interviewing actors and potential crew members. At one point, he recalls, Hanson fired him, but nobody could find him to break the news—in any case, he was re-hired that evening. The project's finances finally achieved relatively stable footing in June, when RTÉ officially withdrew from the production and Euston Films, the film division of Thames Television, stepped into the gap, probably at the behest of David Elstein.[11]

Money remained an issue, however. After a productive meeting with representatives of Euston Films in early July, Parker told Hanson he wanted to observe as much of the filming as possible and 'was taken aback by the tirade about expenses & strain on the budget which this provoked'. He suspected the production team of trying to keep him at a distance, but probably Hanson's stated concerns were his real ones. Parker had to specify which weeks he considered his presence to be indispensable and suffered agonies of frustration when he could not be on location over aspects of the performances he thought he could have improved had he been there. In all, Parker attended about eight of the sixteen weeks of filming, talking with the actors, supervising them in rehearsal when Bicât could not, advising on locations, commenting on daily rushes, and handling any needed changes to the scripts. Bicât tried to 'demystify the directing process', discussing its technical aspects with Parker. 'By the end of the shoot', he remarks, 'Stewart was convinced that he could do it himself. I'm not sure if this is a compliment.'[12]

The scope of *Lost Belongings* made producing it akin to making six very different films while striving to maintain some sense of overall coherence. For example, Alec's episode is a coming-of-age story set against the grim background of Northern Ireland in the early 1970s; the ones dominated by Hugh McBraill belong essentially to the thriller genre; Lenny's is surreal comedy. Meanwhile, the overarching narrative, Deirdre's, is a tragic love story, as well as the tale of a young girl seeking to find her place in the world by coming to terms with her haunted past. Logistical difficulties abounded. With eighty-six speaking parts, casting alone—in London, Belfast, and Dublin—required almost two months. Veteran Northern Irish actor Harry Towb accepted the part of Deirdre's uncle, and Stephen Rea agreed to play Lenny, but most of the other actors were previously unknown to Parker. Casting the young lovers, Deirdre and Niall, proved trickiest of all, since the youth of the characters dictated that the actors playing them would be relatively inexperienced. Gerard O'Hare (Niall) had made a splash earlier that year in the first production of Christina Reid's *Joyriders*, at the Tricycle, but Deirdre was the first starring role for Catherine Brennan, a teenager from the Falls Road area of Belfast, although she had appeared in several television productions in Northern Ireland. Parker and Barry Hanson met her in early April during the latter's first trip to Belfast to see locations mentioned in the scripts, but she did not land the role until nearly three months later. Parker had found her 'quite promising' in April; in a screen test in June, she impressed him with renewed force as 'fierce & vulnerable & right'.[13]

Original plans had called for the *Lost Belongings* production to be based in Dublin, and even after RTÉ dropped out this seemed sensible. Security precautions in Northern Ireland exacerbated the inherent difficulties of film-making. Also, more film production happened in the Republic than in the North, making it easier to find seasoned technical support staff there. Even most of the scenes purportedly set in Belfast were actually filmed in and around Dublin (including the sequence of McBraill escaping from the Maze Prison, recreated by the film crew out of a boatyard and the sewage works in Malahide), although the company did spend 'two precious weeks' in Belfast shooting scenes such as those set in the Ulster Museum. Attempts to add authenticity sometimes backfired, as when members of a loyalist marching band, bused down to help fill out a parade sequence, refused to participate when they realized that they would be playing alongside a Catholic band from the Republic. 'They returned without playing a note', Bicât recalls, 'after putting the Statue of the Virgin Mary in the Gents toilet.'[14]

Primetime had intended to do all production work in Ireland. When RTÉ backed out and Euston Films assumed the main production role, the latter decided to do preparation and filming in Ireland and editing in England, spending six months on each. For an entire year, Bicât lived and breathed *Lost Belongings*, discovering 'a fatigue beyond fatigue and in Ireland a rain beyond rain'. Neither of these seemed to bother the Mexican chief cameraman and director of photography, Gabriel Beristain, who enthused about Irish light and told a reporter that 'There is nothing more beautiful than when you can move the camera through real rain.' Observers commented on the 'incredibly happy aura' around the shoot, and Parker contributed to this. His aversion to early rising made full participation taxing for him, but he relished his role in the production and hated being away from it for any length of time. Throughout the second half of 1986, whether physically on location or not, Parker's thoughts remained with the cast and crew of *Lost Belongings*, and he had difficulty concentrating on any of his other projects.[15]

One that summer involved reworking *Radio Pictures* as a play for the National Theatre. Parker approached the task without excitement, unconvinced the piece had enough heft to meet the more rigorous literary standards of the stage but taking the revision as a technical challenge. The television play had relied on a great deal of inter-cutting between the actors in the studio and the production team in the cubicle, alternating these with crucial scenes set in a club and a restaurant. For the stage script, renamed *Radio Scenery*, Parker consolidated the action in two locations, the cubicle and the studio, envisaging a revolving set that would put the audience in the cubicle looking into the studio for two of the scenes and in the studio looking through the same window into the cubicle for the other two. Each act contains one scene in the cubicle and one in the studio; all the dialogue occurs in real time in one or the other of these places, although one night is understood to have passed between the two acts. The plot remains the same as in the television version, but Parker expanded the piece to stage-play length by adding extra business, which contributes little of substance.[16]

For the stage version, Parker strove to make the members of the production team more than functionaries. The cumulative effect of such changes, paradoxically, was to make the characters less believable than in their earlier incarnations. Whereas the production team in the television play had behaved more or less like an actual BBC production team—making *Radio Pictures*, as Robert Cooper had informed Parker, a cult favourite in the radio drama department—the corresponding characters in *Radio Scenery* seem, for the most part, like a bunch of incompetents. The comedy, dead-pan in the television play, becomes slapstick in the stage version. Parker worried from the start of the revision that 'the rather thin material is fast running out'. It thus came as no surprise when, several months after his September delivery of the script, Peter Hall wrote to say that, although *Radio Scenery* impressed him as a 'crisp and delightful play', none of the directors at the National wished to produce it. Despite half-hearted attempts to secure a production elsewhere, Parker never saw *Radio Scenery* on stage—but, more than the fact that his effort on the rewriting had been wasted, he regretted the time he had spent on it.[17]

Another initiative in 1986 was the writing of a feature film treatment for Barry Hanson's own production company, Telekation International Limited. Hanson had commissioned this on the understanding that he would have twelve months to try to raise development capital. If he secured finance, he could exercise his option on the property by commissioning Parker to write the screenplay. The idea for the project dated to November 1975, when Parker had read Joyce Marlow's *Captain Boycott and the Irish* and proposed a play based on it to the Joint Stock Theatre Group. Marlow's book explores in detail events of 1880 in Ireland, the year in which Irish nationalism acquired a mass following when representatives of the constitutional Home Rule movement, elements of the revolutionary Fenian movement, and large numbers of Irish peasants united (temporarily) on the land question. The Land League, founded by Michael Davitt and led by a young Charles Stewart Parnell, focused these disparate groups' combined efforts against landlordism. With its ultimate aim of peasant proprietorship and intermediate goal of land reform (fair rent, secure tenure, and compensation for tenants' improvements upon sale of land), the League appealed to a wide range of Irish public opinion. Its success in mobilizing people to agitate for radical social transformation in ways that stopped short of physical force particularly interested Parker.[18]

The Land League pioneered the use of a tactic employed by later activists, including, in Parker's lifetime, Martin Luther King, Jr. and Cesar Chávez. 'Boycotting' takes its name from Captain Charles Cunningham Boycott, a minor English landlord and agent for a larger landholder, who served as the target of the League's first well-publicized attempt to use social and economic ostracism as a political weapon. In his Joint Stock proposal, Parker had anticipated treating the episode directly, depicting the inner dynamics of the various parties to the conflict. Revisiting the material eleven years later, Parker shifted his attention from the historical events themselves to a story about the personal concerns of three imaginary characters caught up in them: William Bone, a 'gentleman of the turf' and British spy; his estranged wife Constance, an ardent Land League supporter; and Thaddeus McCoy, Bone's jockey and (unbeknownst to his employer) an unreconstructed Fenian. Parker researched and wrote his treatment for the film in November and December 1986 and revised it in January 1987, then set it aside while Hanson sought script money. In the meantime, he had more pressing concerns— including, urgently, writing the script he had promised to the Field Day Theatre Company.[19]

The first glimmerings of *Pentecost* probably came to Parker in 1982, when he lived in the flat in Golders Green filled with the possessions and permeated by the personality of its deceased former inhabitant. Parker's friend Sam Fannin remembers discussing with him at that time 'the concept of a place being haunted'. The notion put on flesh during the run of *Pratt's Fall* in Glasgow early in 1983 when Anna Davidson, a member of the cast, told Parker about a flat she had bought some years earlier, inclusive of the belongings of the family who lived in it for over fifty years. She had intended to make it her home but could not bear to discard or even to move the contents, which seemed to her to have more right to be there than she had. In 1982, consequently, she sold it to the National Trust, which planned to exhibit it as a representation of working-class life in the city during the twentieth century. Lesley Bruce recalls that the account 'enthralled' Parker, who told Davidson it dovetailed with something he already wanted to write and asked permission to use her story. After this conversation, he recorded in his notebook the idea for a piece he tentatively imagined as a stage play: 'Female antique dealer, buying whole house & contents after owner has died, increasingly obsessed by preserving it for National Trust, discovering life of the woman who'd lived there, finally burning it down deliberately.'[20]

In October 1983, Stephen Rea invited Parker to write a play for Field Day, but, as the latter recorded in his journal, 'no obvious idea' suggested itself in response. A list of current projects in Parker's notebook dated 20 February 1984 indicates that he then thought of the house story as the basis for a film with the working title 'My Old Flames'. Around this time, Rea reiterated his offer of a Field Day slot, and Parker compiled a few possibilities in his notebook: Boycott, *Radio Pictures* (as yet unproduced for television and, as far as Parker then knew, without immediate prospect of being produced), and a play he had been considering for a while about the Czech writer Jaroslav Hašek, author of *The Good Soldier Švejk*.[21] In Belfast in early March 1984, Parker met Rea, Brian Friel, and David Hammond, all members of Field Day's board of directors. Soon after this, he decided to 'work up the House idea to offer to Field Day'.[22]

Two circumstances that spring decisively influenced the final shape of *Pentecost*. First, Parker had learned the previous month that the BBC, after commissioning the pilot episode of *Lost Belongings*, had decided not to make the series, and he now believed the chance of its being produced any time soon to be so remote that he contemplated rethinking it as a novel. Second, he knew that Stephen Rea would expect to take a leading part in any play he wrote for Field Day. Parker had imagined Rea in the role of Lenny Harrigan in *Lost Belongings*. It thus made sense for him to import Lenny's story from *Lost Belongings* into his plans for the Field Day play. This depicted Lenny's adventures working as a researcher for the central BBC on a documentary about Northern Ireland and his increasingly desperate attempts to please his boss, an English lady producer named Gillian Pringle. In his proposal to the BBC for *Lost Belongings*, Parker had described Lenny's episode as being relayed mainly in flashbacks and ending with the start of the Ulster Workers' Council Strike, the politically motivated industrial action by loyalists that forced the dissolution of Northern Ireland's first power-sharing government in 1974 and which symbolized for Parker 'the beginning of the end of Britain's Sunningdale arrangements for a fair and tidy English solution to the whole mess'. The 1974 setting probably entered the Field Day play with Lenny at this juncture in the spring of 1984. Lenny Harrigan and Gillian Pringle both appear on a page of notes for the play written around this time, as does the character of a 'Visitor, returning. Architect? With sack of muesli.' 'Disputed ownership' emerges as the central theme of the play: 'The relativity of tenure. Ghost of the woman who owned it, then Lenny who has inherited it, then the woman who's buying it, and finally the two arrivals [presumably Gillian and the architect], searching for a precarious toehold, ultimately violating the sanctum.' Parker clearly regarded the house as a metaphor for Northern Ireland, and he saw this assortment of characters as 'An ad hoc family, fractured & mutinous.'[23]

The resuscitation of *Lost Belongings* in late summer 1984 also affected *Pentecost*. Field Day had wanted the play to tour in the autumn of 1985, but Parker informed Rea in January 1985 that he could not deliver a script in time and asked to post- pone the production. Parker's writing efforts from January to July 1985 focused on the five remaining scripts of *Lost Belongings*. He finished the Lenny episode in May but shifted the action into 1980, the present time of the series, probably because he now intended to include the UWC Strike in his Field Day play. He did, how- ever, use the plot line about Lenny and the English producer in his television script, which left a hole in his plans for the stage play. Around this time, another major thematic element entered Parker's thinking about the piece: the function of religion in people's lives.[24]

Partly because he had grown up in Northern Ireland, Parker had distanced him- self from organized religion since his teens. The pervasive sectarianism of the North seemed reason enough to avoid such identification. He also rejected the supernatu- ral elements of Christian dogma, believing this made Christian faith impossible for him. His sensibility remained distinctly religious, however. He listened to early church music while writing through the night, and he loved medieval religious drama and the resonant language of the King James version of the Bible. He also thought human beings needed to believe in something greater than themselves, and he perceived a void at the centre of modern, materialist conceptions of life. Plays such as *Nightshade* and *Pratt's Fall* attest to Parker's sense of the spiritual dan- ger of not confronting the existential questions. Nevertheless, he regarded himself as a secular humanist rather than as a Protestant.[25]

In 1984, watching a BBC documentary series called *The Sea of Faith*, Parker heard many of his own views on religion articulated from a surprising quarter. Don Cupitt, architect of the series and author of a book by the same title which Parker bought and read, was the Dean of Emmanuel College, Cambridge, and an Angli- can priest and radical theologian. In the name of 'religious seriousness', he sought 'the full synthesis of faith and modernity'. *The Sea of Faith* consists largely of a survey of important modern and post-modern thinkers, but Cupitt interprets their insights not as leading inevitably to atheism but, rather, as forcing Christianity to redefine itself for a new era. To stop religion from becoming irrelevant to people's daily lives, kept separate from what they really believe, he calls for the 'demytholo- gising' of Christian doctrine and the acceptance of the notion that religion is, and has always been, man-made. Our fundamental beliefs, he argues, are *chosen*, and their 'truth' has less to do with facts than with the influence they have upon the way we live. God similarly undergoes a transformation in Cupitt's 'critical spiritu- ality' from objective to subjective reality. 'The true God is not God as picturesque supernatural fact, but God as our religious ideal', Cupitt declares: '. . . every human being who is serious about existence, who is not content to drift with the crowd towards death but seeks to set himself high ideals and to make his life something of worth, must formulate his own idea of God as the unifying symbol of the life- aim to which he is devoted'. This was the conception of the deity Parker probably had in mind when he confided to Stephen Rea during the second half of 1987 that he feared he had started to believe in God again.[26]

Whether or not Parker had begun considering such a theological context for his Field Day play by the spring of 1985, he spent part of that year's Easter weekend reading *The Sea of Faith*. Cupitt's description of and prescription for the crisis facing contemporary Christianity crystallized for Parker what he already believed. Though his own philosophy was not specifically Christian, Cupitt's fundamental insight that 'What faith is shows what God is' struck a chord. Cupitt lamented that people were losing their actual faith in God 'because the available language about God has been allowed to become too narrow, stale and spiritually obsolete, and no longer functions as a satisfactory vehicle through which people can articulate their highest life-aims'. Here the theologian's concerns brushed up against the writer's 'highest life-aim', and Parker likely felt both challenged and inspired by Cupitt's related observation that humans now live in 'the age of the artist-theologian who offers us a personal vision of the religious life'. At any rate, the play he began to write in January 1987 (after more reprieves from Field Day) bears the impress of such thinking.[27]

The inclusion of religious themes shifted Parker's focus on the characters rather than transforming it, however, since religion and politics are so intertwined in Northern Ireland. Especially on the Protestant/unionist side, the most reactionary forms of religious faith, predicated on what Cupitt would call theological realism, tend to be associated with the most uncompromising political stances. Far more than doctrinal differences between Protestants and Catholics, the belief among extremists from both camps in the objective existence of a transcendent God who takes sides in human affairs factored in the Troubles. For example, Ian Paisley, an evangelical minister and long-time Moderator of the Free Presbyterian Church of Ulster, which he founded in 1951, was also a founder, in 1971, of the hard-line Democratic Unionist Party, which he would lead for over thirty years. Paisley came to prominence as a sworn enemy of ecumenism long before involving himself in secular politics. In religious terms, he was a militant fundamentalist, with close ties to American fundamentalists like Bob Jones. Many of the American churches Paisley visited and preached at through the 1960s opposed the civil rights movement and racial integration, and their views likely influenced his own belief that the cause of militant fundamentalism in Northern Ireland required the defeat of the Catholic civil rights movement that began there in the middle of that decade.[28]

Similar politico-religious ideas featured in the UWC Strike itself. The strikers' influence over the power workers of Northern Ireland, roughly 75 per cent of whom were Protestant, enabled the strike's success, and the mastermind behind the controlled run-down of electricity generation was a power station worker and union organizer from east Belfast named Billy Kelly. Kelly, a Pentecostalist, attributed his inspiration for the strike to the Bible. In a detail Parker recorded among his notes for the Field Day play, Kelly cited to a reporter several biblical references 'which he felt applied to the strike: the Book of Daniel chapters 2, 7 and 12; Ezekiel 36, 37 and 39; the second book of Thessalonians and Revelations [*sic*] chapters

3 and 15'. Recurring themes of these passages include the transience of earthly regimes and the omnipotence of God, the importance of fearing and glorifying God, God's fidelity to His chosen people, and the impending punishment of non-believers.[29]

Outraged loyalist reaction to the Anglo-Irish Agreement, announced on 15 November 1985, had reminded Parker of the atmosphere surrounding the UWC Strike in 1974. This accord represented an attempt by the British and Irish governments to reduce violence and buttress constitutional nationalists in Ireland against the republicans (making worrying electoral gains since their decision, during the hunger strikes, to contest elections while continuing to pursue their armed struggle). The Agreement affirmed that no change in the status of Northern Ireland would take place without the consent of a majority of the population; clarified that there would be no devolution of powers to the North without power-sharing; and established an Intergovernmental Conference, headed by the British Secretary of State for Northern Ireland and the Irish foreign minister and supported by civil servants from both countries, to promote cross-border cooperation and deal with security, legal, and political issues of mutual concern. This last provision, which effectively gave the Irish government an official role in Northern Ireland's affairs as a representative of the interests of the nationalist minority, united all shades of unionist opinion in opposition to the Agreement.[30]

Unionists had hardly expected such a fundamental change in British policy towards Northern Ireland to take place under the leadership of Margaret Thatcher, so unyielding in her approach to the hunger strikers a few years before, and they felt both shocked and betrayed. Two days after the Agreement was announced, Paisley led his congregation in a prayer asking the Almighty to 'deal with the Prime Minister of our country': 'O God, in wrath take vengeance upon this wicked, treacherous lying woman; take vengeance upon her, Oh Lord, and grant that we shall see a demonstration of thy power.' Not content to rely on divine intervention, he and other unionist leaders organized an impressive show of resistance. On 23 November, a crowd numbering perhaps as many as 200,000 converged on Belfast City Hall to express their rejection of the Agreement, and the slogan 'Ulster Says No' came into common use. According to historian Jonathan Bardon, 'Nothing like it had been seen since 1912.'[31]

As a direct result of the British government's unhappy experience with the UWC Strike over a decade earlier, however, the Agreement had been designed to withstand local efforts to nullify it. Unionist politicians had not been informed about the talks that led to the accord, and their involvement in its workings was neither needed nor desired. In 1974, when loyalists took industrial action against the 'Irish Dimension' of the Sunningdale Agreement, they brought down the new power-sharing Northern Ireland government by inducing the unionist members of it to resign. The Anglo-Irish Agreement pointedly excluded all Northern Irish political parties from its operations, which were presented as a matter strictly between the British and Irish governments. Unionists in the mid-1980s had no appreciable bargaining power with either of these entities; indeed, the more trouble they caused, the more justification there seemed to be for the Agreement, and their feelings of infuriated impotence pervaded Northern Ireland throughout the months during and preceding Parker's writing of *Pentecost*.

Despite their lack of leverage, unionists repeatedly expressed their discontent, but the leaders of these protests struggled to maintain discipline among the rank and file. Attempts to demonstrate dignified resolve often resulted in violence and property damage. Protesters injured thirty-eight police officers in December when the Intergovernmental Conference met for the first time, and rioting, looting, vandalism, and intimidation marred a 'day of action' against the Agreement on 3 March 1986, as well as a huge rally on its first anniversary. The head of the RUC, Northern Ireland's police force, later recalled his 'firm determination that there would not be a repeat of 1974 when the subversives and politically motivated strikes bring the whole state down'. Consequently, Bardon reports, the RUC became 'a special object of hatred' although most of its members were Protestant. By May 1986, there had been 368 reported cases of threats to police and their families, and over time hundreds of their homes were attacked.[32]

Militant republicans disliked the Agreement as much as loyalists, and the Provisional IRA also stepped up its attacks on members of the security forces and anyone who dealt with them. This left unionists feeling more embattled than ever, and the resounding defeat in the Republic, in June 1986, of a referendum to amend the constitution to allow divorce in limited cases did nothing to allay Protestant misgivings about the prospect of a united Ireland, however distant. A few weeks earlier, Paisley had called 'a day of prayer for deliverance' from the Agreement, and he took this embarrassing setback for the Irish government as proof that God had heard his appeal. The British government was certainly not listening to him—in February 1987 a petition to the Queen with 400,000 signatures demanding a referendum on the Agreement received no response. Thus, throughout the second half of the 1980s, unionists, in Bardon's words, 'felt more isolated and friendless than at any time in centuries'. The growing prominence of Paisley and the DUP, which by 1987 claimed the allegiance of nearly half of Northern Ireland's Protestants, offered one measure of unionist alienation.[33]

Although Parker set his play in 1974, he maintained in the autumn of 1987 that *Pentecost* was 'really about now, about the process started then which is continued by the Anglo-Irish Agreement. That was the beginning of the serious rift between the loyalists and the English. The beginning of the feeling of rejection on their part, and the hurt—the feeling of being lost'. Seen in this light, the relationships Parker eventually established between the characters in the play acquire added significance. Lenny, a middle-class Catholic, has inherited the house from a maiden aunt after the death of the sitting tenant, Lily Matthews, a Protestant woman who had lived in it since her marriage just after the First World War at the age of 18. Marian, the female antiques dealer buying the house from Lenny, also happens to be his estranged wife who, as a condition of the sale, must agree to finalizing their separation with a divorce. Peter, the architect returning from self-imposed exile in Birmingham to witness what he calls 'The Great Loyalist Insurrection', is a Protestant friend of Lenny's from university. For Gillian Pringle, the English BBC producer who had since found her place opposite Lenny in *Lost Belongings*, Parker

substituted Ruth, a slightly younger friend of Marian's from their days on Northern Ireland's swimming team, who has fled her abusive husband, a member of the
RUC ('You can't even begin to imagine the pressure the police are under', she tells
Marian). Lily appears as a character on stage, although only Marian can see and
hear her. With her unapologetic bigotry—she and her husband were burned out
by a Catholic mob during the sectarian strife of 1921, and her first words to Marian are 'I don't want you in my house'—she embodies the kind of working-class
unionism responsible for the UWC Strike that serves as a backdrop to the living
characters' personal crises. The house itself, 'cluttered, almost suffocated, with the
furnishings and bric-a-brac of the first half of the century', represents her 'desperate, lifelong struggle for cleanliness, tidiness, orderliness—godliness'. Fortress-like,
it lies besieged between Protestant and Catholic ghettos, as well as being under
assault from modernity itself, located as it is in the middle of a redevelopment
zone.[34]

This setting and configuration of characters obviously lend themselves to political interpretation.[35] Parker intended such meanings, but a political reading of *Pentecost* will be only a partial one. Those who view the play solely in these terms often
see its religious themes as tacked on instead of intrinsic. The ending of the play,
especially, where religious language and symbolism are most overt, struck some
early reviewers as a 'coda' rather than a 'resolution'. For Parker himself, however,
the play's spiritual dimension came to supersede the political in importance.
Around the time of the Field Day première, he told an interviewer that the house
in *Pentecost* represented the 'human soul', adding that the play featured people
caught in the void between organized religion and outright disbelief and searching
for a 'third way'. Regarded thus, the final scene represents the culmination of the
play's entire movement, in which Parker translates for the stage Cupitt's argument
about the need for a new Christian spirituality.[36]

Parker probably decided to call his Field Day play *Pentecost* shortly before he
began writing it, since the title does not appear in his notebook in association with
his earlier notes towards the script. Possibly, in reviewing the events of the UWC
Strike, he realized that the Sunday following the end of the strike, 2 June 1974, was
Pentecost Sunday. At any rate, his first set of notes made around the time of composition consists of a series of quotations from the second chapter of the Acts of
the Apostles. This biblical passage describes the descent of the Holy Spirit onto
Jesus's disciples after his death, which ensures that all to whom they preach hear the
good news in their own languages, thereby reversing the damage done at Babel.
Celebrated by Christians as the birthday of the Church, this feast day also prefigures the Second Coming. A play called *Pentecost* thus carries with it associations of
renewal, of division transcended by a unifying spiritual message.[37]

Far from being an afterthought, the ending, in which the four living characters
express a range of attitudes towards Christianity, provides the lens through which
the rest of the play should be viewed. *Pentecost* explores the roles, both malign
and beneficent, that faith can play in a person's life. In particular, Parker poses
the question of how Christianity helps, or does not help, people to deal with
human suffering, both their own and that of others. All the characters in the play

experience great pain. Marian and Lenny still mourn the loss of their son to cot death, a bereavement that prompted the unravelling of their marriage. Ruth suffers not only the beatings of her husband but the memory of her three miscarriages and the knowledge that she may never now be able to have the children she desires. Peter hates what he regards as the narrow-minded lack of generosity and imagination of his own, Protestant, community in Northern Ireland and cannot understand why he feels himself to be 'missing' something by living outside the North. Lily endured agonizing guilt for more than forty years over her brief affair with an English airman while her impotent husband was away in England and also over her secret abandonment of the resulting illegitimate child. Three of the characters—Marian, Lenny, and Peter—are 33, the age of Christ crucified (and the age Parker himself turned in 1974). In three separate scenes, as critic Michael Parker points out, three different characters arrive on stage wounded. Moreover, the number five, associated in Christian symbolism with the five wounds of Christ, pervades the play both thematically and structurally. *Pentecost* has five characters and is divided into five scenes. The Troubles have been going on for five years. Christopher died five years ago at the age of five months (the same length of time the power-sharing executive lasted in 1974). The women in the play have lost, among them, five children. What answer, Parker asks, does Christianity have to any of this? That, Cupitt might say, depends on what sort of Christianity one is talking about.[38]

Lily is identified in the first scene as a Free Presbyterian, an affiliation marking her as a fundamentalist in both religious and political terms. She sees Catholics as 'heathens', and she never accepts Marian's presence in her house or reciprocates any of her friendly overtures. Her life illustrates the destructive effects of 'religious beliefs... understood in a realist and objectified way'. These can, in Cupitt's terms, 'become tools of oppression, producing first a religious psychology that is self-punishing and self-mutilating, and then an ethic that is determined to give others as bad a time as we have given ourselves'. Lily's image of God is that of a stern judge, and she lives in constant consciousness of her own sinful unworthiness. One of the first things the audience learns about Lily is that she lived and died in near-total isolation, a fact that makes the later revelation that she gave birth to a child especially poignant. In early notes for the play, Parker had imagined Lily as capable of having murdered her baby, the badge of her shame, as if to demonstrate how actual evil can result from such a cast of mind. In *Pentecost*, less melodramatically, she admits to having left him lying outside a Baptist church in the hope that some 'moneyed people' would adopt him. Her highest value is loyalty (to God, to her husband, to Ulster), which she misinterprets as fixity, and she spends four decades struggling to maintain the appearance of a virtue she considers irretrievably thrown away. Lily's version of Christianity is literally as well as figuratively life-denying, as Marian (who has found and read her diary) informs the others in the final scene of the play. During the Blitz, instead of staying in the cellar, as she had promised her husband she would do, Lily sat in the parlour, waiting for 'the chosen bomb' to strike her dead. When she escaped unscathed, she interpreted this, not as a sign of God's mercy, but as proof that she had been 'condemned to life'.[39]

Lenny responds to this story with one of the Field Day production's most reliable laugh lines: 'I wonder what it was like here. Before Christianity.' Ruth objects
to his implicit assumption that Christianity has to resemble Lily's brand of Protestantism. She herself belongs to a conservative, evangelical denomination, the
Church of God, which helps to explain why she has remained as long as she has in
an unhappy marriage. Nevertheless, she sees her faith as uplifting and sustaining.
'You don't even know Christianity', she tells Lenny. 'You think it's only denial, but
that's wrong. It's meant to be love and celebration.' Though not an orthodox
believer, Parker agreed with Ruth on this point. He claimed to 'endorse' Christian
values; the problem, for him, derived from the way Christianity was too often
practised in Ireland.[40]

Lenny and Peter, from their different perspectives, probably come closest to
voicing Parker's own opinions on religion, at least the ones he would have held in
1974. Peter, the son of a Methodist minister, represents a more liberal strand of
Protestantism. An apostate both religiously and (as an émigré) culturally, he
rejects with special vehemence a faith that must once have been central to his
identity. He is steeped enough in Christianity to vie with Ruth in quoting from
memory the second chapter of Acts, but he breaks off in disgust when they reach
the line 'And it shall come to pass, that whosoever shall call on the name of the
Lord shall be saved', exclaiming that since 'they're never done calling on the name
of the Lord in this wee province of ours', it 'ought to be the most saved place on
God's earth instead of the most absolutely godforsaken'. A bit later, with vicious
sarcasm, Peter tries to imagine what Jesus Christ would make of Belfast: 'in the
middle of the marching ranks of the Ulster zealots, watching at the elbow of the
holy Catholic Nationalist zealot as he puts a pistol to a man's knee, to a man's
brains, to a man's balls, the Son of God in the polling booth, observing the votes
being cast in support of that...what would Jesus Holy Christ do with us all here,
would you say?'[41]

Lenny, an amiable humanist who has dropped out of the Catholic Church much
as he dropped out of middle-class society by giving up his legal studies to scrape a
living as a jazz musician, thinks he knows:

> he'd close down every church and chapel, temple and tabernacle in the whole island,
> put them to the torch, burn them into rubble, turf the congregations out priests and
> pastors face first, and drive them up into the mountains, up to the boniest, bleakest
> stretches of the Sperrins and the Mournes, and he'd flay them into the rock, until the
> Christianity was scourged out of the very marrows of their bones, he'd expunge reli-
> gion once and for all from off the face of this country, until the people could discover
> no mercy except in each other, no belief except to believe in each other, no forgiveness
> but what the other would forgive, until they cried out in the dark for each other and
> embraced their own humanity...that's the only redemption he'd offer them. Never
> mind believing in Jesus Christ. That's the point at which Jesus Christ might just begin
> to believe in us.[42]

Parker, who likely anticipated that much of his Irish audience would not accept
such a complete rejection of traditional religion, finally, through Marian, articulates a Cupitt-like synthesis of Lenny's (and his own) humanism and Christianity.

Her climactic speeches are given significance by what has preceded them. Marian begins the play as a conventional Catholic who attends Mass and initially resists Lenny's suggestion that they should obtain a divorce since they have no intention of reuniting. Despite such outward conformity in religious matters, she does not seem to draw much spiritual sustenance from whatever beliefs she holds, even asking Lily at one point, 'What makes you think I'm a Catholic?' Marian presents herself in the opening scene as someone whose materialism conflicts with Lenny's socialist idealism, but, as their dialogue makes plain, she is already undergoing a spiritual crisis. Having abruptly decided to sell her antiques shop and her flat, she now seeks inner peace and a larger purpose for her life.[43]

Through the first four scenes of *Pentecost*, Marian thinks these are best attained in solitude, and she makes her initial attempts to find common ground with Lily on the basis of their shared misanthropy and self-loathing. She reacts unsympathetically to the misfortunes that lead Ruth and Lenny to ask her for shelter, and she tolerates Peter's presence only because he has the skills necessary to do a survey of the house that she can present to the National Trust in her bid to convince them to acquire it for a museum of Belfast working-class life. Her instinct for conservation resembles Lily's, and there are signs that Marian could turn into someone like Lily herself. She even begins to sound like her, complaining to Lenny about the 'filth and mess and noise and bickering, in every last corner of the house' and rounding on him when he worries aloud that she might not be fit to be left alone: 'It wouldn't maybe have occurred to you, it wouldn't maybe have penetrated even that dim featherweight brain—that being on my own is the one thing I am fit for?'[44]

Despite Lily's repeated rejection of the idea that she and Marian could have anything in common, their three exchanges, one in each of the play's three middle scenes, gradually work a change in the younger woman. Lily's name recalls the archangel Gabriel, messenger of the Annunciation, who is frequently depicted carrying a lily, symbol of Mary's purity and, through later Christian associations, of death and rebirth. Lily in *Pentecost* serves as the unlikely harbinger of transformation, who, through her negative example, communicates to Marian the need for a new dispensation. During their last conversation, Marian, having read Lily's diary, lays bare the secret that deformed her life. When she accuses Lily of having abandoned her baby, she is rewarded by the sight of the older woman with her defences down at last. Instead of feeling triumphant, though, Marian is overwhelmed by a flood of compassion, offering her absolution and begging, in her turn, 'Forgive me, Lily.'[45]

Marian's newly charitable attitude carries over into the final scene of the play, where she behaves with markedly more understanding and tolerance towards her contemporaries than she has heretofore. She also announces that her earlier plan to hand over the house to the National Trust had been a 'mistaken idea', one that would only have perpetuated 'a crime'. Instead, she says, she will clear it out and live in it, since 'What this house needs most is air and light.' Marian's decision to open the house to new and more beneficial influences is accompanied by her commitment to what Cupitt would call a truly voluntary Christianity, one that

'Religion is an *activity*: it postulates a goal and seeks to attain it.' In
~ers from Lily, not because she is Catholic and Lily was Protestant,
~ makes a conscious choice to put her faith in a different kind of
~rom this decision follows a reaffirmation of the core Christian value of loving one's neighbour as oneself.[46]

Like her biblical namesake, Marian agrees to bear Christ into the world, but
instead of offering herself as a vehicle for a God existing elsewhere, she pronounces
her faith in a wholly human Christian spirituality. 'There is some kind of christ, in
every one of us', she declares, and 'Each of us either honours him, or denies him
and violates him, what we do to him is done to ourselves.' This christ is symbolized
for Marian by her infant son, Christopher, whom she had identified at the end of
Act I with her own soul, 'left for dead'. Thus, as Michael Parker observes, 'christ-
ness' for Marian connotes 'love, hope [and] potential' along with 'fallibility, vulner-
ability and mortality'. For too long, she confesses, Christopher's untimely death
caused her to hate life. Now she is resolved to assign a new meaning to his loss, one
that will help her to reclaim her soul and to live in a life-affirming way. 'Personally,'
she tells the others,

> I want to live now. I want this house to live. We have committed sacrilege enough on
> life, in this place, in these times. We don't just owe it to ourselves, we owe it to our
> dead too...our innocent dead. They're not our masters, they're only our creditors, for
> the life they never knew. We owe them at least that—the fullest life for which they
> could ever have hoped, we carry those ghosts within us, to betray those hopes is the
> real sin against the christ, and I for one cannot commit it one day longer.

The play ends with Ruth, in response to this speech, reading aloud from Acts:
'Therefore did my heart rejoice, and my tongue was glad; moreover also my flesh
shall rest in hope....Thou hast made known to me the ways of life....'[47]

Reading *Pentecost* in light of Don Cupitt's radical theology, it is worth noting
that the question of whether or not Lily is a 'real' ghost is as meaningless as the
question of God's objective existence is for Cupitt. For him, what people claim to
believe is irrelevant compared with how they behave as a result of their faith. Similarly, it does not matter if the ghost of Lily has objective reality, or if she exists only
in Marian's imagination: Marian is changed for the better by their encounters.
Parker likely hoped the same might be said of those who witnessed their interaction. In any case, in contrast to the bleak endings of *Lost Belongings* and *Northern
Star*, he dared in *Pentecost* to posit some basis for belief in the future, tenuous
though it must have seemed in 1987, and to affirm an unfashionable truth. Real
change on the social and political level cannot take place without change on the
individual level—and maybe this individual transformation requires something
more than a calculation of self-interest, something resembling an infusion of the
Holy Spirit. Faith, in Cupitt's sense, requires neither simple acceptance of a 'pre-
established order' nor a complacent assumption that everything will somehow
work out for the best, but the undertaking of a 'pilgrimage' in the direction of 'a
new world and a new human nature which this present era thinks impossible'.
Although it is a history play, *Pentecost* concludes on such a forward-looking note.

In so doing, it answers Parker's call in *Dramatis Personae* for drama that might 'begin to hint at a vision of the future'.[48]

Parker completed a draft of *Pentecost* in late March 1987. During the three months he spent working on the script, he had been attending to the future in other ways as well. The production of *Lost Belongings*, drawing to a close in the same period, had given him the opportunity to work with a new generation of Irish actors. In January and February he had a chance to scan the theatrical horizon when Rough Magic Theatre Company, one of Dublin's most vibrant young ensembles, produced his play *Nightshade*. Founded in 1984, Rough Magic aimed to produce 'new' or 'challenging' work 'that the Irish theatre-goer would not otherwise have the opportunity of seeing'. Parker spent several intense days observing and commenting on rehearsals at the end of January, returning a week later to see a performance. Though such a youthful company inevitably had difficulty grasping all the implications of this death-obsessed play (the actor playing the bereaved undertaker was only 24, for example), the clarity of the production impressed Parker. In terms of story and character, the play came across more forcefully than ever before in this incarnation. Reviewers who remembered the original 1980 Peacock version found this one 'less flashy... but with a shade more flesh on it'. After earning positive reviews in Dublin, the show toured to Wexford, Tralee, Cork, Sligo, Coleraine, and Limerick.[49]

Lynne Parker directed *Nightshade*, enhancing the pleasure of the association with Rough Magic for Stewart. His brother George's daughter, Lynne had become in recent years one of the most important people in his life, someone he connected with both personally and professionally on a profound level. Growing up, she had seen him mainly at Christmas, which he usually spent with his family in Belfast. He and Kate had struck her then as 'exotic creatures... urbane, elegant and fabulously entertaining'. Christmas celebrations in the Parker home took a ritual form, which always included hours of singing, accompanied by Stewart on the guitar, and, on Boxing Day, the performance featuring Lynne and her sister Julie of a playlet by their doting uncle, a new one each year. He also gave each of them a volume of poetry he had written especially for them (Lynne's included a version of the Deirdre legend) and, when they were teenagers, a Pollock's Toy Theatre in which they could stage their own productions with paper cut-outs. They both 'grew up regarding performance as a natural activity' (in addition to Stewart's influence, their grandfather and their Aunt Joan were noted singers and their grandmother an exceptional storyteller) and participated in drama at school and through the drama society of their church. Stewart's transmutation into a professional playwright around this time impressed them, and Lynne recalls the first production of *Spokesong* in 1975 as a revelatory experience: 'I hadn't realized up until then what a play could actually do.'[50]

Lynne's involvement with theatre intensified when she enrolled at Trinity College Dublin, a university she chose for the reputation of its drama group. She stayed with Stewart and Kate in Edinburgh several times during her university career, and these visits marked the start of her 'real relationship' with Stewart. Her frame of reference had grown enough by then to allow her to 'feel more equal to their conversation'. When he and Kate separated in 1982, Stewart and Lynne began to develop an adult friendship. For the first time, she remembers, she 'became aware of him as a vulnerable person', someone 'infinitely more complicated' than she had previously imagined. Lynne had been the first member of Stewart's family to meet Lesley, and she provided a critical link between various phases of his existence. Her decision to devote herself to theatre-making as a 'professional art' brought them closer still, and Rough Magic's production of *Nightshade* inaugurated a collaboration that would continue long after Stewart's death. In years to come, Lynne would be recognized as one of the foremost Irish theatre directors of her generation, and she would use her prestige to bring new exposure to her uncle's work— not because he was her uncle, but because she regarded him as one of the best playwrights of *his* generation, one whose vision, theatrical and otherwise, had ranged ahead of his own time.[51]

Despite the humour pervading his work and the apparent naturalism of his dialogue, a tragic vision lies at the heart of Parker's enduring achievement. In notes towards *Dramatis Personae*, Parker describes tragic vision as that which 'seeks to penetrate reality at a more elevated level than any of the forms of realism', which 'functions in and of its time but pursues a truth which is timeless and universal'. Such a vision 'tries to make coherent the most terrible impulses in the human heart, but ultimately concedes a mystery at the core of it' and 'deals with the life and death of the spirit in a medium which is determinedly secular'. Tragedy, in his view, 'doesn't deal in issues at all'. Rather, 'It deals with the death of the human soul: the destruction of the soul by historical, communal and political forces which are more powerful than the individual will.' A consummate individualist himself, Parker knew as well as anyone how painful it could be to acknowledge such forces, but he sensed that they were 'stronger and more destructive than ever before, because conviction and credulity are once again rampant'.[52]

As a dramatist who wrote for television as well as for the stage, Parker pondered in 1986 the theoretical problems attached to disseminating such a tragic vision via the great popular medium of his age. Television, he feared, was 'inimical' to tragedy owing to its place in the 'inner sanctum' of the spectator. 'People don't wish to feel threatened where they "live"', he acknowledged: 'So television inclines to be relentlessly cheerful, mechanically chirpy and bright-eyed, intimate, domestic, trivialising.' When tragic drama appears on television, he argued, 'people mis-read it: they find cliché and exaggeration in it; whereas novelty and documentary naturalism are precisely what tragedy transcends'. The attempt to present 'an Ulster tragedy' faced the additional difficulty that 'anything set in Ulster is treated as an "issue" drama'.[53]

Parker surely had *Lost Belongings* in mind when he wrote these words, and they indicate that, even before his epic film series had been produced, he worried about how it would be received—thus demonstrating his usual prescience. The series was transmitted, one episode a week, from early April to mid-May 1987. *Lost Belongings* had earned 'the rare accolade' of being shown on both ITV and Channel Four, which put it in the position of having to appeal to the most populist television audience and the most avant-garde tastes at one and the same time. Unfortunately, in director Tony Bicât's opinion, the first showing, at 9 p.m. on a Tuesday night, took place on ITV; each episode was then repeated on Channel Four at 9 p.m. on Saturdays. The programmers would have been better advised, he thought, to present *Lost Belongings* on Channel Four first, since the series had been written and produced in an artistically ambitious way and was designed to appeal more to that audience. In the event, the viewership of approximately four million per week that the series attracted looked small by ITV standards but would have been much more impressive for Channel Four.[54]

One negative effect of the decision to market *Lost Belongings* to a mass audience was that publicity materials evaded the complexity of the material, presenting the Deirdre–Niall relationship as central. 'From the start,' a glossy Thames Television publicity booklet proclaimed, 'their relationship is threatened by the fact that she is Protestant and he a Roman Catholic.' This reduction of Parker's kaleidoscopic drama to what Bicât calls 'a Belfast Romeo and Juliet' story meant that its 'reception was clouded by other lesser works which had treated the Ur-Story of The Province, a love across the religious divide'. As Mark Lawson observed in the *Independent*, 'we've now had enough Niall-and-Deirdre pieces on TV—principally from Graham Reid, Robin Glendinning and Anne Devlin—for Parker to be measured against his predecessors in the genre' (he, at least, regarded *Lost Belongings* as 'among the best of this swelling sub-section of television drama'). 'As far as the English television audience is concerned,' Damien Gorman remarked wearily in the *Irish News*, 'no Catholic has ever gone out with a Catholic, and no Protestant has ever kept company with "one of their own sort".'[55]

This sense of familiarity did nothing to mitigate the biggest problem faced by any series about Northern Ireland: the fact that the Troubles had become, in Parker's words, 'the biggest switch-off subject in British television'. Some reviewers were forthright about their prejudices, with Harry Thompson, for example, complaining, 'There is an extraordinary disposition among television planners to assume that the English/Scottish/Welsh viewers are interested obsessively in plays about Northern Ireland', adding, 'How else can one explain the proliferation of the harsh tones of Belfast on screen, the non-communication which gushes forth in that extraordinary accent, and the frequency with which one is offered stories about "the Troubles"?' Dennis Haywood, another provincial English critic, agreed that 'If TV never crosses the sea to Ireland again—or for a couple of years, at least—to present a play or documentary, it won't be too soon.' Critics such as Mary Kenny of the *Daily Mail* also had trouble distinguishing between *Lost Belongings* and television productions that had exploited the Northern Ireland setting in a sensational fashion. She objected to the larger-than-life aspects of the series, writing, 'I am not sure that [the] story of Deirdre, her beastly Orange uncle, nasty para-military foster-brother, Provo IRA half-brother, her inoffensive lover, her dead parents and all the dreadful events that are bound to befall her are not just a little too pessimistic, even for this background.'[56]

Defensiveness shows in Norman Jenkinson's review of the first episode for the *Belfast Telegraph*. 'It would have been a bonus indeed', he commented, if *Lost Belongings* 'had shown something other than the troubles. As it was, it used every stereotyped character and every incident of violence ever reported.' Apparently unfamiliar with Parker's other work, Jenkinson expressed the wish that 'someone' would 'write a play about the ordinary people of Belfast', conceding that 'This sort of drama series probably goes down very well with cross-channel viewers, who are getting what they expect, and probably don't expect anything different.'[57]

The first episode affronted many viewers. Deirdre's uncle, whose violence and inappropriate advances towards her are dictated by the mythic framework Parker used for the series, is played with superb nastiness by Harry Towb. The character is a particularly unpleasant one, who happens to be a loyalist. A reviewer from the North, like Jenkinson, might decry the characterization as unrepresentative, but he could hardly deny that such people existed. Too often, however, 'mainland' critics decided, based on Roy Connell's prominence in the initial episode, that Parker had made up his mind to portray all Protestants in the series negatively. This liberal English assumption of a republican bias on his part must have annoyed Parker, who had striven to present the widest possible spectrum of attitudes regarding Northern Ireland. Numerous reviews charged him with employing what the *Guardian*'s critic termed 'unhelpful stereotypes'. 'I can quite see', Sally Vincent wrote in *Today*, 'that it was tempting to depict the Ulster Protestant as an ignorant loudmouth who teaches his children to parrot anti-papal propaganda and who keeps a dainty pomander, bearing a portrait of the Queen, over his lav. But was it necessary to make him a pervert and a rapist into the bargain?' Connell, of course, is far from being 'the' only Ulster Protestant in the series, but reviewers frequently jumped to conclusions that fit their pre-existing notions about what the intentions of a Northern Irish dramatist must be. On the basis of the first episode, the reviewer for the *Daily Telegraph* declared that 'Almost everyone, so far, is a stereotype. Unionists are bigots—one is a rapist, already—and the Republicans we have met are romantic and musical....Is "Lost Belongings" going to tell us something like one man's terrorist is another man's freedom fighter? I hope not!' In effect, many critics did what they accused Parker of doing, making generalizations about a whole group based on the actions or personality of one member instead of seeing the individuals he had created.[58]

Having decided in advance what *Lost Belongings* was about, critics sometimes resisted Parker's occasional upending of the conventions of 'Troubles' drama. The Lenny episode, for example, with Stephen Rea's performance as a bumbling free-lance journalist, seemed a 'nosedive' to those who failed to see its relevance to Deirdre's tragic tale. Other reviewers appreciated the way Parker used his audience's preconceptions to draw them into his story, only to challenge what they thought they knew. John Naughton of the *Observer* noted that the episode featuring Deirdre's former neighbour Alec Ferguson (now a classical musician living in London)

opened by tracing what seemed to be merely a trite contrast between the cultivated affluence of Alec's present life and the bedraggled impoverishment of his runaway visitor, but rapidly deepened into an exploration...of how Alec's musical gift provided the magic carpet which enabled him to escape his background, and of what he had actually escaped from. 'Lost Belongings' is turning out to be a bleakly original series, not least because it portrays Prods as victims of their circumstances just as much as the Taigs they revile.[59]

Not all criticism of *Lost Belongings* was political. Opinions differed sharply on the music, composed for the series by Tony Britten and Dave Stewart (of Eurythmics fame). Several reviewers also commented on what John Lyttle of *City Limits* termed the 'style–content dislocation' between the direction and the writing. Bicât's 'creamy, dreamy visual veneer' contrasted strangely, in his view, with Parker's 'working-class Belfast characters'. Moreover, the demands of Parker's scripts, in which several intertwining stories (many of which unfold in flashbacks as well as in the present time of the drama) are presented over six episodes, pushed the limits of viewers' ability to keep up with developments. In those days, television writer Howard Schuman recollects, episodes of British serial drama did not begin with a 'previously on…'-style recap of what had already happened. Writers wrote assuming people would watch and remember everything—a dubious assumption in the case of a multi-dimensional piece like *Lost Belongings*. Claudia Harris, one of the first academic critics of Parker's work, observed that in this series he 'sometimes complicates complexity', reporting that 'Even conscientious viewers had difficulty following the narratives.'[60]

Despite such reservations, critics who watched the whole series generally came down in favour of *Lost Belongings*. Celia Brayfield summed up the critical consensus in her review of the last episode for the *Independent*, writing that '*Lost Belongings* could have been criticised as an over-complex, sprawling drama which was occasionally littered with demeaning cliches.' However, she added, 'It was also a grandly conceived and passionately executed piece which, with all these faults, deserves to rank with the finest achievements of television.' As for the popular response, David Elstein (then director of programmes for Thames Television) informed Parker that the audiences, though 'relatively small' had 'not been out of line with what we would have expected for a series set in Northern Ireland'.[61]

Predictably, the reception of *Lost Belongings*, especially in England, did not satisfy Parker. It did not help that the most negative reviews were of the first episode, leaving Parker to expect six weeks of condemnation by the critics. Lesley Bruce recalls that this initial batch of reviews so upset him that he did not wish to be in London to read the next ones. Openings had always been excruciating for Parker, and the transmission of a television work spread over six weeks seemed to him like one protracted press night. He thus took advantage of the fact that he had found himself, at the end of March 1987, in the unusual position of being 'entirely free of all commitments' to plan a trip to North America, which he had not visited since 1980. Lesley had work obligations that prevented her from accompanying him, but she urged him to go. Parker spent three joyful weeks in the United States and Canada, visiting Ken and June Lambla in North Carolina; Gail and Danny Collins, Irene Lewis, Alfred Gingold and his wife, and Gina Leishman in New York City; and Nancy McKibbin in Ontario. He stayed with Bea MacLeod in Ithaca and spent an afternoon with John Paul. Driving through Clinton, he even surprised Ed Barrett, the man responsible for his hiring by Hamilton College over twenty years before. He returned to London refreshed and rejuvenated, ready to face the test of yet another production.[62]

Practical preparation for *Pentecost* began in late June 1987. Parker met with Patrick Mason, the director, and sat in on auditions in London. Stephen Rea, of course, would play Lenny, a part written for him. (Being Lenny, Rea remembers, felt like being in 'a warm bath'—'acting shouldn't be that easy'.) Eileen Pollock, a veteran of one previous Field Day production, landed the central role of Marian; Barbara Adair, who had recently resumed her first career as an actor after years of working as a school teacher, took the role of Lily; Paula Hamilton was cast as Ruth; and South Africa-reared Jonathan Kent was engaged to play the returning exile Peter. Rehearsals got underway in Derry on 17 August for a 23 September opening. Parker attended throughout the five weeks, rewriting as needed and giving notes to the actors. When Mason had to be away for about six days, Parker filled in for him. Lynne Parker, on hand as an observer and unofficial dialect coach for Kent, found it inspiring to watch her uncle, 'who was obviously so aware of the abstract elements of the play, the philosophy behind it and the intellectual ideas, focus so cleverly on these through the practicalities of the character's behaviour'. Coupled with his experience watching and advising on the production of *Lost Belongings*, Parker's intense involvement with Field Day sharpened his desire to direct his own work.[63]

Parker experienced the concentrated sense of purpose of a Field Day production in Derry as a welcome novelty. The political as well as artistic commitment of everyone involved and the participants' isolation in an unaccustomed environment made for an atmosphere that a London-based production, for example, could never attain. He and Mason stayed together in Magee College housing—a 'monastic' existence, Mason remembers, apart from the drink. Their world consisted largely of the predominantly Catholic Bogside of Derry, still under heavy police and Army surveillance, and Parker joked that he had to go to Belfast for the weekend to relax. *Pentecost* was the first Field Day play to focus on present-day Northern Ireland and to tackle head-on the issue of sectarianism, and this subject-matter heightened the political frisson that always attached to a Field Day project.[64]

As with *Northern Star*, Parker revelled in the opportunity to work with Northern Irish actors on a Northern Irish play that would be seen first by a Northern Irish audience. 'I would rather do a play here than anywhere else in the world', he told an interviewer from the *New York Times*: 'What's great is you draw on the life experiences of actors so directly.' In this case, those experiences conformed in various ways with Parker's own. Hamilton had got her start as an actor in the Shakespeare productions at Sullivan Upper School in Holywood, which Parker had also attended. Pollock had been active in Dramsoc at Queen's University. Adair had worked for the BBC in radio drama and Schools broadcasting. Rea comments that he, Pollock, and Parker all had working-class Protestant roots in Belfast, and sometimes they had to set the English director and Scottish set designer straight on the nuances of Belfast life.[65]

Parker used his conversations with reporters during the rehearsal period to try to guide reaction to *Pentecost*, insisting that, despite the UWC strike in the background, 'the top line of the play is not political at all': 'It's just that I'm using that period as a context for the personal crises that the characters go through. I deliberately chose perhaps one of the worst moments in recent history, for Belfast people.' He had done this, he said, to give his characters 'something to pin themselves against' in their search for 'affirmation...some sort of hope, belief in the future'. He described the play as a personal 'departure':

> It's a much simpler, more conventional, more direct piece than anything I've done before. I don't know whether that may create a certain disappointment in the response to it—because it doesn't have any of the flashiness, or theatricalism that I've gone for in other things. But, I feel that it's an advance for me because I'm actually—very nakedly, and straight-forwardly—presenting fairly powerful emotional relationships. And there's nothing there but the writing.[66]

Many who attended the Field Day opening at the Guildhall in Derry felt the piece's full emotional impact. As Frankie McGinley of the *Donegal Democrat* wrote, 'Not since seeing "Translations"...have I felt so privileged at being at a world premiere.... Parker examines the dark heart of Irish society and seems to find hope.' *Irish Times* critic David Nowlan agreed, calling *Pentecost* 'probably the most important play for Ireland that the Field Day Theatre Company has staged since Friel's classic. Its message is the simplest in history: love thyself and you can begin to love others, and it is couched in all the biblical echoes that all the warring religious factions on this island have used so hatefully well.' Nowlan praised all aspects of the production and declared the play itself 'one of the most stimulating, most satisfying, most touching and most illuminating in years of Irish theatre'.[67]

Other critics questioned this assessment, in terms Parker had anticipated. Colm Tóibín, an enthusiastic reviewer of some of Parker's earlier plays, declared that 'Writers are divided into those whose characters find old diaries in old houses which are full of interest and haunt their minds, and those who don't use this device because it is too hackneyed.... It is odd that Stewart Parker, previously known for his subtlety and originality, has joined the former group.' He deplored the ending, 'full of a false, coy sense of sentimental hope', and faulted the play for wearing 'its Belfast on its sleeve', commenting that 'The North is an interesting place.... It is also a useful place and it is easy to market work from there.' Fintan O'Toole, who had loved *Northern Star*, also disliked the way *Pentecost* ended, charging Parker with having tried, and failed, 'to leap beyond realism into some kind of metaphor of transcendence'. 'We have been led to expect some kind of apocalyptic deliverance', he complained, but 'What we get is an evangelical sermon on the "Christ in ourselves" as the source of change. The problem is that this pentecostal image works only on the level of words. Change is evoked verbally, it doesn't *happen* on stage.'[68]

Parker must have been distressed by such critiques from commentators who had responded to his past work with sympathy and understanding. In their different ways, though, these reviews typify an ambivalence in the Republic towards the

North and, especially, towards Northern Protestantism. O'Toole seemed to find *Pentecost*'s themes alien, regarding the 'territory of the play' as 'literally and imaginatively Protestant'. Parker, he wrote, used 'the language of the Bible with an intensity and fervour that belongs only to the Protestant tradition'. His views were echoed by the *Dublin Opinion* critic, Treacy Fitzgerald, who stated that 'the biblical apocalyptic language becomes oppressive and, for some, a little embarrassing'. A reviewer for the *Munster Express* similarly articulated more bluntly some of Tóibín's reservations about what each perceived as the excessive attention being paid to the Troubles, writing, 'Frankly, many of us down here in the South are sick and tired of the troubles in the North of Ireland and we are constantly assailed in press and on TV and radio, with all the gory details.' Even *Irish Independent* critic Desmond Rushe, who thought *Pentecost* 'Parker's best play to date', referred to it as a 'new Northern problem play'.[69]

Many English critics were also tired of plays set in Northern Ireland. Michael Coveney of the *Financial Times*, for instance, labelled *Pentecost* 'a bit of an overcooked broth': 'The riots and marches outside do not really impinge on the stage action. The allegoric function of the house as a temple of decent Irishness is somewhat emphatic. And the laborious imagery of barrenness in marriage signifying loss of hope on the national scale has been more resoundingly exploited by David Rudkin in *Ashes*.' Despite his jaded view of the piece, Coveney allowed that 'it would be impudent of a mainland critic to guess at the local resonances'. Mary Holland, writing in the *Observer*, was both less reticent and more perceptive, praising Parker's 'brave and harshly funny play about the way the tribal histories of both communities in Northern Ireland cripple the people who live there, stunt their capacity to know themselves and accept one another'. 'Of all his plays,' she remarked, 'this is the most intimate and the most daring in the way he articulates a hope for spiritual regeneration through personal grace. The text of Pentecost preached in a thousand evangelical chapels becomes a plea for the gift of love that may enable people to come to terms with their own past and with each other.' (As a reviewer for the *Irish Press* shrewdly observed of the play's final scene, 'The terminology is Christian, but its essence is Humanist; Christ is to be [found] in individuals, not in creeds.')[70]

The real test of *Pentecost*, however, as Coveney implied, lay in what Northern Irish people made of it, and Northern audiences and reviewers generally found the play true to life, politically relevant, and moving. Gerard Downey in the *Belfast Telegraph* hailed *Pentecost* as 'an absorbing and beautifully crafted piece of work' that presented 'a microcosm of Northern Ireland life at the height of the troubles'. A critic for the *Ulster Herald* concurred that the UWC Strike and its impact on individuals made 'an excellent subject for a play', since 'it caused so much social and domestic chaos that not one family in the Six-Counties was unaffected'. Parker, according to this reviewer, had 'unleashed' his audience's 'most basic emotions—anger, sadness and amusement': 'That we were not presented with any easy solutions, as each character is left to sort out his or her own fate, is a tribute to one of Ireland's finest playwrights.' The reviewer for the *Coleraine Chronicle* 'marvelled' at Parker's 'unpolemical and fair-minded' treatment of 'those disgraceful events of

'1974' but felt less satisfied with the conclusion, arguing that 'the little narrative epiphanies at the end, accompanied by the singing phrases of the Pentecost story itself, demonstrated ultimately not a new hope or insight, but the fact that we are still locked into all the old festering angers and assertions of self'. Jane Coyle in the *Irish News*, on the other hand, replied directly to Fintan O'Toole in her defence of this ending:

> The conclusion is a verbal, rather than a physical, resolution. Parker offers no panacea for the hopeless situation raging outside the house. And he is too much of a realist to suggest, writing this play in 1987 while the battle of the Anglo-Irish Agreement drags on, that such a simplistic formula could ever provide the answer. But what he has done is to draw from the enraged rantings that are heard every Sunday from pulpits all over the North, a message of reconciliation.[71]

The special significance that *Pentecost* had in Northern Ireland provided one theme for Northern reviewers. Derry native Nell McCafferty, writing in the *Sunday News*, began her commentary on the play by noting that there had been far fewer people from the Republic attending the first night in Derry than had come to Field Day openings in years past. The 'family feeling' engendered by this relative lack of outside interest seemed to her 'entirely appropriate to the play', since, for the 'mostly Catholic' audience in the Guildhall, 'It was as though the spouse of a mixed marriage had finally been brought home to be introduced to the in-laws':

> When the Catholic characters spoke, you could feel people relax, and breathe understandingly, as they listened to a language that they well understood. When the [Protestant] characters spoke, the concentration was palpable, with no one wanting to miss a word, particularly when religious belief was mentioned.
> So that's what they think.
> So that's how they see it.

Parker, she remarked, 'left no room for complacency, forcing the audience time and again to have a look at themselves through the characters'. Attenders had 'an uncomfortable night', but many sat on in the Guildhall afterwards, 'talking into the small hours' about the play—especially its end, which to McCafferty's mind betrayed either 'a failure of nerve or Christian optimism'. 'This is a terrific play', she concluded, 'written about us, by one of us.'[72]

On the other side of the sectarian divide, a critic for the Belfast *News Letter* reported that the initial performance in Derry 'held the audience utterly spellbound and enthralled' and pronounced *Pentecost* 'a play for Roman Catholic and Protestant alike'. In another piece that newspaper published a few days later in an attempt to interest Belfast audiences in the play (which would reach the city in mid-October), the reviewer emphasized Parker's local knowledge and the veracity of his characterization:

> through Lily, who could be anyone's Gran from east Belfast, we get the story of a people, proud, Calvinist, atoning through prejudice and confirmed beliefs for sins that have been carefully concealed from church-going neighbours. . . . It is a world and a people and a way of life that Parker, once a part of it himself, knows intimately, and

if he portrays it (and Lily) with often bitter satire, then there is also bitter-sweet love and warm understanding of that world too.

In *Pentecost*, which this critic hazarded would 'go down as one of the great plays of our time', Parker delivered 'a message of hope for a better understanding between people he obviously feels deeply for. . . . counterpointed by tragedy—the tragedy of misunderstanding and ignorance'.[73]

Between late September and mid-December 1987, Field Day toured *Pentecost* to the Dublin Theatre Festival (where the show was housed in the John Player Theatre, site of Parker's *Spokesong* triumph twelve years earlier) and all around Northern Ireland and the Republic.[74] On 8 November, events in Enniskillen underlined the topicality of Parker's drama. An IRA bomb exploded just before a scheduled Remembrance Day wreath-laying ceremony, killing eleven people and injuring sixty-three more. The incident, ironically, helped to improve local community relations by inspiring a backlash against the perpetrators and supporters of violence. Gordon Wilson, whose daughter died, struck a chord that resounded with many when he told an interviewer that he forgave the bombers, adding, 'I shall pray for those people tonight and every night.' Loyalist paramilitaries, which had begun planning retaliatory attacks within hours of the explosion, abandoned the effort after hearing this broadcast—a vivid illustration of the play's suggestion that even unilateral Christian forgiveness could have significant effects. (Three weeks to the day after the bombing, Parker presented Marian's final speech from *Pentecost* as one of a group of Northern Irish writers giving commemorative readings in Enniskillen; the previous weekend, Field Day had visited the town with the play.)[75]

For once in Parker's theatrical career, all the stars aligned. *Pentecost* had a uniformly strong cast, which served the play remarkably well. Patrick Mason's understated direction worked with Parker's dialogue rather than against it, and he involved Parker so thoroughly that the playwright effectively co-directed. Bunny Christie's lovingly detailed set impressed the Belfast *News Letter*'s critic as such 'a perfect re-creation of the familiar east Belfast terrace home' that it 'should go straight into the Folk Museum' after the play's tour. Best of all, the Field Day production gave Parker the opportunity to speak directly and intimately to his own ideal audience: the people of Northern Ireland. Parker attended performances in Derry, Omagh, Armagh, and Belfast and participated in several discussion sessions on the play. The engaged responses to the show in the North energized him tremendously. He did not mind if people hated *Pentecost*, Lesley Bruce recalls, as long as they reacted strongly to it and talked about it. After the disappointing reception of *Heavenly Bodies* the year before, Parker had declared his resolve to stop writing for the stage, at least for the foreseeable future, and he would not have written *Pentecost* if he had not already promised it to Field Day. The success of this production so restored his confidence that he started to think seriously about writing more stage plays.[76]

Parker marked another joyful occasion at the end of 1987: his first Christmas with Lesley in London. In the five years they had been together, they had always celebrated the holiday separately—he with his family in Belfast, she with hers in

England. A profound shift, however, had occurred in the extended Parker family in June 1987 with the death of Stewart's mother, bedridden for years. At Lesley's suggestion, and rather to his own surprise, he persuaded his 75-year-old father to return with him after a trip he made to Ireland in mid-December to accept the 1987 Harvey's Award for Best New Play for *Pentecost*. Herbie remained in Putney for a week, and Stewart delighted in showing him the sights of London. He accompanied his father back to Belfast and stayed a few days visiting family and friends there before flying home on Christmas Eve.[77]

Parker had taken about a month off from new writing after his stint in Derry, concentrating on incorporating rewrites to *Pentecost* and preparing scripts to send to potential directors and publishers. A proposed transfer of the Field Day production into the Royal Court Theatre in London had fallen through when the company realized that the slot offered by Max Stafford-Clark (two weeks as opposed to the previously discussed four) would be too short to allow them to recoup their expenses, so once again Parker was left to try to ensure the future of his work on his own. At the end of October, though, he learned from Barry Hanson that British Screen had approved development money for their proposed feature film, so in mid-November 1987 he began writing the screenplay eventually called *Mayo by Moonlight*, finishing a first draft in early March 1988. This employed as backdrop the Land League's 1880 boycotting agitation, a watershed in the development of Irish nationalism as a mass movement.[78]

The historical figure of Michael Davitt, founder of the League, doubtless held a magnetic appeal for Parker. Evicted with his family as a child from the land they farmed in County Mayo, Davitt grew up in Lancashire, where he lost his right arm in a mill accident at the age of 11. After participating in revolutionary politics as a young man, and spending time in prison, he became a champion of non-violent methods of resistance. Later in life, he associated with James Keir Hardie, an early leader of the British Labour movement, and campaigned for non-sectarian education in Ireland. At a different stage in his own career, Parker would probably have been tempted to make Davitt himself the focus of his drama. Having recently treated the lives of James Joyce, Henry Joy McCracken, and Dion Boucicault, however, he opted in this screenplay to concentrate instead on three fictional characters representing three major interests active in Ireland at the time. William Bone, the British spy, stands for the forces of British coercion; his treacherous sidekick, Thaddeus McCoy, for those who would change Ireland's status by violent means; and Bone's independent wife, Constance, for the moral suasion of the Land League. (In this version of the script, Davitt appears as a mouthpiece for the League, but in notes that Parker made towards a revision in June 1988 he expressed his intention to eliminate Davitt, subsuming his function in the character of Constance.) Through various twists and turns of plot, Bone and McCoy wind up immobilized in a bog, entirely at the mercy of Constance—an upbeat and even comic ending, in contrast to the stand-off between the two men that Parker had described in his original proposal for the film. Through this final image, he suggests that the future of Ireland lies with neither the revolutionaries nor the English masters and their 'legitimate' force, but with the mass of the Irish people.[79]

Around the time he completed the first draft of this screenplay, Parker received the exciting news that Oberon Books, a Birmingham-based publisher, would bring out an edition of his 'history plays': *Northern Star, Heavenly Bodies*, and *Pentecost*. He spent much of the spring and summer of 1988 readying them for the press. The bulk of this work consisted of a thorough revision of *Heavenly Bodies*, but Parker also thought more deeply than he had to date about the plays as a group. The title given to the volume, *Three Plays for Ireland*, reflects the political commitment with which he had approached the writing of each one. In an introduction to the collection written in July 1988, Parker described the plays as a 'Triptych': 'three self-contained groups of figures, from the eighteenth, nineteenth and twentieth centuries respectively, hinged together in a continuing comedy of terrors'. As a Northern Irish playwright, he continued, he had been bequeathed 'a subject for drama which is comprised of multiplying dualities: two islands (the "British Isles"), two Irelands, two Ulsters, two men fighting over a field'. All three plays, he pointed out, contained ghosts, 'uncompleted souls'. 'Plays and ghosts', he averred, 'have a lot in common', since 'The energy which flows from some intense moment of conflict in a particular time and place seems to activate them both.' But whereas 'Plays intend to achieve resolution', 'ghosts appear to be stuck fast in the quest for vengeance'.[80]

In a letter asking a friend to paint a picture for the cover of the book, Parker elaborated further on the connections he perceived between his three last stage plays. He wanted an image of 'Cave-Hill-and-sky' on the front of the volume, he said, in part because 'the three plays in the book are all about people struggling to fly free of the imprisoning circumstances of their history, metaphorically aspiring heavenwards, which is why I have deliberately given all three plays empyreal titles'. Reflecting on his achievement as he prepared this volume for publication cemented Parker's sense of having come to the end of a major phase of his career. Lesley Bruce recalls that he believed he had been dealt the subject of Northern Ireland, like a hand of cards, and he had experienced it as both a burden and a gift. Regardless of how Parker saw this subject-matter at any given time, though, he had felt obliged to treat it. Now, with the completion of *Northern Star, Lost Belongings*, and *Pentecost*, he thought he had finally discharged his duty to his native place. In dedicating the Oberon volume to his niece, Lynne, he symbolically passed the baton to the next generation of Northerners.[81]

Parker's other major writing project of 1988 represented one of the first fruits of his feeling of liberation. In February of that year, he had accepted an invitation from Robert Cooper, now a television drama producer for BBC Northern Ireland, to write a sixty-minute television film—on the understanding that he would be allowed to co-direct it. *Latter-Day Saint* had its roots in a 1966 visit Parker made to Salt Lake City, where he encountered the history and theology of the Church of Jesus Christ of Latter-Day Saints, also known as the Mormons. Mormons believe that in 1823 an angel named Moroni imparted The Book of Mormon, a supplement to the Bible, to their founder, Joseph Smith, and all members of the church are enjoined to help spread this new Gospel. Parker, in late 1987 or early 1988, conceived the idea of a film tracking the progress of a Mormon missionary in

Northern Ireland. Lester, the missionary in question, is, as Parker described him to Cooper, 'young, very short, very dark, earnest, and noticeably odd-looking'. He is also obsessed with St Patrick, with whom he identifies. Parker promised 'a great deal of humour in this fable, but only by default'. His 'efforts', he told Cooper, would 'go to exploring the painful truth and reality of the character and his predicaments, showing the events through his eyes', which would make 'a refreshing change from the usual Ulster perspective, not to mention the usual St. Paddy's Day shamrockery'. Parker researched this screenplay in the spring and early summer of 1988 and produced a rough first draft between July and September.[82]

Compared with the hectic pace he had maintained from mid-1983 through 1987, however, Parker kept his work schedule in 1988 positively leisurely. He allowed himself the luxury of concentrating on one project at a time, not worrying as much as he had in the past about what he would do next. He began making desultory notes towards both a stage play based on his radio play *The Traveller* and a piece about the Northern Irish father of the Brontë sisters. He also felt the urge, as he often did at times of personal crisis or in phases of his career that afforded him more mental space than usual, to return to *Hopdance*, the novel about his amputation, and finish it at last. He had made a deliberate decision, though, to give life priority for a while. His relationship with Lesley had brought him immense happiness, and he wanted to take time to celebrate their life together. His trip to North America in the spring of 1987 had invigorated cherished friendships, and he looked forward to returning with her. In the past couple of years, as well, he had enjoyed travelling to places he had never been before—Norway, the Dordogne valley of France, Greece, Spain—and he eagerly anticipated doing more of that. Especially since the *Pentecost* opening, he had been getting together more often with friends and taking advantage of all London had to offer. He and Lesley lived quietly but intensely, and she remembers feeling almost 'afraid' that such contentment could not possibly last.[83]

Her fears were realized in late summer 1988. For several months, Parker had been suffering from stomach problems. At the beginning of June, a week's worth of stomach pain had driven him to the doctor, who prescribed a course of ulcer medication. Still experiencing symptoms in August, Parker went back to his doctor and undertook a second course of ulcer medicine, which had no more effect than the first one had. Parker visited the doctor once again and specifically requested tests. His physician put him on a waiting list. Feeling worse a week and a half later, Parker returned to the clinic. His own doctor was on holiday, so he saw a different one, who seemed more impressed by the potential gravity of his condition and expedited the tests. On 19 September, at Queen Mary's Hospital in Roehampton, Parker learned that he probably had stomach cancer, a diagnosis confirmed by a biopsy a few days later. Resolved to choose quality over quantity of life, he at first refused chemotherapy but agreed to have surgery. In the operating theatre five days later, however, the surgeon discovered that his cancer had advanced too far to be operable. Parker was told that, although the cancer would be terminal, chemotherapy might buy him a year of quality life. He assented to this suggestion and was sent home for ten days pending his admission to Westminster Hospital for the treatment. During that brief period, his condition deteriorated so rapidly that by the time he was admitted he was too sick to be given the chemotherapy. Until this point, Parker had faced his condition squarely and stoically, telephoning and writing to his closest friends to inform them of the situation and even trying to work on *Hopdance*, but now he asked Lesley not to tell him anything that would make it impossible for him to hope. In the event, he remained in Westminster Hospital until he died, on 2 November, less than two weeks after his forty-seventh birthday.[84]

An overflow crowd attended Parker's funeral at St Brendan's parish church in Sydenham on 10 November 1988. Among floral tributes from organizations including the Lyric Theatre, the Field Day Theatre Company, and the Belfast Festival, a report in the Belfast *News Letter* noted a simple wreath from an anonymous admirer bearing the message 'Stewart, we only met you once through the stage and you made us laugh.' Intimates looked in vain, though, for flashes of Parker's personality in the standard Church of Ireland funeral service. Parker had ceased attending church as a teenager and in his adult life had never been an orthodox Christian. (In hospital, shortly before he died, he had told a nun who offered to pray with him that he was not a believer, though he encouraged her to pray if it would make *her* feel better.) Knowing that people would expect some sort of religious observance on this occasion, however, he had asked his brother to arrange the same service that the family had planned for his mother the previous year.[85]

Parker had been cremated, at his own request, and the directions he left regarding the disposition of his remains come closer to his essential self in their quality of serious joking. An 'Interim will & testament' jotted in his commonplace book in the spring of 1986 expressed his desire 'to have my ashes transported on to the British Rail Ferry at Stranraer, as a last hopeless gesture of support for state ownership, the urn to be dropped over the side, at a mid-way point on the journey to Larne.... thus to be laid to rest in the half-way house in which I was born.' Lynne Parker, who made one of the party accompanying her uncle's ashes to a point in the Channel equidistant from Britain and Ireland, hopes that he 'was swept up into the North Sea' and from thence to the Arctic Circle but concedes that 'More likely he got sucked back to the shores of Ulster and is becalmed off Loyalist North Antrim.'[86]

A few months before Stewart died, Lynne had rung him just to say 'hello'. He informed her that he had been diagnosed with an ulcer, which surprised him because he had just had the 'calmest' year of his life. They talked about her new house, which he had helped her to buy, and he said he looked forward to visiting her in Dublin that autumn, when they could *really* talk. He never made it. Looking back, she feels that 'that was the point at which we just missed each other.... He left before I was properly ready to engage with him and the only way I can do it now is through the plays.'[87]

Most people who loved Parker—and they were legion—experienced a similar sense of frustration. He had died so suddenly, and so full of life, that his physical absence seemed at first a gaping void. In a heartfelt obituary, fellow playwright Frank McGuinness proclaimed that 'If ... the English language has lost an important writer, the Irish people have lost an important man.' But Parker preserved in his writing his own best qualities. His plays are the repository of his spirit—a truth felt keenly by those involved with the London production of *Pentecost*, which opened barely two months after Parker's death. Nicolas Kent, artistic director of the Tricycle Theatre, had asked in the spring of 1988 to produce the play in a year's time. When Parker learned he had cancer, his agent requested that the production be moved up. A fire had left the Tricycle without a venue, but Kent arranged a slot for the company at the Lyric Theatre Studio, Hammersmith. Parker advised on casting but died shortly before rehearsals began. Kent and the actors (Dearbhla Molloy as Marian, Adrian Dunbar as Lenny, Barbara Adair as Lily, Michelle Fairley as Ruth, and Sam Dale as Peter) felt keenly their responsibility to do the play the way Parker would have wanted it done, and, if reviews are a reliable guide, the company lived up to his exacting standards. Parker's voice comes through so clearly in *Pentecost* that friends of the playwright from all over used the London production as an alternative memorial service for him, and Lesley Bruce recalls that she could never hear the end without breaking down. Lynne Parker, too, admits to flinching every time she reads or hears Marian's lines describing her grief over her dead son ('I felt him as a raw scar across my own spirit...'), but she also realizes that Stewart Parker lives on in his work. There, those who knew him can always meet up with him and those wishing to make his acquaintance will find him waiting.[88]

Notes

NOTES TO PREFACE

1. Parker, 'Signposts', *Theatre Ireland*, 11 (Autumn 1985), 28–9.
2. Parker, quoted in Deirdre Purcell, 'The Illusionist', *Sunday Tribune*, 27 September 1987.
3. Seamus Heaney, 'Victorious Ulsterman', *Sunday Independent*, 6 November 1988.
4. Parker, quoted in Raymond Gardner, 'Too Many People Have Writing in the Head...', *Guardian*, 6 December 1976, and in Ciaran Carty, 'Northern Star Rising on the Tide', *Sunday Tribune*, 29 September 1985.
5. Parker, quoted in Bob Willox, 'Parker Pens a Great Play', *News Letter*, 21 February 1977.
6. Parker, letter to Alfred Gingold, 20 October 1975.
7. Parker, *Dramatis Personae* (Belfast: John Malone Memorial Committee, 1986), 13.
8. Parker, quoted in Purcell; Stephen Rea, 23 February 1995.
9. Parker, 'Introduction' to *Over the Bridge*, by Sam Thompson, ed. Stewart Parker (Dublin: Gill and Macmillan, 1970), 14.
10. Belinda McKeon, 'Heavenly Bodies/Peacock Theatre', *Irish Times*, 30 June 2004.
11. Parker, quoted in Purcell.
12. Parker, quoted in Purcell.
13. Anthony Curtis, 'Shilling Lives: An Interview' in Dale Salwak (ed.), *The Literary Biography: Problems and Solutions* (Iowa City: University of Iowa Press, 1996), 126; John Wilson Foster, 'The Critical Condition of Ulster', *Honest Ulsterman*, 79 (Autumn 1985), 54.
14. Parker, *Dramatis Personae*, 17–18.

NOTES TO CHAPTER 1

1. Parker, *The Green Light*, BBC typescript, 1. Parker wrote this piece as an autobiographical Talks Feature for BBC Northern Ireland, recorded it in June 1971, and re-recorded it that August (for reasons unknown to me) with some cuts and changes. John Boyd produced the programme, which was transmitted on Northern Ireland Radio 4 under the title *Self Portrait* on 3 October of the same year. I quote from the typescript rather than the shorter edited version that was aired. The title comes from the end of the talk, where Parker declares that what remains with him from his youth is 'the desire to penetrate the heart of all mystery'. The nature of the 'vision' that 'drifted before me all through childhood and adolescence' is evoked most poignantly for him, he says, by the closing sentences of F. Scott Fitzgerald's *The Great Gatsby*: Gatsby 'believed in the green light, the orgiastic future that year by year recedes before us. It eluded us then, but that's no matter—tomorrow we will run faster, stretch out our arms farther.... So we beat on, boats against the current, borne back ceaselessly into the past' (20).
2. Jonathan Bardon, *Belfast: An Illustrated History* (Belfast: Blackstaff, 1982), 239–41; May Thompson, 30 June 1994; George Parker, 24 June 1995; *Green Light*, 1.
3. Bardon, *Belfast*, 202–3, 193, 243, 234.

4. Bardon, *Belfast*, 234–6.

5. Bardon, *Belfast*, 234, 236–7. The Irish Free State, in contrast, maintained neutrality throughout the war. In Parker's play *Spokesong*, the protagonist was orphaned during the Belfast Blitz. His grandmother, an Irish nationalist, remarks that his parents 'were killed by a German bomb. If Ireland had been a united country it wouldn't have been dropped' (*Spokesong* [New York: Samuel French, 1980], 54).

6. Bardon, *Belfast*, 237–8, 240–2; George and Margaret Parker, 6 April 1994. Herbie's given name was George Herbert Parker, and in notes he will be identified as G. H. Parker. His son, also George Herbert, went by Herb as a boy, but switched to George when he started working—I call him George throughout.

7. Stewart Parker, undated notes on his family; George Parker, 25 February 1995; G. H. Parker, 11 April 1994.

8. G. H. Parker, 11 April 1994; George Parker, 5 and 7 April 1994; Stewart Parker, 'An Ulster Volunteer', *Irish Times*, 6 March 1970; Margaret Parker, 18 October 1998; Julie Parker McMullan, 18 July 1998. Herbie's Parker grandfather was a ship's engineer from Hull who came to Belfast to supervise a contract in the shipyard and stayed; he sailed world-wide on a paddle-wheel vessel called the *Great Eastern*. His maternal grandfather, surnamed Stitt, drove a bread cart. Belle's Lynas grandfather was a shoe-maker who specialized in customized shoes for people with legs deformed by polio. Her maternal grandfather, surnamed Stewart (Stewart Parker was named for him and for James Lynas), served in the British Army.

9. George and Margaret Parker, 6 April 1994 and 28 December 1997; G. H. Parker, 11 April 1994.

10. Parker, quoted in Caroline Walsh, 'Stewart Parker', *Irish Times*, 13 August 1977; G. H. Parker, 10 April 1994; George Parker, 5 April 1994.

11. Parker, untitled and undated (and apparently unfinished) autobiographical fragment, probably written in 1970 or early 1971. This 19-page handwritten manuscript is among Parker's personal papers, but I have not been able to determine exactly when he wrote it or for what purpose. It may represent a first attempt at the radio talk, abandoned when he started writing *The Green Light*.

12. *Green Light*, 13.

13. George Parker, 5 April 1994; *Green Light*, 5.

14. *Green Light*, 14, 18; Joan Parker Clements, 21 June 1995.

15. Carrie Jobes and Molly Crawford, 24 June 1995; G. H. Parker, 11 April 1994; Julie Parker McMullan, 18 July 1998.

16. G. H. Parker, 11 April 1994; George Parker, 5 and 11 April 1994 and 24 June 1995; *Green Light*, 4.

17. G. H. Parker, 11 April 1994; Joan Parker Clements, 9 April 1994; Bill and Bob Granleese, 27 July 1995; Parker, *Green Light*, 15 and quoted in Ciaran Carty, 'Northern Star Rising on the Tide', *Sunday Tribune*, 29 September 1985; Deirdre Purcell, 'The Illusionist', *Sunday Tribune*, 27 September 1987.

18. Bob Granleese, 29 July 1995; Spike Milligan, *The Goon Show Scripts* (London: Woburn, 1972); Bill and Bob Granleese, 27 July 1995.

19. George Parker, 5 April 1994. As a 'fresher' at Queen's University, Parker wrote to the editor of the student newspaper protesting about a negative review another student had published of a Danny Kaye film (Parker, 'Five Pennies', *Gown*, 12 February 1960).

20. Rex Cathcart, *The Most Contrary Region: The BBC in Northern Ireland 1924–1984* (Belfast: Blackstaff, 1984), 157; Robert Welch (ed.), *The Oxford Companion to Irish*

Literature (Oxford: Oxford University Press, 1996), 564; May Neill, letter to author, 23 September 1995; Tony Bradley, 1 November 1994.

21. Private cars were rare in working-class areas until the 1950s (George Parker, 10 April 1994).

22. Parker, *Green Light*, 4 and 'Requiem', a radio feature produced by Brian Barfield of BBC Northern Ireland and broadcast on Radio 3 on 18 August 1973 as part of a programme of Northern Irish writing, *Causeway*; Charles Foran, *The Last House of Ulster* (Toronto: HarperCollins, 1995), 159–60.

23. George and Margaret Parker, 10 April 1994; *Green Light*, 3; Sam Fannin, letter to author, 1 January 1999. In Parker's play *Pentecost*, one of the characters, who has just returned to Belfast from Birmingham, is asked how he managed to pass through the city at the height of the Ulster Workers' Council Strike. He replies, 'I placed my faith in the Ulster Sunday. I believed in my heart, brother—even if the Protestant blackshirts had finally staged a putsch, they would still remember the seventh day and keep it holy. Not to mention rainy, bleak, doom-laden, and utterly devoid of human life' (*Three Plays for Ireland* [Birmingham: Oberon, 1989], 171).

24. Bardon, *Belfast*, 247–8.

25. Bardon, *Belfast*, 251–2; *Green Light*, 7–8, 12; Mary Stewart, principal of Strand Primary School, letter to author (including a photocopy of the school register for the time of Parker's attendance there), 18 November 1998; G. H. Parker, 10 April 1994.

26. Caroline Walsh; Sam McCready, 31 July 1996; *Green Light*, 8.

27. Bill Granleese, 27 July 1995; *Green Light*, 9–10.

28. The Group's historian notes that 'In theory the 10th Belfast has always been open to boys of all religious denominations', but owing to its location in East Belfast and its 'Protestant and Unionist associations', few Catholics would have joined (Andrew J. Totten, *Straight & Ready: A History of the 10th Belfast Scout Group 1908–1988* [privately printed in Belfast by Nelson & Knox, 1989], 26, 31).

29. Parker, *Green Light*, 11 and letter to Andrew Totten, 20 April 1987. The only sport Parker ever really enjoyed was lawn tennis (George Parker, 5 April 1994; Bill and Bob Granleese, 27 July 1995).

30. Bardon, *Belfast*, 253–5.

31. George Parker, 6 April 1994; Sam McCready, 31 July 1996; Parker, *Green Light*, 5–6 and 'Poem for my Mother, on Coming of Age', *Kilkenny Magazine*, 14 (Spring/Summer 1966), 69. While a pupil at Strand, Stewart ate his midday meal at the home of his mother's sister Carrie, whose husband, Edwin Jobes, worked as a shipwright. In 1960, 'Uncle Edwin' took him to the launch of the *Canberra*, the last luxury passenger liner built in Belfast, and, earlier that year, to the original production of *Over the Bridge*, Sam Thompson's play about sectarianism in the shipyards (Parker, 'Where I Was Born', produced by Douglas Carson for the BBC Northern Ireland Schools series *Today and Yesterday in Northern Ireland*, transmitted 11 May 1973 [BBC typescript, 9–11]; Carrie Jobes, 24 June 1995).

32. Margaret Parker, 7 April 1994; Jack Pakenham, 10 July 1995; Robert Crone, 17 November 1998; Sam McCready, 30 July 1996; Brian Garrett, 22 June 1995; Parker, *Green Light*, 15–16 and *Dramatis Personae* (Belfast: John Malone Memorial Committee, 1986), 4, 7.

33. Purcell; *Dramatis Personae*, 3–4.

34. John Frost, letters to author, November and 8 December 1995; J. S. Stevenson, letter to author, 14 December 1998; James Hawthorne, letter to author, 20 July 1995. Parker and Hawthorne would cross paths again years later, when Hawthorne was working in

television production for the BBC. They discussed a project that Hawthorne had in mind, a documentary about John Boyd Dunlop, inventor—in Belfast—of the pneumatic tyre. Although it was never made, the seed had been planted that would blossom in Parker's 1975 play *Spokesong*.

35. May Neill, letters to author, 12 July and 23 September 1995; James Hawthorne, letter to author, 20 July 1995; *Green Light*, 17.

36. James Hawthorne, letter to author, 20 July 1995; Sam McCready, 31 July 1996; Terence Brown, 6 July 1995; Sam Fannin, 23 March 1995; May Neill, letter to author, 12 July 1995; *Green Light*, 17; Joan Parker Clements, 9 April 1994; Brian Rainey, 21 June 1997.

37. Sam McCready, 31 July 1996; Parker, 'Belfast's Women: A Superior Brand of Dynamite', *Evening Standard*, 2 November 1976; Michael Longley, *Tuppenny Stung: Autobiographical Chapters* (Belfast: Lagan Press, 1994), 27; Seamus Heaney, *Preoccupations: Selected Prose 1968–1978* (1980) (London: Faber, 1984), 28; John Wilson Foster, 23 July 1995.

38. Terence Brown, 6 July 1995. This aspect of school life plays an important role in Parker's unpublished novel *The Jest-Book of ST Toile*. See the extract 'OH, OH' in the *Honest Ulsterman*, 23 (May/June 1970), 8–10.

39. Bob Granleese, 27 July 1995.

40. James Hawthorne, letters to author, 20 July and 5 December 1995; May Neill, letter to author, 12 July 1995; John Frost, letter to author, November 1995; Charles Grime, 23 June 1995; Charles Burrowes, 22 June 1995; Terence Brown, 6 July 1995; Parker, quoted in 'Profile: Stewart Parker', *Gown*, 6 October 1961.

41. Deirdre Wilson, *Slave of the Passions* (London: Picador, 1991), 22. Stewart's parents had actually paid, in the pre-Education Act days, to send his brother George to Sullivan. In 1947, when he started, there was a German prisoner-of-war compound behind the school and, as far as he knew, only two other boys from Sydenham enrolled. The three of them would sneak out at lunchtime to escape the 'wartime' meals (rationing continued well into the 1950s) and were reprimanded for kicking a football around the school grounds (*rugby* was the socially approved game). George lasted about two years there before his parents yielded to his pleas to let him have a technical education, at which point he went to work at Shorts. In Parker family lore, when the headmaster of Sullivan learned that a Stewart Parker would be transferring to the school in 1955 he consulted his files and commented that he hoped Stewart would do better than his brother (George Parker, 5 and 6 April 1994; Molly Crawford and Carrie Jobes, 24 June 1995).

42. Sullivan Upper School record card on James Stewart Parker; *Sullivan Upper School Magazine*, 3.8 (Summer 1957), 68–75; Sam McCready, 31 July 1996; Roy Alcorn, 2 July 1994; May Neill, letter to author, 12 July 1995; programmes for the Sullivan Upper School Dramatic Society productions of *Hamlet* (1956), *King Lear* (1957), and *Henry IV, Part I* (1958).

43. 'Profile: Stewart Parker', *Gown*, 6 October 1961; Sam Fannin, 25 March 1995; George and Margaret Parker, 6 April 1994; Parker, quoted in David Simpson, 'The Prolific Pen of Mr Parker', *Belfast Telegraph*, 3 November 1984 and Carty, and *Green Light*, 16.

44. May Neill, letter to author, 12 July 1995. Stewart's essay on 'Spring Cleaning' for the 1957 edition is representative—poised, polished, and virtually empty of content (*Sullivan Upper School Magazine*, 3.8 [Summer 1957], 28–9). Neill found boring the genre that most excited Stewart at the time, science fiction. One of his science fiction stories, 'A Process Called Progress' (in the vein of Aldous Huxley's *Brave New World*) appeared in the school magazine the summer he graduated, 1959.

45. Parker, quoted in Purcell, and undated notes in his youthful handwriting kept in his study with drafts of some of his early poetry.
46. Comfort's 'Third Elegy' was the last poem in the standard grammar school English text, *A Pageant of English Verse*, ed. E. W. Parker (London: Longmans, 1949).
47. Lesley Bruce, 13 April 1994.
48. Joan Parker Clements, 9 April 1994; George and Margaret Parker, 5 and 6 April 1994; Lesley Bruce, 13 April 1994; Parker, 'Time' (manuscript).
49. Julie Parker McMullan, 18 July 1998; Joan Parker Clements, 9 April 1994; George and Margaret Parker, 5 April 1994 and 24 June 1995; G. H. Parker, 10 and 11 April 1994.
50. George Parker, 5 April 1994; G. H. Parker, 11 April 1994; 'Poem for my Mother, on Coming of Age', 69–70.
51. Bill and Bob Granleese, 27 July 1995; *Green Light*, 10, 13–16.

NOTES TO CHAPTER 2

1. Seamus Deane, 21 February 1995; Brian Rainey, 21 June 1997; Tony Bradley, 3 March 1994; Bill Morrison, 7 and 8 June 1994; 'Profile: Stewart Parker', *Gown*, 6 October 1961; Liz Davidson, 8 May 1999; Niki Hill, 'The Way We Were', *Sunday News*, 11 October 1987; Ian Hill, 28 June 1994; George Watson, 6 February 1997; Seamus Heaney, 1 March 1994; Valerie Lilley, 7 June 1994.
2. Jonathan Bardon, *A History of Ulster* (Belfast: Blackstaff, 1992), 618–19; '"Graduates Have Nothing to Fear"', *Gown*, 1 November 1963; Rex Mitchell, 28 June 1994; Ciaran McKeown, 17 November 1998; 'Students and the Course of History', *Gown*, 6 May 1960.
3. 'More and More Students', *Gown*, 9 October 1959; T. W. Moody and J. C. Beckett, *Queen's, Belfast 1845–1949: The History of a University* (London: Faber, 1959), 663.
4. Moody and Beckett, 540–3.
5. Roy Alcorn, 2 July 1994; Tony Bradley, 1 November 1994; Seamus Deane, 21 February 1995; Ian Hill, 28 June 1994; Tony McAuley, 19 November 1998; Alf McCreary, 27 June 1994; Brian Rainey, 21 June 1997; William Harris, 29 October 1998; Philip Hobsbaum, 4 June 1994; Seamus Heaney, 'Further Language', *Studies in the Literary Imagination*, 30.2 (Fall 1997), 9; 'Literific Highlights', *Gown*, 9 October 1959. The Literary and Scientific ('Literific') Society dedicated itself to parliamentary-style debate and was the oldest, largest, and one of the most prominent student organizations at Queen's.
6. See, for example, 'Negroes "Sit-In"', *Gown*, 28 October 1960 and Malcolm Jaffa, 'The Cult of Martin Luther King', *Gown*, 24 November 1961. A few years later, when the Northern Irish civil rights movement began in earnest, its leaders (many of whom—including Austin Currie, Erskine Holmes, Michael Farrell, and Eamonn McCann—had been students at Queen's in this period) took explicit inspiration from the American example (see Bardon's *History of Ulster*, Chapter 14).
7. Liz Dickey, 16 May 1999; Liz Davidson, 10 May 1999.
8. Liz Davidson, 10 May 1999; Roy Alcorn, 2 July 1994; Tony McAuley, 19 November 1998; Ian Hill, 'Excellence at the Empire: Over the Bridge Reviewed', *Gown*, 29 January 1960; Zella Burton, 'Controversial Theatre', *Gown*, 29 January 1960; 'Behind "Q" Censorship', *Gown*, 9 December 1960. The *Gown* article about Paisley was based on a story Raymond Proctor had written for the Queen's magazine *Q*, which had been withdrawn when the printer refused to accept it for fear of losing advertisers—such

were the realities of life in Belfast circa 1960 ('"Q" Faces Censorship', *Gown*, 25 November 1960).

9. Patrick Grant, 22 March 1999; Tony Bradley, 1 November 1994.

10. Brian Walker and Alf McCreary, *Degrees of Excellence: The Story of Queen's, Belfast 1845–1995* (Belfast: Institute of Irish Studies, 1994), 112. The Chancellorship of Queen's was an honorary position; the Vice-Chancellor ran the university.

11. Philip Hobsbaum, 4 June 1994.

12. Tony McAuley, 19 November 1998; George Watson, 6 February 1997; Tony Bradley, 1 November 1994; Patrick Grant, 22 March 1999, and letter to author, 5 April 1999; Peter Butter, 15 March 1999. Students needed Latin and another language to pursue Honours.

13. Tony Bradley, 1 November 1994; George Watson, 6 February 1997; Philip Hobsbaum, 4 June 1994; George McWhirter, 3 May 1995; Laurence Lerner, 17 March 1999; Patrick Grant, 22 March 1999; Liz Davidson, 8 and 10 May 1999; Seamus Deane, 21 February 1995, and 'The Famous Seamus', *New Yorker* (20 March 2000), 63.

14. Peter Butter, 15 March 1999; George McWhirter, 29 May 1995; Heaney, 'Further Language', 7–8; George Watson, 6 February 1997.

15. They tended not, however, to be enrolled in the sciences or engineering, since these courses were particularly demanding and time-intensive.

16. Norman Mailer, 'The White Negro' in Gene Feldman and Max Gartenberg (eds.), *Protest: The Beat Generation and the Angry Young Men* (London: Souvenir Press, 1959), 342–3. This anthology of recent writing on both sides of the Atlantic had been published by New York's Citadel Press in 1958 under the shorter title *The Beat Generation and the Angry Young Men*. It and other works about the Beats were surveyed in *Gown* in October 1960 by a student writing under the name of William Lee Eggleston ('The New Barbarians', *Gown*, 14 October 1960). Bill Morrison, who was close to Parker when they were undergraduates, recalls that 'The White Negro' made a great impression on them at the time. One of Mailer's themes is the potential for creative interchange between the 'hipster' and the Negro, marginalized in a segregated society and thus, according to Mailer, a reservoir of primitive energy and passion. This idea, Morrison says, 'hit us really quite hard . . . we could identify with all that because we had the same kind of sectarian split, although we were all white' (Morrison, 8 June 1994).

17. Bill Morrison, 7 June 1994. The popularity of French existentialism at Queen's probably owed something to the presence in the French department of a scholar who had written pioneering studies of Sartre and Albert Camus (Patrick Grant, letter to author, 5 April 1999).

18. Kenneth Allsop, *The Angry Decade: A Survey of the Cultural Revolt of the Nineteen-Fifties* (London: Peter Owen, 1958), 9, 19.

19. Feldman and Gartenberg, 323–4, 343–4.

20. Feldman and Gartenberg, 13, 356.

21. Bill Morrison, 7 June 1994; Valerie Lilley, 7 June 1994.

22. Programme for the Annual General Meeting of the Queen's University of Belfast Dramatic Society, 1961.

23. Bill Morrison recalls that 'Beckett was an influence on all of us', and Philip Hobsbaum, who directed Parker's MA research at Queen's beginning in 1963, recollects that Parker had read 'a good deal of Joyce' by the time they met (Morrison, 7 June 1994; Hobsbaum, letter to author, 23 February 1999).

24. Parker wrote in 1961 that 'Love's three plays, plus one by Sam Thompson, are the only evidence of successful creative drama here in the last two years'. He found it 'remarkable'

that Love was not a 'regional' playwright, since 'an Ulsterman who writes about anything other than Ulster is hard to come by'. Love, in Parker's view, was 'interested in people behaving as individuals rather than as social animals' (Parker, 'The Triumph of Love', *Interest*, 2.1 [December 1961], 12).

25. Parker, 'Belfast for Beginners', *Interest*, 3.1 (October 1962), 3–5. In this article Parker refers to 'two' theatres in Belfast, presumably the Arts Theatre (which had in the past mounted a programme of international drama but had acquired a new building in 1961 and now pursued a strictly commercial policy) and the Ulster Group Theatre under the management of comedian James Young (which produced mainly working-class domestic farce). The more ambitious Lyric Players Theatre had been around for over ten years but was still amateur and essentially private, operating out of its director's home (see Ophelia Byrne, *The Stage in Ulster from the Eighteenth Century* [Belfast: Linen Hall Library, 1997]).

26. Parker, quoted in Deirdre Purcell, 'The Illusionist', *Sunday Tribune*, 27 September 1987.

27. 'Quidnunc, by Tape Worm', *Gown*, 11 November 1960.

28. Lecturers such as Laurence Lerner, Gamini Salgado, and Philip Hobsbaum also contributed to student publications.

29. After finishing at Queen's, Hamilton became a schoolteacher and within a short time had stopped writing. Morrison recalls that he 'wrote one very strange play about a man who had electrodes put in his brain to take his creativity out. And that was it. The end' (Bill Morrison, 7 June 1994).

30. Bill Morrison, 8 June 1994; 'Profile: Ian J. Hill', *Gown*, 9 October 1959; 'Milestone: Ian and Niki Marry', *Gown*, 6 October 1961.

31. Ian Hill, 'A Way to the Top?', *Gown*, 28 February 1961. Seamus Heaney, now the most celebrated of Parker's contemporaries at Queen's, remained relatively obscure at the time. This was partly a function of personality and individual interests—he did not belong to Dramsoc, for example—but also had much to do with the social dynamics of a particular time and place. Heaney belonged to one of the first waves of Education Act Catholics to hit Queen's, and he and most of his fellows kept their heads down and largely avoided attracting attention to themselves. His undergraduate pen name, 'Incertus', speaks volumes about the position of Northern Catholics in those years.

32. 'Belfast for Beginners', 5.

33. Ciaran McKeown, 17 November 1998; 'Quidnunc? by Tapeworm', *Gown*, 9 December 1960; Angela McCourt and Judy Silver, 'The Second Class Sex', *Gown*, 24 April 1964; George Watson, 6 February 1997; Ian Hill, 28 June 1994; Niki Hill; Liz Davidson, 10 May 1999; Liz Dickey, 16 May 1999; Sybil Allen Poole, 7 June 1999; Tony Bradley, 1 November 1994; Sam Fannin, letter to author, 16 April 1999; Bill Morrison, 7 June 1994. The Student Union has since moved to a building on University Road, and the old Student Union now houses the Queen's Music Department.

34. Tony Bradley, 1 November 1994; Valerie Lilley, 7 June 1994; Roy Alcorn, 2 July 1994; Bill Morrison, 8 June 1994.

35. George Bernard Shaw, *St. Joan* (New York: Penguin, 1951), 65. Parker hesitated to take the role, citing his reluctance to appear in tights, so Alcorn allowed him to wear long underwear and a tunic instead (Roy Alcorn, 2 July 1994).

36. Roy Alcorn, 2 July 1994; Ian Hill, 'Several Points Off Course', *Gown*, 15 January 1960; 'Faces in the Crowd', *Gown*, 4 December 1959; 'Faces in the Crowd', *Gown*, 15 January 1960.

37. Parker, 'Suicide', *Gorgon*, 3 (November 1959), 13; David M. Jenkins, 'Gorgon Reviewed', *Gown*, 4 December 1959; Parker, 'Johnny's Story', *Q*, 18 (Hilary 1960),

7–9; ' "Q" Worth Printing and Buying: But Prose Shows Up Poor Poetry', *Gown*, 11 March 1960.

38. 'Murder in the Cathedral: Drama Festival Plans', *Gown*, 26 February 1960; 'Dramatic Society Carry Off Trophies', *Gown*, 26 April 1960. Queen's Dramsoc was able, because of the unique position of Northern Ireland, to participate in both the all-Ireland Universities' Drama Association Festival and the Student Drama Festival organized by the British National Union of Students. The British finals were held in January, during the Christmas break, the Irish ones in the spring. The directors of student productions were usually referred to as producers, but for clarity's sake I use the more familiar terminology.

39. 'Profile: Bill Morrison', *Gown*, 19 January 1962; Bill Morrison, 7 and 8 June 1994; Valerie Lilley, 7 June 1994; Ian Hill, 28 June 1994; Sam Fannin, 21 March 1995.

40. Programme for the Annual General Meeting of the Queen's University Dramatic Society, 1960; T. S. Eliot, *Sweeney Agonistes: Fragments of an Aristophanic Melodrama* (London: Faber, 1932), 24; Ian Hill, 'Two to Play', *Gown*, 28 October 1960.

41. William Saroyan, *The Hungerers* (New York: Samuel French, 1939), 5–6.

42. Liz Davidson, 8 and 10 May 1999, and letter to author, 25 March 1995; Walker and McCreary, 115.

43. Parker, 'The Decision', *Q*, 19 (December 1960), n.p.

44. Bill Morrison, 7 June 1994; Joan Caldwell McQuoid, 5 July 1999; Parker, 'Editorial', *Interest*, 1.1 (November 1960), 3.

45. Parker, 'Editorial', *Interest*, 1.1; Bill Morrison, 7 June 1994; Morrison and Parker, 'Why?', *Interest*, 1.1 (November 1960), 5.

46. 'Periodicals: Writing Sells Out', *Gown*, 9 November 1962; 'Publications in Trouble', *Gown*, 18 October 1963.

47. Bill Morrison, 7 June 1994; Liz Davidson, letter to author, 25 March 1995; Hugo McCann, 'Experimental Theatre', *Gown*, 25 November 1960; Brian Dale, ' "Dramsoc" Presentation: Three More Plays', *Gown*, 9 December 1960; programme for the Annual General Meeting of the Queen's University Dramatic Society, 1961; 'Morrison's Play for Leeds', *Gown*, 9 December 1960; 'Leeds Win At Home', *Gown*, 17 January 1961.

48. Programme note, *Duet for Laughing Men* (Belfast, Stranmillis Training College, December 1960); Bill Morrison, 7 June 1994.

49. Bill Morrison, 7 June 1994. Parker later wrote a meditation on the potential impact of the tape recorder on poetry, arguing that it might help to 'release' poetry from the page and calling for '[p]oems composed by ear, mind, heart, gut and microphone only' (Parker, 'Tentative Description of a Dinner Given to Promote the Impeachment of William Caxton', *Gorgon* [Christmas 1962], 18–19).

50. Jim Caffrey, 'Was This the Way It Had To Be?', *Gown*, 10 March 1961.

51. Programme for the Annual General Meeting of the Queen's University Dramatic Society, 1961; 'Faces in the Crowd', *Gown*, 21 April 1961; Bill Morrison, 7 June 1994; Niki Hill.

NOTES TO CHAPTER 3

1. George Parker, 9 April 1994; Bill Morrison, 7 June 1994.

2. Caroline Walsh, 'Stewart Parker', *Irish Times*, 13 August 1977; Joan Parker Clements and Margaret Parker, 9 April 1994.

3. Caroline Walsh; George and Margaret Parker and Joan Parker Clements, 9 April 1994.

4. Joan Parker Clements, 9 April 1994; Parker, *Hopdance* manuscript. For nearly a decade after the amputation, Parker worried that his cancer would recur. Only when this apprehension had begun to fade could he acknowledge what a heavy burden he had been carrying since his cancer diagnosis. At this point he felt he must come to terms with the experience by capturing it in prose. In a novel called *Caution in the Traffic, Prudence in the Rain* (later retitled *Hopdance*), he recorded the events of his life before, during, and after the long hospital stay between his second and third years as an undergraduate. In this work, Parker structured his experience for himself in a way that gave it meaning. His alter ego, Tosh, is drifting through life before the cancer is discovered, plagued by the twin 'cankers' of a puzzling pain in his leg and a crippling loneliness. As the story of the amputation and its aftermath unfolds, Tosh begins to allow other people to share his suffering and moves closer to being able to make the great connection he has sought to one other human being. His reflections on writing counterpoint his process of maturation as a person. The amputation, Parker suggests, makes him into a serious writer by forcing him into a more authentic relation to life, which 'Starts with the wound. Ends with the kiss. For the lucky ones.' Parker made no attempt to publish *Hopdance*. Instead, he set it aside, satisfied that it had served a therapeutic purpose. His literary achievement in this novel is considerable, but it is also a unique autobiographical document. Read in conjunction with the reminiscences of those close to him at the time, *Hopdance* affords a vivid portrait of Parker during what might well be considered the most formative year of his life. Further references to it will be signposted in the text.

5. Joan Parker Clements, 9 April 1994.

6. Joan Parker Clements, 9 April 1994; Sam Fannin, letter to author, June 1999.

7. Molly Crawford and Carrie Jobes, 24 June 1995; David Dickson, 9 April 1994.

8. George Parker and Joan Parker Clements, 9 April 1994; Austin Briggs, 15 January 1994.

9. This comes from an essay laying out his aesthetic philosophy that Parker wrote on the fifth anniversary of his amputation, in May 1966. He later incorporated it into the *Hopdance* manuscript.

10. George Parker, 5 and 9 April 1994; G. H. Parker, 10 April 1994; *Hopdance* manuscript.

11. George Parker, 9 April 1994.

12. Liz Davidson, letter to author, 25 March 1995. A mutual friend recalls Parker saying at the time that he thought it would be better for him to meet someone who knew him only as he was now, with one leg (Liz Dickey, 16 May 1999).

13. Joan Parker Clements, 9 April 1994; Bob Granleese, 27 July 1995.

14. Bob Granleese, 27 July 1995. The character of Harrison, a major one in the novel, is based substantially on Bill Morrison.

15. Deirdre Purcell, 'The Illusionist', *Sunday Tribune*, 27 September 1987; Lorraine Brown Fannin, letter to author, 6 March 1995; Seamus Deane, 21 February 1995.

16. 'Profile: Stewart Parker', *Gown*, 6 October 1961.

17. Joan Caldwell McQuoid, 5 July 1999; Liz Davidson, 8 May 1999; Chidiok Tichborne, 'Tichborne's Elegy' in *The Norton Anthology of Poetry*, 3rd edn., ed. Alexander Allison, et al. (New York: Norton, 1983), 105.

18. Joan Parker Clements, 9 April 1994; Bill Morrison, 7 June 1994; *Hopdance* manuscript; Valerie Lilley, 7 June 1994. Marian, one of the characters in Parker's 1987 play *Pentecost*, spent part of her youth in a flat on Magdala Street. When that play opened, Parker told Niki Hill that 'I've been saving Magdala Street for a long time....I was going to get it in somewhere' ('The Way We Were', *Sunday News*, 11 October 1987).

19. Ian Hill, 28 June 1994.
20. Bill Morrison, 7 June 1994.
21. 'Arts Festival Programme', *Gown*, 27 October 1961; 'Arts Festival Proceeds', *Gown*, 24 November 1961; 'Beyond Their Range?', *Gown*, 8 December 1961; Bill Morrison, 7 June 1994; B. Apfel, 'Arts Festival Defended' (letter to the editor from the Festival Organizer), *Gown*, 2 February 1962.
22. M. J. F., 'Arts Festival: Looking Back Indifferently', *Gown*, 19 January 1962; Bill Morrison, 7 June 1994; Niki Hill.
23. Bill Morrison, 7 and 8 June 1994; Valerie Lilley, 7 June 1994.
24. Stewart's brother George and sister-in-law Margaret gave him a transistor radio as a house-warming present when he moved into the Magdala Street flat. This was stolen several months later (George and Margaret Parker, 5 April 1994). The theft features in *Hopdance*, where it comes as a devastating blow to Tosh since the radio had symbolized for him his brother's 'unarticulated anguish and concern...the inconsolable weight of his brother's love'.
25. Sam Fannin, 21 and 22 March 1995; Valerie Lilley, 7 June 1994; Bill Morrison, 7 June 1994.
26. Sam Fannin, 21, 23, and 24 March 1995.
27. Parker, *Dramatis Personae* (Belfast: John Malone Memorial Committee, 1986), 17; John Paul, 17 January 1994.
28. 'Profile: Stewart Parker'. The caption under a photograph of Parker in *Gown* in late 1962 includes the information that he 'has completed the first draft of his novel' (*Gown*, 13 December 1962). Parker wrote *Combo* by hand in a composition book. The manuscript consists of 134 pages of text, preceded by 22 pages of notes. It does not appear to be complete, ending abruptly without fulfilling Parker's schema for the novel. References to the *Combo* manuscript will be signposted in the text.
29. In the *Combo* manuscript, the novel ends with this letter, which seems to be cut off in the middle. Parker's plan for the book, though he did not follow this in every detail, indicates that he intended to conclude with two letters: one from Alan to Walt (at that point he envisaged Alan as the amputee) and one from Ann (who escapes with a broken bone and a pregnancy) to the dead Johnny. There are several possible explanations for the discrepancy: (1) Parker changed his mind about the ending of the novel, (2) he abandoned the project unfinished, or (3) the final pages of the manuscript were mislaid or destroyed by Parker himself or by someone else. The last explanation strikes me as most plausible.
30. George Watson, 6 February 1997.
31. Parker, 'The Broken Lives', *Interest*, 3.6 (May 1963), 17.
32. Brenda Callaghan, 26 June 1994; Sam Fannin, 21 and 22 March 1995, and letter to author, 4 July 1994; Roy Nimmons, letter to author, 10 July 1994; Bob Granleese, 27 and 29 July 1995; Bernard MacLaverty, 5 June 1994; Julie MacRae, 25 February 1995; George and Margaret Parker, 6 April 1994 and 25 February 1995; Joan Parker Clements, 9 April 1994; George Watson, 6 February 1997; Ian Hill, 28 June 1994; Bill Morrison, 7 June 1994; Sylvia Wynne, 9 February 1997.
33. Margaret Parker and Joan Parker Clements, 9 April 1994; G. H. Parker, 10 April 1994; Roy Nimmons, letter to author, 10 July 1994; Ed Barrett, 15 January 1994; Austin Briggs, 15 January 1994.
34. Ed Barrett, 15 January 1994; Austin Briggs, 15 January 1994.
35. In the British system of higher education, undergraduate degrees are rated according to students' performance on comprehensive exams at the end of their courses of study.

The best overall grade is a 1. A 2.1 is a high 2—very good, and sufficient to qualify a student for graduate funding, but not stellar.

36. George Watson, 6 February 1997.
37. Philip Hobsbaum, 4 June 1994.
38. Julie MacRae, 25 February 1995; Tony Bradley, 1 November 1994; Philip Hobsbaum, 4 June 1994; Sam Fannin, 23 March 1995; Tom Adair, 'Across the Watery Vale: Philip Hobsbaum and The Group', *Linen Hall Review*, 4.4 (Winter 1987), 9.
39. Philip Hobsbaum, 4 June 1994 and 'The Belfast Group: A Recollection', *Éire-Ireland*, 32.2 and 3 (Summer/Fall 1997), 173–82; Joan Newmann, 27 June 1994; Nicholas Round, 5 June 1994; 'The Belfast Group: A Symposium', *Honest Ulsterman*, 53 (November/December 1976), 53–63; 'Special Feature: The Belfast Group', *Honest Ulsterman*, 97 (Spring 1994), 3–26; Adair, 9–11. For a detailed discussion of Hobsbaum's background, the workings and early membership of the Group, and its significance, see Heather Clark, *The Ulster Renaissance: Poetry in Belfast 1962–1972* (Oxford: Oxford University Press, 2006). See also Michael Parker, *Seamus Heaney: The Making of the Poet* (Iowa City: University of Iowa Press, 1993).
40. Philip Hosbsbaum, 'Creative Writing' (radio programme recorded 31 May 1966 for BBC Northern Ireland, held in the BBC Radio Archives in Cultra, Northern Ireland, museum number 1951); Seamus Heaney, in 'The Belfast Group: A Symposium', 62; Derek Mahon, 'Poetry in Northern Ireland', *20th-Century Studies*, 4 (November 1970), 91; Michael Parker, *Seamus Heaney*, 58; Clark, 69.
41. Seamus Heaney, in 'The Belfast Group: A Symposium', 62 and 'Victorious Ulsterman', *Sunday Independent*, 6 November 1988; Philip Hobsbaum, 4 June 1994; Michael Longley, in 'The Belfast Group: A Symposium', 56; Jack Pakenham, 10 July 1995.
42. Parker, 'Coming Out', from the Group archive housed in Special Collections at Queen's University Belfast.
43. Philip Hobsbaum, 4 June 1994. 'ST Toile' is 'T. S. Eliot' backwards (John Paul, 17 January 1994). Shortly after Parker left Belfast for the United States in the autumn of 1964, *Interest* published a selection of these pieces presented to the Group under the title 'The Preambles of S T Toile' (*Interest*, 5.1 [November 1964], 18–21).
44. Bill Morrison, 7 and 8 June 1994; John Hamilton, 7 April 1994.
45. Parker, 'The New Stage Club: Theatre in Belfast', *Gown*, 6 December 1963; Sam Fannin, 22 March 1995; Bill Morrison, 7 June 1994; Joan Newmann, 27 June 1994; programme for the New Stage Club production of *Frost at Midnight* by André Obey (Belfast, December 1963).
46. New Stage Club advertising flyer; Stephen Rea, 23 February 1995; Roy Alcorn, 18 June 1995; Sam Fannin, 21 and 22 March 1995, and letters to author, 25 March and 18 April 1994; Sam Thompson, letter to Parker, 10 December 1963; Bill Morrison, 7 June 1994; Parker, letter to Philip Hobsbaum, 7 January 1964.
47. Philip Hobsbaum, 4 June 1994, and letter to author, 9 May 1999; Parker, letter to Hobsbaum, 24 June 1966.
48. Philip Hobsbaum, letter to author, 9 May 1999; J. Stewart Parker, 'The Modern Poet as Dramatist: Some Aspects of Non-Realistic Drama, with Special Reference to Eliot, Yeats and Cummings' (thesis submitted for the degree of Master of Arts, Queen's University Belfast, 1966), 169–70, 166.
49. 'Modern Poet as Dramatist', 174, 187, 206.
50. 'Modern Poet as Dramatist', 213–14. Parker responded to Hobsbaum's initial critique of the *Him* chapter in these terms: 'Thank you very much (sincerely) for the suggestions and disagreements—it is clear to me on re-reading that I went a little overboard

on *Him*, as I tend to do when I find something that excites me' (Parker, letter to Philip Hobsbaum, 10 August 1965).

51. The impact of *Him* upon Parker is perhaps most obvious in his play *Nightshade*, which uses expressionist techniques to dramatize complex psychological adjustments taking place in the characters' minds and which, like Cummings's play, centres on the relations between life, art, and mortality. Parker also adapted some of Cummings's specific theatrical devices for his own ends. For example, in *Spokesong*, he includes a character called the Trick Cyclist who takes a variety of parts in the action and works thematically as the 'spirit of Belfast'. In *Northern Star*, Parker recapitulates the history of the United Irishmen in a sequence of scenes that imitate the styles of previous Irish playwrights and correspond in complex fashion to the ages of man and stages of the revolutionary movement.

52. 'Modern Poet as Dramatist', 176, 198.

53. Philip Hobsbaum, 4 June 1994; Joan Parker Clements, 9 April 1994; George and Margaret Parker, 6 April 1994; G. H. Parker, 10 April 1994; Bob Granleese, 27 July 1995.

NOTES TO CHAPTER 4

1. Stewart Parker, letter to Philip Hobsbaum, 12 August 1964; Margaret Briggs, letter to Frances Pearce, 1 September 1964; *Hamilton College Catalogue 1994–95* (Clinton, New York: Hamilton College, 1994), 5; Marcus Patton, journal, 27 September 1971.

2. Mimi Kingsley, 4 November 1994; Art Skidmore, 9 January 1994; John Paul, 17 January 1994; *Hamilton College Catalogue 1964–1965* (Clinton, New York: Hamilton College, 1964), 75, 5, 105–10, 27, 33, 82; Terry Keenan, 5 November 1994. Skidmore graduated from Hamilton in 1960. His classmate John Nichols vividly portrays the alcoholic social life of the place in his first novel, *The Sterile Cuckoo* (1965), made into a movie with the same title directed by Alan J. Pakula and starring Liza Minelli as the eccentric girlfriend of a young man attending a Hamilton-like college (1969).

3. Austin Briggs, 15 January 1994; *Hamilton College Catalogue 1964–1965*, 85; *Hamiltonian* (college yearbook); *Hamilton Spectator* (college newspaper); Gerard Moses, 5 November 1994; Mimi Kingsley, 3 November 1994; Parker, letter to Philip Hobsbaum, 11 September 1964.

4. Ed Barrett, 15 January and 4 November 1994; Peter Kingsley, 10 July 1999; Mimi Kingsley, 15 January and 3 November 1994; Margaret Briggs, 16 January and 3 November 1994; Austin Briggs, 15 January 1994; Terry and Jane Keenan, 5 November 1994; John Paul, 17 January 1994; Susan Kenney, 13 February 1994; James McConkey, 8 January and 4 November 1994; Gerard Moses, 5 November 1994.

5. Margaret Briggs, 3 November 1994; Dwight Lindley, 15 January 1994; John Paul, e-mail to author, 20 January 2002; Bill Welf, 'J. S. Parker Leaves for Eire', *Hamilton Spectator*, 3 February 1967; Austin Briggs, 15 January 1994; Gerard Moses, 5 November 1994; Parker, 'Belfast's Women: A Superior Brand of Dynamite', *Evening Standard*, 2 November 1976, letters to Philip Hobsbaum, 17 January and 24 July 1965, journal, 1–4 July 1966, and undated autobiographical chronology (kept with *Hopdance* manuscript).

6. *Hamilton College Catalogue 1964–1965*, 49; Parker, letters to Philip Hobsbaum, 11 September 1964 and 17 January and 6 November 1965; Hobsbaum, letter to Parker, 14 May 1965; Austin Briggs, 15 January 1994; Joan Parker Clements, 9 April 1994; Ed Barrett, 4 November 1994.

7. 'Charlatans Name Four Directors', *Hamilton Spectator*, 12 November 1965; Parker, letter to Philip Hobsbaum, 7 December 1965; Peter Yeager, 'Performance Tops Play in Charlatans Thomas Offering', *Hamilton Spectator*, 11 November 1966; Welf; Peter Kingsley, 10 July 1999; Gerard Moses, 5 November 1994; Ivan Marki, 3 November 1994; Terry Keenan, 5 November 1994.

8. Mimi Kingsley, 15 January and 3 November 1994; Austin Briggs, 15 January 1994; Terry and Jane Keenan, 16 January and 5 November 1994; Peter Kingsley, 10 July 1999; Gerard Moses, 5 November 1994; John Paul, 17 January 1994; Lynne Parker, 3 November 2008.

9. Ed Barrett, 15 January 1994; Austin Briggs, 15 January 1994; Peter Kingsley, 10 July 1999; John Paul, 17 January 1994.

10. John Paul, 17 January 1994; William Manchester, *The Glory and the Dream: A Narrative History of America 1932–1972* (New York: Bantam Books, 1975), 1021–5.

11. Peter Kingsley, 11 July 1999; Mimi Kingsley, 15 January 1994; Gerard Moses, 5 November 1994; *Hamilton College Catalogue 1964–1965*, 109.

12. *Hamilton College Catalogue 1966–1967* (Clinton, New York: Hamilton College, 1966), 68–9, 116; Helen Nesbitt, 4 November 1994; Terry and Jane Keenan, 5 November 1994; John Paul, 6 November 1994.

13. Terry and Jane Keenan, 5 November 1994.

14. Parker, letter to Philip Hobsbaum, 17 January 1965. The lines quoted above are compiled from three versions: a typescript of the poem used by Hobsbaum as a Group sheet for discussion of the poem in Parker's absence; the version printed in the *Northern Review*, 1.2 (n.d. [1965]), 18–21; and that in Parker's pamphlet *The Casualty's Meditation* (Belfast: Queen's University Festival Publications, n.d. [1966]).

15. Parker, letter to Philip Hobsbaum, 17 January 1965. Several years later, Parker drew on this incident again for his autobiographical novel *Hopdance*. His alter ego, Tosh, is suddenly restored to himself when the pain-induced delirium lifts three days after his amputation, and here the image is unambiguously positive:

    > For three days he had lain objectified, locked into the silent maelstrom of the casualty. On the third night his eyes were on the window in the ceiling and the blind was up. The moon swam into the window frame. It filled his eyes with a pale beatitude. He stared at it in a long calm astonishment. It was alive with a benign serenity of light. He felt a smile of recognition breaking across his features. He had awakened to his world again.

16. Terry Keenan, 5 November 1994; Parker, letter to Philip Hobsbaum, 24 July 1965.

17. Parker, letters to Philip Hobsbaum, 24 July and 10 August 1965 and 22 March 1966, 'The Preambles of S T Toile', ill. Jim Allen, *Northern Review*, 1.1 (Spring 1965), 12–25, and 'The Casualty Meditates Upon His Journey', *Northern Review*, 1.2; Heather Clark, *The Ulster Renaissance: Poetry in Belfast 1962–1972* (Oxford: Oxford University Press, 2006), 76–9. Clark records that the *Northern Review* ceased publication in 1969.

18. Parker, letters to Philip Hobsbaum, 24 July and 7 December 1965; P. L. Brent (ed.), *Young Commonwealth Poets '65* (London: Heinemann, 1965). Hobsbaum edited the Northern Ireland section of the anthology, and the Parker pieces included were 'Paddy Dies', 'Crutch' (one of the 'fragments' presented as a prose poem), and 'Coming Out'.

19. Parker, 'Poem for my Mother, on Coming of Age' and 'Post Script', *Kilkenny Magazine*, 14 (Spring/Summer 1966), 69–70 and *Casualty's Meditation*. For more on the impact of the Festival pamphlet series, see Clark, 73–4.

20. Philip Hobsbaum, 'Belfast Letter: Nobody's Province', *Spectator* (12 August 1966), 208–9; Parker, letter to Hobsbaum, 22 March 1966.

21. John Paul, 17 January 1994; Gerard Moses, 5 November 1994; Parker, letters to Philip Hobsbaum, 25 September, 6 November, and 7 December 1965 and 22 March 1966.

22. Parker, letters to Philip Hobsbaum, 24 June and 9 October 1966. My account of the trip is based on Parker's contemporary journal entries.

23. Parker, journal, 7, 8, 9, 10 August 1966.

24. Parker, letter to Philip Hobsbaum, 9 October 1966.

25. Parker, 'The Recipient', *Honest Ulsterman*, 2 (June 1968), 18–24; Parker, letters to Philip Hobsbaum, 24 June and 9 October 1966.

26. Parker, *Speaking of Red Indians* (BBC typescript), produced by David A. Turner of the Drama Department, BBC Northern Ireland, and first transmitted by the Northern Ireland Home Service on 24 November 1967.

27. *Red Indians*, 8.

28. *Red Indians*, 16, 13, 17, 5, 18.

29. Peter Kingsley, e-mail to author, 20 July 1999. Mimi Kingsley recalls that Stewart and Kate married to come to the US, since it would be more 'respectable' to arrive as husband and wife (Mimi Kingsley, 15 January 1994). Her mother, Helen Nesbitt, remembers Ed Barrett saying that the young couple never would have married were it not for the Hamilton job offer, but would have lived together instead (Helen Nesbitt, 2 November 1994).

30. Ed Barrett, 15 January 1994.

31. Parker, letter to Philip Hobsbaum, 17 January 1965; Ed Barrett, 15 January 1994; Margaret Briggs, 5 November and 16 January 1994; Austin Briggs, 15 January 1994.

32. John Paul, 17 January and 6 November 1994, and e-mail to author, 20 January 2002.

33. Parker still planned to move to London when he wrote to Hobsbaum on 9 October 1966, but in the same letter he announced his intention to apply to the Arts Council for a grant for the following year, although he did not expect to get one.

34. James McConkey, 8 January and 4 November 1994, and letter to Parker, 2 December 1966; Parker, letter to Ephim Fogel, 8 December 1966; Fogel, letter to Parker, 23 January 1967.

35. Parker, journal, 13 and 23 January 1967.

36. Parker, journal, 8 February 1967. Boyd gave Parker some work reviewing for the weekly arts programme he produced. Parker also wrote one talk, *Heading West* (about his American trip), for Boyd, but most of his assignments in 1967 came from other BBC departments.

37. Tony McAuley, 14 and 19 November 1998. McAuley, who joined the BBC in 1970, recalls that he was only the second Catholic hired as a producer in Northern Ireland. The first, Gerry McCrudden, grew up in Belfast but had gone to London and worked himself up through the ranks of the BBC there before returning to Northern Ireland as a television producer.

38. Sam Fannin, 22 March 1995; Tony McAuley, 14 November 1998.

39. Parker, journal, 16 March 1967.

40. Robert Crone, 17 November 1998. Graduates of Orangefield include popular musician Van Morrison; Gerald Dawe, a poet, critic, and academic; and Brian Keenan, who wrote a best-selling memoir of his experiences as a hostage in Beirut.

41. Robert Crone, 17 November 1998; David Hammond, 30 June 1994. Gerald Dawe recalls that Parker taught his class on the poetry of Sylvia Plath and encouraged Dawe's

own poetic ambitions (Dawe, *The Rest is History* [Newry, Northern Ireland: Abbey Press, 1998], 60).

42. Rex Cathcart, *The Most Contrary Region: The BBC in Northern Ireland 1924–1984* (Belfast: Blackstaff, 1984), 200; Douglas Carson, 21 November 1998; Tony McAuley, 14 November 1998.

43. Robert Crone, 17 November 1998; George Thompson, 'The Ulster Folk Museum' in Michael Longley (ed.), *Causeway: The Arts in Ulster* (Belfast: Arts Council of Northern Ireland, 1971), 153–65; Douglas and Mary Carson, 21 November 1998.

44. Douglas Carson, 21 November 1998; David Hammond, 30 June 1994; Tony McAuley, 14 and 19 November 1998.

45. Douglas Carson, 21 November 1998; Tony McAuley, 14 November 1998.

46. Parker, journal, 3 May 1967. Hamilton's play eventually got what *Gown* termed 'one noisy, press-crowded "private" performance'. Kevin Boyle, 'Queen's Christ Banned', *Gown*, 12 October 1962; Parker, 'Belfast for Beginners', *Interest*, 3.1 (October 1962), 3–4; John Hamilton, 7 April 1994.

47. 'Teasey Leaves Festival', *Gown*, 1 November 1963; Colin Wills, 'Focus…Festival 64', *Gown*, 7 February 1964; Brian Walker and Alf McCreary, *Degrees of Excellence: The Story of Queen's, Belfast 1845–1995* (Belfast: Institute of Irish Studies, 1994), 126; Alf McCreary, 'Twenty-one Entertaining Years', *Belfast Telegraph*, 11 November 1983. Emmerson went on to become Northern Irish flautist James Galway's manager (Sam Fannin, 22 March 1995).

48. Sam Fannin, 22 March 1995; Philip Hobsbaum, 4 June 1994; Walker and McCreary, 126, 123; Michael Emmerson, letter to Parker, 8 May 1967; Tyrone Guthrie, letter to Emmerson, 17 May 1967; Emmerson, letter to Guthrie, 22 May 1967; Emmerson, letter to Parker, 31 May 1967; Parker, letter to Emmerson, 2 June 1967; Parker, draft letter to Guthrie, 6 December 1967; Festival 64 programme.

49. Parker, *The Yahoos' Overthrow* (typescript, 1967) and draft letters to Tyrone Guthrie, 6 December 1967 and n.d. (probably late December 1967 or early January 1968).

50. A 'Deirdre play' is first mentioned in Parker's journal on 23 January 1967.

51. Parker, *The Sensational Real-life Drama of Deirdre Porter* (typescript).

52. 'Five-year Jail Term', *News Letter*, 29 September 1966.

53. Deirdre is the first of a series of (often failed or compromised) artist-figures at the centre of Parker's plays, and the Young Man and his brothers have their counterparts in the song-writing team of *Catchpenny Twist*. Parker never gave up on the Deirdre story itself, eventually using it as the basis of a six-part series of television films, *Lost Belongings*.

54. Parker, journal, 17–31 July 1967 (there is also a mention of this piece under an earlier title, *This Is Your Life In Their Hands*, on 12 May 1967) and *Sam Todd For God*, typescript (the script I have seen is a revised version of the 1967 piece). The inspiration for the play came from Sam Fannin, who saw 'Sam Todd for God', '(as in Clinton for President)…writ large on a gable wall' and 'dragged Stewart out in the car to see it…he was immediately taken by the absurdist potential' (Fannin, letter to author, 10 October 2000).

55. Here Parker sends up the subtitle of the long-running radio saga *The Archers*: 'an everyday story of country folk'.

56. *Sam Todd*, 10, 18–19.

57. *Sam Todd*, 43–6.

58. Parker, journal, 14 August 1967.

NOTES TO CHAPTER 5

1. Adjudicators' Comments on *The Sensational Real-life Drama of Deirdre Porter*, Irish Life Drama Award, 1967; David Turner, letters to Parker, 18 October and 11 December 1967; Parker, journal, 21 October 1967.
2. Michael Emmerson, letter to Parker, 16 September 1967; Parker, journal, 21 October 1967.
3. Parker, draft letter to Tyrone Guthrie, 6 December 1967; Guthrie, letter to Parker, 23 December 1967.
4. Parker, draft letter to Guthrie, n.d. (probably late December 1967 or early January 1968). In June 1968, through the intervention of Professor James Clancy of the Cornell Theatre Arts Department with Peter Zeisler, managing director of the Guthrie Theatre, Parker would spend two weeks in Minneapolis observing rehearsals of a production of *Serjeant Musgrave's Dance* by John Arden. He probably never met Guthrie, though—at least, if he did, he neither noted it in his journal nor mentioned it to Peter Kingsley, in whose parents' house he stayed while in Minneapolis (Clancy, letter to Zeisler, 26 February 1968; Zeisler, letter to Parker, 22 May 1968; Kingsley, 10 July 1999 and e-mail to author, 27 July 2010).
5. Parker, *Maw: A Journey* (Belfast: Queen's University Festival Publications, n.d. [1967]); Seamus Heaney, letter to Parker, 20 October 1967.
6. Parker, 'Texas University Gunman Kills 14' in *Maw*, n.p., and journal, 30 August 1966; William Manchester, *The Glory and the Dream: A Narrative History of America 1932–1972* (New York: Bantam Books, 1974), 1038.
7. Seamus Heaney, letter to Parker, 20 October 1967.
8. Parker noted that 'The earliest fragments must go back at least to 1963. First batch of jests written 63–64. Then a few at Hamilton 64–67. The unifying act of bookmaking was in the 6 weeks of Christmas vacation, December–January 67–68' (Parker, journal, 11 September 1968).
9. Parker, *The Jest-Book of ST Toile*, typescript, 23.
10. *Jest-Book*, 33, 86, 38, 36, 40, 42.
11. *Jest-Book*, 100.
12. Parker, journal, 11 September and 4 October 1968; John Johnson, letters to Parker, 20 July 1965 and 1 October 1968.
13. Two fictional portrayals of the lives of Cornell faculty members and their families around this time are James McConkey, *A Journey to Sahalin* (New York: Coward, McCann & Geoghegan, 1971) and Alison Lurie, *The War Between the Tates* (New York: Random House, 1974). Both depict the sexual anarchy of the period.
14. Paul cannot date the episode with confidence, but cryptic references in Parker's journal lead me to believe it took place in early autumn 1968 (John Paul, 17 January 1994 and 16 July 2001).
15. John Paul, 17 January 1994 and 16 July 2001.
16. Parker, journal, 31 December 1968.
17. Parker, journal, 19 October 1968. Parker read several books with this purpose in mind in January 1969, but it would be many years before his McCracken play got written. *Northern Star*, as he eventually called it, premièred at the Lyric Players Theatre, Belfast, in 1984.
18. Parker was probably familiar with the sympathetic portrayal of Henry Joy McCracken provided in a biography of his sister by Mary McNeill, *The Life and Times of Mary Ann McCracken 1770–1866: A Belfast Panorama*, first published by Allen Figgis in 1960.

19. Manchester, 1047–8, 1070.
20. Richard Curtis, *The Berrigan Brothers: The Story of Daniel and Philip Berrigan* (New York: Hawthorn Books, 1974).
21. Daniel Berrigan, *To Dwell in Peace: An Autobiography* (San Francisco: Harper & Row, 1987), 229 and *The Trial of the Catonsville Nine* (Boston: Beacon Press, 1970), vii; John Paul, 16 July 2001. Day talked with Parker and Paul about a member of her staff who had set fire to himself in emulation of Buddhist monks who self-immolated to protest against the Vietnam War. She had been with him in the hospital as he lay dying, and she assured them he was neither suicidal nor crazy, but merely following his Christian principles in making a sacrifice to call attention to the many people hurt by the war.
22. Parker, journal, 26 October 1968.
23. Neil Hertz, 5 February 1994. Hertz explains that the programme was originally intended to facilitate contact between Cornell students who had been arrested for draft resistance and their alma mater, but, owing to the vagaries of the court system, none of the ex-Cornell students reached Allenwood during the several years of its operation (Hertz, e-mails to author, 29 September and 2 October 1997).
24. Parker, 'School for Revolution', *Irish Times*, 7 April 1970.
25. Manchester, 982–3, 1020–1, 1058–65, 1067, 1079–81, 1127–9.
26. Parker, 'School for Revolution' and journal, 26 February 1969.
27. Parker, journal, 12 and 26 March 1969, and 'School for Revolution'; Manchester, 1149. In Parker's *Lost Belongings*, the protagonist, Deirdre, also writes on toilet paper and flushes it away to avoid discovery.
28. Neil Hertz, 5 February 1994, and e-mail to author, 2 October 1997; Donald Alexander Downs, *Cornell '69: Liberalism and the Crisis of the American University* (Ithaca: Cornell University Press, 1999), 3–4. The older man was admitted on a trial basis but could not adjust to the routine of a student. After trying unsuccessfully to browbeat the Admissions Office into enrolling his son instead, he reverted to selling drugs. The other also got involved in the local drug trade and eventually returned to prison for shooting and killing another dealer.
29. Tony La Vopa, 17 July 1999; Cushing Strout and David I. Grossvogel (eds.), *Divided We Stand: Reflections on the Crisis at Cornell* (Garden City, New York: Doubleday, 1970). See especially the chronology at the front of the volume and Cleveland Donald, Jr, 'Cornell: Confrontation in Black and White', 171, 194–5, 200.
30. Downs argues that the takeover of the Straight had likely been planned in advance in anticipation of an unfavourable decision by the Board on Student Conduct (Downs, 165–70).
31. My account of the Willard Straight takeover is compiled from the Strout and Grossvogel collection, the Downs book, reportage and commentary in the *Cornell Daily Sun*, 18–24 April 1969, and interviews with Neil Hertz (5 February 1994), Tony La Vopa (17 July 1999), and Reeve Parker (14 January 1994).
32. Scott McMillin, letter to author, 14 February 1994; Parker, journal, 22 April 1969.
33. Parker, *Pentecost* in *Three Plays for Ireland* (Birmingham: Oberon, 1989), 184–5.
34. Neil Hertz, 5 February 1994; Reeve Parker, 14 January 1994; Stewart Parker, journal, June 1969 (no specific date, but the entry falls between entries for 4 and 18 June) and 26 November 1968.
35. Alfred Gingold, 12 July 1999.
36. Parker, letter to Ephim Fogel, 10 August 1969.
37. John Paul, 17 January 1994; G. H. Parker, 11 April 1994.
38. Parker, journal, 14–19 August 1969.

NOTES TO CHAPTER 6

1. Tony McAuley, a BBC Northern Ireland Schools producer from 1970 throughout the time that Parker remained in Belfast, recalls him as the first person he knew to try to make a living exclusively as a writer. Denys Hawthorne, BBC Northern Ireland Radio Drama producer in 1971/2, has a similar memory (McAuley, 14 November 1998; Hawthorne, 22 February 1995).

2. Parker, *Three Plays for Ireland* (Birmingham: Oberon, 1989), 184. For the historical sections of this chapter I have drawn on Jonathan Bardon's *A History of Ulster* (Belfast: Blackstaff, 1992) as well as his *Belfast: An Illustrated History* (Belfast: Blackstaff, 1982); Paul Bew and Gordon Gillespie, *Northern Ireland: A Chronology of the Troubles 1968–1993* (Dublin: Gill and Macmillan, 1993); Bob Purdie, *Politics in the Streets: The Origins of the Civil Rights Movement in Northern Ireland* (Belfast: Blackstaff, 1990); an analysis of the first years of the crisis published by the *Sunday Times* in November 1971 ('The Bloody Path Paved with Easy Options', *Sunday Times*, 14 November 1971, 15–19 and 'Two Shots that Killed a Last Bid for Peace', *Sunday Times*, 21 November 1971, 15–18); F. S. L. Lyons, *Ireland Since the Famine*, 2nd edn. (London: Fontana, 1973); Alvin Jackson, *Ireland: 1798–1998* (Oxford: Blackwell, 1999); and R. F. Foster, *Modern Ireland: 1600–1972* (1988) (London: Penguin, 1989).

3. Bardon, *History of Ulster*, 653; Purdie, *Politics in the Streets*, 3, 247–8.

4. 'The Bloody Path Paved with Easy Options', 17; Bew and Gillespie, 19; Bardon, *History of Ulster*, 671.

5. Sam Fannin, 22 March 1995, and letter to author, 24 July 2002; Seán Phillips, letter to author, 5 April 1995; Parker, 'Buntus Belfast', *Irish Times*, 28 January 1970. Entries in Parker's journals indicate that he took Irish classes from October 1969 until December 1971. His teacher, Seán Phillips, recalls him as a 'genuinely interested' and 'certainly better-than-average' student who 'picked up the basics quite quickly' (Phillips, letter to author, 8 August 1995).

6. Parker, 'Buntus Belfast'; 'An Ulster Volunteer', *Irish Times*, 6 March 1970; 'School for Revolution', *Irish Times*, 7 April 1970; 'The Tribe and Thompson', *Irish Times*, 18 June 1970. *Buntús* is the Irish word for 'basics' or 'essentials'. The title of Parker's article plays on the name of a popular beginners' course in spoken Irish, *Buntús Cainte*, or 'The Rudiments of Speech' (Seán Phillips, letter to author, 8 August 1995).

7. 'Tribe and Thompson' and 'Buntus Belfast'.

8. 'Buntus Belfast' and 'Ulster Volunteer'.

9. Parker, interviewed by James P. Mackey for 'Images of Two Traditions' in the BBC Northern Ireland television series *Perspectives*, produced by Father Jim Skelly, recorded 30 May 1987, transmitted 18 October 1987, and 'Ulster Volunteer'.

10. Parker, 'Irish Stereotype' (letter to the editor), *New York Times*, 16 July 1970. Parker uses the phrase 'citizens of Belfast' repeatedly in *Northern Star*, a play focusing on the United Irishmen and the 1798 rebellion, and it evokes a feeling of identification in both Protestant and Catholic members of a local audience. The epithet has the advantage of avoiding national labels entirely to focus on citizenship of a *city* home to unionists and nationalists alike.

11. Parker, journal, 16 April 1970. Perhaps he hoped (forlornly) that Paisley's obvious outrageousness would make him easier to counter than more 'respectable' unionist politicians.

12. Parker, 'Buntus Belfast'.

13. Parker, quoted in Deirdre Purcell, 'The Illusionist', *Sunday Tribune*, 27 September 1987.
14. Parker, 'Introduction' to *Over the Bridge*, by Sam Thompson (Dublin: Gill and Macmillan, 1970), 12.
15. 'Introduction' to *Over the Bridge*, 7–10, 12; May Thompson, 20 June 1995. Thompson's widow recalls that he based Peter O'Boyle in the play on a Catholic worker he himself had helped to escape from a mob. He modelled Davy Mitchell on a shop steward beaten to death for standing up for trade union principles and refusing to work unless the Catholic was allowed to return (May Thompson, 30 June 1994).
16. Hagal Mengel, 'A Lost Heritage: Ulster Drama and the Work of Sam Thompson', Part II, *Theatre Ireland* 2 (1983), 80; Ophelia Byrne, *The Stage in Ulster from the Eighteenth Century* (Belfast: Linen Hall Library, 1997), 47–9; Paddy Devlin, 'The "Over the Bridge" Controversy', *Linen Hall Review*, 2.3 (Autumn 1985), 5–6; 'Introduction' to *Over the Bridge*, 11.
17. 'Introduction' to *Over the Bridge*, 11–12, 7, 14–15; Devlin, 6; Lionel Pilkington, 'Theatre and Cultural Politics in Northern Ireland: The *Over the Bridge* Controversy, 1959', *Éire-Ireland*, 30.4 (Winter 1996), 77; Ray Rosenfield, 'Sam Thompson's "Over the Bridge" in Book Form', *Irish Times*, 8 December 1970.
18. Carrie Jobes, 24 June 1995; Warren Thompson, 16 June 1995; 'Tribe and Thompson'.
19. Mengel, 81; 'Introduction' to *Over the Bridge*, 13–14.
20. Sam Fannin, 22 March 1995; Brian Garrett, 22 June 1995; May Thompson, 30 June 1994; Warren Thompson, 16 June 1995.
21. Rosenfield, ' "Over the Bridge" in Book Form'; Parker, journal, 4 June and 4 December 1970, and letter to Kenneth Jamison, 15 June 1970; Brian Garrett, 22 June 1995; Quidnunc, 'An Irishman's Diary', *Irish Times*, 30 September 1970; May Thompson, 30 June 1994.
22. 'Tribe and Thompson' and 'Introduction' to *Over the Bridge*, 9; Tom McLaughlin, 20 June 2002. McLaughlin, who saw Parker often at this time, remembers his interest in the relationship between theatre and social dynamics and in the idea that drama could make a difference, as he felt *Over the Bridge* had done.
23. Tony McAuley, 14 November 1998; Douglas Carson, 21 November 1998.
24. Parker, 'Your Neighbours', produced by Tony McAuley, BBC Northern Ireland, for the Schools series *Here in Ulster*, transmitted 19 February 1970 (BBC typescript), 7, 12.
25. Parker, journal, 29 January 1970; Tony McAuley, e-mail to author, 5 February 1999.
26. Douglas Carson, 21 November 1998; Tony McAuley, 14 November 1998.
27. Parker, 'Hugh O'Donnell', produced by Tony McAuley, BBC Northern Ireland, for the Schools series *Today and Yesterday in Northern Ireland*, transmitted 21 May 1971 (recording housed in the BBC Radio Archives, Cultra, Northern Ireland, museum reference number 1842).
28. John Malone, 'Schools and Community Relations', *The Northern Teacher* (Winter 1973), 24. See also *Schools Project in Community Relations*, a report published by John Malone in June 1972 and later reprinted by his admirers (Belfast: John Malone Memorial Committee, n.d.).
29. Michael Foley, 12 June 2002; Parker, journal, 8 May 1970, 'Smaller Than Life', review of *The Killer*, by Colin Wilson, *Irish Press*, 27 May 1970, and 'It's a Bad Scene, Mrs. Worthington', *Honest Ulsterman*, 23 (May/June 1970), 15–16.
30. Parker, journal, 19 February and 6 April 1970, and typed proposal for a 90-minute radio play entitled *Hurra! My Boys, For Freedom*, submitted to the BBC in March

1970; Tony McAuley, 14 November 1998; Denys Hawthorne, 22 February 1995; Roger Pine, letter to Parker, 22 June 1970.

31. Parker, journal, September 1967, 26 February 1969, 7 October 1969, 13 February 1970, 7 May 1970, 21 May 1970, 8 February 1971, and 24 February 1971. Tony McAuley believes that Schools scripts then paid about £80 (McAuley, 14 November 1998).

32. Parker, journal, October–November 1969, October–November 1970, March–April 1971, and *Minnie and Maisie and Lily Freed*, produced by John Scotney, BBC Northern Ireland, transmitted 4 August 1971 (BBC transcript).

33. Byrne, 46; *Minnie and Maisie*, 14, 24, 20.

34. *Minnie and Maisie*, 39, 35, and journal, 31 August 1971 and 3 April 1982.

35. Parker, journal, 31 December 1969, 'Pap...Goes the Media', *Irish Times*, 8 February 1971, and 'High Pop', *Irish Times*, 20 April 1970; Joan Newmann, 27 June 1994.

36. Parker, 'What to Rock to for Christmas', *Irish Times*, 15 December 1970, 'Soft Machine', *Irish Times*, 24 August 1970, 'Roots', *Irish Times*, 18 May 1970, and 'Pap...Goes the Media'; Ken and June Lambla, 12 November 1994; Bernard MacLaverty, 16 May 1998; Michael Viney, letter to Stewart Parker, 9 April 1970. A guinea was a monetary unit equal to one pound and one shilling, used before decimalization in 1971. Even after decimalization, professional fees were often described in guineas, although people were actually paid in modern currency (Fannin, letter to author, 28 February 2002, and e-mail to author, 28 June 2002).

37. Parker, *Self Portrait*, produced by John Boyd, BBC Northern Ireland, transmitted 3 October 1971 (BBC typescript). One version I use is a clean copy of this script, probably more or less as written by Parker. The second version, the basis of which is identical to the first, also contains handwritten annotations to reflect what was included in the final product. The various cuts and changes, probably suggested by Boyd, appear to have been motivated sometimes by the desire to clarify a sentence or make it easier to pronounce, sometimes by the need to shorten the piece to fit into a half-hour time frame, and sometimes by a fear that something might prove offensive to solid citizens. I quote from the script as written unless I am making a point about a change itself.

38. *Self Portrait*, 2–3. Michael Foley recalls that F. Scott Fitzgerald was a 'touchstone writer' for Parker. His fondness for the American author, and especially for *Gatsby*, seemed evidence to Foley of a 'romantic streak' Parker usually kept hidden (Foley, 19 June 2002).

39. *Self Portrait*, 2, 6–7.

40. *Self Portrait*, 12–13. In the version broadcast, the last sentence of this passage was toned down to read: 'At the same time, the reflectiveness that went with it made me very aware of the lunacy in this society and saved me from the rabid dogmas that pass for politics here.'

41. *Self Portrait*, 15.

42. *Self Portrait*, 8, 12, 19–20.

43. Brian McKibbin, 11 May 1994; Gerry Thompson, 14 June 1994; Patrick O'Connor, 12 March 1995; David Hammond, 30 June 1994; Tom McLaughlin, 20 June 2002; Ronald Mason, 26 March 1995; Marcus Patton, 6 April 1994; Michael Foley, 19 June 2002.

44. Gerry Thompson, 14 June 1994; John Gilbert, 3 and 4 June 1994; Joanna Mules, 29 June 1994; Michael Foley, 19 June 2002; Sam Fannin, letter to author, 28 February 2002.

45. Michael Foley, 19 June 2002; Michael Longley, 8 April 1994; Tom McLaughlin, 20 June 2002; Aodán Mac Póilin, 9 August 1997; Ronald Mason, 26 March 1995; Brian Garrett, 22 June 1995.

46. David Evans, 25 June 1994; Brenda Callaghan, 26 June 1994; Sam Fannin, 22 March 1995; Tom McLaughlin, 20 June 2002; John Gilbert, 3 June 1994; Marcus Patton, 6 April 1994; Gerry Thompson, 14 June 1994; Pat Scott, 17 June 1995; Tony McAuley, 14 November 1998.

47. Michael Foley, 19 June 2002.

48. Sam Fannin, 21 March 1995; Elgy Gillespie, 9 October 1994; Brenda Callaghan, 26 June 1994; Gina Leishman, 10 October 1994; Michael Foley, 19 June 2002; Ken and June Lambla, 12 November 1994; John Fairleigh, 30 June 1994.

49. Michael Foley, 19 June 2002. Foley even wondered whether Parker's decision not to have children might also be related to his experience with cancer: perhaps he feared on some level that he would not live long enough to raise them.

50. Brenda Callaghan, 26 June 1994. Parker was likely thinking of Methodists like John Malone and Sydney Callaghan when, in *Pentecost*, a character facetiously declares himself one of the Protestant elect and adds, 'my daddy's even a minister of the true faith'. 'You're joking,' his friend replies, 'he's a Methodist. Out on the barricades there, that counts as dangerous left-wing subversion' (*Three Plays for Ireland*, 173).

51. Tom McLaughlin, who took over the flat when the Parkers moved out, found the £5 a week rent expensive; his previous flat had cost only £3 a week (McLaughlin, 20 June 2002).

52. Margaret Parker, 9 April 1994; Marcus Patton, journal, 3 June 1972; Julie Parker McMullan, 18 July 1998. Tom McLaughlin, who met Parker's parents in a pub in Rostrevor, recalls that they seemed relaxed, familiar, and popular there (McLaughlin, 20 June 2002).

53. Margaret Parker, 9 April 1994 and 8 July 2002.

54. Parker named the car Adolf on account of its German origin and temperamental nature. Tom McLaughlin notes that a car was more a necessity than a luxury for Parker, since his artificial leg made it painful for him to walk long distances (McLaughlin, 20 June 2002).

55. American friends who visited Stewart and Kate in the early 1970s were taken to see sights that included stone circles, dolmens, and St Patrick's grave and were everywhere regaled with the lore and legends of that part of the countryside (John Paul, 17 January 1994; Mimi Kingsley, journal, 30 January 1970).

56. Julie Parker McMullan, 18 July 1998; John Paul, 17 January 1994; Terry and Jane Keenan, 5 November 1994; Marcus Patton, journal, 30 October 1971; Mimi Kingsley, journal, 30 January 1970; Margaret Parker, 9 April 1994; Peter Kingsley, 11 July 1999.

57. John Paul, 17 January 1994; Margaret Parker, 8 July 2002; Terry and Jane Keenan, 5 November 1994.

58. Parker, 'Belfast's Women: A Superior Brand of Dynamite', *Evening Standard*, 2 November 1976; Michael Foley, 19 June 2002.

59. Brian Garrett, 22 June 1995; Ken and June Lambla, 12 November 1994; David Evans, 25 June 1994; Brian McKibbin, 11 May 1994; Michael Foley, 12 June 2002; Michael Allen, 24 June 1994; Elgy Gillespie, 9 October 1994.

60. Michael Foley, 19 June 2002; Ray Rosenfield, 'N. I. Arts Body Awards Prizes to Writers', *Irish Times*, 7 December 1971.

NOTES TO CHAPTER 7

1. John Gilbert, 23 June 1994.
2. See Jonathan Bardon, *A History of Ulster* (Belfast: Blackstaff, 1992), 675–8. For the historical sections of this chapter, I shall rely mainly on Bardon; Paul Bew and Gordon Gillespie, *Northern Ireland: A Chronology of the Troubles 1968–1993* (Dublin: Gill and Macmillan, 1993); and other sources as documented.
3. 'Two Shots that Killed a Last Bid for Peace', *Sunday Times*, 21 November 1971, 15.
4. 'The Bloody Path Paved with Easy Options', *Sunday Times*, 14 November 1971, 18–19; Bardon, *History of Ulster*, 678; 'Two Shots that Killed a Last Bid for Peace', 16.
5. Bardon, *History of Ulster*, 679–81; Bew and Gillespie, 31, 33–4; Parker, journal, 9 February 1971; 'Two Shots that Killed a Last Bid for Peace', 17–18.
6. Bardon, *History of Ulster*, 681–5; Bew and Gillespie, 36–7.
7. Marcus Patton, journal, 27 September 1971; Bew and Gillespie, 39; Bardon, *History of Ulster*, 685.
8. Sam Fannin, 25 March 1995; Parker, journal, 2 and 13 September, 6 October, 1 and 12 November, and 7 December 1971; Róisín McAuley, 19 July 2003.
9. Parker, journal, 25 October 1971; 'Sinn Fein [*sic*] Line Challenged in Debate', *Irish Times*, 25 October 1971; 'O'Brien Rejects Rule by the Dead', *Irish Times*, 25 October 1971; Patrick O'Connor, 12 March 1995; Sam Fannin, 22 March 1995.
10. 'Civics', *Irish Times*, 25 October 1971; Parker, 'An Ulster Volunteer', *Irish Times*, 6 March 1970; Bew and Gillespie, 43.
11. Sam Fannin, 25 March 1995.
12. Details of what happened on Bloody Sunday are much disputed, and the basic accounts even of reputable sources differ substantially. For example, Bew and Gillespie estimate the number of marchers at 'nearly 10,000', Bardon gives the participants as 'at least fifteen thousand', while Derry historian Brian Lacy believes that 'about twenty thousand people' were involved. Each writer similarly reports a different number of people injured. All agree, however, on the effect of the shootings: radically increased Catholic and nationalist alienation and a further upsurge in Provisional violence (Bew and Gillespie, 44–5; Bardon, *History of Ulster*, 687–8; Brian Lacy, *Siege City: The Story of Derry and Londonderry* [Belfast: Blackstaff, 1990], 265–6). In June 2010, the report of a twelve-year inquiry headed by Lord Saville confirmed most of what the victims' families had contended from the outset. In a speech apologizing for the shootings on behalf of the British government, then Prime Minister David Cameron acknowledged that the troops should not have been ordered to fire, that no warning was issued, and that 'none of the casualties' had carried a firearm (John F. Burns, 'British Premier Apologizes for "Bloody Sunday" Killings in 1972', *New York Times*, 16 June 2010).
13. Bew and Gillespie, 46–7; Bardon, *History of Ulster*, 688–9.
14. Bew and Gillespie, 47–9; Bardon, *History of Ulster*, 689.
15. Bew and Gillespie, 52; Bardon, *History of Ulster*, 692; Sam Fannin, 25 March 1995.
16. Sam Fannin, 25 March 1995; Alf McCreary, *Survivors* (Belfast: Century Books, 1976), 244; Bardon, *History of Ulster*, 696–9.
17. Bew and Gillespie, 52–4; Bardon, *History of Ulster*, 694, 728; Tom McLaughlin, 20 June 2002.
18. Bardon, *History of Ulster*, 701; Bew and Gillespie, 57; John Gilbert, journal, summer 1972; Nicholas Round, 5 June 1994; Michael Foley, 19 June 2002; Parker, letter to Foley, 18 August 1972; Julie MacRae, 28 June 1994; Tom McLaughlin, 20 June 2002.

19. John Gilbert, 3 June 1994, and journal, October 1971; Stewart Parker, journal, 14 August 1971. Friends at Cornell were aware of Kate's feelings. Neil Hertz, on his own initiative, wrote to the chairman of the English Department to ask whether it might be possible to bring Parker over 'not just for a summer but for the academic year', asserting, 'I know from his recent letters that he isn't very happy with what's going on in Belfast, and that his wife quite hates living there now' (Reeve Parker, 14 January 1994; Hertz, letter to Barry Adams, 27 December 1971).

20. David Evans, 25 June 1994; Marcus Patton, journal, 27 September 1971.

21. McCreary, *Survivors*, 249; Sam Fannin, 22 and 25 March 1995.

22. Tony McAuley, 19 November 1998; McCreary, *Survivors*, 69, 60–1; John Gilbert, letter to Stewart and Kate Parker, 17 July 1972; Parker, journal, 26 October 1971.

23. Tony McAuley, 19 November 1998; McCreary, *Survivors*, 86–7; Patrick O'Connor, 12 March 1995.

24. Patrick O'Connor, 12 March 1995; Brian McKibbin, 11 May 1994; Tony McAuley, 14 and 19 November 1998; Sam Fannin, 25 March 1995.

25. David Evans, 25 June 1994; Nancy McKibbin, 10 May 1994; Nicholas Round, 5 June 1994; Sam Fannin, 22 March 1995; Patrick O'Connor, 12 March 1995; Sara O'Brien, 15 February 2002.

26. Parker, journal, November 1971. The Parkers still spent long weekends in Rostrevor, so they at first thought of the Rugby Road flat as merely their *pied-à-terre* in Belfast, replacing Kate's mother's house, which they had found 'a bit restricting' (Marcus Patton, journal, 27 September 1971). They gradually spent less time in the country and more at Rugby Road.

27. Parker, *Deirdre Porter* (typescript), 46–7.

28. John Gilbert, 3 and 4 June 1994; Marcus Patton, 6 April 1994, letter to author, 19 December 1998, and e-mail to author, 21 July 2003; Julie MacRae, 28 June 1994; *Crab Grass: Poetical Sonatas*, 4 (n.d.); Parker, journal, January 1971.

29. Gerry Thompson, 14 June 1994; Rena McAllister, 22 June 1994; David Evans, 25 June 1994; Patrick O'Connor, 12 March 1995; Brian McKibbin, 11 May 1994; Nancy McKibbin, 10 May 1994; Joanna Mules, 23 June 1994. Many of Parker's friends, including Michael Foley, Gerry Thompson, John Gilbert, and Stephen Rea, tell some version of this story, in which Parker discerned talents in them that ought to be developed and encouraged them to follow their dreams, giving them the courage to believe they could reinvent themselves.

30. Gina Leishman, 10 October 1994; Ken and June Lambla, 12 November 1994. Leishman played several instruments, composed, sang, and tap-danced.

31. Marcus Patton, 10 April 1994; Gina Leishman, 10 October 1994; Gerry Thompson, 14 June 1994; David Evans, 25 June 1994. Evans, too, held Parker in high esteem, as evidenced by the facts that Stewart served as the best man at his wedding in September 1973 and also as godfather to his daughter.

32. Marcus Patton, 13 June 1995 and 10 April 1994; Ken and June Lambla, 11 November 1994.

33. Parker, journal, November 1971–January 1972; John Gilbert, 3 June 1994, journal, December 1971–summer 1972, and letter to Stewart and Kate Parker, 17 July 1972; Marcus Patton, journal, 17 December 1971.

34. Marcus Patton, 6 April 1994, letter to author, 19 December 1998, and e-mail to author, 21 July 2003; Michael Foley, 19 June 2002; John Gilbert, e-mails to author, 5 June and 27 July 2003; *Sir Henry Tonk: A Festschrift in honour of his Next Birthday*

prepared in awe by his colleagues and pupils and containing all known facts (Belfast and Glasgow: Holy Smoke Press, 1994); June Lambla, 12 November 1994.

35. Michael Foley, 19 June 2002; John Gilbert, 3 June 1994, journal, autumn 1971, and e-mail to author, 5 June 2003; Marcus Patton, 10 April 1994; Gerry Thompson, 14 June 1994; Gina Leishman, 10 October 1994; Tony McAuley, 19 November 1998.

36. John Gilbert, 4 June 1994; Marcus Patton, e-mail to author, 21 July 2003.

37. John Gilbert, 4 June 1994, letters to Stewart and Kate Parker, 17 and 31 July 1972, and journal, early 1973; Patrick O'Connor, 12 March 1995.

38. Marcus Patton, 10 April 1994; Steph Pickering, 16 June 1994; John Gilbert, 5 June 1994, and journal (1972–1975).

39. David Hammond, letter to author, 29 July 2002; Brian Barfield, 6 August 2003, and e-mail to author, 23 July 2003; Róisín McAuley, 19 July 2003; John Cronin, 8 and 28 April 1994; Parker, *Lost Belongings* (London: Thames Television, 1987), 163.

40. John Paul, 17 January 1994; Marcus Patton, journal, 9 June 1972; Parker, *The Bus Stories*, ill. Marcus Patton (Belfast: Holy Smoke Press, 1973); Brendan McStravick, 'April Weather on the Buses', *Education Times*, 6 December 1973, 14; David Hammond, 1 July 1994.

41. Denis Smyth, 20 November 1998; Ophelia Byrne, *The Stage in Ulster from the Eighteenth Century* (Belfast: Linen Hall Library, 1997), 54.

42. Parker, journal, 21 September 1970; Louis Muinzer, 23 June 1995; Sara O'Brien, 15 February 2002.

43. Parker, quoted in Joyce McMillan, 'The Nerve & the Energy to Dream', *Scottish Theatre News* (February 1983), 10; Ray Rosenfield, 'N. I. Arts Body Awards Prizes to Writers', *Irish Times*, 7 December 1971.

44. Parker, journal, 3 November 1971 and 28 January 1972; Tony McAuley, 19 November 1998.

45. Parker, journal, September–December 1971. This willingness shown by Parker to tackle a large translation from a language in which he lacked proficiency had a precedent. David Evans remembers that while his father, Estyn, served as Director of the Institute of Irish Studies at Queen's, Parker applied for a fellowship to do a translation of the *Táin*. Evans asked if he knew Irish, and Parker replied that he would learn it (David Evans, 25 June 1994).

46. Parker, journal, June and 31 December 1969, 13 November and 10–11 December 1971. 'Fitts' by Parker were broadcast on the BBC Northern Ireland arts anthology programmes *Soundings* (6 December 1970) and *Causeway* (19 March and 18 August 1973) and BBC Scotland's *New Poetry* (31 January 1973) and *Poetry Now* (28 June 1973). Some of the same poems, and others, were published in *Soundings '72*, ed. Seamus Heaney (Belfast: Blackstaff, 1972), 64; *Crab Grass*, 5 (Summer 1972); and the *Honest Ulsterman*, 34 (June/July/August 1972), 6–7 and 42/3 (March/July 1974), 42. One also featured as a 'poster poem' in an Arts Council of Northern Ireland series, probably in the spring of 1973. Poets collaborated with artists (Parker partnered with Malcolm Bennett) to produce one unified literary and graphic statement. The posters were sold by the Arts Council for 50p each, or £2 for the set of five (cf. *Honest Ulsterman* 42/3).

47. Parker, untitled poems, *Honest Ulsterman*, 34 (June/July/August 1972), 6 and BBC typescript, *New Poetry*, produced by Stewart Conn, BBC Scotland, transmitted 31 January 1973.

48. Parker, untitled poem, BBC typescript, *Poetry Now*, produced by Stewart Conn, BBC Scotland, transmitted 28 June 1973 and untitled poems, BBC typescript, *New Poetry*. Order of poems from undated list of first lines.

49. A number of them may be found in *Paddy Dies* (Co. Donegal, Ireland: Summer Palace Press, 2004), a posthumous volume of Parker's poetry edited by Kate Newmann and Philip Hobsbaum.

50. Parker, quoted in Caroline Walsh, 'Stewart Parker', *Irish Times*, 13 August 1977, journal, 26 February 1970, untitled poem from *New Poetry*, and *Hopdance* manuscript.

51. Parker, quoted in Caroline Walsh and in Niki Hill, 'The Way We Were', *Sunday News* 11 October 1987; *Hopdance* manuscript.

52. *Hopdance* manuscript.

53. Parker, journal, 26 February 1970, 14 January 1971. The decision to change the title came late (Parker, journal, 21 July 1974), and Parker remained attached to the first title, adapting it for a television play unrelated to his amputation, *Iris in the Traffic, Ruby in the Rain*.

54. Parker, journal, 6 January 1975; Caroline Walsh.

55. Parker, journal, 10 January 1972; Lesley Bruce, 14 October 1993.

56. Ken and June Lambla, 11 November 1994. For the history of these planning initiatives, see Bardon's *History of Ulster*, as well as Ron Wiener's *The Rape and Plunder of the Shankill* (Belfast: Notaems Press, 1975), which, despite its sensational title, provides a clear and comprehensive account of developments through the 1960s and early 1970s.

57. Jonathan Bardon, *Belfast: An Illustrated History* (Belfast: Blackstaff, 1982), 268 and *History of Ulster*, 715, 717–18; David McGibbon, 'Sandy Row: A Sketch', photographs by John Gilbert and Dave McCrudden, *Interest* (March 1968), 15–22; John Gilbert, e-mails to author, 5 and 19 June 2003.

58. Wiener, 62; John Gilbert, 11 June 2003, and e-mail to author, 5 June 2003; Joe Mills, 22 June 1995; Brian Trench, 'New Life for the Markets', *Hibernia* (16 September 1977), 9.

59. The history of the motorway project that follows is based mainly on the following sources: Wiener, 51–8; Gerry Thompson, 14 June 1994; The Belfast Urban Study Group, *The B. U. S. Report on the Belfast Urban Motorway* (Belfast: Holy Smoke Press, 1973).

60. Wiener, 59–60; B. M. Rutherford, *Belfast Urban Area Plan: Report of a Public Inquiry* (Belfast: HMSO, 1973), 18; Gerry Thompson, 14 June 1994; Ken and June Lambla, 12 November 1994.

61. *B. U. S. Report on the Belfast Urban Motorway*; Parker, journal, 25 and 30 May, 4 and 18 July, and 6 October 1973 and 5 April 1974; Wiener, 61. Many of the ideas about community-centred urban planning promoted in Belfast by BUS had been promulgated in Jane Jacobs's landmark book *The Death and Life of Great American Cities* (1961). As an activist in New York City, Jacobs had led throughout the mid-1960s (the period when Parker lived in New York State) the successful fight against a proposed Lower Manhattan Expressway.

62. Brian Barfield, 6 August 2003; Parker, 'Safe as Houses: The Great Belfast Urban Motorway Show', *Fortnight*, 72 (19 November 1973), 11–14.

63. Wiener, 65–6; Jeremy Bugler, 'Motorway Fight Unites Belfast's Ghettos', *Observer*, 14 October 1973; Parker, quoted in Candida, 'An Irishwoman's Diary', *Irish Times*, 10 December 1973. Parker would make redevelopment a crucial backdrop to both *Spokesong* and *Pentecost*.

64. *B. U. S. Report on the Belfast Urban Motorway*; Marcus Patton, 6 April 1994; John Gilbert, e-mail to author, 5 June 2003.

65. Marcus Patton, 6 April 1994; Gina Leishman, 10 October 1994; John Gilbert, 3 June 1994.

66. John Gilbert, 3 and 4 June 1994, journal, February 1974, and letter to Brian Walker, August 1979; Gina Leishman, 10 October 1994. All the original inhabitants of the restored No. 9 had left by 1979, and by the beginning of 1980 the lease on it expired and the house reverted to Queen's. The university left it empty and unsecured, and the building was vandalized, robbed, and damaged by flooding after the pipes froze. Queen's still intended to demolish a whole row of houses, but the Rugby Road Residents' Association and other interested parties mounted a successful protest, and the university sold off the dwellings one by one (Dympna Curley, 'Rugby Tackle on QUB "Vandals"', *Belfast Telegraph*, 26 May 1987; John Gilbert, letter to the editor, *Belfast Telegraph*, 3 June 1987; Brian Walker, 8 April 1994).

67. John Fairleigh, 16 June 1995 and 30 June 1994; Ken Lambla, 12 November 1994.

68. Parker, 'School for Revolution', *Irish Times*, 7 April 1970, and journal, 26 July–13 December 1973; John Gilbert, 4 June 1994; David Evans, 25 June 1994; John Fairleigh, 30 June 1994.

69. Brian Barfield, 6 August 2003; Parker, 'Requiem', BBC typescript.

70. Ghosts in one form or another appear in Parker's radio play *The Iceberg* and his stage plays *Spokesong*, *Northern Star*, *Heavenly Bodies*, and *Pentecost*.

71. Parker, journal, 3 July 1973; Seamus Heaney, 'A Postcard from North Antrim' in *Field Work* (1979) (New York: Noonday, 1989), 19; Patrick O'Connor, 12 March 1995; John Gilbert, journal, late June or early July 1973. The character Marian expresses similar sentiments at the end of Parker's play *Pentecost*.

72. Derek Humphry, 'IRA Forces Social Workers to Quit Belfast', *Sunday Times*, 23 September 1973; Wiener, 7–9; John Gilbert, journal, September 1973.

73. Parker, quoted in 'The Artist's Conflict in Ulster', a radio investigation by John Fairleigh, produced by Virginia Hardy, first transmitted 1 October 1973 on the BBC World Service (recording housed in the BBC Radio Archives at Cultra, Northern Ireland, museum number 301).

NOTES TO CHAPTER 8

1. Parker, quoted in Raymond Gardner, 'Too many people have writing in the head...', *Guardian*, 6 December 1976.

2. Parker, quoted in Jonathan Philbin Bowman, 'Party Piece', *In Dublin*, 30 September 1987. For the historical sections of this chapter I rely on Jonathan Bardon, *A History of Ulster* (Belfast: Blackstaff, 1992), 701–14 and 722–5; Paul Bew and Gordon Gillespie, *Northern Ireland: A Chronology of the Troubles 1968–1993* (Dublin: Gill & Macmillan, 1993), 57–8, 60–108; Robert Fisk, *The Point of No Return: The Strike Which Broke the British in Ulster* (London: André Deutsch, 1975); and other sources as documented.

3. Patrick O'Connor, 12 March 1995.

4. Bew and Gillespie, 73–5.

5. Fisk, 47.

6. Fisk, 44–9.

7. Bew and Gillespie, 84; John Gilbert, journal, 17 May 1974.

8. Parker, quoted in Deirdre Purcell, 'The Illusionist', *Sunday Tribune*, 27 September 1987; Fisk, 92; Bew and Gillespie, 84; John Gilbert, journal, 20 May 1974.

9. See Fisk, chapters five and eight, for more on the role of the Army and the police, both reluctant to confront UWC-inspired lawlessness. Usually they ignored it, but in some instances they appeared to offer sympathy and encouragement to the strikers.

10. John Gilbert, journal, 21–2 May 1974.
11. Fisk, 102, 253. Parker would incorporate this section of Wilson's speech verbatim near the beginning of the second act of his play *Pentecost*, set during the UWC Strike.
12. John Gilbert, journal, 25 May 1974.
13. Bardon, *History of Ulster*, 710; Fisk, 125; John Gilbert, journal, 28 May 1974; Parker, journal, 27 May 1974.
14. Bew and Gillespie, 87–8; Bardon, *History of Ulster*, 711; Alvin Jackson, *Ireland: 1798–1998* (Oxford: Blackwell, 1999), 460.
15. Bew and Gillespie, 89–94.
16. Parker, *Dramatis Personae* (Belfast: John Malone Memorial Committee, 1986), 19–20.
17. A. P. W. Malcolmson (ed.), *The Extraordinary Career of the 2nd Earl of Massereene, 1743–1805* (Belfast: HMSO, 1972); Brian Barfield, 6 August 2003; Róisín McAuley, 19 July 2003; Paul Muldoon, 16 June 2003. Sam Fannin called Parker's attention to Malcolmson's book after reading an article about Clotworthy in the *Ulster Tatler* (Fannin, 22 March 1995, and letter to author, 4 November 2003).
18. Parker, *Clotworthy*, Parts I and II, produced by Brian Barfield, BBC Northern Ireland, transmitted 19 and 26 March 1974 (recordings housed in the BBC Radio Archives at Cultra, Northern Ireland, museum numbers 86 and 87).
19. Brian Barfield, 6 August 2003; Parker, journal, March 1974; publicity material for Ixion Productions, April 1975.
20. *The Iceberg* was published in the *Honest Ulsterman*, 50 (Winter 1975), 4–64; I quote from this version of the text. Michael Heffernan's BBC production may be listened to in the BBC Radio Archives at Cultra, Northern Ireland (museum numbers 64 through 66).
21. Jonathan Bardon, *Belfast: An Illustrated History* (Belfast: Blackstaff, 1982), 176; John Updike, 'It Was Sad', *New Yorker* (14 October 1996), 94.
22. Parker, quoted in Gardner.
23. Bardon, *Belfast*, 177 and *History of Ulster*, 455; John Wilson Foster, *The Titanic Complex* (Vancouver, Canada: Belcouver Press, 1997), 76; Parker, *Iceberg*, 7, 32–3, 48.
24. Foster, *Titanic Complex*, 53; *Iceberg*, 55–6.
25. *Iceberg*, 42, 63, 19. Parker initially referred to the play in his journal as 'Titanic' or the 'Titanic play'. Only in late January 1974 did he begin calling it 'Iceberg', a significant change of emphasis. He knew Thomas Hardy's poem 'The Convergence of the Twain' and had copied some lines from it into his notebook: 'And as the smart ship grew/In stature, grace, and hue,/In shadowy silent distance grew the Iceberg too.' There may also, however, have been more subliminal influences at work. As a teenager, Parker loved the works of Aldous Huxley. In *Brave New World*, an architect of the planned society of the future opines that 'The optimum population . . . is modelled on the iceberg—eight-ninths below the water line, one-ninth above' (Aldous Huxley, *Brave New World and Brave New World Revisited* [New York: Harper, 1960], 268).
26. Susan Campbell, 'Radio: Italian Style', *Listener* (16 January 1975), 84; Val Arnold-Forster, 'A Class of Their Own on Radio', *Guardian*, 11 January 1975; Parker, letter to Alfred Gingold, 12 January 1975; Ronald Mason, 26 March 1995; Brian Barfield, 6 August 2003; Róisín McAuley, 19 July 2003; Margaret Windham Heffernan, 31 October 1994.
27. Margaret Windham Heffernan, 31 October 1994.
28. Parker, letters to Alfred Gingold, 12 January 1975 and 22 February 1976; Margaret Windham Heffernan, 31 October 1994.

29. Heffernan did die prematurely, in 1985, after an altercation in a restaurant with a drunken man—ironically, a Northern Irish Protestant—who was rowdily mocking Heffernan's accent at a neighbouring table. The man punched Heffernan in response to a request that he quieten down, triggering a heart attack (Margaret Windham Heffernan, 31 October 1994). Paul Muldoon captures the essence of Heffernan's personality in 'The Soap-Pig', an elegy for him published in *Meeting the British* (Winston-Salem, North Carolina: Wake Forest University Press, 1987), 32–6.

30. Parker, journal, 27 January and 24 May 1975, and letter to Alfred Gingold, 12 January 1975.

31. Stephen Rea, 23 February 1995; Sam McCready, 12 October 2003; Christie Hickman, 'Stephen Rea, Fringe Actor Par Excellence', *Drama* (Autumn 1983), 23–5; Charles Hunter, 'Stephen Rea: Actor-Manager with a Mission', *Irish Times*, 19 September 1987; Fintan O'Toole, 'Stephen Rea: The Great Leap from the Abbey', *Sunday Tribune*, 23 September 1984; Alex Renton, 'Ireland's Leading Rebel', *Illustrated London News* (January 1989), 60–1; Alan Riding, 'Cast in the Middle of the Long Conflict in Northern Ireland', *New York Times*, 15 February 1998; Tony Clayton-Lea, 'The Understated Actor', *Cara* (Aer Lingus magazine) 33.3 (May/June 2000), 28–32; Malachi O'Doherty, 'On the Eve of Pentecost', *Hype* (November 1987), 29–30.

32. Stephen Rea, 23 February 1995; Parker, journal, 7 March 1975.

33. Michael Foley, 19 June 2002; Parker, journal, 6 January 1975.

34. Bea MacLeod, 14 January 1994; Nancy Cole, 17 March 1999; John Paul, 17 January 1994; Parker, journal, 5 August 1974. This production prefigured Parker's television play *Radio Pictures*, which centres on the recording of a radio play.

35. Bardon, *Belfast*, 135.

36. For more comprehensive descriptions of twentieth-century Northern Irish theatre see Ophelia Byrne, *The Stage in Ulster from the Eighteenth Century* (Belfast: Linen Hall Library, 1997); Roy Connolly, *The Evolution of the Lyric Players Theatre, Belfast: Fighting the Waves* (Lewiston, New York: Edwin Mellen, 2000); and Sam Hanna Bell, *The Theatre in Ulster: A Survey of the Dramatic Movement in Ulster from 1902 Until the Present Day* (Totowa, New Jersey: Rowman and Littlefield, 1972). See also Mark Carruthers and Stephen Douds (eds.), *Stepping Stones: The Arts in Ulster 1971–2001* (Belfast: Blackstaff, 2001), especially the essays by Ophelia Byrne and David Grant.

37. Byrne, 49–50.

38. Sam Hanna Bell, 112.

39. In constructing the following account of the Lyric Theatre, I relied on the published sources cited above, along with Mary O'Malley's memoir *Never Shake Hands with the Devil* (Dublin: Elo, 1990). I also gleaned insights from interviews with a number of people, especially Denis Smyth, Sam McCready, and Ciaran McKeown.

40. Denis Smyth, 20 November 1998; Mary O'Malley, 37, 118, 125–8.

41. Connolly, 46–9; Sylvia Wynne, 9 February 1997; Sam Hanna Bell, 100.

42. Byrne, 59; Parker, review of the Lyric Theatre's production of three plays by W. B. Yeats for *The Arts: A Monthly Review*, BBC Northern Ireland, transmitted 22 June 1967, introduced by Peter Devlin, produced (probably) by John Boyd (script held at the BBC Written Archives Centre in Reading, England).

43. Ciaran McKeown, 17 November 1998; Sam McCready, 12 October 2003; Sybil Allen Poole, 7 June 1999; Parker, 'Signposts', *Theatre Ireland*, 11 (Autumn 1985), 27.

44. Ciaran McKeown, 17 November 1998; Mary O'Malley, 213, 215; Byrne, 60–1; Christopher Fitz-Simon, 28 May 1999.

45. 'Signposts', 27; Denis Smyth, 11 April 1994 and 20 November 1998; Sam McCready, 31 July 1996.

46. Parker, journal, 27 October 1969; Mary O'Malley, 239; Connolly, 9, 104, 141–2, 150.

47. Kate Ireland, 'Theatre: Much Ado About Nothing and Lovers at the Lyric Theatre, Belfast', *Honest Ulsterman*, 24 (July/August 1970), 14–17 and 'Theatre II', *Honest Ulsterman*, 26 (November/December 1970), 22–3; Stewart Parker, 'Theatre I', *Honest Ulsterman*, 26 (November/December 1970), 21–2 and journal, 5–12 and 27 September 1969.

48. Frank Ormsby, 3 June 2002; Michael Foley, 19 June 2002; Brian Barfield, 6 August 2003, and e-mail to author, 23 July 2003.

49. The title originated with Mícheál Mac Liammóir, the legendary Irish actor, director, and producer, who had served with O'Malley on an advisory board of the Abbey Theatre. Parker and his friends sometimes referred to her this way among themselves: the expression captures her imperiousness, her Catholic nationalism, and her reverence for the plays of the great Irish poet (Sam McCready, 12 October 2003; Róisín McAuley, 19 July 2003).

50. 'Signposts', 27; Connolly, 272.

51. Connolly, 174–80. Sam Thompson's son Warren remembers running into Parker at the Lyric after a performance of one of Boyd's plays, probably *The Flats*. Parker said he thought the play awful; he planned to leave the theatre quickly before Boyd asked him how he had liked it, since he did not have the heart to tell him (Warren Thompson, 16 June 1995).

52. Frank Ormsby, 17 November 1998, and 'The Write-An-Ulster-Play Kit', *Honest Ulsterman*, 36 (November/December 1972), 2–3. Haire, born in Belfast, was living in England at the time.

53. 'Signposts', 27–9. The following narrative of Parker's efforts to get *Spokesong* produced derives from his journal and other sources as documented.

54. Parker and Michael Heffernan, draft proposal to Arts Council of Northern Ireland, 27 January 1975.

55. Parker, journal, 29 March and 10 May 1975; Brian Garrett, letter to Messrs. Dunlop Limited, 3 April 1975.

56. Ciaran McKeown, 19 November 1998; Mary O'Malley, 278, 283–5; Connolly, 106, 110; Alf McCreary, 'Twenty-one Entertaining Years', *Belfast Telegraph*, 11 November 1983; Parker, draft letter to Frank Murphy, 16 April 1975, and journal, 7 April 1975.

57. Parker, journal, 29 April and 13 May 1975.

58. Mary O'Malley, 285, 288; Connolly, 188, 192, 194, 196.

59. Parker, journal, 14 and 15 May 1975.

60. Parker, journal, 15 May 1975. John Gilbert, whose opinions on the subject almost certainly conformed to Parker's, wrote to the *Listener* to complain about Haire's 'outsider's view...passing for an insider's view' and branding his play 'a commodity which relies on a stereotyped view of our situation' (Gilbert, letter to the editor, *Listener* [29 May 1975], 709).

61. Parker, journal, 20 May 1975, and 'Signposts', 29; Stephen Rea, 23 February 1995.

62. Parker, journal, 22, 25, and 28 July 1975, and 'Signposts', 29.

63. Parker, journal, 14 August and 1 September 1975.

64. Parker and Heffernan, draft proposal to Arts Council of Northern Ireland, 27 January 1975.

65. Parker, quoted in Robert Berkvist, 'A Freewheeling Play About Irish History', *New York Times*, 11 March 1979 and in Caroline Walsh, 'Stewart Parker', *Irish Times*, 13 August 1977; *Spokesong* (New York: Samuel French, 1980), 31.

66. John Gilbert, 23 June 1994; Mark Phelan, 14 May 2008; Kate Newmann (ed.), *Dictionary of Ulster Biography* (Belfast: Institute of Irish Studies, 1993), 166. For years after *Spokesong* first opened in Dublin, when it was being produced by theatres around the world, MacRae would receive the occasional phone call from an actress playing Daisy, who had been directed by Parker to talk with her and listen to her 'intonations' (Julie MacRae, 28 June 1994).

67. *Spokesong*, 52, 27.

68. Parker, letters to Michael Foley, 4 July 1972, and John Gilbert, 5 July 1972, quoted in Berkvist, journal, 3 January and 1 February 1975, and *Spokesong* 8, 33, 10.

69. Parker, notebook, probably August 1974, and *Spokesong*, 35, 42, 19. For this last aspect of Frank's thinking, Parker was at least partially indebted to the American author Robert Pirsig, whose *Zen and the Art of Motorcycle Maintenance* he read with great excitement and reviewed in autumn 1974 for the BBC's *Bookends* programme (Parker, journal, 13 September and 5 November 1974; John Cronin, 8 April 1994). References to the book in John Gilbert's journal indicate that he was similarly taken with it.

70. Parker, quoted in Berkvist, and 'Signposts', 28.

71. Parker, journal, 15 February and 18 March 1975, and draft letter to John Ford, 2 April 1975.

72. Parker, journal, 6 May 1975.

73. *Spokesong*, 61–2.

74. Parker, journal, 17 July 1975, and *Spokesong*, 65, 70–1.

75. *Spokesong*, 59, 69, 73. For a more extensive reading of *Spokesong* (and *The Iceberg*), see my ' "Ireland, the Continuous Past": Stewart Parker's Belfast History Plays' in Stephen Watt, Eileen Morgan, and Shakir Mustafa (eds.), *A Century of Irish Drama: Widening the Stage* (Bloomington: Indiana University Press, 2000), 256–74.

76. Parker, journal, 21 April, 2 June, and 1 July 1975, 'Grand Old Alleyman', *Irish Times*, 11 July 1975, quoted in Berkvist, and letters to Jimmy Kennedy, 29 July and 6 August 1975; Kennedy, letters to Parker, 11 July and 1 and 12 August 1975.

77. Parker, journal, 1 and 6 August 1975; Mary O'Malley, 273, 287; Ken and June Lambla, 11 November 1994.

78. Parker, letter to Alfred Gingold, 20 October 1975, and 'Signposts', 29.

79. Parker, journal, 11 August and 5 October 1975; Ken and June Lambla, 11 November 1994.

80. Parker, journal, 6 and 7 October 1975, and letter to Alfred Gingold, 20 October 1975; Kane Archer, ' "Spokesong" Turns Up A Few Surprises', *Irish Times*, 7 October 1975; Mary Mac Goris, 'Ride in the North but Hardly a Play?', *Irish Independent*, 7 October 1975; Mary Higgins, 'Bicycle Made for Touché', *Irish Press*, 7 October 1975; John Peter, 'Delightful Debut', *Sunday Times*, 12 October 1975; John Barber, 'Bicycle Play Witty and Nostalgic', *Daily Telegraph*, 11 October 1975.

81. Niall Stokes, 'Bikes and Belfast', *Hibernia* (17 October 1975), 23; Parker, journal, 17 October 1975 and 23–4 September 1976.

82. Parker, journal, 10, 13, 15, and 16 October 1975; John Boyd, 27 June 1994.

83. Parker, journal, 29 October–7 November and 5 and 18 December 1975.

84. Parker, journal, 10 September and 30 October 1975; Marc Berlin, 22 March 1994.

85. Paul Muldoon, 16 June 2003; Brian Barfield, 6 August 2003.

86. Parker, journal, 26 November and 27 October 1975, and *The Joyous Wheel*, read by Stewart Parker, Allan McClelland, Pitt Wilkinson, Barry McGovern, and Máire Ní

Ghráinne, produced by Brian Barfield, recorded on 8 and 9 October 1975, and first transmitted 12 October 1975 (recording housed in the BBC Radio Archives at Cultra, Northern Ireland, museum number 311).

87. Denys Hawthorne, 22 February 1995; Parker, journal, 15 March 1974, and 'I'm a Wallflower, You're a Weed', *Honest Ulsterman*, 30 (September/October 1971), 20–2.

88. Parker, *Private Grounds*, produced by Gerry McCrudden, BBC Northern Ireland, transmitted 21 November 1975 (BBC camera script), 39.

89. Gerry McCrudden, 19 August 2003; Parker, journal, 11 January, 21 and 24 April, 7 May, 4 and 24 June, and 3, 7, 16, 18, and 20–3 July 1975.

90. Parker, journal, 14 October and 21 and 26 November 1975; Kate Parker, letters to John Gilbert, 25 November and 1 December 1975.

91. Parker, journal, 26 and 27 November 1975; Kate Parker, letter to John Gilbert, 1 December 1975.

92. Parker, *Herod the Great*, produced by Paul Muldoon, BBC Northern Ireland, transmitted 27 December 1975 (BBC typescript), 17 (recording housed in the BBC Radio Archives at Cultra, Northern Ireland, museum number 1988).

93. Parker, journal, 31 December 1975; *Sir Henry Tonk: A Festschrift in honour of his Next Birthday prepared in awe by his colleagues and pupils and containing all known facts* (Belfast: Holy Smoke Press, 1994), 32, 119–20, 133, 136; Ken and June Lambla, 11 November 1994; Marcus Patton, 6 April 1994; Steph Pickering, e-mail to author, 18 January 2004; Robin Morton, 'Gorilla Made Monkey Out of Revellers', *Belfast Telegraph*, 2 January 1976.

NOTES TO CHAPTER 9

1. Rob Ritchie (ed.), *The Joint Stock Book: The Making of a Theatre Collective* (London: Methuen, 1987); David Self, 'Joint Stock Theatre Group', entry in *The Continuum Companion to Twentieth Century Theatre*, ed. Colin Chambers (London: Continuum, 2002), 408.

2. Joyce Marlow, *Captain Boycott and the Irish* (New York: E. P. Dutton, 1973); Jonathan Bardon, *A History of Ulster* (Belfast: Blackstaff, 1992), 366.

3. Parker, notebook, probably 12 January 1976, and draft letter to Max Stafford-Clark, 6 November 1975.

4. Parker, '*Boycott*: a summary', prepared for the Joint Stock Theatre Group on 19 January 1976.

5. George Parker, 5 April 1994; Stewart Parker, notebook.

6. Sam Fannin, 22 March 1995, and letters to author, 25 September 1994 and 29 February 2004; Vincent Power, *Send 'Em Home Sweatin': The Showband Story* (Cork: Cork University Press, 2000), 410–13; Gerry Smyth, *Noisy Ireland: A Short History of Irish Popular Music* (Cork: Cork University Press, 2005), 11–17. Nelson's surname recalls Belfast band leader Dave Glover, who has claimed responsibility for the term 'showband' (see Smyth, 138).

7. Sam Fannin, 24 March 1995; Parker, *I'm A Dreamer Montreal*, radio play, produced by Michael Heffernan, BBC Northern Ireland, transmitted 20 July 1977 (BBC typescript), 11, 13.

8. Sam Fannin, 22 March 1995. Fannin's band played gigs on both sides of the sectarian divide, which could foster a dangerous confusion. Once, Fannin remembers, he was playing with McIntyre at a republican pub in Sligo. At the end of the evening, McIntyre, 'a spacer', turned to him, told him to play the national anthem, and launched into

'God Save the Queen'. Fannin quickly drowned him out with the drum introduction to 'The Soldier's Song'.

9. *I'm A Dreamer Montreal* (radio), 45; Sam Fannin, letter to author, 25 September 1994.

10. Parker, letter to Alfred Gingold, 22 February 1976, and journal, 3 and 16 February 1976.

11. Parker, journal, 29 February 1976, and quoted in *Studio Three* discussion on 'Theatre in Ulster Today', presented by Michael Barnes and produced by Brian Barfield for BBC Northern Ireland, transmitted 29 February 1976 (recording housed in the BBC Radio Archives at Cultra, Northern Ireland, museum number 2049).

12. Parker, journal, 2 March 1976, and quoted in 'The Belfast Group: A Symposium', *Honest Ulsterman*, 53 (November/December 1976), 59; Joan Newmann, 27 June 1994. The references in the opening of Parker's symposium piece are to James Simmons and Seamus Heaney.

13. Parker, 'Author's Notes', *Catchpenny Twist: A Charade in Two Acts* (New York: Samuel French, 1984), 94–5. Although Parker revised the play between early drafts and the version Samuel French published, the basic outline of the plot remained the same. Most revision consisted of rearranging and trimming scenes and sharpening the dialogue. I have confined my quotation from the published text to passages that remained substantially the same as in a draft dating from April 1977.

14. One example early in 1976 was his review of *Clive: Inside the Record Business*, an account of the early career of a record executive named Clive Davis who, Parker concluded, raised in his memoir 'bigger questions about the role and position of art in a consumer society than he himself is prepared to entertain' (Parker, 'Music Business', *Irish Times*, 22 January 1976).

15. 'Author's Notes', *Catchpenny Twist*, 95.

16. Paul Bew and Gordon Gillespie, *Northern Ireland: A Chronology of the Troubles 1968–1993* (Dublin: Gill and Macmillan, 1993), 102–3; John Wyver, 'Irish Eyes', *Time Out* (2–8 December 1977), 13; Parker, quoted in Caroline Walsh, 'Stewart Parker', *Irish Times*, 13 August 1977, and 'Author's Notes', *Catchpenny Twist*, 93–4; Power, 266–71.

17. *Catchpenny Twist* (and 'Author's Notes'), 95, 23, 31.

18. Parker, journal, 25 February 1976, and *Catchpenny Twist*, 72, 86.

19. 'Author's Notes', *Catchpenny Twist*, 94.

20. *Catchpenny Twist*, 91. In an earlier version of the ending, Parker had similarly aimed to shock his audience while keeping the action more naturalistic. Marie Kyle, who has read the article mentioning Roy and Martyn's brief career writing martyr-ballads on commission, marches in with two of her colleagues in the republican movement, who proceed to knee-cap them.

21. Max Stafford-Clark, letter to Parker, 21 January 1976; Graham Cowley, letter to Frank Murphy, 12 April 1976.

22. Parker, journal, 5 May 1976; Lesley Bruce, letter to author, 8 December 2003. Stafford-Clark confirmed on 18 May 1976 what Parker had already assumed: Joint Stock could not now afford to do the show. Parker, however, filed away the Boycott idea for future reference. One of the last pieces he completed, shortly before his death, was a film screenplay, *Mayo by Moonlight*, set in the same historical period and drawing on some of the same events.

23. Parker, journal, 13 May 1976.

24. Parker, letters to Alfred Gingold, 1 November 1976, and Bea MacLeod, 28 September 1976, and journal, 17 May 1976; John Gilbert, journal, 23 September 1976; Dan Crawford, 2 June 1994; Lesley Bruce, 1 March 1995.

25. The volume that sparked Parker's interest in Boucicault was almost certainly *The Dolmen Boucicault*, ed. David Krause (Dublin: Dolmen, 1964). In addition to Krause's lively biographical note, the book contains three of Boucicault's plays: *The Colleen Bawn, Arrah na Pogue*, and *The Shaughraun*. In 1976, as he noted in his journal, Parker listened to a radio feature on Boucicault (25 April), saw *The Shaughraun* at the Abbey (8 July), and watched *London Assurance* on television (10 October).

26. Parker, journal, 3–4 June 1976.

27. Parker, notebook, entries probably dating from 4 December 1975 and 25 May 1976.

28. Andrew Parkin, 'Metaphor as Dramatic Structure in Plays by Stewart Parker', in Masaru Sekine (ed.), *Irish Writers and the Theatre* (Gerrards Cross, Bucks.: Colin Smythe, 1986), 135–6.

29. Parker, journal, 3–4 August 1976.

30. Parker, journal, 23 June and 6 and 10 July 1976.

31. Parker, journal, 23 July 1976.

32. Parker, journal, 30–1 July 1976.

33. Parker, journal, 31 August 1976. One or both of them had been considering this option even before the trip to Edinburgh. At least a week preceding these conversations with Kate and Marcus, Stewart had told John Gilbert he was thinking about moving to Edinburgh (Gilbert, journal, 24 August 1976).

34. Marcus Patton, 10 April 1994; Steph Pickering, 16 June 1994; Parker, journal, 1 September 1975.

35. Parker, letter to Alfred Gingold, 1 November 1976, and journal, 2, 9, and 11 August 1976; Dan Crawford, 2 June 1994.

36. Parker, journal, 18 August and 7–8 September 1976; John Gilbert, journal, 9 September 1976.

37. Parker, journal, 14, 15, 16, 19, and 25 September 1976, and letter to Bea MacLeod, 28 September 1976; B. A. Young, 'Spokesong', *Financial Times*, 15 September 1976; John Barber, 'Witty Musical With View of Torn Ulster', *Daily Telegraph*, 15 September 1976; Michael Billington, 'Spokesong', *Guardian*, 15 September 1976; Ann McFerran, '"Spokesong"', *Time Out* (16 September 1976); Milton Shulman, 'Two Wheels Good…', *Evening Standard*, 15 September 1976; Ned Chaillet, 'Spokesong: Kings Head', *The Times*, 15 September 1976; Victoria Radin, 'In God's Country', *Observer*, 19 September 1976; Rosemary Say, 'In Suspense', *Sunday Telegraph*, 19 September 1976; Kenneth Hurren, 'Tandem', *Spectator* (25 September 1976), 29.

38. Dan Crawford, 2 June 1994; John Gilbert, journal, 23 September 1976; Parker, journal, 23–4 September 1976.

39. Parker, letter to Alfred Gingold, 1 November 1976, and journal, 27 September 1976; Joan Rodker, letter to Parker, 24 September 1976; Barry Hanson, letter to Parker, 28 September 1976; Andrew Brown, letter to Parker, 28 September 1976; David Aukin, letter to Parker, 1 October 1976.

40. Parker, journal, 1 October 1976; Simon Farquhar, e-mail to author, 14 January 2004. Farquhar has researched the history of the *Play for Today* programme. See Irene Shubik, *Play for Today: The Evolution of Television Drama*, 2nd edn. (Manchester: Manchester University Press, 2000), for an account of the development of the programme by one of its first producers.

41. Rex Cathcart, *The Most Contrary Region: The BBC in Northern Ireland 1924–1984* (Belfast: Blackstaff, 1984), 262; Lesley Bruce, 16 October 1993; Wyver, 'Irish Eyes'. Parker's play *Private Grounds* had been produced by BBC Northern Ireland as an Arts feature rather than as television drama.

42. Parker, journal, 2–4 October 1976.

43. Parker, journal, 12 October 1976.

44. Parker, journal, 18 October 1976.

45. Kate Parker, letter to John Gilbert, 25 October 1976; Stewart Parker, journal, 20 October and 8 November 1976 and 19 January 1977.

46. Parker, letter to Alfred Gingold, 1 November 1976; Sam Fannin, 25 March 1995, and letter to author, 29 February 2004.

47. Parker, letter to John Gilbert, 1 August 1972; Denys Hawthorne, 22 February 1995.

48. Parker, *The Actress and the Bishop* (typescript), 40.

49. Michael Billington, 'The Actress and the Bishop', *Guardian*, 11 December 1976; Parker, letter to Alfred Gingold, 28 January 1977.

50. Parker, journal, 21 and 23 November 1976 and 4 and 7 January 1977, and letter to Alfred Gingold, 28 January 1977.

51. Parker, letter to Alfred Gingold, 15 December 1976.

52. Parker, letter to Bea MacLeod, 16 December 1976, and journal, 15 and 31 December 1976.

53. Parker, journal, 21, 24, and 28 January and 11 February 1977.

54. Douglas Blake, 'Vaudeville: "Spokesong"', *The Stage and Television Today*, 3 March 1977. See also B. A. Young, 'Spokesong', *Financial Times*, 17 February 1977; John Elsom, 'Back Brake', *Listener* (24 February 1977), 249; John Barber, 'Stage Set Afire by Belfast Bike Maniac', *Daily Telegraph*, 18 February 1977.

55. Dan Crawford, 2 June 1994; Parker, journal, 12–15 February 1977, and letter to John Gilbert, 21 February 1977.

56. In addition to reviews cited above, see, for example, Irving Wardle, 'Spokesong', *The Times*, 17 February 1977; Bernard Levin, 'No Laughing Matter', *Sunday Times*, 20 February 1977; Sheridan Morley, 'Song of the Spokes', *Punch* (23 February 1977), 330.

57. Parker, journal, 19 March 1977.

58. Parker, journal, 28 February 1977.

59. Parker, journal, 5 March 1977.

60. Parker, journal, 24 February, 4 July, and 11 January 1977; Kate Parker, letter to John Gilbert, 25 October 1976; Stewart Parker, letter to John Gilbert, 22 January 1977.

61. Parker, journal, 8 and 25 March 1977, and letter to Jimmy Kennedy, 28 March 1977.

62. Parker, journal, 29 and 30 March 1977; Jimmy Kennedy, letters to Parker, 30 March, 6 April, and 13 April 1977; Parker, draft letters to Kennedy, 2 and 9 April 1977.

63. Parker, journal, 26 April–13 May 1977; Bew and Gillespie, 118–21; Bardon, *History of Ulster*, 732.

64. Parker, journal, 19 February 1976; *Montserrat*, official tourist brochure in Parker's possession, published in 1976 or 1977; Brian McGinn, 'How Irish is Montserrat?', *Irish Roots*, 1 (1994), 20+ and 'How Irish is Montserrat?' (Part 3), *Irish Roots*, 4 (1994), 20+.

65. Parker, journal, 4 May 1977.

66. Parker, journal, 30 May and 7 and 14 June 1977, and letter to Alfred Gingold, 2 July 1977.

67. Parker, journal, 22 and 30 July 1977.
68. Parker, journal, 24 and 25 August 1977.
69. Parker, journal, 26 August 1977; David Nowlan, '"Catchpenny Twist" at the Peacock', *Irish Times*, 26 August 1977; Con Houlihan, 'Recycling the Gags and Laughs', *Irish Press*, 26 August 1977; Desmond Rushe, 'Parker Play Has Telling Insight', *Irish Independent*, 26 August 1977; Frances O'Rourke, 'No Happy Endings', *Sunday Press*, 28 August 1977; Desmond MacAvock, 'Charade with a Message', *Evening Press*, 26 August 1977; Gus Smith, 'The Music Scores at the Peacock', *Sunday Independent*, 28 August 1977.
70. Parker, journal, 8 and 6 October 1977.
71. Parker, journal, 30 August and 6 October 1977.
72. Parker, letter to Alfred Gingold, 28 October 1977.
73. Stewart Parker, letter to John Gilbert, 22 January 1977; Kate Parker, letter to John Gilbert, 10 January 1977; Julie MacRae, 24 February 1995; Brian Walker, 8 April 1994; Angélique Day, 26 June 1994.
74. Parker, journal, 12 August and 22–4 September 1977; John Gilbert, journal, 22 January 1977.
75. Parker, journal, 27 September 1977.
76. Parker, journal, 25 April 1977.
77. Parker, journal, 30 September, 1 and 3 October, and 16 and 24 November 1977, and quoted in Wyver, 'Irish Eyes'; Jennifer Johnston, 'Situation Comedy', *Radio Times* (3 December 1977), 10; Memo from Janet Quigg, Assistant Information Officer, Northern Ireland, to various BBC authorities, 6 December 1977.
78. Parker, journal, 15 December 1977.
79. Parker, journal, 3 and 16 December 1977.
80. Parker, journal, 23 and 31 December 1977.
81. Brian McGinn writes, 'In addition to honoring St Patrick on 17 March, Montserratians also honour slaves executed after an abortive revolt on 17 March 1768....In this case, the targets of the slave plot were Irish planters who, had everything gone right, might have been too inebriated to resist' (McGinn, 'How Irish is Montserrat?' *Irish Roots*, 1 [1994], 22).
82. Parker, journal, 5, 11, and 16 January 1978.
83. Parker, letter to Shaun Davey, 21 November 1978, and *Kingdom Come* (typescript), 58; Michael Billington, 'Kingdom Come', *Guardian*, 18 January 1978; Irving Wardle, 'Witty and Agile Lyrics Among Exotic Foliage', *The Times*, 18 January 1978.
84. Keith Nurse, 'King's Head: Kingdom Come', *Daily Telegraph*, 19 January 1978; Michael Coveney, 'Kingdom Come', *Financial Times*, 18 January 1978; Billington, 'Kingdom Come'; Parker, journal, 18 January 1978.
85. Parker, journal, 24 and 29 January 1978.
86. Robert Cushman, 'Basho and the Tidal Wave', *Observer*, 22 January 1978; Conor Cruise O'Brien, 'A Song of Disembafflement', *Observer*, 29 January 1978; Parker, letter to Shaun Davey, 4 February 1978. A few days after returning to Belfast, Parker would offer O'Brien his sincere thanks:

> When I departed for New Haven a month ago, I was in a state of near despair about my work....The struggle to make theatrical sense of my own experience of my own country—eight months of concentrated work in this particular instance—seemed to have gone for nothing. All [the London critics] wanted, apparently, were the stale and stultifying clichés—bombs, booze, blarney and the mean back streets.

> I don't know how to express the effect of your essay…except to say that it put new heart into me. To have one's intentions understood is a great reward. To have one's entertainment enjoyed is in itself a great joy. To experience a consummation of these responses as expressed by someone with access to the public press is, in my own career, unprecedented. (Parker, draft letter to Conor Cruise O'Brien, 22 February 1978)

87. Parker, journal, 8 February 1978; Julie MacRae, 24 February 1995.
88. Parker, journal, 9 February 1978.
89. Parker, journal, 10 February 1978; Richard Eder, '"Spokesong", by Stewart Parker, Belfast Drama, at Long Wharf', *New York Times*, 11 February 1978; Clive Barnes, 'Dazzling "Spokesong" Rewarding', *New York Post*, 14 February 1978.
90. Parker, journal, 19 February 1978.

NOTES TO CHAPTER 10

1. Parker, journal, 13 April 1978, and letter to Bea MacLeod, 26 April 1978.
2. David Pauker, inter-office memos to Marc Berlin, 22 February and 31 March 1978, letters to Parker, 7 March and 4 and 21 April 1978, and letter to Berlin, 28 March 1978; Parker, journal, 1 April 1978.
3. Parker, letter to Bea MacLeod, 26 April 1978; programme for the Long Wharf Theatre production of *Spokesong* (New Haven, 1978), 15; David Pauker, letter to Parker, 21 April 1978; Jimmy Kennedy, letter to Parker, 12 June 1978; Kenneth Frankel, letter to Parker, 11 April 1978.
4. Parker, letter to Shaun Davey, 27 June 1978; Steph Pickering, 17 June 1994.
5. Parker, letter to Alfred Gingold, 6 September 1978; Noeleen Dowling, 6 July 1994; Marilyn Imrie, 15 March 1995.
6. *Hearth: A Review of Projects Completed 1978–1993* (Belfast: Hearth, 1994), 5; David and Karen Maxwell, 17 June 1994; Parker, letter to Bea MacLeod, 26 April 1978.
7. Steph Pickering, 16 June 1994, and e-mails to author, 25 and 27 June 2004; Jennie Renton, 5 April 2007.
8. Simon Winchester, 'The Irish Eyes Which Have Little Time For Smiling', *Guardian*, 4 August 1977; Parker, journal, 4 August 1977, and letter to Alfred Gingold, 28 October 1977.
9. Parker later included many of these elements in a six-part series of television films with the same title that was finally aired in 1987.
10. Parker, journal, 25 March 1977, letter to Andrew Totten, 20 April 1987, and *Catchpenny Twist* (New York: Samuel French, 1984), 8.
11. Parker, journal, 21, 25, and 26 June 1978, and letter to Shaun Davey, 27 June 1978.
12. Parker, letters to Alfred Gingold, 6 September 1978, and Shaun Davey, 5 September 1978.
13. Parker, letter to Shaun Davey, 5 September 1978.
14. Parker, journal, 3–10 August and 5 September 1978.
15. Parker, journal, 20 September and 5 and 6 October 1978.
16. Clive Barnes, 'Parker's "Catchpenny" Adds an Interesting Twist', *New York Post*, 18 November 1978; Parker, letter to Shaun Davey, 2 November 1978.
17. Parker, letter to Shaun Davey, 2 November 1978.
18. David Pauker, letters to Parker, 5 July 1978, and Hugh Alexander, 11 September 1978.
19. Parker, *I'm a Dreamer Montreal* (Thames Television typescript), 87–93; Ronald Hastings, television guide, *Daily Telegraph*, 6 March 1979.

20. Parker, letter to Bea MacLeod, 28 September 1976, and journal, 30 October and 16 November 1978.
21. Parker, letter to Shaun Davey, 2 November 1978, and journal, 25 October 1978.
22. Parker, letter to Shaun Davey, 2 November 1978, and journal, 3 November 1978.
23. Shaun Davey, 7 July 1994, and letter to Parker, 8 November 1978; Parker, letter to Davey, 21 November 1978.
24. Shaun Davey, letter to Parker, 4 December 1978; Parker, journal, 7 December 1978.
25. Parker, letter to Joan Rodker, 8 December 1978, and journal, 15 December 1978.
26. Parker, journal, 21 November and 3 and 7 December 1978.
27. Parker, journal, 9, 4, 5, 7, and 11 January 1979. Hogmanay is the last day of the year, a traditional occasion for celebration in Scotland (and in Parker's circle). One is 'first-footed' when one welcomes into one's home the first visitor of the New Year.
28. David Pauker, letter to Paul Libin, 10 January 1979.
29. Parker, journal, 13–14 and 16 February 1979.
30. Parker, journal, 24 February 1979.
31. The Collinses were Connecticut-based journalists Parker had met through Fairleigh and got to know better during the productions of *Spokesong* and *Catchpenny Twist* in New Haven and Hartford. Gail Collins later became the editorial page editor of the *New York Times* (Gail Collins, 28 September 2004).
32. Parker, letter to Bea MacLeod, n.d. [late May or early June 1979]. The most powerful New York critics, Richard Eder and Clive Barnes, repeated their endorsements of the play and production, though Eder qualified his and Barnes acknowledged that 'The whole look of the play and its fulfilment emerged much more forcibly in New Haven' (Eder, 'Stage: "Spokesong" Spins Cycle of Belfast', *New York Times*, 16 March 1979; Barnes, 'Spine-tingling "Spokesong" Sings of Cycles and Bombs', *New York Post*, 16 March 1979). Douglas Watt, who had not liked the play in New Haven, still did not like it, and *Variety* published a snide review a few days later. Mixed reviews appeared in the *New Yorker* and *New York* magazines (Watt, ' "Spokesong" Lets the Air Out of Its Tires', *Daily News*, 16 March 1979; 'Hobe.', 'Show On Broadway: Spokesong', *Variety*, 21 March 1979; Brendan Gill, 'In Praise of Wheels', *New Yorker* [26 March 1979], 53–4; John Simon, 'From Wheel to Woe', *New York* [2 April 1979], 85).
33. Parker, journal, 26 March 1979.
34. Parker, 'State of Play', *Canadian Journal of Irish Studies*, 7.1 (June 1981), 6–9.
35. 'State of Play', 9.
36. 'State of Play', 10–11.
37. Parker, journal, 5, 9, and 11 May 1979.
38. Parker, journal, 14 May 1979.
39. Marc Berlin, 22 March 1994; Colm Tóibín, 'Grim Laughter', *Hibernia* (1 May 1980); Robert Cooper, 'Riveting Exchanges' in *Stewart Parker*, supplement to *Fortnight*, 278 (1989), v.
40. Parker, quoted in Robert Ottaway (ed.), 'Highlights of Your BBC Week: Radio and Television', *Radio Times* (14–20 February 1981), 5.
41. Parker, *The Kamikaze Ground Staff Reunion Dinner* in *Best Radio Plays of 1980* (London: Eyre Methuen, 1981), 19–20, 35, 25, 29.
42. *Kamikaze Ground Staff*, 29–31, 38.
43. Parker, journal, 19 October 1979; Ronald Mason, letter to Parker, 8 January 1980; John Tydeman, letter to Parker, 17 December 1979.
44. Parker, draft letter to Hugh Alexander, 9 August 1979; Alexander, letter to Parker, 6 September 1979; Marc Berlin, 22 March 1994.

45. Parker, journal, 9 May, 29 August, and 4 December 1975, and notebook, probably 9 May, 29 August, and 4 December 1975. *Nightshade* and Losey's version of *The Go-Between* share elements besides a preoccupation with sex, death, and love: a precocious child coming of age, a shocking secret revealed, and a magician, to name a few.

46. Parker, quoted in Robert Allen, 'Stewart Parker: Playwright from a Lost Tribe', *Irish Times*, 31 January 1987, and in Maev Kennedy, 'Tortoise at Work', *Irish Times*, 17 September 1985.

47. J. Stewart Parker, 'The Modern Poet as Dramatist: Some Aspects of Non-Realistic Drama, with Special Reference to Eliot, Yeats and Cummings' (thesis submitted for the degree of Master of Arts, Queen's University, Belfast, 1966), 190.

48. Parker, journal, 20 December 1976, and notebook, probably August 1976; Colin Murray Parkes, *Bereavement: Studies of Grief in Adult Life* (New York: International Universities Press, 1972), 78. Lynne Parker, artistic director of Dublin's Rough Magic Theatre Company and the playwright's niece, has a rule of thumb for directing formidably difficult Parker plays such as *Nightshade* or *Northern Star*. She looks first for the human relationships and problems in these plays of ideas, in the belief that if audiences do not care about the people they see on stage, they will not care about the ideas either. I am following her lead in my analysis of *Nightshade*.

49. Parker, *Nightshade* (Dublin: Co-op Books, 1980), 15–16, and *Dramatis Personae* (Belfast: John Malone Memorial Committee, 1986).

50. *Nightshade*, 26, 41–2, 36.

51. *Nightshade*, 54, 44.

52. *Nightshade*, 9–12.

53. *Nightshade*, 37.

54. *Nightshade*, 43, 56, 62. In *Bereavement*, Parkes cites studies documenting an increased mortality rate, especially from heart disease, among people who have recently lost a close relative to death (Parkes, 16–17). If Quinn has, in fact, had a heart attack, it is anybody's guess as to whether he recovers or not. Lynne Parker suggests another possible scenario: 'Much of the play deals with the limbo of a death unresolved—not come to terms with or surrounded by mystery—and I think it possible that Quinn's final state is…an equivalent of this. By this I mean that he could have had a stroke.' The 'state of suspended animation and impasse' a stroke could entail would be in keeping with the 'no-man's-land described in the play' (Lynne Parker, e-mail to author, 13 June 2000).

55. The stories of Jacob and the Angel and of Sleeping Beauty were among Parker's five 'sacred texts' (discussed more fully in Chapter 7 of this book). He identified the biblical story with his 'condition (lame)' and the fairy tale with his 'poetic soul'. In September 1979, while chiefly occupied with writing the first draft of *Nightshade*, Parker agreed to write a pantomime to be performed at the Opera House in Belfast in 1980; he intended to adapt *Sleeping Beauty*. Although he ultimately withdrew from the project, citing pressure of other work, the incident provides additional evidence of the story's powerful appeal to him (Parker, journal, 11 September 1979; Michael Barnes, letter to Parker, 16 January 1980).

56. *Nightshade*, 27–8.

57. *Nightshade*, 37, 62.

58. *Nightshade*, 52–3.

59. *Nightshade*, 21, 28.

60. *Nightshade*, 39, 61.

61. *Nightshade*, 36.

62. Parker, notebook, probably August 1976, and *Nightshade*, 44; Julie MacRae, 24 February 1995; Lynne Parker, 18 October 1993.

63. *Nightshade*, 30, 32. This speech recalls a quotation from a 1970 report of the Irish Medico-Social Research Board that Parker intended to use as an epigraph to *Hopdance*: 'When we die, we do not just die of the disease we have, we die of our whole life.'

64. Robert Allen; Parker, journal, 10 October 1979; Lesley Bruce, 18 October 1993.

65. Chris Parr, letter to Parker, 23 April 1979; Parker, journal, 30 October 1979.

66. Peter Gill, letter to Parker, 6 December 1979; Max Stafford-Clark, letters to Parker, 13 and 20 November 1979; Irene Lewis, letter to Parker, 30 January 1980.

67. Extracts from Christopher Ewart-Biggs Memorial Fund Appeal, enclosed in a letter from Jane Ewart-Biggs to Parker, 17 October 1979. Lesley Bruce recalls that of all the prizes Parker won in his lifetime he remained proudest of this one (Bruce, 9 March 1994).

68. Parker, journal, 9 November and 2, 6, and 3 December 1979.

69. Parker, journal, 28 December 1979.

70. Parker, journal, 21 February and 2 March 1980; Michael Billington, 'Catchpenny Twist', *Guardian*, 22 February 1980; John Peter, 'Innocents in an Irish Minefield', *Sunday Times*, 2 March 1980; Michael Coveney, 'Catchpenny Twist', *Financial Times*, 22 February 1980. See also Ann McFerran, theatre listing, *Time Out* (29 February–6 March 1980); Ned Chaillet, 'Catchpenny Twist', *The Times*, 25 February 1980; Milton Shulman, 'No Escape…', *Evening Standard*, 22 February 1980; Robert Cushman, 'Belfast Songsters', *Observer*, 24 February 1980; and R. S., 'Irish Stew', *Sunday Telegraph*, 24 February 1980.

71. Julie MacRae, 28 June 1994; Parker, journal, 28 January 1980, and one-line précis from a handwritten list of brief descriptions of his plays made for his agents in the early 1980s.

72. Parker, journal, 11 February 1980.

73. Parker, journal, 12 February 1980.

74. Parker, journal, 12 and 13 March 1980.

75. Parker, letter to Bea MacLeod, 4 June 1980, and *Tall Girls Have Everything*, typescript.

76. Parker, journal, 13, 14, and 25 March 1980.

77. Nancy McKibbin, 10 May 1994; Steph Pickering, 16 June 1994.

78. That summer the theatre would have to close temporarily when the roof actually did cave in (Parker, journal, 10 July 1980).

79. Parker, journal, 24 March 1980.

80. Parker, journal, 9, 28, and 24 April and 1 May 1980.

81. Parker, journal, 27 March and 21 April 1980; David Pauker, letter to Parker, 1 May 1980; Parker, letter to Bea MacLeod, 4 June 1980.

82. Parker, journal, 31 July and 4, 5, 12, and 14 August 1980; programme for the Peacock production of *Nightshade* (Dublin, 1980).

83. Parker, journal, 12, 15, and 23 September 1980.

84. Parker, journal, 27 September and 7 October 1980; Shaun Davey, 7 July 1994.

85. Parker, journal, 8 and 9 October 1980; Lesley Bruce, 15 October 1993.

86. Sam Fannin, 25 March 1995.

87. Michael Coveney, 'Dublin Theatre Festival: Translations', *Financial Times*, 13 October 1980; John Barber, 'Curious Grave Jokes', *Daily Telegraph*, 14 October 1980; Parker, journal, 14 October 1980; John Finegan, 'Fantasies in a Funeral Parlour', *Evening Herald*, 10 October 1980; Emmanuel Kehoe, 'Nightshade', *Sunday Press*, 12 October

1980; Con Houlihan, 'Thoughts of What Might Have Been...', *Evening Press*, 10 October 1980; Ned Chaillet, 'Where New Plays Are the Main Attraction', *The Times*, 17 October 1980; Michael Sheridan, 'Heavy Dose of Deadly "Nightshade"', *Irish Press*, 10 October 1980.

88. David McKenna, untitled review, *In Dublin* (17–30 October 1980); Colm Tóibín, 'Parker Pens a Rare Delight', *Hibernia* (16 October 1980); David Nowlan, '"Nightshade" at the Peacock', *Irish Times*, 10 October 1980. Other good reviews included Tony Hennigan, 'Death as a Sinister Illusion', *Irish Independent*, 10 October 1980 and Gus Smith, 'Enter McKenna—the Magician', *Sunday Independent*, 12 October 1980.

89. Douglas Kennedy, 24 October 1993; Maev Kennedy; Parker, journal, 18 and 21 October 1980.

90. Parker, journal, 23 and 30 October 1980.

91. Parker, journal, 23 and 27 October 1980.

92. Parker, journal, 7 November 1980.

93. Martin O'Brien, 'Nightshade—an Exhilarating Conundrum', *Belfast Telegraph*, 11 November 1980; JR, 'Play to Be Seen', *News Letter*, 11 November 1980; Ian Hill, 'Festival', *Guardian*, 14 November 1980; Parker, journal, 10, 11, and 14 November 1980.

94. Parker, journal, 13, 15, 16, and 17 November 1980.

95. Parker, quoted in Jeananne Crowley, 'Belfast Revisited', *Radio Times* (21–7 November 1981), 15.

96. Parker, 'Me & Jim', *Irish University Review*, 12.1 (Spring 1982), 32.

97. Julie MacRae, 28 June 1994; Parker, draft letter to Stephen Frears, 4 and 5 December 1980.

98. Parker, *Iris in the Traffic, Ruby in the Rain* in *Irish University Review*, 28.2 (Autumn/Winter 1998), 345.

99. Parker, journal, 28 November 1980, and draft letter to Stephen Frears, 4 and 5 December 1980.

100. Parker, journal, 16 and 19 December 1980; Lesley Bruce, 6 June 2007.

101. Parker, notebook, probably July or August 1976.

102. Patrick O'Connor, 12 March 1995; Sam Fannin, letter to author, 4 July 2004; Parker, 'Edinburgh: Festive and Steadfast City', *New York Times*, 21 February 1982, and journal, 20 June 1979 and 18 July 1980.

NOTES TO CHAPTER 11

1. Parker's play was aired for the first time on 16 December 1979 and repeated by the BBC on 27 April 1980. The award year ran for twelve months from December 1979.

2. *Best Radio Plays of 1980* (London: Eyre Methuen, 1981); Nick Hern, letter to Parker, 12 January 1981; Parker, journal, 5 January 1981.

3. Rob Buckler, letter to Parker, 27 November 1979.

4. Parker admired the artistry of this sequence but worried that it might 'just serve to confuse people further' (journal, 16 January 1981).

5. Parker, journal, 10–13, 15, 17, 18, and 20 February 1981; Jennifer Selway, 'The Week in View', *Observer*, 15 February 1981; Clive James, 'Bomb-happy Colonels', *Observer*, 22 February 1981.

6. Parker, journal, 15 and 26 January 1981.

7. Parker, journal, 3–5 and 11 March 1981.

8. Parker, journal, 14 March 1981.

9. Parker, journal, 11–12 February and 28–30 March 1981.

10. Parker, journal, 16 June and 7 May 1981.

11. Parker, journal, 15 and 24 June and 7 and 16 July 1981; Liz Parker, 'Why Don't More Women Buy Books?' *Guardian*, 7 July 1981; 'Why a Busy Woman Has No Time for Books' (letters to the editor), *Guardian*, 16 July 1981.

12. John J. O'Meara (ed. and trans.), *The Voyage of Saint Brendan: Journey to the Promised Land* (Atlantic Highlands, New Jersey: Humanities Press, 1976); *The Oxford Companion to Irish Literature*, ed. Robert Welch (Oxford: Oxford University Press, 1996), 390; J. C. J. Metford, *Dictionary of Christian Lore and Legend* (London: Thames and Hudson, 1983), 54; Parker, *The Green Light*, typescript, 5.

13. O'Meara, xiv; Parker, journal, April and May 1967; Geoffrey Ashe, *Land to the West: St Brendan's Voyage to America* (London: Collins, 1962).

14. John Paul, 6 November 1994; Parker, journal, September–December 1971; Ray Rosenfield, 'N. I. Arts Body Awards Prizes to Writers', *Irish Times*, 7 December 1971.

15. Entry for (Giles) Timothy Severin, *Who's Who 2004* (New York: Palgrave Macmillan, 2004), 1974; Tim Severin, *The Brendan Voyage*, illus. Trondur Patursson (New York: McGraw-Hill, 1978); Parker, journal, 9 July 1978 and 29 July 1980.

16. Lesley Bruce, 20 March 1995.

17. I have based my description of the Vinland Map controversy on the account given by the Norwegian cartographical historian Kirsten A. Seaver in *Maps, Myths, and Men: The Story of the Vinland Map* (Stanford: Stanford University Press, 2004). Seaver, who doubts the map's authenticity, presents an exhaustive survey of the many issues surrounding it, as well as a convincing guess as to the map's author: Father Josef Fischer, S. J., a distinguished historian of cartography who, Seaver speculates, drew the map to amuse himself in retirement and to provide 'proof' of several of his pet theories about both the Norse in Greenland and North America and the worldwide reach and influence of the medieval Catholic Church.

18. Wilcomb E. Washburn, 'Preface', *Proceedings of the Vinland Map Conference*, ed. Wilcomb E. Washburn (Chicago: University of Chicago Press, 1971), ix.

19. Helen Wallis, quoted in Seaver, 97.

20. The genders of the characters were part of Parker's plan for *Pratt's Fall* from the start. A note made around the same time as his first one for the play sets out this outline for it: 'Man who discovers map. Woman who lives w/ him, keeper of maps in museum. They write a book together. Defend it at international conference. She propounding theory. He conjuring scenes from Voyage. Denouement—she discovers he forged it' (Parker, notebook, probably autumn 1976).

21. Parker, *Pratt's Fall* in *Plays: 1* (London: Methuen, 2000), 259. Parker made a few significant changes to *Pratt's Fall* between his initial draft and this version, and these will be discussed as relevant. Much of his revision, however, focused on polishing individual speeches. In quoting from the play, I shall confine myself as far as possible to passages that remained substantially the same from draft to draft and shall cite the published version.

22. *Pratt's Fall*, 269–70. In an early draft of the play, the phrase 'nostalgia for faith' is attributed to Mahoney. In the published version, the words are Victoria's, but Mahoney concurs with her analysis.

23. *Pratt's Fall*, 283, 302.

24. Parker, synopsis of *Pratt's Fall*, May 1980, and journal, 20 November and 12 December 1980.
25. *Pratt's Fall*, 262. In the early draft, Godfrey describes them as 'extremists'.
26. *Pratt's Fall*, 251, 273.
27. Parker, notebook, probably the spring of 1985.
28. *Pratt's Fall*, 325–6.
29. *Pratt's Fall*, 331.
30. Parker, journal, 5, 20, and 28 August 1981; David Aukin, letter to Parker, 26 August 1981.
31. Parker, journal, 28–9 and 31 August and 4 September 1981.
32. Parker, journal, 1 and 7 September 1981.
33. Parker, journal, 17 and 20 October 1981, and letter to Nancy and Brian McKibbin, 6 May 1982.
34. Lesley Bruce, 14 October 1993 and 6 June 2007.
35. Parker, journal, 30 November 1981. *Iris in the Traffic, Ruby in the Rain* was transmitted on 24 November 1981 on BBC1.
36. John Wyver, 'Television', *City Limits* (20–6 November 1981), 55; Jennifer Selway, 'The Week in View', *Observer*, 22 November 1981; Anne Campbell Dixon, 'Television—Tuesday', *Daily Telegraph*, 24 November 1981; 'Television/Radio', *Guardian*, 24 November 1981; Bill Carter, 'But Some Are More Equal', *Sunday Times*, 22 November 1981.
37. Parker, journal, 27 and 29 November 1981; Dennis Hackett, 'Equality Myth', *The Times*, 25 November 1981; Russell Davies, 'Crusading with Cliff', *Sunday Times*, 29 November 1981; John Naughton, 'Breaking Eggs', *Listener* (26 November 1981), 662–3; Keith Baker, 'Younger Than Yesterday', *Belfast Telegraph*, 28 November 1981.
38. Parker, journal, 2, 4, and 7–8 December 1981.
39. David Aukin, letters to Parker, 14 December 1981 and 11 January 1982; Parker, journal, 4 and 14 January 1982.
40. Parker, journal, 15 December and 15, 19, and 21 January 1982.
41. Parker, journal, 9 February 1982.
42. Parker, journal, 16–18 February 1982.
43. Parker, 'Me & Jim', *Irish University Review*, 12.1 (Spring 1982), 33–4.
44. Parker, notebook, 1974, and journal, 9 January 1980, 6 June 1981, and 26 January and 6 March 1982.
45. Richard Ellmann, *James Joyce* (Oxford: Oxford University Press, 1959), 1.
46. Parker, synopsis of *Joyce in June*, undated (but written 12 June 1981).
47. Synopsis of *Joyce in June*.
48. Parker, *Joyce in June* (BBC typescript), 132.
49. *Joyce in June*, 6, 8, 10, and 12.
50. *Joyce in June*, 10–11.
51. Lesley Bruce, 6 June 2007; Parker, letter to Nancy and Brian McKibbin, 6 May 1982; Corinna Honan, 'They've Made Dad's Tragedy into a Comedy', *Daily Mail*, 6 October 1984; Ann Pacey, 'The Great Money Chase', *Sunday Mirror*, 7 October 1984.
52. Honan; Parker, quoted in Patricia Finney, 'Take Tim Curry and Run', *Evening Standard*, 5 October 1984; Lesley Bruce, 17 October 1993.
53. Parker, *Blue Money*, typescript, 18.
54. *Blue Money*, 49, 81, and journal, 21 April 1982.
55. Parker, journal, 9 and 24 March 1982, and letter to Nancy and Brian McKibbin, 6 May 1982.

56. Parker, journal, 18 March 1982, and letter to Nancy and Brian McKibbin, 6 May 1982.

57. Parker, letter to Nancy and Brian McKibbin, 6 May 1982, and journal, 4 and 7 May 1982.

58. Parker, journal, 10–13 May 1982; Lesley Bruce, 6 June 2007.

59. Parker, journal, 24 February, 16 and 17 April, and 24 May 1982, and letters to Bea MacLeod, 30 November 1982, and Nancy and Brian McKibbin, 30 July 1982; Lesley Bruce, 30 March 1994, 20 March 1995, and 6 June 2007; Sam Fannin, 22 March 1995, and letters to author, 25 September 1994 and 2 July 2007.

60. Parker, journal, 26 February 1982, and letter to Nancy and Brian McKibbin, 6 May 1982.

61. Parker, journal, 4 August 1977 and 18, 21, and 28 June 1982; Stephen Rea, 23 February 1995. For a comprehensive account of the early years of the Field Day Theatre Company, see my *Acting Between the Lines: The Field Day Theatre Company and Irish Cultural Politics 1980–1984* (Oxford: Oxford University Press, 1994).

62. Parker, journal, 18 June 1982, and letter to Nancy and Brian McKibbin, 30 July 1982.

63. Lesley Bruce, 6 June 2007; Parker, letter to Nancy and Brian McKibbin, 30 July 1982.

64. Lesley Bruce, 6 June 2007.

65. Parker, letter to Nancy and Brian McKibbin, 30 July 1982, and journal, 17 June 1982.

66. Parker, journal, 28 July 1982.

67. From there she continued on to Julie MacRae in Vancouver; the McKibbins in Dundas, Ontario; Bea MacLeod in Ithaca; a holiday home owned by Gina Leishman's father in Yorkshire; the Maxwells in Edinburgh; and John Gilbert and his wife in Glasgow. Eventually she settled in her own flat in Glasgow.

68. Ann Hasson, 22 February 1995.

69. Parker, letter to Nancy and Brian McKibbin, 30 July 1982.

70. Parker, journal, 22 July 1982; Ken and June Lambla, 11 November 1994; Gina Leishman, 10 October 1994; Nancy McKibbin, 10 May 1994; Bea MacLeod, 14 and 17 January 1994; Steph Pickering, 16 June 1994; David and Karen Maxwell, 17 June 1994; John Gilbert, 3 June 1994; Marcus Patton, 6 April 1994.

71. Parker, letter to Nancy and Brian McKibbin, 30 July 1982, and journal, 6 August 1982.

72. Parker, journal, 26, 3, and 10 August 1982 and 5 January 1983.

NOTES TO CHAPTER 12

1. Parker, journal, 5 October 1984.

2. Howard Schuman, 15 November 2007; Peter Farago, 15 June 1994; Sam Fannin, 27 November 2007.

3. Lesley Bruce, 6 June 2007, and 10 and 13 November 2007.

4. Parker, journal, 17 June 1982, and 2 and 5 January 1983.

5. John Paul, 17 January 1994; Nancy Cole, 17 March 1999.

6. Margaret Windham Heffernan, 31 October 1994; Parker, *Radio Pictures* (BBC rehearsal script, 1985), 32, 34.

7. *Radio Pictures*, 85, 102, 12, 20.

8. Parker, journal, 27 January 1983, and *Radio Pictures*, 46, 96–7.

9. Parker, letter to Bea MacLeod, 30 November 1982.

10. Lesley Bruce, 23 October 1993 and 6 June 2007; Marilyn Imrie, 15 March 1995; Joyce McMillan, 'Theatre', *Sunday Standard*, 30 January 1983; Mary Brennan, 'Pratt's Fall', *Herald*, 27 January 1983. See also Joseph Farrell, 'Tron, Glasgow: Pratt's Fall', *Scotsman*, 28 January 1983; Cordelia Oliver, 'Pratt's Fall', *Guardian*, 29 January 1983; 'A Hilarious Sort of History', *Jewish Echo*, 8 February 1983.

11. Programme for the Birmingham Repertory's production of *Nightshade* (1983); Peter Farago, 15 June 1994; Anthony Masters, 'Thrilling Chasms of Mood and Style', *The Times*, 3 June 1983; Eric Shorter, 'Deathly Delight', *Daily Telegraph*, 2 June 1983; Lesley Bruce, 16 November 2007.

12. Parker, journal, 11 October 1981; Ciaran McKeown, 17 and 19 November 1998; Roy Connolly, *The Evolution of the Lyric Players Theatre, Belfast: Fighting the Waves* (Lewiston, New York: Edwin Mellen, 2000).

13. Ciaran McKeown, e-mail to author, 22 November 1997.

14. Parker, draft letter to Leon Rubin, 10 August 1982; Ciaran McKeown, 19 November 1998, and e-mail to author, 22 November 1997.

15. Terence Brown, 'History's Nightmare: Stewart Parker's *Northern Star*', *Theatre Ireland*, 13 (1987), 40–1; Parker, *Northern Star* in *Three Plays for Ireland* (Birmingham: Oberon, 1989), 13, 64.

16. Kevin Whelan, *The Tree of Liberty: Radicalism, Catholicism and the Construction of Irish Identity 1760–1830* (Notre Dame, Indiana: University of Notre Dame Press, 1996), 133.

17. *Northern Star*, 16.

18. *Northern Star*, 59.

19. Jonathan Bardon, *A History of Ulster* (Belfast: Blackstaff, 1992), 220; *Northern Star*, 65.

20. John Smith, quoted in Edna C. Fitzhenry, *Henry Joy McCracken* (Dublin: Talbot, 1936), 148; *Northern Star*, 73.

21. *Northern Star*, 18, 16.

22. Parker, programme note for the Lyric Players Theatre production of *Northern Star* (Belfast, 1984) and quoted in Ciaran Carty, 'Northern Star Rising On the Tide', *Sunday Tribune*, 29 September 1985.

23. *Northern Star*, 59, 29, 55.

24. Parker, *Northern Star*, 17, and quoted in Carty; Fintan O'Toole, 'Second Opinion', *Irish Times*, 12 October 1996.

25. *Northern Star*, 72–3.

26. *Northern Star*, 54.

27. *Northern Star*, 56–8.

28. *Northern Star*, 14–15, 75.

29. Parker, journal, 13 September and 14 and 25 November 1983.

30. Sean McCarthy, 11 October 2007; Patrick Mason, 7 July 1994; programme for the Western Union inaugural tour (1983); Parker, journal, 1 October 1983. Western Union folded after this initial venture because McCarthy became ill and moved back to Scotland.

31. Parker, journal, 24 May 1983, and letter to Julie Barber, 13 June 1983; Barber, letter to Parker, 10 June 1983; minutes of the Field Day board meeting held on 5 June 1983 (box 52, folder 1 of the Tom Paulin papers—MSS 880—held at the Manuscript, Archives, and Rare Book Library of Emory University, Atlanta, Georgia). For more about the David Rudkin incident, see my *Acting Between the Lines: The Field Day Theatre Company*

and Irish Cultural Politics 1980–1984 (Oxford: Oxford University Press, 1994), 191–203.

32. Stephen Rea, letter to Parker, 16 October 1983; Parker, journal, 19 October 1983.

33. Rob Buckler, letter to Parker, 28 April 1980; Parker, letter to Buckler, 27 January 1981.

34. Parker, journal, 1 July, 11 and 15 September, and 6 October 1981 and 15 June 1982; Alexandra Cann (London Management), record of conversation with Parker, 29 September 1981; Lesley Bruce, e-mail to author, 21 October 2007.

35. Parker, *The Traveller* (BBC transcript), 43. *The Traveller* was produced by Robert Cooper and transmitted 30 January 1985 on Radio 3.

36. Parker, notebook, probably 2 January 1983.

37. Parker himself was 42 when he wrote *The Traveller*, but he likely anticipated (correctly) that he would be 43 when it was aired.

38. *Traveller*, 9.

39. *Traveller*, 4.

40. Walter de la Mare, 'The Listeners' in Sir Arthur Quiller-Couch (ed.), *The Oxford Book of English Verse 1250–1918* (Oxford: Oxford University Press, 1939), 1107.

41. *Traveller*, 9, 18; Dante Alighieri, *Inferno* (trans. John Ciardi) in *The Norton Anthology of World Masterpieces*, ed. Maynard Mack, et al. (New York: Norton, 1997), 1018.

42. Parker, journal, 13–17 June 1984 and 30 January and 2 February 1985, and notebook, 11 January 1988; Gillian Reynolds, 'Radio/Showpiece BBC', *Daily Telegraph*, 5 February 1985; Mervyn Jones, 'Holding Out', *Listener* (7 February 1985), 36; Robert Cooper, 8 March 1995, and letter to Parker, 24 April 1985.

43. Parker, journal, 6 November 1981, 8 January, 9 February, and 4 August 1982, 28 June 1983, and 18 and 22 January 1984, and letter to Nancy McKibbin, 5 May 1984; Irving Wardle, 'Theatre in London', *The Times*, 18 January 1984; Michael Billington, 'Nightshade', *Guardian*, 18 January 1984; Michael Ratcliffe, 'Kremlin Charade', *Observer*, 22 January 1984.

44. Parker, journal, 25 January, 3 and 20 February, and 14 March 1984.

45. Parker, journal, 11 May 1982, 7 March and 10 July 1983, and 3 and 17 February 1984; Howard Schuman, 15 November 2007.

46. Parker, journal, 23 March 1984; Strongbow investment brochure, tax year 1984/85; Sam Fannin, letter to author, 5 July 2005; Peter Ormrod, 'My Wall of Death' and 'The Wall of Death' (typescripts).

47. Parker, journal, 6 and 25 April 1984; Carty; John Coates, 'Catching Ireland's Secret Exporters', *Sunday Times*, 10 June 1984.

48. Parker, journal, 31 May and 7–10 June 1984, and *Eat the Peach* notebook, May 1984.

49. Transcript of conversation between Peter Ormrod and Connie Kiernan (May 1984); Parker, *Eat the Peach*, typescript of second draft.

50. Parker, draft letter to Jeremy Isaacs, 11 February 1986, and journal, 8 September 1984.

51. Parker, journal, 3 June 1983, 28 January, 23 May, 25 and 27 September, and 1 October 1984, and 28 January 1985.

52. David Simpson, 'The Prolific Pen of Mr Parker', *Belfast Telegraph*, 3 November 1984; Mary Kenny, 'Cash and Curry are a Red Hot Mix', *Daily Mail*, 8 October 1984; Lucy Hughes-Hallett, 'Weekend View', *Standard*, 8 October 1984; Nancy Banks-Smith, 'Private on Parade', *Guardian*, 8 October 1984; Peter Ackroyd, 'Ambiguous Talents', *The Times*, 8 October 1984; Lesley Bruce, 10 November 2007; Parker, journal, 7 October 1984.

53. Lesley Bruce, 13 November 2007; Ciaran McKeown, e-mail to the author, 22 November 1997; Parker, journal, 25 January, 30 March, and August through October 1984.

54. Parker, journal, 6 and 7 November 1984; CMC, 'Stewart Classic', *News Letter*, 8 November 1984; Jane Bell, 'Reflective Star', *Belfast Telegraph*, 8 November 1984; David Nowlan, '"Northern Star" at Belfast Lyric Theatre', *Irish Times*, 9 November 1984; Ian Hill, 'Northern Star', *Guardian*, 16 November 1984; John Peter, 'Taking Comedy to Extremes', *Sunday Times*, 18 November 1984; Fintan O'Toole, 'Tensions in Past and Present Tense', *Sunday Tribune*, 2 December 1984; 'Northern Vigour' (leader), *Irish Times*, 10 November 1984.

55. Maev Kennedy, 'Tortoise at Work', *Irish Times*, 17 September 1985; Sam Fannin, 27 November 2007; Ian Hill, e-mail to author, 28 November 2007; Barry White, leader, *Belfast Telegraph*, 12 November 1984.

56. Simpson; Jane Coyle, 'Northern Star is Born in Belfast', *Irish News* 15 November 1984.

57. Jane Bell; Ian Hill, 'Northern Star'; Parker, quoted in Coyle, 'Northern Star Is Born'.

58. Robert Allen, 'Stewart Parker: Playwright From a Lost Tribe', *Irish Times*, 31 January 1987; Parker, journal, 10, 11, and 15 November and 7 December 1984.

59. Parker, journal, 14, 15, and 20 January 1985.

60. Celia Brayfield, 'Sound Effect', *The Times*, 17 July 1985; Lucy Hughes-Hallett, 'Last Night's View', *Evening Standard*, 17 July 1985; Parker, journal, 25 February 1985.

NOTES TO CHAPTER 13

1. Parker, journal, 12 and 26 January 1981.

2. Parker, draft letter to Rob Buckler, 27 January 1981. Parker adapted many of the details of Alec's story line from Irish flautist James Galway's autobiography, which he had read (Lynne Parker, 22 October 1993). Galway's experience demonstrated how a working-class boy from a loyalist neighbourhood in Belfast could go from playing in a local flute band to being a world-class star of classical music. Galway had been born in 1939, however, and left Northern Ireland well before the Troubles began. The paramilitary dimension of the story is purely Parker's invention. Nor does the character of Alec, as Parker later wrote him, bear much resemblance to Galway, who, judging from his own account of his life, took pride in his working-class roots. Parker eventually called the film 'Buck Alec', a name borrowed from one of the neighbourhood characters mentioned in Galway's memoir. See James Galway, *An Autobiography* (New York: St Martin's Press, 1979).

3. Parker, draft letter to Rob Buckler, 27 January 1981.

4. Paul Bew and Gordon Gillespie, *Northern Ireland: A Chronology of the Troubles 1968–1993* (Dublin: Gill and Macmillan, 1993), 148, 156; Padraig O'Malley, *Biting at the Grave: The Irish Hunger Strikes and the Politics of Despair* (Belfast: Blackstaff, 1990), 7; Parker, journal, 7 May 1981.

5. Parker, journal, 16, 18, and 19 September 1982, and 'Proposals for a television film serial in six parts, each of fifty minutes', typescript, probably written September 1982; Howard Schuman, 15 November 2007; Lesley Bruce, 18 November 2007.

6. 'Proposals for a television film serial in six parts'.

7. Parker, 'Introduction' to *Lost Belongings* (London: Thames Television, 1987), 5.

8. Parker, 'Proposals for a television film serial in six parts', 'Introduction' to *Lost Belongings*, 3, and journal, 24 January 1981 and 23 and 24 March 1982.

9. 'Proposals for a television film serial in six parts'.

10. Parker, 'Introduction' to *Lost Belongings*, 5–6, and journal, 21 and 23 September 1983 and February 1984.

11. Lez Cooke, *British Television Drama: A History* (London: British Film Institute, 2003), 129; Howard Schuman, 15 November 2007; Sylvia Harvey, 'Channel Four Television: From Annan to Grade', *British Television: A Reader*, ed. Edward Buscombe (Oxford: Oxford University Press, 2000), 104–5; Parker, journal, 16 August 1984.

12. Cooke, 115, 118, 130, 150; Parker, journal, 30 January 1985.

13. Cooke, 96, 138–42.

14. Cooke, 129–34, 138; Tony Bicât, 14 March 1994.

15. Howard Schuman, 15 November 2007; Cooke, 150; Parker, journal, 22 and 26 July and 18 September 1985, interviewed by Cherry Ripe, Australian Broadcasting Corporation, transmitted 7 January 1989, and quoted in Nick Smurthwaite, 'Out of the Land of Myths and Legends', *The Stage and Television Today*, 2 April 1987, 24.

16. The oldest surviving version of the Deirdre legend is translated by Thomas Kinsella in *The Tain* (London: Oxford University Press, 1970), 8–20 and by Jeffrey Gantz in *Early Irish Myths and Sagas* (London: Penguin, 1981), 256–67. A translation of the medieval version of the story may be found in an edition by Eleanor Hull of *The Cuchullin Saga in Irish Literature* (London: David Nutt, 1898), 22–53. Parker relied primarily on the older telling of the story, but he borrowed much incidental detail from the medieval one.

17. Parker, interviewed by James P. Mackey for 'Images of Two Traditions', a programme in the BBC Northern Ireland television series *Perspectives*, produced by Father Jim Skelly, recorded in Belfast on 30 May 1987, transmitted 18 October 1987.

18. *Perspectives* interview.

19. Parker, *Lost Belongings*, 15, 44, and 51. In the Ulster Cycle of tales, the Red Branch is an order of warriors under the patronage of King Conchobor.

20. *Lost Belongings*, 115–17.

21. *Lost Belongings*, 229–32.

22. *Lost Belongings*, 52, 297, 299, and 'Introduction' to *Lost Belongings*, 7.

23. Parker, journal, 24 July 1985, and *Lost Belongings*, 293, 295–6, 298.

24. Parker, journal, 16, 18, and 21 March, 10 April, and 4 June 1985.

25. Paddy Woodworth, 'Wrangles Hit "Peach" Movie', *Sunday Press*, 19 May 1985; Strongbow company brochure (probably February 1985); Parker, journal, 5 February 1985; 'Strongbow: The Ultimate Gamble', *Aspect* (March 1985), 54–5; Frank Fitzgibbon, 'Kelleher and Collins Go to the Movies', *Success* (March 1985), 22–5; Philip Molloy, 'A Peach with Little Flavour', *Irish Press*, 18 March 1986.

26. Parker, journal, 6 February and 14–16 March 1985, and letter to John Kelleher, 18 March 1985.

27. John Kelleher, letter to Parker, 19 March 1985; Parker, journal, 17–18 and 23 March, 1, 4, and 9 April, and 4 May 1985; Stephen Rea, quoted in Woodworth.

28. Parker, journal, 25 July 1985.

29. Parker, journal, 14 March 1986; Molloy.

30. Parker, quoted in Ciaran Carty, 'Northern Star Rising on the Tide', *Sunday Tribune*, 29 September 1985; David Collins, quoted in Woodworth.

31. Andrew Stephen, 'Did Britain Let the Side Down?', *Sunday Times* magazine (4 March 1984), 18–23; Parker, journal, 4 March 1984.

32. Parker, journal, 17 January and 7 February 1985, and letter to Alfred Gingold and Helen Rogan, 10 February 1985.

33. Parker, journal, 14 March, 15 April, and 1 May 1985.

34. Parker, sixteen-page treatment for a film entitled *The Life of Rawley* (typescript, 3 September 1985), 15–16.

35. Parker, journal, 18 September and 4 October 1985 and 11 March 1986; Ian McArthur, letter to Parker, 4 March 1986.

36. Lesley Bruce, letter to Nancy McKibbin, 16 August 1985; Lucy Hughes-Hallett, 'Last Night's View', *Evening Standard*, 17 July 1985; Maureen Paton, 'Mad, Mad World of the Radio Set', *Daily Express*, 17 July 1985; Sean Day-Lewis, 'Studio Scenes', *Daily Telegraph*, 17 July 1985; Barry Took, 'Good Sports', *Listener* (11 July 1985), 43–4; Parker, journal, 30 March 1985.

37. Celia Brayfield, 'Sound Effect', *The Times* 17 July 1985; Lesley Bruce, letter to Nancy McKibbin, 16 August 1985; Parker, journal, 9 August 1985.

38. Michael Hastings, letter to Parker, 13 June 1985; Patrick Sandford, letter to Parker, 12 February 1985; Valerie Osborne, letter to Marc Berlin, 16 September 1985. The Northern tour of *Northern Star* included Derry, Omagh, Portadown, Newry, Coleraine, and Armagh.

39. David Nowlan, ' "Northern Star" at the Olympia', *Irish Times*, 24 September 1985; Gus Smith, 'Parker's Compassion and Nobility', *Sunday Independent*, 29 September 1985; Desmond Rushe, 'A History Lesson In a Relevant and Compelling Work', *Irish Independent*, 24 September 1985; Martin Cropper, 'Brilliant Pastiche', *The Times*, 26 September 1985; Michael Ratcliffe, 'Ireland's Comedy of Terrors', *Observer*, 6 October 1985; William A. Henry III, 'Acts of History', *Time* (21 October 1985).

40. Gus Smith, 'Parker's Compassion'; Parker, journal, 3 October, 29 June, 13 November, and 1 December 1985.

41. Parker, journal, 3, 16, and 17 December 1985.

42. Parker, journal, 4 September and 24 December 1985; Clare Fox and Eddie Kulukundis, letter to Parker, 23 December 1985.

43. Parker, letter to Alfred Gingold and Helen Rogan, 3 March 1985, and journal, 30 July, 25 June, and 10 December 1985; Tony Bicât, 14 March 1994.

44. Tony Bicât, 14 March 1994; Parker, journal, 27 January 1986.

45. Howard Schuman, 15 November 2007; Cooke, 118–19; Barry Hanson, 'The 1970s: Regional Variations' in Jonathan Bignell, Stephen Lacey, and Madeleine Macmurraugh-Kavanagh (eds.), *British Television Drama: Past, Present and Future* (Basingstoke: Palgrave Macmillan, 2000), 58–63; Parker, journal, 20 February 1986. Hanson's credits, as script editor and producer, included ground-breaking plays and serials such as *Penda's Fen* (BBC1, 1974), *Gangsters* (BBC1, 1975), and *Out* (Thames, 1978).

46. Parker, journal, 11 September 1985.

47. Parker's first and most important source of information on Dion Boucicault was David Krause (ed.), *The Dolmen Boucicault* (Dublin: Dolmen, 1964), which contains Boucicault's three most famous Irish plays and a biographical introduction. He also relied on Richard Fawkes, *Dion Boucicault: A Biography* (London: Quartet, 1979)—and on Fawkes himself, whom he met in the course of his research for *Heavenly Bodies*. Parker summed up his own views on Boucicault in 'The Philosophy of Pleasure', a programme note he wrote for the National Theatre's 1988/89 production of *The Shaughraun*.

48. Dion Boucicault, 'The Drama and Its Critics' (letter), *Spirit of the Times*, 31 May 1879, 407; David Krause, 'The Theatre of Dion Boucicault: A Short View of His Life and Art', *The Dolmen Boucicault*, 9–47; 'The Philosophy of Pleasure'. I will continue to refer here only to sources Parker knew about in late 1985 and early 1986, when he was writing *Heavenly Bodies*, and to his own remarks on Boucicault. For a discussion incorporating more recent critical commentary, see my 'Stewart Parker's *Heavenly Bodies*:

Dion Boucicault, Show Business, and Ireland', *Modern Drama*, 43.3 (Fall 2000), 404–20.

49. Krause, 13.
50. Parker, proposal to Thames Television for a series entitled *The Gaslight Moon, or A Tumult in the Drawing Room* (typescript, November 1976).
51. Parker, programme note for the Birmingham Repertory Theatre production of *Heavenly Bodies* (1986).
52. Parker, journal, 19 and 20 September 1985. The legendary foundation of *Joyce in June* is Don Giovanni. The Exile of the Sons of Uisliu is, of course, the tale underlying *Lost Belongings*. The mythological basis of *I'm a Dreamer Montreal* is less evident, but Parker told an interviewer in 1987 that he had been thinking of the story of Orpheus and Eurydice (Smurthwaite).
53. Most of what little information is available on Patterson was compiled by Harry Bradshaw, who spent several years researching his career and was responsible for an RTÉ radio feature on him (Bradshaw, 27 January 1999, and script of *The Rambler from Clare*, produced by Kieran Sheedy and transmitted by RTÉ on 10 June 1976). Parker possessed a copy of Bradshaw's radio script on Patterson as well as a few outline biographies of uncertain origin.
54. Krause, 11–12; Parker, journal, 29 November 1985.
55. Parker, *Heavenly Bodies* in *Three Plays for Ireland* (Birmingham: Oberon, 1989), 85; Krause, 38. The published version of *Heavenly Bodies* differs from the one produced in Birmingham in 1986, which was overloaded and a bit confusing. Parker's basic conception of the play did not change, but he made significant cuts in the script, clarified the central dramatic conflict, and polished individual speeches. I will quote from the published version of the play but confine myself to passages that do not differ substantially from the earlier draft. Statements I make about the structure of the play hold true for both versions.
56. Dion Boucicault, 'The Decline of the Drama', *North American Review*, 125 (September/October 1877), 236; *Heavenly Bodies*, 106, 110, 132.
57. Fawkes, 5, 11.
58. *Heavenly Bodies*, 121.
59. *Heavenly Bodies*, 134.
60. *Heavenly Bodies*, 141, 143–4.
61. *Heavenly Bodies*, 144.
62. Parker, letter to John Boyd, 29 January 1968 (held in the John Boyd collection at the Linen Hall Library, Belfast). In addition to the works by David Krause and Richard Fawkes cited above, sources consulted by Parker included, but were probably not limited to, Townsend Walsh, *The Career of Dion Boucicault* (1915) (New York: Benjamin Blom, 1967); Charles Lamb Kinney, *The Life and Career of Dion Boucicault* (New York: Graphic Company, 1883); Robert Hogan, *Dion Boucicault* (New York: Twayne, 1969); William Paul Steele, *The Character of Melodrama* (Orono, Maine: University of Maine Press, 1968); and Eric Molin and Robin Goodefellowe (eds.), *Dion Boucicault, The Shaughraun: A Documentary Life, Letters and Selected Works* (United States of America: Proscenium Press, 1979).
63. Parker, journal, 13 December 1985.
64. Parker, journal, 11 March 1986.
65. Parker, journal, 15, 17, 21, 23, and 18 March 1986.
66. Parker, journal, 25 March and 3 and 4 April 1986.
67. Parker, journal, 26 and 27 April 1986; Martin Cropper, 'Heavenly Bodies', *The Times*, 24 April 1986; B. A. Young, 'Heavenly Bodies/Birmingham Rep', *Financial Times*,

24 April 1986; John Peter, 'The Making of a Romantic Lead', *Sunday Times*, 4 May 1986; Michael Ratcliffe, 'A Saucy Night at Spithead', *Observer*, 27 April 1986.

68. Parker, journal, 28 April and 3 May 1986; Lesley Bruce, 21 October 1993; Ann Fitz-Gerald, 'Birmingham: Heavenly Bodies', *The Stage and Television Today*, 22 May 1986; Cropper, 'Heavenly Bodies'.

69. Parker, journal, 4, 29, and 31 May, and draft letter to Nicolas Kent, 2 June 1986.

NOTES TO CHAPTER 14

1. Parker, journal, 11 and 14 May 1986; Robert Crone and John Malone, *The Human Curriculum* (Belfast: Farset Co-Operative Press, 1983); Robert Crone, 17 November 1998; H. R. Cathcart, letter to Parker, 5 July 1985.

2. Parker, *Dramatis Personae* (Belfast: John Malone Memorial Committee, 1986), 3–4, 6.

3. *Dramatis Personae*, 7, 13, 15–16.

4. *Dramatis Personae*, 17–18.

5. *Dramatis Personae*, 18.

6. *Dramatis Personae*, 18–19.

7. *Dramatis Personae*, 19.

8. Parker, notes for *Dramatis Personae* contained in the commonplace book he began keeping in 1986, journal, 9 November 1985, and *Dramatis Personae*, 19–20.

9. Tony Bicât, 14 March 1994, and 'A Walk with Stewart' (typescript, 1995).

10. Parker, journal, 28 February and 29 April 1986, and 'Introduction' to *Lost Belongings* (London: Thames Television, 1987), 8; Tony Bicât, 14 March 1994, and 'A Walk with Stewart'.

11. Parker, journal, 12 December 1985 and 17 March, 19 May, and 6, 12, 17, and 25 June 1986; Tony Bicât, 14 March 1994, and 'A Walk with Stewart'.

12. Parker, journal, 2 and 23 July and 15 August 1986, and 'Introduction' to *Lost Belongings*, 8; Tony Bicât, 14 March 1994, and 'A Walk with Stewart'.

13. Tony Bicât, 14 March 1994, and 'A Walk with Stewart'; Parker, journal, 2 April and 25 June 1986.

14. Tony Bicât, 14 March 1994, and 'A Walk with Stewart'; Charles Hunter, 'Putting the Deirdre Myth on Film', *Irish Times*, 17 September 1986.

15. Tony Bicât, 14 March 1994, and 'A Walk with Stewart'; Hunter, 'Putting the Deirdre Myth on Film'.

16. Parker, *Radio Scenery* (typescript, 1986).

17. Robert Cooper, letter to Parker, 9 September 1985; Parker, journal, 31 July 1986; Peter Hall, letter to Parker, 4 December 1986.

18. Marc Berlin, letter to Barry Hanson, 27 October 1986; Joyce Marlow, *Captain Boycott and the Irish* (New York: E. P. Dutton, 1973); Parker, draft letter to Max Stafford-Clark, 6 November 1975.

19. Parker, '*Boycott*: a summary', written for the Joint Stock Theatre Group (typescript, 1976), and proposal for an original screenplay with the working title 'Horseman, Pass By' (typescript, January 1987).

20. Sam Fannin, letter to author, 25 September 1994; Parker, notebook, early 1983; Lesley Bruce, 21 October 1993; description of 'The Tenement House' in *Guide to Over 100 Properties* (Edinburgh: National Trust for Scotland, 1994), 48.

21. Parker, journal, 19 October 1983, and notebook, February and March 1984. At this time, contrary to his later assertion in the introduction to *Three Plays for Ireland* (a volume containing *Northern Star*, *Heavenly Bodies*, and *Pentecost*), Parker had not conceived

of *Pentecost* as completing a 'triptych' begun by the other two. He did see his plays about McCracken and Boucicault as part of a 'common enterprise', but he grouped them in his mind with his projected Hašek play as 'The History Plays', dealing with eighteenth-, nineteenth-, and twentieth-century Man respectively: 'A revolutionary. A showman. A writer.' (Parker, 'Introduction' to *Three Plays for Ireland* [Birmingham: Oberon, 1989], 9, and undated notes found in Parker's study.)

22. Parker, journal, 6, 8, and 14 March 1984.
23. Parker, journal, 10 February 1984, 'Proposals for a television film serial in six parts, each of fifty minutes' (typescript, September 1982), and notebook, probably March 1984. I discuss the UWC Strike, and Parker's experience of it, in Chapter 8.
24. Parker, journal, 22 February 1984 and 20 January and 21 May 1985.
25. Lesley Bruce, 16 October 1993 and 28 July 2008.
26. Lesley Bruce, 16 October 1993 and 28 July 2008; http://www.doncupitt.com; Don Cupitt, *The Sea of Faith* (London: BBC, 1984; paperback edition 1985), 229, 228, 12, 19, 249, 270, 247; Stephen Rea, 23 February 1995.
27. Lesley Bruce, 28 July 2008; Cupitt, 258, 247, 245; Parker, journal, 6 April and 6 October 1985 and 27 May 1986.
28. Jonathan Bardon, *A History of Ulster* (Belfast: Blackstaff, 1992); Richard Jordan, 'The Second Coming of Paisley: From Premillennial Crusader to Amillennial Politician', talk delivered at the annual meeting of the American Conference for Irish Studies in Davenport, Iowa, 18 April 2008, and 'The Interposition of Paisleyism: Irish Civil Rights and Segregation', talk delivered at the annual meeting of the American Conference for Irish Studies in State College, Pennsylvania, 8 May 2010.
29. Robert Fisk, *The Point of No Return: The Strike Which Broke the British in Ulster* (London: André Deutsch, 1975), 34, 166–71, 28, 175; Parker, notebook, late 1986 or early 1987. Extracts from the Bible and from Fisk's book, including the one about Kelly just cited, were included in the programme for the Field Day production at Parker's request (programme for the Field Day production of *Pentecost* [1987]; Parker, journal, 3 August 1987).
30. For my account of the Anglo-Irish Agreement and the unionist reaction it provoked, I am relying on Bardon, *History of Ulster*, 753–77; Paul Bew and Gordon Gillespie, *Northern Ireland: A Chronology of the Troubles 1968–1993* (Dublin: Gill and Macmillan, 1993), 187–207; Michael Parker, *Northern Irish Literature, 1975–2006* (Basingstoke: Palgrave Macmillan, 2007), 46–52; and Paul Arthur and Keith Jeffery, *Northern Ireland Since 1968* (Oxford: Blackwell, 1988), 16–20.
31. Bew and Gillespie, 189; Bardon, *History of Ulster*, 758.
32. Bew and Gillespie, 193, 196, 198, 202; Bardon, *History of Ulster*, 762.
33. Bardon, *History of Ulster*, 764, 757; Arthur and Jeffery, 53, 55–6.
34. Parker, quoted in Deirdre Purcell, 'The Illusionist', *Sunday Tribune*, 27 September 1987, and *Pentecost* in *Three Plays for Ireland*, 171, 161, 155, 147.
35. I offered my own political/historical reading of the play in ' "Ireland, the Continuous Past": Stewart Parker's Belfast History Plays' in Stephen Watt, Eileen Morgan, and Shakir Mustafa (eds.), *A Century of Irish Drama: Widening the Stage* (Bloomington and Indianapolis: Indiana University Press, 2000), 256–74.
36. Michael Coveney, 'Pentecost/Guildhall, Londonderry', *Financial Times*, 25 September 1987; Parker, interview with Seamus McKee for the BBC Northern Ireland arts programme *Saturday Supplement*, produced by Judith Elliott and transmitted on 26 September 1987 (housed at the BBC Radio Archives in Cultra, Northern Ireland, museum number 4903).

37. J. C. J. Metford, *Dictionary of Christian Lore and Legend* (London: Thames and Hudson, 1983), 195.

38. *Pentecost*, 199; Michael Parker, *Northern Irish Literature*, 258; Metford, 100.

39. *Pentecost*, 157, 195, 202; Cupitt, 211–12. In a note for the play he then called 'House On Fire', probably dating to July 1985, Parker wrote 'they discover the skeleton of a baby hidden away in a cupboard' (in *Pentecost*, in contrast, Marian finds a child's christening gown hidden in Lily's underwear drawer). In a later note, likely made shortly before he began writing *Pentecost*, Parker expressed indecision about what happened to Lily's baby: 'the three women have all lost children—Ruth through miscarriages, Lily through murder, (or stillbirth), Marian through death in the cot'. While none of this establishes conclusively that Parker intended Lily herself to be the murderer of her child, I believe this interpretation fits best with Lily's character and the rest of the play. There is a difference only of degree between a woman who would kill her baby to conceal her infidelity and one who would keep her abandonment of her child a secret until her death several decades later, whereas a Lily whose child was murdered by someone else (Alfie in a jealous rage, perhaps?) would be a fundamentally different person (Parker, notebook, probably July 1985 and late 1986 or early 1987).

40. Parker, *Pentecost*, 202, 174, 204, and interviewed by Cherry Ripe for the Australian Broadcasting Corporation, recorded 16 August 1988 and transmitted 7 January 1989; Alex Renton, 'Crossing the Troubled Borders of Irish Drama', *Independent*, 27 November 1987.

41. *Pentecost*, 173, 205–6.

42. *Pentecost*, 153, 163, 206–7.

43. *Pentecost*, 193.

44. *Pentecost*, 191.

45. *Pentecost*, 197.

46. *Pentecost*, 202; Cupitt, 265.

47. *Pentecost*, 181, 207–8; Michael Parker, *Northern Irish Literature*, 107.

48. Cupitt, 190; *Dramatis Personae*, 19.

49. Programme for the Rough Magic Theatre Company production of *Nightshade* (1987); Lynne Parker, letter to author, 6 August 2008; David Nowlan, '"Nightshade" at the Project', *Irish Times*, 5 February 1987; Colm Tóibín, 'Powerful H-Block Drama', *Sunday Independent*, 8 February 1987.

50. Lynne Parker, letter to author, 6 August 2008; Julie Parker McMullan, 18 July 1998.

51. Lynne Parker, letter to author, 6 August 2008.

52. Parker, 'A Commonplace Book, 1986–'.

53. 'A Commonplace Book, 1986–'.

54. W. Stephen Gilbert, 'Mixing It', *Listener* (2 April 1987), 27; Lesley Bruce, 16 November 2007; Tony Bicât, 14 March 1994; David Elstein, letter to Parker, 22 May 1987.

55. *Lost Belongings* publicity booklet (Thames Television, 1987); Tony Bicât, 'A Walk With Stewart'; Mark Lawson, 'Singing in the Pain', *Independent*, 8 April 1987; Damien Gorman, 'Points Victory for Fight Game', *Irish News*, 11 April 1987.

56. Parker, quoted in John Lyttle, 'Everyday People', *City Limits* (9 April 1987); Harry Thompson, 'The Embittered Cliche Persists', *Journal, Newcastle upon Tyne*, 11 April 1987; Dennis Haywood, 'Dennis Haywood's Viewpoint...On Last Night's TV', *Yorkshire Evening Post*, 8 April 1987; Mary Kenny, 'All So Believable...and That's the *Real* Tragedy', *Daily Mail*, 8 April 1987.

57. Norman Jenkinson, 'Nothing Out of the Ordinary', *Belfast Telegraph*, 11 April 1987.

58. Hugh Hebert, 'The Bands on the Run', *Guardian*, 8 April 1987; Sally Vincent, 'Victims of Circumstance', *Today*, 8 April 1987; Jenny Rees, 'Love in a Violent Climate', *Daily Telegraph*, 8 April 1987.

59. Peter McGarry, 'A Nosedive for Drama', *Coventry Evening Telegraph*, 29 April 1987; John Naughton, '"You Brute, You Beast"', *Observer*, 19 April 1987.

60. W. Stephen Gilbert; John Lyttle, 'Lost Belongings', *City Limits* (2 April 1987); Howard Schuman, 15 November 2007; Claudia W. Harris, 'A Living Mythology', *Theatre Ireland*, 13 (November 1987), 17.

61. Celia Brayfield, 'The Brutal Lost Litany', *Independent*, 13 May 1987; David Elstein, letter to Parker, 22 May 1987.

62. Tony Bicât, 14 March 1994, and 'A Walk with Stewart'; Lesley Bruce, 16 October 1993; Parker, journal, 27 March 1987; John Paul, 17 January 1994; Ed Barrett, 15 January 1994.

63. Parker, journal, June through September 1987; programme for the Field Day production of *Pentecost* (1987); Stephen Rea, 23 February 1995; Lynne Parker, letter to author, 6 August 2008.

64. Patrick Mason, 7 July 1994.

65. Parker, quoted in Francis X. Clines, 'Theater Crosses Borders in Ireland, Fueled by the Troubles and a Love of Language', *New York Times*, 27 September 1987; Jane Coyle, 'Drama as Girl Meets Girl', *Irish News*, 22 October 1987; programme for the Field Day production of *Pentecost*; Stephen Rea, 23 February 1995.

66. Parker, quoted in Jonathan Philbin Bowman, 'Party Piece', *In Dublin* (30 September 1987).

67. Frankie McGinley, 'A Good Play', *Donegal Democrat*, 2 October 1987; David Nowlan, '"Pentecost" at the Guildhall, Derry', *Irish Times*, 24 September 1987.

68. Colm Tóibín, 'A Coy Despatch from the Front Line', *Sunday Independent*, 4 October 1987; Fintan O'Toole, 'Death and the Insurrection', *Sunday Tribune*, 27 September 1987.

69. O'Toole, 'Death and the Insurrection'; Treacy Fitzgerald, 'Pentecost on Tour', *Dublin Opinion* (October 1987); 'Tabs on Theatre', *Munster Express*, 6 November 1987; Desmond Rushe, 'Optimistic Pentecost is Parker at his Best', *Irish Independent*, 29 September 1987.

70. Coveney, 'Pentecost/Guildhall, Londonderry'; Mary Holland, 'The Belfast Bible', *Observer*, 27 September 1987; 'Echoing Lost Lives', *Irish Press*, 25 September 1987.

71. Gerard Downey, '"Pentecost" Shows Parker at His Best', *Belfast Telegraph*, 24 September 1987; E. McA., 'Emotionally-Stunning Production', *Ulster Herald*, 17 October 1987; The Spectator, 'A Play of Real Interest, Performed with Love and Zest', *Coleraine Chronicle*, 21 November 1987; Jane Coyle, 'Well-Deserved Pat On the Back', *Irish News*, 29 September 1987.

72. Nell McCafferty, 'A Night Meeting the Family', *Sunday News*, 4 October 1987. Stephen Rea recalls that, the following year, Parker expressed an interest in writing a musical for Field Day in collaboration with McCafferty (Rea, 23 February 1995).

73. CF, 'Play Strips Ulster Bare', *News Letter*, 24 September 1987; 'Play Probes the Protestant Tradition', *News Letter*, 28 September 1987.

74. Stops included Monaghan, Downpatrick, Strabane, Cookstown, Omagh, Armagh, Belfast, Waterford, Cork, Ennis, Sligo, Ballybofey, Antrim, Coleraine, Maghera, Newry, Ballycastle, Enniskillen, Galway, Limerick, Newcastle West, Listowel, and Tralee (Field Day publicity flyer, 1987).

75. Bardon, *History of Ulster*, 775–7; Bew and Gillespie, 208; Michael Longley, 29 March 1994; Frank McGuinness, 'Stewart Parker', *Independent*, 5 November 1988.

76. 'Play Probes the Protestant Tradition'; Parker, journal, 24 September and 9–12 October 1987; Lesley Bruce, 15, 21, and 28 October 1993.

77. Parker, journal, December 1987; Lesley Bruce, 15 November 2007.

78. Lesley Bruce, 20 October 1993; Parker, journal, 3–6 and 30 October and 16 November 1987 and 4 March 1988. There is a popular Irish song called 'Moonlight in Mayo'—Parker plays on this as well as on the fact that many perpetrators of vigilante violence in the period treated by the screenplay used the sobriquet 'Captain Moonlight'.

79. Marlow, 71–6, 227, 276; Parker, *Mayo by Moonlight* (typescript, 1988), notes towards a second draft of the screenplay (17 June 1988), and proposal for an original screenplay with the working title 'Horseman, Pass By'.

80. Parker, journal, 2 March and 7 July 1988, and 'Introduction' to *Three Plays for Ireland*, 9.

81. Parker, letter to Joanna Mules, 29 July 1988; Lesley Bruce, 15 October 1993 and 10 March 1994. A photograph of the Cave Hill by John Gilbert, another friend of Parker, was ultimately used on the cover of *Three Plays for Ireland*.

82. Parker, letter to Robert Cooper, 9 February 1988; Marc Berlin, letter to Alannah Hensler, 20 May 1988; Hensler, letter to Berlin, 3 June 1988; Parker, journal, 11–13 August 1966 and March–September 1988, and notebook, second half of 1987 or early 1988.

83. Parker, notebook, 1988, and journal, 13 July 1988; Lesley Bruce, 16 and 21 October 1993 and 10 November 2007.

84. Parker, journal, 1988; Lesley Bruce, 25 March 1994.

85. Bulletin from the funeral service of Stewart Parker; 'Final Curtain Call for Parker', *News Letter*, 11 November 1988; Lesley Bruce, 21 October 1993; George Parker, 25 February 1995.

86. Lesley Bruce, 20 October 1993; 'A Commonplace Book, 1986–'; Lynne Parker, e-mail to author, 13 September 2008.

87. Lynne Parker, e-mail to author, 13 September 2008.

88. McGuinness; Parker, journal, 3 June 1988; Lesley Bruce, 15 and 21 October 1993 and 10 March 1994; Lynne Parker, e-mail to author, 13 September 2008.

References

INTERVIEWS AND CONVERSATIONS WITH THE AUTHOR

Alcorn, Roy, Ballymoney, Northern Ireland, 2 July 1994.
——Telephone, 18 June 1995.
Allen, Michael, Belfast, 24 June 1994.
Barfield, Brian, Telephone, 6 August 2003.
Barrett, Ed, Clinton, New York, 15 January 1994.
——Clinton, New York, 4 November 1994.
Berlin, Marc, London, 22 March 1994.
Bicât, Tony, London, 14 March 1994.
Boyd, John, Belfast, 27 June 1994.
Bradley, Tony, Telephone, 3 March 1994.
——Burlington, Vermont, 1 November 1994.
Bradshaw, Harry, Telephone, 27 January 1999.
Briggs, Austin, Clinton, New York, 15 January 1994.
Briggs, Margaret, Clinton, New York, 16 January 1994.
——Clinton, New York, 3 November 1994.
——Clinton, New York, 5 November 1994.
Brown, Terence, Cork, 6 July 1995.
Bruce, Lesley, London, 14 October 1993.
——London, 15 October 1993.
——London, 16 October 1993.
——London, 17 October 1993.
——London, 18 October 1993.
——London, 20 October 1993.
——London, 21 October 1993.
——London, 23 October 1993.
——London, 28 October 1993.
——London, 9 March 1994.
——London, 10 March 1994.
——London, 25 March 1994.
——London, 30 March 1994.
——London, 13 April 1994.
——London, 1 March 1995.
——London, 20 March 1995.
——Telephone, 6 June 2007.
——London, 10 November 2007.
——London, 13 November 2007.
——London, 15 November 2007.
——London, 16 November 2007.
——London, 18 November 2007.
——Telephone, 28 July 2008.
Burrowes, Charles, Telephone, 22 June 1995.
Butter, Peter, Telephone, 15 March 1999.

Callaghan, Brenda, Belfast, 26 June 1994.

Carson, Douglas, Belfast, 21 November 1998.

Carson, Mary, Belfast, 21 November 1998.

Clements, Joan Parker, Rostrevor, Northern Ireland, 9 April 1994.

——Telephone, 21 June 1995.

Cole, Nancy, Telephone, 17 March 1999.

Collins, Gail, Atlanta, Georgia, 28 September 2004.

Cooper, Robert, London, 8 March 1995.

Crawford, Dan, London, 2 June 1994.

Crawford, Molly, Belfast, 24 June 1995.

Crone, Robert, Belfast, 17 November 1998.

Cronin, John, Telephone, 8 April 1994.

——Belfast, 28 April 1994.

Davey, Shaun, County Wicklow, Ireland, 7 July 1994.

Davidson, Liz, Telephone, 8 May 1999.

——Telephone, 10 May 1999.

Day, Angélique, Belfast, 26 June 1994.

Deane, Seamus, Derry, 21 February 1995.

Dickey, Liz, Telephone, 16 May 1999.

Dickson, David, Ballynahinch, Northern Ireland, 9 April 1994.

Dowling, Noeleen, Dublin, 6 July 1994.

Evans, David, Belfast, 25 June 1994.

Fairleigh, John, Belfast, 30 June 1994.

——Belfast, 16 June 1995.

Fannin, Sam, Murcia, Spain, 21 March 1995.

——Murcia, Spain, 22 March 1995.

——Murcia, Spain, 23 March 1995.

——Murcia, Spain, 24 March 1995.

——Murcia, Spain, 25 March 1995.

——Telephone, 27 November 2007.

Farago, Peter, London, 15 June 1994.

Fitz-Simon, Christopher, Bloomington, Indiana, 28 May 1999.

Foley, Michael, Telephone, 12 June 2002.

——Telephone, 19 June 2002.

Foster, John Wilson, Vancouver, Canada, 23 July 1995.

Garrett, Brian, Belfast, 22 June 1995.

Gilbert, John, Glasgow, 3 June 1994.

——Glasgow, 4 June 1994.

——Glasgow, 5 June 1994.

——Glasgow, 23 June 1994.

——Telephone, 11 June 2003.

Gillespie, Elgy, San Francisco, 9 October 1994.

Gingold, Alfred, Brooklyn, New York, 12 July 1999.

Granleese, Bill, Langley, British Columbia, Canada, 27 July 1995.

Granleese, Bob, Langley, British Columbia, Canada, 27 July 1995.

——Telephone, 29 July 1995.

Grant, Patrick, Telephone, 22 March 1999.

Grime, Charles, Telephone, 23 June 1995.

Hamilton, John, Bangor, Northern Ireland, 7 April 1994.

Hammond, David, Telephone, 30 June 1994.

——Telephone, 1 July 1994.

Harris, William, Research Triangle Park, North Carolina, 29 October 1998.

Hasson, Ann, Derry, 22 February 1995.

Hawthorne, Denys, Derry, 22 February 1995.

Heaney, Seamus, Telephone, 1 March 1994.

Heffernan, Margaret Windham, Boston, 31 October 1994.

Hertz, Neil, Telephone, 5 February 1994.

Hill, Ian, Belfast, 28 June 1994.

Hobsbaum, Philip, Glasgow, 4 June 1994.

Imrie, Marilyn, London, 15 March 1995.

Jobes, Carrie, Belfast, 24 June 1995.

Keenan, Jane, Syracuse, New York, 5 November 1994.

Keenan, Terry, Telephone, 16 January 1994.

——Syracuse, New York, 5 November 1994.

Kennedy, Douglas, London, 24 October 1993.

Kenney, Susan, Telephone, 13 February 1994.

Kingsley, Mimi, Clinton, New York, 15 January 1994.

——Clinton, New York, 3 November 1994.

——Clinton, New York, 4 November 1994.

Kingsley, Peter, New York City, 10 July 1999.

——New York City, 11 July 1999.

La Vopa, Tony, Research Triangle Park, North Carolina, 17 July 1999.

Lambla, June, Charlotte, North Carolina, 11 November 1994.

——Charlotte, North Carolina, 12 November 1994.

Lambla, Ken, Charlotte, North Carolina, 11 November 1994.

——Charlotte, North Carolina, 12 November 1994.

Leishman, Gina, San Francisco, 10 October 1994.

Lerner, Laurence, Telephone, 17 March 1999.

Lilley, Valerie, Liverpool, 7 June 1994.

Lindley, Dwight, Telephone, 15 January 1994.

Longley, Michael, Telephone, 29 March 1994.

——Belfast, 8 April 1994.

McAllister, Rena, Glasgow, 22 June 1994.

McAuley, Róisin, Telephone, 19 July 2003.

McAuley, Tony, Belfast, 14 November 1998.

——Belfast, 19 November 1998.

McCarthy, Sean, Telephone, 11 October 2007.

McConkey, James, Telephone, 8 January 1994.

——Trumansburg, New York, 4 November 1994.

McCready, Sam, Baltimore, Maryland, 30 July 1996.

——Baltimore, Maryland, 31 July 1996.

——Telephone, 12 October 2003.

McCreary, Alf, Belfast, 27 June 1994.

McCrudden, Gerry, Telephone, 19 August 2003.

McKeown, Ciaran, Belfast, 17 November 1998.

——Belfast, 19 November 1998.

McKibbin, Brian, Toronto, 11 May 1994.
McKibbin, Nancy, Toronto, 10 May 1994.
McLaughlin, Tom, Telephone, 20 June 2002.
MacLaverty, Bernard, Glasgow, 5 June 1994.
——Atlanta, Georgia, 16 May 1998.
MacLeod, Bea, Ithaca, New York, 14 January 1994.
——Ithaca, New York, 17 January 1994.
McMullan, Julie Parker, Dublin, 18 July 1998.
Mac Póilin, Aodán, Belfast, 9 August 1997.
McQuoid, Joan Caldwell, Telephone, 5 July 1999.
MacRae, Julie, Belfast, 28 June 1994.
——Belfast, 24 February 1995.
——Belfast, 25 February 1995.
McWhirter, George, Vancouver, Canada, 3 May 1995.
——Vancouver, Canada, 29 May 1995.
Marki, Ivan, Telephone, 3 November 1994.
Mason, Patrick, Dublin, 7 July 1994.
Mason, Ronald, London, 26 March 1995.
Maxwell, David, Edinburgh, 17 June 1994.
Maxwell, Karen, Edinburgh, 17 June 1994.
Mills, Joe, Belfast, 22 June 1995.
Mitchell, Rex, Belfast, 28 June 1994.
Morrison, Bill, Liverpool, 7 June 1994.
——Liverpool, 8 June 1994.
Moses, Gerard, Syracuse, New York, 5 November 1994.
Muinzer, Louis, Telephone, 23 June 1995.
Muldoon, Paul, Telephone, 16 June 2003.
Mules, Joanna, Belfast, 23 June 1994.
——Belfast, 29 June 1994.
Nesbitt, Helen, Clinton, New York, 2 November 1994.
——Clinton, New York, 4 November 1994.
Newmann, Joan, Belfast, 27 June 1994.
O'Brien, Sara, Telephone, 15 February 2002.
O'Connor, Patrick, Faversham, Kent, 12 March 1995.
Ormsby, Frank, Belfast, 17 November 1998.
——Telephone, 3 June 2002.
Pakenham, Jack, Telephone, 10 July 1995.
Parker, G. H., Belfast, 10 April 1994.
——Belfast, 11 April 1994.
Parker, George, Belfast, 5 April 1994.
——Belfast, 6 April 1994.
——Belfast, 7 April 1994.
——Belfast, 9 April 1994.
——Belfast, 10 April 1994.
——Belfast, 11 April 1994.
——Belfast, 25 February 1995.
——Belfast, 24 June 1995.
——Telephone, 28 December 1997.
Parker, Lynne, London, 18 October 1993.

Parker, Lynne, London, 22 October 1993.
—— Dublin, 3 November 2008.
Parker, Margaret, Belfast, 6 April 1994.
—— Belfast, 7 April 1994.
—— Belfast, 9 April 1994.
—— Belfast, 10 April 1994.
—— Belfast, 25 February 1995.
—— Belfast, 24 June 1995.
—— Telephone, 28 December 1997.
—— Telephone, 18 October 1998.
—— Telephone, 8 July 2002.
Parker, Reeve, Ithaca, New York, 14 January 1994.
Patton, Marcus, Belfast, 6 April 1994.
—— Belfast, 10 April 1994.
—— Belfast, 13 June 1995.
Paul, John, Ithaca, New York, 17 January 1994.
—— Ithaca, New York, 6 November 1994.
—— Telephone, 16 July 2001.
Phelan, Mark, Belfast, 14 May 2008.
Pickering, Steph, Edinburgh, 16 June 1994.
—— Edinburgh, 17 June 1994.
Poole, Sybil Allen, Telephone, 7 June 1999.
Rainey, Brian, Quebec, Canada, 21 June 1997.
Rea, Stephen, Derry, 23 February 1995.
Renton, Jennie, Telephone, 5 April 2007.
Round, Nicholas, Telephone, 5 June 1994.
Schuman, Howard, London, 15 November 2007.
Scott, Pat, Belfast, 17 June 1995.
Skidmore, Art, Telephone, 9 January 1994.
Smyth, Denis, Belfast, 11 April 1994.
—— Belfast, 20 November 1998.
Thompson, Gerry, Brighton, 14 June 1994.
Thompson, May, Belfast, 30 June 1994.
—— Belfast, 20 June 1995.
Thompson, Warren, Belfast, 16 June 1995.
Tomelty, Frances, London, 13 November 2007.
Walker, Brian, Belfast, 8 April 1994.
Watson, George, Aberdeen, 6 February 1997.
Wynne, Sylvia, London, 9 February 1997.

WRITTEN COMMUNICATION WITH THE AUTHOR

Barfield, Brian, E-mail, 23 July 2003.
Bruce, Lesley, Letter, 8 December 2003.
—— E-mail, 21 October 2007.
Davidson, Liz, Letter, 25 March 1995.
Fannin, Lorraine Brown, Letter, 6 March 1995.
Fannin, Sam, Letter, 25 March 1994.
—— Letter, 18 April 1994.

—— Letter, 4 July 1994.
—— Letter, 25 September 1994.
—— Letter, 1 January 1999.
—— Letter, 16 April 1999.
—— Letter, June 1999.
—— Letter, 10 October 2000.
—— Letter, 28 February 2002.
—— E-mail, 28 June 2002.
—— Letter, 24 July 2002.
—— Letter, 4 November 2003.
—— Letter, 29 February 2004.
—— Letter, 4 July 2004.
—— Letter, 5 July 2005.
—— Letter, 2 July 2007.
Farquhar, Simon, E-mail, 14 January 2004.
Frost, John, Letter, November 1995.
—— Letter, 8 December 1995.
Gilbert, John, E-mail, 5 June 2003.
—— E-mail, 19 June 2003.
—— E-mail, 27 July 2003.
Grant, Patrick, Letter, 5 April 1999.
Hammond, David, Letter, 29 July 2002.
Hawthorne, James, Letter, 20 July 1995.
—— Letter, 5 December 1995.
Hertz, Neil, E-mail, 29 September 1997.
—— E-mail, 2 October 1997.
Hill, Ian, E-mail, 28 November 2007.
Hobsbaum, Philip, Letter, 23 February 1999.
—— Letter, 9 May 1999.
Kingsley, Peter, E-mail, 20 July 1999.
McAuley, Tony, E-mail, 5 February 1999.
McKeown, Ciaran, E-mail, 22 November 1997.
McMillin, Scott, Letter, 14 February 1994.
Neill, May, Letter, 12 July 1995.
—— Letter, 23 September 1995.
Nimmons, Roy, Letter, 10 July 1994.
Parker, Lynne, E-mail, 13 June 2000.
—— Letter, 6 August 2008.
—— E-mail, 13 September 2008.
Patton, Marcus, Letter, 19 December 1998.
—— E-mail, 21 July 2003.
Paul, John, E-mail, 20 January 2002.
Phillips, Seán, Letter, 5 April 1995.
—— Letter, 8 August 1995.
Pickering, Steph, E-mail, 18 January 2004.
—— E-mail, 25 June 2004.
—— E-mail, 27 June 2004.
Stevenson, J. S., Letter, 14 December 1998.
Stewart, Mary, Letter, 18 November 1998.

UNPUBLISHED LETTERS BY STEWART PARKER

Draft letter to Hugh Alexander, 9 August 1979.

Letter to Julie Barber, 13 June 1983.

Letter to John Boyd, 29 January 1968 (held in the John Boyd collection at the Linen Hall Library, Belfast).

Letter to Rob Buckler, 27 January 1981.

Letter to Robert Cooper, 9 February 1988.

Letter to Shaun Davey, 4 February 1978.

——27 June 1978.

——5 September 1978.

——2 November 1978.

——21 November 1978.

Letter to Michael Emmerson, 2 June 1967.

Letter to Ephim Fogel, 8 December 1966.

——10 August 1969.

Letter to Michael Foley, 4 July 1972.

——18 August 1972.

Draft letter to John Ford, 2 April 1975.

Draft letter to Stephen Frears, 4 and 5 December 1980.

Letter to John Gilbert, 5 July 1972.

——1 August 1972.

——22 January 1977.

——21 February 1977.

Letter to Alfred Gingold, 12 January 1975.

——20 October 1975.

——22 February 1976.

——1 November 1976.

——15 December 1976.

——28 January 1977.

——2 July 1977.

——28 October 1977.

——6 September 1978.

——and Helen Rogan, 10 February 1985.

——and Helen Rogan, 3 March 1985.

Draft letter to Tyrone Guthrie, 6 December 1967.

——n.d. (probably late December 1967 or early January 1968).

Letter to Philip Hobsbaum, 7 January 1964.

——12 August 1964.

——11 September 1964.

——17 January 1965.

——24 July 1965.

——10 August 1965.

——25 September 1965.

——6 November 1965.

——7 December 1965.

——22 March 1966.

——24 June 1966.

——9 October 1966.

Draft letter to Jeremy Isaacs, 11 February 1986.

Letter to Kenneth Jamison, 15 June 1970.
Letter to John Kelleher, 18 March 1985.
Letter to Jimmy Kennedy, 29 July 1975.
—— 6 August 1975.
—— 28 March 1977.
Draft letter to Jimmy Kennedy, 2 April 1977.
—— 9 April 1977.
Draft letter to Nicolas Kent, 2 June 1986.
Letter to Nancy and Brian McKibbin, 6 May 1982.
—— 30 July 1982.
Letter to Nancy McKibbin, 5 May 1984.
Letter to Bea MacLeod, 28 September 1976.
—— 16 December 1976.
—— 26 April 1978.
—— n.d. (late May or early June 1979).
—— 4 June 1980.
—— 30 November 1982.
Letter to Joanna Mules, 29 July 1988.
Draft letter to Frank Murphy, 16 April 1975.
Draft letter to Conor Cruise O'Brien, 22 February 1978.
Letter to Joan Rodker, 8 December 1978.
Draft letter to Leon Rubin, 10 August 1982.
Draft letter to Max Stafford-Clark, 6 November 1975.
Letter to Andrew Totten, 20 April 1987.

OTHER UNPUBLISHED CORRESPONDENCE

Alexander, Hugh, Letter to Stewart Parker, 6 September 1979.
Aukin, David, Letter to Stewart Parker, 1 October 1976.
—— 26 August 1981.
—— 14 December 1981.
—— 11 January 1982.
Barber, Julie, Letter to Stewart Parker, 10 June 1983.
Barnes, Michael, Letter to Stewart Parker, 16 January 1980.
Berlin, Marc, Letter to Barry Hanson, 27 October 1986.
—— Letter to Alannah Hensler, 20 May 1988.
Briggs, Margaret, Letter to Frances Pearce, 1 September 1964.
Brown, Andrew, Letter to Stewart Parker, 28 September 1976.
Bruce, Lesley, Letter to Nancy McKibbin, 16 August 1985.
Buckler, Rob, Letter to Stewart Parker, 27 November 1979.
—— 28 April 1980.
Cathcart, H. R. Letter to Stewart Parker, 5 July 1985.
Clancy, James, Letter to Peter Zeisler, 26 February 1968.
Cooper, Robert, Letter to Stewart Parker, 24 April 1985.
—— 9 September 1985.
Cowley, Graham, Letter to Frank Murphy, 12 April 1976.
Davey, Shaun, Letter to Stewart Parker, 8 November 1978.
—— 4 December 1978.
Elstein, David, Letter to Stewart Parker, 22 May 1987.

Emmerson, Michael, Letter to Stewart Parker, 8 May 1967.
—— Letter to Tyrone Guthrie, 22 May 1967.
—— Letter to Stewart Parker, 31 May 1967.
—— 16 September 1967.
Ewart-Biggs, Jane, Letter to Stewart Parker, 17 October 1979.
Fogel, Ephim, Letter to Stewart Parker, 23 January 1967.
Fox, Clare and Eddie Kulukundis, Letter to Stewart Parker, 23 December 1985.
Frankel, Kenneth, Letter to Stewart Parker, 11 April 1978.
Garrett, Brian, Letter to Messrs. Dunlop Limited, 3 April 1975.
Gilbert, John, Letter to Stewart Parker, 17 July 1972.
—— 31 July 1972.
—— Letter to Brian Walker, August 1979.
Gill, Peter, Letter to Stewart Parker, 6 December 1979.
Guthrie, Tyrone, Letter to Michael Emmerson, 17 May 1967.
—— Letter to Stewart Parker, 23 December 1967.
Hall, Peter, Letter to Stewart Parker, 4 December 1986.
Hanson, Barry, Letter to Stewart Parker, 28 September 1976.
Hastings, Michael, Letter to Stewart Parker, 13 June 1985.
Heaney, Seamus, Letter to Stewart Parker, 20 October 1967.
Hensler, Alannah, Letter to Marc Berlin, 3 June 1988.
Hern, Nick, Letter to Stewart Parker, 12 January 1981.
Hertz, Neil, Letter to Barry Adams, 27 December 1971.
Hobsbaum, Philip, Letter to Stewart Parker, 14 May 1965.
Johnson, John, Letter to Stewart Parker, 20 July 1965.
—— 1 October 1968.
Kelleher, John, Letter to Stewart Parker, 19 March 1985.
Kennedy, Jimmy, Letter to Stewart Parker, 11 July 1975.
—— 1 August 1975.
—— 12 August 1975.
—— 30 March 1977.
—— 6 April 1977.
—— 13 April 1977.
—— 12 June 1978.
Lewis, Irene, Letter to Stewart Parker, 30 January 1980.
McArthur, Ian, Letter to Stewart Parker, 4 March 1986.
McConkey, James, Letter to Stewart Parker, 2 December 1966.
Mason, Ronald, Letter to Stewart Parker, 8 January 1980.
Osborne, Valerie, Letter to Marc Berlin, 16 September 1985.
Parker, Kate, Letter to John Gilbert, 25 November 1975.
—— 1 December 1975.
—— 25 October 1976.
—— 10 January 1977.
Parr, Chris, Letter to Stewart Parker, 23 April 1979.
Pauker, David, Letter to Hugh Alexander, 11 September 1978.
—— Memo to Marc Berlin, 22 February 1978.
—— Letter to Marc Berlin, 28 March 1978.
—— Memo to Marc Berlin, 31 March 1978.
—— Letter to Paul Libin, 10 January 1979.
—— Letter to Stewart Parker, 7 March 1978.

——4 April 1978.
——21 April 1978.
——5 July 1978.
——1 May 1980.
Pine, Roger, Letter to Stewart Parker, 22 June 1970.
Quigg, Janet, Memo to various BBC authorities, 6 December 1977.
Rea, Stephen, Letter to Stewart Parker, 16 October 1983.
Rodker, Joan, Letter to Stewart Parker, 24 September 1976.
Sandford, Patrick, Letter to Stewart Parker, 12 February 1985.
Stafford-Clark, Max, Letter to Stewart Parker, 21 January 1976.
——13 November 1979.
——20 November 1979.
Thompson, Sam, Letter to Stewart Parker, 10 December 1963.
Turner, David, Letter to Stewart Parker, 18 October 1967.
——11 December 1967.
Tydeman, John, Letter to Stewart Parker, 17 December 1979.
Viney, Michael, Letter to Stewart Parker, 9 April 1970.
Zeisler, Peter, Letter to Stewart Parker, 22 May 1968.

OTHER WRITINGS BY STEWART PARKER

'Time' (manuscript, n.d.).
'Spring Cleaning', *Sullivan Upper School Magazine*, 3.8 (Summer 1957), 28–9.
'Suicide', *Gorgon*, 3 (November 1959), 12–13.
'Five Pennies' (letter to the editor), *Gown*, 12 February 1960.
'Johnny's Story', *Q*, 18 (Hilary 1960), 7–9.
'Editorial', *Interest*, 1.1 (November 1960), 3.
'The Decision', *Q*, 19 (December 1960), n.p.
'The Triumph of Love', *Interest*, 2.1 (December 1961), 12.
'Belfast for Beginners', *Interest*, 3.1 (October 1962), 3–5.
Combo (manuscript, 1962).
'Tentative Description of a Dinner Given to Promote the Impeachment of William Caxton',
    Gorgon (Christmas 1962), 18–19.
'The Broken Lives', *Interest*, 3.6 (May 1963), 17.
Group sheets held in Special Collections, main library of Queen's University, Belfast (type-
    scripts, 1963–).
'The New Stage Club: Theatre in Belfast', *Gown*, 6 December 1963.
'The Preambles of S T Toile', *Interest*, 5.1 (November 1964), 18–21.
'The Preambles of S T Toile', ill. Jim Allen, *Northern Review*, 1.1 (Spring 1965), 12–25.
'The Casualty Meditates Upon His Journey', *Northern Review*, 1.2 (n.d. [1965]), 18–21.
'Poem for my Mother, on Coming of Age', *Kilkenny Magazine*, 14 (Spring/Summer 1966), 69–70.
'Post Script', *Kilkenny Magazine*, 14 (Spring/Summer 1966), 70.
'The Modern Poet as Dramatist: Some Aspects of Non-Realistic Drama, with Special Refer-
    ence to Eliot, Yeats and Cummings' (thesis submitted for the degree of Master of Arts,
    Queen's University, Belfast, 1966).
The Casualty's Meditation (Belfast: Queen's University Festival Publications, n.d. [1966]).
Review of the Lyric Theatre's production of three plays by W. B. Yeats for the BBC Northern
    Ireland radio series *The Arts: A Monthly Review*, produced (probably) by John Boyd, transmitted
    on 22 June 1967 (script held at the BBC Written Archives Centre in Reading, England).

The Sensational Real-life Drama of Deirdre Porter (typescript, n.d.).

Sam Todd For God (typescript, n.d.).

The Yahoos' Overthrow (typescript, 1967).

Maw: A Journey (Belfast: Queen's University Festival Publications, n.d. [1967]).

Speaking of Red Indians, produced by David A. Turner, BBC Northern Ireland, transmitted 24 November 1967 on Northern Ireland Radio 4 (BBC transcript).

'The Recipient', *Honest Ulsterman*, 2 (June 1968), 18–24.

The Jest-Book of ST Toile (typescript, 1968).

'Buntus Belfast', *Irish Times*, 28 January 1970.

'Your Neighbours', produced by Tony McAuley, BBC Northern Ireland, for the Schools series *Here in Ulster*, transmitted 19 February 1970 on Northern Ireland Radio 4 (BBC typescript).

'An Ulster Volunteer', *Irish Times*, 6 March 1970.

Proposal for a ninety-minute radio play entitled *Hurra! My Boys, For Freedom* (typescript, 1970).

'School for Revolution', *Irish Times*, 7 April 1970.

'High Pop', *Irish Times*, 20 April 1970.

'Roots', *Irish Times*, 18 May 1970.

'Smaller Than Life', *Irish Press*, 27 May 1970.

'It's a Bad Scene, Mrs. Worthington', *Honest Ulsterman*, 23 (May/June 1970), 15–16.

'OH, OH', *Honest Ulsterman*, 23 (May/June 1970), 8–10.

'The Tribe and Thompson', *Irish Times*, 18 June 1970.

'Irish Stereotype' (letter to the editor), *New York Times*, 16 July 1970.

'Soft Machine', *Irish Times*, 24 August 1970.

'Theatre I', *Honest Ulsterman*, 26 (November/December 1970), 21–2.

'Introduction' to *Over the Bridge*, by Sam Thompson, ed. Stewart Parker, ill. Jack McManus (Dublin: Gill and Macmillan, 1970), 7–15.

'What to Rock to for Christmas', *Irish Times*, 15 December 1970.

'Pap…Goes the Media', *Irish Times*, 8 February 1971.

'Hugh O'Donnell', produced by Tony McAuley, BBC Northern Ireland, for the Schools series *Today and Yesterday in Northern Ireland*, transmitted 21 May 1971 on Northern Ireland Radio 4 (recording housed in the BBC Radio Archives, Cultra, Northern Ireland, museum number 1842).

Untitled autobiographical fragment (manuscript, n.d. [probably 1970 or 1971]).

The Green Light (BBC typescript, 1971).

Minnie and Maisie and Lily Freed, produced by John Scotney, BBC Northern Ireland, transmitted 4 August 1971 on Radio 4 (BBC transcript).

'I'm a Wallflower, You're a Weed', *Honest Ulsterman*, 30 (September/October 1971), 20–2.

Self Portrait, BBC typescript of edited radio talk (originally entitled *The Green Light*), produced by John Boyd, BBC Northern Ireland, transmitted 3 October 1971 on Northern Ireland Radio 4 (held at the BBC Written Archives Centre in Reading, England).

Untitled poems, *Honest Ulsterman*, 34 (June/July/August 1972), 6–7.

Untitled poems included in *New Poetry*, a radio anthology produced by Stewart Conn for BBC Scotland, transmitted 31 January 1973 on Radio 4 Scotland (BBC typescript).

'Where I Was Born', produced by Douglas Carson, BBC Northern Ireland, for the Schools series *Today and Yesterday in Northern Ireland*, transmitted 11 May 1973 on Northern Ireland Radio 4 (BBC typescript).

Untitled poems included in *Poetry Now*, a radio anthology produced by Stewart Conn for BBC Scotland, transmitted 28 June 1973 on Radio 3 (BBC typescript).

'Requiem', produced by Brian Barfield, BBC Northern Ireland, as part of a programme in an anthology series of Northern Irish writing called *Causeway*, transmitted 18 August 1973 on Radio 3 (BBC typescript; recording housed in the BBC Radio Archives in Cultra, Northern Ireland, museum number 1567).

Hopdance (manuscript).

'Safe as Houses: The Great Belfast Urban Motorway Show', *Fortnight*, 72 (19 November 1973), 11–14.

The Bus Stories, ill. Marcus Patton (Belfast: Holy Smoke Press, 1973).

Clotworthy, in two parts, produced by Brian Barfield, BBC Northern Ireland, transmitted 19 and 26 March 1974 (recording housed in the BBC Radio Archives at Cultra, Northern Ireland, museum numbers 86 and 87).

The Iceberg, produced by Michael Heffernan, BBC Northern Ireland, transmitted 7 January 1975 on Radio 3 (recording housed in the BBC Radio Archives at Cultra, Northern Ireland, museum numbers 64 through 66).

The Iceberg in *Honest Ulsterman*, 50 (Winter 1975), 4–64.

and Michael Heffernan, Draft proposal to the Arts Council of Northern Ireland, 27 January 1975.

'Grand Old Alleyman', *Irish Times*, 11 July 1975.

The Joyous Wheel, produced by Brian Barfield, BBC Northern Ireland, transmitted 12 October 1975 (recording housed in the BBC Radio Archives at Cultra, Northern Ireland, museum number 311).

Private Grounds, produced by Gerry McCrudden, BBC Northern Ireland, transmitted 21 November 1975 (BBC camera script).

Herod the Great, produced by Paul Muldoon, BBC Northern Ireland, transmitted 27 December 1975 on Radio Ulster (BBC typescript; recording housed in the BBC Radio Archives at Cultra, Northern Ireland, museum number 1988).

'Boycott: a summary', prepared for the Joint Stock Theatre Group (typescript, 1976).

'Music Business', *Irish Times*, 22 January 1976.

'Belfast's Women: A Superior Brand of Dynamite', *Evening Standard*, 2 November 1976.

Proposal to Thames Television for a series entitled *The Gaslight Moon, or A Tumult in the Drawing Room* (typescript, November 1976).

The Actress and the Bishop (typescript, 1976).

I'm a Dreamer Montreal, produced by Michael Heffernan, BBC Northern Ireland, transmitted 20 July 1977 (BBC typescript).

Kingdom Come (typescript, 1977).

I'm a Dreamer Montreal, produced by Rob Buckler for Thames Television, directed by Brian Farnham, transmitted 6 March 1979 on ITV (Thames Television typescript).

Treatment for Thames Television for a six-part television series called *Kingdom Come* (typescript, December 1978).

Tall Girls Have Everything (typescript, 1980).

Synopsis of *Pratt's Fall* (typescript, May 1980).

Nightshade (Dublin: Co-op Books, 1980).

Spokesong (New York: Samuel French, 1980).

The Kamikaze Ground Staff Reunion Dinner in *Best Radio Plays of 1980* (London: Eyre Methuen, 1981), 7–38.

Synopsis of *Joyce in June* (typescript, June 1981).

'State of Play', *Canadian Journal of Irish Studies*, 7.1 (June 1981), 5–11.

'Edinburgh: Festive and Steadfast City', *New York Times*, 21 February 1982.

'Me & Jim', *Irish University Review*, 12.1 (Spring 1982), 32–4.

Joyce in June, produced by Terry Coles, directed by Donald McWhinnie, transmitted 30 December 1982 on BBC2 (BBC typescript).

'Proposals for a television film serial in six parts, each of fifty minutes' (typescript, September 1982).

Blue Money, produced by June Roberts and Jo Apted for Blue Money Productions and London Weekend Television, directed by Colin Bucksey, transmitted 7 October 1984 on ITV (rehearsal script).

Catchpenny Twist: A Charade in Two Acts (New York: Samuel French, 1984).

The Traveller, produced and directed by Robert Cooper, BBC Manchester, transmitted 30 January 1985 on Radio 3 (BBC transcript).

Eat the Peach, second draft (typescript, October 1984).

Programme note for the Lyric Players Theatre production of *Northern Star* (Belfast, November 1984).

Radio Pictures, produced by Rosemary Hill, directed by Nicholas Renton, transmitted 16 July 1985 on BBC2 (rehearsal script).

Treatment for a film entitled *The Life of Rawley* (typescript, September 1985).

'Signposts', *Theatre Ireland*, 11 (Autumn 1985), 27–9.

Programme note for the Birmingham Repertory Theatre production of *Heavenly Bodies* (1986).

Radio Scenery (typescript, 1986).

Dramatis Personae (Belfast: John Malone Memorial Committee, 1986).

Proposal for an original screenplay with the working title 'Horseman, Pass By' (typescript, January 1987).

Lost Belongings (London: Thames Television, 1987).

Interviewed by Seamus McKee for the BBC Northern Ireland arts programme *Saturday Supplement*, produced by Judith Elliott, transmitted 26 September 1987 (recording housed in the BBC Radio Archives at Cultra, Northern Ireland, museum number 4903).

Interviewed by James P. Mackey for 'Images of Two Traditions', a programme in the BBC Northern Ireland television series *Perspectives*, produced by Father Jim Skelly, transmitted 18 October 1987.

Mayo by Moonlight (typescript, 1988).

Notes towards a second draft of *Mayo by Moonlight* (17 June 1988).

Commonplace book (1986–).

Undated handwritten notes on his family.

'The Philosophy of Pleasure', programme note for the National Theatre production of *The Shaughraun* by Dion Boucicault (London, 1988/89).

Interviewed by Cherry Ripe for the Australian Broadcasting Corporation, recorded 16 August 1988, transmitted 7 January 1989.

Three Plays for Ireland (Birmingham: Oberon, 1989).

Iris in the Traffic, Ruby in the Rain in *Irish University Review*, 28.2 (Autumn/Winter 1998), 319–46.

Plays: 1, introd. Lynne Parker (London: Methuen, 2000).

Plays: 2, introd. Stephen Rea (London: Methuen, 2000).

Paddy Dies, ed. Kate Newmann and Philip Hobsbaum (Co. Donegal, Ireland: Summer Palace Press, 2004).

Dramatis Personae & Other Writings, ed. Gerald Dawe, Maria Johnston, and Clare Wallace (Prague: Litteraria Pragensia, 2008).

High Pop: The Irish Times Column 1970–1976, ed. and introd. Gerald Dawe and Maria Johnston (Belfast: Lagan Press, 2008).

Television Plays, ed. and introd. Clare Wallace (Prague: Litteraria Pragensia, 2008).

OTHER RARE OR UNPUBLISHED SOURCES

Adjudicators' comments on *The Sensational Real-life Drama of Deirdre Porter*, Irish Life Drama Award, 1967.

Belfast Urban Study Group, *The B. U. S. Report on the Belfast Urban Motorway* (Belfast: Holy Smoke Press, 1973).

Bicât, Tony, 'A Walk with Stewart' (typescript, 1995).

Bulletin for the funeral service of Stewart Parker (St Brendan's Parish Church, Sydenham, 10 November 1988).

Cann, Alexandra, Record of conversation with Stewart Parker, 29 September 1981.

Christopher Ewart-Biggs Memorial Fund Appeal, n.d. [probably 1979].

Cornell Daily Sun (Cornell University student newspaper, Ithaca, New York).

Crab Grass: Poetical Sonatas, 4 (n.d.).

Gilbert, John, Journal.

Gown (Queen's University student newspaper, Belfast).

Hamilton College Catalogue 1964–1965 (Clinton, New York: Hamilton College, 1964).

Hamilton College Catalogue 1966–1967 (Clinton, New York: Hamilton College, 1966).

Hamilton College Catalogue 1994–95 (Clinton, New York: Hamilton College, 1994).

Hamiltonian (yearbook of Hamilton College, Clinton, New York).

Hamilton Spectator (Hamilton College student newspaper, Clinton, New York).

Hearth: A Review of Projects Completed 1978–1993 (Belfast: Hearth, 1994).

Kingsley, Mimi, Journal.

Minutes of the Field Day Theatre Company board meeting held on 5 June 1983 (box 52, folder 1 of the Tom Paulin papers—MSS 880—held at the Manuscript, Archives, and Rare Book Library of Emory University, Atlanta, Georgia).

Montserrat (official tourist brochure, 1976 or 1977).

New Stage Club advertising flyer (Belfast, 1963).

Ormrod, Peter, 'My Wall of Death' and 'The Wall of Death' (typescripts).

Patton, Marcus, Journal.

Programme for the Annual General Meeting of the Queen's University of Belfast Dramatic Society, 1960.

Programme for the Annual General Meeting of the Queen's University of Belfast Dramatic Society, 1961.

Programme for the Birmingham Repertory Theatre production of *Nightshade* (1983).

Programme for Festival 64 (Queen's University, Belfast, 1964).

Programme for the Field Day Theatre Company production of *Pentecost* (1987 tour).

Programme for the Long Wharf Theatre production of *Spokesong* (New Haven, Connecticut, 1978).

Programme for the Lyric Players Theatre production of *Northern Star* (Belfast, 1984).

Programme for the New Stage Club production of *Frost at Midnight* by André Obey (Belfast, 1963).

Programme for the Peacock production of *Nightshade* (Dublin: Abbey Theatre, 1980).

Programme for the Queen's University of Belfast Dramatic Society production of *A Kind of Nothing*, by Bill Morrison (Leeds, National Student Drama Festival, January 1961).

Programme for the Rough Magic Theatre Company production of *Nightshade* (Dublin, 1987).

Programme for the Student Christian Movement in Queen's University and Stranmillis Training College production of *Twentieth Century Lullaby*, by Cedric Mount, *Duet for Laughing Men*, by Stewart Parker, and *The Terrible Meek*, by Charles Rann Kennedy (Belfast, Stranmillis Training College, 1960).

Programme for the Sullivan Upper School Dramatic Society production of *Hamlet* (Holywood, Northern Ireland, 1956).

Programme for the Sullivan Upper School Dramatic Society production of *King Lear* (Holywood, Northern Ireland, 1957).

Programme for the Sullivan Upper School Dramatic Society production of *Henry IV, Part I* (Holywood, Northern Ireland, 1958).

Programme for the Western Union production of *Pratt's Fall*, by Stewart Parker and *Our Jane*, by Michael Skelly (1983 tour).

Publicity material for Ixion Productions, 1975.

Publicity booklet for *Lost Belongings* (Thames Television, 1987).

Publicity flyer (Field Day Theatre Company, 1987).

Sir Henry Tonk: A Festschrift in honour of his Next Birthday prepared in awe by his colleagues and pupils and containing all known facts (Belfast and Glasgow: Holy Smoke Press, 1994).

Strongbow investment brochure, tax year 1984/85.

Sullivan Upper School record card on James Stewart Parker.

Transcript of conversation between Peter Ormrod and Connie Kiernan (typescript, May 1984).

Wiener, Ron, *The Rape and Plunder of the Shankill* (Belfast: Notaems Press, 1975).

OTHER PUBLISHED SOURCES

Ackroyd, Peter, 'Ambiguous Talents', *The Times*, 8 October 1984.

Adair, Tom, 'Across the Watery Vale: Philip Hobsbaum and The Group', *Linen Hall Review*, 4.4 (Winter 1987), 9–11.

Allen, Robert, 'Stewart Parker: Playwright from a Lost Tribe', *Irish Times*, 31 January 1987.

Allison, Alexander, et al. (eds.), *The Norton Anthology of Poetry*, 3rd edn. (New York: Norton, 1983).

Allsop, Kenneth, *The Angry Decade: A Survey of the Cultural Revolt of the Nineteen-Fifties* (London: Peter Owen, 1958).

Anon., 'An Irishman's Diary', *Irish Times*, 19 September 1975.

—— 'Arts Festival Proceeds', *Gown*, 24 November 1961.

—— 'Arts Festival Programme', *Gown*, 27 October 1961.

—— 'Behind "Q" Censorship', *Gown*, 9 December 1960.

—— (ed.), 'The Belfast Group: A Symposium', *Honest Ulsterman*, 53 (November/December 1976), 53–63.

—— 'Beyond Their Range?', *Gown*, 8 December 1961.

—— 'The Bloody Path Paved with Easy Options', *Sunday Times*, 14 November 1971, 15–19.

—— Caption under a photograph of Stewart Parker, *Gown*, 13 December 1962.

—— 'Charlatans Name Four Directors', *Hamilton Spectator*, 12 November 1965.

—— 'Civics' (leader), *Irish Times*, 25 October 1971.

—— 'Dramatic Society Carry Off Trophies', *Gown*, 26 April 1960.

—— 'Echoing Lost Lives', *Irish Press*, 25 September 1987.

—— 'Faces in the Crowd', *Gown*, 4 December 1959.

—— 'Faces in the Crowd', *Gown*, 15 January 1960.

—— 'Faces in the Crowd', *Gown*, 21 April 1961.

—— 'Final Curtain Call for Parker', *News Letter*, 11 November 1988.

—— 'Five-year Jail Term', *News Letter*, 29 September 1966.

—— ' "Graduates Have Nothing to Fear" ', *Gown*, 1 November 1963.

—— *Guide to Over 100 Properties* (Edinburgh: National Trust for Scotland, 1994).

—— 'A Hilarious Sort of History', *Jewish Echo*, 8 February 1983.

—— 'Leeds Win at Home', *Gown*, 17 January 1961.

—— 'Literific Highlights', *Gown*, 9 October 1959.

—— 'Milestone: Ian and Niki Marry', *Gown*, 6 October 1961.

—— 'More and More Students', *Gown*, 9 October 1959.

—— 'Morrison's Play for Leeds', *Gown*, 9 December 1960.

—— 'Murder in the Cathedral: Drama Festival Plans', *Gown*, 26 February 1960.

—— 'Negroes "Sit-In" ', *Gown*, 28 October 1960.

—— 'Northern Vigour' (leader), *Irish Times*, 10 November 1984.

—— 'O'Brien Rejects Rule by the Dead', *Irish Times*, 25 October 1971.

—— 'Periodicals: Writing Sells Out', *Gown*, 9 November 1962.

—— 'Play Probes the Protestant Tradition', *News Letter*, 28 September 1987.

—— 'Profile: Bill Morrison', *Gown*, 19 January 1962.

—— 'Profile: Ian J. Hill', *Gown*, 9 October 1959.

—— 'Profile: Stewart Parker', *Gown*, 6 October 1961.

—— 'Publications in Trouble', *Gown*, 18 October 1963.

—— ' "Q" Faces Censorship', *Gown*, 25 November 1960.

—— ' "Q" Worth Printing and Buying: But Prose Shows Up Poor Poetry', *Gown*, 11 March 1960.

—— 'Quidnunc, by Tape Worm', *Gown*, 11 November 1960.

—— 'Quidnunc? by Tapeworm', *Gown*, 9 December 1960.

—— 'Sinn Fein [*sic*] Line Challenged in Debate', *Irish Times*, 25 October 1971.

—— 'Special Feature: The Belfast Group', *Honest Ulsterman*, 97 (Spring 1994), 3–26.

—— 'Strongbow: The Ultimate Gamble', *Aspect* (March 1985), 54 + .

—— 'Students and the Course of History', *Gown*, 6 May 1960.

—— 'Tabs on Theatre', *Munster Express*, 6 November 1987.

—— 'Teasey Leaves Festival', *Gown*, 1 November 1963.

—— 'Television/Radio', *Guardian*, 24 November 1981.

—— 'Two Shots that Killed a Last Bid for Peace', *Sunday Times*, 21 November 1971, 15–18.

—— *Who's Who 2004* (New York: Palgrave Macmillan, 2004).

Apfel, B., 'Arts Festival Defended' (letter to the editor), *Gown*, 2 February 1962.

Archer, Kane, ' "Spokesong" Turns Up A Few Surprises', *Irish Times*, 7 October 1975.

Arnold-Forster, Val, 'A Class of Their Own on Radio', *Guardian*, 11 January 1975.

Arthur, Paul and Keith Jeffery, *Northern Ireland Since 1968* (Oxford: Blackwell, 1988).

Ashe, Geoffrey, *Land to the West: St. Brendan's Voyage to America* (London: Collins, 1962).

Baker, Keith, 'Younger Than Yesterday', *Belfast Telegraph*, 28 November 1981.

Banks-Smith, Nancy, 'Private on Parade', *Guardian*, 8 October 1984.

Barber, John, 'Bicycle Play Witty and Nostalgic', *Daily Telegraph*, 11 October 1975.

—— 'Witty Musical With View of Torn Ulster', *Daily Telegraph*, 15 September 1976.

—— 'Stage Set Afire by Belfast Bike Maniac', *Daily Telegraph*, 18 February 1977.

—— 'Curious Grave Jokes', *Daily Telegraph*, 14 October 1980.

Bardon, Jonathan, *Belfast: An Illustrated History* (Belfast: Blackstaff, 1982).

—— *A History of Ulster* (Belfast: Blackstaff, 1992).

Barnes, Clive, 'Dazzling "Spokesong" Rewarding', *New York Post*, 14 February 1978.

—— 'Parker's "Catchpenny" Adds an Interesting Twist', *New York Post*, 18 November 1978.

Barnes, Clive, 'Spine-tingling "Spokesong" Sings of Cycles and Bombs', *New York Post*, 16 March 1979.

Barnes, Michael (presenter), 'Theatre in Ulster Today', radio discussion for *Studio Three*, produced by Brian Barfield, BBC Northern Ireland, transmitted 29 February 1976 (recording housed in the BBC Radio Archives at Cultra, Northern Ireland, museum number 2049).

Bell, Jane, 'Reflective Star', *Belfast Telegraph*, 8 November 1984.

Bell, Sam Hanna, *The Theatre in Ulster: A Survey of the Dramatic Movement in Ulster from 1902 Until the Present Day* (Totowa, New Jersey: Rowman and Littlefield, 1972).

Berkvist, Robert, 'A Freewheeling Play About Irish History', *New York Times*, 11 March 1979.

Berrigan, Daniel, *The Trial of the Catonsville Nine* (Boston: Beacon Press, 1970).

—— *To Dwell in Peace: An Autobiography* (San Francisco: Harper & Row, 1987).

Bew, Paul and Gordon Gillespie, *Northern Ireland: A Chronology of the Troubles 1968–1993* (Dublin: Gill and Macmillan, 1993).

Billington, Michael, 'Spokesong', *Guardian*, 15 September 1976.

—— 'The Actress and the Bishop', *Guardian*, 11 December 1976.

—— 'Kingdom Come', *Guardian*, 18 January 1978.

—— 'Catchpenny Twist', *Guardian*, 22 February 1980.

—— 'Nightshade', *Guardian*, 18 January 1984.

Blake, Douglas, 'Vaudeville: "Spokesong" ', *The Stage and Television Today*, 3 March 1977.

Boucicault, Dion, 'The Decline of the Drama', *North American Review*, 125 (September/October 1877), 235–45.

—— 'The Drama and Its Critics' (letter to the editor), *Spirit of the Times*, 31 May 1879, 407.

—— *The Dolmen Boucicault*, ed. David Krause (Dublin: Dolmen, 1964).

Bowman, Jonathan Philbin, 'Party Piece', *In Dublin* (30 September 1987).

Boyle, Kevin, 'Queen's Christ Banned', *Gown*, 12 October 1962.

Bradshaw, Harry, *The Rambler from Clare*, radio feature produced by Kieran Sheedy and transmitted 10 June 1976 by RTÉ.

Brayfield, Celia, 'Sound Effect', *The Times*, 17 July 1985.

—— 'The Brutal Lost Litany', *Independent*, 13 May 1987.

Brennan, Mary, 'Pratt's Fall', *Herald*, 27 January 1983.

Brent, P. L. (ed.), *Young Commonwealth Poets '65* (London: Heinemann, 1965).

Brown, Terence, 'History's Nightmare: Stewart Parker's *Northern Star*', *Theatre Ireland*, 13 (1987), 40–1.

Bugler, Jeremy, 'Motorway Fight Unites Belfast's Ghettos', *Observer*, 14 October 1973.

Burton, Zella, 'Controversial Theatre', *Gown*, 29 January 1960.

Byrne, Ophelia, *The Stage in Ulster from the Eighteenth Century* (Belfast: Linen Hall Library, 1997).

Caffrey, Jim, 'Was This the Way It Had To Be?', *Gown*, 10 March 1961.

Campbell, Susan, 'Radio: Italian Style', *Listener* (16 January 1975).

Candida, 'An Irishwoman's Diary', *Irish Times*, 10 December 1973.

Carruthers, Mark and Stephen Douds (eds.), *Stepping Stones: The Arts in Ulster 1971–2001* (Belfast: Blackstaff, 2001).

Carter, Bill, 'But Some Are More Equal', *Sunday Times*, 22 November 1981.

Carty, Ciaran, 'Northern Star Rising on the Tide', *Sunday Tribune*, 29 September 1985.

Cathcart, Rex, *The Most Contrary Region: The BBC in Northern Ireland 1924–1984* (Belfast: Blackstaff, 1984).

Chaillet, Ned, 'Spokesong: King's Head', *The Times*, 15 September 1976.

—— 'Catchpenny Twist', *The Times*, 25 February 1980.

—— 'Where New Plays Are the Main Attraction', *The Times*, 17 October 1980.

Clark, Heather, *The Ulster Renaissance: Poetry in Belfast 1962–1972* (Oxford: Oxford University Press, 2006).

Clayton-Lea, Tony, 'The Understated Actor', *Cara* (Aer Lingus magazine), 33.3 (May/June 2000), 28–32.

Clines, Francis X., 'Theater Crosses Borders in Ireland, Fueled by the Troubles and a Love of Language', *New York Times*, 27 September 1987.

CMC, 'Stewart Classic', *News Letter*, 8 November 1984.

Coates, John, 'Catching Ireland's Secret Exporters', *Sunday Times*, 10 June 1984.

Connolly, Roy, *The Evolution of the Lyric Players Theatre, Belfast: Fighting the Waves* (Lewiston, New York: Edwin Mellen, 2000).

Cooke, Lez, *British Television Drama: A History* (London: British Film Institute, 2003).

Cooper, Robert, 'Riveting Exchanges' in John Fairleigh (ed.), *Stewart Parker*, supplement to *Fortnight*, 278 (1989), v.

Coveney, Michael, 'Kingdom Come', *Financial Times*, 18 January 1978.

—— 'Catchpenny Twist', *Financial Times*, 22 February 1980.

—— 'Dublin Theatre Festival: Translations', *Financial Times*, 13 October 1980.

—— 'Pentecost/Guildhall, Londonderry', *Financial Times*, 25 September 1987.

Coyle, Jane, 'Northern Star is Born in Belfast', *Irish News*, 15 November 1984.

—— 'Well-Deserved Pat On the Back', *Irish News*, 29 September 1987.

—— 'Drama as Girl Meets Girl', *Irish News*, 22 October 1987.

Crone, Robert and John Malone, *The Human Curriculum* (Belfast: Farset Co-Operative Press, 1983).

Cropper, Martin, 'Brilliant Pastiche', *The Times*, 26 September 1985.

—— 'Heavenly Bodies', *The Times*, 24 April 1986.

Crowley, Jeananne, 'Belfast Revisited', *Radio Times* (21–27 November 1981), 13–15.

Cupitt, Don, *The Sea of Faith* (London: BBC, 1984; paperback edition 1985).

—— www.doncupitt.com.

Curley, Dympna, 'Rugby Tackle on QUB "Vandals"', *Belfast Telegraph*, 26 May 1987.

Curtis, Anthony, 'Shilling Lives: An Interview' in Dale Salwak (ed.), *The Literary Biography: Problems and Solutions* (Iowa City: University of Iowa Press, 1996), 121–9.

Curtis, Richard, *The Berrigan Brothers: The Story of Daniel and Philip Berrigan* (New York: Hawthorn Books, 1974).

Cushman, Robert, 'Basho and the Tidal Wave', *Observer*, 22 January 1978.

—— 'Belfast Songsters', *Observer*, 24 February 1980.

Dale, Brian, '"Dramsoc" Presentation: Three More Plays', *Gown*, 9 December 1960.

Davies, Russell, 'Crusading with Cliff', *Sunday Times*, 29 November 1981.

Dawe, Gerald, *The Rest is History* (Newry, Northern Ireland: Abbey Press, 1998).

Day-Lewis, Sean, 'Studio Scenes', *Daily Telegraph*, 17 July 1985.

Deane, Seamus, 'The Famous Seamus', *New Yorker* (20 March 2000), 54–79.

Devlin, Paddy, 'The "Over the Bridge" Controversy', *Linen Hall Review*, 2.3 (Autumn 1985), 4–6.

Dixon, Anne Campbell, 'Television—Tuesday', *Daily Telegraph*, 24 November 1981.

Downey, Gerard, '"Pentecost" Shows Parker at His Best', *Belfast Telegraph*, 24 September 1987.

Downs, Donald Alexander, *Cornell '69: Liberalism and the Crisis of the American University* (Ithaca: Cornell University Press, 1999).

Eder, Richard, ' "Spokesong", by Stewart Parker, Belfast Drama, at Long Wharf', *New York Times*, 11 February 1978.

—— 'Stage: "Spokesong" Spins Cycle of Belfast', *New York Times*, 16 March 1979.

Eggleston, William Lee, 'The New Barbarians', *Gown*, 14 October 1960.

Eliot, T. S., *Sweeney Agonistes: Fragments of an Aristophanic Melodrama* (London: Faber, 1932).

Ellmann, Richard, *James Joyce* (Oxford: Oxford University Press, 1959).

Elsom, John, 'Back Brake', *Listener* (24 February 1977).

Evans, Angela, et al., 'Why a Busy Woman Has No Time for Books' (letters to the editor), *Guardian*, 16 July 1981.

F., C., 'Play Strips Ulster Bare', *News Letter*, 24 September 1987.

F., M. J., 'Arts Festival: Looking Back Indifferently', *Gown*, 19 January 1962.

Fairleigh, John, 'The Artist's Conflict in Ulster', a radio investigation produced by Virginia Hardy, first transmitted 1 October 1973 on the BBC World Service (recording housed in the BBC Radio Archives at Cultra, Northern Ireland, museum number 301).

—— (ed.), *Stewart Parker*, supplement to *Fortnight*, 278 (1989).

Farrell, Joseph, 'Tron, Glasgow: Pratt's Fall', *Scotsman*, 28 January 1983.

Fawkes, Richard, *Dion Boucicault: A Biography* (London: Quartet, 1979).

Feldman, Gene and Max Gartenberg (eds.), *Protest: The Beat Generation and the Angry Young Men* (London: Souvenir Press, 1959).

Finegan, John, 'Fantasies in a Funeral Parlour', *Evening Herald*, 10 October 1980.

Finney, Patricia, 'Take Tim Curry and Run', *Evening Standard*, 5 October 1984.

Fisk, Robert, *The Point of No Return: The Strike Which Broke the British in Ulster* (London: André Deutsch, 1975).

FitzGerald, Ann, 'Birmingham: Heavenly Bodies', *The Stage and Television Today*, 22 May 1986.

Fitzgerald, Treacy, 'Pentecost on Tour', *Dublin Opinion* (October 1987).

Fitzgibbon, Frank, 'Kelleher and Collins Go to the Movies', *Success* (March 1985), 22–5.

Fitzhenry, Edna C., *Henry Joy McCracken* (Dublin: Talbot, 1936).

Foran, Charles, *The Last House of Ulster* (Toronto: HarperCollins, 1995).

Foster, John Wilson, 'The Critical Condition of Ulster', *Honest Ulsterman*, 79 (Autumn 1985), 38–55.

—— *The Titanic Complex* (Vancouver, Canada: Belcouver Press, 1997).

Foster, R. F., *Modern Ireland: 1600–1972* (1988) (London: Penguin, 1989).

Galway, James, *An Autobiography* (New York: St. Martin's Press, 1979).

Gantz, Jeffrey, *Early Irish Myths and Sagas* (London: Penguin, 1981).

Gardner, Raymond, 'Too many people have writing in the head...', *Guardian*, 6 December 1976.

Gilbert, John, Letter to the editor, *Listener* (29 May 1975), 709.

—— Letter to the editor, *Belfast Telegraph*, 3 June 1987.

Gilbert, W. Stephen, 'Mixing It', *Listener* (2 April 1987), 27.

Gill, Brendan, 'In Praise of Wheels', *New Yorker* (26 March 1979), 53–4.

Gorman, Damien, 'Points Victory for Fight Game', *Irish News*, 11 April 1987.

Hackett, Dennis, 'Equality Myth', *The Times*, 25 November 1981.

Hanson, Barry, 'The 1970s: Regional Variations' in Jonathan Bignell, Stephen Lacey, and Madeleine Macmurraugh-Kavanagh (eds.), *British Television Drama: Past, Present and Future* (Basingstoke: Palgrave Macmillan, 2000), 58–63.

Harris, Claudia W., 'A Living Mythology', *Theatre Ireland*, 13 (November 1987), 15–17.

Harvey, Sylvia, 'Channel Four Television: From Annan to Grade' in Edward Buscombe (ed.), *British Television: A Reader* (Oxford: Oxford University Press, 2000).

Hastings, Ronald, Television guide, *Daily Telegraph*, 6 March 1979.

Haywood, Dennis, 'Dennis Haywood's Viewpoint…On Last Night's TV', *Yorkshire Evening Post*, 8 April 1987.

Heaney, Seamus (ed.), *Soundings '72* (Belfast: Blackstaff, 1972).

—— *Field Work* (1979) (New York: Noonday, 1989).

—— *Preoccupations: Selected Prose 1968–1978* (1980) (London: Faber, 1984).

—— 'Victorious Ulsterman', *Sunday Independent*, 6 November 1988.

—— 'Further Language', *Studies in the Literary Imagination*, 30.2 (Fall 1997), 7–16.

Hennigan, Tony, 'Death as a Sinister Illusion', *Irish Independent*, 10 October 1980.

Henry, William A. (III), 'Acts of History', *Time* (21 October 1985).

Herbert, Hugh, 'The Bands on the Run', *Guardian*, 8 April 1987.

Hickman, Christie, 'Stephen Rea, Fringe Actor Par Excellence', *Drama* (Autumn 1983), 23–5.

Higgins, Mary, 'Bicycle Made for Touché', *Irish Press*, 7 October 1975.

Hill, Ian, 'Several Points Off Course', *Gown*, 15 January 1960.

—— 'Excellence at the Empire: Over the Bridge Reviewed', *Gown*, 29 January 1960.

—— 'Two to Play', *Gown*, 28 October 1960.

—— 'A Way to the Top?', *Gown*, 28 February 1961.

—— 'Festival', *Guardian*, 14 November 1980.

—— 'Northern Star', *Guardian*, 16 November 1984.

Hill, Niki, 'The Way We Were', *Sunday News*, 11 October 1987.

'Hobe.', 'Show On Broadway: Spokesong', *Variety*, 21 March 1979.

Hobsbaum, Philip, 'Creative Writing', radio programme recorded and transmitted by BBC Northern Ireland on 31 May 1966 (recording housed in the BBC Radio Archives at Cultra, Northern Ireland, museum number 1951).

—— 'Belfast Letter: Nobody's Province', *Spectator* (12 August 1966), 208–9.

—— 'The Belfast Group: A Recollection', *Éire-Ireland*, 32.2 and 3 (Summer/Fall 1997), 173–82.

Hogan, Robert, *Dion Boucicault* (New York: Twayne, 1969).

Holland, Mary, 'The Belfast Bible', *Observer*, 27 September 1987.

Honan, Corinna, 'They've Made Dad's Tragedy into a Comedy', *Daily Mail*, 6 October 1984.

Houlihan, Con, 'Recycling the Gags and Laughs', *Irish Press*, 26 August 1977.

—— 'Thoughts of What Might Have Been…', *Evening Press*, 10 October 1980.

Hughes-Hallett, Lucy, 'Weekend View', *Standard*, 8 October 1984.

—— 'Last Night's View', *Evening Standard*, 17 July 1985.

Hull, Eleanor, *The Cuchullin Saga in Irish Literature* (London: David Nutt, 1898).

Humphry, Derek, 'IRA Forces Social Workers to Quit Belfast', *Sunday Times*, 23 September 1973.

Hunter, Charles, 'Putting the Deirdre Myth on Film', *Irish Times*, 17 September 1986.

—— 'Stephen Rea: Actor-Manager with a Mission', *Irish Times*, 19 September 1987.

Hurren, Kenneth, 'Tandem', *Spectator* (25 September 1976), 29.

Huxley, Aldous, *Brave New World and Brave New World Revisited* (New York: Harper, 1960).

Ireland, Kate [Kate Parker], 'Theatre: Much Ado About Nothing and Lovers at the Lyric Theatre, Belfast', *Honest Ulsterman*, 24 (July/August 1970), 14–17.

—— 'Theatre II', *Honest Ulsterman*, 26 (November/December 1970), 22–3.

Jackson, Alvin, *Ireland: 1798–1998* (Oxford: Blackwell, 1999).

Jaffa, Malcolm, 'The Cult of Martin Luther King', *Gown*, 24 November 1961.

James, Clive, 'Bomb-happy Colonels', *Observer*, 22 February 1981.

Jenkins, David M., 'Gorgon Reviewed', *Gown*, 4 December 1959.

Jenkinson, Norman, 'Nothing Out of the Ordinary', *Belfast Telegraph*, 11 April 1987.

Johnston, Jennifer, 'Situation Comedy', *Radio Times* (3 December 1977), 10.

Jones, Mervyn, 'Holding Out', *Listener* (7 February 1985), 36.

Jordan, Richard, 'The Second Coming of Paisley: From Premillennial Crusader to Amillennial Politician', talk delivered at the annual meeting of the American Conference for Irish Studies in Davenport, Iowa, 18 April 2008.

—— 'The Interposition of Paisleyism: Irish Civil Rights and Segregation', talk delivered at the annual meeting of the American Conference for Irish Studies in State College, Pennsylvania, 8 May 2010.

Kehoe, Emmanuel, 'Nightshade', *Sunday Press*, 12 October 1980.

Kennedy, Maev, 'Tortoise at Work', *Irish Times*, 17 September 1985.

Kenny, Mary, 'Cash and Curry are a Red Hot Mix', *Daily Mail*, 8 October 1984.

—— 'All So Believable…and That's the *Real* Tragedy', *Daily Mail*, 8 April 1987.

Kinney, Charles Lamb, *The Life and Career of Dion Boucicault* (New York: Graphic Company, 1883).

Kinsella, Thomas, *The Tain* (London: Oxford University Press, 1970).

Krause, David (ed.), *The Dolmen Boucicault* (Dublin: Dolmen, 1964).

Lacy, Brian, *Siege City: The Story of Derry and Londonderry* (Belfast: Blackstaff, 1990).

Lawson, Mark, 'Singing in the Pain', *Independent*, 8 April 1987.

Levin, Bernard, 'No Laughing Matter', *Sunday Times*, 20 February 1977.

Longley, Michael (ed.), *Causeway: The Arts in Ulster* (Belfast: Arts Council of Northern Ireland, 1971).

—— *Tuppenny Stung: Autobiographical Chapters* (Belfast: Lagan Press, 1994).

Lurie, Alison, *The War Between the Tates* (New York: Random House, 1974).

Lyons, F. S. L., *Ireland Since the Famine*, 2nd edn. (London: Fontana, 1973).

Lyttle, John, 'Lost Belongings', *City Limits* (2 April 1987).

—— 'Everyday People', *City Limits* (9 April 1987).

McA., E., 'Emotionally-Stunning Production', *Ulster Herald*, 17 October 1987.

MacAvock, Desmond, 'Charade with a Message', *Evening Press*, 26 August 1977.

McCafferty, Nell, 'A Night Meeting the Family', *Sunday News*, 4 October 1987.

McCann, Hugo, 'Experimental Theatre', *Gown*, 25 November 1960.

McConkey, James, *A Journey to Sahalin* (New York: Coward, McCann & Geoghegan, 1971).

McCourt, Angela and Judy Silver, 'The Second Class Sex', *Gown*, 24 April 1964.

McCreary, Alf, *Survivors* (Belfast: Century Books, 1976).

—— 'Twenty-one Entertaining Years', *Belfast Telegraph*, 11 November 1983.

McFerran, Ann, ' "Spokesong" ', *Time Out* (16 September 1976).

—— Theatre listing, *Time Out* (29 February–6 March 1980).

McGarry, Peter, 'A Nosedive for Drama', *Coventry Evening Telegraph*, 29 April 1987.

McGibbon, David, 'Sandy Row: A Sketch', photographs by John Gilbert and Dave McCrudden, *Interest* (March 1968), 15–22.

McGinley, Frankie, 'A Good Play', *Donegal Democrat*, 2 October 1987.

McGinn, Brian, 'How Irish is Montserrat?', *Irish Roots*, 1 (1994), 20+ .

—— 'How Irish is Montserrat?' (Part 3), *Irish Roots*, 4 (1994), 20+ .

Mac Goris, Mary, 'Ride in the North but Hardly a Play?' *Irish Independent*, 7 October 1975.

McGuinness, Frank, 'Stewart Parker', *Independent*, 5 November 1988.

McKenna, David, Review of *Nightshade*, by Stewart Parker, *In Dublin* (17–30 October 1980).

McKeon, Belinda, 'Heavenly Bodies/Peacock Theatre', *Irish Times*, 30 June 2004.

McMillan, Joyce, 'Theatre', *Sunday Standard*, 30 January 1983.

—— 'The Nerve & the Energy to Dream', *Scottish Theatre News* (February 1983), 9–13.

McNeill, Mary, *The Life and Times of Mary Ann McCracken 1770–1866: A Belfast Panorama* (1960) (Belfast: Blackstaff, 1988).

McStravick, Brendan, 'April Weather on the Buses', *Education Times*, 6 December 1973, 14.

Mack, Maynard, et al. (eds.), *The Norton Anthology of World Masterpieces* (New York: Norton, 1997).

Mahon, Derek, 'Poetry in Northern Ireland', *20th-Century Studies*, 4 (November 1970), 89–93.

Malcolmson, A. P. W. (ed.), *The Extraordinary Career of the 2nd Earl of Massereene, 1743–1805* (Belfast: HMSO, 1972).

Malone, John M., *Schools Project in Community Relations* (1972) (Belfast: John Malone Memorial Committee, n.d.).

—— 'Schools and Community Relations', *The Northern Teacher* (Winter 1973), 19–30.

Manchester, William, *The Glory and the Dream: A Narrative History of America 1932–1972* (New York: Bantam Books, 1975).

Marlow, Joyce, *Captain Boycott and the Irish* (New York: E. P. Dutton, 1973).

Masters, Anthony, 'Thrilling Chasms of Mood and Style', *The Times*, 3 June 1983.

Mengel, Hagal, 'A Lost Heritage: Ulster Drama and the Work of Sam Thompson', Part II, *Theatre Ireland*, 2 (1983), 80–2.

Metford, J. C. J., *Dictionary of Christian Lore and Legend* (London: Thames and Hudson, 1983).

Milligan, Spike, *The Goon Show Scripts* (London: Woburn, 1972).

Molin, Eric and Robin Goodefellowe (eds.), *Dion Boucicault, The Shaughraun: A Documentary Life, Letters and Selected Works* (United States of America: Proscenium Press, 1979).

Molloy, Philip, 'A Peach with Little Flavour', *Irish Press*, 18 March 1986.

Moody, T. W. and J. C. Beckett, *Queen's, Belfast 1845–1949: The History of a University* (London: Faber, 1959).

Morley, Sheridan, 'Song of the Spokes', *Punch* (23 February 1977), 330.

Morrison, Bill and Stewart Parker, 'Why?', *Interest*, 1.1 (November 1960), 4–5.

Morton, Robin, 'Gorilla Made Monkey Out of Revellers', *Belfast Telegraph*, 2 January 1976.

Muldoon, Paul, *Meeting the British* (Winston-Salem, North Carolina: Wake Forest University Press, 1987).

Naughton, John, 'Breaking Eggs', *Listener* (26 November 1981), 662–3.

—— 'You Brute, You Beast', *Observer*, 19 April 1987.

Newmann, Kate (ed.), *Dictionary of Ulster Biography* (Belfast: Institute of Irish Studies, 1993).

Newton, Francis [Eric J. Hobsbawm], *The Jazz Scene* (1959) (New York: Da Capo Press, 1975).

Nowlan, David, ' "Catchpenny Twist" at the Peacock', *Irish Times*, 26 August 1977.

—— ' "Nightshade" at the Peacock', *Irish Times*, 10 October 1980.

—— ' "Northern Star" at Belfast Lyric Theatre', *Irish Times*, 9 November 1984.

—— ' "Northern Star" at the Olympia', *Irish Times*, 24 September 1985.

—— ' "Nightshade" at the Project', *Irish Times*, 5 February 1987.

Nowlan, David, ' "Pentecost" at the Guildhall, Derry', *Irish Times*, 24 September 1987.

Nurse, Keith, 'King's Head: Kingdom Come', *Daily Telegraph*, 19 January 1978.

O'Brien, Conor Cruise, 'A Song of Disembafflement', *Observer*, 29 January 1978.

O'Brien, Martin, 'Nightshade—an Exhilarating Conundrum', *Belfast Telegraph*, 11 November 1980.

O'Doherty, Malachi, 'On the Eve of Pentecost', *Hype* (November 1987), 29–30.

O'Malley, Mary, *Never Shake Hands with the Devil* (Dublin: Elo, 1990).

O'Malley, Padraig, *Biting at the Grave: The Irish Hunger Strikes and the Politics of Despair* (Belfast: Blackstaff, 1990).

O'Meara, John J. (ed. and trans.), *The Voyage of Saint Brendan: Journey to the Promised Land* (Atlantic Highlands, New Jersey: Humanities Press, 1976).

O'Rourke, Frances, 'No Happy Endings', *Sunday Press*, 28 August 1977.

O'Toole, Fintan, 'Stephen Rea: The Great Leap from the Abbey', *Sunday Tribune*, 23 September 1984.

—— 'Tensions in Past and Present Tense', *Sunday Tribune*, 2 December 1984.

—— 'Death and the Insurrection', *Sunday Tribune*, 27 September 1987.

—— 'Second Opinion', *Irish Times*, 12 October 1996.

Oliver, Cordelia, 'Pratt's Fall', *Guardian*, 29 January 1983.

Ormsby, Frank, 'The Write-An-Ulster-Play Kit', *Honest Ulsterman*, 36 (November/December 1972), 2–3.

Ottaway, Robert (ed.), 'Highlights of Your BBC Week: Radio and Television', *Radio Times* (14–20 February 1981), 5.

Pacey, Ann, 'The Great Money Chase', *Sunday Mirror*, 7 October 1984.

Parker, E. W. (ed.), *A Pageant of English Verse* (London: Longmans, 1949).

Parker, Liz [Kate Parker], 'Why Don't More Women Buy Books?', *Guardian*, 7 July 1981.

Parker, Michael, *Seamus Heaney: The Making of the Poet* (Iowa City: University of Iowa Press, 1993.

—— *Northern Irish Literature, 1975–2006* (Basingstoke: Palgrave Macmillan, 2007).

Parkes, Colin Murray, *Bereavement: Studies of Grief in Adult Life* (New York: International Universities Press, 1972).

Parkin, Andrew, 'Metaphor as Dramatic Structure in Plays by Stewart Parker' in Masaru Sekine (ed.), *Irish Writers and the Theatre* (Gerrards Cross, Bucks.: Colin Smythe, 1986), 135–50.

Paton, Maureen, 'Mad, Mad World of the Radio Set', *Daily Express*, 17 July 1985.

Peter, John, 'Delightful Debut', *Sunday Times*, 12 October 1975.

—— 'Innocents in an Irish Minefield', *Sunday Times*, 2 March 1980.

—— 'Taking Comedy to Extremes', *Sunday Times*, 18 November 1984.

—— 'The Making of a Romantic Lead', *Sunday Times*, 4 May 1986.

Pilkington, Lionel, 'Theatre and Cultural Politics in Northern Ireland: The *Over the Bridge* Controversy, 1959', *Éire-Ireland*, 30.4 (Winter 1996), 76–93.

Power, Vincent, *Send 'Em Home Sweatin': The Showband Story* (Cork: Cork University Press, 2000).

Purcell, Deirdre, 'The Illusionist', *Sunday Tribune*, 27 September 1987.

Purdie, Bob, *Politics in the Streets: The Origins of the Civil Rights Movement in Northern Ireland* (Belfast: Blackstaff, 1990).

Quidnunc, 'An Irishman's Diary', *Irish Times*, 30 September 1970.

Quiller-Couch, Sir Arthur (ed.), *The Oxford Book of English Verse 1250–1918* (Oxford: Oxford University Press, 1939).

R., J., 'Play to Be Seen', *News Letter*, 11 November 1980.

Radin, Victoria, 'In God's Country', *Observer*, 19 September 1976.

Ratcliffe, Michael, 'Kremlin Charade', *Observer*, 22 January 1984.

—— 'Ireland's Comedy of Terrors', *Observer*, 6 October 1985.

—— 'A Saucy Night at Spithead', *Observer*, 27 April 1986.

Rees, Jenny, 'Love in a Violent Climate', *Daily Telegraph*, 8 April 1987.

Renton, Alex, 'Crossing the Troubled Borders of Irish Drama', *Independent*, 27 November 1987.

—— 'Ireland's Leading Rebel', *Illustrated London News* (January 1989), 60–1.

Reynolds, Gillian, 'Radio/Showpiece BBC', *Daily Telegraph*, 5 February 1985.

Richtarik, Marilynn, *Acting Between the Lines: The Field Day Theatre Company and Irish Cultural Politics 1980–1984* (Oxford: Oxford University Press, 1994).

—— 'Stewart Parker's *Heavenly Bodies*: Dion Boucicault, Show Business, and Ireland', *Modern Drama*, 43.3 (Fall 2000), 404–20.

—— ' "Ireland, the Continuous Past": Stewart Parker's Belfast History Plays' in Stephen Watt, Eileen Morgan, and Shakir Mustafa (eds.), *A Century of Irish Drama: Widening the Stage* (Bloomington and Indianapolis: Indiana University Press, 2000), 256–74.

Riding, Alan, 'Cast in the Middle of the Long Conflict in Northern Ireland', *New York Times*, 15 February 1998.

Ritchie, Rob (ed.), *The Joint Stock Book: The Making of a Theatre Collective* (London: Methuen, 1987).

Rosenfield, Ray, 'Sam Thompson's "Over the Bridge" in Book Form', *Irish Times*, 8 December 1970.

—— 'N. I. Arts Body Awards Prizes to Writers', *Irish Times*, 7 December 1971.

Rushe, Desmond, 'Parker Play Has Telling Insight', *Irish Independent*, 26 August 1977.

—— 'A History Lesson In a Relevant and Compelling Work', *Irish Independent*, 24 September 1985.

—— 'Optimistic Pentecost is Parker at his Best', *Irish Independent*, 29 September 1987.

Rutherford, B. M., *Belfast Urban Area Plan: Report of a Public Inquiry* (Belfast: HMSO, 1973).

S., R., 'Irish Stew', *Sunday Telegraph*, 24 February 1980.

Saroyan, William, *The Hungerers* (New York: Samuel French, 1939).

Say, Rosemary, 'In Suspense', *Sunday Telegraph*, 19 September 1976.

Seaver, Kirsten A., *Maps, Myths, and Men: The Story of the Vinland Map* (Stanford: Stanford University Press, 2004).

Self, David, 'Joint Stock Theatre Group', entry in *The Continuum Companion to Twentieth Century Theatre*, ed. Colin Chambers (London: Continuum, 2002), 408.

Selway, Jennifer, 'The Week in View', *Observer*, 15 February 1981.

—— 'The Week in View', *Observer*, 22 November 1981.

Severin, Tim, *The Brendan Voyage*, ill. Trondur Patursson (New York: McGraw-Hill, 1978).

Shaw, George Bernard, *St. Joan* (New York: Penguin, 1951).

Sheridan, Michael, 'Heavy Dose of Deadly "Nightshade" ', *Irish Press*, 10 October 1980.

Shorter, Eric, 'Deathly Delight', *Daily Telegraph*, 2 June 1983.

Shubik, Irene, *Play for Today: The Evolution of Television Drama*, 2nd edn. (Manchester: Manchester University Press, 2000).

Shulman, Milton, 'Two Wheels Good…', *Evening Standard*, 15 September 1976.

—— 'No Escape…', *Evening Standard*, 22 February 1980.

Simon, John, 'From Wheel to Woe', *New York* (2 April 1979), 85.

Simpson, David, 'The Prolific Pen of Mr Parker', *Belfast Telegraph*, 3 November 1984.

Smith, Gus, 'The Music Scores at the Peacock', *Sunday Independent*, 28 August 1977.

—— 'Enter McKenna—the Magician', *Sunday Independent*, 12 October 1980.

—— 'Parker's Compassion and Nobility', *Sunday Independent*, 29 September 1985.

Smurthwaite, Nick, 'Out of the Land of Myths and Legends', *The Stage and Television Today* (2 April 1987), 24.

Smyth, Gerry, *Noisy Ireland: A Short History of Irish Popular Music* (Cork: Cork University Press, 2005).

Spectator, The, 'A Play of Real Interest, Performed with Love and Zest', *Coleraine Chronicle*, 21 November 1987.

Steele, William Paul, *The Character of Melodrama* (Orono, Maine: University of Maine Press, 1968).

Stephen, Andrew, 'Did Britain Let the Side Down?', *Sunday Times* magazine (4 March 1984), 18–23.

Stokes, Niall, 'Bikes and Belfast', *Hibernia* (17 October 1975), 23.

Strout, Cushing and David I. Grossvogel (eds.), *Divided We Stand: Reflections on the Crisis at Cornell* (Garden City, New York: Doubleday, 1970).

Thompson, George, 'The Ulster Folk Museum' in *Causeway: The Arts in Ulster*, ed. Michael Longley (Belfast: Arts Council of Northern Ireland, 1971), 153–65.

Thompson, Harry, 'The Embittered Cliche Persists', *Journal, Newcastle upon Tyne*, 11 April 1987.

Thompson, Sam, *Over the Bridge*, ed. Stewart Parker, ill. Jack McManus (Dublin: Gill and Macmillan, 1970).

Tóibín, Colm, 'Grim Laughter', *Hibernia* (1 May 1980).

—— 'Parker Pens a Rare Delight', *Hibernia* (16 October 1980).

—— 'Powerful H-Block Drama', *Sunday Independent*, 8 February 1987.

—— 'A Coy Despatch from the Front Line', *Sunday Independent*, 4 October 1987.

Took, Barry, 'Good Sports', *Listener* (11 July 1985), 43–4.

Totten, Andrew J., *Straight & Ready: A History of the 10th Belfast Scout Group 1908–1988* (Belfast: Nelson & Knox, 1989).

Trench, Brian, 'New Life for the Markets', *Hibernia* (16 September 1977), 9.

Updike, John, 'It Was Sad', *New Yorker* (14 October 1996), 94–8.

Vincent, Sally, 'Victims of Circumstance', *Today*, 8 April 1987.

Walker, Brian and Alf McCreary, *Degrees of Excellence: The Story of Queen's, Belfast 1845–1995* (Belfast: Institute of Irish Studies, 1994).

Walsh, Caroline, 'Stewart Parker', *Irish Times*, 13 August 1977.

Walsh, Townsend, *The Career of Dion Boucicault* (1915) (New York: Benjamin Blom, 1967).

Wardle, Irving, 'Spokesong', *The Times*, 17 February 1977.

—— 'Witty and Agile Lyrics Among Exotic Foliage', *The Times*, 18 January 1978.

—— 'Theatre in London', *The Times*, 18 January 1984.

Washburn, Wilcomb E. (ed.), *Proceedings of the Vinland Map Conference* (Chicago: University of Chicago Press, 1971).

Watt, Douglas, ' "Spokesong" Lets the Air Out of Its Tires', *Daily News*, 16 March 1979.

Welch, Robert (ed.), *The Oxford Companion to Irish Literature* (Oxford: Oxford University Press, 1996).

Welf, Bill, 'J. S. Parker Leaves for Eire', *Hamilton Spectator*, 3 February 1967.

Whelan, Kevin, *The Tree of Liberty: Radicalism, Catholicism and the Construction of Irish Identity 1760–1830* (Notre Dame, Indiana: University of Notre Dame Press, 1996).

White, Barry, Leader, *Belfast Telegraph*, 12 November 1984.

Willox, Bob, 'Parker Pens a Great Play', *News Letter*, 21 February 1977.

Wills, Colin, 'Focus…Festival 64', *Gown*, 7 February 1964.

Wilson, Deirdre, *Slave of the Passions* (London: Picador, 1991).

Winchester, Simon, 'The Irish Eyes Which Have Little Time for Smiling', *Guardian*, 4 August 1977.

Woodworth, Paddy, 'Wrangles Hit "Peach" Movie', *Sunday Press*, 19 May 1985.

Wyver, John, 'Irish Eyes', *Time Out* (2–8 December 1977), 13.

—— 'Television', *City Limits* (20–26 November 1981), 55.

Yeager, Peter, 'Performance Tops Play in Charlatans Thomas Offering', *Hamilton Spectator*, 11 November 1966.

Young, B. A., 'Spokesong', *Financial Times*, 15 September 1976.

—— 'Spokesong', *Financial Times*, 17 February 1977.

—— 'Heavenly Bodies/Birmingham Rep', *Financial Times*, 24 April 1986.

Index